# A
# TESTAMENT OF HOPE

## The Essential Writings
## and Speeches
## of Martin Luther King, Jr.

Edited by

James Melvin Washington

WITHDRAWN

D0063994

HarperOne
*An Imprint of HarperCollinsPublishers*

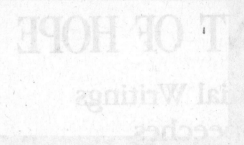

HarperOne

HarperCollins books may be purchased for educational, business, or sales promotional use. For information please write: Special Markets Department, HarperCollins Publishers, 10 East 53rd Street, New York, NY 10022.

HarperCollins Web site: http://www.harpercollins.com

HarperCollins®, 📖®, and HarperOne™ are trademarks of HarperCollins Publishers.

FIRST HARPERCOLLINS PAPERBACK EDITION PUBLISHED IN 1991

**Library of Congress Cataloging-in-Publication Data**

King, Martin Luther, Jr., 1929–1968.
    A testament of hope : the essential writings and speeches of
Martin Luther King, Jr. / edited by James Melvin Washington. —
1st HarperCollins pbk. ed.
      p. cm.
    Includes bibliographical references and index.
    ISBN: 978–0–06–064691–2
      1. Afro-Americans—Civil rights.  2. United States—Race relations.
I. Washington, James Melvin.  II. Title.
E185.97.K5A25    1991
323.1'196073—dc20                      90–48203

09  10  11  12  RRD(H)  50  49  48

Martin Luther King, Jr., was the conscience of his generation. A southerner, a black man, he gazed on the great wall of segregation and saw that the power of love could bring it down.

From the pain and exhaustion of his fight to free all people from the bondage of separation and injustice, he wrung his eloquent statement of his dream of what America could be.

He helped us overcome our ignorance of one another. He spoke out against a war he felt was unjust, as he had spoken out against laws that were unfair.

He made our nation stronger because he made it better. Honored by kings, he continued to his last days to strive for a world where the poorest and humblest among us could enjoy the fulfillment of the promises of our founding fathers.

His life informed us, his dreams sustain us yet.

—Citation of the posthumous award of the
Presidential Medal of Freedom to the
Reverend Dr. Martin Luther King, Jr.,
4 July 1977

# Contents

## POLITICAL: WEDGED BETWEEN DEMOCRACY AND BLACK NATIONALISM

## PART II / FAMOUS SERMONS AND PUBLIC ADDRESSES

## PART III / HISTORIC ESSAYS

# PART IV / INTERVIEWS

# PART V / BOOKS

# APPENDIX / ADDITIONAL INTERVIEW

# Editor's Introduction

## Martin Luther King, Jr., Martyred Prophet for a Global Beloved Community of Justice, Faith, and Hope

I am deeply honored to present this collection of Martin Luther King's writings to the public. Working with King's writings, and with his associates, I have sought a clear image of this complex man. Who was he, and why did he so seize the imagination of America? Why did he elicit such love and such hatred? What formed him, and to whom shall we look for leadership now that he is gone?

When King was martyred in 1968, America lost its most effective prophet. Oppressed people, both at home and abroad, lost their most articulate voice. His prophetic words mirrored a twentieth-century America that had acquired global power, but one that had also sacrificed some of its most treasured values on the altar of institutional racism, economic injustice, and international influence. He was not the first religious American social reformer to offer jeremiads about a promise unfulfilled. Indeed, he stood firmly in the mainstream of this American dissenting tradition. Yet, paradoxically, he was both a unique personality and a representative of his people precisely because he belonged to this tradition.

This was a tradition that included abolitionists and many other varieties of progressive social reformers. Many Americans do not understand or have forgotten how indebted we are to the stubborn tradition of the loyal opposition in American history. The opposition's determination to put righteousness, conscience, and morality before social and political expediency helped to shape some of our most fundamental values and institutions.

From time to time, there were moments when this loyal opposition reflected the prevailing national mood. But few dissenters helped create the mood as King did. With the help of the media, King showed the nation from Montgomery to Selma that the cancer of racial bigotry had infected America's cherished democratic and moral tradition. Many in the nation felt that they were being judged unfairly. But many more concluded that the people themselves could not avoid being the defendants in King's stinging indictments against our complacency. He prosecuted our banal acceptance of social, political, and economic evils. As a consequence, many of us were moved to work against the forces that undermined our precious values. He in turn became our conscience and our advocate. He became a prophet of the people and to the people. What President Lyndon Baines Johnson said in 1965 about all the participants in the civil rights movement also applies to King: "And who among us can say we would have made the same progress were it not for his persistent bravery and his faith in American democracy."

King would not want us to laud him without recognizing those millions of his supporters at home and abroad. Among this host, he would and did emphasize the centrality of the black churches as his citadel of spiritual and material support.

Most of us are sadly unaware however that the black church movement, King's primary spiritual and social mooring, nurtured its own dissenting tradition. For those of us who are aware, it is still ironic that this tradition could so rapidly produce a world historical figure like Martin Luther King, Jr. We cannot tell this story here in detail. But some broad strokes should serve our purpose.

King's roots are indeed in the religion of his black slave forebears. The slaves and free blacks forged in the New World a new compact between their African cultural heritage and their need for a spiritual genealogy.

This new religion provided psychic and spiritual sustenance for a people in the grip of oppression. But freedom fighters in the South as well as the North resisted as best they could. Out of this dissenting tradition came the determination to resist oppression that is reflected in the slave spirituals:

Go down, Moses
Go down to Egyptland
Go tell ol' Pharaoh,
Let my people go!

Many people, black and white, came to view Martin Luther King, Jr., as a modern Moses despite the fact that he was a religious leader out of the black middle class. They embraced this view, often unaware that middle-class black leaders did not arise overnight. They had to be nurtured. Many middle-class black and white missionaries and teachers joined forces after the Civil War to build a viable black middle class. They hoped that these youngsters would in turn lead their people to greater freedom. There followed, however, the long years of virtual disenfranchisement and jim crow segregation, with painfully slow advances in economic and political power. During those years, black churches grew strong. They shepherded black Christians who were fighting illiteracy and violent oppression. They were the heart of the black communities in both the North and the South.

Like most organizations, like white churches, black churches also developed, formed factions and alliances, split, recongregated, and multi-

plied. Among the demominations, Baptists and Methodists predominat-
ed. Despite the rapid development and expansions of congregational
alliances, the black church movement was seldom able to amass solidarity across denominational grouping, because of continuous internal
struggles for power.[1] Although caustic, Edward Franklin Frazier's judgment about the social and political effectiveness of the black middle
class can also be applied to the black church movement. He said, "Shut
up within a world where serious matters are not taken seriously, middle-
class Negroes carry on a serious struggle for status and recognition."[2]
However, Frazier failed to account for the activistic tradition within the
black middle class. He saw black middle-class activism as primarily the
preserve of an older generation of middle-class black America. But that
view did not account for the younger, militant members of the black
middle class, such as Martin Luther King, Jr. King himself criticized the
lack of social interest on the part of many middle-class black Americans
in the 1950s. He was especially disappointed with those in the black
church movement who had not responded quickly to the new opportunity for social change.

Although he often criticized black Christians for their complacency,
King never disowned either the black church movement or his own early faith commitments. He deepened their intellectual grounding, but he
never belittled the faith of the people or their powerful spirituality. In
fact, he tells story after story of how black people of faith, such as Mother Pollard,[3] emboldened and inspired him to press forward. In his famous "Letter from Birmingham City Jail," he declared, "I am grateful
to God that, through the influence of the Negro church, the way of nonviolence became an integral part of our struggle."

When he penned this letter in a Birmingham jail cell, King knew that
scores of black Christians, both lay and clergy, had risked their lives for
the cause, and that scores of black churches had been burned, vandal-
ized, and bombed throughout the South. He told *Playboy* interviewers
that when black ministers "finally decided to entrust our movement
with their support," they became "a glorious example in the history of
Christendom. For never in Christian history, within a Christian country,
have Christian churches been on the receiving end of such naked brutality and violence as we are witnessing here in America today. Not since
the days of the Christians in the catacombs has God's house, as a symbol,
weathered such attack as Negro churches." King's comments are not an
exaggeration. When the public finally receives a full history of the black
church movement, the roots of this Christian movement's *theologia cru-
cis* will be most evident.

Throughout the course of their history, black congregations suffered
greatly under the persecution of white terrorists who murdered their
members, leaders, and neighbors. These racists destroyed black proper-
ties while espousing platitudes about justice and freedom for all. In fact,

while this tragic drama was in process, most white moderates—with the exception of those such as Reinhold Niebuhr, who early encouraged blacks to embrace nonviolent resistance—had the audacity to insist that black Christians should be paragons of the faith. The later "black power" disdain for hypocritical white liberalism was not without some ethical justification. However, such accusers had trouble explaining the altruism and martyrdom of white liberals such as Jonathan Daniels, James Reeb, and Viola Liuzzo.

With many black and white Christians and progressive activists behind King, SCLC became a mighty moral force for social reform. King's rise to social power marked the end of American Christendom's—and especially the black church movement's—often passive and sometimes cynical indifference to this persecution. More educated, militant, and worldly-wise ministers, such as Oliver Leon Brown, Archibald Carey, Edwin R. Edmonds, Theodore Jemison, Dearing E. King, Adam Clayton Powell, Jr., Kelly Miller Smith, Frederick Sampson, Gardner Calvin Taylor, Wyatt Tee Walker, and Frank Williams were being called to strategic black pastorates throughout the South as well as the North. They were able to strike a happy balance between a bourgeois black social gospel tradition and the old-time religion founded in the slave quarters. Martin Luther King, Jr., quickly became a member of this new generation of black religious leaders because he also refused to alienate himself from the struggles of the black masses.

Several social factors besides their own extraordinary ability contributed to the successful rise of these religious leaders to social power. Martin Luther King, Jr., himself pointed out five factors that brought about tremendous psychic and social changes within black America. The rapid migration of the general black population from the rural South to the urban North had been steadily increasing since the devastating economic depressions of 1907 and 1929. Moreover, amazingly rapid educational advance expanded the ranks of the black middle class. Indeed, practically all the major black leaders of the civil rights movement were graduates of black colleges and universities such as Fisk, Howard, Tuskegee, Virginia Union, and Morehouse. These institutions were organized shortly after the end of the Civil War. The tireless labor of post-Civil War missionaries and teachers in the South, as well as the generous philanthropy of several American foundations and Northern religious denominations, became a mighty force for social reform, and struck a powerful blow against the crippling effects of illiteracy.

As a consequence of urban migration and the creation of a sophisticated black middle class, blacks in urban America, both North and South, were in a good position to improve their economic lot. This improvement was especially strengthened after the nation quickly recovered from its post-World War II recession, and entered into its longest and wealthiest period of economic well-being. On the political front, no factor bolstered black self-determination and pride more than the successful effort of the Reverend Leon Oliver Brown and the National Association for the Advancement of Colored People (NAACP) in obtaining the historic 17 May 1954 Supreme Court decision to desegregate America's public schools. The Topeka Board of Education had required Linda Brown, the pastor's nine-year-old daughter, to walk two blocks in order to catch a school bus that took her to an all-black school two miles from her home when an all-white school was closer. Brown, pastor of the Saint Mark African Methodist Episcopal Church in Topeka, Kansas, filed a suit against the board, and won.

The final factor King attributes to what he called the rising tide of racial consciousness, a renewed African American "awareness that his struggle for freedom is a part of a worldwide struggle. He has watched developments in Asia and Africa with rapt attention." Indeed, King observed, by 1962 approximately thirty modern independent African nations had acquired political freedom from European domination. That fact was not lost on black American audiences.

During the 1950s and 1960s, the British Empire crumbled slowly but steadily. In the United States, this period was the heyday of a paranoid anticommunism fostered by Republican senator Joseph McCarthy of Wisconsin. McCarthy led a new surge of repression against America's minorities. "Insolent" (read *brave*) black soldiers returning from brilliant successes such as the Battle of the Bulge enraged the racists, who were determined to "keep the niggers in their place." But they were too late. A new day had arrived for black America.

Many black leaders now affirmed that a "New Negro" movement was afoot. Black leaders have often used this phrase to gather and focus black support. Indeed, the black leaders, and a few liberal whites, who had organized the Niagara Movement in 1905 in response to racial riots in Springfield, Illinois, had also hailed the advent of a "New Negro." By 1909 they had reorganized themselves into the now famous National Association for the Advancement of Colored People (NAACP), which began a major legal assault against jim crow segregation. The tough-minded black professional crusade saw many victories scored by the students of Charles Houston, a major black legal scholar who taught at Howard University, such as Supreme Court Justice Thurgood Marshall. They were often joined in this crusade, as well as in others, by the National Urban League, which was formed in 1912. They did not see major changes, however, until the liberal New Deal judges appointed by President Franklin Delano Roosevelt began to change the ethics of the American judiciary.

But for many the pace of this middle-class reform movement was too slow. The black masses were becoming increasingly restless. Black Americans were deeply angered by the McCarthyist victimization of black cultural heroes such as novelist Richard Wright and singer Paul

Robeson. The red-baiting ideologues of Americanism such as J. Edgar Hoover, Strom Thurmond, and later George C. Wallace, used McCarthyist tactics in an effort to undermine the civil rights movement. King himself was accused of being procommunist, and he constantly weathered unwarranted FBI abrogations of his constitutional right to privacy. But Hoover's vendetta did not succeed in undoing King's monumental contribution to the moral, social, political, and spiritual history of the twentieth century.

## PROPHET OF THE PEOPLE

Those of us who were both King's contemporaries and his sympathizers believed that some strange providence guided the course of his life. Many of us came to believe that Dr. King's leadership embodied the *Zeitgeist*, the spirit of the times, a powerful moment in the career of the struggle for freedom. We wanted to believe that God was on our side, and we believed that King's life, and the movement he led, constituted a powerful "testament of hope." Author James Baldwin said that Martin Luther King, Jr., "has succeeded, in a way no Negro before him has managed to do, to carry the battle into the individual heart and make its resolution the province of the individual will. He has made it a matter, on both sides of the racial fence, of self-examination."[4] King believed that God was calling on both black and white Americans to examine their consciences about the state of race relations.

He believed the bitterness and hatred shared by both races was a malignant cancer nurtured by white injustice and black fatalism. This injustice and this resignation in turn bred social hatred and political cynicism. In despair, African Americans built a psychic defense system around various doctrines of black moral superiority and the spiritual and cultural power of African people. Meanwhile, white Americans were busily expanding a *Herrenvolk* democracy that was being undermined by racism. These spiritual and political tribalisms divided the nation, each sustained by two quite different understandings of the providence that each believed seem to be abundantly blessing the United States. White Americans apparently felt they were indeed the showcase of God's blessings; and black Americans felt they too were on their way to a Promised Land—one similar to the one white America now occupied. Both sides quoted the Bible.

The chief ideologues were outspoken conservative and liberal preachers. Conservative evangelical preachers boldly announced that communism and liberalism threatened American economic and social well-being in the period after World War II. One of them, Jerry Falwell, declared, in the middle of King's civil rights campaign in Selma, Alabama, that "I must personally say that I do question the sincerity and non-violent intentions of some civil rights leaders such as Dr. Martin Luther King, Jr., Mr. James Farmer, and others, who are known to have left-wing associations."[5] Falwell had a black counterpart in the Reverend Dr. Joseph Harrison Jackson, president of the National Baptist Convention, U.S.A. (the denomination with which King had been affiliated until 1961, when he sided with a seceding group called the Progressive National Baptist Convention).[6] Conservative black preachers usually had little trouble getting either an audience or support. Progressive black preachers had to work harder to get their white compatriots to move from discussion to action. Benjamin E. Mays (King's mentor, and onetime president of Morehouse College) recalled that the progressive integrated Southern Regional Council was "exceedingly cautious and timid, stepping lightly so as not to disturb the status quo of a segregated society."[7]

Progressive black leaders did feel that they had to press their white friends to endorse attempts to overthrow jim crow segregationist policies. And no part of the middle-class black leadership felt the need and pressure to overthrow segregation more than did black ministers. They counseled the victims of this infamous system. They buried the victims of white mob violence. They labored to relieve the psychic and economic depression largely caused by racist injustice. And they were among the first to openly denounce and actively oppose racist oppression.

For all their personal foibles and disadvantages, black preachers managed to create and sustain the only consistent tradition of prophetic ministry in America. In the days of slavery (1619–1863), they were often denied the free exercise of their ministerial gifts. And in the era of Jim Crow segregation, disenfranchisement, and lynchings (1863–1965), they were derided and accused of retarding social progress by presiding over separate black congregations and denominations.

Martin Luther King's ardent supporter and good friend, Gardner C. Taylor, pastor of Brooklyn's historic Concord Baptist Church of Christ, once characterized Martin Luther King, Jr., as heir to a long lineage of black preachers who had been "maligned and caricatured as merchants of escapism." Despite such pressures, they forged important institutions and movements with the tools of a powerful faith in God, a legendary preaching tradition, and the tenacious loyalty and encouragement of ordinary black church members. Martin Luther King, Jr., was a product of this company of prophets, and he accepted his "call" to be a part of this ministry even before he finished college. As the son of a black preacher, he had an obligation to give serious consideration to becoming one himself. The pressure was especially great in his case because his maternal great-grandfather, grandfather, and his father were all black Baptist preachers. King became one of the outstanding preachers of our era. And his life was his greatest sermon.

## THE LIFE OF A PROPHET

Martin Luther King, Jr., was born in Atlanta, Georgia, on 15 January 1929. His parents were the Reverend Martin Luther King, Sr., and Mrs. Alberta Williams King. Between 1935 and 1944, he attended David T. Howard Elementary School, Atlanta University Laboratory School, and Booker T. Washington High School. He passed a special examination to enter Morehouse College without finishing high school, and attended Morehouse between 1944 and 1948.

In the meantime, the Ebenezer Baptist Church in Atlanta, whose senior pastor was King's father, also licensed the son to preach, in 1947, when he was only 18 and ordained him to the Christian ministry on 25 February 1948. He graduated from Morehouse College with a bachelor's degree in sociology in June 1948. That September he entered Crozer Theological Seminary in Chester, Pennsylvania, a seminary affiliated with what was then called the Northern Baptist Convention (now called the American Baptist Churches in the USA). In 1951 he obtained his bachelor's degree in divinity at the head of his class. Encouraged by his seminary professors, he applied for the doctorate in systematic theology at Boston University School of Theology. He earned this degree within five years, and received it on 5 June 1955.

Within that five-year period, two events in his life were to be far more important than the doctorate in shaping his destiny. First, he married Coretta Scott of Marion, Alabama, on 18 June 1953. When they met in Boston, she was a recent graduate of Antioch College who was pursuing graduate study in singing at the New England Conservatory of Music. Before he finished his dissertation, the historic Dexter Avenue Baptist Church of Montgomery, Alabama, invited him to become their twentieth pastor. On 31 October 1954, amid much local fanfare, Martin and Coretta King were installed as the First Family of this prestigious black Baptist church.

The second event took place on 1 December 1955. Mrs. Rosa Parks, a forty-two-year-old black seamstress, took an action that shook the racist South and signaled to African Americans that the time had come at last to unequivocally reply "No!" to racial segregation and discrimination. While riding the public bus from her job at the Montgomery Fair department store, this tired black worker was approached by a white man who boarded the bus and who remained standing rather than sit next to a black woman. The bus driver demanded that she surrender her seat, as the jim crow laws of Alabama required. Rosa Parks said, "No." She was arrested. The fight to vindicate her ignited the civil rights movement of the 1960s. Her "No" became the indignant rallying cry for black people throughout America.

Martin Luther King, Jr., later described her action thus: "She was not 'planted' there by the NAACP, or any other organization; she was planted there by her personal sense of dignity and self-respect. She was anchored to that seat by the accumulated indignities of days gone by and the boundless aspirations of generations yet unborn. She was a victim of both the forces of history and the forces of destiny. She had been tracked down by the *Zeitgeist*—the spirit of the time."[8]

Rosa Parks was saying no to an age of white terrorism that sought to dominate and control African Americans by lynchings. This age began after the Civil War and the Reconstruction, as racists wrested the vote away from black people by all manner of illegal means. For a time after World War II, the lynchings and burnings had somewhat abated, thanks to such groups as the Southern Regional Council and the NAACP. But in *Brown* v. *Topeka, Kansas Board of Education* on 17 May 1954, the U.S. Supreme Court mandated public school desegregation "with all deliberate speed." Immediately, white racists such as the members of the White Citizen's Council and the Ku Klux Klan (KKK) intensified violence against blacks. In Mississippi alone, three known cases of white terrorism had recently received great attention in the black press. The Reverend George W. Lee was lynched at Belzoni, Mississippi, after he and Gus Courts attempted to register to vote in Humphreys County. Lamar Smith was lynched at Brookhaven. And—most infamously of all—the fourteen-year-old boy Emmett Till was lynched in Money, Mississippi. What Rosa Parks did was brave indeed, given such a context!

For 381 days, Dr. King, as president of the Montgomery Improvement Association, led a successful nonviolent black boycott against the Montgomery, Alabama, public bus system. In this boycott, the force of his personality and his deeply spiritual, intelligent preaching against violence and for justice made him an internationally known Christian proponent of nonviolent social change. He felt a decisive moment in history had arrived. He declared, "after prayerful consideration I am convinced that the psychological moment has come when a concentrated drive against injustice can bring great tangible gains."[9] King decided to institutionalize his newly acquired social power by founding the Southern Christian Leadership Conference in 1957. He resigned from his Montgomery parish in January 1960, and became the co-pastor of his father's church, Ebenezer Baptist Church, so that he could work full-time on his SCLC activities.

We could merely add here that Dr. King delivered (before the nationally televised March On Washington on 28 August 1963) the historic keynote address we know as his "I Have a Dream" speech; that he received the 1964 Nobel Prize for Peace; and that he was assassinated in Memphis, Tennessee, on 4 April 1968. But such a terse narrative would not disclose the historical significance of the period between the publication of Dr. King's *Stride Toward Freedom* in 1958 and his death in 1968. In this brief span of time, the United States experienced a moral, religious, and political revolution whose tremors were felt around the world.

## THE CHALLENGE TO AMERICA'S CONSCIENCE

As the British Empire rapidly crumbled, the United States scrambled to catch as many of the windfalls as possible. But its own domestic problems revealed John Foster Dulles's moralizing imperialism to be blatantly hypocritical.

America had always claimed to be the hope of the world. As early as 1630, John Winthrop, first governor of the newly formed Massachusetts Bay Colony and a seemingly insignificant servant of England's expanding mercantilist interests in America, quoted Jesus' Sermon on the Mount as the moral authorization for his holy commonwealth. He said aboard the little ship, *Arabella*, that "we are a city upon a hill." The New Puritans were to be the new moral and religious beacon light for an unrighteous world lost in a hopeless wilderness of sin and decadence. But as the religious historian Sydney Eckman Ahlstrom reminds us, "radical inequality and massive forms of oppression have been features—fundamental features—of the 'American way of life.' "[10] Nevertheless, this moral and religious heritage spawned a continuous tradition of social reform movements that attacked America's emerging "culture of consumption" from within. Reformers, from Rhode Island's Roger Williams to Martin Luther King, Jr., urged the nation to be faithful to this moral heritage. This tenacious tradition has also had many martyrs, including Elijah Lovejoy, John Brown, Abraham Lincoln, Martin Luther King, Jr., and many more. These heroes and heroines believed that America could not only be great but also good. They saw something fundamentally noble about a nation of people who believe character should be a corporate as well as an individual virtue. However, consensus faded when the nation sought to unpack the contents of its national moral creed. The national ambivalence cost the reformers their lives. Yet the heritage lives on, as the American dream, as the promise engraved on the Statue of Liberty, as Martin Luther King's dream. It remains for us to resolve our internal conflicts and to realize this dream.

How did King fit into this heritage? How did it mold him? Four grand threads seem to have interwoven the tapestry of King's life and thought: (1) an understanding of providence, (2) an humble sense of his own pastoral power, (3) a deep commitment to an understanding of the prophet as "a drum major for righteousness," and (4) a solid understanding of the global implications in the African American quest for justice.

In one of his many poignant sermons, Martin Luther King, Jr., described himself as "a drum major for righteousness." Surely the designation of the third Monday in January as a national holiday (Martin Luther King Day) signals an acceptance of King, albeit reluctantly, as a national hero. Whether this symbolic act is seen as an example of shrewd political subversion or a majestic act of national repentance for the violation of sacred beliefs in democracy, justice, freedom, and peace, depends greatly on how thoroughly America will address those injustices that Martin Luther King, Jr., gave his life to eradicate.

King believed some great modern innocence had been assaulted by the merchants of materialism and bigotry. He believed the universalist religious dream of one *world* under God had been victimized by the racist nationalism that brazenly paraded the banner "ONE NATION UNDER GOD." It is difficult to appreciate King's achievement if we do not understand that his dilemma was that he saw both the need for and the danger of nationalism. He certainly was an Americanist, but not a nationalist ideologue. He was faithful to his country so long as his country was faithful to the vision of what King often called "the beloved community." Some black leaders, such as Malcolm X, argued that King's vision was only a tragic fantasy. If so, that fantasy was shared by many children of African slaves and a nation of voluntary European immigrants.

The symbolic victory of this national holiday presents a new opportunity to broaden the cultural and social revolution that black America started. Many black leaders correctly perceived, in the words of Professor Charles H. Long of the University of North Carolina, that America is "a hermeneutical situation." This cadre includes Frederick Douglass, W. E. B. DuBois, Langston Hughes, and James Baldwin.

No other black leader, however, has quite equaled the rich social and religious artistry of Martin Luther King, Jr. He was indeed a world historical figure. He captured the spotlight of history precisely at the right time, and responded with a blueprint for what America could become if it trusted its democratic legacy. His dream proved to be too threatening. It implied a massive redistribution of wealth and resources. He was murdered. But his dream still excites our social and political imaginations. It beckons us to work, to realize the dream that America can indeed be a truly pluralistic society, and that planet Earth can be a place in the universe where peace, justice, and freedom are the dominant ethos. By calling his vision a *dream*, King reformulated a great hypothesis that the founders of this republic held dear, and that the twentieth century yearns to see made real in the twenty-first century. He believed, to use the words of James Baldwin in a recent open letter to Bishop Desmond Tutu, that "black freedom will make white freedom possible. Indeed, *our* freedom, which we have been forced to buy at so high a price, is the only hope of freedom that they have."[11] The fall of the racist foundations of Western imperialism seems imminent. The goal of creating a world where "all God's children" will be free still remains firmly planted in the hearts of tireless workers around the world who struggle for a better day—the struggle for a day when, to use the words of an old traditional African American prayer, "the wicked shall cease from troubling, and the weary shall be at rest." As long as we are blessed, every now and then, with a Martin Luther King, Jr., our struggle is not in vain.

## THE STATE OF KING STUDIES

The several recent studies of the life and thought of Martin Luther King, Jr., all show a certain degree of confusion about what I consider to be his essentially religious personality. They invent labels that attempt to capture his essence. He has been called "charismatic, the moral conscience of the nation, man with a hard head, militant conservative, anarchist, apostate, leftist, communist, a fool, a fool for Christ, De Lawd, martyr," etc. Some of these labels are complimentary, others seek to be objective, and still others are downright derogatory.[12] As all great world historical figures, King has become the subject of intellectual archaeologists seeking to map the deep caverns of modern life and thought.

The most controversial dimension of King studies involves the FBI wiretap tapes of King and his associates. The use of these tapes for scholarly research has already been hindered by close associates of Dr. King, such as the Reverends Walter Fauntroy, Wyatt Tee Walker, and Andrew Young, who joined with other former colleagues in asking a federal court to enjoin the public from using those tapes until the twenty-first century.

No one has worked more diligently to use these tapes than Professor David Garrow of the City University of New York. But he has been enjoined from using the tapes of Dr. King and his closest associates, and he has primarily succeeded in securing extensive interviews with King associates outside of the inner circle. The success of this approach is evident in the publication of his Pulitzer Prize–winning book, *Bearing the Cross: Martin Luther King, Jr., and the Southern Christian Leadership Conference* (1986). We have learned much from Garrow's gargantuan effort to preserve the humanity and historical significance of King and SCLC.

Taylor Branch's *Parting the Waters: America During the King Years* (1988), another worthy recipient of a Pulitzer Prize, offers a stunningly eloquent and insightful portrayal of the religious and social network that nurtured and supported King and his public image. Numerous other analyses of King and various aspects of the civil rights movement, including biographies and autobiographies of various civil rights figures, have been published since these excellent studies by Garrow and Branch. In fact Branch promises a sequel to his first book, which stops at 1963. [Section VIII of the Selected Bibliography lists only those works primarily related to the public ministry of Dr. King.]

None of these publications, however, has created as much of a commotion as the late Ralph David Abernathy's autobiography. He was King's closest associate and one of his best friends. Many lamented what seemed to be a friend's betrayal. As scholars, journalists, politicians, and other citizens continue to debate the propriety of examining the private life of public figures, many who still believe in the necessity for public heroes will continue to defend King, the hero, against King, the human being. Both protagonists and antagonists of the heroic persona will be required by the psychic and material vicissitudes that are pressing against and beyond the turnstile of a new millennium to reconsider the role of ethics, myth, and history in assessments of Dr. King's personal and public life. But fairness and empathy should require all evaluators to remember that Dr. King bequeathed to both his biological and spiritual heirs nothing more nor less than what he called "a committed life." Dr. King, and the unheralded prophetic martyrs of the civil rights movement, have unintentionally placed all of us strangely and uncomfortably in their debt.

Many scholars are contributing to the repayment of this debt by bringing their analytical powers and research skills to the vigorous effort to preserve the memories and meanings of the civil rights movement. Since Dr. King was this movement's most prominent leader, it is understandable that he has been the primary focus of such scholarly endeavors. Noting this trend, Eric Foner of Columbia University outlined the agenda confronting scholars interested in the civil rights era in his review of Stephen B. Oates's fine biography of King, titled *Let the Trumpet Sound: The Life of Martin Luther King, Jr.* (1982). He warned against the danger of equating "a mass movement with a single individual" and added, "Mr. Oates never penetrates the black community to provide a sense of the resources, both personal and institutional, that sustained those humble men and women who walked the streets of Montgomery and filled the jails of Birmingham." The spirituality of the civil rights movement begs for our attention.[13]

Mrs. Coretta Scott King and the Center for Nonviolent Social Change in Atlanta took the major initiative in organizing the sponsorship of a critical, multivolume series of books titled *The Martin Luther King, Jr., Papers.* For this historic venture, the center deserves the support of all who wish to preserve King's memory. It will undoubtedly become a major contribution to American scholarship, under the distinguished editorship of Clayborne Carson of Stanford University, and will be published by the University of California Press. This enterprise promises a definitive record of the involvement of King and the SCLC in the civil rights movement.

Despite these prodigious efforts, the story of the role of the black church movement's involvement in the civil rights struggle demands a separate study. The hesitance of African American church leaders to share information and insights with people outside the church is founded on the painful experience of being repeatedly misunderstood by both black and white scholars who do not take the history and the religious culture of the black church seriously enough to investigate its taproots.

In fact, few of the recent studies of King's life and thought offer insights into his rich religious background and imagination. The most notable exceptions are the two books and three articles written respectively by Kenneth Smith in collaboration with Ira Zepp, Jr., John J. Ansbro, James McClendon, and James H. Cone.[14] Smith and Zepp rather single-mindedly sought to demonstrate that King was deeply indebted to liberal evangelical theology, which they claimed he first learned at Crozer Theological Seminary. Ansbro, on the other hand, offers a finely woven overview of the impact of mainstream white theologians on King's theological liberalism, and his social and political philosophy. McClendon's article is the best representative of a series of articles written to defend the legitimacy of King as an important American theologian. James H. Cone's articles, written in his usual bold tone, chide the American intellectual establishment for ignoring the importance of the black church movement on King's life and thought, and suggest lines of interpretation that he plans to develop in later publications. We eagerly await the publication of his comparative analysis of the theologies of King and Malcolm X, titled *King and Malcolm and America* (Orbis Books, 1991).

## THE RATIONALE FOR THIS COLLECTION OF KING'S WRITINGS

Given the preceding discussion, it might be asked why this collection of documents is necessary. The general public and students in various colleges, universities, and seminaries need a handy set of the published writings of King. I discovered in my research that King's staff often either actually wrote or made heavy contributions to some of the published writings. I agree with Stephen B. Oates's comment about this delicate issue in regard to King's 1961 speech, which is printed in this anthology as "If the Negro Wins, Labor Wins." Oates said, "Perhaps Levison helped him to draft it," and he adds parenthetically that Bayard Rustin may also have helped him, "but the language, style, and sense of history are King's."[15]

The documents in this anthology, however, were *primarily* written by King, whose arduous schedule limited the amount of time available for the intricate work involved in carefully producing texts. They reflect the view that King and his close associates agreed should be given to the American public. As such, these published documents represent the public stance of King as president of the Southern Christian Leadership Conference. We need to recall both what he or his representatives said, what he meant to say, and what he wanted to say. The more indepth scholarship of scholars such as Garrow and Clayborne promises to reveal what King meant and wanted to say, but could not say because of the press of events or because of judgments about how the American public would receive his more private views. The resolution of such hermeneutical problems in King studies will occupy the time and energy of many scholars in the years to come. For now, this anthology seeks to offer a canonical presentation of the public witness of this physically diminutive spiritual giant.

This collection of King's writings is organized chronologically within certain specified topics. The purpose of this arrangement is twofold. First, it allows the reader to get a rapid overview of the kinds of reading publics King and his staff felt would be receptive to his message. Second, we can acquire a profile of the essential issues and events that shaped the development of his public theology and philosophy, both from the documents themselves and from the editor's headnotes and footnotes for each document. The section headings highlight this agenda.

The Selected Bibliography at the end of this book offers an introduction to further readings that grapple with this important theological and historical debate.

## ACKNOWLEDGMENTS

Tom Dorsaneo, marketing director at Harper & Row San Francisco, was one of the first to conceive of this book. Roy M. Carlisle, my conscientious and inspiring editor of Harper & Row San Francisco, deserves credit not only for the conception, but also for the delivery of the final product. Madison Shockley, Dana Fenton, and Mark Taylor provided important research assistance with grace and speed. Betty Bolden, Paul A. Byrnes, Kirk A. Moll, and Seth Kasten, staff members of Union Theological Seminary's magnificent Walter Burke Library graciously provided much assistance.

Professor David Garrow of the City University of New York, D. Louise Cook, director of the library at the Martin Luther King, Jr., Center for Nonviolent Social Change, both kindly provided fugitive documents and clarified how King and his staff worked together to produce his writings. Their commitment to scholarly integrity and to King's memory is admirable.

Many friends and colleagues in the academy, as well as the clergy, greatly influenced my interpretation, but should not be blamed for errors either in interpretation or fact. Among this number I especially appreciate conversations I've had with Nathaniel Everett Ellis, Professors John W. Blassingame, James H. Cone, Edwin R. Edmonds, James A. Forbes, Jr., Henry and Ella Mitchell, Peter Paris, Albert J. Raboteau, Edwin S. Redkey, Leslie Rout, Williams Scott, Cornel West, Preston Noah Williams, David Wills, Gayraud S. Wilmore; and the Reverend Drs. Gardner C. Taylor, William T. Crutcher, John Dixon Elder, Richard Gay, Carolyn Knight, Suzan Johnson, David Licorish, Nimrod Reynold, John L. Scott, Kelley Miller Smith (deceased), Frederick Sampson, Frederick Steen, Frederick Jerome Streets, Wyatt Tee Walker, and Obie Wright, Jr. The vital work of research scholars such as Drs.

Randall K. Burkett and Genna Rae McNeil were most helpful. Richard Newman, a tireless laborer in the field of African American Religious History, deserves a special note of gratitude for his assistance in locating documents and giving wise advice.

None of this would have been possible, however, without the confidence and encouragement so generously bestowed on me by Dame Coretta Scott King, whom many of us cherish as the First Lady of the civil rights movement. Both Mrs. King, and her daughter and my good friend, Yolanda King, provided me with precious insights and grand memories of the depths of human compassion. I hope that with this publication the nation will officially pause to assess its conscience, and to thank Dr. King and his family for sacrificing so much. May we become worthy of the trust and the Dream!

## NOTES

1. For discussions of the history, theology, and politics of the black church movement, see Carter G. Woodson, *The History of the Negro Church* (Washington, D.C.: Associated Publishers, 1921); E. Franklin Frazier and C. Eric Lincoln, *The Negro Church in America / The Black Church Since Frazier* (New York: Schocken Books, 1974); George A. Singleton, *The Romance of African Methodism* (New York: Exposition Press, 1952); William J. Walls, *The African Methodist Episcopal Church: Reality of the Black Church* (Charlotte, N.C.: A.M.E. Zion Book Concern, 1974); Gayraud S. Wilmore, *Black Religion and Black Radicalism: An Interpretation of the Religious History of Afro-American People*, 2nd ed., rev. and enl. (Maryknoll, N.Y.: Orbis Books, 1983); Joseph Harrison Jackson, *A Story of Christian Activism: The History of the National Baptist Convention, U.S.A., Inc.* (Nashville: Townsend Press, 1980); Leroy Fitts, *A History of Black Baptists* (Nashville: Broadman Press, 1985); and James Melvin Washington, *Frustrated Fellowship: Black Baptist Quest for Social Power* (Macon, Ga.: Mercer University Press, 1986). Other significant works, by scholars such as Randall Burkett, Carol V. R. George, Richard Newman, Albert J. Raboteau, Edwin S. Redkey, Milton C. Sernett, Lester B. Scherer, Michal Sobel, Clarence Walker, and David Wills, that grapple with various aspects of African American religious history should also be consulted.
2. E. Franklin Frazier, "The Negro Middle Class and Desegregation" (1957), in G. Franklin Edwards, ed., *E. Franklin Frazier on Race Relations* (Chicago and London: University of Chicago Press, 1968), 306.
3. See his Mother Pollard story in the excerpt from "Strength to Love" titled, "Antidotes for Fear."
4. James Baldwin, "The Highroad of Destiny," in C. Eric Lincoln, ed., *Martin Luther King, Jr.: A Profile* (New York: Hill and Wang, 1970), 111.
5. Quoted from the complete text of Falwell's sermon delivered before his Thomas Road Baptist Church congregation in Lynchburg, Virginia, at the evening service of 21 March 1965, and titled, "Ministers and Marches" in Perry Deane Young, *God's Bullies: Native Reflections on Preachers and Politics* (New York: Holt, Rinehart and Winston, 1982), 310.
6. See Joseph H. Jackson, *Unholy Shadows and Freedom's Holy Light* (Nashville: Townsend Press, 1967); Peter J. Paris, *Black Leaders in Conflict* (New York: Pilgrim Press, 1978); and Paris's *The Social Teaching of the Black Churches* (Philadelphia: Fortress Press, 1985).
7. Benjamin E. Mays, *Born to Rebel: An Autobiography* (New York: Scribner's, 1971), 220.
8. Martin Luther King, Jr., *Stride Toward Freedom: The Montgomery Story* (New York: Harper & Row, 1958), 29.
9. Quoted in Coretta Scott King, *My Life With Martin Luther King, Jr.* (New York: Holt,

Rinehart and Winston, 1969), 183.

10. Sydney E. Ahlstrom, "The Radical Turn in Theology and Ethics: Why It Occurred in the 1960s," THE ANNALS of the American Academy of Political and Social Science 387 (January 1970): 10.

11. James Baldwin, "Letter to the Bishop," New Statesman (23 August 1985): 9.

12. For an early attempt to profile cross currents at stake in this debate, see C. Eric Lincoln, ed., Martin Luther King, Jr.: A Profile (New York: Hill and Wang, 1970). For a thoroughly derogatory examination from the right-wing Evangelical camp, see James D. Bales, The Martin Luther King Story (Tulsa, Okla.: Christian Crusade Publications, 1967).

13. Eric Foner, "The Man Who Had the Dream," New York Times Book Review (12 September 1982): 14, 58. A discussion of recent and traditional political uses of African American spirituality can be found in James Melvin Washington, "Jesse Jackson and the Symbolic Politics of Black Christendom," The ANNALS of the American Academy of Political and Social Science 480 (July 1985): 89–105.

14. Kenneth Smith, Ira Zepp, Jr., Search for the Beloved Community: The Thinking of Martin Luther King, Jr. (Valley Forge, Pa.: Judson Press, 1974); John J. Ansbro, Martin Luther King, Jr.: The Making of a Mind (Maryknoll, N.Y.: Orbis Books, 1982); James William McClendon, "Martin Luther King, Jr.: Politician or American Church Father?" Journal of Ecumenical Studies 8 (Winter 1971): 115ff.; and two articles by James H. Cone, titled, "Martin Luther King, Jr.: The Source of His Courage to Face Death," Concilium 183 (March 1983): 418–27, and "Martin Luther King, Jr.: Black Theology—Black Church," Theology Today 40/4 (1984): 409–20.

15. Stephen B. Oates, Let the Trumpet Sound: The Life of Martin Luther King, Jr. (New York: Harper & Row, 1982), 521, notes for pages 186–87.

# PART I: PHILOSOPHY

## Religious: Nonviolence

# Nonviolence and Racial Justice

*This article appeared in* Christian Century, *the premier liberal Protestant journal, shortly after almost 100 black clergymen came to the Ebenezer Baptist Church in Atlanta in response to a call from the Reverends Fred Shuttlesworth, Charles K. Steele, and Dr. King. They met on 10–11 January 1957, formed the Southern Christian Leadership Conference (SCLC), and elected King as its first president. This article outlines King's hope that nonviolent direct action could become the philosophy around which committed Christians could rally in order to defeat the "evil" of segregation. With the encouragement and editorial assistance of two very important activist pacifists—the Reverend Glenn E. Smiley, national field secretary of the Fellowship of Reconciliation, and Bayard Rustin, then executive secretary of the War Resisters' League—King sought to use this philosophy through SCLC to focus and direct the new black struggle for equality. As the president of the Montgomery Improvement Association, he argued that this tactic had been used successfully in MIA's nonviolent boycott against that city's bus company. After 381 days of the black boycott, the U.S. Supreme Court on 13 November 1956 affirmed the 4 June decision handed down by a panel of three judges on the U.S. District Court, who ruled against the local and state segregation laws of Alabama.*

It is commonly observed that the crisis in race relations dominates the arena of American life. This crisis has been precipitated by two factors: the determined resistance of reactionary elements in the South to the Supreme Court's momentous decision outlawing segregation in the public schools, and the radical change in the Negro's evaluation of himself. While southern legislative halls ring with open defiance through "interposition" and "nullification," while a modern version of the Ku Klux Klan has arisen in the form of "respectable" white citizens' councils, a revolutionary change has taken place in the Negro's conception of his own nature and destiny. Once he thought of himself as an inferior and patiently accepted injustice and exploitation. Those days are gone.

The first Negroes landed on the shores of this nation in 1619, one year ahead of the Pilgrim Fathers. They were brought here from Africa and, unlike the Pilgrims, they were brought against their will, as slaves. Throughout the era of slavery the Negro was treated in inhuman fashion. He was considered a thing to be used, not a person to be respected.

He was merely a depersonalized cog in a vast plantation machine. The famous Dred Scott decision of 1857 well illustrates his status during slavery. In this decision the Supreme Court of the United States said, in substance, that the Negro is not a citizen of the United States; he is merely property subject to the dictates of his owner.

After his emancipation in 1863, the Negro still confronted oppression and inequality. It is true that for a time, while the army of occupation remained in the South and Reconstruction ruled, he had a brief period of eminence and political power. But he was quickly overwhelmed by the white majority. Then in 1896, through the Plessy *v.* Ferguson decision, a new kind of slavery came into being. In this decision the Supreme Court of the nation established the doctrine of "separate but equal" as the law of the land. Very soon it was discovered that the concrete result of this doctrine was strict enforcement of the "separate," without the slightest intention to abide by the "equal." So the Plessy doctrine ended up plunging the Negro into the abyss of exploitation where he experienced the bleakness of nagging injustice.

## A PEACE THAT WAS NO PEACE

Living under these conditions, many Negroes lost faith in themselves. They came to feel that perhaps they were less than human. So long as the Negro maintained this subservient attitude and accepted the "place" assigned him, a sort of racial peace existed. But it was an uneasy peace in which the Negro was forced patiently to submit to insult, injustice and exploitation. It was a negative peace. True peace is not merely the absence of some negative force—tension, confusion or war; it is the presence of some positive force—justice, good will and brotherhood.

Then circumstances made it necessary for the Negro to travel more. From the rural plantation he migrated to the urban industrial community. His economic life began gradually to rise, his crippling illiteracy gradually to decline. A myriad of factors came together to cause the Negro to take a new look at himself. Individually and as a group, he began to reevaluate himself. And so he came to feel that he was somebody. His religion revealed to him that God loves all his children and that the important thing about a man is "not his specificity but his fundamentum," not the texture of his hair or the color of his skin but the quality of his soul.

This new self-respect and sense of dignity on the part of the Negro undermined the South's negative peace, since the white man refused to accept the change. The tension we are witnessing in race relations today can be explained in part by this revolutionary change in the Negro's evaluation of himself and his determination to struggle and sacrifice until the walls of segregation have been fully crushed by the battering rams of justice.

## QUEST FOR FREEDOM EVERYWHERE

The determination of Negro Americans to win freedom from every form of oppression springs from the same profound longing for freedom that motivates oppressed peoples all over the world. The dynamic beat of deep discontent in Africa and Asia is at bottom a quest for freedom and human dignity on the part of people who have long been victims of colonialism. The struggle for freedom on the part of oppressed people in general and of the American Negro in particular has developed slowly and is not going to end suddenly. Privileged groups rarely give up their privileges without strong resistance. But when oppressed people rise up against oppression there is no stopping point short of full freedom. Realism compels us to admit that the struggle will continue until freedom is a reality for all the oppressed peoples of the world.

Hence the basic question which confronts the world's oppressed is: How is the struggle against the forces of injustice to be waged? There are two possible answers. One is resort to the all too prevalent method of physical violence and corroding hatred. The danger of this method is its futility. Violence solves no social problems; it merely creates new and more complicated ones. Through the vistas of time a voice still cries to every potential Peter, "Put up your sword!" The shores of history are white with the bleached bones of nations and communities that failed to follow this command. If the American Negro and other victims of oppression succumb to the temptation of using violence in the struggle for justice, unborn generations will live in a desolate night of bitterness, and their chief legacy will be an endless reign of chaos.

## ALTERNATIVE TO VIOLENCE

The alternative to violence is nonviolent resistance. This method was made famous in our generation by Mohandas K. Gandhi, who used it to free India from the domination of the British empire. Five points can be made concerning nonviolence as a method in bringing about better racial conditions.

First, this is not a method for cowards; it *does* resist. The nonviolent resister is just as strongly opposed to the evil against which he protests as is the person who uses violence. His method is passive or nonaggressive in the sense that he is not physically aggressive toward his opponent. But his mind and emotions are always active, constantly seeking to persuade the opponent that he is mistaken. This method is passive physically but strongly active spiritually; it is nonaggressive physically but dynamically aggressive spiritually.

A second point is that nonviolent resistance does not seek to defeat or humiliate the opponent, but to win his friendship and understanding. The nonviolent resister must often express his protest through noncooperation or boycotts, but he realizes that noncooperation and boycotts are not ends themselves; they are merely means to awaken a sense of moral shame in the opponent. The end is redemption and reconciliation. The aftermath of nonviolence is the creation of the beloved community, while the aftermath of violence is tragic bitterness.

A third characteristic of this method is that the attack is directed against forces of evil rather than against persons who are caught in those forces. It is evil we are seeking to defeat, not the persons victimized by evil. Those of us who struggle against racial injustice must come to see that the basic tension is not between races. As I like to say to the people in Montgomery, Alabama: "The tension in this city is not between white people and Negro people. The tension is at bottom between justice and injustice, between the forces of light and the forces of darkness. And if there is a victory it will be a victory not merely for fifty thousand Negroes, but a victory for justice and the forces of light. We are out to defeat injustice and not white persons who may happen to be unjust."

A fourth point that must be brought out concerning nonviolent resistance is that it avoids not only external physical violence but also internal violence of spirit. At the center of nonviolence stands the principle of love. In struggling for human dignity the oppressed people of the world must not allow themselves to become bitter or indulge in hate campaigns. To retaliate with hate and bitterness would do nothing but intensify the hate in the world. Along the way of life, someone must have sense enough and morality enough to cut off the chain of hate. This can be done only by projecting the ethics of love to the center of our lives.

## THE MEANING OF 'LOVE'

In speaking of love at this point, we are not referring to some sentimental emotion. It would be nonsense to urge men to love their oppressors in an affectionate sense. "Love" in this connection means understanding good will. There are three words for love in the Greek New Testament. First, there is *eros*. In Platonic philosophy *eros* meant the yearning of the soul for the realm of the divine. It has come now to mean a sort of aesthetic or romantic love. Second, there is *philia*. It meant intimate affectionateness between friends. *Philia* denotes a sort of reciprocal love: the person loves because he is loved. When we speak of loving those who oppose us we refer to neither *eros* nor *philia*; we speak of a love which is expressed in the Greek word *agape*. *Agape* means nothing sentimental or basically affectionate; it means understanding, redeeming good will for all men, an overflowing love which seeks nothing in return. It is the love of God working in the lives of men. When we love on the *agape* level we love men not because we like them, not because their attitudes and ways appeal to us, but because God loves them. Here we rise to the position of loving the person who does the evil deed while hating the deed he does.

Finally, the method of nonviolence is based on the conviction that the universe is on the side of justice. It is this deep faith in the future that causes the nonviolent resister to accept suffering without retaliation. He knows that in his struggle for justice he has cosmic companionship. This belief that God is on the side of truth and justice comes down to us from the long tradition of our Christian faith. There is something at the very center of our faith which reminds us that Good Friday may reign for a day, but ultimately it must give way to the triumphant beat of the Easter drums. Evil may so shape events that Caesar will occupy a palace and Christ a cross, but one day that same Christ will rise up and split history into A.D. and B.C., so that even the life of Caesar must be dated by his name. So in Montgomery we can walk and never get weary, because we know that there will be a great camp meeting in the promised land of freedom and justice.

This, in brief, is the method of nonviolent resistance. It is a method that challenges all people struggling for justice and freedom. God grant that we wage the struggle with dignity and discipline. May all who suffer oppression in this world reject the self-defeating method of retaliatory violence and choose the method that seeks to redeem. Through using this method wisely and courageously we will emerge from the bleak and desolate midnight of man's inhumanity to man into the bright daybreak of freedom and justice.

*Christian Century* 74 (6 February 1957): 165–67.

# 2

# The Most Durable Power

*This excerpt is from a sermon King preached in Montgomery, Alabama, on 6 November 1956, just seven days before the U.S. Supreme Court ruled against Alabama's bus segregation laws.*

Always be sure that you struggle with Christian methods and Christian weapons. Never succumb to the temptation of becoming bitter. As you press on for justice, be sure to move with dignity and discipline, using only the weapon of love. Let no man pull you so low as to hate him. Always avoid violence. If you succumb to the temptation of using violence in your struggle, unborn generations will be the recipients of a long and desolate night of bitterness, and your chief legacy to the future will be an endless reign of meaningless chaos.

In your struggle for justice, let your oppressor know that you are not attempting to defeat or humiliate him, or even to pay him back for injustices that he has heaped upon you. Let him know that you are merely seeking justice for him as well as yourself. Let him know that the festering sore of segregation debilitates the white man as well as the Negro. With this attitude you will be able to keep your struggle on high Christian standards.

Many persons will realize the urgency of seeking to eradicate the evil of segregation. There will be many Negroes who will devote their lives to the cause of freedom. There will be many white persons of good will and strong moral sensitivity who will dare to take a stand for justice. Honesty impels me to admit that such a stand will require willingness to suffer and sacrifice. So don't despair if you are condemned and persecuted for righteousness' sake. Whenever you take a stand for truth and justice, you are liable to scorn. Often you will be called an impractical idealist or a dangerous radical. Sometimes it might mean going to jail. If such is the case you must honorably grace the jail with your presence. It might even mean physical death. But if physical death is the price that some must pay to free their children from a permanent life of psychological death, then nothing could be more Christian.

I still believe that standing up for the truth of God is the greatest thing in the world. This is the end of life. The end of life is not to be happy. The end of life is not to achieve pleasure and avoid pain. The end of life is to do the will of God, come what may.

I still believe that love is the most durable power in the world. Over the centuries men have sought to discover the highest good. This has been the chief quest of ethical philosophy. This was one of the big questions of Greek philosophy. The Epicureans and the Stoics sought to answer it; Plato and Aristotle sought to answer it. What is the *summum bonum* of life? I think I have discovered the highest good. It is love. This principle stands at the center of the cosmos. As John says, "God is love." He who loves is a participant in the being of God. He who hates does not know God.

*Christian Century* 74 (5 June 1957): 708. Copyright © 1957 The Christian Century Foundation from the 5 June 1957 issue. Renewed. Used by permission.

# 3

# The Power of Nonviolence

*Invited by the Young Men's Christian Association (YMCA) and the Young Women's Christian Association (YWCA) at the University of California at Berkeley, King spoke on 4 June 1957 before a packed audience of eager students. This excerpt is from that address.*

From the very beginning there was a philosophy undergirding the Montgomery boycott, the philosophy of nonviolent resistance. There was always the problem of getting this method over because it didn't make sense to most of the people in the beginning. We had to use our mass meetings to explain nonviolence to a community of people who had never heard of the philosophy and in many instances were not sympathetic with it. We had meetings twice a week on Mondays and on Thursdays, and we had an institute on nonviolence and social change. We had to make it clear that nonviolent resistance is not a method of cowardice. It does resist. It is not a method of stagnant passivity and deadening complacency. The nonviolent resister is just as opposed to the evil that he is standing against as the violent resister but he resists without violence. This method is nonaggressive physically but strongly aggressive spiritually.

## NOT TO HUMILIATE BUT TO WIN OVER

Another thing that we had to get over was the fact that the nonviolent resister does not seek to humiliate or defeat the opponent but to win his friendship and understanding. This was always a cry that we had to set before people that our aim is not to defeat the white community, not to humiliate the white community, but to win the friendship of all of the persons who had perpetrated this system in the past. The end of violence or the aftermath of violence is bitterness. The aftermath of nonviolence is reconciliation and the creation of a beloved community. A boycott is never an end within itself. It is merely a means to awaken a sense of shame within the oppressor but the end is reconciliation, the end is redemption.

Then we had to make it clear also that the nonviolent resister seeks to attack the evil system rather than individuals who happen to be caught up in the system. And this is why I say from time to time that the struggle in the South is not so much the tension between white people and Negro people. The struggle is rather between justice and injustice, between the forces of light and the forces of darkness. And if there is a victory it will not be a victory merely for fifty thousand Negroes. But it will be a victory for justice, a victory for good will, a victory for democracy.

Another basic thing we had to get over is that nonviolent resistance is also an internal matter. It not only avoids external violence or external physical violence but also internal violence of spirit. And so at the center of our movement stood the philosophy of love. The attitude that the only way to ultimately change humanity and make for the society that we all long for is to keep love at the center of our lives. Now people used to ask me from the beginning what do you mean by love and how is it that you can tell us to love those persons who seek to defeat us and those persons who stand against us; how can you love such persons? And I had to make it clear all along that love in its highest sense is not a sentimental sort of thing, not even an affectionate sort of thing.

## *AGAPE* LOVE

The Greek language uses three words for love. It talks about *eros*. *Eros* is a sort of aesthetic love. It has come to us to be a sort of romantic love and it stands with all of its beauty. But when we speak of loving those who oppose us we're not talking about *eros*. The Greek language talks about *philia* and this is a sort of reciprocal love between personal friends. This is a vital, valuable love. But when we talk of loving those who oppose you and those who seek to defeat you we are not talking about *eros* or *philia*. The Greek language comes out with another word and it is *agape*. *Agape* is understanding, creative, redemptive good will for all men. Biblical theologians would say it is the love of God working in the minds of men. It is an overflowing love which seeks nothing in return. And when you come to love on this level you begin to love men not because they are likable, not because they do things that attract us, but because God loves them and here we love the person who does the evil deed while hating the deed that the person does. It is the type of love that stands at the center of the movement that we are trying to carry on in the Southland—*agape*.

## SOME POWER IN THE UNIVERSE THAT WORKS FOR JUSTICE

I am quite aware of the fact that there are persons who believe firmly in nonviolence who do not believe in a personal God, but I think every person who believes in nonviolent resistance believes somehow that the universe in some form is on the side of justice. That there is something unfolding in the universe whether one speaks of it as an unconscious process, or whether one speaks of it as some unmoved mover, or whether someone speaks of it as a personal God. There is something in the universe that unfolds for justice and so in Montgomery we felt somehow that as we struggled we had cosmic companionship. And this was one of the things that kept the people together, the belief that the universe is on the side of justice.

God grant that as men and women all over the world struggle against evil systems they will struggle with love in their hearts, with understanding good will. *Agape* says you must go on with wise restraint and calm reasonableness but you must keep moving. We have a great opportunity in America to build here a great nation, a nation where all men live together as brothers and respect the dignity and worth of all human personality. We must keep moving toward that goal. I know that some people are saying we must slow up. They are writing letters to the North and they are appealing to white people of good will and to the Negroes saying slow up, you're pushing too fast. They are saying we must adopt a policy of moderation. Now if moderation means moving on with wise restraint and calm reasonableness, then moderation is a great virtue that all men of good will must seek to achieve in this tense period of transition. But if moderation means slowing up in the move for justice and capitulating to the whims and caprices of the guardians of the deadening status quo, then moderation is a tragic vice which all men of good will must condemn. We must continue to move on. Our self-respect is at stake; the prestige of our nation is at stake. Civil rights is an eternal moral issue which may well determine the destiny of our civilization in the ideological struggle with communism. We must keep moving with wise restraint and love and with proper discipline and dignity.

## THE NEED TO BE "MALADJUSTED"

Modern psychology has a word that is probably used more than any other word. It is the word "maladjusted." Now we all should seek to live a well adjusted life in order to avoid neurotic and schizophrenic personalities. But there are some things within our social order to which I am proud to be maladjusted and to which I call upon you to be maladjusted. I never intend to adjust myself to segregation and discrimination. I never intend to adjust myself to mob rule. I never intend to adjust myself to the tragic effects of the methods of physical violence and to tragic militarism. I call upon you to be maladjusted to such things. I call upon you to be as maladjusted as Amos who in the midst of the injustices of his day cried out in words that echo across the generation, "Let judgment run down like waters and righteousness like a mighty stream." As maladjusted as Abraham Lincoln who had the vision to see that this nation could not exist half slave and half free. As maladjusted as Jefferson, who in the midst of an age amazingly adjusted to slavery could cry out, "All men are created equal and are endowed by their Creator with certain inalienable rights and that among these are life, liberty and the pursuit of happiness." As maladjusted as Jesus of Nazareth who dreamed a dream of the fatherhood of God and the brotherhood of man. God grant that we will be so maladjusted that we will be able to go out and change our world and our civilization. And then we will be able to move from the bleak and desolate midnight of man's inhumanity to man to the bright and glittering daybreak of freedom and justice.

*Intercollegian* (May 1958): 8ff.

# An Experiment in Love

*King relied heavily on the systematic analysis of the Christian concept of "love"*
*in the work of Anders Nygren, a noted Swedish theologian. In his important*
*study titled* Agape and Eros *(1953), Nygren argued that the New Testament*
*concept of love, transliterated from the Greek as "agape," is the most powerful*
*creative force in the universe. It is God's love for humanity. According to Nygren,*
*"*Agape *does not recognize value, but creates it.* Agape *loves and imparts value*
*by loving. The man who is loved by God has not value in himself; what gives him*
*value is precisely the fact that God loves him." Paul Tillich, on the other hand,*
*argued quite correctly that the New Testament defines love in terms of* eros *as*
*well as* agape. *King, a Tillichian scholar, overlooks critical discussions of Ny-*
*gren's interpretation, and actually misinterprets Nygren's view at a number of*
*points. But, as Harold Bloom is fond of saying, every translation and interpreta-*
*tion involves some degree of "misprison." That is, it involves some creative form*
*of often unintentional misinterpretation. Fortunately, King's interpretation both*
*of the New Testament concept of love and Nygren's analysis of it introduced a*
*fresh application of the concept from the standpoint of Christian social ethics*
*when he argues in this article that "*Agape *is a willingness to go to any length to*
*restore community."*

From the beginning a basic philosophy guided the movement. This
guiding principle has since been referred to variously as nonviolent resistance, noncooperation, and passive resistance. But in the first days of
the protest none of these expressions was mentioned: the phrase most
often heard was "Christian love." It was the Sermon on the Mount,
rather than a doctrine of passive resistance, that initially inspired the
Negroes of Montgomery to dignified social action. It was Jesus of Nazareth that stirred the Negroes to protest with the creative weapon of
love.

As the days unfolded, however, the inspiration of Mahatma Gandhi
began to exert its influence. I had come to see early that the Christian
doctrine of love operating through the Gandhian method of nonviolence was one of the most potent weapons available to the Negro in his
struggle for freedom. About a week after the protest started, a white
woman who understood and sympathized with the Negroes' efforts
wrote a letter to the editor of the *Montgomery Advertiser* comparing the
bus protest with the Gandhian movement in India. Miss Juliette Mor-

gan, sensitive and frail, did not long survive the rejection and condemnation of the white community, but long after she died in the summer of
1957 the name of Mahatma Gandhi was well known in Montgomery.
People who had never heard of the little brown saint of India were now
saying his name with an air of familiarity. Nonviolent resistance had
emerged as the technique of the movement, while love stood as the regulating ideal. In other words, Christ furnished the spirit and motivation,
while Gandhi furnished the method.

One of the glories of the Montgomery movement was that Baptists,
Methodists, Lutherans, Presbyterians, Episcopalians, and others all
came together with a willingness to transcend denominational lines. Although no Catholic priests were actively involved in the protest, many of
their parishioners took part. All joined hands in the bond of Christian
love. Thus the mass meetings accomplished on Monday and Thursday
nights what the Christian Church had failed to accomplish on Sunday
mornings.

In my weekly remarks as president of the resistance committee, I
stressed that the use of violence in our struggle would be both impractical and immoral. To meet hate with retaliatory hate would do nothing
but intensify the existence of evil in the universe. Hate begets hate; violence begets violence; toughness begets a greater toughness. We must
meet the forces of hate with the power of love; we must meet physical
force with soul free. Our aim must never be to defeat or humiliate the
white man, but to win his friendship and understanding.

In a real sense, Montgomery's Negroes showed themselves willing to
grapple with a new approach to the crisis in race relations. It is probably
true that most of them did not believe in nonviolence as a philosophy of
life, but because of their confidence in their leaders and because nonviolence was presented to them as a simple expression of Christianity in
action, they were willing to use it as a technique. Admittedly, nonviolence in the truest sense is not a strategy that one uses simply because it
is expedient at the moment; nonviolence is ultimately a way of life that
men live by because of the sheer morality of its claim. But even granting
this, the willingness to use nonviolence as a technique is a step forward.
For he who goes this far is more likely to adopt nonviolence later as a
way of life.

It must be emphasized that nonviolent resistance is not a method for
cowards; it does resist. If one uses this method because he is afraid or
merely because he lacks the instruments of violence, he is not truly nonviolent. This is why Gandhi often said that if cowardice is the only alternative to violence, it is better to fight. He made this statement conscious
of the fact that there is always another alternative: no individual or
group need submit to any wrong, nor need they use violence to right
that wrong; there is the way of nonviolent resistance. This is ultimately
the way of the strong man. It is not a method of stagnant passivity. The

phrase "passive resistance" often gives the false impression that this is a sort of "do-nothing method" in which the resister quietly and passively accepts evil. But nothing is further from the truth. For while the nonviolent resister is passive in the sense that he is not physically aggressive toward his opponent, his mind and emotions are always active, constantly seeking to persuade his opponent that he is wrong. The method is passive physically but strongly active spiritually. It is not passive non-resistance to evil, it is active nonviolent resistance to evil.

A second basic fact that characterizes nonviolence is that it does not seek to defeat or humiliate the opponent, but to win his friendship and understanding. The nonviolent resister must often express his protest through noncooperation or boycotts, but he realizes that these are not ends themselves; they are merely means to awaken a sense of moral shame in the opponent. The end is redemption and reconciliation. The aftermath of nonviolence is the creation of the beloved community, while the aftermath of violence is tragic bitterness.

A third characteristic of this method is that the attack is directed against forces of evil rather than against persons who happen to be doing the evil. It is evil that the nonviolent resister seeks to defeat, not the persons victimized by evil. If he is opposing racial injustice, the nonviolent resister has the vision to see that the basic tension is not between races. As I like to say to the people in Montgomery: "The tension in this city is not between white people and Negro people. The tension is, at bottom, between justice and injustice, between the forces of light and the forces of darkness. And if there is a victory, it will be a victory not merely for fifty thousand Negroes, but a victory for justice and the forces of light. We are out to defeat injustice and not white persons who may be unjust."

A fourth point that characterizes nonviolent resistance is a willingness to accept suffering without retaliation, to accept blows from the opponent without striking back. "Rivers of blood may have to flow before we gain our freedom, but it must be our blood," Gandhi said to his countrymen. The nonviolent resister is willing to accept violence if necessary, but never to inflict it. He does not seek to dodge jail. If going to jail is necessary, he enters it "as a bridegroom enters the bride's chamber."

One may well ask: "What is the nonviolent resister's justification for this ordeal to which he invites men, for this mass political application of the ancient doctrine of turning the other cheek?" The answer is found in the realization that unearned suffering is redemptive. Suffering, the nonviolent resister realizes, has tremendous educational and transforming possibilities. "Things of fundamental importance to people are not secured by reason alone, but have to be purchased with their suffering," said Gandhi. He continues: "Suffering is infinitely more powerful than the law of the jungle for converting the opponent and opening his ears which are otherwise shut to the voice of reason."

A fifth point concerning nonviolent resistance is that it avoids not only external physical violence but also internal violence of spirit. The nonviolent resister not only refuses to shoot his opponent but he also refuses to hate him. At the center of nonviolence stands the principle of love. The nonviolent resister would contend that in the struggle for human dignity, the oppressed people of the world must not succumb to the temptation of becoming bitter or indulging in hate campaigns. To retaliate in kind would do nothing but intensify the existence of hate in the universe. Along the way of life, someone must have sense enough and morality enough to cut off the chain of hate. This can only be done by projecting the ethic of love to the center of our lives.

In speaking of love at this point, we are not referring to some sentimental or affectionate emotion. It would be nonsense to urge men to love their oppressors in an affectionate sense. Love in this connection means understanding, redemptive good will. When we speak of loving those who oppose us, we refer to neither *eros* nor *philia*; we speak of a love which is expressed in the Greek word *agape*. *Agape* means understanding, redeeming good will for all men. It is an overflowing love which is purely spontaneous, unmotivated, groundless, and creative. It is not set in motion by any quality or function of its object. It is the love of God operating in the human heart.

*Agape* is disinterested love. It is a love in which the individual seeks not his own good, but the good of his neighbor (1 Cor. 10:24). *Agape* does not begin by discriminating between worthy and unworthy people, or any qualities people possess. It begins by loving others *for their sakes*. It is an entirely "neighbor-regarding concern for others," which discovers the neighbor in every man it meets. Therefore, *agape* makes no distinction between friends and enemy; it is directed toward both. If one loves an individual merely on account of his friendliness, he loves him for the sake of the benefits to be gained from the friendship, rather than for the friend's own sake. Consequently, the best way to assure oneself that love is disinterested is to have love for the enemy-neighbor from whom you can expect no good in return, but only hostility and persecution.

Another basic point about *agape* is that it springs from the *need* of the other person—his need for belonging to the best in the human family. The Samaritan who helped the Jew on the Jericho Road was "good" because he responded to the human need that he was presented with. God's love is eternal and fails not because man needs his love. Saint Paul assures us that the loving act of redemption was done "while we were yet sinners"—that is, at the point of our greatest need for love. Since the white man's personality is greatly distorted by segregation, and his soul is greatly scarred, he needs the love of the Negro. The Negro must love the white man, because the white man needs his love to remove his tensions, insecurities, and fears.

*Agape* is not a weak, passive love. It is love in action. *Agape* is love seeking to preserve and create community. It is insistence on community even when one seeks to break it. *Agape* is a willingness to go to any length to restore community. It doesn't stop at the first mile, but it goes the second mile to restore community. It is a willingness to forgive, not seven times, but seventy times seven to restore community. The cross is the eternal expression of the length to which God will go in order to restore broken community. The resurrection is a symbol of God's triumph over all the forces that seek to block community. The Holy Spirit is the continuing community creating reality that moves through history. He who works against community is working against the whole of creation. Therefore, if I respond to hate with a reciprocal hate I do nothing but intensify the cleavage in broken community. I can only close the gap in broken community by meeting hate with love. If I meet hate with hate, I become depersonalized, because creation is so designed that my personality can only be fulfilled in the context of community. Booker T. Washington was right: "Let no man pull you so low as to make you hate him." When he pulls you that low he brings you to the point of defying creation, and thereby becoming depersonalized.

In the final analysis, *agape* means a recognition of the fact that all life is interrelated. All humanity is involved in a single process, and all men are brothers. To the degree that I harm my brother, no matter what he is doing to me, to that extent I am harming myself. For example, white men often refuse federal aid to education in order to avoid giving the Negro his rights; but because all men are brothers they cannot deny Negro children without harming their own. They end, all efforts to the contrary, by hurting themselves. Why is this? Because men are brothers. If you harm me, you harm yourself.

A sixth basic fact about nonviolent resistance is that it is based on the conviction that the universe is on the side of justice. Consequently, the believer in nonviolence has deep faith in the future. This faith is another reason why the nonviolent resister can accept suffering without retaliation. For he knows that in his struggle for justice he has cosmic companionship. It is true that there are devout believers in nonviolence who find it difficult to believe in a personal God. But even these persons believe in the existence of some creative force that works for universal wholeness. Whether we call it an unconscious process, an impersonal Brahman, or a Personal Being of matchless power and infinite love, there is a creative force in this universe that works to bring the disconnected aspects of reality into a harmonious whole.

---

This article is actually an excerpt from pages 66–71 of Martin Luther King, Jr., *Stride Toward Freedom: The Montgomery Circle* (New York: Harper & Row, 1958) which appeared in *Jubilee* (September 1958): 13–16. [Although this article is cited in most King bibliographies as beginning on page 11, it actually begins on page 13. Pages 11–13 contain rather extensive comments from the editor of *Jubilee*. In fact, this article and his *Stride Toward Freedom: The Montgomery Story* were both published in September 1958.]

# 5

# Speech Before the Youth March for Integrated Schools

*On 18 April 1959, King, along with several other civil rights leaders, including Daisy Bates, Harry Belafonte, A. Philip Randolph, Jackie Robinson, and Roy Wilkins, spoke before 26,000 black high school and college students who had come to the nation's capital to demonstrate their support for the 1954 Supreme Court decision against racial segregation in the nation's public schools. This was the second consecutive year that such a march was held. The first march, with 10,000 students present, was held on 25 October 1958. Liberal Senator Paul Douglass of Illinois had the texts of the march's speeches placed in the* Congressional Record.

As I stand here and look out upon the thousands of Negro faces, and the thousands of white faces, intermingled like the waters of a river, I see only one face—the face of the future.

Yes; as I gaze upon this great historic assembly, this unprecedented gathering of young people, I cannot help thinking—that a hundred years from now the historians will be calling this not the "beat" generation, but the generation of integration.

The fact that thousands of you came here to Washington and that thousands more signed your petition proves that this generation will not take "No" for an answer—will not take double talk for an answer—will not take gradualism for an answer. It proves that the only answer you will settle for is—total desegregation and total equality—now.

I know of no words eloquent enough to express the deep meaning, the great power, and the unconquerable spirit back of this inspiringly original, uniquely American march of young people. Nothing like it has ever happened in the history of our nation. Nothing, that is, except the last youth march. What this march demonstrates to me, above all else, is that you young people, through your own experience, have somehow discovered the central fact of American life—that the extension of democracy for all Americans depends upon complete integration of Negro Americans.

By coming here you have shown yourselves to be highly alert, highly responsible young citizens. And very soon the area of your responsibility will increase, for you will begin to exercise your greatest privilege as an American—the right to vote. Of course, you will have no difficulty exercising this privilege—if you are white.

But I wonder if you can understand what it feels like to be a Negro, living in the South, where, by attempting to exercise this right, you may be taking your life in your hands.

The denial of the vote not only deprives the Negro of his constitutional rights—but what is even worse—it degrades him as a human being. And yet, even this degradation, which is only one of many humiliations of everyday life, is losing its ability to degrade. For the southern Negro is learning to transform his degradation into resistance. Nonviolent resistance. And by so doing he is not only achieving his dignity as a human being, he is helping to advance democracy in the South. This is why my colleagues and I in the Southern Leadership Conference are giving our major attention to the campaign to increase the registration of Negro voters in the South to three million. Do you realize what would happen in this country if we were to gain three million southern Negro votes? We could change the composition of Congress. We could have a Congress far more responsive to the voters' will. We could have all schools integrated—north and south. A new era would open to all Americans. Thus, the Negro, in his struggle to secure his own rights is destined to enlarge democracy for all people, in both a political and a social sense.

Indeed in your great movement to organize a march for integrated schools you have actually accomplished much more. You have awakened on hundreds of campuses throughout the land a new spirit of social inquiry to the benefit of all Americans.

This is really a noble cause. As June approaches, with its graduation ceremonies and speeches, a thought suggests itself. You will hear much about careers, security, and prosperity. I will leave the discussion of such matters to your deans, your principals, and your valedictorians. But I do have a graduation thought to pass along to you. Whatever career you may choose for yourself—doctor, lawyer, teacher—let me propose an avocation to be pursued along with it. Become a dedicated fighter for civil rights. Make it a central part of your life.

It will make you a better doctor, a better lawyer, a better teacher. It will enrich your spirit as nothing else possibly can. It will give you that rare sense of nobility that can only spring from love and selflessly helping your fellow man. Make a career of humanity. Commit yourself to the noble struggle for equal rights. You will make a greater person of yourself, a greater nation of your country, and a finer world to live in.

*Congressional Record* 105 (20 May 1959): 8696–97.

# 6

# My Trip to the Land of Gandhi

*Between 2 February and 10 March, Dr. and Mrs. King toured India with Dr. Lawrence D. Reddick, a black professor of history at Alabama State University in Montgomery, to study Gandhi's philosophy and techniques of nonviolence. They were guests of Prime Minister Jawaharlal Nehru, one of Gandhi's disciples.*

For a long time I had wanted to take a trip to India. Even as a child the entire Orient held a strange fascination for me—the elephants, the tigers, the temples, the snake charmers and all the other storybook characters.

While the Montgomery boycott was going on, India's Gandhi was the guiding light of our technique of nonviolent social change. We spoke of him often. So as soon as our victory over bus segregation was won, some of my friends said: "Why don't you go to India and see for yourself what the Mahatma, whom you so admire, has wrought."

In 1956 when Pandit Jawaharlal Nehru, India's prime minister, made a short visit to the United States, he was gracious enough to say that he wished that he and I had met and had his diplomatic representatives make inquiries as to the possibility of my visiting his country some time soon. Our former American ambassador to India, Chester Bowles, wrote me along the same lines.

But every time that I was about to make the trip, something would interfere. At one time it was my visit by prior commitment to Ghana. At another time my publishers were pressing me to finish writing *Stride Toward Freedom*. Then along came Mrs. Izola Ware Curry. When she struck me with that Japanese letter opener on that Saturday afternoon in September as I sat autographing books in a Harlem store, she not only knocked out the travel plans that I had but almost everything else as well.

After I recovered from this near-fatal encounter and was finally released by my doctors, it occurred to me that it might be better to get in the trip to India before plunging too deeply once again into the sea of the southern segregation struggle.

I preferred not to take this long trip alone and asked my wife and my friend, Lawrence Reddick, to accompany me. Coretta was particularly interested in the women of India and Dr. Reddick in the history and government of that great country. He had written my biography, *Crusader Without Violence*, and said that my true test would come when the people who knew Gandhi looked me over and passed judgment upon me and the Montgomery movement. The three of us made up a sort of three-headed team with six eyes and six ears for looking and listening.

The Christopher Reynolds Foundation made a grant through the American Friends Service Committee to cover most of the expenses of the trip and the Southern Christian Leadership Conference and the Montgomery Improvement Association added their support. The Gandhi Memorial Trust of India extended an official invitation, through diplomatic channels, for our visit.

And so on February 3, 1959, just before midnight, we left New York by plane. En route we stopped in Paris with Richard Wright, an old friend of Reddick's, who brought us up to date on European attitudes on the Negro question and gave us a taste of the best French cooking.

We missed our plane connection in Switzerland because of fog, arriving in India after a roundabout route, two days late. But from the time we came down out of the clouds at Bombay on February 10, until March 10, when we waved goodbye at the New Delhi airport, we had one of the most concentrated and eye-opening experiences of our lives. There is so much to tell that I can only touch upon a few of the high points.

At the outset, let me say that we had a grand reception in India. The people showered upon us the most generous hospitality imaginable. We were graciously received by the prime minister, the president and the vice-president of the nation: members of Parliament, governors and chief ministers of various Indian states; writers, professors, social reformers and at least one saint. Since our pictures were in the newspapers very often it was not unusual for us to be recognized by crowds in public places and on public conveyances. Occasionally I would take a morning walk in the large cities, and out of the most unexpected places someone would emerge and ask: "Are you Martin Luther King?"

Virtually every door was open to us. We had hundreds of invitations that the limited time did not allow us to accept. We were looked upon as brothers with the color of our skins as something of an asset. But the strongest bond of fraternity was the common cause of minority and colonial peoples in America, Africa and Asia struggling to throw off racialism and imperialism.

We had the opportunity to share our views with thousands of Indian people through endless conversations and numerous discussion sessions. I spoke before university groups and public meetings all over India. Because of the keen interest that the Indian people have in the race problem these meetings were usually packed. Occasionally interpreters were used, but on the whole I spoke to audiences that understood English.

The Indian people love to listen to the Negro spirituals. Therefore,

Coretta ended up singing as much as I lectured. We discovered that autograph seekers are not confined to America. After appearances in public meetings and while visiting villages we were often besieged for autographs. Even while riding planes, more than once pilots came into the cabin from the cockpit requesting our signatures.

We got a good press throughout our stay. Thanks to the Indian papers, the Montgomery bus boycott was already well known in that country. Indian publications perhaps gave a better continuity of our 381-day bus strike than did most of our papers in the United States. Occasionally I meet some American fellow citizen who even now asks me how the bus boycott is going, apparently never having read that our great day of bus integration, December 21, 1956, closed that chapter of our history.

We held press conferences in all of the larger cities—Delhi, Calcutta, Madras and Bombay—and talked with newspapermen almost everywhere we went. They asked sharp questions and at times appeared to be hostile but that was just their way of bringing out the story that they were after. As reporters, they were scrupulously fair with us and in their editorials showed an amazing grasp of what was going on in America and other parts of the world.

The trip had a great impact upon me personally. It was wonderful to be in Gandhi's land, to talk with his son, his grandsons, his cousins and other relatives; to share the reminiscences of his close comrades, to visit his ashrama, to see the countless memorials for him and finally to lay a wreath on his entombed ashes at Rajghat. I left India more convinced than ever before that nonviolent resistance is the most potent weapon available to oppressed people in their struggle for freedom. It was a marvelous thing to see the amazing results of a nonviolent campaign. The aftermath of hatred and bitterness that usually follows a violent campaign was found nowhere in India. Today a mutual friendship based on complete equality exists between the Indian and British people within the commonwealth. The way of acquiescence leads to moral and spiritual suicide. The way of violence leads to bitterness in the survivors and brutality in the destroyers. But, the way of nonviolence leads to redemption and the creation of the beloved community.

The spirit of Gandhi is very much alive in India today. Some of his disciples have misgivings about this when they remember the drama of the fight for national independence and when they look around and find nobody today who comes near the stature of the Mahatma. But any objective observer must report that Gandhi is not only the greatest figure in India's history but that his influence is felt in almost every aspect of life and public policy today.

India can never forget Gandhi. For example, the Gandhi Memorial Trust (also known as the Gandhi Smarak Nidhi) collected some $130 million soon after the death of "the father of the nation." This was perhaps the largest, spontaneous, mass monetary contribution to the memory of a single individual in the history of the world. This fund, along with support from the Government and other institutions, is resulting in the spread and development of Gandhian philosophy, the implementing of his constructive program, the erection of libraries and the publication of works by and about the life and times of Gandhi. Posterity could not escape him even if it tried. By all standards of measurement, he is one of the half-dozen greatest men in world history.

I was delighted that the Gandhians accepted us with open arms. They praised our experiment with the nonviolent resistance technique at Montgomery. They seem to look upon it as an outstanding example of the possibilities of its use in Western civilization. To them as to me it also suggests that nonviolent resistance *when planned and positive in action* can work effectively even under totalitarian regimes.

We argued this point at some length with the groups of African students who are today studying in India. They felt that nonviolent resistance could only work in a situation where the resisters had a potential ally in the conscience of the opponent. We soon discovered that they, like many others, tended to confuse passive resistance with nonresistance. This is completely wrong. True nonviolent resistance is not unrealistic submission to evil power. It is rather a courageous confrontation of evil by the power of love, in the faith that it is better to be the recipient of violence than the inflictor of it, since the latter only multiplies the existence of violence and bitterness in the universe, while the former may develop a sense of shame in the opponent, and thereby bring about a transformation and change of heart.

Nonviolent resistance does call for love, but it is not a sentimental love. It is a very stern love that would organize itself into collective action to right a wrong by taking on itself suffering. While I understand the reasons why oppressed people often turn to violence in their struggle for freedom, it is my firm belief that the crusade for independence and human dignity that is now reaching a climax in Africa will have a more positive effect on the world, if it is waged along the lines that were first demonstrated in that continent by Gandhi himself.

India is a vast country with vast problems. We flew over the long stretches, from north to south, east to west; took trains for shorter jumps and used automobiles and jeeps to get us into the less accessible places.

India is about a third the size of the United States but has almost three times as many people. Everywhere we went we saw crowded humanity—on the roads, in the city streets and squares, even in the villages.

Most of the people are poor and poorly dressed. The average income per person is less than seventy dollars per year. Nevertheless, their turbans for their heads, loose-flowing, wrap-around *dhotis* that they wear instead of trousers and the flowing saris that the women wear instead of dresses are colorful and picturesque. Many Indians wear part native and part Western dress.

We think that we in the United States have a big housing problem, but in the city of Bombay, for example, over a half-million people sleep out of doors every night. These are mostly unattached, unemployed or partially employed males. They carry their bedding with them like foot soldiers and unroll it each night in any unoccupied space they can find—on the sidewalk, in a railroad station or at the entrance of a shop that is closed for the evening.

The food shortage is so widespread that it is estimated that less than thirty percent of the people get what we would call three square meals a day. During our great depression of the 1930s, we spoke of "a third of a nation" being "ill-housed, ill clad and ill fed." For India today, simply change one third to two-thirds in that statement and that would make it about right.

As great as is unemployment, under-employment is even greater. Seventy percent of the Indian people are classified as agricultural workers and most of these do less than two hundred days of farm laber per year because of the seasonal fluctuations and other uncertainties of mother nature. Jobless men roam the city streets.

Great ills flow from the poverty of India but strangely there is relatively litle crime. Here is another concrete manifestation of the wonderful spiritual quality of the Indian people. They are poor, jammed together and half starved but they do not take it out on each other. They are a kindly people. They do not abuse each other—verbally or physically—as readily as we do. We saw but one fist fight in India during our stay.

In contrast to the poverty-stricken, there are Indians who are rich, have luxurious homes, landed estates, fine clothes and show evidence of overeating. The bourgeoise—white, black or brown—behaves about the same the world over.

And then there is, even here, the problem of segregation. We call it race in America; they call it caste in India. In both places it means that some are considered inferior, treated as though they deserve less.

We were surprised and delighted to see that India has made greater progress in the fight against caste "untouchability" than we have made here in our own country against race segregation. Both nations have federal laws against discrimination (acknowledging, of course, that the decision of our Supreme Court is the law of our land). But after this has been said, we must recognize that there are great differences between what India has done and what we have done on a problem that is very similar. The leaders of India have placed their moral power behind their law. From the Prime Minister down to the village councilmen, everybody declares publicly that untouchability is wrong. But in the United States some of our highest officials decline to render a moral judgment on segregation and some from the South publicly boast of their determination to maintain segregation. This would be unthinkable in India.

Moreover, Gandhi not only spoke against the caste system but he acted against it. He took "untouchables" by the hand and led them into the temples from which they had been excluded. To equal that, President Eisenhower would take a Negro child by the hand and lead her into Central High School in Little Rock.

Gandhi also renamed the untouchables, calling them "Harijans" which means "children of God."

The government has thrown its full weight behind the program of giving the Harijans an equal chance in society—especially when it comes to job opportunities, education, and housing.

India's leaders, in and out of government, are conscious of their country's other great problems and are heroically grappling with them. The country seems to be divided. Some say that India should become westernized and modernized as quickly as possible so that she might raise her standards of living. Foreign capital and foreign industry should be invited in, for in this lies the salvation of the almost desperate situation.

On the other hand, there are others—perhaps the majority—who say that Westernization will bring with it the evils of materialism, cutthroat competition and rugged individualism; that India will lose her soul if she takes to chasing Yankee dollars; and that the big machine will only raise the living standards of the comparative few workers who get jobs but that the greater number of people will be displaced and will thus be worse off than they are now.

Prime Minister Nehru, who is at once an intellectual and a man charged with the practical responsibility of heading the government, seems to steer a middle course between these extreme attitudes. In our talk with him he indicated that he felt that some industrialization was absolutely necessary; that there were some things that only big or heavy industry could do for the country but that if the state keeps a watchful eye on the developments, most of the pitfalls may be avoided.

At the same time, Mr. Nehru gives support to the movement that would encourage and expand the handicraft arts such as spinning and weaving in home and village and thus leave as much economic self-help and autonomy as possible to the local community.

There is a great movement in India that is almost unknown in America. At its center is the campaign for land reform known as Bhoodan. It would solve India's great economic and social change by consent, not by force. The Bhoodanists are led by the saints Vinoba Bhave and Jayaprakash Narayan, a highly sensitive intellectual, who was trained in American colleges. Their ideal is self-sufficiency. Their program envisions:

1. *Persuading* large landowners to give up some of their holding to landless peasants;

2. *Persuading* small landowners to give up their individual ownership for common cooperative ownership by the villages;

3. *Encouraging* farmers and villagers to spin and weave the cloth for their own clothes during their spare time from their agricultural pursuits.

Since these measures would answer the questions of employment, food and clothing, the village could then, through cooperative action, make just about everything that it would need or get it through bartering and exchange from other villages. Accordingly, each village would be virtually self-sufficient and would thus free itself from the domination of the urban centers that are today like evil lodestones drawing the people away from the rural areas, concentrating them in city slums and debauching them with urban vices. At least this is the argument of the Bhoodanists and other Gandhians.

Such ideas sound strange and archaic to Western ears. However, the Indians have already achieved greater results than we Americans would ever expect. For example, millions of acres of land have been given up by rich landlords and additional millions of acres have been given up to cooperative management by small farmers. On the other hand, the Bhoodanists shrink from giving their movement the organization and drive that we in America would venture to guess that it must have in order to keep pace with the magnitude of the problems that everybody is trying to solve.

Even the government's five-year plans fall short in that they do not appear to be of sufficient scope to embrace their objectives. Thus, the three five-year plans were designed to provide twenty-five million new jobs over a fifteen-year period but the birth rate of India is six million per year. This means that in fifteen years there will be nine million more people (less those who have died or retired) looking for the fifteen million new jobs. In other words, if the planning were one hundred percent successful, it could not keep pace with the growth of problems it is trying to solve.

As for what should be done, we surely do not have the answer. But we do feel certain that India needs help. She must have outside capital and technical know-how. It is in the interest of the United States and the West to help supply these needs and *not attach strings to the gifts.*

Whatever we do should be done in a spirit of international brotherhood, not national selfishness. It should be done not merely because it is diplomatically expedient, but because it is morally correct. At the same time, it will rebound to the credit of the West if India is able to maintain her democracy while solving her problems.

It would be a boon to democracy if one of the great nations of the world, with almost four hundred million people, proves that it is possible to provide a good living for everyone without surrendering to a dictatorship of either the "right" or "left." Today India is a tremendous force for peace and nonviolence, at home and abroad. It is a land where the idealist and the intellectual are yet respected. We should want to help India preserve her soul and thus help to save our own.

Ebony (July 1959): 84–86, 88–90, 92. This article was written with the editorial assistance of Reddick, who also did the primary research for King's Stride Toward Freedom.

# 7

# The Social Organization
# of Nonviolence

*Although King had been introduced to various philosophies of nonviolence while a student at Morehouse College and Crozer Theological Seminary, his trip to India consummated his conversion to nonviolence. One of the first serious challenges to that philosophy, and to the legal gradualism of the NAACP, was the emerging militancy among young African Americans. The editorial hand of Bayard Rustin assisted King in taking a stance against Robert Williams, a die-hard advocate of militant black self-defense. Williams, the local president of the NAACP in Monroe County, North Carolina, and an ex-marine, formed, drilled, and armed blacks to defend themselves. Both the NAACP and SCLC strongly denounced Williams's endorsement of violence.*

Paradoxically, the struggle for civil rights has reached a stage of profound crisis, although its outward aspect is distinctly less turbulent and victories of token integration have been won in the hard-resistance areas of Virginia and Arkansas.

The crisis has its origin in a decision rendered by the Supreme Court more than a year ago which upheld the pupil placement law. Though little noticed then, this decision fundamentally weakened the historic 1954 ruling of the Court. It is imperceptibly becoming the basis of a *de facto* compromise between the powerful contending forces.

The 1954 decision required for effective implementation resolute federal action supported by mass action to undergird all necessary changes. It is obvious that federal action by the legislative and executive branches was half-hearted and inadequate. The activity of Negro forces, while heroic in some instances, and impressive in other sporadic situations, lacked consistency and militancy sufficient to fill the void left by government default. The segregationists were swift to seize these advantages, and unrestrained by moral or social conscience, defied the law boldly and brazenly.

The net effect of this social equation has led to the present situation, which is without clearcut victory for either side. Token integration is a developing pattern. This type of integration is merely an affirmation of a principle without the substance of change.

It is, like the Supreme Court decision, a pronouncement of justice, but by itself does not insure that the millions of Negro children will be educated in conditions of equality. This is not to say that it is without value. It has substantial importance. However, it fundamentally changes the outlook of the whole movement, for it raises the prospect of long, slow change without a predictable end. As we have seen in northern cities, token integration has become a pattern in many communities and remained frozen, even though environmental attitudes are substantially less hostile to full integration than in the South.

## THREE VIEWS OF VIOLENCE

This then is the danger. Full integration can easily become a distant or mythical goal—major integration may be long postponed, and in the quest for social calm a compromise firmly implanted in which the real goals are merely token integration for a long period to come.

The Negro was the tragic victim of another compromise in 1878, when his full equality was bargained away by the federal government and a condition somewhat above slave status but short of genuine citizenship became his social and political existence for nearly a century.

There is reason to believe that the Negro of 1959 will not accept supinely any such compromises in the contemporary struggle for integration. His struggle will continue, but the obstacles will determine its specific nature. It is axiomatic in social life that the imposition of frustrations leads to two kinds of reactions. One is the development of a wholesome social organization to resist with effective, firm measures any efforts to impede progress. The other is a confused, anger-motivated drive to strike back violently, to inflict damage. Primarily, it seeks to cause injury to retaliate for wrongful suffering. Secondarily, it seeks real progress. It is punitive—not radical or constructive.

The current calls for violence have their roots in this latter tendency. Here one must be clear that there are three different views on the subject of violence. One is the approach of pure nonviolence, which cannot readily or easily attract large masses, for it requires extraordinary discipline and courage. The second is violence exercised in self-defense, which all societies, from the most primitive to the most cultured and civilized, accept as moral and legal. The principle of self-defense, even involving weapons and bloodshed, has never been condemned, even by Gandhi, who sanctioned it for those unable to master pure nonviolence. The third is the advocacy of violence as a tool of advancement, organized as in warfare, deliberately and consciously. To this tendency many Negroes are being tempted today. There are incalculable perils in this approach. It is not the danger or sacrifice of physical being which is primary, though it cannot be contemplated without a sense of deep concern for human life. The greatest danger is that it will fail to attract

Negroes to a real collective struggle, and will confuse the large uncommitted middle group, which as yet has not supported either side. Further, it will mislead Negroes into the belief that this is the only path and place them as a minority in a position where they confront a far larger adversary than it is possible to defeat in this form of combat. When the Negro uses force in self-defense he does not forfeit support—he may even win it, by the courage and self-respect it reflects. When he seeks to initiate violence he provokes questions about the necessity for it, and inevitably is blamed for its consequences. It is unfortunately true that however the Negro acts, his struggle will not be free of violence initiated by his enemies, and he will need ample courage and willingness to sacrifice to defeat this manifestation of violence. But if he seeks it and organizes it, he cannot win. Does this leave the Negro without a positive method to advance? Mr. Robert Williams would have us believe that there is no effective and practical alternative. He argues that we must be cringing and submissive or take up arms. To so place the issue distorts the whole problem. There are other meaningful alternatives.

The Negro people can organize socially to initiate many forms of struggle which can drive their enemies back without resort to futile and harmful violence. In the history of the movement for racial advancement, many creative forms have been developed—the mass boycott, sit-down protests and strikes, sit-ins—refusal to pay fines and bail for unjust arrests—mass marches—mass meetings—prayer pilgrimages, etc. Indeed, in Mr. Williams' own community of Monroe, North Carolina, a striking example of collective community action won a significant victory without use of arms or threats of violence. When the police incarcerated a Negro doctor unjustly, the aroused people of Monroe marched to the police station, crowded into its halls and corridors, and refused to leave until their colleague was released. Unable to arrest everyone, the authorities released the doctor and neither side attempted to unleash violence. This experience was related by the doctor who was the intended victim.

There is more power in socially organized masses on the march than there is in guns in the hands of a few desperate men. Our enemies would prefer to deal with a small armed group rather than with a huge, unarmed but resolute mass of people. However, it is necessary that the mass-action method be persistent and unyielding. Gandhi said the Indian people must "never let them rest," referring to the British. He urged them to keep protesting daily and weekly, in a variety of ways. This method inspired and organized the Indian masses and disorganized and demobilized the British. It educates its myriad participants, socially and morally. All history teaches us that like a turbulent ocean beating great cliffs into fragments of rock, the determined movement of people incessantly demanding their rights always disintegrates the old order.

It is this form of struggle—non-cooperation with evil through mass actions—"never letting them rest"—which offers the more effective road for those who have been tempted and goaded to violence. It needs the bold and the brave because it is not free of danger. It faces the vicious and evil enemies squarely. It requires dedicated people, because it is a backbreaking task to arouse, to organize, and to educate tens of thousands for disciplined, sustained action. From this form of struggle more emerges that is permanent and damaging to the enemy than from a few acts of organized violence.

Our present urgent necessity is to cease our internal fighting and turn outward to the enemy—using every form of mass action yet known—create new forms—and resolve never to let them rest. This is the social lever which will force open the door to freedom. Our powerful weapons are the voices, the feet, and the bodies of dedicated, united people, moving without rest toward a just goal. Greater tyrants than southern segregationists have been subdued and defeated by this form of struggle. We have not yet used it, and it would be tragic if we spurn it because we have failed to perceive its dynamic strength and power.

## CASHING IN ON WAR?

I am reluctant to inject a personal defense against charges by Mr. Williams that I am inconsistent in my struggle against war and too weak-kneed to protest nuclear war. Merely to set the record straight, may I state that repeatedly, in public addresses and in my writings, I have unequivocally declared my hatred for this most colossal of all evils and I have condemned any organizer of war, regardless of his rank or nationality. I have signed numerous statements with other Americans condemning nuclear testing and have authorized publication of my name in advertisements appearing in the largest-circulation newspapers in the country, without concern that it was then "unpopular" to so speak out.

*Liberation* (October 1959): 5–6.

# 8

# Pilgrimage to Nonviolence

*This article updated King's autobiographical discussion of how he came to the intellectual decision to embrace nonviolence. It appeared in* Christian Century *as part of its famous series on "How My Mind Has Changed," where world-renowned theologians are given the opportunity to reflect on or update their theological views.*

Ten years ago I was just entering my senior year in theological seminary. Like most theological students I was engaged in the exciting job of studying various theological theories. Having been raised in a rather strict fundamentalistic tradition, I was occasionally shocked as my intellectual journey carried me through new and sometimes complex doctrinal lands. But despite the shock the pilgrimage was always stimulating, and it gave me a new appreciation for objective appraisal and critical analysis. My early theological training did the same for me as the reading of Hume did for Kant: it knocked me out of my dogmatic slumber.

At this stage of my development I was a thoroughgoing liberal. Liberalism provided me with an intellectual satisfaction that I could never find in fundamentalism. I became so enamored of the insights of liberalism that I almost fell into the trap of accepting uncritically everything that came under its name. I was absolutely convinced of the natural goodness of man and the natural power of human reason.

I

The basic change in my thinking came when I began to question some of the theories that had been associated with so-called liberal theology. Of course there is one phase of liberalism that I hope to cherish always: its devotion to the search for truth, its insistence on an open and analytical mind, its refusal to abandon the best light of reason. Liberalism's contribution to the philological-historical criticism of biblical literature has been of immeasurable value and should be defended with religious and scientific passion.

It was mainly the liberal doctrine of man that I began to question. The more I observed the tragedies of history and man's shameful inclination to choose the low road, the more I came to see the depths and strength of sin. My reading of the works of Reinhold Niebuhr made me

35

aware of the complexity of human motives and the reality of sin on every level of man's existence. Moreover, I came to recognize the complexity of man's social involvement and the glaring reality of collective evil. I came to feel that liberalism had been all too sentimental concerning human nature and that it leaned toward a false idealism.

I also came to see that liberalism's superficial optimism concerning human nature caused it to overlook the fact that reason is darkened by sin. The more I thought about human nature the more I saw how our tragic inclination for sin causes us to use our minds to rationalize our actions. Liberalism failed to see that reason by itself is little more than an instrument to justify man's defensive ways of thinking. Reason, devoid of purifying power of faith, can never free itself from distortions and rationalizations.

In spite of the fact that I had to reject some aspects of liberalism, I never came to an all-out acceptance of neo-orthodoxy. While I saw neo-orthodoxy as a helpful corrective for a liberalism that had become all too sentimental, I never felt that it provided an adequate answer to the basic questions. If liberalism was too optimistic concerning human nature, neo-orthodoxy was too pessimistic. Not only on the question of man but also on other vital issues neo-orthodoxy went too far in its revolt. In its attempt to preserve the transcendence of God, which had been neglected by liberalism's overstress of his immanence, neo-orthodoxy went to the extreme of stressing a God who was hidden, unknown and "wholly other." In its revolt against liberalism's overemphasis on the power of reason, neo-orthodoxy fell into a mood of antirationalism and semifundamentalism, stressing a narrow, uncritical biblicism. This approach, I felt, was inadequate both for the church and for personal life.

So although liberalism left me unsatisfied on the question of the nature of man, I found no refuge in neo-orthodoxy. I am now convinced that the truth about man is found neither in liberalism nor in neo-orthodoxy. Each represents a partial truth. A large segment of Protestant liberalism defined man only in terms of his essential nature, his capacity for good. Neo-orthodoxy tended to define man only in terms of his existential nature, his capacity for evil. An adequate understanding of man is found neither in the thesis of liberalism nor in the antithesis of neo-orthodoxy, but in a synthesis which reconciles the truths of both.

During the past decade I also gained a new appreciation for the philosophy of existentialism. My first contact with this philosophy came through my reading of Kierkegaard and Nietzsche. Later I turned to a study of Jaspers, Heidegger and Sartre. All of these thinkers stimulated my thinking; while finding things to question in each, I nevertheless learned a great deal from study of them. When I finally turned to a serious study of the works of Paul Tillich I became convinced that existentialism, in spite of the fact that it had become all too fashionable, had grasped certain basic truths about man and his condition that could not be permanently overlooked.

Its understanding of the "finite freedom" of man is one of existentialism's most lasting contributions, and its perception of the anxiety and conflict produced in man's personal and social life as a result of the perilous and ambiguous structure of existence is especially meaningful for our time. The common point in all existentialism, whether it is atheistic or theistic, is that man's existential situation is a state of estrangement from his essential nature. In their revolt against Hegel's essentialism, all existentialists contend that the world is fragmented. History is a series of unreconciled conflicts and man's existence is filled with anxiety and threatened with meaninglessness. While the ultimate Christian answer is not found in any of these existential assertions, there is much here that the theologian can use to describe the true state of man's existence.

Although most of my formal study during this decade has been in systematic theology and philosophy, I have become more and more interested in social ethics. Of course my concern for social problems was already substantial before the beginning of this decade. From my early teens in Atlanta I was deeply concerned aboout the problem of racial injustice. I grew up abhorring segregation, considering it both rationally inexplicable and morally unjustifiable. I could never accept the fact of having to go to the back of a bus or sit in the segregated section of a train. The first time that I was seated behind a curtain in a dining car I felt as if the curtain had been dropped on my selfhood. I had also learned that the inseparable twin of racial injustice is economic injustice. I saw how the systems of segregation ended up in the exploitation of the Negro as well as the poor whites. Through these early experiences I grew up deeply conscious of the varieties of injustice in our society.

## II

Not until I entered theological seminary, however, did I begin a serious intellectual quest for a method to eliminate social evil. I was immediately influenced by the social gospel. In the early fifties I read Rauschenbusch's *Christianity and the Social Crisis,* a book which left an indelible imprint on my thinking. Of course there were points at which I differed with Rauschenbusch. I felt that he had fallen victim to the nineteenth century "cult of inevitable progress," which led him to an unwarranted optimism concerning human nature. Moreover, he came perilously close to identifying the kingdom of God with a particular social and economic system—a temptation which the church should never give in to. But in spite of these shortcomings Rauschenbusch gave to American Protestantism a sense of social responsibility that it should never lose. The gospel at its best deals with the whole man, not only his soul but his body, not only his spiritual well-being, but his material well-being. Any religion that professes to be concerned about the souls of men and is not concerned about the slums that damn them, the economic conditions that strangle them and the social conditions that cripple them is a spiritually moribund religion awaiting burial.

After reading Rauschenbusch I turned to a serious study of the social and ethical theories of the great philosophers. During this period I had almost despaired of the power of love in solving social problems. The "turn the other cheek" philosophy and the "love your enemies" philosophy are only valid, I felt, when individuals are in conflict with other individuals; when racial groups and nations are in conflict a more realistic approach is necessary. Then I came upon the life and teachings of Mahatma Gandhi. As I read his works I became deeply fascinated by his campaigns of nonviolent resistance. The whole Gandhian concept of *satyagraha* (*satya* is truth which equals love, and *graha* is force; *satyagraha* thus means truth-force or love-force) was profoundly significant to me. As I delved deeper into the philosophy of Gandhi my skepticism concerning the power of love gradually diminished, and I came to see for the first time that the Christian doctrine of love operating through the Gandhian method of nonviolence was one of the most potent weapons available to oppressed people in their struggle for freedom. At this time, however, I had a merely intellectual understanding and appreciation of the position, with no firm determination to organize it in a socially effective situation.

When I went to Montgomery, Alabama, as a pastor in 1954, I had not the slightest idea that I would later become involved in a crisis in which nonviolent resistance would be applicable. After I had lived in the community about a year, the bus boycott began. The Negro people of Montgomery, exhausted by the humiliating experiences that they had constantly faced on the buses, expressed in a massive act of noncooperation their determination to be free. They came to see that it was ultimately more honorable to walk the streets in dignity than to ride the buses in humiliation. At the beginning of the protest the people called on me to serve as their spokesman. In accepting this responsibility my mind, consciously or unconsciously, was driven back to the Sermon on the Mount and the Gandhian method of nonviolent resistance. This principle became the guiding light of our movement. Christ furnished the spirit and motivation while Gandhi furnished the method.

The experience in Montgomery did more to clarify my thinking on the question of nonviolence than all of the books that I had read. As the days unfolded I became more and more convinced of the power of nonviolence. Living through the actual experience of the protest, nonviolence became more than a method to which I gave intellectual assent; it became a commitment to a way of life. Many issues I had not cleared up intellectually concerning nonviolence were now solved in the sphere of practical action.

A few months ago I had the privilege of traveling to India. The trip had a great impact on me personally and left me even more convinced of the power of nonviolence. It was a marvelous thing to see the amazing results of a nonviolent struggle. India won her independence, but without violence on the part of Indians. The aftermath of hatred and bitterness that usually follows a violent campaign is found nowhere in India. Today a mutual friendship based on complete equality exists between the Indian and British people within the commonwealth.

I do not want to give the impression that nonviolence will work miracles overnight. Men are not easily moved from their mental ruts or purged of their prejudiced and irrational feelings. When the underprivileged demand freedom, the privileged first react with bitterness and resistance. Even when the demands are couched in nonviolent terms, the initial response is the same. I am sure that many of our white brothers in Montgomery and across the South are still bitter toward Negro leaders, even though these leaders have sought to follow a way of love and nonviolence. So the nonviolent approach does not immediately change the heart of the oppressor. It first does something to the hearts and souls of those committed to it. It gives them new self-respect; it calls up resources of strength and courage that they did not know they had. Finally, it reaches the opponent and so stirs his conscience that reconciliation becomes a reality.

## III

During recent months I have come to see more and more the need for the method of nonviolence in international relations. While I was convinced during my student days of the power of nonviolence in group conflicts within nations, I was not yet convinced of its efficacy in conflicts between nations. I felt that while war could never be a positive or absolute good, it could serve as a negative good in the sense of preventing the spread and growth of an evil force. War, I felt, horrible as it is, might be preferable to surrender to a totalitarian system. But more and more I have come to the conclusion that the potential destructiveness of modern weapons of war totally rules out the possibility of war ever serving again as a negative good. If we assume that mankind has a right to survive then we must find an alternative to war and destruction. In a day when sputniks dash through outer space and guided ballistic missiles are carving highways of death through the stratosphere, nobody can win a war. The choice today is no longer between violence and nonviolence. It is either nonviolence or nonexistence.

I am no doctrinaire pacifist. I have tried to embrace a realistic pacifism. Moreover, I see the pacifist position not as sinless but as the lesser evil in the circumstances. Therefore I do not claim to be free from the moral dilemmas that the Christian nonpacifist confronts. But I am convinced that the church cannot remain silent while mankind faces the threat of being plunged into the abyss of nuclear annihilation. If the church is true to its mission it must call for an end to the arms race.

In recent months I have also become more and more convinced of the reality of a personal God. True, I have always believed in the personality of God. But in past years the idea of a personal God was little more than a metaphysical category which I found theologically and philosophically satisfying. Now it is a living reality that has been validated in the experiences of everyday life. Perhaps the suffering, frustration and agonizing moments which I have had to undergo occasionally as a result of my involvement in a difficult struggle have drawn me closer to God. Whatever the cause, God has been profoundly real to me in recent months. In the midst of outer dangers I have felt an inner calm and known resoures of strength that only God could give. In many instances I have felt the power of God transforming the fatigue of despair into the buoyancy of hope. I am convinced that the universe is under the control of a loving purpose and that in the struggle for righteousness man has cosmic companionship. Behind the harsh appearances of the world there is a benign power. To say God is personal is not to make him an object among other objects or attribute to him the finiteness and limitations of human personality; it is to take what is finest and noblest in our consciousness and affirm its perfect existence in him. It is certainly true that human personality is limited, but personality as such inolves no necessary limitations. It simply means self-consciousness and self-direction. So in the truest sense of the word, God is a living God. In him there is feeling and will, responsive to the deepest yearnings of the human heart: this God both evokes and answers prayers.

The past decade has been a most exciting one. In spite of the tensions and uncertainties of our age something profoundly meaningful has begun. Old systems of exploitation and oppression are passing away and new systems of justice and equality are being born. In a real sense ours is a great time in which to be alive. Therefore I am not yet discouraged about the future. Granted that the easygoing optimism of yesterday is impossible. Granted that we face a world crisis which often leaves us standing amid the surging murmur of life's restless sea. But every crisis has both its dangers and its opportunities. Each can spell either salvation or doom. In a dark, confused world the spirit of God may yet reign supreme.

This article is a restatement of Chapter 6 of Martin Luther King, Jr., *Stride Toward Freedom: The Montgomery Story* (New York: Harper & Row, 1958) which appeared in *Christian Century* 77 (13 April 1960): 439–41.

# 9

# Suffering and Faith

*The editors of* Christian Century, *aware that King constantly received numerous threats against his life, urged him to comment on his view of suffering. His remarks are quite brief, both because of his schedule and because he was unwilling to appear as someone with "a martyr complex."*

Some of my personal sufferings over the last few years have also served to shape my thinking. I always hesitate to mention these experiences for fear of conveying the wrong impression. A person who constantly calls attention to his trials and sufferings is in danger of developing a martyr complex and of making others feel that he is consciously seeking sympathy. It is possible for one to be self-centered in his self-denial and self-righteous in his self-sacrifice. So I am always reluctant to refer to my personal sacrifices. But I feel somewhat justified in mentioning them in this article because of the influence they have had in shaping my thinking.

Due to my involvement in the struggle for the freedom of my people, I have known very few quiet days in the last few years. I have been arrested five times and put in Alabama jails. My home has been bombed twice. A day seldom passes that my family and I are not the recipients of threats of death. I have been the victim of a near-fatal stabbing. So in a real sense I have been battered by the storms of persecution. I must admit that at times I have felt that I could no longer bear such a heavy burden, and have been tempted to retreat to a more quiet and serene life. But every time such a temptation appeared, something came to strengthen and sustain my determination. I have learned now that the Master's burden is light precisely when we take his yoke upon us.

My personal trials have also taught me the value of unmerited suffering. As my sufferings mounted I soon realized that there were two ways that I could respond to my situation: either to react with bitterness or seek to transform the suffering into a creative force. I decided to follow the latter course. Recognizing the necessity for suffering I have tried to make of it a virtue. If only to save myself from bitterness, I have attempted to see my personal ordeals as an opportunity to transform myself and heal the people involved in the tragic situation which now obtains. I have lived these last few years with the conviction that unearned suffering is redemptive.

There are some who still find the cross a stumbling block, and others consider it foolishness, but I am more convinced than ever before that it is the power of God unto social and individual salvation. So like the Apostle Paul I can now humbly yet proudly say, "I bear in my body the marks of the Lord Jesus." The suffering and agonizing moments through which I have passed over the last few years have also drawn me closer to God. More than ever before I am convinced of the reality of a personal God.

# 10

# Love, Law, and Civil Disobedience

*This is a transcription of Dr. King's address before the annual meeting of the Fellowship of the Concerned on 16 November 1961. This interracial fellowship was affiliated with the Southern Regional Council, which was formed in 1944 after Dr. Gordon Blaine Hancock, a noted black Baptist pastor, journalist, and professor, wrote an article titled "Interracial Hypertension," in which he chided Southern liberals for their tolerance of racial bigotry and segregation. It succeeded the Commission on Interracial Cooperation, which was organized in 1919. They agreed to work to improve "economic, civic, and racial conditions in the South . . . [and] to attain through research and action programs the ideals and practices of equal opportunity." Under the leadership of stalwart white liberals such as Will Alexander, Howard Odum, and moderates such as Mrs. Jessie Daniel Ames, the commission provided a forum for progressives on the "race question" to discuss issues and devise strategies for challenging Southern segregation. But, as Dr. Benjamin E. Mays, King's mentor and former president of Atlanta's Morehouse College, said, "Negroes carried the ball in the movement." They had to continually prod this increasingly effective organization to be more aggressive. King and his staff knew that the source of many criticisms against the student "sit-ins" and "freedom rides" came from members of this group who preferred a more gradual approach. His task at this meeting was to persuade veteran white liberals, at the invitation of Mrs. Dorothy Rogers Tilly, to see the student movement as a natural outgrowth of their own work and of his own campaign. Mrs. Tilly was married to Milton E. Tilly, an Atlanta businessman, and was a former member of President Truman's Committee on Civil Rights.*

Members of the Fellowship of the Concerned, of the Southern Regional Council, I need not pause to say how very delighted I am to be here today, and to have the opportunity of being a little part of this very significant gathering. I certainly want to express my personal appreciation to Mrs. Tilly and the members of the Committee, for giving me this opportunity. I would also like to express just a personal word of thanks and appreciation for your vital witness in this period of transition which we are facing in our Southland, and in the nation, and I am sure that as a result of this genuine concern, and your significant work in communities all across the South, we have a better South today and I am sure will have a better South tomorrow with your continued endeavor and I do want to express my personal gratitude and appreciation to you of the Fellowship of the Concerned for your significant work and for your forthright witness.

Now, I have been asked to talk about the philosophy behind the student movement. There can be no gainsaying of the fact that we confront a crisis in race relations in the United States. This crisis has been precipitated on the one hand by the determined resistance of reactionary forces in the South to the Supreme Court's decision in 1954 outlawing segregation in the public schools. And we know that at times this resistance has risen to ominous proportions. At times we find the legislative halls of the South ringing loud with such words as interposition and nullification. And all of these forces have developed into massive resistance. But we must also say that the crisis has been precipitated on the other hand by the determination of hundreds and thousands and millions of Negro people to achieve freedom and human dignity. If the Negro stayed in his place and accepted discrimination and segregation, there would be no crisis. But the Negro has a new sense of dignity, a new self-respect and new determination. He has reevaluated his own intrinsic worth. Now this new sense of dignity on the part of the Negro grows out of the same longing for freedom and human dignity on the part of the oppressed people all over the world; for we see it in Africa, we see it in Asia, and we see it all over the world. Now we must say that this struggle for freedom will not come to an automatic halt, for history reveals to us that once oppressed people rise up against that oppression, there is no stopping point short of full freedom. On the other hand, history reveals to us that those who oppose the movement for freedom are those who are in privileged positions who very seldom give up their privileges without strong resistance. And they very seldom do it voluntarily. So the sense of struggle will continue. The question is how will the struggle be waged.

Now there are three ways that oppressed people have generally dealt with their oppression. One way is the method of acquiescence, the method of surrender; that is, the individuals will somehow adjust themselves to oppression, they adjust themselves to discrimination or to segregation or colonialism or what have you. The other method that has been used in history is that of rising up against the oppressor with corroding hatred and physical violence. Now of course we know about this method in Western civilization because in a sense it has been the hallmark of its grandeur, and the inseparable twin of western materialism. But there is a weakness in this method because it ends up creating many more social problems than it solves. And I am convinced that if the Negro succumbs to the temptation of using violence in his struggle for freedom and justice, unborn generations will be the recipients of a long and desolate night of bitterness. And our chief legacy to the future will be an endless reign of meaningless chaos.

But there is another way, namely the way of nonviolent resistance. This method was popularized in our generation by a little man from India, whose name was Mohandas K. Gandhi. He used this method in a magnificent way to free his people from the economic exploitation and the political domination inflicted upon them by a foreign power.

This has been the method used by the student movement in the South and all over the United States. And naturally whenever I talk about the student movement I cannot be totally objective. I have to be somewhat subjective because of my great admiration for what the students have done. For in a real sense they have taken our deep groans and passionate yearnings for freedom, and filtered them in their own tender souls, and fashioned them into a creative protest which is an epic known all over our nation. As a result of their disciplined, nonviolent, yet courageous struggle, they have been able to do wonders in the South, and in our nation. But this movement does have an underlying philosophy, it has certain ideas that are attached to it, it has certain philosophical precepts. These are the things that I would like to discuss for the few moments left.

I would say that the first point or the first principle in the movement is the idea that means must be as pure as the end. This movement is based on the philosophy that ends and means must cohere. Now this has been one of the long struggles in history, the whole idea of means and ends. Great philosophers have grappled with it, and sometimes they have emerged with the idea, from Machiavelli on down, that the end justifies the means. There is a great system of thought in our world today, known as commmunism. And I think that with all of the weakness and tragedies of communism, we find its greatest tragedy right here, that it goes under the philosophy that the end justifies the means that are used in the process. So we can read or we can hear the Lenins say that lying, deceit, or violence, that many of these things justify the ends of the classless society.

This is where the student movement and the nonviolent movement that is taking place in our nation would break with communism and any other system that would argue that the end justifies the means. For in the long run, we must see that the end represents the means in process and the ideal in the making. In other words, we cannot believe, or we cannot go with the idea that the end justifies the means because the end is preexistent in the means. So the idea of nonviolent resistance, the philosophy of nonviolent resistance, is the philosophy which says that the means must be as pure as the end, that in the long run of history, immoral destructive means cannot bring about moral and constructive ends.

There is another thing about this philosophy, this method of nonviolence which is followed by the student movement. It says that those who adhere to or follow this philosophy must follow a consistent principle of noninjury. They must consistently refuse to inflict injury upon another. Sometimes you will read the literature of the student movement and see that, as they are getting ready for the sit-in or stand-in, they will read something like this, "If you are hit do not hit back, if you are cursed do not curse back." This is the whole idea, that the individual who is engaged in a nonviolent struggle must never inflict injury upon another. Now this has an external aspect and it has an internal one. From the external point of view it means that the individuals involved must avoid external physical violence. So they don't have guns, they don't retaliate with physical violence. If they are hit in the process, they avoid external physical violence at every point. But it also means that they avoid internal violence of spirit. This is why the love ethic stands so high in the student movement. We have a great deal of talk about love and nonviolence in this whole thrust.

Now when the students talk about love, certainly they are not talking about emotional bosh, they are not talking about merely a sentimental outpouring; they're talking something much deeper, and I always have to stop and try to define the meaning of love in this context. The Greek language comes to our aid in trying to deal with this. There are three words in the Greek language for love; one is the word *eros*. This is a beautiful type of love, it is an aesthetic love. Plato talks about it a great deal in his Dialogue, the yearning of the soul for the realm of the divine. It has come to us to be a sort of romantic love, and so in a sense we have read about it and experienced it. We've read about it in all the beauties of literature. I guess in a sense Edgar Allan Poe was talking about *eros* when he talked about his beautiful Annabelle Lee, with the love surrounded by the halo of eternity. In a sense Shakespeare was talking about *eros* when he said "Love is not love which alters when it alteration finds, or bends with the remover to remove; O'no! It is an ever fixed mark that looks on tempests and is never shaken, it is the star to every wandering bark." (You know, I remember that because I used to quote it to this little lady when we were courting; that's *eros*.) The Greek language talks about *philia* which was another level of love. It is an intimate affection between personal friends, it is a reciprocal love. On this level you love because you are loved. It is friendship.

Then the Greek language comes out with another word which is called the *agape*. *Agape* is more than romantic love, *agape* is more than friendship. *Agape* is understanding, creative, redemptive, good will to all men. It is an overflowing love which seeks nothing in return. Theologians would say that it is the love of God operating in the human heart. So that when one rises to love on this level, he loves men not because he likes them, not because their ways appeal to him, but he loves every man because God loves him. And he rises to the point of loving the person who does an evil deed while hating the deed that the person does. I think this is what Jesus meant when he said "love your enemies." I'm very happy that he didn't say like your enemies, because it is pretty difficult to like some people. Like is sentimental, and it is pretty difficult to like someone bombing your home; it is pretty difficult to like somebody threatening your children; it is difficult to like congressmen who spend all of their time trying to defeat civil rights. But Jesus says love them, and love is greater than like. Love is understanding, redemptive, creative, good will for all men. And it is this idea, it is this whole ethic of love which is the idea standing at the basis of the student movement.

There is something else: that one seeks to defeat the unjust system, rather than individuals who are caught in that system. And that one goes on believing that somehow this is the important thing, to get rid of the evil system and not the individual who happens to be misguided, who happens to be misled, who was taught wrong. The thing to do is to get rid of the system and thereby create a moral balance within society.

Another thing that stands at the center of this movement is another idea: that suffering can be a most creative and powerful social force. Suffering has certain moral attributes involved, but it can be a powerful and creative social force. Now, it is very interesting at this point to notice that both violence and nonviolence agree that suffering can be a very powerful social force. But there is this difference: violence says that suffering can be a powerful social force by inflicting the suffering on somebody else: so this is what we do in war, this is what we do in the whole violent thrust of the violent movement. It believes that you achieve some end by inflicting suffering on another. The nonviolent say that suffering becomes a powerful social force when you willingly accept that violence on yourself, so that self-suffering stands at the center of the nonviolent movement and the individuals involved are able to suffer in a creative manner, feeling that unearned suffering is redemptive, and that suffering may serve to transform the social situation.

Another thing in this movement is the idea that there is within human nature an amazing potential for goodness. There is within human nature something that can respond to goodness. I know somebody's liable to say that this is an unrealistic movement if it goes on believing that all people are good. Well, I didn't say that. I think the students are realistic enough to believe that there is a strange dichotomy of disturbing dualism within human nature. Many of the great philosophers and thinkers through the ages have seen this. It caused Ovid the Latin poet to say, "I see and approve the better things of life, but the evil things I do." It caused even Saint Augustine to say "Lord, make me pure, but not yet." So that that is in human nature. Plato, centuries ago said that the human personality is like a charioteer with two headstrong horses, each wanting to go in different directions, so that within our own individual lives we see this conflict and certainly when we come to the collective life of man, we see a strange badness. But in spite of this there is something in human nature that can respond to goodness. So that man is neither innately good nor is he innately bad; he has potentialities for both. So in this sense, Carlyle was right when he said that, "there are depths in man which go down to the lowest hell, and heights which reach the highest heaven, for are not both heaven and hell made out of him, ever-lasting miracle and mystery that he is?" Man has the capacity to be good, man has the capacity to be evil.

And so the nonviolent resister never lets this idea go, that there is something within human nature than can respond to goodness. So that a Jesus of Nazareth or a Mohandas Gandhi, can appeal to human beings and appeal to that element of goodness within them, and a Hitler can appeal to the element of evil within them. But we must never forget that there is something within human nature that can respond to goodness, that man is not totally depraved; to put it in theological terms, the image of God is never totally gone. And so the individuals who believe in this movement and who believe in nonviolence and our struggle in the South, somehow believe that even the worst segrationist can become an integrationist. Now sometimes it is hard to believe that this is what this movement says, and it believes it firmly, that there is something within human nature that can be changed, and this stands at the top of the whole philosophy of the student movement and the philosophy of nonviolence.

It says something else. It says that it is as much a moral obligation to refuse to cooperate with evil as it is to cooperate with good. Noncooperation with evil is as much a moral obligation as the cooperation with good. So that the student movement is willing to stand up courageously on the idea of civil disobedience. Now I think this is the part of the student movement that is probably misunderstood more than anything else. And it is a difficult aspect, because on the one hand the students would say, and I would say, and all the people who believe in civil rights would say, obey the Supreme Court's decision of 1954 and at the same time, we would disobey certain laws that exist on the statutes of the South today.

This brings in the whole question of how can you be logically consistent when you advocate obeying some laws and disobeying other laws. Well, I think one would have to see the whole meaning of this movement at this point by seeing that the students recognize that there are two types of laws. There are just laws and there are unjust laws. And they would be the first to say obey the just laws, they would be the first to say that men and women have a moral obligation to obey just and right laws. And they would go on to say that we must see that there are unjust laws. Now the question comes into being, what is the difference, and who determines the difference, what is the difference between a just and an unjust law?

Well, a just law is a law that squares with a moral law. It is a law that squares with that which is right, so that any law that uplifts human personality is a just law. Whereas that law which is out of harmony with the moral is a law which does not square with the moral law of the universe. It does not square with the law of God, so for that reason it is unjust and any law that degrades the human personality is an unjust law.

Well, somebody says that that does not mean anything to me; first, I don't believe in these abstract things called moral laws and I'm not too religious, so I don't believe in the law of God; you have to get a little more concrete, and more practical. What do you mean when you say that a law is unjust, and a law is just? Well, I would go on to say in more concrete terms that an unjust law is a code that the majority inflicts on the minority that is not binding on itself. So that this becomes difference made legal. Another thing that we can say is that an unjust law is a code which the majority inflicts upon the minority, which that minority had no part in enacting or creating, because that minority had no right to vote in many instances, so that the legislative bodies that made these laws were not democratically elected. Who could ever say that the legislative body of Mississippi was democratically elected, or the legislative body of Alabama was democratically elected, or the legislative body even of Georgia has been democratically elected, when there are people in Terrell County and in other counties because of the color of their skin who cannot vote? They confront reprisals and threats and all of that; so that an unjust law is a law that individuals did not have a part in creating or enacting because they were denied the right to vote.

Now the same token of just law would be just the opposite. A just law becomes saneness made legal. It is a code that the majority, who happen to believe in that code, compel the minority, who don't believe in it, to follow, because they are willing to follow it themselves, so it is saneness made legal. Therefore the individuals who stand up on the basis of civil disobedience realize that they are following something that says that there are just laws and there are unjust laws. Now, they are not anarchists. They believe that there are laws which must be followed; they do not seek to defy the law, they do not seek to evade the law. For many individuals who would call themselves segregationists and who would hold on to segregation at any cost seek to defy the law, they seek to evade the law, and their process can lead on into anarchy. They seek in the final analysis to follow a way of uncivil disobedience, not civil disobedience. And I submit that the individual who disobeys the law, whose conscience tells him it is unjust and who is willing to accept the penalty by staying in jail until that law is altered, is expressing at the moment the very highest respect for law.

This is what the students have followed in their movement. Of course there is nothing new about this; they feel that they are in good company and rightly so. We go back and read the Apology and the Crito, and you see Socrates practicing civil disobedience. And to a degree academic freedom is a reality today because Socrates practiced civil disobedience. The early Christians practiced civil disobedience in a superb manner, to a point where they were willing to be thrown to the lions. They were willing to face all kinds of suffering in order to stand up for what they knew was right even though they knew it was against the laws of the Roman Empire.

We could come up to our own day and we see it in many instances. We must never forget that everything that Hitler did in Germany was "legal." It was illegal to aid and comfort a Jew, in the days of Hitler's Germany. But I believe that if I had the same attitude then as I have now I would publicly aid and comfort my Jewish brothers in Germany if Hitler were alive today calling this an illegal process. If I lived in South Africa today in the midst of the white supremacy law in South Africa, I would join Chief Luthuli and others in saying break these unjust laws. And even let us come up to America. Our nation in a sense came into being through a massive act of civil disobedience for the Boston Tea Party was nothing but a massive act of civil disobedience. Those who stood up against the slave laws, the abolitionists, by and large practiced civil disobedience. So I think these students are in good company, and they feel that by practicing civil disobedience they are in line with men and women through the ages who have stood up for something that is morally right.

Now there are one or two other things that I want to say about this student movement, moving out of the philosophy of nonviolence, something about what it is a revolt against. On the one hand it is a revolt against the negative peace that has encompassed the South for many years. I remember when I was in Montgomery, Alabama, one of the white citizens came to me one day and said—and I think he was very sincere about this—that in Montgomery for all of these years we have been such a peaceful community, we have had so much harmony in race relations and then you people have started this movement and boycott, and it has done so much to disturb race relations, and we just don't love the Negro like we used to love them, because you have destroyed the harmony and the peace that we once had in race relations. And I said to him, in the best way I could say and I tried to say it in nonviolent terms, we have never had peace in Montgomery, Alabama, we have never had peace in the South. We have had a negative peace, which is merely the absence of tension; we've had a negative peace in which the Negro patiently accepted his situation and his plight, but we've never had true peace, we've never had positive peace, and what we're seeking now is to develop this positive peace. For we must come to see that peace is not merely the absence of some negative force, it is the presence of a positive force. True peace is not merely the absence of tension, but it is the presence of justice and brotherhood. I think this is what Jesus meant when he said, "I come not to bring peace but a sword." Now Jesus didn't mean he came to start war, to bring a physical sword, and he didn't mean, I come not to bring positive peace. But I think what Jesus was saying in substance was this, that I come not to bring an old negative peace, which makes for stagnant passivity and deadening complacency, I come to bring something different, and whenever I come, a conflict is precipitated, between the old and the new, whenever I come a struggle takes place between justice and injustice, between the forces of light and the forces of darkness. I come not to bring a negative peace, but a positive peace, which is brotherhood, which is justice, which is the Kingdom of God.

And I think this is what we are seeking to do today, and this movement is a revolt against a negative peace and a struggle to bring into being a positive peace, which makes for true brotherhood, true integration, true person-to-person relationships. This movement is also revolt against what is often called tokenism. Here again many people do not understand this, they feel that in this struggle the Negro will be satisfied with tokens of integration, just a few students and a few schools here and there and a few doors open here and there. But this isn't the meaning of the movement and I think that honesty impels me to admit it everywhere I have an opportunity, that the Negro's aim is to bring about complete integration in American life. And he has come to see that token integration is little more than token democracy, which ends up with many new evasive schemes and it ends up with new discrimination, covered up with such niceties of complexity. It is very interesting to discover that the movement has thrived in many communities that had token integration. So this reveals that the movement is based on a principle that integration must become real and complete, not just token integration.

It is also a revolt against what I often call the myth of time. We hear this quite often, that only time can solve this problem. That if we will only be patient, and only pray—which we must do, we must be patient and we must pray—but there are those who say just do these things and wait for time, and time will solve the problem. Well the people who argue this do not themselves realize that time is neutral, that it can be used constructively or destructively. At points the people of ill will, the segregationists, have used time much more effectively than the people of good will. So individuals in the struggle must come to realize that it is necessary to aid time, that without this kind of aid, time itself will become an ally of the insurgent and primitive forces of social stagnation. Therefore, this movement is a revolt against the myth of time.

There is a final thing that I would like to say to you, this movement is a movement based on faith in the future. It is a movement based on a philosophy, the possibility of the future bringing into being something real and meaningful. It is a movement based on hope. I think this is very important. The students have developed a theme song for their movement, maybe you've heard it. It goes something like this, "We shall overcome, deep in my heart, I do believe, we shall overcome," and then they go on to say another verse, "We are not afraid, we are not afraid today, deep in my heart I do believe, we shall overcome." So it is out of this deep faith in the future that they are able to move out and adjourn the councils of despair, and to bring new light in the dark chambers of pessimism. I can remember the times that we've been together, I remember that night in Montgomery, Alabama, when we had stayed up all night discussing the Freedom Rides, and that morning came to see that it was necessary to go on with the Freedom Rides, that we would not in all good conscience call an end to the Freedom Rides at that point. And I remember the first group got ready to leave, to take a bus for Jackson, Mississippi, we all joined hands and started singing together. "We shall overcome, we shall overcome." And something within me said, now how is it that these students can sing this, they are going down to Mississippi, they are going to face hostile and jeering mobs, and yet they could sing, "We shall overcome." They may even face physical death, and yet they could sing, "We shall overcome." Most of them realized that they would be thrown into jail, and yet they could sing, "We shall overcome, we are not afraid." Then something caused me to see at that moment the real meaning of the movement. That students had faith in the future. That the movement was based on hope, that this movement had something within it that says somehow even though the arc of the moral universe is long, it bends toward justice. And I think this should be a challenge to all others who are struggling to transform the dangling discords of our Southland into a beautiful symphony of brotherhood. There is something in this student movement which says to us, that we shall overcome. Before the victory is won some may have to get scarred up, but we shall overcome. Before the victory of brotherhood is achieved, some will maybe face physical death, but we shall overcome. Before the victory is won, some will lose jobs, some will be called communists, and reds, merely because they believe in brotherhood, some will be dismissed as dangerous rabblerousers and agitators merely because they're standing up for what is right, but we shall overcome. That is the basis of this movement, and as I like to say, there is something in this universe that justifies Carlyle in saying no lie can live forever. We shall overcome because there is something in this universe which justifies William Cullen Bryant in saying truth crushed to earth shall rise again. We shall overcome because there is something in this universe that justifies James Russell Lowell in saying, truth forever on the scaffold, wrong forever on the throne. Yet that scaffold sways the future, and behind the dim unknown standeth God within the shadows keeping watch above His own. With this faith in the future, with this determined struggle, we will be able to emerge from the bleak and desolate midnight of man's inhumanity to man, into the bright and glittering daybreak of freedom and justice. Thank you.

*New South* (December 1961): 3ff. A version of this address was reprinted in Philip S. Foner, ed., *The Voice of Black America: Major Speeches by Negroes in the United States, 1797–1971* (New York: Simon & Schuster, 1972), pp. 943–53 as "The Philosophy of the Student Nonviolent Movement." [Further information about Mrs. Dorothy Rogers Tilly can be found in John Patrick McDowell, *The Social Gospel in the South: The Woman's Home Mission Movement in the Methodist Episcopal Church, South, 1886–1939* (Baton Rouge and London: Louisiana State University Press, 1982), pp. 96–97. Further discussions of the work of the Southern Regional Council can be found in Benjamin E. Mays, *Born to Rebel: An Autobiography* (New York: Scribner's, 1971), pp. 213–20, and Raymond Gavins, *The Perils and Prospects of Southern Black Leadership: Gordon Blaine Hancock, 1884–1970* (Durham, N.C.: Duke University Press, 1977), pp. 129–60.]

# Nonviolence: The Only Road to Freedom

*Amid urban riots, a new wave of strident militancy within black America, stiff competition for funds and political influence from other civil rights organizations, and the signs that the nation's attention was increasingly being diverted from the civil rights movement, King and his editorial staff defended SCLC's position that nonviolent resistance was the only effective strategy for social change available to black people.*

The year 1966 brought with it the first public challenge to the philosophy and strategy of nonviolence from within the ranks of the civil rights movement. Resolutions of self-defense and Black Power sounded forth from our friends and brothers. At the same time riots erupted in several major cities. Inevitably a link was made between the two phenomena though movement leadership continued to deny any implications of violence in the concept of Black Power.

The nation's press heralded these incidents as an end of the Negro's reliance on nonviolence as a means of achieving freedom. Articles appeared on "The Plot to get Whitey," and, "Must Negroes fight back?" and one had the impression that a serious movement was underway to lead the Negro to freedom through the use of violence.

Indeed, there was much talk of violence. It was the same talk we have heard on the fringes of the nonviolent movement for the past ten years. It was the talk of fearful men, saying that they would not join the nonviolent movement because they would not remain nonviolent if attacked. Now the climate had shifted so that it was even more popular to talk of violence, but in spite of the talk of violence there emerged no action in this direction. One reporter pointed out in a recent New Yorker article, that the fact that Beckwith, Price, Rainey, and Collie Leroy Wilkins remain alive is living testimony to the fact that the Negro remains nonviolent. And if this is not enough, a mere check of the statistics of casualties in the recent riots shows that the vast majority of persons killed in riots are Negroes. All the reports of sniping in Los Angeles's expressways did not produce a single casualty. The young demented white student at the University of Texas has shown what damage a sniper can do when he is serious. In fact, this one young man killed more people in one day than all the Negroes have killed in all the riots in all the cities since the Harlem riots of 1964. This must raise a serious question about the violent intent of the Negro, for certainly there are many ex-GIs within our ghettos, and no small percentage of those recent migrants from the South have demonstrated some proficiency hunting squirrels and rabbits.

I can only conclude that the Negro, even in his bitterest moments, is not intent on killing white men to be free. This does not mean that the Negro is a saint who abhors violence. Unfortunately, a check of the hospitals in any Negro community on any Saturday night will make you painfully aware of the violence within the Negro community. Hundreds of victims of shooting and cutting lie bleeding in the emergency rooms, but there is seldom if ever a white person who is the victim of Negro hostility.

I have talked with many persons in the ghettos of the North who argue eloquently for the use of violence. But I observed none of them in the mobs that rioted in Chicago. I have heard the street-corner preachers in Harlem and in Chicago's Washington Park, but in spite of the bitterness preached and the hatred espoused, none of them has ever been able to start a riot. So far, only the police through their fears and prejudice have goaded our people to riot. And once the riot starts, only the police or the National Guard have been able to put an end to them. This demonstrates that these violent eruptions are unplanned, uncontrollable temper tantrums brought on by long-neglected poverty, humiliation, oppression and exploitation. Violence as a strategy for social change in America is nonexistent. All the sound and fury seems but the posturing of cowards whose bold talk produces no action and signifies nothing.

I am convinced that for practical as well as moral reasons, nonviolence offers the only road to freedom for my people. In violent warfare, one must be prepared to face ruthlessly the fact that there will be casualties by the thousands. In Vietnam, the United States has evidently decided that it is willing to slaughter millions, sacrifice some two hundred thousand men and twenty billion dollars a year to secure the freedom of some fourteen million Vietnamese. This is to fight a war on Asian soil, where Asians are in the majority. Anyone leading a violent conflict must be willing to make a similar assessment regarding the possible casualties to a minority populaton confronting a well-armed, wealthy majority with a fanatical right wing that is capable of exterminating the entire black population and which would not hesitate such an attempt if the survival of white Western materialism were at stake.

Arguments that the American Negro is a part of a world which is two-thirds colored and that there will come a day when the oppressed people of color will rise together to throw off the yoke of white oppression are at least fifty years away from being relevant. There is no colored nation, including China, which now shows even the potential of leading a revolution of color in any international proportion. Ghana, Zambia, Tanzania and Nigeria are fighting their own battles for survival against poverty, illiteracy and the subversive influence of neocolonialism, so that they offer no hope to Angola, Southern Rhodesia and South Africa, and much less to the American Negro.

The hard cold facts of racial life in the world today indicate that the hope of the people of color in the world may well rest on the American Negro and his ability to reform the structures of racist imperialism from within and thereby turn the technology and wealth of the West to the task of liberating the world from want.

This is no time for romantic illusions about freedom and empty philosophical debate. This is a time for action. What is needed is a strategy for change, a tactical program which will bring the Negro into the mainstream of American life as quickly as possible. So far, this has only been offered by the nonviolent movement.

Our record of achievement through nonviolent action is already remarkable. The dramatic social changes which have been made across the South are unmatched in the annals of history. Montgomery, Albany, Birmingham and Selma have paved the way for untold progress. Even more remarkable is the fact that this progress occurred with a minimum of human sacrifice and loss of life.

Not a single person has been killed in a nonviolent demonstration. The bombings of the 16th Street Baptist Church occurred several months after demonstrations stopped. Rev. James Reeb, Mrs. Viola Liuzzo and Jimmie Lee Jackson were all murdered at night following demonstrations. And fewer people have been killed in ten years of action across the South than were killed in three nights of rioting in Watts. No similar changes have occurred without infinitely more sufferings, whether it be Gandhi's drive for independence in India or any African nation's struggle for independence.

## THE QUESTION OF SELF-DEFENSE

There are many people who very honestly raise the question of self-defense. This must be placed in perspective. It goes without saying that people will protect their homes. This is a right guaranteed by the Constitution and respected even in the worst areas of the South. But the mere protection of one's home and person against assault by lawless night riders does not provide any positive approach to the fears and conditions which produce violence. There must be some program for establishing law. Our experience in places like Savannah and Macon, Georgia, has been that a drive which registers Negroes to vote can do more to provide protection of the law and respect for Negroes by even racist sheriffs than anything we have seen.

In a nonviolent demonstration, self-defense must be approached from quite another perspective. One must remember that the cause of the demonstration is some exploitation or form of oppression that has made it necessary for men of courage and good will to demonstrate against the evil. For example, a demonstration against the evil of *de facto* school segregation is based on the awareness that a child's mind is crippled daily by inadequate educational opportunity. The demonstrator agrees that it is better for him to suffer publicly for a short time to end the crippling evil of school segregation than to have generation after generation of children suffer in ignorance.

In such a demonstration, the point is made that schools are inadequate. This is the evil to which one seeks to point; anything else detracts from that point and interferes with confrontation of the primary evil against which one demonstrates. Of course, no one wants to suffer and be hurt. But it is more important to get at the cause than to be safe. It is better to shed a little blood from a blow on the head or a rock thrown by an angry mob than to have children by the thousands grow up reading at a fifth- or sixth-grade level.

It is always amusing to me when a Negro man says that he can't demonstrate with us because if someone hit him he would fight back. Here is a man whose children are being plagued by rats and roaches, whose wife is robbed daily at overpriced ghetto food stores, who himself is working for about two-thirds the pay of a white person doing a similar job and with similar skills, and in spite of all this daily suffering it takes someone spitting on him or calling him a nigger to make him want to fight.

Conditions are such for Negroes in America that all Negroes ought to be fighting aggressively. It is as ridiculous for a Negro to raise the question of self-defense in relation to nonviolence as it is for a soldier on the battlefield to say he is not going to take any risks. He is there because he believes that the freedom of his country is worth the risk of his life. The same is true of the nonviolent demonstrator. He sees the misery of his people so clearly that he volunteers to suffer in their behalf and put an end to their plight.

Furthermore, it is extremely dangerous to organize a movement around self-defense. The line between defensive violence and aggressive or retaliatory violence is a fine line indeed. When violence is tolerated even as a means of self-defense there is grave danger that in the fervor of emotion the main fight will be lost over the question of self-defense.

When my home was bombed in 1955 in Montgomery, many men wanted to retaliate, to place an armed guard on my home. But the issue there was not my life, but whether Negroes would achieve first-class treatment on the city's buses. Had we become distracted by the question of my safety we would have lost the moral offensive and sunk to the level of our oppressors.

I must continue by faith or it is too great a burden to bear and violence, even in self-defense, creates more problems than it solves. Only a refusal to hate or kill can put an end to the chain of violence in the world and lead us toward a community where men can live together without fear. Our goal is to create a beloved community and this will require a qualitative change in our souls as well as a quantitative change in our lives.

## STRATEGY FOR CHANGE

The American racial revolution has been a revolution to "get in" rather than to overthrow. We want a share in the American economy, the housing market, the educational system and the social opportunities. This goal itself indicates that a social change in America must be nonviolent.

If one is in search of a better job, it does not help to burn down the factory. If one needs more adequate education, shooting the principal will not help, or if housing is the goal, only building and construction will produce that end. To destroy anything, person or property, can't bring us closer to the goal that we seek.

The nonviolent strategy has been to dramatize the evils of our society in such a way that pressure is brought to bear against those evils by the forces of good will in the community and change is produced.

The student sit-ins of 1960 are a classic illustration of this method. Students were denied the right to eat at a lunch counter, so they deliberately sat down to protest their denial. They were arrested, but this made their parents mad and so they began to close their charge accounts. The students continued to sit in, and this further embarrassed the city, scared away many white shoppers and soon produced an economic threat to the business life of the city. Amid this type of pressure, it is not hard to get people to agree to change.

So far, we have had the Constitution backing most of the demands for change, and this has made our work easier, since we could be sure that the federal courts would usually back up our demonstrations legally. Now we are approaching areas where the voice of the Constitution is not clear. We have left the realm of constitutional rights and we are entering the area of human rights.

The Constitution assured the right to vote, but there is no such assurance of the right to adequate housing, or the right to an adequate income. And yet, in a nation which has a gross national product of 750 billion dollars a year, it is morally right to insist that every person has a decent house, an adequate education and enough money to provide basic necessities for one's family. Achievement of these goals will be a lot more difficult and require much more discipline, understanding, organization and sacrifice.

It so happens that Negroes live in the central city of the major cities of the United States. These cities control the electoral votes of the large states of our nation. This means that though we are only ten percent of the nation's population, we are located in such a key position geographically—the cities of the North and black belts of the South—that we are able to lead a political and moral coalition which can direct the course of the nation. Our position depends upon a lot more than political power, however. It depends upon our ability to marshal moral power as well. As soon as we lose the moral offensive, we are left with only our ten percent of the power of the nation. This is hardly enough to produce any meaningful changes, even within our own communities, for the lines of power control the economy as well and once the flow of money is cut off, progress ceases.

The past three years have demonstrated the power of a committed, morally sound minority to lead the nation. It was the coalition molded through the Birmingham movement which allied the forces of the churches, labor and the academic communities of the nation behind the liberal issues of our time. All of the liberal legislation of the past session of Congress can be credited to this coalition. Even the presence of a vital peace movement and the campus protest against the war in Vietnam can be traced back to the nonviolent action movement led by the Negro. Prior to Birmingham, our campuses were still in a state of shock over the McCarthy era and Congress was caught in the perennial deadlock of southern Democrats and midwestern Republicans. Negroes put the country on the move against the enemies of poverty, slums and inadequate education.

## TECHNIQUES OF THE FUTURE

When Negroes marched, so did the nation. The power of the nonviolent march is indeed a mystery. It is always surprising that a few hundred Negroes marching can produce such a reaction across the nation. When marches are carefully organized around well-defined issues, they represent the power which Victor Hugo phrased as the most powerful force in the world, "an idea whose time has come." Marching feet announce that time has come for a given idea. When the idea is a sound one, the cause a just one, and the demonstration a righteous one, change will be forthcoming. But if any of these conditions are not present, the power for change is missing also. A thousand people demonstrating for the right to use heroin would have little effect. By the same token, a group of ten thousand marching in anger against a police station and cussing out the chief of police will do very little to bring respect, dignity and unbiased law enforcement. Such a demonstration would only produce fear and bring about an addition of forces to the station and more oppressive methods by the police.

Marches must continue in the future, and they must be the kind of marches that bring about the desired result. But the march is not a "one shot" victory-producing method. One march is seldom successful, and as my good friend Kenneth Clark points out in *Dark Ghetto*, it can serve merely to let off steam and siphon off the energy which is necessary to produce change. However, when marching is seen as a part of a program to dramatize an evil, to mobilize the forces of good will, and to generate pressure and power for change, marches will continue to be effective.

Our experience is that marches must continue over a period of thirty to forty-five days to produce any meaningful results. They must also be of sufficient size to produce some inconvenience to the forces in power or they go unnoticed. In other words, they must demand the attention of the press, for it is the press which interprets the issue to the community at large and thereby sets in motion the machinery for change.

Along with the march as a weapon for change in our nonviolent arsenal must be listed the boycott. Basic to the philosophy of nonviolence is the refusal to cooperate with evil. There is nothing quite so effective as a refusal to cooperate economically with the forces and institutions which perpetuate evil in our communities.

In the past six months simply by refusing to purchase products from companies which do not hire Negroes in meaningful numbers and in all job categories, the Ministers of Chicago under SCLC's Operation Breadbasket have increased the income of the Negro community by more than two million dollars annually. In Atlanta the Negroes' earning power has been increased by more than twenty million dollars annually over the past three years through a carefully disciplined program of selective buying and negotiations by the Negro minister. This is nonviolence at its peak of power, when it cuts into the profit margin of a business in order to bring about a more just distribution of jobs and opportunities for Negro wage earners and consumers.

But again, the boycott must be sustained over a period of several weeks and months to assure results. This means continuous education of the community in order that support can be maintained. People will work together and sacrifice if they understand clearly why and how this sacrifice will bring about change. We can never assume that anyone understands. It is our job to keep people informed and aware.

Our most powerful nonviolent weapon is, as would be expected, also our most demanding, that is organization. To produce change, people must be organized to work together in units of power. These units might be political, as in the case of voters' leagues and political parties; they may be economic units such as groups of tenants who join forces to form a tenant union or to organize a rent strike; or they may be laboring units of persons who are seeking employment and wage increases.

More and more, the civil rights movement will become engaged in the task of organizing people into permanent groups to protect their own interests and to produce change in their behalf. This is a tedious task which may take years, but the results are more permanent and meaningful.

In the future we will be called upon to organize the unemployed, to unionize the businesses within the ghetto, to bring tenants together into collective bargaining units and establish cooperatives for purposes of building viable financial institutions within the ghetto that can be controlled by Negroes themselves.

There is no easy way to create a world where men and women can live together, where each has his own job and house and where all children receive as much education as their minds can absorb. But if such a world is created in our lifetime, it will be done in the United States by Negroes and white people of good will. It will be accomplished by persons who have the courage to put an end to suffering by willingly suffering themselves rather than inflict suffering upon others. It will be done by rejecting the racism, materialism and violence that has characterized Western civilization and especially by working toward a world of brotherhood, cooperation and peace.

*Ebony* 21 (October 1966): 27–30.

# 12

# A Gift of Love

*This anecdotal piece accents the role of love in the black freedom movement, and was part of a Christmas series on that theme.*

This Christmas I remember the little black children of Grenada, Mississippi, beaten by grown men as they walked to school. I remember a baby, attacked by rats in a Chicago slum. I remember a young Negro, murdered by a gang in Cicero, Illinois, where he was looking for a job; and a white minister in Georgia, forced out of his sacred office because he spoke for human dignity. I remember, too, farm workers in Mississippi, risking their lives and their livelihood to march out of the cotton fields and vote for freedom and democracy.

This I remember, especially in this season of giving, for these people have followed the example and spirit of Christ Himself. They have given mankind a priceless "Gift of Love."

I am thinking now of some teenage boys in Chicago. They have nicknames like "Tex," and "Pueblo," and "Goat," and "Teddy." They hail from the Negro slums. Forsaken by society, they once proudly fought and lived for street gangs like the Vice Lords, the Roman Saints, the Rangers.

But this year, they gave us all the gift of nonviolence, which is indeed a gift of love.

I met these boys and heard their stories in discussions we had on some long, cold nights last winter at the slum apartment I rent in the West Side ghetto of Chicago. I was shocked at the venom they poured out against the world. At times I shared their despair and felt a hopelessness that these young Americans could ever embrace the concept of nonviolence as the effective and powerful instrument of social reform.

All their lives, boys like this have known life as a madhouse of violence and degradation. Some have never experienced a meaningful family life. Some have police records. Some dropped out of the incredibly bad slum schools, then were deprived of honorable work, then took to the streets.

To the young victim of the slums, this society has so limited the alternatives of his life that the expression of his manhood is reduced to the ability to defend himself physically. No wonder it appears logical to him to strike out, resorting to violence against oppression. That is the only way he thinks he can get recognition.

And so, we have seen occasional rioting—and, much more frequently and consistently, brutal acts and crimes by Negroes against Negroes. In many a week in Chicago, as many or more Negro youngsters have been killed in gang fights as were killed in the riots there last summer.

The Freedom Movement has tried to bring a message to boys like Tex. First, we explained that violence can be put down by armed might and police work, that physical force can never solve the underlying social problems. Second, we promised them we could prove, by example, that nonviolence works.

The young slum dweller has good reason to be suspicious of promises. But these young people in Chicago agreed last winter to give nonviolence a test. Then came the very long, very tense, hot summer of 1966, and the first test for many Chicago youngsters: the Freedom March through Mississippi. Gang members went there in carloads.

Those of us who had been in the movement for years were apprehensive about the behavior of the boys. Before the march ended, they were to be attacked by tear gas. They were to be called upon to protect women and children on the march, with no other weapon than their own bodies. To them, it would be a strange and possibly nonsensical way to respond to violence.

But they reacted splendidly! They learned in Mississippi, and returned to teach in Chicago, the beautiful lesson of acting against evil by renouncing force.

And in Chicago, the test was sterner. These marchers endured not only the filthiest kind of verbal abuse, but also barrages of rocks and sticks and eggs and cherry bombs. They did not reply in words or violent deeds. Once again, their only weapon was their own bodies. I saw boys like Goat leap into the air to catch with their bare hands the bricks and bottles that were sailed toward us.

It was through the Chicago marches that our promise to them—that nonviolence achieves results—was redeemed, and their hopes for a better life were rekindled. For they saw, in Chicago, that a humane police force—in contrast to police in Mississippi—could defend the exercise of constitutional rights as well as enforce the law in the ghetto.

They saw, in prosperous white American communities, that hatred and bigotry could and should be confronted, exposed, and dealt with. They saw, in the very heart of a great city, that men of power could be made to listen to the tramp of marching feet and the call for freedom and justice, and use their power to work for a truly Open City for all.

Boys like Teddy, a child of the slums, saw all this because they decided to rise above the cruelties of those slums and to work and march, peacefully, for human dignity. They revitalized my own faith in nonviolence. And these poverty-stricken boys enriched us all with a gift of love.

*McCall's* 94 (December 1966): 146–47.

# 13

# Showdown for Nonviolence

*Dr. King had already been assassinated by James Earl Ray in Memphis, Tennessee, on 4 April 1968 when this article appeared. The worst period of racial rioting in U.S. history erupted. This article prophesied that these riots would occur because "America is reaping the harvest of hate and shame planted through generations of educational denial, political disfranchisement and economic exploitation of its black population."*

The policy of the federal government is to play russian roulette with riots; it is prepared to gamble with another summer of disaster. Despite two consecutive summers of violence, not a single basic cause of riots has been corrected. All of the misery that stoked the flames of rage and rebellion remains undiminished. With unemployment, intolerable housing and discriminatory education a scourge in Negro ghettos, Congress and the administration still tinker with trivial, halfhearted measures.

Yet only a few years ago, there was discernible, if limited, progress through nonviolence. Each year, a wholesome, vibrant Negro self-confidence was taking shape. The fact is inescapable that the tactic of nonviolence, which had then dominated the thinking of the civil rights movement, has in the last two years not been playing its transforming role. Nonviolence was a creative doctrine in the South because it checkmated the rabid segregationists who were thirsting for an opportunity to physically crush Negroes. Nonviolent direct action enabled the Negro to take to the streets in active protest, but it muzzled the guns of the oppressor because even he could not shoot down in daylight unarmed men, women and children. This is the reason there was less loss of life in ten years of southern protest than in ten days of northern riots.

Today, the northern cities have taken on the conditions we faced in the South. Police, national guard and other armed bodies are feverishly preparing for repression. They can be curbed not by unorganized resort to force by desperate Negroes but only by a massive wave of militant nonviolence. Nonviolence was never more relevant as an effective tactic than today for the North. It also may be the instrument of our national salvation.

I agree with the President's National Advisory Commission on Civil Disorders that our nation is splitting into two hostile societies and that the chief destructive cutting edge is white racism. We need, above all, effective means to force Congress to act resolutely—but means that do not involve the use of violence. For us in the Southern Christian Leadership Conference, violence is not only morally repugnant, it is pragmatically barren. We feel there is an alternative both to violence and to useless timid supplications for justice. We cannot condone either riots or the equivalent evil of passivity. And we know that nonviolent militant action in Selma and Birmingham awakened the conscience of white America and brought a moribund, insensitive Congress to life.

The time has come for a return to mass nonviolent protest. Accordingly, we are planning a series of such demonstrations this spring and summer, to begin in Washington, D.C. They will have Negro and white participation, and they will seek to benefit the poor of both races.

We will call on the government to adopt the measures recommended by its own commission. To avoid, in the commission's words, the tragedy of "continued polarization of the American community and ultimately the destruction of basic democratic values," we must have "national action—compassionate, massive and sustained, backed by the resources of the most powerful and the richest nation on earth."

The demonstrations we have planned are of deep concern to me, and I want to spell out at length what we will do, try to do, and believe in. My staff and I have worked three months on the planning. We believe that if this campaign succeeds, nonviolence will once again be the dominant instrument for social change—and jobs and income will be put in the hands of the tormented poor. If it fails, nonviolence will be discredited, and the country may be plunged into holocaust—a tragedy deepened by the awareness that it was avoidable.

We are taking action after sober reflection. We have learned from bitter experience that our government does not correct a race problem until it is confronted directly and dramatically. We also know, as official Washington may not, that the flash point of Negro rage is close at hand.

Our Washington demonstration will resemble Birmingham and Selma in duration. It will be more than a one-day protest—it can persist for two or three months. In the earlier Alabama actions, we set no time limits. We simply said we were going to struggle there until we got a response from the nation on the issues involved. We are saying the same thing about Washington. This will be an attempt to bring a kind of Selma-like movement, Birmingham-like movement, into being, substantially around the economic issues. Just as we dealt with the social problem of segregation through massive demonstrations, and we dealt with the political problem—the denial of the right to vote—through massive demonstrations, we are now trying to deal with the economic problems—the right to live, to have a job and income—through massive protest. It will be a Selma-like movement on economic issues.

We remember that when we began direct action in Birmingham and Selma, there was a thunderous chorus that sought to discourage us. Yet today, our achievements in these cities and the reforms that radiated from them are hailed with pride by all.

We've selected fifteen areas—ten cities and five rural districts—from which we have recruited our initial cadre. We will have two hundred poor people from each area. That would be about three thousand to get the protests going and set the pattern. They are important, particularly in terms of maintaining nonviolence. They are being trained in this discipline now.

In areas where we are recruiting, we are also stimulating activities in conjunction with the Washington protest. We are planning to have some of these people march to Washington. We may have half the group from Mississippi, for example, go to Washington and begin the protest there, while the other half begins walking. They would flow across the South, joining the Alabama group, the Georgia group, right on up through South and North Carolina and Virginia. We hope that the sound and sight of a growing mass of poor people walking slowly toward Washington will have a positive, dramatic effect on Congress.

Once demonstrations start, we feel, there will be spontaneous supporting activity taking place across the country. This has usually happened in campaigns like this, and I think it will again. I think people will start moving. The reasons we didn't choose California and other areas out West are distance and the problem of transporting marchers that far. But part of our strategy is to have spontaneous demonstrations take place on the West Coast.

A nationwide nonviolent movement is very important. We know from past experience that Congress and the president won't do anything until you develop a movement around which people of goodwill can find a way to put pressure on them, because it really means breaking that coalition in Congress. It's still a coalition-dominated, rural-dominated, basically southern Congress. There are Southerners there with committee chairmanships, and they are going to stand in the way of progress as long as they can. They get enough right-wing midwestern or northern Republicans to go along with them.

This really means making the movement powerful enough, dramatic enough, morally appealing enough, so that people of goodwill, the churches, labor, liberals, intellectuals, students, poor people themselves begin to put pressure on congressmen to the point that they can no longer elude our demands.

Our idea is to dramatize the whole economic problem of the poor. We feel there's a great deal that we need to do to appeal to Congress itself. The early demonstrations will be more geared toward educational purposes—to educate the nation on the nature of the problem and the crucial aspects of it, the tragic conditions that we confront in the ghettos.

After that, if we haven't gotten a response from Congress, we will branch out. And we are honest enough to feel that we aren't going to get any instantaneous results from Congress, knowing its recalcitrant nature on this issue, and knowing that so many resources and energies are being used in Vietnam rather than on the domestic situation. So we don't have any illusions about moving Congress in two or three weeks. But we do feel that, by starting in Washington, centering on Congress and departments of the government, we will be able to do a real educational job.

We call our demonstration a campaign for jobs and income because we feel that the economic question is the most crucial that black people, and poor people generally, are confronting. There is a literal depression in the Negro community. When you have mass unemployment in the Negro community, it's called a social problem; when you have mass unemployment in the white community, it's called a depression. The fact is, there is a major depression in the Negro community. The unemployment rate is extremely high, and among Negro youth, it goes up as high as forty percent in some cities.

We need an economic bill of rights. This would guarantee a job to all people who want to work and are able to work. It would also guarantee an income for all who are not able to work. Some people are too young, some are too old, some are physically disabled, and yet in order to live, they need income. It would mean creating certain public-service jobs, but that could be done in a few weeks. A program that would really deal with jobs could minimize—I don't say stop—the number of riots that could take place this summer.

Our whole campaign, therefore, will center on the job question, with other demands, like housing, that are closely tied to it. We feel that much more building of housing for low-income people should be done. On the educational front, the ghetto schools are in bad shape in terms of quality, and we feel that a program should be developed to spend at least a thousand dollars per pupil. Often, they are so far behind that they need more and special attention, the best quality education that can be given.

These problems, of course, are overshadowed by the Vietnam war. We'll focus on the domestic problems, but it's inevitable that we've got to bring out the question of the tragic mix-up in priorities. We are spending all of this money for death and destruction, and not nearly enough money for life and constructive development. It's inevitable that the question of the war will come up in this campaign. We hear all this talk about our ability to afford guns and butter, but we have come to see that this is a myth, that when a nation becomes involved in this kind of war, when the guns of war become a national obsession, social needs inevitably suffer. And we hope that as a result of our trying to dramatize this and getting thousands and thousands of people moving around this issue, that our government will be forced to reevaluate its policy abroad in order to deal with the domestic situation.

The American people are more sensitive than Congress. A Louis Harris poll has revealed that fifty-six percent of the people feel that some kind of program should come into being to provide jobs to all who want to work. We had the WPA when the nation was on the verge of bankruptcy; we should be able to do something when we're sick with wealth. That poll also showed that fifty-seven percent of the people felt the slums should be eradicated and the communities rebuilt by those who live in them, which would be a massive job program.

We need to put pressure on Congress to get things done. We will do this with First Amendment activity. If Congress is unresponsive, we'll have to escalate in order to keep the issue alive and before it. This action may take on disruptive dimensions, but not violent in the sense of destroying life or property: it will be militant nonviolence.

We really feel that riots tend to intensify the fears of the white majority while relieving its guilt, and so open the door to greater repression. We've seen no changes in Watts, no structural changes have taken place as the result of riots. We are trying to find an alternative that will force people to confront issues without destroying life or property. We plan to build a shantytown in Washington, patterned after the bonus marches of the thirties, to dramatize how many people have to live in slums in our nation. But essentially, this will be just like our other nonviolent demonstrations. We are not going to tolerate violence. And we are making it very clear that the demonstrators who are not prepared to be nonviolent should not participate in this. For the past six weeks, we've had workshops on nonviolence with the people who will be going to Washington. They will continue through the spring. These people will form a core of the demonstration and will later be the marshals in the protests. They will be participating themselves in the early stages, but after two or three weeks, when we will begin to call larger numbers in, they will be the marshals, the ones who will control and discipline all of the demonstrations.

We plan to have a march for those who can spend only a day or two in Washington, and that will be toward the culminating point of the campaign. I hope this will be a time when white people will rejoin the ranks of the movement.

Demonstrations have served as unifying forces in the movement; they have brought blacks and whites together in very practical situations, where philosophically they may have been arguing about Black Power. It's a strange thing how demonstrations tend to solve problems. The other thing is that it's little known that crime rates go down in almost every community where you have demonstrations. In Montgomery, Alabama, when we had a bus boycott, the crime rate in the Negro community went down sixty-five percent for a whole year. Anytime we've had demonstrations in a community, people have found a way to slough off their self-hatred, and they have had a channel to express their longings and a way to fight nonviolently—to get at the power structure, to know you're doing something, so you don't have to be violent to do it.

We need this movement. We need it to bring about a new kind of togetherness between blacks and whites. We need it to bring allies together and to bring the coalition of conscience together.

A good number of white people have given up on integration too. There are a lot of "White Power" advocates, and I find that people do tend to despair and engage in debates when nothing is going on. But when action is taking place, when there are demonstrations, they have a quality about them that leads to a unity you don't achieve at other times.

I think we have come to the point where there is no longer a choice now between nonviolence and riots. It must be militant, massive nonviolence, or riots. The discontent is so deep, the anger so ingrained, the despair, the restlessness so wide, that something has to be brought into being to serve as a channel through which these deep emotional feelings, these deep angry feelings, can be funneled. There has to be an outlet, and I see this campaign as a way to transmute the inchoate rage of the ghetto into a constructive and creative channel. It becomes an outlet for anger.

Even if I didn't deal with the moral dimensions and question of violence versus nonviolence, from a practical point of view, I don't see riots working. But I am convinced that if rioting continues, it will strengthen the right wing of the country, and we'll end up with a kind of right-wing takeover in the cities and a Fascist development, which will be terribly injurious to the whole nation. I don't think America can stand another summer of Detroit-like riots without a development that could destroy the soul of the nation, and even the democratic possibilities of the nation.

I'm committed to nonviolence absolutely. I'm just not going to kill anybody, whether it's in Vietnam or here. I'm not going to burn down any building. If nonviolent protest fails this summer, I will continue to preach it and teach it, and we at the Southern Christian Leadership Conference will still do this. I plan to stand by nonviolence because I have found it to be a philosophy of life that regulates not only my dealings in the struggle for racial justice but also my dealings with people, with my own self. I will still be faithful to nonviolence.

But I'm frank enough to admit that if our nonviolent campaign doesn't generate some progress, people are just going to engage in more violent activity, and the discussion of guerrilla warfare will be more extensive.

In any event, we will not have been the ones who will have failed. We will place the problems of the poor at the seat of government of the wealthiest nation in the history of mankind. If that power refuses to acknowledge its debt to the poor, it will have failed to live up to its promise to insure "life, liberty and the pursuit of happiness" to its citizens.

If this society fails, I fear that we will learn very shortly that racism is a sickness unto death.

We welcome help from all civil rights organizations. There must be a diversified approach to the problem, and I think both the NAACP and the Urban League play a significant role. I also feel that CORE and SNCC have played very significant roles. I think SNCC's recent conclusions are unfortunate. We have not given up on integration. We still believe in black and white together. Some of the Black Power groups have temporarily given up on integration. We have not. So maybe we are the bridge, in the middle, reaching across and connecting both sides.

The fact is, we have not had any insurrection in the United States because an insurrection is planned, organized, violent rebellion. What we have had is a kind of spontaneous explosion of anger. The fact is, people who riot don't want to riot. A study was made recently by some professors at Wayne State University. They interviewed several hundred people who participated in the riot last summer in Detroit, and a majority of these people said they felt that my approach to the problem—nonviolence—was the best and most effective.

I don't believe there has been a massive turn to violence. Even the riots have had an element of nonviolence to persons. But for a rare exception, they haven't killed any white people, and Negroes could, if they wished, kill by the hundreds. That would be insurrection. But the amazing thing is that the Negro has vented his anger on property, not persons, even in the emotional turbulence of riots.

But I'm convinced that if something isn't done to deal with the very harsh and real economic problems of the ghetto, the talk of guerrilla warfare is going to become much more real. The nation has not yet recognized the seriousness of it. Congress hasn't been willing to do anything about it, and this is what we're trying to face this spring. As committed as I am to nonviolence, I have to face this fact: if we do not get a positive response in Washington, many more Negroes will begin to think and act in violent terms.

I hope, instead, that what comes out of these nonviolent demonstrations will be an economic bill of rights for the disadvantaged, requiring about ten or twelve billion dollars. I hope that a specific number of jobs is set forth, that a program will emerge to abolish unemployment, and that there will be another program to supplement the income of those whose earnings are below the poverty level. These would be measures of success in our campaign.

It may well be that all we'll get out of Washington is to keep Congress from getting worse. The problem is to stop it from moving backward. We started out with a poverty bill at 2.4 billion dollars, and now it's back to 1.8 billion. We have a welfare program that's dehumanizing, and then Congress adds a Social Security amendment that will bar literally thousands of children from any welfare. Model cities started out; it's been cut back. Rent subsidy, an excellent program for the poor, cut down to nothing. It may be that because of these demonstrations, we will at least be able to hold on to some of the things we have.

There is an Old Testament prophecy of the "sins of the Fathers being visited upon the third and fourth generations." Nothing could be more applicable to our situation. America is reaping the harvest of hate and shame planted through generations of educational denial, political disfranchisement and economic exploitation of its black population. Now, almost a century removed from slavery, we find the heritage of oppression and racism erupting in our cities, with volcanic lava of bitterness and frustration pouring down our avenues.

Black Americans have been patient people, and perhaps they could continue patient with but a modicum of hope; but everywhere, "time is winding up," in the words of one of our spirituals, "corruption in the land, people take your stand; time is winding up." In spite of years of national progress, the plight of the poor is worsening. Jobs are on the decline as a result of technological change, schools North and South are proving themselves more and more inadequate to the task of providing adequate education and thereby entrance into the mainstream of the society. Medical care is virtually out of reach of millions of black and white poor. They are aware of the great advances of medical science—heart transplants, miracle drugs—but their children still die of preventable diseases, and even suffer brain damage due to protein deficiency.

In Mississippi, children are actually starving, while large landowners have placed their land in the soil bank and receive millions of dollars annually not to plant food and cotton. No provision is made for the life and survival of the hundreds of thousands of sharecroppers who now have no work and no food. Driven off the land, they are forced into tent cities and ghettos of the North, for our Congress is determined not to stifle the initiative of the poor (though they clamor for jobs) through welfare handouts. Handouts to the rich are given more sophisticated nomenclature such as parity, subsidies and incentives to industry.

White America has allowed itself to be indifferent to race prejudice and economic denial. It has treated them as superficial blemishes, but now awakes to the horrifying reality of a potentially fatal disease. The urban outbreaks are "a fire bell in the night," clamorously warning that the seams of our entire social order are weakening under strains of neglect.

The American people are infected with racism—that is the peril. Paradoxically, they are also infected with democratic ideals—that is the hope. While doing wrong, they have the potential to do right. But they do not have a millennium to make changes. Nor have they a choice of continuing in the old way. The future they are asked to inaugurate is not so unpalatable that it justifies the evils that beset the nation. To end poverty, to extirpate prejudice, to free a tormented conscience, to make a tomorrow of justice, fair play and creativity—all these are worthy of the American ideal.

We have, through massive nonviolent action, an opportunity to avoid a national disaster and create a new spirit of class and racial harmony. We can write another luminous moral chapter in American history. All of us are on trial in this troubled hour, but time still permits us to meet the future with a clear conscience.

_Look_ 32 (16 April 1968): 23–25.

# Social: Integration

# 14

# Our Struggle

*This article was an early attempt to describe and assess the importance of the Montgomery struggle.*

The segregation of Negroes, with its inevitable discrimination, has thrived on elements of inferiority present in the masses of both white and Negro people. Through forced separation from our African culture, through slavery, poverty, and deprivation, many black men lost self-respect.

In their relations with Negroes, white people discovered that they had rejected the very center of their own ethical professions. They could not face the triumph of their lesser instincts and simultaneously have peace within. And so, to gain it, they rationalized—insisting that the unfortunate Negro, being less than human, deserved and even enjoyed second-class status.

They argued that his inferior social, economic and political position was good for him. He was incapable of advancing beyond a fixed position and would therefore be happier if encouraged not to attempt the impossible. He is subjugated by a superior people with an advanced way of life. The "master race" will be able to civilize him to a limited degree, if only he will be true to his inferior nature and stay in his place.

White men soon came to forget that the southern social culture and all its institutions had been organized to perpetuate this rationalization. They observed a caste system and quickly were conditioned to believe that its social results, which they had created, actually reflected the Negro's innate and true nature.

In time many Negroes lost faith in themselves and came to believe that perhaps they really were what they had been told they were—something less than men. So long as they were prepared to accept this role, racial peace could be maintained. It was an uneasy peace in which the Negro was forced to accept patiently injustice, insult, injury and exploitation.

Gradually the Negro masses in the South began to reevaluate themselves—a process that was to change the nature of the Negro community and doom the social patterns of the South. We discovered that we had never really smothered our self-respect and that we could not be at one with ourselves without asserting it. From this point on, the South's terrible peace was rapidly undermined by the Negro's new and courageous thinking and his ever-increasing readiness to organize and to act. Conflict and violence were coming to the surface as the white South desperately clung to its old patterns. The extreme tension in race relations in the South today is explained in part by the revolutionary change in the Negro's evaluation of himself and of his destiny and by his determination to struggle for justice. *We Negroes have replaced self-pity with self-respect and self-depreciation with dignity.*

When Mrs. Rosa Parks, the quiet seamstress whose arrest precipitated the nonviolent protest in Montgomery, was asked why she had refused to move to the rear of a bus, she said: "It was a matter of dignity; I could not have faced myself and my people if I had moved."

## THE NEW NEGRO

Many of the Negroes who joined the protest did not expect it to succeed. When asked why, they usually gave one of three answers: "I didn't expect Negroes to stick to it," or, "I never thought we Negroes had the nerve," or, "I thought the pressure from the white folks would kill it before it got started."

In other words, our nonviolent protest in Montgomery is important because it is demonstrating to the Negro, North and South, that many of the stereotypes he has held about himself and other Negroes are not valid. Montgomery has broken the spell and is ushering in concrete manifestations of the thinking and action of the new Negro.

We now know that:

### WE CAN STICK TOGETHER

In Montgomery, forty-two thousand of us have refused to ride the city's segregated buses since December 5. Some walk as many as fourteen miles a day.

### OUR LEADERS DO NOT HAVE TO SELL OUT

Many of us have been indicted, arrested, and "mugged." Every Monday and Thursday night we stand before the Negro population at the prayer meetings and repeat: "It is an honor to face jail for a just cause."

### THREATS AND VIOLENCE DO NOT NECESSARILY INTIMIDATE THOSE WHO ARE SUFFICIENTLY AROUSED AND NONVIOLENT

The bombing of two of our homes has made us more resolute. When a handbill was circulated at a White Citizens Council meeting stating that Negroes should be "abolished" by "guns, bows and arrows, sling shots and knives," we responded with even greater determination.

### OUR CHURCH IS BECOMING MILITANT

Twenty-four ministers were arrested in Montgomery. Each has said publicly that he stands prepared to be arrested again. Even upper-class Negroes who reject the "come to Jesus" gospel are now convinced that the church has no alternative but to provide the nonviolent dynamics for social change in the midst of conflict. The thirty thousand dollars used for the car pool, which transports over twenty thousand Negro workers, school children and housewives, has been raised in the churches. The churches have become the dispatch centers where the people gather to wait for rides.

## WE BELIEVE IN OURSELVES

In Montgomery we walk in a new way. We hold our heads in a new way. Even the Negro reporters who converged on Montgomery have a new attitude. One tired reporter, asked at a luncheon in Birmingham to say a few words about Montgomery, stood up, thought for a moment, and uttered one sentence: "Montgomery has made me proud to be a Negro."

## ECONOMICS IS PART OF OUR STRUGGLE

We are aware that Montgomery's white businessmen have tried to "talk sense" to the bus company and the city commissioners. We have observed that small Negro shops are thriving as Negroes find it inconvenient to walk downtown to the white stores. We have been getting more polite treatment in the white shops since the protest began. We have a new respect for the proper use of our dollar.

## WE HAVE DISCOVERED A NEW AND POWERFUL WEAPON— NONVIOLENT RESISTANCE

Although law is an important factor in bringing about social change, there are certain conditions in which the very effort to adhere to new legal decisions creates tension and provokes violence. We had hoped to see demonstrated a method that would enable us to continue our struggle while coping with the violence it aroused. Now we see the answer: face violence if necessary, but refuse to return violence. If we respect those who oppose us, they may achieve a new understanding of the human relations involved.

## WE NOW KNOW THAT THE SOUTHERN NEGRO HAS COME OF AGE, POLITICALLY AND MORALLY

Montgomery has demonstrated that we will not run from the struggle, and will support the battle for equality. The attitude of many young Negroes a few years ago was reflected in the common expression, "I'd rather be a lamp post in Harlem than Governor of Alabama." Now the idea expressed in our churches, schools, pool rooms, restaurants and homes is: "Brother, stay here and fight nonviolently. 'Cause if you don't let them make you mad, you can win." The official slogan of the Montgomery Improvement Association is "Justice without Violence."

## THE ISSUES IN MONTGOMERY

The leaders of the old order in Montgomery are not prepared to negotiate a settlement. This is not because of the conditions we have set for returning to the buses. The basic question of segregation in intrastate travel is already before the courts. Meanwhile we ask only for what in Atlanta, Mobile, Charleston and most other cities of the South is considered the southern pattern. We seek the right, under segregation, to seat ourselves from the rear forward on a first come, first served basis. In addition, we ask for courtesy and the hiring of some Negro bus drivers on predominantly Negro routes.

A prominent judge of Tuscaloosa was asked if he felt there was any connection between Autherine Lucy's effort to enter the University of Alabama and the Montgomery nonviolent protest. He replied, "Autherine is just one unfortunate girl who doesn't know what she is doing, but in Montgomery it looks like all the niggers have gone crazy."

Later the judge is reported to have explained that "of course the good niggers had undoubtedly been riled up by outsiders, Communists and agitators." It is apparent that at this historic moment most of the elements of the white South are not prepared to believe that "our Negroes could of themselves act like this."

## MISCALCULATION OF THE WHITE LEADERS

Because the mayor and city authorities cannot admit to themselves that we have changed, every move they have made has inadvertently increased the protest and united the Negro community.

[1955]

*Dec. 1*      They arrested Mrs. Parks, one of the most respected Negro women in Montgomery.

*Dec. 3*      They attempted to intimidate the Negro population by publishing a report in the daily paper that certain Negroes were calling for a boycott of the buses. They thereby informed the thirty thousand Negro readers of the planned protest.

*Dec. 5*      They found Mrs. Parks guilty and fined her fourteen dollars. This action increased the number of those who joined the boycott.

*Dec. 5*      They arrested a Negro college student for "intimidating passengers." Actually, he was helping an elderly woman cross the street. This mistake solidified the college students' support of the protest.

Two policemen on motorcycles followed each bus on its rounds through the Negro community. This attempt at psychological coercion further increased the number of Negroes who joined the protest.

In a news telecast at 6:00 P.M., a mass meeting planned for that evening was announced. Although we had expected only five hundred people at the meeting, over five thousand attended.

*Dec. 6*    They began to intimidate Negro taxi drivers. This led to the setting up of a car pool and a resolution to extend indefinitely our protest, which had originally been called for one day only.

*Dec. 7*    They began to harass Negro motorists. This encouraged the Negro middle class to join the struggle.

*Dec. 8*    The lawyer for the bus company said, "We have no intention of hiring Negro drivers now or in the forseeable future." To us this meant never. The slogan then became, "Stay off the buses until we win."

*Dec. 9*    The mayor invited Negro leaders to a conference, presumably for negotiation. When we arrived, we discovered that some of the men in the room were white supremacists and members of the White Citizens Council. The mayor's attitude was made clear when he said, "Comes the first rainy day and the Negroes will be back in the buses." The next day it did rain, but the Negroes did not ride the buses.

At this point over forty-two thousand Montgomery Negroes had joined the protest. After a period of uneasy quiet, elements in the white community turned to further police intimidation and to violence.

[1956]

*Jan. 26*    I was arrested for traveling thirty miles per hour in a twenty-five-mile zone. This arrest occurred just two hours before a mass meeting. So, we had to hold seven mass meetings to accommodate the people.

*Jan. 30*    My home was bombed.

*Feb. 1*    The home of E. D. Nixon, one of the protest leaders and former state president of the NAACP, was bombed. This brought moral and financial support from all over the state.

*Feb. 22*    Eighty-nine persons, including the twenty-four ministers, were arrested for participating in the nonviolent protests.

Every attempt to end the protest by intimidation, by encouraging Negroes to inform, by force and violence, further cemented the Negro community and brought sympathy for our cause from men of good will all over the world. The great appeal for the world appears to lie in the fact that we in Montgomery have adopted the method of nonviolence.

In a world in which most men attempt to defend their highest values by the accumulation of weapons of destruction, it is morally refreshing to hear five thousand Negroes in Montgomery shout "Amen" and "Halleluh" when they are exhorted to "pray for those who oppose you," or pray "Oh Lord, give us strength of body to keep walking for freedom," and conclude each mass meeting with: "Let us pray that God shall give us strength to remain nonviolent though we may face death."

## THE LIBERAL DILEMMA

And death there may be. Many white men in the South see themselves as a fearful minority in an ocean of black men. They honestly believe with one side of their minds that Negroes are depraved and disease-ridden. They look upon any effort at equality as leading to "mongrelization." They are convinced that racial equality is a Communist idea and that those who ask for it are subversive. They believe that their caste system is the highest form of social organization.

The enlightened white southerner, who for years has preached gradualism, now sees that even the slow approach finally has revolutionary implications. Placing straws on a camel's back, no matter how slowly, is dangerous. This realization has immobilized the liberals and most of the white church leaders. They have no answer for dealing with or absorbing violence. They end in begging for retreat, lest "things get out of hand and lead to violence."

Writing in *Life*, William Faulkner, Nobel prize-winning author from Mississippi, recently urged the NAACP to "stop now for a moment." That is to say, he encouraged Negroes to accept injustice, exploitation and indignity for a while longer. It is hardly a moral act to encourage others patiently to accept injustice which he himself does not endure.

In urging delay, which in this dynamic period is tantamount to retreat, Faulkner suggests that those of us who press for change now may not know that violence could break out. He says we are "dealing with a fact: the fact of emotional conditions of such fierce unanimity as to scorn the fact that it is a minority and which will go to any length and against any odds at this moment to justify and, if necessary, defend that condition and its right to it."

We southern Negroes believe that it is essential to defend the right of equality now. From this position we will not and cannot retreat. Fortunately, we are increasingly aware that we must not try to defend our position by methods that contradict the aim of brotherhood. We in Montgomery believe that the only way to press on is by adopting the philosophy and practice of nonviolent resistance.

This method permits a struggle to go on with dignity and without the need to retreat. It is a method that can absorb the violence that is inevitable in social change whenever deep-seated prejudices are challenged.

If, in pressing for justice and equality in Montgomery, we discover that those who reject equality are prepared to use violence, we must not despair, retreat, or fear. Before they make this crucial decision, they must remember: whatever they do, we will not use violence in return. We hope we can act in the struggle in such a way that they will see the error of their approach and will come to respect us. Then we can all live together in peace and equality.

The basic conflict is not really over the buses. Yet we believe that, if the method we use in dealing with equality in the buses can eliminate injustice within ourselves, we shall at the same time be attacking the basis of injustice—man's hostility to man. This can only be done when we challenge the white community to re-examine its assumptions as we are now prepared to reexamine ours.

We do not wish to triumph over the white community. That would only result in transferring those now on the bottom to the top. But, if we can live up to nonviolence in thought and deed, there will emerge an interracial society based on freedom for all.

*Liberation* 1 (April 1956): 3–6.

# 15

# Walk for Freedom

*The Reverend Glenn E. Smiley, a white minister, was responsible for helping King produce these reflections on the use of nonviolent resistance in Montgomery. In fact, when Dr. King became the president of the Montgomery Improvement Association, he did not recognize that he was using nonviolent resistance. Both Smiley and Bayard Rustin were primarily responsible for convincing him that he should interpret the movement in the light of the principles and techniques of nonviolent resistance.*

The present protest here in Montgomery on the part of the Negro citizens, grows out of many experiences—experiences that have often been humiliating and have led to deep resentment. The Negro citizens of Montgomery compose about seventy-five percent of the bus riders. In riding buses, they have confronted conditions which have made for a great deal of embarrassment, such as having to stand over empty seats, having to pay fares at the front door and going out to the back to get on, and then the very humiliating experience of being arrested for refusing to get up and give a seat to a person of another race.

These conditions and those experiences have now reached the point that the Negro citizens are tired, and this tiredness was expressed on December 5, when more than ninety-nine percent of the Negro bus riders decided not to ride the buses, in a protest against these unjust conditions. This protest has lasted now for many, many weeks and it is still in process.

From the beginning, we have insisted on nonviolence. This is a protest—a *nonviolent* protest against injustice. We are depending on moral and spiritual forces. To put it another way, this is a movement of passive resistance, and the great instrument is the instrument of love. We feel that this is our chief weapon, and that no matter how long we are involved in the protest, no matter how tragic the experiences are, no matter what sacrifices we have to make, we will not let anybody drag us so low as to hate them.

Love *must* be at the forefront of our movement if it is to be a successful movement. And when we speak of love, we speak of understanding, good will toward *all* men. We speak of a creative, a redemptive sort of love, so that as we look at the problem, we see that the real tension is not between the Negro citizens and the white citizens of Montgomery, but it is a conflict between justice and injustice, between the forces of light and the forces of darkness, and if there is a victory—and there *will* be a victory—the victory will not be merely for the Negro citizens and a defeat for the white citizens, but it will be a victory for justice and a defeat of injustice. It will be a victory for goodness in its long struggle with the forces of evil.

## VIOLENCE IS IMMORAL

This is a spiritual movement, and we intend to keep these things in the forefront. We know that violence will defeat our purpose. We know that in our struggle in America and in our specific struggle here in Montgomery, violence will not only be impractical but immoral. We are outnumbered; we do not have access to the instruments of violence. Even more than that, not only is violence impractical, but it is *immoral*; for it is my firm conviction that to seek to retaliate with violence does nothing but intensify the existence of evil and hate in the universe.

Along the way of life, someone must have *sense* enough and morality enough to cut off the chain of hate and evil. The greatest way to do that is through love. I believe firmly that love is a transforming power that can lift a whole community to new horizons of fair play, good will and justice.

## LOVE VS. BOMBS

Love is our great instrument and our great weapon, and that alone. On January 30 my home was bombed. My wife and baby were there; I was attending a meeting. I first heard of the bombing at the meeting, when someone came to me and mentioned it, and I tried to accept it in a very calm manner. I first inquired about my wife and daughter; then after I found out that they were all right, I stopped in the midst of the meeting and spoke to the group, and urged them not to be panicky and not to do anything about it because that was not the way.

I immediately came home and, on entering the front of the house, I noticed there were some five hundred to a thousand persons. I came in the house and looked it over and went back to see my wife and to see if the baby was all right, but as I stood in the back of the house, hundreds and hundreds of people were still gathering, and I saw there that violence was a possibility.

It was at that time that I went to the porch and tried to say to the people that we could not allow ourselves to be panicky. We could not allow ourselves to retaliate with any type of violence, but that we were still to confront the problem with *love*.

One statement that I made—and I believe it very firmly—was: "He who lives by the sword will perish by the sword." I urged the people to continue to manifest love, and to continue to carry on the struggle with the same dignity and with the same disicpline that we had started out with. I think at that time the people did decide to go home, things did get quiet, and it ended up with a great deal of calmness and a great deal of discipline, which I think our community should be proud of and which I was very proud to see because our people were determined not to retaliate with violence.

## "STAND UP TO THE FINISH"

Some twenty-six of the ministers and almost one hundred of the citizens of the city were indicted in this boycott. But we realized in the beginning that we would confront experiences that make for great sacrifices, experiences that are not altogether pleasant. We decided among ourselves that we would stand up to the finish, and that is what we are determined to do. In the midst of the indictments, we still hold to this nonviolent attitude, and this primacy of love.

## PRAY FOR JUSTICE

Even though convicted, we will not retaliate with hate, but will still stand with love in our hearts, and stand resisting injustice, with the same determination with which we started out. We need a great deal of encouragement in this movement. Of course one thing that we are depending on, from not only other communities but from our own community, is prayer. We ask people everywhere to pray that God will guide us, pray that justice will be done and that righteousness will stand. And I think through these prayers we will be strengthened; it will make us feel the unity of the nation and the presence of Almighty God. For as we said all along, this is a spiritual movement.

*Fellowship* 22 (May 1956): 5–7.

# 16

# The Current Crisis
# in Race Relations

*Written for a Christian publication, this article highlights King's accent on the implications of the New Testament conception of the believer's responsibility to love one's neighbor. The theological justification for his dual emphasis on nonviolence and integration is expressed here when he asserts that "the aftermath of nonviolence is the creation of the beloved community, while the aftermath of violence is tragic bitterness."*

In American life there is today a real crisis in race relations. This crisis has been precipitated, on the one hand, by the determined resistance of reactionary elements in the South to the Supreme Court's momentous decision against segregation in the public schools. Many states have risen in open defiance. Legislative halls of the South ring loud with such words as "interposition" and "nullification." The Ku Klux Klan is on the march again, determined to preserve segregation at any cost. Then there are the White Citizens Councils. All of these forces have conjoined to make for massive resistance.

The crisis has been precipitated, on the other hand, by the radical change in the Negro's evaluation of himself. There would probably be no crisis in race relations if the Negro continued to think of himself in inferior terms and patiently accepted injustice and exploitation. But it is at this very point that the change has come. For many years the Negro tacitly accepted segregation. He was the victim of stagnant passivity and deadening complacency. The system of slavery and segregation caused many Negroes to feel that perhaps they were inferior. This is the ultimate tragedy of segregation. It not only harms one physically, but it injures one spiritually. It scars the soul and distorts the personality. It inflicts the segregator with a false sense of superiority while inflicting the segregated with a false sense of inferiority. But through the forces of history something happened to the Negro. He came to feel that he was somebody. He came to feel that the important thing about a man is not the color of his skin or the texture of his hair, but the texture and quality of his soul. With this new sense of dignity and new self-respect a new Negro emerged. So there has been a revolutionary change in the Negro's evaluation of his nature and destiny, and a determination to achieve freedom and human dignity.

This determination springs from the same longing for freedom that motivates oppressed people all over the world.

The deep rumblings of discontent from Asia and Africa are at bottom a quest for freedom and human dignity on the part of the people who have long been the victims of colonialism and imperialism. The struggle for freedom on the part of oppressed people in general and the American Negro in particular is not suddenly going to disappear. It is sociologically true that privileged classes rarely ever give up their privileges without strong resistance. It is also true that once oppressed people rise up against their oppression there is no stopping point short of full freedom. So realism impels us to admit that the struggle will continue until freedom is a reality for all of the oppressed peoples of the world.

## STRUGGLE

Since the struggle will continue, the basic question which confronts the oppressed peoples of the world is this: How will the struggle against the forces of injustice be waged?

There are two possible answers. One is to resort to the all too prevalent method of physical violence and corroding hatred. Violence nevertheless solves no social problem; it merely creates new and more complicated ones. Occasionally violence is temporarily successful, but never permanently so. It often brings temporary victory, but never permanent peace. If the American Negro and other victims of oppression succumb to the temptation of using violence in the struggle for justice, unborn generations will be the recipients of a long and desolate night of bitterness, and their chief legacy to the future will be an endless reign of meaningless chaos.

## NONVIOLENCE

The alternative to violence is the method of nonviolent resistance.

This method is nothing more and nothing less than Christianity in action. It seems to me to be the Christian way of life in solving problems of human relations. This method was made famous in our generation by Mohandas K. Gandhi, who used it to free his country from the domination of the British Empire. This method has also been used in Montgomery, Alabama, under the leadership of the ministers of all denominations, to free fifty thousand Negroes from the long night of bus segregation. Several basic things can be said about nonviolence as a method in bringing about better racial conditions.

First, this is not a method of cowardice or stagnant passivity; it does resist. The nonviolent resister is just as opposed to the evil against which he is protesting as the person who used violence. It is true that this method is passive or aggressive in the sense the the nonviolent resister is not aggressive physically toward his opponent, but his mind and emotions are always active, constantly seeking to persuade the opponent that he is mistaken. This method is passive physically, but it is strongly active spiritually; it is nonaggressive physically, but dynamically aggressive spiritually.

A second basic fact about this method is that it does not seek to defeat or humiliate the opponent, but to win his friendship and understanding. The nonviolent resister must often voice his protest through noncooperation or boycotts, but he realizes that noncooperation and boycotts are not ends within themselves; they are means to awaken a sense of moral shame within the opponent. The end is redemption and reconciliation.

The aftermath of nonviolence is the creation of the beloved community, while the aftermath of violence is tragic bitterness.

## AGAINST EVIL

A third fact that characterizes the method of nonviolence is that the attack is directed to forces of evil, rather than persons caught in the forces. It is evil that we are seeking to defeat, not the persons victimized with evil. Those of us who struggle against racial injustice must come to see that the basic tension is not between races. As I like to say to the people in Montgomery, Alabama: "The tension in this city is not between white people and Negro people. The tension is at bottom between justice and injustice, between the forces of light and the forces of darkness. And if there is a victory it will be a victory, not merely for fifty thousand Negroes, but a victory for justice and the forces of life. We are out to defeat injustice and not white persons who may happen to be unjust."

## INTERNAL VIOLENCE

A fourth point that must be brought out concerning the method of nonviolence is that this method not only avoids external physical violence, but also internal violence of spirit. At the center of nonviolence stands the principle of love. In struggling for human dignity the oppressed people of the world must not succumb to the temptation of becoming bitter or indulging in hate campaigns. To retaliate with hate and bitterness would do nothing but intensify the existence of hate in our world. We have learned through the grim realities of life and history that hate and violence solve nothing. They only serve to push us deeper and deeper into the mire. Violence begets violence; hate begets hate; and toughness begets a greater toughness. It is all a descending spiral, and the end is destruction—for everybody. Along the way of life, someone must have enough sense and morality to cut off the chain of hate by projecting the ethics of love into the center of our lives.

In speaking of love, I am not referring to some sentimental and affectionate emotion. It would be nonsense to urge men to love their oppressors in an affectionate sense. Love in this connection means understanding good will as expressed in the Greek word *agape*. This means nothing sentimental or basically affectionate; it means understanding, redeeming good will for all men, an ever-owing love which seeks nothing in return. It is spontaneous, unmotivated, groundless, and creative. It is the love of God operating in the human heart. When we rise to love on the *agape* level, we rise to the position of loving the person who does the evil deed, while hating the deed that the person does.

A fifth basic fact about the method of nonviolent resistance is that it is based on the conviction that the universe is on the side of justice. It is this deep faith in the future that causes the nonviolent resister to accept suffering without retaliation. He knows that in his struggle for justice he has cosmic companionship. Now I am aware of the fact that there are devout believers in nonviolence who find it difficult to believe in a personal God. But even these persons believe in the existence of some creative force that works for togetherness, a creative force in this universe that works to bring the disconnected aspects of reality into a harmonious whole. There is a creative power in the universe that works to bring low gigantic mountains of evil and pull down prodigious hilltops of injustice.

## FAITH

This is the faith that keeps the nonviolent resister going through all of the tension and suffering that he must inevitably confront.

Those of us who call the name of Jesus Christ find something at the center of our faith which forever reminds us that God is on the side of truth and justice. Good Friday may occupy the throne for a day, but ultimately it must give way to the triumph of Easter. Evil may so shape events that Caesar will occupy a palace and Christ a cross, but that same Christ arose and split history into A.D. and B.C., so that even the life of Caesar must be dated by his name. Yes, "the arc of the moral universe is long, but it bends toward justice." There is something in this universe which justifies William Cullen Bryant in saying, "Truth crushed to earth will rise again." So in Montgomery, Alabama, we can walk and never get weary, because we know that there will be a great camp meeting in the promised land of freedom and justice.

## MORAL DILEMMA

I cannot close this article without saying that the problem of race is indeed America's greatest moral dilemma.

The churches are called upon to recognize the urgent necessity of taking a forthright stand on this crucial issue. If we are to remain true to the gospel of Jesus Christ, we cannot rest until segregation and discrimination are banished from every area of American life. Many churches have already taken a stand. The National Council of Churches has condemned segregation over and over again, and has requested its constituent denominations to do likewise. Most of the major denominations have endorsed that action. Many individual ministers, even in the South, have stood up with dauntless courage. High tribute and appreciation is due the ninety ministers of Atlanta, Georgia, who so courageously signed the noble statement calling for compliance with the law and a reopening of the channels of communication between the races.

All of these things are admirable and deserve our highest praise. But we must admit that these courageous stands from the church are still far too few. The sublime statements of the major denominations on the question of human relations move all too slowly to the local churches in actual practice. All too many ministers are still silent. It may well be that the greatest tragedy of this period of social transition is not the glaring noisiness of the so-called bad people, but the appalling silence of the so-called good people. It may be that our generation will have to repent not only for the diabolical actions and vitriolic words of the children of darkness, but also for the crippling fears and tragic apathy of the children of light.

What we need is a restless determination to make the ideal of brotherhood a reality in this nation and all over the world.

There are certain technical words which tend to become stereotypes and cliches after a certain period of time. Psychologists have a word which is probably used more frequently than any other word in modern psychology. It is the word "maladjusted." In a sense all of us must live the well-adjusted life in order to avoid neurotic and schizophrenic personalities. But there are some things in our social system to which all of us ought to be maladjusted. I never intend to adjust myself to the viciousness of mob rule. I never intend to adjust myself to the evils of segregation and the crippling effects of discrimination. I never intend to adjust myself to the inequalities of an economic system which takes necessities from the masses to give luxuries to the classes. I never intend to become adjusted to the madness of militarism and the self-defeating method of physical violence.

It may be that the salvation of the world lies in the hands of the maladjusted. The challenge to us is to be maladjusted—as maladjusted as the prophet Amos, who in the midst of the injustices of his day, could cry out in words that echo across the centuries, "Let judgment run down like waters and righteousness like a mighty stream"; as maladjusted as Lincoln, who had the vision to see that this nation could not survive half slave and half free; as maladjusted as Jefferson, who in the midst of an age amazingly adjusted to slavery could cry out in words lifted to cosmic proportions, "All men are created equal, and are endowed by their Creator with certain unalienable rights, that among these are Life, Liberty and the pursuit of Happiness"; as maladjusted as Jesus who could say to the men and women of his generation, "Love your enemies, bless them that curse you, do good to them that hate you, and pray for them that despitefully use you."

The world is in desperate need of such maladjustment. Through such courageous maladjustment we will be able to emerge from the bleak and desolate midnight of man's inhumanity to man into the bright and glittering daybreak of freedom and justice.

*New South* (March 1958): 8–12. [This was the last time King and his editorial staff reprinted this article. Apparently it first appeared in *Presbyterian Outlook*. His editors also published it under the following titles: "Out of Segregation's Long Night: An Interpretation of a Racial Crisis," *The Churchman* 172 (February 1958): 7ff., and "Out of the Long Night of Segregation," *Advance* 150 (28 February 1958): 14ff.]

# 17

# Who Speaks for the South?

*King argued that white liberals such as Lillian E. Smith and Harry Ashmore*
*speak for the South, rather than radical white racists such as Marvin Griffin,*
*then governor of Georgia. He argued that the liberals speak for a silent majority*
*who allow themselves to be dominated by a vocal, bigoted minority.*

The history of our nation is the history of a long and tireless effort to broaden the franchise of American citizens. At the very birth of our nation, a great struggle had to be made to secure the ballot for people who did not own property. Even among the Founding Fathers there were men who felt that only those who owned property should have the right to vote. Over this issue a mighty struggle took place. When, after many long years, this fight was successfully won, a great effort was made by women seeking to obtain the franchise. Again after weary decades of agitation, the Nineteenth Amendment to the Constitution opened a new chapter in the lives of women and in the life of our nation.

Thus, we see that from 1789 to 1920 disenfranchised Americans fought and won their basic right to vote. However, for the Negroes of the South, there was still no ballot. Whether they owned property or were penniless, whether male or female, these American victories in the extension of democracy did not affect them.

But this history does provide a profound lesson for the voiceless Negroes. It teaches us how a struggle is won. We see that the poor men of 1776 did not accept disenfranchisement without protest. In a legal manner, these pioneers fought as hard for the vote as they had fought as minutemen at Lexington and Concord.

Later when women decided the time had come for them to vote, they were far from submissive or silent. They cried out in the halls of government. They agitated in their homes. They protested in the streets. And they were jailed. But they pressed on. Their voices were vigorous, even strident, but they were always effective. Through their courage, their steadfastness, their unity and their willingness to sacrifice, they won the right to vote.

From these women we have learned how social changes take place through struggle. In this same tradition of determination, of confidence in the justice of a cause, Negroes must now demand the right to vote. And these qualities of courage, perseverance, unity, sacrifice, plus a nonviolence of spirit are the weapons we must depend upon if we are to vote with freedom.

America must begin the struggle for democracy *at home*. The advocacy of free elections in Europe by American officials is hypocrisy when free elections are not held in great sections of America. To Negro Americans it is ironic to be governed, to be taxed, to be given orders, but to have no representation in a nation that would defend the right to vote abroad. We have a duty to deliver our nation from this snare and this delusion.

Let us make our intentions crystal clear. We must and we will be free. We want freedom now. We want the right to vote now. We do not want freedom fed to us in teaspoons over another 150 years. Under God we were born free. Misguided men robbed us of our freedom. We want it back; we would keep it forever. This is not idle chatter, for we know that sacrifice is involved, that brutality will be faced, that savage conduct will need to be endured, that slick trickery will need to be overcome, but we are resolutely prepared for all of this. We are prepared to meet whatever comes with love, with firmness and with unyielding nonviolence. We are prepared to press on unceasingly and persistently, to obtain our birthright and to hand it down to our children and to their children's children.

Already this struggle has had its sacred martyrs: the Reverend George Washington Lee, shot and killed in Mississippi; Mr. and Mrs. Harry Moore, bombed and murdered here in Florida; Emmett Till, a mere boy, unqualified to vote, but seemingly used as a victim to terrorize Negro citizens and keep them from the polls. While the blame for the grisly mutilation of Till has been placed upon two cruel men, the ultimate responsibility for this and other tragic events must rest with the American people themselves. It rests with all of us, black and white, who call ourselves civilized men. For democracy demands responsibility, courage, and the will to freedom from all men.

There is blood on the hands of those who halt the progress of our nation and frustrate the advancement of its people by coercion and violence. But despite this, it is our duty to pray for those who mistreat us. We must pray for a change of attitude in all those who violate human dignity and who rob men, women and little children of human decency. We must pray for ourselves that we shall have the strength to move forward each day, knowing that our every act can emancipate us and can add compassion to the heart of our nation. We must pray for the power that comes from loving our neighbor as we love ourselves.

Because all men are one, the revolution for American freedom affected the entire world. In the same manner, freedom for the American Negro will affect the lives of all the people in the South for the better, just as the absence of Negro freedom has affected the lives of all Americans for the worse. This can be seen from the tragic consequences, the insecurities, that have emerged from the disenfranchisement of Negroes in the South.

The ghastly results have not been borne alone by the Negro. Poor white men, women and children, bearing the scars of ignorance, deprivation, and poverty, are evidence of the fact that harm to one is injury to all. They, too, are victims of the one-party system that has developed in the South, a system that denies free political choice and real political expression to millions of white voters. With a limited electorate, capable of being manipulated, reactionary men gained access to the highest legislative bodies of government. Today, because the Negro cannot vote, Congress is dominated by southern senators and representatives who are not elected in a fair nor in a legal manner. The strategic position of these men, as chairmen of the most important committees in the House and Senate, enables them to filibuster and to bottle up legislation urgently needed for the economic and social welfare of all Americans, Negro and white. Hence, it may clearly be seen that it is not the Negro alone who suffers but the nation as a whole.

Governor Griffin, who recently called for a poll tax to reduce the Negro vote in Georgia, Senator Eastland, and men who hold their views do not, I am thoroughly confident, speak for the South. They speak only for a willful but vocal minority. This group is not the South. I believe that voices like those of Miss Lillian E. Smith of Georgia, Mr. Harry Ashmore of Arkansas, and the ever-growing list of the white Christian ministers, such as the group that recently issued a statement in Atlanta, Georgia—these voices represent the true and basic sentiments of millions of southerners, whose voices are yet unheard, whose course is yet unclear and whose courageous acts are yet unseen.

In the name of God, in the interest of human dignity and for the cause of democracy, I appeal to these millions to gird their courage, to speak out and to act on their basic convictions. In their hearts the white southerners know the loyalty, the courage and the democratic responsibility of the Negro people. Beyond this, they know that we are dedicated to nonviolence. Just as I have urged Negroes to face the calculated risk involved in resisting injustice nonviolently, I implore the white southerner of good will to face the calculated risk that working openly for justice and freedom demand.

We southerners, Negro and white, must no longer permit our heritage to be dishonored before the world. And the South should know that the effort of Negroes to vote is not merely a matter of exercising rights guaranteed by the United States Constitution. The question is beyond rights. We have a duty to perform. We have a moral obligation to carry out. We have the duty to remove from political domination a small minority that cripples the economic and social institutions of our country and thereby degrades and impoverishes everyone.

---

*Liberation* 2 (March 1958): 13–14.

# 18

# The Burning Truth in the South

*On 1 February 1960, Joseph McNeill, Ezell Blair, Jr., Franklin McCain, and David Richmond, freshmen at North Carolina Agricultural and Technical College in Greensboro, decided to protest against department store lunch counter discrimination. Department stores would allow blacks to buy goods, but would not allow them to sit down to eat at the lunch counters. By the end of the following September, over 70,000 students, both black and white, had participated in similar demonstrations across the country. Mrs. Ella Baker, the executive secretary of SCLC, was enthusiastic about this amazing display of youth participation in the civil rights movement. She encouraged Dr. King to endorse this movement and to help the students organize the Student Nonviolent Coordinating Committee (SNCC).*

An electrifying movement of Negro students has shattered the placid surface of campuses and communities across the South. Though confronted in many places by hoodlums, police guns, tear gas, arrests, and jail sentences, the students tenaciously continue to sit down and demand equal service at variety store lunch counters, and extend their protest from city to city. In communities like Montgomery, Alabama, the whole student body rallied behind expelled students and staged a walkout while state government intimidation was unleashed with a display of military force appropriate to a wartime invasion. Nevertheless, the spirit of self-sacrifice and commitment remains firm, and the state governments find themselves dealing with students who have lost the fear of jail and physical injury.

It is no overstatement to characterize these events as historic. Never before in the United States has so large a body of students spread a struggle over so great an area in pursuit of a goal of human dignity and freedom.

The suddenness with which this development burst upon the nation has given rise to the description "spontaneous." Yet it is not without clearly perceivable causes and precedents. First, we should go back to the ending of World War II. Then, the new will and determination of the Negro were irrevocably generated. Hundreds of thousands of young Negro men were mustered out of the armed forces, and with their honorable discharge papers and GI Bill of Rights grants, they received a promise from a grateful nation that the broader democracy for which they had fought would begin to assume reality. They believed in this promise and acted in the conviction that changes were guaranteed. Some changes did appear—but commensurate neither with the promise nor the need.

Struggles of a local character began to emerge, but the scope and results were limited. Few Americans outside the immediately affected areas even realized a struggle was taking place. One perceptible aspect was the steady, significant increase in voting registration which took place, symbolizing the determination of the Negro, particularly the veteran, to make his rights a reality. The number of registered voters reached a point higher than exists today.

The United States Supreme Court decision of 1954 was viewed by Negroes as the delivery of part of the promise of change. In unequivocal language the Court affirmed that "separate but equal" facilities are inherently unequal, and that to segregate a child on the basis of his race is to deny that child equal protection of the law. This decision brought hope to millions of disinherited Negroes who had formerly dared only to dream of freedom. But the implementation of the decision was not to be realized without a sharp and difficult struggle. Through five years of turmoil some advances were achieved. The victory is far from complete, but the determination by Negroes that it will be won is universal.

What relation have these events to the student sit-downs? It was the young veteran who gave the first surge of power to the postwar civil rights movements. It was the high school, college, and elementary school young people who were in the front line of the school desegregation struggle. Lest it be forgotten, the opening of hundreds of schools to Negroes for the first time in history required that there be young Negroes with the moral and physical courage to face the challenges and, all too frequently, the mortal danger presented by mob resistance.

There were such young Negroes in the tens of thousands, and no program for integration failed for want of students. The simple courage of students and their parents should never be forgotten. In the years 1958 and 1959 two massive Youth Marches to Washington for Integrated Schools involved some forty thousand young people who brought with them nearly five hundred thousand signatures on petitions gathered largely from campuses and youth centers. This mass action infused a new spirit of direct action challenging government to act forthrightly.

Hence for a decade young Negroes have been steeled by both deeds and inspiration to step into responsible action. These are the precedents for the student struggle of today.

Many related, interacting social forces must be understood if we are to understand history as it is being made. The arresting upsurge of Africa and Asia is remote neither in time nor in space to the Negro of the

South. Indeed, the determination of Negro Americans to win freedom from all forms of oppression springs from the same deep longing that motivates oppressed peoples all over the world.

However inadequate forms of education and communication may be, the ordinary Negro Jim Smith knows that in primitive jungle villages in India still illiterate peasants are casting a free ballot for their state and federal legislators. In one after another of the new African states black men form the government, write the laws, and administer the affairs of state. But in state after state in the United States the Negro is ruled and governed without a fragment of participation in civic life. The contrast is a burning truth which has molded a deep determination to end this intolerable condition.

Negroes have also experienced sharp frustrations as they struggle for the realization of promises expressed in hollow legislative enactments or empty electoral campaign oratory. Conferences from the lowest levels of officialdom up to the chief executive in the White House result in the clarification of problems—but not their solution. Studies by many commissions, unhappily devoid of power, continue to pose problems without any concrete results that could be translated into jobs, education, equality of opportunity, and access to the fruits of an historic period of prosperity. In "the affluent society," the Negro has remained the poor, the underprivileged, and the lowest class. Court actions are often surrounded by a special type of red tape that has made for long drawn-out processes of litigation and evasive schemes. The Negro has also become aware that token integration was not a start in good faith but a new form of discrimination covered up with certain niceties.

It was inevitable, therefore, that a more direct approach would be sought—one which would contain the promise of some immediate degree of success based upon the concrete act of the Negro. Hence, a period began in which the emphasis shifted from the slow court process to direct action in the form of bus protests, economic boycotts, mass marches to and demonstrations in the nation's capital and state capitals.

One may wonder why the present movement started with the lunch counters. The answer lies in the fact that here the Negro has suffered indignities and injustices that cannot be justified or explained. Almost every Negro has experienced the tragic inconveniences of lunch counter segregation. He cannot understand why he is welcomed with open arms at most counters in the store, but is denied service at a certain counter because it happens to be selling food and drink. In a real sense the "sit-ins" represent more than a demand for service; they represent a demand for respect.

It is absurd to think of this movement as being initiated by Communists or some other outside group. This movement is an expression of the longing of a new Negro for freedom and human dignity. These students were anchored to lunch counter seats by the accumulated indignities of days gone by and the boundless aspirations of generations yet unborn.

In this new method of protest a new philosophy provided a special undergirding—the philosophy of nonviolence. It was first modestly and quietly projected in one community, Montgomery, when the threat of violence became real in the bus protest. But it burst from this limited arena, and was embraced by masses of people across the nation with fervor and consistency.

The appeal of nonviolence has many facets:

First—It proclaims the sincere and earnest wish of the Negro that though changes must be accomplished, there is no desire to use or tolerate force. Thus, it is consistent with the deeply religious traditions of Negroes.

Second—It denies that vengeance for past oppression motivates the new spirit of determined struggle.

Third—It brings to the point of action a great multitude who need the assurance that a technique exists which is suitable and practical for a minority confronting a majority often vicious and possessed of effective weapons of combat.

Fourth—Many Negroes recognize the necessity of creating discord to alter established community patterns, but they strongly desire that controls be built it, so that neither they nor their adversaries would find themselves engaged in mutual destruction.

Fifth—Having faith that the white majority is not an undifferentiated whole, Negro leaders have welcomed a moral appeal which can reach the emotions and intellect of significant white groups.

The appeal of the philosophy of nonviolence encompasses these many requirements. The key significance of the student movement lies in the fact that from its inception, everywhere, it has combined direct action of non-violence.

This quality has given it the extraordinary power and discipline which every thinking person observes. It has discredited the adversary, who knows how to deal with force but is bewildered and panicky in the face of the new techniques. Time will reveal that the students are learning lessons not contained in their textbooks. Hundreds have already been expelled, fined, imprisoned, and brutalized, and the numbers continue to grow. But with the punishments, something more is growing. A generation of young people has come out of decades of shadows to face naked state power; it has lost its fears, and experienced the majestic dignity of a direct struggle for its own liberation. These young people have connected up with their own history—the slave revolts, the incomplete revolution of the Civil War, the brotherhood of colonial colored men in Africa and Asia. They are an integral part of the history which is reshaping the world, replacing a dying order with modern democracy. They are doing this in a nation whose own birth spread new principles and shattered a medieval social society then dominating most of the globe.

It is extremely significant that in many places the Negro students have found white allies to join in their actions. It is equally significant that on a mass scale students and adults in the North and elsewhere have organized supporting actions, many of which are still only in their early stages.

The segregationists now face some hard alternatives: They can continue to seek to maintain segregated facilities. In this event they must live with discord or themselves initiate, and be responsible for, violence with all its evil consequences. They may close the facilities as they have done in many places. But this will not end the movement; rather, it will spread to libraries, public parks, schools, and the like, and these too will have to be closed, thus depriving both white and Negro of necessary cultural and recreational institutions. This would be a step backward for the whole of society. Or finally, they can accept the principle of equality. In this case they still have two alternative approaches. They may make the facilities equally bad for both white and Negro or equally good. Thus finally the simple logic and justice in their own interests should direct them to the only acceptable solution—to accept equality and maintain it on the best level for both races.

The outcome of the present struggle will be some time in unfolding, but the line of its direction is clear. It is a final refutation of the time-honored theory that the Negro prefers segregation. It would be futile to deplore, as many do, the tensions accompanying the social changes. Tension and conflict are not alien nor abnormal to growth but are the natural results of the process of changes. A revolution is occurring in both the social order and the human mind. One hundred eighty-four years ago a bold group of men signed the Declaration of Independence. If their struggle had been lost they had signed their own death warrant. Nevertheless, though explicitly regretting that King George had forced them to this extreme by a long "train of abuses," they resolutely acted and a great new society was born. The Negro students, their parents, and their allies are acting today in that imperishable tradition.

*Progressive* 24 (May 1960): 8–10.

# 19

# An Address Before
# the National Press Club

*In this address before a meeting of the National Press Club in Washington, D.C., on 19 July 1962, Dr. King defended his commitment to nonviolent resistance and integration, and outlined his hopes for the future of race relations in America.*

Mr. Chairman, distinguished dais guests, members of the National Press Club, ladies and gentlemen, I warmly welcome the opportunity to address such a distinguished group of journalists. For a period I felt that circumstance would make it impossible for me to occupy this significant platform at this particular time. Just last week I was convicted in the city court of Albany, Georgia, for participating in a peaceful march protesting segregated conditions in that community. I decided, on the basis of conscience, not to pay the fine of $178, but to serve the jail sentence of forty-five days. Rev. Ralph D. Abernathy and I were notified that some unknown donor had paid our fines and that we had to leave the jail. As the *Atlanta Constitution* suggested the other day, we have now reached a new landmark in race relations. We have witnessed persons being ejected from lunch counters during the sit-ins, and thrown into jails during the freedom rides. But for the first time, we witnessed persons being kicked out of jail.

Victor Hugo once said that there is nothing more powerful in all the world than an idea whose time has come.

Anyone sensitive to the present moods, morals, and trends in our nation, must know that the time for racial justice has come. The issue is not whether segregation and discrimination will be eliminated but how they will pass from the American scene.

During the past decade some intelligent leadership in the South recognized inevitability. Others, however, vainly tried to stop the wind from blowing and the tides from flowing. The recalcitrant forces authored such concepts as nullification and interposition, along with uglier evils such as bombings, mob violence, and economic reprisals. But the idea whose time had come moved on, and over the rubble left by the violence of the mobsters, many communities resumed their normal activities and moved out on a new basis of partial integration. To be sure, the changes have been unevenly distributed and in some communities even a small beginning is barely perceptible. Yet, enough has been accomplished to make the pattern of the future sharply clear. The illusions of the diehards have been shattered, and, in most instances, they have made a hurried retreat from the reckless notions of ending public education and closing parks, lunch counters, and other public facilities.

But in the tradition of the old guard which dies but does not surrender, a new hastily constructed roadblock has appeared in the form of planned and institutionalized tokenism. Many areas of the South are retreating to a position which will permit a handful of Negroes to attend all-white schools or the employment in lily-white factories of one Negro to a thousand white employees. Thus, we have advanced in some areas from all-out unrestrained resistance to a sophisticated form of delay embodied in tokenism. In a sense, this is one of the most difficult problems that our movement confronts. But I am confident that this tactic will prove to be as vain a hope as the earlier quest to utilize massive resistance to inhibit even a scintilla of change.

Now, what of the future? Will it be marked by the same types of action as the past periods? This question is not easy to answer with precision. Certainly there will continue to be resistance. But in spite of this, I am convinced that the opponents of desegregation are fighting a losing battle. The old South has gone, never to return again. Many of the problems that we are confronting in the South today grow out of the futile attempt of the white South to maintain a system of human values that came into being under a feudalistic plantation system and which cannot survive in a day of democratic equalitarianism.

First, if the South is to grow economically it must continue to industrialize. We see signs of this vigorous industrialization, with a concomitant urbanization, throughout every southern state. Day after day, the South is receiving new multimillion-dollar industries. With the growth of industry the folkways of white supremacy will gradually pass away.

This growth of industry will also increase the purchasing power of the Negro, and this augmented purchasing power will result in improved medical care, greater educational opportunities, and more adequate housing. Each of these developments will result in a further weakening of segregation.

In spite of screams of "over my dead body will any change come," one must not overlook the changes that have come to the South as a result of federal action. There are always those individuals who argue that legislation, court orders, and executive decrees from the federal government are ineffective because they cannot change the heart. They contend that you cannot legislate morals. It may be true that morality cannot be legislated, but behavior can be regulated. The law may not change the heart, but it can restrain the heartless. It will take education and religion to change bad internal attitudes, but legislation and court orders can control the external effects of bad internal attitudes. Federal court decrees have altered transportation patterns and changed educational mores. The habits, if not the hearts, of people have been, and are being, altered every day by federal action. These major social changes have a cumulative force conditioning other segments of life.

More and more the voice of the church is being heard. It is still true that the church is the most segregated major institution in America. As a minister of the gospel I am ashamed to have to affirm that eleven o'clock on Sunday morning, when we stand to sing "In Christ There Is No East nor West," is the most segregated hour of America, and the Sunday school is the most segregated school of the week. But in spite of this appalling fact, we are beginning to shake the lethargy from our souls. Here and there churches are courageously making attacks on segregation, and actually integrating their congregation. Several parochial and church-related schools of the South are throwing off the traditional yoke of segregation. As the church continues to take a forthright stand on this issue, the transition from a segregated to an integrated society will be infinitely smoother.

Probably the most powerful force that is breaking down the barriers of segregation is the new determination of the Negro himself. For many years the Negro tacitly accepted segregation. He was often the victim of stagnant passivity and deadening complacency. While there were always solo voices in the Negro community crying out against segregation, conditions of fear and apathy made it difficult to develop a mass chorus. But through the forces of history something happened to the Negro. The social upheavals of two world wars, the Great Depression, and the spread of the automobile have made it both possible and necessary for the Negro to move away from his former isolation on the rural plantation. The decline of agriculture and parallel growth of industry have drawn large numbers of Negroes to urban centers and brought about a gradual improvement in their economic status. New contacts have led to a broadened outlook and new possibilities for educational advance. Once plagued with a tragic sense of inferiority resulting from the crippling effects of slavery and segregation, the Negro has now been driven to reevaluate himself. He has come to feel that he is somebody. With this new sense of somebodiness and self-respect, a new Negro has emerged with a new determination to achieve freedom and human dignity whatever the cost may be.

This is the true meaning of the struggle that is taking place in the South today. One cannot understand the Montgomery bus boycott, the sit-ins, and the Albany, Georgia, movement without understanding that there is a new Negro on the scene with a new sense of dignity and destiny. Thousands of Negroes have come to see that it is ultimately more honorable to suffer in dignity than accept segregation in humiliation.

A special feature of our struggle is its universal quality. Every social strata is involved—lower, middle, and upper class. Every age—children, teenagers, adults, and senior citizens. The whole nation was startled by the Montgomery bus protest in 1956—chiefly because every Negro allied himself in the cause with firm discipline. The same universal involvement is now appearing in Albany, Georgia. Last December more than seven hundred Negroes from this community willingly went to jail to create an effective protest. I shall never forget this experience in which elderly women over seventy, young teenagers and middle-aged adults crowded the jail cells—some with professional degrees in medicine, law and education; some simple housekeepers and laborers; others from business—all differences of age and social status, but all united around one objective. This is a powerful growing force which no society may wisely ignore.

Fortunately, the Negro has been willing to grapple with a creative and powerful force in his struggle for racial justice, namely, nonviolent resistance. This does not mean that a new method has come into being to serve as a substitute for litigation and legislation. Certainly we must continue to work through the courts and legislative channels. But those who adhere to the method of nonviolent direct action recognize that legislation and court orders tend only to declare rights; they can never thoroughly deliver them. Only when the people themselves begin to act are rights on paper given lifeblood. A catalyst is needed to breathe life experience into a judicial decision by the persistent exercise of the rights until they become usual and ordinary in human contact.

The method of nonviolent resistance is effective in that it has a way of disarming the opponent, it exposes his moral defenses, it weakens his morale and at the same time it works on his conscience.

It also makes it possible for the individual to struggle to secure moral ends through moral means. One of the most persistent philosophical debates of the centuries has been over the question of ends and means. There have been those from Machiavelli on down who have argued that the end justifies the means. This, I feel, is one of the greatest tragedies of communism. Read Lenin as he says, "lying, deceit, and violence are justifiable means to bring about the end of a classless society." This is where nonviolence breaks with communism and any other method which contends that the end justifies the means. In a real sense, the means represent the ideal in the making and the end in process. So in the long run destructive means cannot bring about constructive ends, because the end is preexistent in the means.

Nonviolent resistance also provides a creative force through which men can channelize their discontent. It does not require that they abandon their discontent. This discontent is sound and healthy. Nonviolence saves it from degenerating into morbid bitterness and hatred. Hate is always tragic. It is as injurious to the hater as it is to the hated. It distorts the personality and scars the soul. Psychiatrists are telling us now that many of the inner conflicts and strange things that happen in the subconscious are rooted in hate. So they are now saying, "Love or perish." This is the beauty of nonviolence. It says you can struggle without hating; you can fight war without violence.

It is my great hope that as the Negro plunges deeper into the quest for freedom, he will plunge even deeper into the philosophy of nonviolence. As a race we must work passionately and unrelentingly for first-class citizenship, but we must never use second-class methods to gain it. We must never succumb to the temptation of using violence in the struggle, for if this happens, unborn generations will be the recipients of a long and desolate night of bitterness and our chief legacy to the future will be an endless reign of meaningless chaos.

I feel that this way of nonviolence is vital because it is the only way to reestablish the broken community. It is the method which seeks to implement the just law by appealing to the conscience of the great decent majority who through blindness, fear, pride, or irrationality have allowed their consciences to sleep.

The nonviolent resisters can summarize their message in the following simple terms: We will take direct action against injustice without waiting for other agencies to act. We will not obey unjust laws or submit to unjust practices. We will do this peacefully, openly, cheerfully because our aim is to persuade. We adopt the means of nonviolence because our end is a community at peace with itself. We will try to persuade with our words, but if our words fail, we will try to persuade with our acts. We will always be willing to talk and seek fair compromise, but we are ready to suffer when necessary and even risk our lives to become witnesses to the truth as we see it.

This approach to the problem is not without successful precedent. We have the magnificent example of Gandhi who challenged the might of the British Empire and won independence for his people by using only the weapons of truth, noninjury, courage, and soul force. Today we have the noble example of thousands of Negro students who have challenged the principalities of segregation. Their courageous and disciplined activities have come as a refreshing oasis in a desert sweltering with the heat of injustice. They have taken the whole nation back to those great wells of democracy which were dug deep by the Founding Fathers in the formulation of the Constitution and the Declaration of Independence. One day all of America will be proud of their achievements.

Along with our continued efforts in nonviolent direct action, we are determined to extend our exercise of constitutional privileges to areas heretofore neglected, particularly in the exercise of the ballot. We are embarked upon a campaign to involve millions of Negroes in the use of the franchise. Some of our workers have already suffered violence and arrests for these efforts, but we will continue. We believe that with our intensified actions a correspondingly expanded federal government program of vigorous law enforcement is indispensable. A number of administrative initiatives have been useful, and the present Justice Department has certainly moved with forthrightness and concern in the sensitive area of voter registration. But the coming period will undoubtedly require that the Justice Department utilize the Civil Rights Act of 1960 extensively and seek court-appointed referees in thousands of communities in which the right to vote is flagrantly and brutally denied to Negroes. The majesty of federal law must assert its supremacy over the reign of evil and illegality dominating defiant southern communities.

I have spent most of my time talking about the problem as it exists in the South. But I hope this is not interpreted as my feeling that the problem is merely southern. Indeed no section of our country can boast of clean hands in the area of brotherhood. Segregation may exist in the South in overt and glaring forms, but it exists in the North in hidden and subtle forms. Housing and employment discrimination are often as prominent in the North as they are in the South. In short, the racial issue that we confront in America is not a sectional but a national problem.

I must also clear up another impression which may have been conveyed. I have talked about the emerging new order of integration, and the forces that are at work to assure its realization. From this one may conclude that I am laboring under the impression that the problem is about solved now, and that man can sit complacently by the wayside and wait on the coming of the inevitable. Nothing could be further from the truth. Human progress is neither automatic nor inevitable. The Darwinian theory of evolution is valid in the biological realm, but when a Hubert Spencer seeks to apply it to the whole of society there is very little evidence for it. Even a superficial look at history reveals that no social advance rolls in on the wheels of inevitability; it comes through the tireless efforts and persistent work of dedicated individuals. Without this hard work, time itself becomes an ally of the primitive forces of irrational emotionalism and social stagnation. We have already suffered unnecessary delays in the civil rights struggle because of this lack of vigorous and positive action.

To outline the problem is to chart the course of the Negro freedom movement. We have come to the day when a piece of freedom is not enough for us as human beings nor for the nation of which we are part. We have been given pieces, but unlike bread, a slice of which does diminish hunger, a piece of liberty no longer suffices. Freedom is like life. You cannot be given life in installments. You cannot be given breath but no body, nor a heart but no blood vessels. Freedom is one thing—you have it all, or you are not free.

Our goal is freedom. I believe we will win it because the goal of the nation is freedom. Yet we are not passively waiting for a deliverance to come from others moved by their pity for us. Our destiny is bound up with the destiny of America—we built it for two centuries without wages, we made cotton king, we built our homes and homes for our masters and suffered injustice and humiliation—but out of a bottomless vitality continued to live and grow. If the inexpressible cruelties of slavery could not extinguish our existence, the opposition we now face will surely fall. We feel that we are the conscience of America—we are its troubled soul—we will continue to insist that right be done because both God's will and the heritage of our nation speak through our echoing demands.

We are simply seeking to bring into full realization the American dream—a dream yet unfulfilled. A dream of equality of opportunity, of privilege and property widely distributed; a dream of a land where men no longer argue that the color of a man's skin determines the content of his character; the dream of a land where every man will respect the dignity and worth of human personality—this is the dream. When it is realized, the jangling discords of our nation will be transformed into a beautiful symphony of brotherhood, and men everywhere will know that America is truly the land of the free and the home of the brave.

*Congressional Record* 108 (20 July 1962): 14247–49.

# 20

# The Case Against "Tokenism"

*The veteran civil rights leader here argued that "token integration" would not satisfy African Americans, because "a new sense of somebodiness" had revolutionized blacks' self-conception about their role in American society.*

A few weeks ago, I was convicted in the City Court of Albany, Georgia, for participating in a peaceful march protesting segregated conditions in that community. I decided, on the basis of conscience, not to pay the fine of $178 but to serve the jail sentence of forty-five days. Just as I was about to get adjusted to my new home, Rev. Ralph D. Abernathy and I were notified that some unknown donor had paid our fines and that we had to leave the jail. As the *Atlanta Constitution* suggested shortly after, we have now reached a new landmark in race relations. We have witnessed persons being ejected from lunch counters during the sit-ins and thrown into jails during the freedom rides. But for the first time we witnessed persons being kicked out of jail. [Just over a week ago, while holding a prayer protest outside the city hall in Albany, Georgia, Dr. King was arrested again and returned to jail.]

Victor Hugo once said that there is nothing more powerful in all the world than an idea whose time has come. Anyone sensitive to the present moods, morals and trends in our nation must know that the time for racial justice has come. The issue is not *whether* segregation and discrimination will be eliminated but *how* they will pass from the scene.

During the past decade, some intelligent leaders in the South have recognized inevitability. Others, however, have tried vainly to stop the wind from blowing and the tides from flowing. These recalcitrant forces authored concepts like nullification and interposition, along with such uglier evils as bombings, mob violence and economic reprisals. But the idea whose time had come moved on. Over the rubble left by the violence of mobsters, many communities resumed their normal activities on a new basis of partial integration.

These changes have been unevenly distributed and in some communities may be barely perceptible, yet enough has been accomplished to make the pattern of the future sharply clear. The illusions of the diehards have been shattered and, in most instances, they have made a hurried retreat from the reckless notions of ending public education and closing parks, lunch counters and other public facilities.

But in the tradition of old guards, who would die rather than surrender, a new and hastily constructed roadblock has appeared in the form of planned and institutionalized tokenism. Many areas of the South are retreating to a position where they will permit a handful of Negroes to attend all-white schools or allow the employment in lily-white factories of one Negro to a thousand whites. Thus, we have advanced in some places from all-out, unrestrained resistance to a sophisticated form of delaying tactics, embodied in tokenism. In a sense, this is one of the most difficult problems that the integration movement confronts. But I am confident that this strategem will prove as fruitless as the earlier attempt to mobilize massive resistance to even a scintilla of change.

What of the future? Will it be marked by the same actions as in the past? This is not easy to answer with precision. Certainly there will still be resistance—but I am convinced the old South has gone, never to return. Many of the problems today are due to a futile attempt by the white South to maintain a system of human values that came into being under a feudalistic plantation system and that cannot survive in a democratic age.

If the South is to grow economically, it must continue to industrialize. Day after day, the South is receiving new, multimillion-dollar industries and with the growth of urban society the folkways of white supremacy will gradually pass away. The arrival of industry will increase the purchasing power of the Negro and with that will come improved medical care, greater educational opportunities and more adequate housing. And every such development will result in a further weakening of segregation.

In spite of screams of "over my dead body will any change come," the changes that have come to the South as a result of federal action must not be overlooked. There are always those who will argue that legislation, court orders and executive decrees from the federal government are ineffective because they cannot change the heart. They contend that you cannot legislate morals. But while it may be true that morality cannot be legislated, behavior can be regulated.

The law may not change the heart—but it can restrain the heartless. It will take education and religion to change bad internal attitudes—but legislation and court orders can control their external effects. Federal court decrees have, for example, altered transportation patterns and changed educational mores—so that the habits, if not the hearts, of people are being altered every day by federal action. And these major social changes have a cumulative force conditioning other segments of life.

More and more, the voice of the church is being heard—although it is still true that the church is the most segregated major institution in America. As a minister of the gospel, I am ashamed to say that eleven o'clock on Sunday morning—when we stand to sing "In Christ There Is

No East Nor West"—is the most segregated hour of America, and that Sunday school is the most segregated school of the week. But in spite of this appalling fact, the nation is beginning to shake the lethargy from its soul.

Here and there, churches are courageously making attacks on segregation and even integrating their congregations. Several parochial and church-related schools of the South are also throwing off the incubus, and as the church continues to take a forthright stand on this issue, the transition from a segregated to an integrated society will be infinitely smoother.

Probably the most powerful force, however, in breaking down the barriers of segregation is the new determination of the Negro himself. For many years the Negro tacitly accepted them. He was often the victim of stagnant passivity and deadening complacency. While there were always lone voices in the Negro community crying out against segregation, conditions of fear and apathy made it difficult for them to develop into a mass chorus. But through the forces of history something happened to the Negro.

The social upheavals of two world wars, the Great Depression and the spread of the automobile made it both possible and necessary for the Negro to move away from his former isolation on the rural plantation. The decline of agriculture and the parallel growth of industry have drawn large numbers of Negroes to urban centers and brought about a gradual improvement in their economic status. New contacts have led to a broadened outlook and new possibilities for educational advance. Once plagued with a tragic sense of inferiority, resulting from the crippling effects of slavery and segregation, the Negro has now been driven to reevaluate himself.

He has come to feel that he *is* somebody. And with this new sense of "somebodiness" and self-respect, a new Negro has emerged with a new determination to achieve freedom and human dignity whatever the cost may be.

This is the true meaning of the struggle that is taking place in the South today. One cannot understand the Montgomery bus boycott, the sit-ins and the Albany, Georgia, movement without understanding that there is a new Negro on the scene with a new sense of dignity and destiny. Thousands of Negroes have come to see that it is ultimately more honorable to suffer in dignity than accept segregation in humiliation.

A special feature of our struggle is its universal quality. Every social stratum is involved—lower, middle and upper class—and every age—children, teenagers, adults and senior citizens. The whole nation was startled by the Montgomery bus protest in 1956, chiefly because every Negro allied himself with the cause in firm discipline.

The same universal involvement is now appearing in Albany, Georgia. Last December more than seven hundred Negroes from this community willingly went to jail to create an effective protest. I shall never forget the experience of seeing women over seventy, teenagers and middle-aged adults crowding the cells—some with professional degrees in medicine, law and education; some simple housekeepers and laborers and others from business. All were different in age and social status—but all were united in one objective. Negro solidarity is a powerful growing force which no society may wisely ignore.

Fortunately, the Negro has been willing to use a creative and powerful force in his struggle for racial justice—namely, nonviolent resistance. This is not meant as a substitute for litigation and legislation, which must continue. But those who adhere to the method of nonviolent, direct action recognize that legislation and court orders tend only to declare rights—they can never thoroughly deliver them.

Only when the people themselves begin to act are rights on paper given lifeblood. Life is breathed into a judicial decision by the persistent exercise of legal rights until they become usual and ordinary in human experience.

The method of nonviolent resistance is effective in that it has a way of disarming opponents. It exposes their moral defenses, weakens their morale and at the same time works on their conscience. It makes it possible for the individual to struggle for moral ends through moral means.

One of the most persistent philosophical debates throughout the centuries has been over the question of ends and means. There have been those, like Machiavelli, who have argued that the end justifies the means. This, I feel, is one of the greatest tragedies of communism. Read Lenin as he says "Lying, deceit and violence are justifiable means to bring about the aim of a classless society."

This is where the principle of nonviolence breaks with communism and any other method which holds to the same belief. In a real sense, the means represent the ideal in the making—the end in process. So, in the long run, destructive means cannot bring about constructive ends because the ends are preexistent in the means.

Nonviolent resistance also provides a creative force through which men can channelize their discontent. It does not require that they abandon it, for this kind of discontent is sound and healthy. Nonviolence simply saves it from degenerating into morbid bitterness and hatred. Hate is always tragic. It is as injurious to the hater as it is to the hated. It distorts the personality and scars the soul. Psychiatrists, believing that many of man's inner conflicts are rooted in hate, are now saying "Love or perish." And this is the beauty of nonviolence. It says you can struggle without hating; you can fight war without violence.

It is my great hope that as the Negro plunges deeper into the quest for freedom he will plunge even deeper into the philosophy of nonviolence. As a race, Negroes must work passionately and unrelentingly for first-class citizenship—but they must never use second-class methods to gain it. They must never succumb to the temptation of using violence in the struggle.

I feel that this way of nonviolence is vital because it is the only way to reestablish the broken community. It is the method which seeks to implement just law by appealing to the conscience of the great decent majority who through blindness, fear, pride or irrationality have allowed their consciences to sleep.

The nonviolent resisters can summarize their message in the following simple terms. We will take direct action against injustice without waiting for other agencies to act. We will not obey unjust laws or submit to unjust practices. We will do this peacefully, openly, cheerfully—because our aim is to persuade. We adopt the means of nonviolence because our end is a community at peace with itself. We will try to persuade with our words—but if our words fail we will try to persuade with our acts. We will always be willing to talk and seek fair compromise but we are ready to suffer when necessary and even risk our lives to become witnesses to the truth as we see it.

Along with continued efforts in nonviolent direct action, the movement is determined to extend the exercise of neglected constitutional privileges—particularly in the exercise of the ballot. A campaign has been started to involve millions of Negroes in the use of the franchise. Negro workers have already suffered violence and arrests for these efforts but the campaign will continue.

I believe that beside this intensified effort, an expanded federal government program of vigorous law enforcement is also indispensable. A number of administrative initiatives have already been useful and the present Justice Department has certainly moved with forthrightness and concern in the sensitive area of voter registration. But the coming period will undoubtedly require the Justice Department to utilize the Civil Rights Act of 1960 extensively and seek court-appointed referees in thousands of communities in which the right to vote is flagrantly and brutally denied to Negroes. The majesty of federal law must assert its supremacy over the reign of evil dominating defiant southern communities.

So far, I have discussed only the problem as it exists in the South. But this is not to suggest that the problem is merely southern. No section of the country can boast of clean hands. Segregation may exist in the South in overt and glaring forms but it exists in the North in hidden and subtle ways. Discrimination in housing and employment is often as bad in the North as it is anywhere. The racial issue confronting America is not a sectional issue but a national problem.

Nor must anyone assume that the problem is almost solved and that people can therefore sit complacently by the wayside and await the coming of the inevitable. Human progress is neither automatic nor inevitable. The Darwinian theory of evolution is valid in biology but when a

Herbert Spencer seeks to apply it to the whole of society there is little evidence to support it.

The most superficial look at history shows that no social advance rolls in on the wheels of inevitability. It comes through the tireless efforts and persistent work of dedicated individuals. Without this hard work, time itself becomes an ally of primitive forces and social stagnation. Unnecessary delays have already been suffered in the civil rights struggle through a lack of vigorous action.

To outline the problem is to chart the course of the Negro freedom movement. A piece of freedom is no longer enough for human beings nor for the nation of which Negroes are part. They have been given pieces—but unlike bread, a slice of liberty does not finish hunger. Freedom is like life. It cannot be had in installments. Freedom is indivisible—we have it all, or we are not free.

The Negroes' goal is freedom. I believe we will win it because the goal of the nation is freedom. Yet we are not passively waiting for deliverance to come from others out of pity. Our destiny is bound up with the destiny of America—we built it for two centuries without wages; we made cotton king; we built our homes and homes for our masters and suffered injustice and humiliation. But out of a bottomless vitality we continued to live and grow.

If the inexpressible cruelties of slavery could not extinguish our existence, the opposition we now face will surely fail. We feel that we are the conscience of America—we are its troubled soul. We will continue to insist that right be done because both God's will and the heritage of our nation speak through our echoing demands.

*New York Times Magazine* (5 August 1962): 11ff.

# 21

# Bold Design for a New South

*This is the third annual report on the state of civil rights in America that Dr. King wrote for the progressive newsjournal,* Nation.

An arresting paradox emerged in 1962. History will doubtless judge the year as marking a favorable turning point in the struggle for equality, yet it was also the year that civil rights was displaced as the dominant issue in domestic politics. Although thundering events in Oxford, Mississippi, and Albany, Georgia, captured public attention, there was a perceptible diminishing in the concern of the nation to achieve a just solution of the problem.

Part of the blame must be laid to the administration's cautious tactics. Early in the year, the president backed away from the Senate fight to amend Rule 22, the so-called filibuster rule; had he entered the fray, the amendment would probably have passed and the greatest obstacle to the passage of civil rights legislation would have been smashed. (Despite this experience, the President again remained aloof, under similar circumstances, in January of this year, and again the amendment failed to carry.) True, 1962 was the year of the Cuban crisis, which understandably tended to dwarf all other issues. Yet even in the shadow of Cuba, such issues as trade legislation and tax reform took the play away from civil rights in editorial columns, public debate and headlines.

The administration's circumscribed actions in the civil rights field was generally accepted by the public; even liberal forces proved watchful rather than anxious, hopeful rather than insistent. The demand for progress was somehow drained of its moral imperative, and the issue no longer commanded the conscience of the nation as it had in previous years.

The decline of civil rights as the number one domestic issue was a direct consequence, I believe, of the rise and public acceptance of "tokenism." The American people have not abandoned the quest for equal rights; rather, they have been persuaded to accept token victories as indicative of genuine and satisfactory progress.

An impressive list of government actions took place in 1962 affecting job opportunities, voting rights, desegregation of public facilities, the appointment of Negroes to official posts, housing discrimination, etc. In fairness, it must be said that this administration has outstripped all previous ones in the breadth of its civil rights activities. Yet the movement, instead of breaking out into the open plains of progress, remains constricted and confined. A sweeping revolutionary force is pressed into a narrow tunnel.

This is inevitable when sharply limited goals are set as objectives in place of substantial accomplishments. While merely seven percent of Negro children in the South attend integrated schools, the major battle of the year was over one Negro in a Mississippi university. Two thousand school districts remain segregated after nearly a decade of litigation based upon Supreme Court decisions.

Hundreds of southern communities continue to segregate public facilities, yet even after the immense efforts and sacrifices of the weary Negro citizens of Albany, Georgia, the government enters the fray only at the periphery, filing an *amicus curiae* brief in a lawsuit.

Negro unemployment has mounted to double the proportion of white unemployment, and government action produces a handful of jobs in industries possessing government contracts.

Housing discrimination confines Negroes to slums, North and South, and an executive order forbidding it affects the smallest possible area.

If tokenism were our goal, this administration has adroitly moved us towards its accomplishment. But tokenism can now be seen not only as a useless goal, but as a genuine menace. It is a palliative which relieves emotional distress, but leaves the disease and its ravages unaffected. It tends to demobilize and relax the militant spirit which alone drives us forward to real change.

Tokenism was the inevitable outgrowth of the administration's design for dealing with discrimination. The administration sought to demonstrate to Negroes that it has concern for them, while at the same time it has striven to avoid inflaming the opposition. The most cynical view holds that it wants the vote of both and is paralyzed by the conflicting needs of each. I am not ready to make a judgment condemning the motives of the administration as hypocritical. I believe that it sincerely wishes to achieve change, but that it has misunderstood the forces at play. Its motives may better be judged when and if it fails to correct mistakes as they are revealed by experience.

The day for assessing that experience is at hand. Token gains may well halt our progress, rather than further it. The time has come when the government must commit its immense resources squarely on the side of the quest for freedom. This is not a struggle in which government is a mere mediator. Its laws are being violated.

In a dispute between capital and labor, the government may assume the role of mediator when the simple determination of wages is the issue. But it did not assume this role in the thirties, when the issue was a basic right—the freedom of labor to organize and be represented. Then a law of stern and sweeping power put the government wholly on labor's side. A National Labor Relations Board legislated and enforced labor rights in every nook and cranny of the nation, bending the most powerful corporations into compliance.

Negro rights have no comparable government bastion. Negroes are isolated in communities which daily violate their constitutional privileges with total impunity. The government cannot merely mediate, because basic legal rights are involved. The scale on which violations exist is so vast that limited approaches will never reach the evil; only enforcement machinery of vast proportions will be equal to the task.

Government has not accepted the philosophy of tokenism in defense of economic planning. We have created scientific and industrial miracles: computers solve in minutes problems humans would require hundreds of years to calculate; man-made instruments guide missiles millions of miles into space, measuring and analyzing the components of other worlds. Yet in a luncheonette in a southern town, the government cannot make the Constitution function for human rights.

The government cannot merely mediate because the national interest is deeply involved. The widespread, blatant and persistent denial of human rights in huge regions of our nation constitutes our gravest weakness before world tribunals and world opinion. Our national interest compels us to do more than seek tokens of justice.

I stated at the outset that while 1962 was the year in which civil rights receded as the primary domestic issue, it was also a year that marked a favorable turning point in this area. In what sense can 1962 be considered "favorable"?

The Kennedy administration may have embraced tokenism as a least common denominator, acceptable to the whole South. But the fact is that this approach is tactically and strategically unsound; the South is not, today, one whole. It is already split, fissured into two parts; one is ready for extensive change, the other adamantly opposed to any but the most trivial alterations. The administration should not seek to fashion policies for the latter; it should place its weight behind the *dynamic* South, encouraging and facilitating its progressive development.

The simple and arresting truth that became clear in 1962 is that significant elements of the South have come to see that segregation has placed the whole region socially, educationally, and economically behind the rest of the nation. What is the evidence for this? The following are quotations from the leading white newspaper of the South, the *Atlanta Constitution*:

*We have stopped justifying and begun rectifying racial wrongs. We have traded self-deception for self-respect. . . .*

*This is the South we are proud of—a land of gentlemen, plain-spoken, manly and respectful of their people . . . not a swampland of the deceitful where weaselers dodge and cavil and speak half-truths to the unknowing. . . .*

*As a Negro is freed from force, the white man is freed from guilt; as narrow political systems pass, our people broaden; as schooling improves, factory pay-rolls will multiply and as America grows, the South will more than match her. For here on the final frontier, greatness is setting in. . . .*

In the same week these challenging words were written as a declaration of independence of a new South, the governor of North Carolina declared in plain-spoken terms that discrimination in employment in his state must go.

This is the moment for government to drive a wedge into the splitting South, spreading it open. Negroes and enlightened whites have already built alliances which are registering momentous gains in in the electoral arena. In 1962, Georgia, on the basis of a Negro-white *de facto* alliance, elected a moderate governor, a moderate mayor in Atlanta, a moderate congressman from the most populous county, and sent a Negro to the state senate for the first time in nearly a hundred years.

The South is fissuring along a seam which divides the industrializing regions from the stagnating, backward, agricultural areas. This is significant because the new social and political attitudes are rooted in economic necessity. New industry will not come where dying customs create social tensions, second-rate education and cities without the cultural institutions required for the technical personnel of modern industry.

In short: communities have learned that they cannot live in the past and enjoy the fruits of the present. More and more southerners are speaking out, telling plain truths to the bitter and the blind. Enlightened self-interest makes them accept the Negro's drive for freedom as an ally rather than an enemy.

There will still be differences of opinion in the South. Yet the present direction is forward and the areas in which blind conflict rages are narrowing. We will continue to know jails at first hand because change will not come easily in many places. Nevertheless, we will negotiate desegregation into oblivion in one community as we batter its stubborn walls in another.

The crystallizing of this new social revolution confronts the administration with the responsibility to pattern programs in bold designs. In place of timorous steps suitable for the Old South, the goverment should turn to the New South, giving it the aid it needs.

The administration is at a historic crossroad. It has at stake its moral commitment, and with it its political fortunes. It will not weaken its international posture, but strengthen it, if it takes the road to democratization of the South in active unity with the enlightened South—white and Negro. It will not suffer domestically, because its fate in the large northern cities will turn on the Negro electorate and these cities will determine who occupies the White House.

The president has called for civil rights legislation in the present session of Congress in the face of earlier counsels of despair—the hostility of Congress, he was told, made any such proposals futile. The president's specific program includes some constructive measures. Regarding voting and registration, he has again introduced the proposal that completion of six grades of school should be accepted as evidence of literacy, qualifying the applicant for registration. Thousands of potential voters can be benefited by such a law. He has further proposed a mechanism for bypassing obstructive local registrars by specifying objective standards under which federal registrars may be appointed to qualify voters.

A legislative struggle this year need not be a quixotic exercise in futility. The obstructive coalition of southern Democrats and conservative Republicans can be split on this issue. The Republicans cannot afford to block civil rights legislation which the president earnestly sponsors, and southern Democrats cannot defeat it if they are isolated; if, however, the president is lethargic, the Republicans can be tranquil. They can content themselves merely with criticizing the president in the absence of real challenge. If civil rights is elevated to the urgency that trade, tax and military legislation enjoys, 1963 can be a year of achievement and not another annual experience with frustration.

These are practical political considerations all dictating one road. Yet above it all, a greater imperative demands fulfillment. Throughout our history, the moral decision has always been the correct decision. From our determination to be free in 1776, to our shedding of the evil of chattel slavery in 1863, to our decision to stand against the wave of fascism in the 1930s, we grew and became stronger in our commitment to the democratic tradition. The correct decision in 1963 will make it a genuine turning point in human rights. One hundred years ago a president, tortured by doubts, finally ended slavery and a new American society took shape. Lincoln had hoped the slavery issue could be relegated to secondary place, but life thrust it into the center of history. There segregation, the evil heritage of slavery, still remains.

*Nation* 196 (30 March 1963): 259–62. The Nation Magazine, Nation Associates, Inc., copyright © 1963.

# 22

# The Ethical Demands for Integration

*Dr. King offered this eloquent defense of his philosophy of integration in this speech he delivered in Nashville, Tennessee, on 27 December 1962, before a church conference.*

The problem of race and color prejudice remains America's greatest moral dilemma. When one considers the impact it has upon our nation, internally and externally, its resolution might well determine our destiny. History has thrust upon our generation an indescribably important task—to complete a process of democratization which our nation has too long developed too slowly, but which is our most powerful weapon for world respect and emulation. How we deal with this crucial situation will determine our moral health as individuals, our cultural health as a region, our political health as a nation, and our prestige as a leader of the free world. The shape of the world today does not afford us the luxury of an anemic democracy. The price that America must pay for the continued oppression of the Negro is the price of its own destruction. The hour is late; the clock of destiny is ticking out; we must act now before it is too late.

## "FANATICAL DEATH THROES"

Happily, we have made some meaningful strides in breaking down the barriers of racial segregation. Ever since 1954, when the Supreme Court examined the legal body of segregation and pronounced it constitutionally dead, the system has been on the wane. Even the devout die-hards who used to cry "never," are now saying "later." Much of the tumult and the shouting interspersed with tirades against "race-mixing," "mongrelization of the races," and "outside agitators" represent the fanatical death throes of a dying system. As minimal as may be the "across-the-board" statistics, desegregation is in process. The bells of history are definitely tolling for segregation. I am convinced that in less than ten years desegregation will be a reality throughout the South.

## DESEGREGATION NOT ENOUGH

However, when the *desegregation* process is one hundred percent complete, the human relations dilemma of our nation will still be monumental unless we launch now the parallel thrust of the *integration* process. Although the terms desegregation and integration are often used interchangeably, there is a great deal of difference between the two. In the context of what our national community needs, *desegregation* alone is empty and shallow. We must always be aware of the fact that our ultimate goal is integration, and that desegregation is only a first step on the road to the good society. Perhaps this is the point at which we should define our terms.

## INTEGRATION THE ULTIMATE GOAL

The word *segregation* represents a system that is prohibitive; it denies the Negro equal access to schools, parks, restaurants, libraries and the like. *Desegregation* is eliminative and negative, for it simply removes these legal and social prohibitions. Integration is creative, and is therefore more profound and far-reaching than desegregation. Integration is the positive acceptance of desegregation and the welcomed participation of Negroes into the total range of human activities. Integration is genuine intergroup, interpersonal doing. Desegregation then, rightly, is only a short-range goal. Integration is the ultimate goal of our national community. Thus, as America pursues the important task of respecting the "letter of the law," i.e., compliance with desegregation decisions, she must be equally concerned with the "spirit of the law," i.e., commitment to the democratic dream of integration.

We do not have to look very far to see the pernicious effects of a desegregated society that is not integrated. It leads to "physical proximity without spiritual affinity." It gives us a society where men are physically desegregated and spiritually segregated, where elbows are together and hearts are apart. It gives us special togetherness and spiritual apartness. It leaves us with a stagnant equality of sameness rather than a constructive equality of oneness.

Therefore, our topic leads us to an analysis of the "oughtness" of integration. On the basis of what is right, why is integration an *end* and desegregation only a *means*? In the context of justice, freedom, morality and religion, what are the basic ethical demands of integration?

## THE WORTH OF PERSONS

There must be a recognition of the sacredness of human personality. Deeply rooted in our political and religious heritage is the conviction that every man is an heir to a legacy of dignity and worth. Our Hebraic-

Christian tradition refers to this inherent dignity of man in the Biblical term *the image of God*. This innate worth referred to in the phrase the image of God is universally shared in equal portions by all men. There is no graded scale of essential worth; there is no divine right of one race which differs from the divine right of another. Every human being has etched in his personality the indelible stamp of the Creator.

This idea of the dignity and worth of human personality is expressed eloquently and unequivocably in the Declaration of Independence. "All men," it says, "are created equal. They are endowed by their Creator with certain inalienable rights, among these are life, liberty and the pursuit of happiness." Never has a sociopolitical document proclaimed more profoundly and eloquently the sacredness of human personality.

Frederick Douglas stated the same truth in his lecture on the Constitution of the United States. He says: "Its language is, 'We the people'; not we the white people, not even we the citizens, not we the privileged class, not we the high, not we the low, but we the people . . . we the human inhabitants; and if Negroes are people they are included in the benefits for which the Constitution of America was ordained and established."

Segregation stands diametrically opposed to the principle of the sacredness of human personality. It debases personality. Immanuel Kant said in one formulation of the *Categorical Imperative* that "all men must be treated as *ends* and never as mere *means*." The tragedy of segregation is that it treats men as means rather than ends, and thereby reduces them to things rather than persons. To use the words of Martin Buber, segregation substitutes an "I-it" relationship for the "I-thou" relationship. The colloquialism of the southern landed gentry that referred to slaves and/or Negro labor as "hands" betrays the "thing" quality assigned to Negroes under the system. Herein lies the root of paternalism that persists even today. The traditional southerner is fond of "his Negro" as he is of a pet or a finely-tooled fire arm. "It" serves a purpose or gets a job done. The only concern is performance, not well-being.

But man is not a thing. He must be dealt with, not as an "animated tool," but as a person sacred in himself. To do otherwise is to depersonalize the potential person and desecrate what he is. So long as the Negro is treated as a means to an end, so long as he is seen as anything less than a person of sacred worth, the image of God is abused in him and consequently and proportionately lost by those who inflict the abuse. Only by establishing a truly integrated society can we return to the Negro the quality of "thouness" which is his due because of the nature of his being.


## LIFE DEMANDS FREEDOM

A second ethical demand of integration is a recognition of the fact that a denial of freedom to an individual is a denial of life itself. The very character of the life of man demands freedom. In speaking of freedom at this point I am not talking of the freedom of a thing called the will. The very phrase, freedom of the will, abstracts freedom from the person to make it an object; and an object almost by definition is not free. But freedom cannot thus be abstracted from the person, who is always subject as well as object and who himself still does the abstracting. So I am speaking of the freedom of man, the whole man, and not one faculty called the will.

Neither am I implying that there are no limits to freedom. Always freedom is within predestined structure. Thus a man is free to go north from Atlanta to Washington or south from Atlanta to Miami. But he is not free to go north to Miami or south to Washington, except by a long round-the-world journey; and he is not free to go to both cities at one and the same time. We are always both free and destined. Freedom is the chosen fulfillment of our destined nature.

With these qualifications we return to the assertion that the essence of man is found in freedom. This is what Paul Tillich means when he declares, "Man is man because he is free," or what Tolstoy implies when he says, "I cannot conceive of a man not being free unless he is dead."

## WHAT IS FREEDOM?

What is freedom? It is, first, the capacity to deliberate or weigh alternatives. "Shall I be a teacher or a lawyer?" "Shall I vote for this candidate or the other candidate?" "Shall I be a Democrat, Republican or Socialist?" Second, freedom expresses itself in decision. The word decision like the word incision involves the image of cutting. Incision means to cut in, decision means to cut off. When I make a decision I cut off alternatives and make a choice. The existentialists say we must choose, that we are choosing animals; and if we do not choose we sink into thinghood and the mass mind. A third expression of freedom is responsibility. This is the obligation of the person to respond if he is questioned about his decisions. No one else can respond for him. He alone must respond, for his acts are determined by the centered totality of his being.

From this analysis we can clearly see the evilness of segregation. It cuts off one's capacity to deliberate, decide and respond.

The absence of freedom is the imposition of restraint on my deliberation as to what I shall do, where I shall live, how much I shall earn, the kind of tasks I shall pursue. I am robbed of the basic quality of man-ness. When I cannot choose what I shall do or where I shall live or how I shall survive, it means in fact that someone or some system has already made these a priori decisions for me, and I am reduced to an animal. I do not live; I merely exist. The only resemblances I have to real life are the motor responses and functions that are akin to humankind. I cannot adequately assume responsibility as a person because I have been made a party to a decision in which I played no part in making.

Now to be sure, this is hyperbole in some degree but only to underscore what actually happens when a man is robbed of his freedom. The very nature of his life is altered and his being cannot make the full circle of personhood because that which is basic to the character of life itself has been diminished.

## "SOCIAL LEPROSY"

This is why segregation has wreaked havoc with the Negro. It is sometimes difficult to determine which are the deepest—the physical wounds or the psychological wounds. Only a Negro can understand the social leprosy that segregation inflicts upon him. The suppressed fears and resentments, and the expressed anxieties and sensitivities make each day of life a turmoil. Every confrontation with the restrictions imposed is another emotional battle in a never-ending war. He is shackled in his waking moments to tiptoe stance, never quite knowing what to expect next and in his subconscious he wrestles with this added demon.

Is there any argument to support the withdrawing of life-quality from groups because of the color of their skin, or the texture of their hair or any external characteristic which has nothing at all to do with life-quality? Certainly not on the grounds of morality, justice or religion. Nothing can be more diabolical than a deliberate attempt to destroy in any man his will to be a man and to withhold from him that something that constitutes his true reserve. Desegregation then is not enough for it only travels a part of the distance. It vouchsafes the lack of restriction against one's freedom but it does not prohibit the blocking of his total capacity. Only integration can do this, for it unchains the spirit and the mind and provides for the highest degree of life-quality freedom. I may do well in a *desegregated* society but I can never know what my total capacity is until I live in an *integrated* society. I cannot be free until I have had the opportunity to fulfill my total capacity untrammeled by any artificial hindrance or barrier.

Integration demands that we recognize that a denial of freedom is a denial of life itself.

## THE UNITY OF HUMANITY

A third ethical demand of integration is a recognition of the solidarity of the human family. Integration seems almost inevitably desirable and practical because basically we are all one. Paul's declaration that God "hath made of one blood" all nations of the world is more anthropological fact than religious poetry. The physical differences between the races are insignificant when compared to the physical identities. The world's foremost anthropologists all agree that there is no basic difference in the racial groups of our world. Most deny the actual existence of what we have known as "race." There are four major blood types and all four are found in every racial group. There are no superior and inferior races.

The next truth is evidential in the history of mankind. Not only are all men alike (generically speaking), but man is by nature a societal creature. Aside from the strength and weakness found in *Homo sapiens*, man has been working from the beginning at the great adventure of "community." Whenever Cro-magnon man, under whatever strange impulse, put aside his stone ax and decided to mutually cooperate with his caveman neighbor, it marked the most creative turn of events in his existence. That seemingly elementary decision set in motion what we now know as civilization. At the heart of all that civilization has meant and developed is "community"—the mutually cooperative and voluntary venture of man to assume a semblance of responsibility for his brother. What began as the closest answer to a desperate need for survival from the beast of prey and the danger of the jungle was the basis of present-day cities and nations. Man could not have survived without the impulse which makes him the societal creature he is.

The universe is so structured that things do not quite work out rightly if men are not diligent in their concern for others. The self cannot be self without other selves. I cannot reach fulfillment without thou. Social psychologists tell us that we cannot truly be persons unless we interact with other persons. All life is interrelated. All men are caught in an inescapable network of mutuality, tied in a single garment of destiny. This is what John Donne meant.

## GOD AND HUMAN WORTH

Now let me hasten to say that while all of the three aforementioned points are basic, they represent Christianity's minimal declaration of human unity. In the final analysis, says the Christian ethic, every man must be respected because God loves him. The worth of an individual does not lie in the measure of his intellect, his racial origin, or his social position. Human worth lies in relatedness to God. An individual has value because he has value to God. Whenever this is recognized, "whiteness" and "blackness" pass away as determinants in a relationship and "son" and "brother" are substituted.

For me, this is a welcome conference. In the last few years we have had to face admittedly some very sharp changes in our customs and mores in the South. They have been difficult changes, not only to whites, but also at times to Negroes.

## ". . . BECAUSE IT IS RIGHT!"

Nevertheless, as difficult as the changes may be, it is change produced by that which is right. Yet it is this simple truth that has escaped the focus of the nation's and the South's attention. It is sad that the moral dimension of integration has not been sounded by the leaders of government and the nation. They staunchly supported the principle of the Court's decision but their rationale fell short of being prophetic. They sounded the note that has become the verse, chorus and refrain of the so-called calm and reasonable moderates—*we must obey the law!* The temper of acceptance might be far different if only our leaders would say publicly to the nation—"We must obey the mandate of the Court *because it is right!*"

This conference places the issue of national morality squarely before us. Desegregation is not enough; integration alone is consonant with our national purpose.

Let me hasten to say that despite the tremendous difficulties that integration imposes, nonetheless, work toward its implementation is not to be abandoned for the sake of approximating the more accessible goal of desegregation. Further a word of caution might be said to those who would argue that desegregation should be abandoned and all of our energies invested in the integration process. It is not an "either-or," it is a "both-and," undertaking. Desegregation is the necessary step in the right direction if we are to achieve integration. Desegregation will not change attitudes but it will provide the contact and confrontation necessary by which integration is made possible and attainable.

## DESEGREGATION IS "ENFORCEABLE" BUT INTEGRATION IS NOT

I can summarize all that I have been saying by affirming that the demands of desegregation are enforceable demands while the demands of integration fall within the scope of unenforceable demands.

Some time ago Dr. Harry Emerson Fosdick made an impressive distinction between enforceable and unenforceable obligations. The former are regulated by the codes of society and the vigorous implementation of law-enforcement agencies. Breaking these obligations, spelled out on thousands of pages in law books, has filled numerous prisons. But unenforceable obligations are beyond the reach of the laws of society. They concern inner attitudes, genuine person-to-person relations, and expressions of compassion which law books cannot regulate and jails cannot rectify. Such obligations are met by one's commitment to an inner law, written on the heart. Man-made laws assure justice, but a higher law produces love. No code of conduct ever compelled a father to love his children or a husband to show affection to his wife. The law court may force him to provide bread for the family, but it cannot make him provide the bread of love. A good father is obedient to the unenforceable.

## LAW CAN HELP

Let us never succumb to the temptation of believing that legislation and judicial decrees play only minor roles in solving this problem. Morality cannot be legislated, but behavior can be regulated. Judicial decrees may not change the heart, but they can restrain the heartless. The law cannot make an employer love an employee, but it can prevent him from refusing to hire me because of the color of my skin. The habits, if not the hearts of people, have been and are being altered everyday by legislative acts, judicial decisions and executive orders. Let us not be misled by those who arue that segregation cannot be ended by the force of law.

But acknowledging this, we must admit that the ultimate solution to the race problem lies in the willingness of men to obey the unenforceable. Court orders and federal enforcement agencies are of inestimable value in achieving desegregation, but desegregation is only a partial, though necessary step toward the final goal which we seek to realize, genuine intergroup and interpersonal living. Desegregation will break down the legal barriers and bring men together physically, but something must touch the hearts and souls of men so that they will come together spiritually because it is natural and right. A vigorous enforcement of civil rights laws will bring an end to segregated public facilities which are barriers to a truly desegregated society, but it cannot bring an end to fears, prejudice, pride, and irrationality, which are the barriers to a truly integrated society. Those dark and demonic responses will be removed only as men are possessed by the invisible, inner law which etches on their hearts the conviction that all men are brothers and that love is mankind's most potent weapon for personal and social transformation. True integration will be achieved by true neighbors who are willingly obedient to unenforceable obligations.

## THE DISCIPLINE OF NONVIOLENCE

I cannot conclude without saying that integration places certain ethical demands upon those who have been on the oppressed end of the old order. Perhaps this is why it is my personal conviction that the most potent instrument the Negro community can use to gain total emancipation in America is that of nonviolent resistance. The evidence of the last few years supports my faith that through the use of nonviolence much can be done to raise the Negro to a sense of self-respect and human dignity. The Gandhian concept of noninjury parallels the Hebraic-Christian teaching of the sacredness of every human being.

In the context of the Negro's thrust for the full exercise of constitutional privilege, nonviolence has introduced the additive that has helped the Negro stand taller. When a library is declared to be desegregated, the presence and practice of nonviolence allows him to seek the use of the facilities without fear and apprehension. More than this, it has instilled in him the verve to challenge segregation and discrimination in whatever form it exists. Nonviolence in so many ways has given the Negro a new sense of "somebodyness." The impact of the nonviolent discipline has done a great deal toward creating in the mind of the Negro a new image of himself.

It has literally exalted the person of the Negro in the South in the face of daily confrontations that scream at him that he is inferior or less than because of the accident of his birth.

## HOW NONVIOLENCE HELPS

Nonviolence helps the individuals to adhere to proper means and proper goals. The nonviolent technique is double-barreled; not only has the Negro developed a new image of himself employing its practices, but it has also thwarted the growth of bitterness. In a very large measure, nonviolence has helped to diminish long-repressed feelings of anger and frustration. In the course of respecting the discipline of the nonviolent way, the Negro has learned that he must respect the adversary who inflicts the system upon him and he develops the capacity to hate segregation but to love the segregationist. He learns in the midst of his determined efforts to destroy the system that has shackled him so long, that a commitment to nonviolence demands that he respect the personhood of his opponent. Thus, nonviolence exalts the pesonality of the *segregator* as well as the *segregated*. The common denominator of the flux of social change in the South is the growing awareness on the part of the respective opponents that mutually they confront the eternality of the basic worth of every member of the human family.

*Religion and Labor* (May 1963): 1, 3–4, 7–8.

# 23

# Behind the Selma March

On 2 January 1965, Dr. King, who had just received the Nobel Prize for Peace in Oslo, Norway, on 10 December 1964, announced that a new, and more militant, phase of his civil rights campaign would be initiated in Selma, Alabama. From its inception, SCLC sought to secure both social and political rights for black Americans. On that fateful January day, King said, "We are not asking, we are demanding the ballot." Selma, located in Dallas County, Alabama, was then under the jurisdiction of Sheriff James G. Clark, an avid, shrewd segregationist. Rather than immediately respond to Dr. King's usual tactic of "dramatizing" racism before the television cameras, he admonished his deputies to enforce Alabama's segregationist voter registration laws with the least amount of brutality. Despite the unmerciful beating of the Reverend James Bevel and the murder of Jimmie Lee Jackson, Clark denied King the drama he needed to accent the painful reality of black disenfranchisement. King proved to be more determined than even Clark suspected. Clark finally felt compelled to arrest King, along with 770 other demonstrators, on 1 February. Many of these demonstrators were children. By 3 February, Clark had arrested 500 more demonstrators. The jails of Dallas County were bursting. Clark became increasingly frustrated, and so did King. But the national conscience had not been aroused. President Lyndon Baines Johnson, FBI director J. Edgar Hoover, and many others, tried to pressure King to be "reasonable." On 6 March, Dr. King called for a march from Selma to Montgomery in order to carry the campaign for voting rights to the steps of the state capitol. That was on a Saturday, the day before the first Sunday of the month. For most earnest black Baptists, the first Sunday of a month is comparable to the Jewish celebration of Yom Kippur. Scholars have questioned King's sincerity when he and Ralph Abernathy, his chief lieutenant, experienced great vocational conflict between their clerical responsibilities to administer the Lord's Supper and baptism on the first Sunday and their civil rights activism. From his church office at Ebenezer Baptist Church in Atlanta, Dr. King gave his approval for the Reverend Hosea Williams in Selma to lead several hundred demonstrators to the Edmund Pettus Bridge, as evidence of SCLC's determination to march to Montgomery. King believed they would simply be arrested for violating Governor George Wallace's ban against the march. No one expected a bloodbath to ensue. After all, Clark had been shrewd thus far. But state law enforcement officers were in charge now. Combined with innumerable white vigilante ruffians, they produced one of the most tragic depictions of white racism ever captured on film. Black and white demonstrators were beaten unmercifully. The cameras allowed the entire nation to be eyewitnesses to this hideous spectacle.

In his address to the joint session of Congress, President Johnson made one of the most eloquent, unequivocal, and passoniate pleas for human rights ever made by a president of the United States. He revealed a great understanding of the depth and dimension of the problem of racial justice. His tone and his delivery were disarmingly sincere. His power of persuasion has been nowhere more forcefully seen. We are happy to know that our struggle in Selma has gone far beyond the issue of the right to vote and has focused the attention of the nation on the vital issue of equality in human rights.

During the course of our struggle to achieve voting rights for Negroes in Selma, Alabama, it was reported that a "delicate understanding" or "agreement" had existed between myself, Alabama state officials, and the federal government to avoid the scheduled march to Montgomery on Tuesday, March 9.

It was interpreted in some quarters, on the basis of news reports of my testimony in support of our petition to the federal district court in Montgomery for an injunction against state officials, that I worked with the federal government to throttle the indignation of white clergymen and Negroes and their courageous determination to take a stand, so that Selma could present a superficially calm face to the millions of Americans whose eyes and minds were trained on it at that particular moment.

I am concerned about this perversion of the facts and for the record would like to sketch in the background of the events leading to the confrontation of marchers and Alabama state troopers at Pettus Bridge in Selma, and our subsequent peaceful turning back.

The goal of the demonstrations in Selma, as elsewhere, is to dramatize the existence of injustice and to bring about the presence of justice by methods of nonviolence. Long years of experience indicate to us that Negroes can achieve this goal when four things occur:

1. Nonviolent demonstrators go into the streets to exercise their constitutional rights.

2. Racists resist by unleashing violence against them.

3. Americans of conscience in the name of decency demand federal intervention and legislation.

4. The administration, under mass pressure, initiates measures of immediate intervention and remedial legislation.

The working out of this process has never been simple or tranquil. When nonviolent protests were countered by local authorities with harassment, intimidation, and brutality, the federal government has always first asked the Negro to desist and leave the streets, rather than bring pressure to bear on those who commit the criminal acts. We have always been compelled to reject vigorously such federal requests and have rather relied on our allies, the millions of Americans across the nation, to bring pressure on the federal government for protective action in our behalf. Our position has always been that there is a wrong and right side to the question of full freedom and equality for millions of Negro Americans and that the federal government does not belong in the middle on this issue.

During our nonviolent direct-action campaigns we have always been advised, and again were so advised in Selma, that violence may ensue. Herein lies a dilemma: Of course there always exists the likelihood that, because of the hostility to our demonstrations, acts of lawlessness may be precipitated. We realize that we must exercise extreme caution so that our direct-action program is not conducted in a manner that might be considered provocative or an invitation to violence. Accordingly, each situation must be studied in detail; the strength and temper of our adversaries must be estimated and any change in any of these factors will affect the details of our strategy. Nevertheless, we often must begin a march without knowing when or where it will actually terminate.

How were these considerations applied to our plans for the march from Selma to Montgomery?

My associates and friends are constantly concerned about my personal safety, and in the light of recent threats of death, many of them urged me not to march Sunday for fear that my presence in the line would lead to assassination attempts. However, as a matter of conscience, I cannot always respond to the wishes of my staff and associates; in this case, I had made the decision to lead the march on Sunday and was prepared to do so in spite of any possible danger to my person.

In working out a time schedule, I had to consider my church responsibilities. Because I am so frequently out of my pulpit and because my life is so full of emergencies, I am always on the horns of a dilemma. I had been away for two straight Sundays and therefore felt that I owed it to my parishioners to be there. It was arranged that I take a chartered plane to Montgomery after the morning service and lead the march out of Selma, walking with a group for three or four hours, and take the chartered flight back in order to be on hand for the Communion Service at 7:30 P.M.

When Governor Wallace issued his ban on the march, it was my view and that of most of my associates that the state troopers would deal with the problem by arresting all of the people in the line. We never imagined that they would use the brutal methods to which they actually resorted to repress the march. I therefore concluded that if I were arrested it would be impossible for me to get back to the evening service to administer the Lord's Supper and baptism. Because of this situation, my staff urged me to stay in Atlanta and lead a march on Monday morning. This I agreed to do. I was prepared to go to jail on Monday but at the same time I would have met my church responsibilities. If I had had any idea that the state troopers would use the kind of brutality they did, I would have felt compelled to give up my church duties altogether to lead the line. It was one of those developments that none of us anticipated. We felt that the state troopers, who had been severely criticized over their terrible acts two weeks earlier even by conservative Alabama papers, would never again engage in this kind of violence. I shall never forget my agony of conscience for not being there when I heard of the dastardly acts perpetrated against nonviolent demonstrators that Sunday. As a result, I felt that I had to lead a march on the following Tuesday and decided to spend Monday mobilizing for it.

The march on Tuesday illustrated the dilemma we often face. Not to try to march again would have been unthinkable. However, whether we were marching to Montgomery or to a limited point within the city limits of Selma could not be determined in advance; the only certain thing was that we had to begin so that a confrontation with injustice would take place, in full view of the millions looking on throughout this nation.

The next question was whether the confrontation had to be a violent one; here the responsibility of weighing all factors and estimating the consequences rests heavily on the civil rights leaders. It is easy to decide on either extreme. To go forward recklessly can have terrible consequences in terms of human life and also can cause friends and supporters to lose confidence if they feel a lack of responsibility exists. On the other hand, it is ineffective to guarantee that no violence will occur by the device of not marching or undertaking token marches avoiding direct confrontation.

We determined to seek the middle course. We would march until we faced the troopers. We would not disengage until they made clear that they were going to use force. We would disengage then, having made our point, revealing the continued presence of violence, and showing clearly who are the oppressed and who the oppressors, hoping, finally, that the national administration in Washington would feel and respond to the shocked reactions with action.

On Tuesday, March 9, Judge Frank M. Johnson of the federal district court in Montgomery issued an order enjoining me and the local Selma leadership of the nonviolent voting rights movement from peacefully marching to Montgomery. The issuance of Judge Johnson's order caused disappointment and bitterness to all of us. We had looked to the federal judiciary in Alabama to prevent the unlawful interference with our program to expand elective franchise for Negroes throughout the black belt.

I consulted with my lawyers and trusted advisors both in Selma and other parts of the country and discussed what course of action we should take. Information came in that troopers of the Alabama State Police and Sheriff James Clark's possemen would be arrayed in massive force across Highway 80 at the foot of Pettus Bridge in Selma. I reflected upon the role of the federal judiciary as a protector of the rights of

Negroes. I also gave thoughtful consideration to the hundreds of clergymen and other persons of good will who had come to Selma to make a witness with me in the cause of justice by participating in our planned march to Montgomery. Taking all of this into consideration, I decided that our plans had to be carried out and that I would lead our march to a confrontation with injustice to make a witness to our countrymen and the world of our determination to vote and be free.

As my associates and I were spiritually preparing ourselves for the task ahead, Governor Leroy Collins, chairman of the newly created Community Relations Service under the Civil Rights Act of 1964, and John Doar, Acting Assistant Attorney General, Civil Rights Division, came to see me to dissuade me from the course of action which we had painfully decided upon.

Governor Collins affirmed and restated the commitment of President Johnson to the achievement of full equality for all persons without regard to race, color, or creed, and his commitment to securing the right to vote for all persons eligible to do so. He very strongly urged us not to march. I listened attentively to both Mr. Doar and Governor Collins. I explained to them why, as a matter of conscience, I felt it was necessary to seek a confrontation with injustice on Highway 80. I asked them to try to understand that I would rather die on the highway in Alabama than make a butchery of my conscience by compromising with evil. The Reverend Fred Shuttlesworth said to the Governor that instead of urging us not to march, he should urge the state troopers not to be brutal toward us and not attempt to stop our peaceful march. Governor Collins realized at this point that we were determined to march and left the room, saying that he would do what he could to prevent the state troopers from being violent.

It is important to stress once again that no prearranged agreement existed. Whether Governor Collins and other officials from the federal government talked with Mr. Lingo and the officials in Alabama is something that I do not know.

All I do know is that just as we started to march, Governor Collins rushed to me and said that he felt everything would be all right. He gave me a small piece of paper indicating a route that I assume Mr. Baker, Public Safety Director of Selma, wanted us to follow. It was the same route that had been taken on Sunday. The press, reporting this detail, gave the impression that Governor Collins and I had sat down and worked out some compromise. There were no talks or agreements between Governor Collins and me beyond the discussions I have just described. I held on to my decision to march despite the fact that many people in the line were concerned about breaking the court injunction issued by one of the strongest and best judges in the South. I felt that we had to march at least to the point where the troopers brutalized the people on Sunday even if it would mean a recurrence of violence, arrest, or even death. As a nonviolent leader, I could not advocate breaking through a human wall set up by the policemen. While we desperately desired to proceed to Montgomery, we knew before we started our march that this human wall set up on Pettus Bridge would make it impossible for us to go beyond it. It was not that we didn't intend to go on to Montgomery, but that, in consideration of our commitment to nonviolent action, we knew we could not go under the present conditions.

As to our next step:

As soon as we had won legal affirmation of our right to march to Montgomery, the next phase hinged on the successful completion of our mission to petition the governor to take meaningful measures to abolish voting restrictions, the poll tax, and police brutality.

*Saturday Review* 48 (3 April 1965): 16–17, 57. See Charles E. Fager, *Selma, 1965* (New York: Scribner's, 1974); and David J. Garrow, *Protest at Selma: Martin Luther King, Jr., and the Voting Rights Act of 1965* (New Haven: Yale University Press, 1978).

# Political: Wedged Between Democracy and Black Nationalism

# 24

# Facing the Challenge
# of a New Age

*Dr. King's struggle to mediate between his own middle-class and Christian com-*
*mitment to nonviolent resistance and to integration are evident in this edited*
*version of his address before the First Annual Institute on Non-Violence and*
*Social Change, which was held in Montgomery, Alabama, in December 1956.*

Those of us who live in the twentieth century are privileged to live in
one of the most momentous periods of human history. It is an exciting
age filled with hope. It is an age in which a new social order is being
born. We stand today between two worlds—the dying old and the
emerging new.

Now I am aware of the fact that there are those who would contend
that we live in the most ghastly period of human history. They would argue that the rhythmic beat of the deep rumblings of discontent from
Asia, the uprisings in Africa, the nationalistic longings of Egypt, the roar-
ing cannons from Hungary, and the racial tensions of America are all indicative of the deep and tragic midnight which encompasses our civilization. They would argue that we are retrogressing instead of progressing.
But far from representing retrogression and tragic meaninglessness, the
present tensions represent the necessary pains that accompany the birth
of anything new. Long ago the Greek philosopher Heraclitus argued that
justice emerges from the strife of opposites, and Hegel, in modern philosophy, preached a doctrine of growth through struggle. It is both historically and biologically true that there can be no birth and growth without
birth and growing pains. Whenever there is the emergence of the new we
confront the recalcitrance of the old. So the tensions which we witness in
the world today are indicative of the fact that a new world order is being
born and an old order is passing away.

We are all familiar with the old order that is passing away. We have
lived with it for many years. We have seen it in its international aspect,
in the form of colonialism and imperialism. There are approximately
two billion four hundred million (2,400,000,000) people in this world,
and the vast majority of these people are colored—about one billion six
hundred million (1,600,000,000) of the people of the world are colored.

Fifty years ago, or even twenty-five years ago, most of these one billion six hundred million people lived under the yoke of some foreign power. We could turn our eyes to China and see there six hundred million men and women under the pressing yoke of British, Dutch, and French rule. We could turn our eyes to Indonesia and see a hundred million men and women under the domination of the Dutch. We could turn to India and Pakistan and notice four hundred million brown men and women under the pressing yoke of the British. We could turn our eyes to Africa and notice there two hundred million black men and women under the pressing yoke of the British, the Dutch and the French. For years all of these people were dominated politically, exploited economically, segregated and humiliated.

But there comes a time when people get tired. There comes a time when people get tired of being trampled over by the iron feet of oppression. There comes a time when people get tired of being plunged across the abyss of exploitation where they experience the bleakness of nagging despair. There comes a time when people get tired of being pushed out of the glittering sunlight of life's July and left standing in the piercing chill of an Alpine November. So in the midst of their tiredness these people decided to rise up and protest against injustice. As a result of their protest more than one billion three hundred million (1,300,000,000) of the colored peoples of the world are free today. They have their own governments, their own economic systems, and their own educational systems. They have broken loose from the Egypt of colonialism and imperialism, and they are now moving through the wilderness of adjustment toward the promised land of cultural integration. As they look back they see the old order of colonialism and imperialism passing away and the new order of freedom and justice coming into being.

We have also seen the old order in our own nation, in the form of segregation and discrimination. We know something of the long history of this old order in America. It had its beginning in the year 1619 when the first Negro slaves landed on the shores of this nation. They were brought here from the soils of Africa. And unlike the Pilgrim Fathers who landed at Plymouth a year later, they were brought here against their wills. Throughout slavery the Negro was treated in a very inhuman fashion. He was a thing to be used, not a person to be respected. He was merely a depersonalized cog in a vast plantation machine. The famous Dred Scott Decision of 1857 well illustrates the status of the Negro during slavery. In this decision the Supreme Court of the United States said, in substance, that the Negro is not a citizen of the United States; he is merely property subject to the dictates of his owner. Then came 1896. It was in this year that the Supreme Court of this nation, through the *Plessy v. Ferguson* decision, established the doctrine of separate-but-equal as the law of the land. Through this decision segregation gained legal and moral sanction. The end result of the Plessy doctrine was that it led to a strict enforcement of the "separate," with hardly the slightest attempt to abide by the "equal." So the Plessy doctrine ended up making for tragic inequalities and ungodly exploitation.

Living under these conditions, many Negroes came to the point of losing faith in themselves. They came to feel that perhaps they were less than human. The great tragedy of physical slavery was that it led to mental slavery. So long as the Negro maintained this subservient attitude and accepted this "place" assigned to him, a sort of racial peace existed. But it was an uneasy peace in which the Negro was forced patiently to accept insult, injustice and exploitation. It was a negative peace. True peace is not merely the absence of some negative force—tension, confusion, or war; it is the presence of some positive force—justice, good will and brotherhood. And so the peace which existed between the races was a negative peace devoid of any positive and lasting quality.

Then something happened to the Negro. Circumstances made it necessary for him to travel more. His rural plantation background was gradually being supplanted by migration to urban and industrial communities. His economic life was gradually rising to decisive proportions. His cultural life was gradually rising through the steady decline of crippling illiteracy. All of these factors conjoined to cause the Negro to take a new look at himself. Negro masses began to reevaluate themselves. The Negro came to feel that he was somebody. His religion revealed to him that God loves all of His children, and that every man, from a bass black to a treble white, is significant on God's keyboard. So he could now cry out with the eloquent poet:

> Fleecy locks and black complexion
> Cannot forfeit nature's claim.
> Skin may differ, but affection
> Dwells in black and white the same.
> And were I so tall as to reach the pole
> Or to grasp the ocean at a span,
> I must be measured by my soul.
> The mind is the standard of the man.

With this new self-respect and new sense of dignity on the part of the Negro, the South's negative peace was rapidly undermined. And so the tension which we are witnessing in race relations today can be explained, in part, by the revolutionary change in the Negro's evaluation of himself, and his determination to struggle and sacrifice until the walls of segregation have finally been crushed by the battering rams of surging justice.

Along with the emergence of a "New Negro," with a new sense of dignity and destiny, came that memorable decision of May 17, 1954. In this decision the Supreme Court of this nation unanimously affirmed that the old Plessy doctrine must go. This decision came as a legal and sociological death blow to an evil that had occupied the throne of

American life for several decades. It affirmed in no uncertain terms that separate facilities are inherently unequal and that to segregate a child because of his race is to deny him equal protection of the law. With the coming of this great decision we could gradually see the old order of segregation and discrimination passing away, and the new order of freedom and justice coming into being. Let nobody fool you, all of the loud noises that you hear today from the legislative halls of the South in terms of "interposition" and "nullification," and of outlawing the NAACP are merely the death groans from a dying system. The old order is passing away, and the new order is coming into being. We are witnessing in our day the birth of a new age, with a new structure of freedom and justice.

Now as we face the fact of this new, emerging world, we must face the responsibilities that come along with it. A new age brings with it new challenges. Let us consider some of the challenges of this new age.

First, we are challenged to rise above the narrow confines of our individualistic concerns to the broader concerns of all humanity. The new world is a world of geographical togetherness. This means that no individual or nation can live alone. We must all learn to live together, or we will be forced to die together. This new world of geographical togetherness has been brought about, to a great extent, by man's scientific and technological genius. Man through his scientific genius has been able to dwarf distance and place time in chains; he has been able to carve highways through the stratosphere. And so it is possible today to eat breakfast in New York City and dinner in Paris, France. Bob Hope has described this new jet age in which we live. It is an age in which we will be able to get a nonstop flight from Los Angeles, California, to New York City, and if by chance we develop hiccups on taking off, we will "hic" in Los Angeles and "cup" in New York City. It is an age in which one will be able to leave Tokyo on Sunday morning and, because of time difference, arrive in Seattle, Washington, on the preceding Saturday night. When your friends meet you at the airport in Seattle inquiring when you left Tokyo, you will have to say, "I left tomorrow." This, in a very humorous sense, says to us that our world is geographically one. Now we are faced with the challenge of making it spiritually one. Through our scientific genius we have made of the world a neighborhood; now through our moral and spiritual genius we must make of it a brotherhood. We are all involved in the single process. Whatever affects one directly affects all indirectly. We are all links in the great chain of humanity. This is what John Donne meant when he said years ago:

No man is an island, entire of it selfe; every man is a piece of the Continent, a part of the maine; if a clod bee washed away by the Sea, Europe is the lesse, as well as if a Promontorie were, as well as if a Mannor of thy friends or of thine owne were; any mans' death diminishes me, because I am involved in Mankinde; And therefore never send to know for whom the bell tolls; it tolls for thee.

A second challenge that the new age brings to each of us is that of achieving excellency in our various fields of endeavor. In the new age many doors will be opening to us that were not opened in the past, and the great challenge which we confront is to be prepared to enter these doors as they open. Ralph Waldo Emerson said in an essay back in 1871:

If a man can write a better book, or preach a better sermon, or make a better mouse trap than his neighbor, even if he builds his house in the woods the world will make a beaten path to his door.

In the new age we will be forced to compete with people of all races and nationalities. Therefore, we cannot aim merely to be good Negro teachers, good Negro doctors, good Negro ministers, good Negro skilled laborers. We must set out to do a good job, irrespective of race, and do it so well that nobody could do it better.

Whatever your life's work is, do it well. Even if it does not fall in the category of one of the so-called big professions, do it well. As one college president said, "A man should do his job so well that the living, the dead, and the unborn could do it no better." If it falls your lot to be a street sweeper, sweep streets like Michelangelo painted pictures, like Shakespeare wrote poetry, like Beethoven composed music; sweep streets so well that all the host of Heaven and earth will have to pause and say, "Here lived a great street sweeper, who swept his job well." As Douglas Mallock says:

> If you can't be a pine on the top of the hill
> Be a scrub in the valley—but be
> The best little scrub by the side of the hill,
> Be a bush if you can't be a tree.
>
> If you can't be a highway just be a trail
> If you can't be the sun be a star;
> It isn't by size that you win or fail—
> Be the best of whatever you are.

A third challenge that stands before us is that of entering the new age with understanding good will. This simply means that the Christian virtues of love, mercy and forgiveness should stand at the center of our lives. There is the danger that those of us who have lived so long under the yoke of oppression, those of us who have been exploited and trampled over, those of us who have had to stand amid the tragic midnight of injustice and indignities will enter the new age with hate and bitterness. But if we retaliate with hate and bitterness, the new age will be nothing but a duplication of the old age. We must blot out the hate and injustice of the old age with the love and justice of the new. This is why I believe so firmly in nonviolence. Violence never solves problems. It only creates new and more complicated ones. If we succumb to the temptation of using violence in our struggle for justice, unborn generations will be the recipients of a long and desolate night of bitterness, and our chief legacy to the future will be an endless reign of meaningless chaos.

We have before us the glorious opportunity to inject a new dimension of love into the veins of our civilization. There is still a voice crying out in terms that echo across the generations, saying: Love your enemies, bless them that curse you, pray for them that despitefully use you, that you may be the children of your Father which is in Heaven.

This love might well be the salvation of our civilization. This is why I am so impressed with our motto for the week, "Freedom and Justice through Love." Not through violence; not through hate; no, not even through boycotts; but through love. It is true that as we struggle for freedom in America we will have to boycott at times. But we must remember as we boycott that a boycott is not an end within itself; it is merely a means to awaken a sense of shame within the oppresssor and challenge his false sense of superiority. But the end is reconciliation; the end is redemption; the end is the creation of the beloved community. It is this type of spirit and this type of love that can transform opposers into friends. It is this type of understanding good will that will transform the deep gloom of the old age into the exuberant gladness of the new age. It is this love which will bring about miracles in the hearts of men.

Now I realize that in talking so much about love it is very easy to become sentimental. There is the danger that our talk about love will merely be empty words devoid of any practical and true meaning. But when I say love those who oppose you I am not speaking of love in a sentimental or affectionate sense. It would be nonsense to urge men to love their oppressors in an affectionate sense. When I refer to love at this point I mean understanding good will. The Greek languages comes to our aid at this point. The Greek language has three words for love. First it speaks of love in terms of *eros*. Plato used this word quite frequently in his dialogues. *Eros* is a type of esthetic love. Now it has come to mean a sort of romantic love. I guess Shakespeare was thinking in terms of *eros* when he said:

> Love is not love
> which alters when it alteration finds,
> or bends with the remover to remove.
> O no, it is an ever fixed mark
> that looks on tempests and is never shaken.
> It is a star to every wandering bark. . . .

This is *eros*. And then the Greek talks about *philia*. *Philia* is a sort of intimate affectionateness between personal friends. It is a sort of reciprocal love. On this level a person loves because he is loved. Then the Greek language comes out with another word which is the highest level of love. It speaks of it in terms of *agape*. *Agape* means nothing sentimental or basically affectionate. It means understanding, redeeming good will for all men. It is an overflowing love which seeks nothing in return. It is the love of God working in the lives of men. When we rise to love on the *agape* level we love men not because we like them, not because their attitudes and ways appeal to us, but because God loves us. Here we rise to the position of loving the person who does the evil deed while hating the deed that the person does. With this type of love and understanding good will we will be able to stand amid the radiant glow of the new age with dignity and discipline. Yes, the new age is coming. It is coming mighty fast.

Now the fact that this new age is emerging reveals something basic about the universe. It tells us something about the core and heartbeat of the cosmos. It reminds us that the universe is on the side of justice. It says to those who struggle for justice, "You do not struggle alone, but God struggles with you." This belief that God is on the side of truth and justice comes down to us from the long tradition of our Christian faith. There is something at the very center of our faith which reminds us that Good Friday may occupy the throne for a day, but ultimately it must give way to the triumphant beat of the drums of Easter. Evil may so shape events that Caesar will occupy a palace and Christ a cross, but one day that same Christ will rise up and split history into A.D. and B.C., so that even the life of Caesar must be dated by His name. There is something in this universe that justifies Carlyle in saying, "No lie can live forever." There is something in this universe which justifies William Cullen Bryant in saying, "Truth crushed to earth will rise again." There is something in this universe that justifies James Russell Lowell in saying:

> Truth forever on the scaffold
> Wrong forever on the throne
> Yet that scaffold sways the future
> And behind the dim unknown stands God
> Within the shadows keeping watch above his own.

And so here in Montgomery, after more than eleven long months, we can walk and never get weary, because we know there is a great camp meeting in the promised land of freedom and justice.

Before closing I must correct what might be a false impression. I am afraid that if I close at this point many will go away misinterpreting my whole message. I have talked about the new age which is fastly coming into being. I have talked about the fact that God is working in history to bring about this new age. There is the danger, therefore, that after hearing all of this you will go away with the impression that we can go home, sit down, and do nothing, waiting for the coming of the inevitable. You will somehow feel that this new age will roll in on the wheels of inevitability, so there is nothing to do but wait on it. If you get that impression you are the victims of an illusion wrapped in superficiality. We must speed up the coming of the inevitable.

Now it is true, if I may speak figuratively, that Old Man Segregation is on his deathbed. But history has proven that social systems have a great last-minute breathing power, and the guardians of a status quo are always on hand with their oxygen tents to keep the old order alive. Segregation is still a fact in America. We still confront it in the South in its glaring and conspicuous forms. We still confront it in the North in its hidden and subtle forms. But if democracy is to live, segregation must die. Segregation is a glaring evil. It is utterly unchristian. It relegates the segregated to the status of a thing rather than elevates him to the status of a person. Segregation is nothing but slavery covered up with certain niceties of complexity. Segregation is a blatant denial of the unity which we all have in Christ Jesus.

So we must continue the struggle against segregation in order to speed up the coming of the inevitable. We must continue to gain the ballot. This is one of the basic keys to the solution of our problem. Until we gain political power through possession of the ballot we will be convenient tools of unscrupulous politicians. We must face the appalling fact that we have been betrayed by both the Democratic and Republican parties. The Democrats have betrayed us by capitulating to the whims and caprices of the southern dixiecrats. The Repulicans have betrayed us by capitulating to the blatant hypocrisy of right-wing reactionary northerners. This coalition of southern Democrats and northern right-wing Republicans defeats every proposed bill on civil rights. Until we gain the ballot and place proper public officials in office this condition will continue to exist. In communities where we confront difficulties in gaining the ballot, we must use all legal and moral means to remove these difficulties.

We must continue to struggle through legalism and legislation. There are those who contend that integration can come only through education, for no other reason than that morals cannot be legislated. I choose, however, to be dialectical at this point. It is neither education nor legislation; it is both legislation and education. I quite agree that it is impossible to change a man's internal feelings merely through law. But this really is not the intention of the law. The law does not seek to change one's internal feelings; it seeks rather to control the external effects of those internal feelings. For instance, the law cannot make a man love—religion and education must do that—but it can control his efforts to lynch. So in order to control the external effects of prejudiced internal feelings, we must continue to struggle through legislation.

Another thing that we must do in pressing on for integration is to invest our finances in the cause of freedom. Freedom has always been an expensive thing. History is a fit testimony to the fact that freedom is rarely gained without sacrifice and self-denial. So we must donate large sums of money to the cause of freedom. We can no longer complain that we do not have the money. Statistics reveal that the economic life of the Negro is rising to decisive proportions. The annual income of the American Negro is now more than sixteen billion dollars, almost equal to the national income of Canada. So we are gradually becoming economically independent. It would be a tragic indictment on both the self-respect and practical wisdom of the Negro if history reveals that at the height of the twentieth century the Negro spent more for frivolities than for the cause of freedom. We must never let it be said that we spend more for the evanescent and ephemeral than for the eternal values of freedom and justice.

Another thing that we must do in speeding up the coming of the new age is to develop intelligent, courageous and dedicated leadership. This is one of the pressing needs of the hour. In this period of transition and growing social change, there is a dire need for leaders who are calm and yet positive, leaders who avoid the extremes of "hot-headedness" and "Uncle Tomism." The urgency of the hour calls for leaders of wise judgment and sound integrity—leaders not in love with money, but in love with justice; leaders not in love with publicity, but in love with humanity; leaders who can subject their particular egos to the greatness of the cause. To paraphrase Holland's words:

> God give us leaders!
> A time like this demands strong minds, great hearts,
> true faith and ready hands;
> Leaders whom the lust of office does not kill;
> Leaders whom the spoils of life cannot buy;
> Leaders who possess opinions and a will;
> Leaders who have honor; leaders who will not lie;
> Leaders who can stand before a demagogue
> and damn his treacherous flatteries without winking!
> Tall leaders, sun crowned, who live above the fog
> in public duty and private thinking.

Finally, if we are to speed up the coming of the new age we must have the moral courage to stand up and protest against injustice wherever we find it. Wherever we find segregation we must have the fortitude to passively resist it. I realize that this will mean suffering and sacrifice. It might even mean going to jail. If such is the case we must be willing to fill up the jail houses of the South. It might even mean physical death. But if physical death is the price that some must pay to free their children from a permanent life of psychological death, then nothing could be more honorable. Once more it might well turn out that the blood of the martyr will be the seed of the tabernacle of freedom.

Someone will ask, how will we face the acts of cruelty and violence that might come as results of our standing up for justice? What will be our defense? Certainly it must not be retaliatory violence. We must find our defense in the amazing power of unity and courage that we have demonstrated in Montgomery. Our defense is to meet every act of violence toward an individual Negro with the facts that there are thousands of others who will present themselves in his place as potential victims. Every time one schoolteacher is fired for standing up courageously for justice, it must be faced with the fact that there are four thousand more to be fired. If the oppressors bomb the home of one Negro for his courage, this must be met with the fact that they must be required to bomb the homes of fifty thousand more Negroes. This dynamic unity, this amazing self-respect, this willingness to suffer, and this refusal to hit back will soon cause the oppressor to become ashamed of his own methods. He will be forced to stand before the world and his God splattered with the blood and reeking with the stench of his Negro brother.

There is nothing in all the world greater than freedom. It is worth paying for; it is worth losing a job; it is worth going to jail for. I would rather be a free pauper than a rich slave. I would rather die in abject poverty with my convictions than live in inordinate riches with the lack of self-respect. Once more every Negro must be able to cry out with his forefathers: "Before I'll be a slave, I'll be buried in my grave and go home to my Father and be saved."

If we will join together in doing all of these things we will be able to speed up the coming of the new world—a new world in which men will live together as brothers; as world in which men will beat their swords into ploughshares and their spears into pruning hooks; a world in which men will no longer take necessities from the masses to give luxuries to the classes; a world in which all men will respect the dignity and worth of all human personality. Then we will be able to sing from the great tradition of our nation:

> My Country 'tis of thee,
> Sweet land of liberty,
> Of thee I sing;
> Land where my fathers died;
> Land of the pilgrim's pride;
> From every mountain side
> Let Freedom ring!

This must become literally true. Freedom must ring from every mountainside. Yes, let it ring from the snow-capped Rockies of Colorado, from the prodigious hilltops of New Hampshire, from the mighty Alleghenies of Pennsylvania, from the curvaceous slopes of California. But not only that. Let freedom ring from every mountainside—from every molehill in Mississippi, from Stone Mountain of Georgia, from Lookout Mountain of Tennessee, yes, and from every hill and mountain of Alabama. From every mountainside let freedom ring. When this day finally comes, "The morning stars will sing together and the sons of God will shout for joy."

*Phylon* 28 (April 1957): 24–34.

# 25

# The Rising Tide
# of Racial Consciousness

*This is an abridged version of a speech that Dr. King gave at the Golden Anniversary Conference of the National Urban League.*

What are the factors that have led to this new sense of dignity and self-respect on the part of the Negro? First, we must mention the population shift from rural to urban life. For many years the vast majority of Negroes were isolated on the rural plantation. They had very little contact with the world outside their geographical boundaries. But gradually circumstances made it possible and necessary for them to migrate to new and larger centers—the spread of the automobile, the Great Depression, and the social upheavals of the two world wars. These new contacts led to a broadened outlook. These new levels of communication brought new and different attitudes.

A second factor that has caused the Negroes' new self-consciousness has been rapid educational advance. Over the years there has been a steady decline of crippling illiteracy. At emancipation only five percent of the Negroes were literate; today more than ninety-five percent are literate. Constant streams of Negro students are finishing colleges and universities every year. More than sixteen hundred Negroes have received the highest academic degree bestowed by an American university. These educational advances have naturally broadened his thinking. They have given the Negro not only a larger view of the world, but also a larger view of himself.

A third factor that produced the new sense of pride in the Negro was the gradual improvement of his economic status. While the Negro is still the victim of tragic economic exploitation, significant strides have been made. The annual collective income of the Negro is now approximately eighteen billion dollars, which is more than the national income of Canada and all of the exports of the United States. This augmented purchasing power has been reflected in more adequate housing, improved medical care, and greater educational opportunities. As these changes have taken place they have driven the Negro to change his image of himself.

A fourth factor that brought about the new sense of pride in the Negro was the Supreme Court's decision outlawing segregation in the public schools. For all men of good will May 17, 1954, came as a joyous daybreak to end the long night of enforced segregation. In simple, eloquent, and unequivocal language the court affirmed that "separate but equal" facilities are inherently unequal and that to segregate a child on the basis of his race is to deny that child equal protection of the law. This decision brought hope to millions of disinherited Negroes who had formerly dared only to dream of freedom. Like an exit sign that suddenly appeared to one who had walked through a long and desolate corridor, this decision came as a way out of the darkness of segregation. It served to transform the fatigue of despair into the buoyancy of hope. It further enhanced the Negro's sense of dignity.

A fifth factor that has accounted for the new sense of dignity on the part of the Negro has been the awareness that his struggle for freedom is a part of a worldwide struggle. He has watched developments in Asia and Africa with rapt attention. On these vast prodigious continents dwell two-thirds of the world's people. For years they were exploited economically, dominated politically, segregated and humiliated by foreign powers. Thirty years ago there were only three independent countries in the whole of Africa—Liberia, Ethiopia, and South Africa. By 1962, there may be as many as thirty independent nations in Africa. These rapid changes have naturally influenced the thinking of the American Negro. He knows that his struggle for human dignity is not an isolated event. It is a drama being played on the stage of the world with spectators and supporters from every continent.

## DETERMINATION AND RESISTANCE

This growing self-respect has inspired the Negro with a new determination to struggle and sacrifice until first-class citizenship becomes a reality. This is at bottom the meaning of what is happening in the South today. Whether it is manifested in nine brave children of Little Rock walking through jeering and hostile mobs, or fifty thousand people of Montgomery, Alabama, substituting tired feet for tired souls and walking the streets of that city for 381 days, or thousands of courageous students electrifying the nation by quietly and nonviolently sitting at lunch counters that have been closed to them because of the color of their skin, the motivation is always the same—the Negro would rather suffer in dignity than accept segregation in humiliation.

This new determination on the part of the Negro has not been welcomed by some segments of the nation's population. In some instances it has collided with tenacious and determined resistance. This resistance has risen at times to ominous proportions. A few states have reacted in open defiance. The legislative halls of the South ring loud with such words as "interposition" and "nullification." Many public officials are going to the absurd and fanatical extreme of closing the schools rather than to comply with the law of the land. This resistance to the Negroes' aspirations expresses itself in the resurgence of the Ku Klux Klan and the birth of White Citizens Councils.

The resistance to the Negroes' aspirations expresses itself not only in obvious methods of defiance, but in the subtle and skillful method of truth distortion. In an attempt to influence the minds of northern and southern liberals, the segregationists will cleverly disseminate half-truths. Instead of arguing for the validity of segregation and racial inferiority on the basis of the Bible, they set their arguments on cultural and sociological grounds. The Negro is not ready for integration, they say; because of academic and cultural lags on the part of the Negro, the integration of schools will pull the white race down. They are never honest enough to admit that the academic and cultural lags in the Negro community are themselves the result of segregation and discrimination. The best way to solve any problem is to remove the cause. It is both rationally unsound and sociologically untenable to use the tragic effects of segregation as an argument for its continuation.

The great challenge facing the nation today is to solve this pressing problem and bring into full realization the ideals and dreams of our democracy. How we deal with this crucial situation will determine our political health as a nation and our prestige as a leader of the free world. The price that America must pay for the continued oppression of the Negro is the price of its own destruction. The hour is late; the clock of destiny is ticking out. We must act now! It is a trite yet urgently true observation that if America is to remain a first-class nation, it cannot have second-class citizens.

Our primary reason for bringing an end to racial discrimination in America must not be the Communist challenge. Nor must it be merely to appeal to Asian and African peoples. The primary reason for our uprooting racial discrimination from our society is that it is morally wrong. It is a cancerous disease that prevents us from realizing the sublime principles of our Judeo-Christian tradition. Racial discrimination substitutes an "I-it" relationship for the "I-thou" relationship. It relegates persons to the status of things. Whenever racial discrimination exists it is a tragic expression of man's spiritual degeneracy and moral bankruptcy. Therefore, it must be removed not merely because it is diplomatically expedient, but because it is morally compelling.

## A NATIONAL PROBLEM

The racial issue that we confront in America is not a sectional but a national problem. Injustice anywhere is a threat to justice everywhere. Therefore, no American can afford to be apathetic about the problem of racial justice. It is a problem that meets every man at his front door.

There is need for strong and aggressive leadership from the federal government. There is a pressing need for a liberalism in the North that is truly liberal, that firmly believes in integration in its own community as well as in the deep South. There is need for the type of liberal who not only rises up with righteous indignation when a Negro is lynched in Mississippi, but will be equally incensed when a Negro is denied the right to live in his neighborhood, or join his professional association, or secure a top position in his business. This is no day to pay mere lip service to integration; we must pay life service to it.

There are several other agencies and groups that have significant roles to play in this all-important period of our nation's history; the problem of racial injustice is so weighty in detail and broad in extent that it requires the concerted efforts of numerous individuals and institutions to bring about a solution.

## THE PRIMARY RESPONSIBILITY

In the final analysis if first-class citizenship is to become a reality for the Negro he must assume the primary responsibility for making it so. The Negro must not be victimized with the delusion of thinking that others should be more concerned than himself about his citizenship rights.

In this period of social change the Negro must work on two fronts. On the one hand we must continue to break down the barrier of segregation. We must resist all forms of racial injustice. This resistance must always be on the highest level of dignity and discipline. It must never degenerate to the crippling level of violence. There is another way—a way as old as the insights of Jesus of Nazareth and as modern as the methods of Mahatma Gandhi. It is a way not for the weak and cowardly but for the strong and courageous. It has been variously called passive resistance, nonviolent resistance, or simply Christian love. It is my great hope that, as the Negro plunges deeper into the quest for freedom, he will plunge deeper into the philosophy of nonviolence. As a race we must work passionately and unrelentingly for first-class citizenship, but we must never use second-class methods to gain it. Our aim must be not to defeat or humiliate the white man, but to win his friendship and understanding. We must never become bitter nor should we succumb to the temptation of using violence in the struggle, for if this happens, unborn generations will be the recipients of a long and desolate night of bitterness and our chief legacy to the future will be an endless reign of meaningless chaos.

I feel that this way of nonviolence is vital because it is the only way to reestablish the broken community. It is the method which seeks to implement the just law by appealing to the conscience of the great decent majority who through blindness, fear, pride, or irrationality have allowed their consciences to sleep.

The nonviolent resisters can summarize their message in the following simple terms: we will take direct action against injustice without waiting for other agencies to act. We will not obey unjust laws or submit to unjust practices. We will do this peacefully, openly, and cheerfully because our aim is to persuade. We adopt the means of nonviolence because our end is a community at peace with itself. We will try to persuade with our words, but, if our words fail, we will try to persuade with our acts. We will always be willing to talk and seek fair compromise, but we are ready to suffer when necessary and even risk our lives to become witnesses to the truth as we see it.

I realize that this approach will mean suffering and sacrifice. It may mean going to jail. If such is the case the resister must be willing to fill the jail houses of the South. It may even mean physical death. But if physical death is the price that a man must pay to free his children and his white brethren from a permanent death of the spirit, then nothing could be more redemptive. This is the type of soul force that I am convinced will triumph over the physical force of the oppressor.

This approach to the problem of oppression is not without successful precedent. We have the magnificent example of Gandhi who challenged the might of the British Empire and won independence for his people by using only the weapons of truth, noninjury, courage, and soul force. Today we have the example of thousands of Negro students in the South who have courageously challenged the principalities of segregation. These young students have taken the deep groans and the passionate yearnings of the Negro people and filtered them in their own souls and fashioned them in a creative protest which is an epic known all over our nation. For the last few months they have moved in a uniquely meaningful orbit imparting light and heat to distant satellites. Through their nonviolent direct action they have been able to open hundreds of formerly segregated lunch counters in almost eighty cities. It is no overstatement to characterize these events as historic. Never before in the United States has so large a body of students spread a struggle over so great an area in pursuit of a goal of human dignity and freedom. I am convinced that future historians will have to record this student movement as one of the greatest epics of our heritage.

Let me mention another front on which we must work that is equally significant. The Negro must make a vigorous effort to improve his personal standards. The only answer that we can give to those who through blindness and fear would question our readiness and capability is that our lagging standards exist because of the legacy of slavery and segregation, inferior schools, slums, and second-class citizenship, and not because of an inherent inferiority. The fact that so many Negroes have made lasting and significant contributions to the cultural life of America in spite of these crippling restrictions is sufficient to refute all of the myths and half-truths disseminated by the segregationist.

Yet we cannot ignore the fact that our standards do often fall short. One of the sure signs of maturity is the ability to rise to the point of self-criticism. We have been affected by our years of economic deprivation and social isolation. Some Negroes have become cynical and disillusioned. Some have so conditioned themselves to the system of segregation that they have lost that creative something called *initiative*. So many have used their oppression as an excuse for mediocrity. Many of us live above our means, spend money on nonessentials and frivolities, and fail to give to serious causes, organizations, and educational institutions that so desperately need funds. Our crime rate is far too high.

## CONSTRUCTIVE ACTION

Therefore there is a pressing need for the Negro to develop a positive program through which these standards can be improved. After we have analyzed the sociological and psychological causes of these problems, we must seek to develop a constructive program to solve them. We must constantly stimulate our youth to rise above the stagnant level of mediocrity and seek to achieve excellence in their various fields of endeavor. Doors are opening now that were not open in the past, and the great challenge facing minority groups is to be ready to enter these doors as they open. No greater tragedy could befall us at this hour but that of allowing new opportunities to emerge without the concomitant preparedness to meet them.

We must make it clear to our young people that this is an age in which they will be forced to compete with people of all races and nationalities. We cannot aim merely to be good Negro teachers, good Negro doctors, or good Negro skilled laborers. We must set out to do a good job irrespective of race. We must seek to do our life's work so well that nobody could do it better. The Negro who seeks to be merely a good Negro, whatever he is, has already flunked his matriculation examination for entrance into the university of integration.

This then must be our present program: nonviolent resistance to all forms of racial injustice, even when this means going to jail; and bold, constructive action to end the demoralization caused by the legacy of slavery and segregation. The nonviolent struggle, if conducted with the dignity and courage already shown by the sit-in students of the South, will in itself help end the demoralization; but a new frontal assault on the poverty, disease, and ignorance of a people too long deprived of the God-given rights of life, liberty, and the pursuit of happiness will make the victory more certain.

We must work assiduously and with determined boldness to remove from the body politic this cancerous disease of discrimination which is preventing our democratic and Christian health from being realized. Then and only then will we be able to bring into full realization the dream of our American democracy—a dream yet unfulfilled. A dream of equality of opportunity, of privilege and property widely distributed; a dream of a land where men will not take necessities from the many to give luxuries to the few; a dream of a land where men to not argue that the color of a man's skin determines the content of his character; a dream of a place where all our gifts and resources are held not for ourselves alone but as instruments of service for the rest of humanity; the dream of a country where every man will respect the dignity and worth of all human personality, and men will dare to live together as brothers—that is the dream. Whenever it is fulfilled we will emerge from the bleak and desolate midnight of man's inhumanity to man into the bright and glowing daybreak of freedom and justice for all of God's children.

*YWCA Magazine* (December 1960): 4–6.

# 26

# Equality Now: The President Has the Power

*This was the first annual report that Dr. King printed in the* Nation *on the state of the civil rights movement.*

The new administration has the opportunity to be the first in one hundred years of American history to adopt a radically new approach to the question of civil rights. It must begin, however, with the firm conviction that the principle is no longer in doubt. The day is past for tolerating vicious and inhuman opposition on a subject which determines the lives of twenty million Americans. We are no longer discussing the wisdom of democracy over monarchism—and we would not permit hoodlum royalists to terrorize the streets of our major cities or the legislative halls of our states. We must decide that in a new era, there must be new thinking. If we fail to make this positive decision, an awakening world will conclude that we have become a fossil nation, morally and politically; and no floods of refrigerators, automobiles or color television sets will rejuvenate our image.

The second element in a new approach is the recognition by the federal government that it has sufficient power at its disposal to guide us through the changes ahead. The intolerably slow pace of civil rights is due at least as much to the limits which the federal government has imposed on its own actions as it is to the actions of the segregationist opposition.

If we examine the total of all judicial, executive and legislative acts of the past three decades and balance them against the sum needed to achieve fundamental change, two startling conclusions are inescapable. The first is the hopeless inadequacy of measures adopted—pitifully insufficient in scope and limited in conception. The second conclusion is even more disturbing. Federal action has been not only inadequate; viewed as a whole, it has also been self-nullifying. In 1954, the Supreme Court declared school segregation to be unconstitutional. Yet, since then federal executive agencies and vast federal legislative programs have given millions of dollars yearly to educational institutions which continue to violate the Supreme Court decision.

Further, the federal government collects taxes from all citizens, Negro and white, which it is Constitutionally obligated to use for the benefit of all; yet, billions of these tax dollars have gone to support housing programs and hospital and airport construction in which discrimination is an open and notorious practice. Private firms which either totally exclude Negroes from the work force, or place them in discriminatory status, receive billions of dollars annually in government contracts. The federal government permits elections and seats representatives in its legislative chambers in disregard of the fact the millions of Negro citizens have no vote. It directly employs millions in its various agencies and departments, yet its employment practices, especially in Southern states, are rife with discrimination.

These illustrations can be multiplied many times. The shocking fact is that while the government moves sluggishly, and in patchwork fashion, to achieve equal rights for all citizens, in the daily conduct of its own massive economic and social activities it participates directly and indirectly in the denial of these rights. We must face the tragic fact that the federal government is the nation's highest investor in segregation.

Therefore, a primary goal of a well-meaning administration should be a thorough examination of its own operations and the development of a rigorous program to wipe out immediately every vestige of federal support and sponsorship of discrimination. Such a program would serve not only to attack the problem centrally, where results can be produced, but collaterally to educate and influence the whole American populace, especially in the deep South of massive resistance. It would also be the first step in the evolution of federal leadership to guide the entire nation to its new democratic goals.

There is impressive precedent in recent history for massive governmental mobilization to create new conditions. As a consequence of economic crisis in the early thirties, the federal government, under the leadership of President Kennedy's party, undertook to change fundamental economic relationships. Every person in the nation was affected. In a bewilderingly brief period, wages were regulated at new levels, unemployment insurance created, relief agencies set up, public works planned and executed. Regulatory legislation covering banking, the stock market and money market was immediately enacted. Laws protecting trade-union organization were brought into being and administrative agencies to interpret and enforce the labor laws were created. Along with this broad assault on the depression went an educational campaign to facilitate the changes in public psychology requisite to the acceptance of such formidable alternatives to old thought patterns. The nation which five years earlier viewed federal intervention on any level as collectivism or socialism, in amazingly swift transition, supported the new role of government as appropriate and justified.

These breathtaking, fundamental changes took place because a leadership emerged that was both determined and bold, that rejected inhibitions imposed by old traditions and habits. It utilized all agencies and organs of government in a massive drive to change a situation which imperiled the very existence of our society.

Viewed in this light, an administration with good will, sincerely desirous of eliminating discrimination from American life, could accomplish its goal by mobilizing the immense resources of the organs of government and throwing them into every area where the problem appears. There are at least three vital areas in which the president can work to bring about effective solutions.

First, there is the legislative area. The president could take the offensive, despite southern opposition, by fighting for a really far-reaching legislative program. With resolute presidential leadership, a majority in both houses could be persuaded to pass meaningful laws. A determined majority-party leadership possesses the means to carry the reluctant along—and to hasten the end of the political careers, or the privileges, of those who prove unyielding. The influence the president can exert upon Congress when, with crusading zeal, he summons support from the nation has been demonstrated more than once int he past.

An example of an area in which a vigorous president could significantly influence Congress is that of voter registration. The Civil Rights Commission has revealed that "many Negro American citizens find it difficult, and often impossible, to vote." It went on to assert that these voting denials are accomplished through the creation of legal impediments, administrative obstacles, and the fear of economic reprisal and physical harm. A truly decisive president would work passionately and unrelentingly to change these shameful conditions. He would take such a creative general proposal as that made by the Civil Rights Commission of 1959 on Federal Registrars to insure the right to vote, and would campaign "on the Hill" and across the nation until Congress acted. He would also have the courage to insist that, in compliance with the Fourteenth Amendment, a state's representation in Congress be reduced in proportion to the number of citizens denied the right to vote because of race.

This approach would help us eliminate the defeatist psychology engendered by the alliance of dixiecrats and northern reactionaries in Congress. The same alliance, existing in even greater strength, failed in the past to stop legislation that altered patterns just as deeply embedded in American mores as racial discrimination. It is leadership and determination that counts—and these have been lacking of recent years.

A second area in which the president can make a significant contribution toward the elimination of racial discrimination is that of moral persuasion. The president is the embodiment of the democratic personality of the nation, both domestically and internationally. His own personal conduct influences and educates. If he were to make it known that he would not participate in any activities in which segregation exists, he would set a clear example for Americans everywhere, of every age, on a simple, easily understood level.

The calling of White House conferences of Negro and white leaders could be extremely useful. The president could serve the great purpose of opening the channels of communication between the races. Many white southerners who, for various reasons, fear to meet with Negro leaders in their own communities would participate unhesitatingly in a biracial conference called by the president.

It is appropriate to note here that, even in the hard-core South, a small but growing number of whites are breaking with the old order. These people believe in the morality as well as the constitutionality of integration. Their still, small voices often go unheard amid the louder shouts of defiance, but they are active in the field. They often face problems of ostracism and isolation as a result of their stand. Their isolation and difficulties would be lessened if they were among the invitees to the White House to participate in a conference on desegregation.

No effort to list the president's opportunities to use the prestige of his office to further civil rights could be adequate; from fireside chats to appearances at major events, the list is endless. All that is needed at the outset is a firm resolve to make the presidency a weapon for this democratic objective; the opportunities would then arise by themselves.

But beyond the legislative area and the employment of presidential prestige, a weapon of overwhelming significance lies in the executive itself. It is no exaggeration to say that the president could give segregation its death blow through a stroke of the pen. The power inherent in executive orders has never been exploited; its use in recent years has been microscopic in scope and timid in conception.

Historically, the executive has promulgated orders of extraordinary range and significance. The Emancipation Proclamation was an executive order. The integration of the armed forces grew out of President Truman's Executive Order 8891. Executive orders could require the immediate end to all discrimination in any housing accommodations financed with federal aid. Executive orders could prohibit any contractor dealing with any federal agency from practicing discrimination in employment by requiring (a) cancellation of existing contracts, (b) and/or barring violators from bidding, (c) and/or calling in of government loans of federal funds extended to violators, (d) and/or requiring renegotiation of payment to exact financial penalties where violations appear after performance of a contract. With such effective penalties, enforcement of fair employment practices would become self-imposed by those enjoying billions of dollars in contracts with federal agencies.

An executive order could also bring an immediate end to the discriminatory employment policies of federal agencies and departments. It is no secret that, despite statutes to the contrary, Negroes are almost totally excluded from skilled, clerical and supervisory jobs in the federal government. A recent report of the President's Committee on Government Employment states: "That there is discrimination in federal employment is unquestionably true." A basic reason for this is that there have never been any sanctions imposed for violations of the law. In a real sense, a president can eliminate discrimination in federal employment, just as it was eliminated in the military services, by setting up adequately staffed committees with authority to punish those who violate official government policy from the inside.

We can easily see how an end to discriminatory practices in federal agencies would have tremendous value in changing attitudes and behavior patterns. If, for instance, the law enforcement personnel in the FBI were integrated, many persons who now defy federal law, might come under restraints from which they are presently free. If other law enforcement agencies under the Treasury Department, such as the Internal Revenue Service, the Bureau of Narcotics, the Alcohol Tax Unit, the Secret Service and Customs had an adequate number of field agents, investigators and administrators who were Negro, there would be a greater respect for Negroes as well as the assurance that prejudicial behavior in these agencies toward citizens would cease.

Another area in which an executive order can bring an end to a considerable amount of discrimination is that of health and hospitalization. Under the Hill-Burton Act, the federal government grants funds to the states for the construction of hospitals. Since this program began in 1948, more than one hundred million dollars a year has gone to the states in direct aid. The government also makes grants to the states for mental health, maternal and child-care services, and for programs designed to control tuberculosis, cancer, and heart disease. In spite of this sizable federal support, it is a known fact that most of the federally financed and approved health and hospitalization programs in the South are operated on a segregated basis. In many instances, the southern Negroes are denied access to them altogether.

The president could wipe out these shameful conditions almost overnight by simply ordering his Secretary of Health, Education and Welfare not to approve grants to states whose plans authorize segregation or denial of service on the basis of race. This type of sanction would bring even the most recalcitrant southerners into line.

There is hardly any area in which executive leadership is needed more than in housing. Here the Negro confronts the most tragic expression of discrimination; he is consigned to ghettos and overcrowded conditions. And here the North is as guilty as the South.

Unfortunately, the federal government has participated directly and indirectly in the perpetuation of housing discrimination. Through the Federal Housing Administration (FHA), the Public Housing Administration (PHA), Urban Renewal Administration (URA), and the Veterans Administration Loan Program, the federal government makes possible most of the building programs in the United States. Since its creation in 1934, the FHA alone has insured more than thirty-three billion dollars in mortgages involving millions of homes. As a result of PHA programs, more than two million people presently live in more than two thousand low-rent housing projects in forty-four states and the District of Columbia. The URA, which was established in 1954 to help cities eliminate slum and blighted areas, has approved projects in more than 877 localities. The GI Bill of Rights authorizes the Veterans Administration to make loans outright to veterans for the construction of homes. This program has become so extensive that there have been years in which thirty percent of all new urban dwelling units were built with the help of VA loan guarantees.

While most of these housing programs have anti-discrimination clauses, they have done little to end segregated housing. It is a known fact that FHA continues to finance private developers who openly proclaim that none of their homes will be sold to Negroes. The urban renewal program has, in many instances, served to accentuate, even to initiate, segregated neighborhoods. (Since a large percentage of the people to be relocated are Negroes, they are more than likely to be relocated in segregated areas.)

A president seriously concerned about this problem could direct the housing administrator to require all participants in federal housing programs to agree to a policy of "open occupancy." Such a policy could be enforced by (a) making it mandatory for all violators to be excluded from future participation in federally financed housing programs and (b) by including a provision in each contract giving the government the right to declare the entire mortgage debt due and payable upon breach of the agreement.

These are merely illustrations of acts possible of multiplication in many other fields.

Executive policy could reshape the practices and programs of other agencies and departments whose activities affect the welfare of millions. The Department of Health, Education and Welfare could be directed to coordinate its resources to give special aid in those areas of the country where assistance might change local attitudes. The department could give valuable assistance to local school boards without any additional legislative enactments.

The Department of Agriculture—which doubtless considers civil rights issues as remote from its purview—could fruitfully reappraise its present operations with a view to taking certain steps that require no new legislative powers. The department could be of tremendous assistance to Negro farmers who are now denied credit simply because of their desire to exercise their citizenship rights. To wipe out this kind of discrimination would be to transform the lives of hundreds of thousands of Negroes on the land. A department zealous to implement democratic ideals might become a source of security and help to struggling farmers rather than a symbol of hostility and discrimination on the federal level.

A Justice Department that is imbued with a will to create justice has vast potential. The employment of powerful court orders, enforced by sizable numbers of federal marshals, would restrain lawless elements now operating with inexcusable license. It should be remembered that in early American history it was the federal marshal who restored law in frontier communities when local authority broke down.

In the opinion of many authorities executive power, operating through the attorney general, opens many hitherto untried avenues for executive action in the field of school desegregation. There are existing laws under which the attorney general could go into court and become a force in the current school struggles. Atrophy is not alone a medical phenomenon; it has its counterpart in social and political life. Long years of ignoring this area of law and executive power have led, indeed, to atrophy; nothing is done, nothing is studied, though new situations arise constantly where existing laws could reasonably be utilized.

Space will not permit a spelling out of all the measures by which every federal body could contribute to the enforcement of civil rights. This is the task of a master plan. Nor is it necessary to detail a legislative program, nor to list still unused powers inherent in the judiciary. Justices J. Skelley Wright and W. A. Bootle in Louisiana and Georgia respectively have given examples of the ability of a single federal district judge to handle the unconstitutional maneuverings of state legislatures.

The purpose of this review is to emphasize that a recognition of the potentials of federal power is a primary necessity if the fight for full racial equality is to be won. With it, however, must go another indispensable factor—the recognition by the government of its moral obligation to solve the problem.

A recent visit to India revealed to me the vast opportunities open to a government determined to end discrimination. When it confronted the problem of centuries-old discrimination against the "untouchables," India began its thinking at a point that we have not yet reached. Probing its moral responsibilities, it concluded that the country must atone for the immense injustices imposed upon the untouchables. It therefore made provision not alone for equality, but for special treatment to enable the victims of discrimination to leap the gap from backwardness to competence. Thus, millions of rupees are set aside each year to provide scholarships, financial grants and special employment opportunities for the untouchables. To the argument that this is a new form of discrimination inflicted upon the majority population, the Indian people respond by saying that this is their way of atoning for the injustices and indignities heaped in the past upon their seventy million untouchable brothers.

Although discrimination has not yet been eliminated in India, the atmosphere there differs sharply from that in our country. In India, it is a crime punishable by imprisonment to practice discrimination against an untouchable. But even without this coercion, so successfully has the government made the issue a matter of moral and ethical responsibility that no government figure or political leader on any level would dare defend discriminatory practices. One could wish that we here in the United States had reached this level of morality.

To coordinate the widespread activities on the civil rights front, the president should appoint a Secretary of Integration. The appointee should be of the highest qualifications, free from partisan political obligations, imbued with the conviction that the government of the most powerful nation on earth cannot lack the capacity to accomplish the rapid and complete solution to the problem of racial equality.

These proposals for federal action do not obviate the necessity for the people themselves to act, of course. An administration of good faith can be strengthened immeasurably by determined popular action. This is the great value of the nonviolent direct-action movement that has engulfed the South. On the one hand, it gives large numbers of people a method of securing moral ends through moral means. On the other hand, it gives support and stimulation to all those agencies which have the power to bring about meaningful change. Thousands of courageous students, sitting peacefully at lunch counters, can do more to arouse the administration to positive action than all of the verbal and written commentaries on governmental laxity put together.

When our government determines to ally itself with those of its citizens who are crusading for their freedom within our borders, and lends the might of its resources creatively and unhesitatingly to the struggle, the blight of discrimination will begin rapidly to fade.

History has thrust upon the present administration an indescribably important destiny—to complete a process of democratization which our nation has taken far too long to develop, but which is our most powerful weapon for earning world respect and emulation. How we deal with this crucial problem of racial discrimination will determine our moral health as individuals, our political health as a nation, our prestige as a leader of the free world. I can think of few better words for the guidance of the new administration than those which concluded the 1946 report of the President's Commission on Civil Rights: "The United States is not so strong, the final triumph of the democratic ideal not so inevitable that we can ignore what the world thinks of us or our record." These words are even more apt today than on the day they were written.

Nation 192 (4 February 1961): 91–95. The Nation Magazine, Nation Associates, Inc. © 1961.

# 27

# The Time for Freedom
# Has Come

*A new generation of black youth became so committed to the cause for black free-*
*dom that they courageously went to jail to demonstrate their determination.*
*Many abandoned their middle-class disdain for civil disobedience. They came to*
*view arrest for the sake of liberation as a mark of honor. Dr. King here explained*
*why that was the case.*

On a chill morning in the autumn of 1956, an elderly, toilworn Negro
woman in Montgomery, Alabama, began her slow, painful four-mile
walk to her job. It was the tenth month of the Montgomery bus boycott,
which had begun with a life expectancy of one week. The old woman's
difficult progress led a passerby to inquire sympathetically if her feet
were tired. Her simple answer became the boycotter's watchword. "Yes,
friend, my feet is real tired, but my soul is rested."

Five years passed and once more Montgomery arrested the world's attention. Now the symbolic segregationist is not a stubborn, rude bus
driver. He emerges in 1961 as a hoodlum stomping the bleeding face of
a freedom rider. But neither is the Negro today an elderly woman whose
grammar is uncertain; rather, he is college-bred, Ivy League-clad,
youthful, articulate and resolute. He has the imagination and drive of
the young, tamed by discipline and commitment. The nation and the
world have reacted with astonishment at these students cast from a new
mold, unaware that a chain reaction was accumulating explosive force
behind a strangely different facade.

Generating these changes is a phenomenon Victor Hugo described in
these words: "There is no greater power on earth than an idea whose
time has come." In the decade of the sixties the time for freedom for
the Negro has come. This simple truth illuminates the motivations, the
tactics and the objectives of the students' daring and imaginative
movement.

The young Negro is not in revolt, as some have suggested, against a
single pattern of timid, fumbling, conservative leadership. Nor is his
conduct to be explained in terms of youth's excesses. He is carrying forward a revolutionary destiny of a whole people consciously and deliber-

ately. Hence the extraordinary willingness to fill the jails as if they were honors classes and the boldness to absorb brutality, even to the point of death, and remain nonviolent. His inner strength derives from his goal of freedom and the leadership role he has grasped even at a time when some of his white counterparts still grope in philosophical confusion searching for a personal goal with human values, searching for security from economic instability, and seeking relief from the haunting fear of nuclear destruction.

The campuses of Negro colleges are infused with a dynamism of both action and philosophical discussion. The needs of a surging period of change have had an impact on all Negro groups, sweeping away conventional trivialities and escapism.

Even in the thirties, when the college campus was alive with social thought, only a minority was involved in action. Now, during the sit-in phase, when a few students were suspended or expelled, more than one college saw the total student body involved in a walkout protest. This is a change in student activity of profound significance. Seldom, if ever, in American history has a student movement engulfed the whole student body of a college.

In another dimension, an equally striking change is altering the Negro campuses. Not long ago the Negro collegian imitated the white collegian. In attire, in athletics, in social life, imitation was the rule. For the future, he looked to a professional life cast in the image of the middle-class white professional. He imitated with such energy that Gunnar Myrdal described the ambitious Negro as "an exaggerated American."

Today the imitation has ceased. The Negro collegian now initiates. Groping for unique forms of protest, he created the sit-ins and freedom rides. Overnight his white fellow students began to imitate him. As the movement took hold, a revival of social awareness spread across campuses from Cambridge to California. It spilled over the boundaries of the single issue of desegregation and encompassed questions of peace, civil liberties, capital punishment and others. It penetrated the ivy-covered walls of the traditional institutions as well as the glass and stainless-steel structures of the newly-established colleges.

A consciousness of leadership, a sense of destiny have given maturity and dedication to this generation of Negro students which have few precedents. As a minister, I am often given promises of dedication. Instinctively I examine the degree of sincerity. The striking quality in Negro students I have met is the intensity and depth of their commitment. I am no longer surprised to meet attractive, stylishly dressed young girls whose charm and personality would grace a junior prom and to hear them declare in unmistakably sincere terms, "Dr. King, I am ready to die if I must."

Many of the students, when pressed to express their inner feelings, identify themselves with students in Africa, Asia and South America.

The liberation struggle in Africa has been the greatest single international influence on American Negro students. Frequently I hear them say that if their African brothers can break the bonds of colonialism, surely the American Negro can break Jim Crow.

African leaders such as President Kwame Nkrumah of Ghana, Governor General Nnamdi Azikiwe of Nigeria, Dr. Tom Mboya of Kenya and Dr. Hastings Banda of Nyasaland are popular heroes on most Negro college campuses. Many groups demonstrated or otherwise protested when the Congo leader, Patrice Lumumba, was assassinated. The newspapers were mistaken when they interpreted these outbursts of indignation as "Communist-inspired."

Part of the impatience of Negro youth stems from their observation that change is taking place rapidly in Africa and other parts of the world, but comparatively slowly in the South. When the United States Supreme Court handed down its historic desegregation decision in 1954, many of us, perhaps naively, thought that great and sweeping school integration would ensue. Yet, today, seven years later, only seven percent of the Negro children of the South have been placed in desegregated schools. At the current rate it will take ninety-three more years to desegregate the public schools of the South. The collegians say, "We can't wait that long" or simply, "We won't wait!"

Negro students are coming to understand that education and learning have become tools for shaping the future and not devices of privilege for an exclusive few. Behind this spiritual explosion is the shattering of a material atom.

The future of the Negro college student has long been locked within the narrow walls of limited opportunity. Only a few professions could be practiced by Negroes and, but for a few exceptions, behind barriers of segregation in the North as well as the South. Few frustrations can compare with the experience of struggling with complex academic subjects, straining to absorb concepts which may never be used, or only half-utilized under conditions insulting to the trained mind.

A Negro intern blurted out to me shortly after his patient died, "I wish I were not so well trained because then I would never know how many of these people need not die for lack of proper equipment, adequate post-operative care and timely admission. I'm not practicing good medicine. I'm presiding over tragedies which the absence of good medicine creates."

The Negro lawyer knows his practice will bulk large with criminal cases. The law of wills, of corporations, of taxation will only infrequently reach his office because the clientele he serves has had little opportunity to accumulate property. In his courtroom experience in the South, his clients and witnesses will probably be segregated and he, as well as they, will seldom be referred to as "Mister." Even worse, all too often he knows that the verdict was sealed the moment the arrest was made.

These are but a few examples of the real experience of the Negro professional, seen clearly by the student who has been asked to study with serious purpose. Obviously his incentive has been smothered and weakened. But today, more than ever, the Negro realizes that, while studying, he can also act to change the conditions which cripple his future. In the struggle to desegregate society he is altering it directly for himself as well as for future generations.

There is another respect in which the Negro student is benefiting, and simultaneously contributing to, society as a whole. He is learning social responsibility; he is learning to earn, through his own direct sacrifice, the result he seeks. There are those who would make him soft, pliable and conformist—a mechanical organization man or an uncreative status seeker. But the experience of Negro youth is as harsh and demanding as that of the pioneer on the untamed frontier. Because his struggle is complex, there is no place in it for the frivolous or rowdy. Knowledge and discipline are as indispensable as courage and self-sacrifice. Hence the forging of priceless qualities of character is taking place daily as a high moral goal is pursued.

Inevitably there will emerge from this caldron a mature man, experienced in life's lessons, socially aware, unafraid of experimentation and, most of all, imbued with the spirit of service and dedication to a great ideal. The movement therefore gives to its participants a double education—academic learning from books and classes, and life's lessons from responsible participation in social action. Indeed, the answer to the quest for a more mature, educated American, to compete successfully with the young people of other lands, may be present in this new movement.

Of course, not every student in our struggle has gained from it. This would be more than any humanly designed plan could realize. For some, the opportunity for personal advantage presented itself and their character was not equal to the challenge. A small percentage of students have found it convenient to escape from their own inadequacies by identifying with the sit-ins and other activities. They are, however, relatively few because this is a form of escape in which the flight from responsibility imposes even greater responsibilities and risks.

It is not a solemn life, for all of its seriousness. During a vigorous debate among a group of students discussing the moral and practical soundness of nonviolence, a majority rejected the employment of force. As the minority dwindled to a single student, he finally declared, "All I know is that, if rabbits could throw rocks, there would be fewer hunters in the forest."

This is more than a witty remark to relieve the tensions of serious and even grim discussion. It expresses some of the pent-up impatience, some of the discontent and some of the despair produced by minute corrections in the face of enormous evil. Students necessarily have conflicting reactions. It is understandable that violence presents itself as a quick, effective answer for a few.

For the large majority, however, nonviolent, direct action has emerged as the better and more successful way out. It does not require that they abandon their discontent. This discontent is a sound, healthy social response to the injustice and brutality they see around them. Nonviolence offers a method by which they can fight the evil with which they cannot live. It offers a unique weapon which, without firing a single bullet, disarms the adversary. It exposes his moral defenses, weakens his morale, and at the same time works on his conscience.

Another weapon which Negro students have employed creatively in their nonviolent struggle is satire. It has enabled them to avoid corrosive anger while pressing the cutting edge of ridicule against the opponent. When they have been admonished to "go slow," patiently to wait for gradual change, with a straight face they will assure you that they are diligently searching for the happy medium between the two extremes of moderation and gradualism.

It is perhaps the special quality of nonviolent direct action, which sublimates anger, that explains why so few students are attracted to extreme nationalist sects advocating black supremacy. The students have anger under controlling bonds of discipline. Hence they can answer appeals for cooling-off periods by advocating cooling-off for those who are hot with anger and violence.

Much has been made of the willingness of these devotees of nonviolent social action to break the law. Paradoxically, although they have embraced Thoreau's and Gandhi's civil disobedience on a scale dwarfing any past experience in American history, they do respect law. They feel a moral responsibility to obey just laws. But they recognize that there are also unjust laws.

From a purely moral point of view, an unjust law is one that is out of harmony with the moral law of the universe. More concretely, an unjust law is one in which the minority is compelled to observe a code that is not binding on the majority. An unjust law is one in which people are required to obey a code that they had no part in making because they were denied the right to vote.

In disobeying such unjust laws, the students do so peacefully, openly and nonviolently. Most important, they willingly accept the penalty, whatever it is, for in this way the public comes to reexamine the law in question and will thus decide whether it uplifts or degrades man.

This distinguishes their positon on civil disobedience from the "uncivil disobedience" of the segregationist. In the face of laws they consider unjust, the racists seek to defy, evade and circumvent the law, and they are unwilling to accept the penalty. The end result of their defiance is anarchy and disrespect for the law. The students, on the other hand, believe that he who openly disobeys a law, a law conscience tells him is unjust, and then willingly accepts the penalty, gives evidence thereby that he so respects that law that he belongs in jail until it is changed. Their appeal is to the conscience.

Beyond this, the students appear to have perceived what an older generation overlooked in the role of law. The law tends to declare rights—it does not deliver them. A catalyst is needed to breathe life experience into a judicial decision by the persistent exercise of the rights until they become usual and ordinary in human conduct. They have offered their energies, their bodies to effect this result. They see themselves the obstetricians at the birth of a new order. It is in this manner that the students have related themselves to and materialized "the idea whose time has come."

In a sense, the victories of the past two years have been spectacular and considerable. Because of the student sitters, more than 150 cities in the South have integrated their lunch counters. Actually, the current breakthroughs have come about partly as a result of the patient legal, civil and social ground clearing of the previous decades. Then, too, but slowly, the national government is realizing that our so-called domestic race relations are a major force in our foreign relations. Our image abroad reflects our behavior at home.

Many liberals, of the North as well as the South, when they list the unprecedented programs of the past few years, yearn for a "cooling-off" period; not too fast, they say, we may lose all that we have gained if we push faster than the violent ones can be persuaded to yield.

This view, though understandable, is a misreading of the goals of the young Negroes. They are not after "mere tokens" of integration ("tokenism," they call it); rather theirs is a revolt against the whole system of Jim Crow and they are prepared to sit-in, kneel-in, wade-in and stand-in until every waiting room, rest room, theatre and other facility throughout the nation that is supposedly open to the public is in fact open to Negroes, Mexicans, Indians, Jews or what have you. Theirs is total commitment to this goal of equality and dignity. And for this achievement they are prepared to pay the costs—whatever they are—in suffering and hardship as long as may be necessary.

Indeed, these students are not struggling for themselves alone. They are seeking to save the soul of America. They are taking our whole nation back to those great wells of democracy which were dug deep by the Founding Fathers in the formulation of the Constitution and the Declaration of Independence. In sitting down at the lunch counters, they are in reality standing up for the best in the American dream. They courageously go to the jails of the South in order to get America out of the dilemma in which she finds herself as a result of the continued existence of segregation. One day historians will record this student movement as one of the most significant epics of our heritage.

But should we, as a nation, sit by as spectators when the social unrest seethes? Most of us recognize that the Jim Crow system is doomed. If so, would it not be the wise and human thing to abolish the system surely and swiftly? This would not be difficult, if our national government would exercise its full powers to enforce federal laws and court decisions and do so on a scale commensurate with the problems and with an unmistakable decisiveness. Moreover, we would need our religious, civic and economic leaders to mobilize their forces behind a real, honest-to-goodness "End Jim Crow Now" campaign.

This is the challenge of these young people to us and our ideals. It is also an expression of their new-found faith in themselves as well as in their fellow man.

In an effort to understand the students and to help them understand themselves, I asked one student I know to find a quotation expressing his feeling of our struggle. He was an inarticulate young man, athletically expert and far more poetic with a basketball than with words, but few would have found the quotation he typed on a card and left on my desk early one morning:

*I sought my soul, but my soul I could not see,*
*I sought my God, but he eluded me,*
*I sought my brother, and I found all three.*

---

# 28

# In A Word: Now

*The foreboding tone of this 1963 article reflects the depressing degree to which the forces that opposed racial justice became increasingly entrenched. Governor George Wallace of Alabama signaled how stubborn white racists had become in his inaugural address: "I draw the line in the dust and toss the gauntlet before the feet of tyranny, and I say segregation now, segregation tomorrow, segregation forever." From March through April, Dr. King led demonstrations in Birmingham, Alabama. From 3 to 5 May, the nation witnessed the horror of the police brutality against the demonstrators when the infamous Eugene ("Bull") Connor, Birmingham's public safety director, kept ordering his officers to turn fire hoses and police dogs against the young adults and children who marched in these demonstrations. The television cameras captured the stark ugliness of white racism. By 20 May, the U.S. Supreme Court ruled that the segregation ordinances of Birmingham were unconstitutional. But Governor Wallace and other segregationists became more determined. Wallace stood in front of the door of the University of Alabama rather than allow black students to register. President John Fitzgerald Kennedy "federalized" the Alabama National Guard to ensure compliance with the court order mandating that these students be admitted. Other segregationists were not as open as Wallace. In the darkness of the early morning hours, one of them fired a rifle into the home of Medgar Evers, a veteran civil rights leader, and killed him instantly. Despite these events and riots in black ghettos such as Harlem, Dr. King and other major black civil rights leaders led the historic March on Washington on 28 August. Soon after the beautiful mall stretching between the Lincoln Memorial and the Washington Monument was cleared of the debris left by thousands of inspired marchers, four little black girls were killed by a time bomb as they were attending Sunday school at the Sixteenth Street Baptist Church in Birmingham, Alabama.*

Victor Hugo once said that progress is the mode of man; that when it is blocked, just as an obstacle in a river makes the water foam, so an obstacle to progress makes humanity seethe.

Any plan for the future, therefore, which seeks to calm troubled waters will have to sweep barriers away, rather than pour oil over turbulent tides.

The hundreds of thousands who marched in Washington marched to level barriers. They summed up everything in a word—NOW. What is the content of NOW?

Everything, not some things, in the president's civil rights bill is part of NOW.

Immediate and effective federal action to curb the shocking police brutality in the South is an urgent part of NOW. Just lately, the Department of Justice has indicted leaders of the civil rights movement in Albany, Georgia, and Birmingham, Alabama, alleging that false statements were made under oath. This zealousness to punish Negroes for statements is in sharp contrast to the inaction of the same department in hundreds of cases of extreme police brutality.

The right to vote is part of NOW. To walk unafraid to the ballot box and cast a free vote remains still a myth in most of the South.

Unemployment is a form of brutality, especially violent for those who live on the edge of poverty. Negroes have twice as much of it as others. NOW means jobs, FEPC training, leveling obstacles of discrimination and the creation of new jobs by public works.

These are some of the imperatives of NOW. If they are met, the passionate determination Negroes have recently made so manifest can be mellowed without being compromised. Then slower, long-range planning can begin.

The far-reaching solutions for lifting the "weight of centuries" will necessarily involve systematic liquidation of ghetto life, loans and grants to provide equal opportunities for the unequally equipped, adult education, remedial clinics for damaged families and individuals and integrated housing construction on a scale commensurate with the extent of slums, rather than with the extent of budgets.

The present spontaneous, largely disorganized and spasmodic methods of piecemeal approaches, differing from city to city, and with a variety of tempos, will have to give way to broad national planning. A nation which could put more than eleven million men in arms in a few short years, which poured torrents of sophisticated munitions from hundreds of thousands of coordinated facilities and deployed them in war, has the capacity to master a problem of much less complexity. It needs only the same will it possessed when it felt its existence threatened.

The long-deferred issue of second-class citizenship has become our nation's first-class crisis. We can deal with it now, or we can drive a seething humanity to a desperation it tried, asked and hoped to avoid.

*New York Times Magazine* (29 September 1963): 91–92.

# 29

# Hammer on Civil Rights

*This was Dr. King's fourth annual report on the state of the civil rights struggle.*

Exactly one hundred years after Abraham Lincoln wrote the Emancipation Proclamation for them, Negroes wrote their own document of freedom in their own way. In 1963, the civil rights movement coalesced around a technique for social change, nonviolent direct action. It elevated jobs and other economic issues to the summit, where earlier it had placed discrimination and suffrage. It thereby forged episodic social protest into the hammer of social revolution.

Within a few months, more than one thousand American cities and towns were shaken by street demonstrations, and more than twenty thousand nonviolent resisters went to jail. Nothing in the Negro's history, save the era of Reconstruction, equals in intensity, breadth and power this matchless upheaval. For weeks it held spellbound, not only this country, but the entire world. What had moved the nation's foundations was a genuinely new force in American life. Negro power had matured and was dynamically asserting itself.

The impact of this new strength, expressed on a new level, means among other things that the civil rights issue can never again be thrust into the background. There will not be "One hundred years of litigation," that cynical threat of the segregationists. Nor will there be easy compromises which divert and stagnate the movement. The problem will now be faced and solved or it will without pause torment and agonize the political and social life of the nation.

In the past two decades, the contemporary world entered a new era characterized by multifaceted struggles for human rights. Continents erupted under the pressures of a billion people pressing in from the past to enter modern society. In nations of both the East and the West, long-established political and social structures were fissured and changed. The issues of human rights and individual freedom challenged forms of government as dissimilar as those of the Soviet Union, colonial Africa, Asia, Latin America and the United States.

The Negro freedom movement reflects this world upheaval within the United States. It is a component of a world era of change, and that is the source of its strength and durability. Against this background the civil rights issue confronts the Eighty-eighth Congress and the presidential campaign of 1964.

Earlier civil rights legislation was cautiously and narrowly drawn, designed primarily to anticipate and avoid Negro protest. It had a double and contradictory objective: to limit change and yet to muffle protest. The earlier legislation was conceived and debated under essentially calm conditions. The bill now pending in Congress is the child of a storm, the product of the most turbulent motion the nation has ever known in peacetime.

Congress has already recognized that this legislation is imbued with an urgency from which there is no easy escape. The new level of strength in the civil rights movement is expressed in plans it has already formulated to intervene in the congressional deliberations at the critical and necessary points. It is more significantly expressed in plans to guarantee the bill's implementation when it is enacted. And reserve plans exist to exact political consequences if the bill is defeated or emasculated.

As had been foreseen, the bill survived intact in the House. It has now moved to the Senate, where a legislative confrontation reminiscent of Birmingham impends. Bull Connor became a weight too heavy for the conscience of Birmingham to bear. There are men in the Senate who now plan to perpetuate the injustices Bull Connor so ignobly defended. His weapons were the high-pressure hose, the club and the snarling dog; theirs is the filibuster. If America is as revolted by them as it was by Bull Connor, we shall emerge with a victory.

The keys to victory in Birmingham were the refusal to be intimidated; the indomitable spirit of Negroes to endure; their willingness to fill the jails; their ability to love their children—and take them by the hand into battle; to leave on that battlefield six murdered Negro children, to suffer the grief, and resist demoralization and provocation by violence.

Argument will inevitably be made that in the Senate cloture is the only weapon available to subdue the filibuster. And cloture requires that a two-thirds majority be mustered before a simple majority can legislate. In thirty-five years, the only time that cloture has been successfully invoked was against a fragile liberal group opposed by the administration regulars and almost the entire Republican delegation. That is hardly a convincing precedent for the success of cloture in the present fight.

On the other hand, if proponents of the civil rights measure will adopt some of the burning spirit of this new period, they can match their tenacity with that of the filibusterers. The dixiecrats can be worn down by an endurance that surpasses theirs. What one group of men dedicated to a dying cause can do, another group, if they are as deeply committed to justice, should be able to do. When the southern obstructionists find themselves at the end of their physical and moral resources, cloture may be employed gently to end their misery.

It is not too much to ask, 101 years after Emancipation, that senators who must meet the challenge of the filibuster do so in the spirit of the heroes of Birmingham. They must avoid the temptation to compromise the bill as a means of ending the filibuster. They can use the Birmingham method by keeping the Senate in continuous session, by matching the ability of the segregationists to talk with their capacity to outlast them. Nonviolent action to resist can be practiced in the Senate as well as in the streets.

There could be no more fitting tribute to the children of Birmingham than to have the Senate for the first time in history bury a civil rights filibuster. The dead children cannot be restored, but living children can be given a life. The assassins who still walk the streets will still be unpunished, but at least they will be defeated.

The important point is that if the filibuster is not beaten by a will to wear it out, the dixiecrats will be justified in believing that they face, not an implacable adversary, but merely a nagging opponent. Negroes are not going to be satisfied with half a loaf of the legislation now pending. The civil rights forces in the Senate will have to find the strength to win a full victory. Anything less will be regarded as a defeat in the context of today's political realities.

While attention is now properly focused on legislation, it is still useful to widen our perspective by stepping back a little. For the past several years Negro rights have been imperiled and impeded by a confusion of tactics. In the earlier years of the administration of President Kennedy, executive power was advocated as a more effective weapon than legislative action. It was argued then that laws existed, but were not adequately exercised; that a broad application of executive power could effect many significant changes. The Civil Rights Commission, easily the most underrated agency of government, began its life in political isolation because neither side respected it. In one of its early reports it declared that the federal government was the single heaviest financial supporter of segregation. Much of this evil, the commission indicated, could be cured by executive action.

President Kennedy did begin a new use of his presidential power by exposing the little-observed practices of many government bureaus. Changes of some significance began to alter the profile of certain agencies. His Committee on Fair Employment headed by then Vice President Johnson, opened jobs and upgraded opportunities for Negroes in many plants in the South. Though the tempo was slow and the goal distant, the direction was right.

President Kennedy, also, after considerable delay, issued an order prohibiting segregation in government-financed housing. It was conspicuously flawed with compromise and to this date has not significantly altered any housing patterns. Nevertheless, it was another example of the application of presidential power, and if timidity of conception or execution limited the effect, still a new path was chopped through the thicket. Alert and aggressive civil rights forces have an opportunity to pave a highway over it. These examples of executive action illustrate that gain is possible even in the absence of legislation.

However, before a serious drive was mounted in this direction, the unfolding of massive and revolutionary direct action restored legislation to the head of the list, and virtually all public attention has since focused on Congress.

Perhaps unintentionally, one method became posed against the other; the investigation and use of executive power receded as the legislative battle crowded into the limelight. But there is no reason why the civil rights movement should abandon one weapon as it flourishes another. It would amount to negligence to allow the creative use of executive power to wither because gains are possible on the legislative stage. More than that, when the legislation becomes law, its vitality and power will depend as much on its implementation as on the strength of its declarations.

Legislative enactments, like court decisions, declare rights, but do not automatically deliver them. Ultimately, executive action determines what force and effect legislation will have. The elusive benefit of legislation is illustrated by the fact that for some years federal law has authorized the appointment of federal registrars where voting rights are denied. Yet to date not one registrar has enrolled one voter from among the millions of eligible Negroes who remain disenfranchised. An even more striking example of executive vacuum, as Dr. Howard Zinn has pointed out, is that civil rights legislation passed in 1866 is still not enforced in the South. The United States Criminal Code Title 10, sections 241 and 242, make it a crime for officials to deprive persons of their constitutional rights, and for any persons to conspire to that end. The numberless violations of that law stand in sharp contrast to the infrequency with which the Justice Department has attempted to invoke it.

The simple fact is that federal law is so extensively defied in the South that it is no exaggeration to say that the federal union is barely a reality. For the southern Negro it is more a tragic myth. He has been exploited, jailed and even murdered, by deeds which federal writ can reach, but his oppression continues essentially unrelieved.

The most tragic and widespread violations occur in the areas of police brutality and the enforcement against the Negro of obviously illegal state statutes. For many white Americans in the North there is little comprehension of the grossness of police behavior and its wide practice. The Civil Rights Commission, after a detailed, scholarly and objective study, declared it to be one of the worst manifestations of the Negro's oppression. The public becomes aware of it only during episodes of nonviolent demonstration, and often concludes that what they have witnessed is an atypical incident of excessive conduct. That the behavior is habitual, not exceptional, is a fact little understood.

Police brutality, with community support, or at best indifference, is a daily experience for Negroes in all too many areas of the South. They live in a police state which, paradoxically, maintains itself within a democratic republic. Under these conditions, an occasional lawsuit by the federal government, which may drag for years through the courts, is no remedy. Indeed, it is sometimes worse than nothing. It demonstrates the futility and weakness of federal power.

People often wonder why southern demonstrations tend to sputter out after a vigorous beginning and heroic sacrifice. The answer, simply and inescapably, is that naked force has defeated the Negro. A ruling state apparatus, accustomed for generations to act with impunity against him, is able to employ every element of unchecked power. A slow-moving federal suit, or sporadic and frequently ineffectual federal mediation, is scarcely more adequate to support the Negro in such a one-sided engagement than would be a pat on the back.

Negroes have found nonviolent direct action to be a miraculous method of curbing force, but it is not a cure-all. When the glare of a thousand spotlights illuminates the misdeeds of southern police, their guns and clubs are temporarily muzzled. Yet so shameless are the mores of the feudal South that even in the presence of millions of witnesses police still employ such barbaric weapons as the cattle prod and the high-pressure hose. Moreover, when a deed can be cloaked in night, the depravity of conduct is bottomless. The blasting to death of four Sunday school children is such an example. Assassinations, mutilations, floggings and bombings are others.

When the armored car of the Birmingham police rumbled into the spotlight, it was regarded as a grotesque but rare example of local police power run wild. In the past weeks the mayor of Jackson, Mississippi, has boasted of the armor he has accumulated for next summer. It includes "Thompson's Tank," a thirteen-thousand-pound armored battle wagon, carrying a task force of twelve men armed with shotguns, tear gas and submachine guns. The mobile equipment also includes three troop lorries, two searchlight tanks and three giant trailer trucks, nearly five hundred men, plus a reserve pool of deputies, state troopers, civilian city employees and neighborhood citizen patrols. This local army awaits nonviolent demonstrators with undisguised hostility and the familiar trigger-happy eagerness for confrontation.

The inevitable conclusion is that as Negroes have marshaled extraordinary courage to employ nonviolent direct action, they have been left—by the most powerful federal government in the world—almost solely to their own resources to face a massively equipped army. They have endured violence to reveal their plight and to protest it; their government has been able to muster only the minimum courage and determination to aid them.

This contradiction cries out for resolution. Legislation, commissions, biracial committees, cannot change a community when those in the seats of power locally are aware that they can organize and employ force while the federal power temporizes. There are governments in some areas of the world today that have no effective control in some regions of their country. The United States a century ago did not have control of areas dominated by unsubdued Indian tribes. But we are nearing the year 2000 and our national power almost defies description. Yet it cannot enforce elementary law even in a dusty rural southern village.

It is not my intention, in presenting these stark facts, to make a blanket condemnation of this administration or its predecessor. The Kennedy administration initiated the pending bill and, at this writing, the Johnson administration has fought off weakening amendments. It would be not only unrealistic, but unfair, to ignore the complexities that face and frequently confound national leaders who have inherited a hundred years of evasions, compromises, and malevolence. Nevertheless, to understand difficulties should not be a preparation for surrendering to them.

Along with the fight to add legislation to the law books, the intolerable conditions of the South require that the administration look in a new way to its powers and their use. The president and the heads of every relevant agency should allocate the time to study the question; they should literally throw away the key to the room until answers are uncovered.

An example of the creative innovations that might be forthcoming is the assignment in recent years of federal marshals in situations unsuitable for troops. Earlier, no one had thought of using the marshals as a civil rights measure. Yet the federal marshal is well known even to school children; he attained legendary fame in the taming of the West and is exalted today in books, movies and television.

It is a challenge to wonder what the organization of a marshal's corps might do to bring law into the South. Up to now, however creative the idea to use them may have been, they have too often been hastily withdrawn and their recruitment revealed as an emergency measure with no thought that they might remain on the scene for as long as resistance to law required.

Above all, the federal government must not overlook the fact that the heroics of some southern officials are more impressive for stagecraft than for determination. The battle-clad brigades are designed to terrorize Negroes and to generate alarming illusions of warfare in the timid onlookers, North and South. They will not freeze the blood of Negroes who have cast out their fears. They should not intimidate a federal power that has not hesitated to commit its forces on fronts around the world.

Still another example of creative search through the legal corridors of the federal law was the discovery that the Interstate Commerce Commission had power to require desegregation of interstate buses and terminals. This right of law in support of the freedom ride movement made possible a relative degree of progress; at the same time, a project that had been born to violence ended in peaceful victory.

Finally, many new elements of the South are as appalled by these histrionics as are citizens of the North. They would welcome the curbing of the updated, iron-booted Klansmen. There is genuinely a new South, but it cannot surface without the shelter of federal power and order. The dignity of the federal government would be radiantly enhanced if it arrayed a trained, self-confident force of federal marshals against these armed usurpers who have stomach for battle only with the unarmed and nonviolent.

The country abounds in specialists and experts in law enforcement. If the administration would summon to the White House a conference of experts to deliberate with the highest officials of government, it could not fail to produce practical and effective answers. The administration participants should include not only the president but also the National Security Council.

Some of the other participants in a White House session might be the heads of the Treasury law enforcement agencies. There is a need to know what is going on in conspiratorial racist circles. Many of the shocking bombings might have been avoided if such knowledge had been available. Something must certainly be done to capture those who have with utter impunity caused dozens of bombings across the South. The law enforcement agencies of Treasury are suggested because the Bureau of Narcotics is extensively experienced in working within secret groups and obtaining effective results. And the alcohol-tax unit of Internal Revenue is probably more familiar with the rural South than is any other agency, because for years it has been tracking down "moonshiners."

These examples are cited, not as outstanding or special, but to suggest that the scope of inquiry should be so wide that no possible key will be overlooked in the search for solutions. If determination is expressed at the highest level, and if it is realized that the prevalent lawlessness of the South must come to an end, the victory cannot fail. The massive power of the federal government, applied with imagination, can make this problem yield.

The necessity for a new approach to the executive power is not a matter of choice. The newfound strength of the civil rights movement will not vanish or wither. Negroes have learned the strength of their own power and will unleash it again and again. The surge of their revolution must inevitably engulf the nation once more, and if effective methods have not been devised, chaos can result from future confrontations dealt with indecisively. Now is the time to anticipate needs, not when the flames of conflict are raging. This is the lesson the past teaches us. This is the test to which concerned national leaders are put—not by civil rights leaders as such, but by conditions too brutal to be endured, and by justice too long delayed to be justified.

*Nation* 198 (9 March 1964): 230–34. The Nation Magazine, Nation Associates, Inc. © 1964.

# 30

# Negroes Are Not Moving Too Fast

*In the midst of the 1964 presidential campaign, many pundits warned that if the fast pace of the civil rights struggle was not slowed there would be a "white backlash." Dr. King responded to this fear.*

America is fortunate that the strength and militancy of Negro protest have been tempered by a sense of responsibility. This advantage can be dissipated if some current myths are not eliminated. The first such myth is that the Negro is going ahead too far, too fast. Another popular, erroneous idea is that the Negro will happily take whatever he can get, no matter how little. There also are dangerous myths about the "white backlash," which was so much talked about in the campaign just finished. And then there are myths about how the Negro riots occurred last summer. The white leadership—the power structure—must face up to the fact that its sins of omission and commission have challenged our policy of nonviolence.

Among many white Americans who have recently achieved middle-class status or regard themselves close to it, there is a prevailing belief that Negroes are moving too fast and that their speed imperils the security of whites. Those who feel this way refer to their own experience and conclude that while they waited long for their chance, the Negro is expecting special advantages from the government.

It is true that many white Americans struggle to attain security. It is also a hard fact that none had the experience of Negroes. No one else endured chattel slavery on American soil. No one else suffered discrimination so intensely or so long as the Negroes. In one or two generations the conditions of life for white Americans altered radically. For Negroes, after three centuries, wretchedness and misery still afflict the majority.

Anatole France one said, "The law, in its majestic equality, forbids all men to sleep under bridges—the rich as well as the poor." There could scarcely be a better statement of the dilemma of the Negro today. After a decade of bitter struggle, multiple laws have been enacted proclaiming his equality. He should feel exhilaration as his goal comes into sight.

But the ordinary black man knows that Anatole France's sardonic jest expresses a very bitter truth. Despite new laws, little has changed in his life in the ghettos. The Negro is still the poorest American—walled in by color and poverty. The law pronounces him equal, abstractly, but his conditions of life are still far from equal to those of other Americans.

More important than all of these facts is that the gap between Negroes and whites is not narrowing as so many believe. It is growing wider. The technological revolution expressed in automation and cybernetics is edging the Negro and certain poor whites into a socially superfluous role, into permanent uselessness and hopeless impoverishment.

In 1964, the nation's production has hit historic heights. Yet U.S. government statistics reveal that the unemployment rate of Negro youth averages thirty-three percent. In some of the northern ghettos the rate of unemployment of youth is fifty percent. These figures of unemployment dwarf even those of the depression of the 1930s, and they shed some light on why there was such a high proportion of young people in last summer's riots. Despair made them active participants.

Charges that Negroes are going "too fast" are both cruel and dangerous. The Negro is not going nearly fast enough, and claims to the contrary only play into the hands of those who believe that violence is the only means by which the Negro will get anywhere.

Another, more enduring myth is that the Negro has waited so long that any improvement will satisfy him. A beginning sincerely made is one thing, but a token beginning that is an end in itself is quite another thing, and Negroes will not be deluded into accepting one for the other. The tragedy of the present is that many newly prosperous Americans contemplate that the unemployable Negro shall live out his life in rural and urban slums, silently and apathetically. This thinking is wrong. Walter Lippmann has summed up the facts behind the folly in these words: "The Negro minority is too large to be subdued. . . . Negro grievances are too real, their cause too just, to allow the great white majority to acquiesce in the kind of terrorism and brutality that would be needed to silence them."

Federal, state and municipal governments toy with meager and inadequate solutions while the alarm and militancy of the Negro rises. A section of the white population, perceiving Negro pressure for change, misconstrues it as a demand for privileges rather than as a desperate quest for existence. The ensuing white backlash intimidates government officials who are already too timorous, and, when the crisis demands vigorous measures, a paralysis ensues.

And this exposes the folly of so much that has been said about the white backlash itself.

The most popular explanation for the backlash is that it is a response to Negro "aggressiveness" and "excessive demands." It is further attributed to an overzealous government which is charged with so favoring Negro demands that it has stimulated them beyond reason.

These are largely half-truths and, as such, whole lies. A multitude of polls conducted during the past two years reveals that even during the buildup of the white backlash, a majority of Americans approved the reforms Negroes have sought. The high point of white support occurred at the time of the historic march on Washington in 1963. Significantly, there was no white backlash then. Instead, there was respect and sympathy which resulted in substantial white participation in the Washington march. It is therefore demonstrable that militancy is not the basis for white resentment on a mass scale. Something happened after the summer of 1963 which must explain the backlash. It is here that Negro acts of commission and omission contributed to the ugly result in various communities.

Whites must bear the heaviest guilt for the present situation, but it would be both unwise and unjust to gloss over Negro culpability. In the first place, it must be admitted that the principal Negro leadership in effect abruptly abdicated, though not intentionally. For many years Negro actions had a sporadic quality, and as a result, the leadership neither planned ahead nor maintained itself at the helm at all times. All leaders, including myself, continued to work vigorously, but we failed to assert the leadership the movement needed. Into this vacuum there flowed less-experienced and frequently irresponsible elements. For month after month the initiative was held by these people, and the response of the main leadership was either a negative reaction or disdain.

The irresponsibles were free to initiate a new, distorted form of action. The principal distortion was the substitution of small, unrepresentative forces for the huge, mass, total-community movements we had always organized. Our reliance on mass demonstrations, intended to isolate and expose the evildoer by the mass presence of his victims, was a key element in our tactics. It showed to the white majority that Negroes in large numbers were committed and united. We also designed in each case a concrete program which was expressed in clear terms so that it might stand examination.

In contrast, the sporadic, fragmentary forays of the new groups had no perceptible objectives except to disrupt the lives of both Negroes and whites, including whites who were our friends and allies. When a mere handfull of well-intentioned but tragically misguided young people blocked the doorways to New York City's Board of Education, or threatened to stop traffic to the World's Fair, or charged into the streets to spread garbage, and to halt traffic on bridges, they were reducing the imposing grandeur of the movement to cheap chaos. The mass movement of millions was overnight exposed to ridicule and debasement.

On reflection, it was insufficient, at the time, for the principal leadership merely to withhold support of such conduct and perversion of our aims and methods. We were under a duty to attack it boldly and vigorously. Action is not in itself a virtue; its goals and its forms determine its value.

In a period of turbulence, mistakes, which under other circumstances might have been contained, are frequently made worse by unexpected developments. This occurred when some elements who had never been a part of the civil rights movement erupted in violence in the subways and on the streets in New York and other cities. The headlines of a sensation-seeking press enlarged essentially small events to the level of catastrophes.

These exaggerations obscured the fact that crime lives in the heart of all large cities. The irritating deeds of certain irresponsible civil rights forces, and the senseless violence in which the perpetrators were Negro, merged in the minds of many people. For a large section of the population, Negroes became a menace. The physical safety of people who must use the streets and subways is closer to them than the abstract questions of justice for a minority, however appalling its grievances. Civil rights leaders cannot control crime. They can control the demonstrations they initiate, however. They have a responsibility to maintain discipline and guidance that no one is able to confuse constructive protest with criminal acts, which all condemn.

The ghetto has hidden many things from whites, and not the least of these is the rampant racketeering that has a sanctuary in the slums and corrupts the ghetto's already miserable life. The mayors of troubled cities who look only into Negro excesses for the causes of unrest would do well to look critically into their own law enforcement agencies.

In 1963, at the time of the Washington march, the whole nation talked of Negro freedom and the Negro began to believe in its reality. Then shattered dreams and the persistence of grinding poverty drove a small but desperate group of Negroes into the swamp of senseless violence. Riots solved nothing, but they stunned the nation. One of the questions they evoked was doubt about the Negro's attachment to the doctrine of nonviolence.

Ironically, many important civic leaders began to lecture Negroes to adhere to nonviolence. It is important to recall that *Negroes* created the theory of nonviolence as it applies to American conditions. For years they fought within their own ranks to achieve its acceptance. They had to overcome the accusation that nonviolence counseled love for murderers. Only after dozens of Birminghams, large and small, was it acknowledged that it took more courage to employ nonviolent direct action than impetuous force.

Yet a distorted understanding of nonviolence began to emerge among white leaders. They failed to perceive that nonviolence can exist only in a context of justice. When the white power structure calls upon the Negro to reject violence but does not impose upon itself the task of creating necessary social change, it is in fact asking for submission to injustice. Nothing in the theory of nonviolence counsels this suicidal course.

The simple fact is that there cannot be nonviolence and tranquility, without significant reforms of the evils that endangered the peace in the first place. It is the effort of the power structure to benefit from nonviolence without yielding meaningful change that is responsible for the rise of elements who would discredit it.

Is the dilemma impossible for resolution? The best course for the Negro happens to be the best course for whites as well and for the nation as a whole.

There must be a grand alliance of Negro and white. This alliance must consist of the vast majorities of each group. It must have the objective of eradicating social evils which oppress both white and Negro. The unemployment which afflicts one third of Negro youth also affects over twelve and one-half percent of white youth. It is not only more moral for both races to work together but more logical.

One argument against a grand alliance holds that the shortage of jobs creates a natural climate of competition which tends to divide, not unify. If those who need jobs regard them as bones thrown to hungry animals, a destructive competition would seem inevitable. However, Negroes certainly do not want nor could they find the path to freedom by taking jobs from the white man. Instead, they want the white man to collaborate with them in making new jobs. This is the key point. Our economy, our resources are well able to provide full employment.

It has also been argued that while alliances for economic advancement can be achieved, several "subjective questions" such as housing and schools will be more stubborn. But these questions are based upon myth, not reality. Just as Negroes would be foolish to seek to overcome ninety percent of the population by organizing their ten percent in hostile combat, whites would be equally foolish to think that the Negroes' ten percent is capable of crowding the schools and neighborhoods of ninety percent.

The majority of Negroes want an alliance with white Americans to tackle the social injustices that afflict *both* of them. If a few Negro extremists and white extremists manage to divide their people, the tragic result will be the ascendancy of extreme reaction which exploits all people. For some Americans deluded by myths, the candidacy of a Goldwater seemed a solution for their ills. Essentially he identified big government, radicalism and bureaucracy as the cause of all evils. Civil rights legislation, in his view, is not a social necessity—it is merely oppressive big government. He ignored the towering presence of discrimination and segregation, but vividly exaggerated crime in the streets. The poverty of the Negroes, he implied, is due to want of ambition and industry. The picture that emerged to delight the racist was that of undeserving, shiftlesss, criminally dangerous radicals who have manipulated government for their selfish ends, but whose grievances are largely fanciful, and will wither away if left to the states.

Our nation has absorbed many minorities from all nations of the world. In the beginning of this century, in a single decade, almost nine million immigrants were drawn into our society. Many reforms were necessary—labor laws and social welfare measures—to achieve this result. We accomplished these changes in the past because there was a will to do it, and because the nation became greater and stronger in the process. Our country has the need and capacity for further growth, and today there are enough Americans, Negro and white, with faith in the future, with compassion, and will to repeat the bright experience of our past.

*Saturday Evening Post* 237 (7 November 1964): 8–9.

# 31

# Civil Right No. 1: The Right to Vote

*This article appeared in the Sunday, 14 March 1965, issue of the* New York Times. *President Johnson delivered his historic address on his pending Voting Rights Bill the next day.*

Few people in America realize the seriousness of the burden imposed upon our democracy by the disenfranchisement of Negroes in the Deep South. In Mississippi only about twenty-six thousand out of a voting-age population of some 450,000 Negroes have been allowed to register. The situation in Alabama and Louisiana is almost as bad, though previous state administrations of a more liberal inclination did permit the registration of approximately 150,000 Negro voters in Louisiana and 111,000 in Alabama. In recent years, however, under Wallace in Alabama and former governor Jimmy Davis of Louisiana, the plan has been to freeze Negro registration at a level which can be successfully negated by sure segregationist voting strength.

This has led to a crisis not only for the Negro in the South but for Negroes in the swollen ghettos of the North. Northern cities are inheriting the results of northern indifference to southern racism and exploitation as the victims of oppression migrate there in search of freedom. If they had had the ballot, Negroes might have had a chance to lead a decent life in their southern homelands, where many owned small plots of land and participated in a stable pattern of community life that at least promised survival and a minimum of emotional security. This is more than is promised by the slums of New York, Chicago and other cities, which are already teeming with bitterness and constantly kept at boiling point by the misery of rats, filth, unemployment and *de facto* segregation.

But the evils of disenfranchisement burden our cities in other ways as well as by mass migration. Southern seniority in Congress, resting as it does on the "whites only" ballot box, maintains power in the hands of our nation's most reactionary politicians. Bills providing for the welfare of our nation, from Medicare to education, must run the gauntlet of southern power before they are enacted—and many never are.

Voting as a badge of full citizenship has always had a special meaning to the Negro, but in 1965 the denial of the right to vote cuts painfully and deeply into his new sense of personal dignity. It is salt on his wounded pride. For today he looks beyond the borders of his own land and sees the decolonization and liberation of Africa and Asia; he sees colored peoples, yellow, black and brown, ruling over their own new nations. He sees colored statesmen voting on vital issues of war and peace at the United Nations at a time when he is not even permitted to vote for the office of sheriff in his local county.

In 1964, however, the Negro voter participated as a significant partner in a ballot landslide that repudiated a Republican party which had allowed itself to be captured by racism and reaction. He was the key to the Democratic victory in several southern states, and he thereby proved that voting is more than a badge of citizenship and dignity—it is an effective tool for change.

Voting is the foundation stone for political action. With it the Negro can eventually vote out of office public officials who bar the doorway to decent housing, public safety, jobs and decent integrated education. It is now obvious that the basic elements so vital to Negro advancement can only be achieved by seeking redress from government at local, state, and federal levels. To do this the vote is essential.

When the full power of the ballot is available to my people, it will not be exercised merely to advance our cause alone. We have learned in the course of our freedom struggle that the needs of twenty million Negroes are not truly separable from those of the nearly two hundred million whites and Negroes in America, all of whom will benefit from a color-blind land of plenty that provides for the nourishment of each man's body, mind and spirit. Our vote would place in Congress true representatives of the people who would legislate for the Medicare, housing, schools and jobs required by all men of any color.

In Selma, Alabama, thousands of Negroes are courageously providing dramatic witness to the evil forces that bar our way to the all-important ballot box. They are laying bare for all the nation to see, for all the world to know, the nature of segregationist resistance. The ugly pattern of denial flourishes with insignificant differences in thousands of Alabama, Louisiana, Mississippi and other southern communities. Once it is exposed, and challenged by the marching feet of Negro citizens, the nation will take action to cure this cancerous sore. What is malignant in Selma must be removed by congressional surgery so that all citizens may freely exercise their right to vote without delays, harassment, economic intimidation and police brutality. Selma is to 1965 what Birmingham was to 1963.

The pattern of denial depends upon four main roadblocks. First, there is the Gestapo-like control of county and local government in the South by the likes of Sheriff Jim Clark of Selma, Alabama, and Sheriff

Rainey of Philadelphia, Mississippi. There is a carefully cultivated mystique behind the power and brutality of these men. The gun, the club and the cattle prod reinforce the fear that is the main barrier to voting—a barrier erected by 345 years' exposure to the psychology and brutality of slavery and legal segregation. It is a fear rooted in feelings of inferiority.

But the fear is also real, as the broken bodies and bloody heads of citizens in Selma and Marion bear witness. And the snakes placed on people standing in line were not hallucinations, as hundreds, including the press, can testify. Nor was it a sick imagination that conjured up the vision of a public official, sworn to uphold the law, who forced an inhuman march upon hundreds of Negro children; who ordered the Reverend James Bevel to be chained to his sickbed; who clubbed a Negro woman registrant, and who callously inflicted repeated brutalities and indignities upon nonviolent Negroes peacefully petitioning for their constitutional right to vote.

Would a fiction writer have the temerity to invent a character wearing a sheriff's badge at the head of a helmeted posse who punched a clergyman in the mouth and then proudly boasted: "If I hit him, I don't know it. One of the first things I ever learned was not to hit a nigger with your fist because his head is too hard. Of course, the camera might make me out to be a liar. I do have a sore finger."

Yet such a man actually exists in Sheriff Clark. He was voted into office in Dallas County by an electorate that includes only 635 out of fifteen thousand Negroes of voting age. In contrast, out of 14,440 whites of voting age, 9,543 have been registered. So far, thirty-four hundred Negroes have been arrested in Selma, placing ten times as many in Selma jails as are on the voters' roll.

The second factor in the pattern of Negro disenfranchisement is the abuse of local and state laws to impede the exercise of suffrage rights. Southern officials, knowing they cannot jail citizens for seeking the right to vote, instead claim that Negroes are guilty of other "offenses." In Selma, for instance, more than three thousand arrests have been made on such charges as "breach of peace," "contempt of court," "disorderly conduct," "unlawful assembly," "contributing to the delinquency of minors," and "criminal provocation."

Aside from the obvious intimidation involved in arrest and jail, three thousand Negro citizens now face years of expensive and frustrating litigation before these "charges" are defeated and their right to vote vindicated.

After so many years of intimidation, the Negro community has learned that its salvation lies in united action. When one Negro stands up, he is run out of town. But when a thousand stand up together the situation is drastically altered. Abuse of the law by local police power is expressly designed to frustrate such united action, and so long as these mass arrests are made on trumped-up "charges" the path to the registrar's office is obstructed.

The third factor in abridging Negro voting rights is the registrar himself, administering complex registration procedures designed specifically to slow up and frustrate Negro applicants. As Burke Marshall, former assistant attorney general in charge of the civil rights division, has pointed out:

"The Negro voting problem . . . is more than a legal issue. For it takes courage, patience and massive effort before a significant number of Negro residents are ready to break the pattern of their lives by attempting to register to vote, and when the effort is unsuccessful because of discrimination, delay, intimidation or of the failure of Negro applicants themselves, the promised federal rights again become illusory."

Where the will to keep Negro registration to a minimum is strong, Mr. Marshall said, "the latitude for discrimination is almost endless. The delaying practices that can be used are virtually infinite."

Using them, the white hierarchy of Selma has succeeded in limiting Negro registration to the snail's pace of about 145 persons a year. At this rate it would take about 103 years to register the fifteen thousand eligible Negro voters of Dallas County—not counting those who will reach voting age in that period or who may move into the county. A weapon for delay is the decision to open the registration office on only two days per month. Long lines of Negroes have waited without success merely to enter the office to apply for registration.

After thirteen private and government lawsuits were instituted, however, minimal corrective measures were ordered by Judge Daniel H. Thomas of the federal district court of Mobile. Although he found a "pattern of discrimination," he refused to order the registrar's office to open more frequently. Instead, he set up a new procedure containing many of the same seeds of discouragement and frustration. Negroes seeking to register may "sign up" on a public "appearance sheet," and a federal voting referee has now been appointed to process the applications. In the meantime every Negro who has signed the appearance sheet must be ready to endure an ordeal by economic retaliation and personal intimidation perfected by racists over many decades.

It is a shining tribute to Negro determination, therefore, that despite this harassment, including being made to wait in the pouring rain, 266 persons—most of them Negroes—completed their registration applications in Selma on March 1, an all-time record for the county.

But it must also be said that the concept of a federal referee appointed by the court looks good only on the surface. We happen to know something, for instance, about the referee appointed for adjacent Perry County. He has just about as discriminatory a record as the county-appointed registrar and we are already contesting his pattern of misconduct. He is a native of Greene County, which is also in the "black belt" and has as bitter a heritage of segregation as Perry and Dallas counties, with even fewer Negroes registered.

Moreover, the appointment of a voting referee provides no assurance of speedy processing for the thousands of applications that will flood his office. The act of 1960 that permitted the courts to appoint referees allows for a legal challenge to each person registered by the referee and thus offers ample opportunities for delay, which is the key to southern tactics.

Delays feed the dangers that beset Negroes. Every day means more murder and brutality, more suffering from inferior education, more dreary hours in the long night of economic exploitation and more of the deadly despair brought on by personal humiliation.

The whole program of delay can be appreciated if one recognizes that the white community is almost one hundred percent registered and eligible to vote whereas Negro voters are added almost one by one to the voters' roll. If it takes a century more to redeem the Fifteenth Amendment's promise, the white southern official could not care less.

The fourth roadblock on the way to Negro suffrage is the literacy test, administered by the registrars and designed to be difficult. The Justice Department has been able to establish in hundreds of counties that these tests are not administered fairly. There are many instances of "fair-skinned" Negroes and white persons being helped to register, while in Selma ministers and teachers have been rejected six and seven times. (An interesting sidelight on this is that Selma's deputy registrar handed out twenty or more vouchers for prospective voters on which the word was spelled "vocher.") Although a federal court has now ordered Selma to scrap a most technical and difficult literacy test, the order applies only to Selma, so that the legal battle will have to be waged county by county. Again, time is the enemy operating on the side of the "white only" ballot box.

It is surely ironical that the states which have labored so diligently to keep the Negro masses ignorant through inferior segregated education now require "literacy" as a prerequisite for voting. You hardly need much formal training to know who as sheriff will treat you like a human being and who will crack your skull!

The deliberate nature of our legal process is being abused. Legal redress for Negroes entails expensive court actions whose victories are the signal not for the capitulation of segregationists but rather for further bouts with new delaying tactics. Even the recent action of the attorney general in Alabama to strike at statewide measures, while welcome, cannot bring redress here and now. The delays inherent in test cases, where the U.S. Supreme Court must ultimately rule, make sadly pertinent the comment of Chief Justice Earl Warren in the school desegregation cases: "Justice delayed is justice denied."

Clearly, the heart of the voting problem lies in the fact that the machinery for enforcing this basic right is in the hands of state-appointed officials answerable to the very people who believe they can continue to wield power in the South only so long as the Negro is disenfranchised. No matter how many loopholes are plugged, no matter how many irregularities are exposed, it is plain that the federal government must withdraw this control from the states or else set up machinery for policing it effectively.

The patchwork reforms brought about by the laws of 1957, 1960, and 1964 have helped, but the denial of suffrage has gone on too long, has caused too deep a hurt for Negroes to wait out the time required by slow, piecemeal enforcement procedures. What is needed is the new voting rights legislation promised for this session of Congress.

As I told our people in Dallas County two weeks ago, "We are going to bring a voting bill into being in the streets of Selma. President Johnson has a mandate from the American people. He must go out and get a voting bill this time that will end the necessity for any more voting bills."

Certainly, no community in the history of the Negro struggle has responded with the enthusiasm of Selma and her neighboring town of Marion, Alabama. Where Birmingham depended largely upon students and unemployed adults, Selma has involved fully forty percent of the Negro population in active demonstrations, and at least half the Negro population of Marion was arrested on one day.

Seldom has there been so complete a representation of every facet of community life. Teachers and students, clergy and laity—all joined the long march of freedom. This is significant because it means that, once the demonstrations are over, a limited political organization will be left in being to direct the drive for votes and other rights. This could well be the pattern of the future, for it is plain that the 1964 Civil Rights Act has given new confidence to the nonviolent movement.

But it is also clear that the voting sections of the existing act are inadequate, as I have stressed in my recent meetings with President Johnson. I urge Congress to enact a voting rights bill including these basic principles:

(1) Registration machinery so automatic that it eliminates varying standards and undue discretion on the part of hostile state registrars, and requires only elementary biographical details from applicants. This was recommended by the U.S. Civil Rights Commission after it completed its studies in Alabama, Louisiana and the black belt.

(2) The abolition of literacy tests in those areas where Negroes have been disadvantaged by generations of inferior, segregated education.

(3) Application of the law to all elections, federal and state, and especially to local elections for sheriff, school boards, etc.

(4) Enforcement of the law by federal registrars appointed by and responsible to the president.

(5) Such legislation, while directed against oppressive areas like Selma, must be versatile enough to overcome more sophisticated resistance in cities like New Orleans, Chicago, New York or Miami.

One of the difficult lessons we have learned is that you cannot depend upon American institutions to function without pressure. Any real change in the status quo depends on continued creative action to sharpen the conscience of the nation and establish a climate in which even the most recalcitrant elements are forced to admit that change is necessary.

To this end, we are committed to keep up the pressure for the adoption of a civil rights act of 1965. We know that Americans of good will have learned that no nation can long continue to flourish or to find its way to a better society while it allows any one of its citizens, let alone vast numbers in eleven southern states, to be denied the right to participate in the most fundamental of all privileges of democracy—the right to vote.

At a time when the Supreme Court has said that the law of the land demands "one man, one vote," so that all state legislatures may be democratically structured, it would be a mockery indeed if this were not followed without delay by an insistence upon "one vote for every man."

*New York Times Magazine* (14 March 1965): 26–27ff.

# 32

# Next Stop: The North

*After the passage of the 1965 Voting Rights Bill on 6 August 1965, just days after the tragic riots in the Watts section of Los Angeles, California, SCLC sought to redirect its attention to the plight of urban African Americans.*

The flames of Watts illuminated more than the western sky; they cast light on the imperfections in the civil rights movement and the tragic shallowness of white racial policy in the explosive ghettos.

Ten years ago in Montgomery, Alabama, seething resentment caused a total Negro community to unite to level a powerful system of injustice. The nation and the world were electrified by their new method of struggle—mass, nonviolent direct action. In the succeeding years the power of this method shook the nation from its somnolence and complacency, changed embedded customs, wrote historic legislation, and gave a whole generation vibrant ideals. In the decade the arena widened, the conflict intensified, and the stakes rose in importance, yet the method was undeviatingly nonviolent.

Yet on the tenth anniversary of nonviolence as a theory of social change, with its success acknowledged and applauded around the world, a segment of a Negro community united to protest injustice, but this time by means of violence.

The paradox is striking, but it can be understood: our movement has been essentially regional, not national—the confrontation of opposing forces met in climactic engagements only in the South. The issues and their solution were similarly regional and the changes affected only the areas of combat.

It is in the South that Negroes in this past decade experienced the birth of human dignity—eating in restaurants, studying in schools, traveling in public conveyances side by side with whites for the first time in a century. Every day southern Negroes perceive, and are reminded of, the fruits of their struggle. The changes are not only dramatic but are cumulative and dynamic, moving constantly toward broader application.

In the North, on the other hand, the Negro's repellent slum life was altered not for the better but for the worse. Oppression in the ghettos intensified. To the homes of ten years ago, squalid then, were added ten years of decay. School segregation did not abate but increased. Above all, unemployment for Negroes swelled and remained unaffected by general economic expansion. As the nation, Negro and white, trembled with outrage at police brutality in the South, police misconduct in the North was rationalized, tolerated, and usually denied.

The northern ghetto dweller lived in a schizophrenic social milieu. He supported and derived pride from southern struggles and accomplishment. Yet the civil rights revolution appeared to be draining energy from the North, energy that flowed south to transform life there while stagnation blanketed northern Negro communities. It was a decade of role reversal. The North, heretofore vital, atrophied, and the traditionally passive South burst with dynamic vibrancy.

If the struggle had been on a national front, the changes in the North would have been kaleidoscopic. To match the South in relative change, the North in the decade should have been well on its way to the dissolution of ghettos; unemployment due to discrimination should have disappeared; tensions with the police should have been modified or eradicated by long-tested institutions, and interracial relationships should have been so commonplace that they should no longer have attracted comment or attention. In short, the North needed and was ready for profound progress and, relatively, the changes should have far surpassed those in the South. In fact, however, the North, at best, stood still as the South caught up.

Civil rights leaders had long thought that the North would benefit derivatively from the southern struggle. They assumed that without massive upheavals certain systematic changes were inevitable as the whole nation reexamined and searched its conscience. This was a miscalculation. It was founded on the belief that opposition in the North was not intransigent; that it was flexible and was, if not fully, at least partially hospitable to corrective influences. We forgot what we knew daily in the South—freedom is not given, it is won by struggle.

In my travels in the North I was increasingly becoming disillusioned with the power structures there. I encountered the tragic and stubborn fact that in virtually no major city was there a mayor possessing statesmanship, understanding, or even strong compassion on the civil rights question. Many of them sat on platforms with all the imposing regalia of office to welcome me to their cities, and showered praise on the heroism of southern Negroes. Yet when the issues were joined concerning local conditions only the language was polite; the rejection was firm and unequivocal. All my experience indicated that hope of voluntary understanding was chimerical; there was blindness, obtuseness, and rigidity that would only be altered by a dynamic movement. Ironically, Mayor Ivan Allen of Atlanta and many other southern public officials, with all their conflicts, came much further in human relations than mayors of the major northern cities. Many political leaders in the South had only yesterday been implacable segregationists but found the inner resources to change their convictions. More than that, they had the courage and integrity to speak bluntly to their constituents and furnished the leadership for them to make necessary constructive changes.

Another inescapable contrast is in the role of national and local governments. The national administrations increasingly became more and more responsive to pressures from the South. As our movement, pursuing techniques of creative nonviolence, encountered savage and brutal responses, all branches of the federal government moved to face the challenge with increasing responsibility and firmness. Beyond this, a deeper human understanding of underlying causes became clearer to them and a true sense of identity and alliance emerged. In the North, in marked contrast, municipal and state laws were enacted without passion or evident conviction. Feeble and anemic enforcement amid political machinations made them all but ineffectual. It was worse than tokenism; it was trifling with life-and-death issues with unfeeling clumsiness and opportunism.

What was the culpability of Negro leaders? Southern Negro leaders remained substantially regional forces although inspirationally they emerged as national figures. Further, they projected solutions principally for southern conditions in framing proposals for national legislation. Finally, they took more from the North in support than they put into it. They found themselves overwhelmed with the responsibility of a movement of revolutionary dimensions and could not assume national command even had their leadership been desired. Northern Negro leaders were content to support the South and many did so devotedly. Others tended to coast with gradualism because the issues being sought in the South had long been solved in the North.

The key error of both Negro and white leadership was in expecting the ghettos to stand still and in underestimating the deterioration that increasingly embittered its life.

The white population is a stranger to the ghetto. Negroes are not only hemmed in in it; whites are shut out of it.

Unemployment and pitiful wages are at the bottom of ghetto misery. Life-sapping poverty roots Negroes in the decayed tenements where rats and filth become inseparable parts of the structures. But dirt alone could not crush a people, especially those who are so widely employed in disposing of it. Unemployment and insecure employment more effectively undermine family life. Not only are the Negroes in general the first to be cast into the jobless army, but the Negro male precedes his wife in unemployment. As a consequence, he lives in a matriarchal society within the larger culture, which is patriarchal. The cruelest blow to his integrity as a man are laws which deprive a family of Aid to Dependent Children support if a male resides in the home. He is then forced to abandon his family so that they may survive. He is coerced into irresponsibility by his responsible love for his family. But even ensuring food on the table is insufficient to secure a constructive life for the children. They are herded into ghetto schools and pushed through grades of schooling without learning. Their after-school life is spent in neglected, filthy streets that abound in open crime. The most grievous charge against municipal police is not brutality, though it exists. Permissive crime in ghettos is the nightmare of the slum family. Permissive crime is the name for the organized crime that flourishes in the ghetto—designed, directed, and cultivated by white national crime syndicates operating numbers, narcotics, and prostitution rackets freely in the protected sanctuaries of the ghettos. Because no one, including the police, cares particularly about ghetto crime, it pervades every area of life. The Negro child who learns too little about books in his pathetic schools, learns too much about crime in the streets around him. Even when he and his family resist its corruption, its presence is a source of fear and of moral debilitation.

Against this caricature of the American standard of living is the immediate proximity of the affluent society. In the South there is something of shared poverty, Negro and white. In the North, white existence, only steps away, glitters with conspicuous consumption. Even television becomes incendiary when it beams pictures of affluent homes and multitudinous consumer products to an aching poor, living in wretched hovels.

In these terms Los Angeles could have expected riots because it is the luminous symbol of luxurious living for whites. Watts is closer to it, and yet farther from it, than any other Negro community in the country. The looting in Watts was a form of social protest very common through the ages as a dramatic and destructive gesture of the poor toward symbols of their needs.

Los Angeles could have expected the holocaust when its officials tied up federal aid in political manipulation; when the rate of Negro unemployment soared above the depression levels of the thirties; when the population density of Watts became the worst in the nation. Yet even these tormenting physical conditions are less than the full story. California in 1964 repealed its law forbidding racial discrimination in housing. It was the first major state in the country to take away gains Negroes had won at a time when progress was visible and substantial elsewhere, and especially in the South. California by this callous act voted for ghettos. The atrociousness of some deeds may be concealed by legal ritual, but their destructiveness is felt with bitter force by its victims. Victor Hugo understood this when he said, "If a soul is left in darkness, sins will be committed. The guilty one is not he who commits the sin, but he who causes the darkness."

Out of these many causes the Negro freedom movement will be altering its course in the period to come. Conditions in the North will come into focus and sharpened conflict will unfold.

The insistent question is whether that movement will be violent or nonviolent. It cannot be taken for granted that Negroes will adhere to nonviolence under any conditions. When there is rocklike intransigence or sophisticated manipulation that mocks the empty-handed petitioner, rage replaces reason. Nonviolence is a powerful demand for reason and justice. If it is rudely rebuked it is not transformed into resignation and passivity. Southern segregationists in many places yielded to it because they realized alternatives could be more destructive. Northern white leadership has relied too much on tokens, substitutes, and Negro patience. The end of this road is clearly in sight. The cohesive, potentially explosive Negro community in the North has a short fuse and a long train of abuses. Those who argue that it is hazardous to give warnings, lest the expression of apprehension lead to violence, are in error. Violence has already been practiced too often, and always because remedies were postponed. It is now the task of responsible people to indicate where and why spontaneous combustion is accumulating.

The southern Negro created mass nonviolent direct action and made history with it and will go on to far greater gains, holding it firmly as his peaceful sword.

The North, on the other hand, has for several years been spontaneously testing violence. There are many who are arguing that positive gains have followed riots. They hold that in the complexities of urban life the tricks of sophisticated segregation cannot be defeated except by the power of violence. They are so close to white society but so alienated from it and consumed with revulsion toward its hypocrisies that they are disinterested in integration. Black nationalism is more fitted to their angry mood.

I do not believe this thinking will dominate the movement, however. I think it will fail, not because northern Negroes will settle for a no-win tranquillity and calm; it will fail because they can be convinced there is a more effective method and a more moral one—nonviolent direct action.

This method has never been utilized on a large or protracted scale in the North. But in the South it will mobilize Negroes for action more effectively than appeals to violence. Ultimately rioting has the serious defect that it can be terminated by greater force. The number available for violence is relatively small and can be countered. Conversely, nonviolence can mobilize numbers so huge there is no counterforce. Its power is such that it can be sustained by the will of its supporters not merely for days but even for extended periods.

If one hundred thousand Negroes march in a major city to a strategic location, they will make municipal operations difficult to conduct; they will exceed the capacity of even the most reckless mayor to use force against them; and they will repeat this action daily, if necessary. Without harming persons or property they can draw as much attention to their grievances as the outbreak at Watts, and they will have asserted their unwavering determination while retaining their dignity and discipline.

The critical task will be to convince Negroes driven to cynicism that nonviolence can win. Many municipal government leaders will have no more imagination than to scorn it and ridicule it. Nonetheless, though they will be serving the trend to violence, they will not influence the bulk of Negroes who, I am confident, will embrace nonviolence. In the South we are taunted, mocked, and abused beyond belief. A hundred political commentators interred nonviolence into a premature grave.

Yet in 1965 there is a new South, still far from democratic consistency or harmony, but equally distant from the plantation-overseer South. The northern Negro knows this because he helped to bring it into being. He has yet to use nonviolent direct action; he has not even examined its special tactical application in his different community. He may even be reluctant in his urban sophistication to embrace its moral simplicities. But his wisdom is not less than his southern brothers and a power that could break the savagery of southern segregation commands respect and induces emulation. The rushing history of change has been late to reach the North but it is now on a fixed northerly course. The urban slums need not be destroyed by flames; earnest people of good will can decree their end nonviolently—as atrocious relics of a persisting unjust past.

*Saturday Review* (13 November 1965): 33–35, 105. 1965 Saturday Review Magazine. Reprinted by permission.

# PART II: FAMOUS SERMONS AND PUBLIC ADDRESSES

# 33

# Give Us the Ballot—
# We Will Transform the South

*Dr. King delivered this keynote address in front of the Lincoln Memorial during the Prayer Pilgrimage for Freedom on 17 May 1957, the third anniversary of the Supreme Court's famous school desegregation decision.*

Three years ago the Supreme Court of this nation rendered in simple, eloquent and unequivocal language a decision which will long be stenciled on the mental sheets of succeeding generations. For all men of good will, this May 17 decision came as a joyous daybreak to end the long night of enforced segregation. It came as a great beacon light of hope to millions of distinguished people throughout the world who had dared only to dream of freedom. It came as a legal and sociological deathblow to the old Plessy doctrine of "separate-but-equal." It came as a reaffirmation of the good old American doctrine of freedom and equality for all people.

Unfortunately, this noble and sublime decision has not gone without opposition. This opposition has often risen to ominous proportions. Many states have risen up in open defiance. The legislative halls of the South ring loud with such words as "interposition" and "nullification." Methods of defiance range from crippling economic reprisals to the tragic reign of violence and terror. All of these forces have conjoined to make for massive resistance.

But, even more, all types of conniving methods are still being used to prevent Negroes from becoming registered voters. The denial of this sacred right is a tragic betrayal of the highest mandates of our democratic traditions and it is democracy turned upside down.

So long as I do not firmly and irrevocably possess the right to vote I do not possess myself. I cannot make up my mind—it is made up for me. I cannot live as a democratic citizen, observing the laws I have helped to enact—I can only submit to the edict of others.

So our most urgent request to the president of the United States and every member of Congress is to give us the right to vote.

Give us the ballot and we will no longer have to worry the federal government about our basic rights.

Give us the ballot and we will no longer plead to the federal government for passage of an antilynching law; we will by the power of our vote write the law on the statute books of the southern states and bring an end to the dastardly acts of the hooded perpetrators of violence.

Give us the ballot and we will transform the salient misdeeds of bloodthirsty mobs into the calculated good deeds of orderly citizens.

Give us the ballot and we will fill our legislative halls with men of good will, and send to the sacred halls of Congress men who will not sign a Southern Manifesto,* because of their devotion to the manifesto of justice.

Give us the ballot and we will place judges on the benches of the South who will "do justly and love mercy," and we will place at the head of the southern states governors who have felt not only the tang of the human, but the glow of the divine.

Give us the ballot and we will quietly and nonviolently, without rancor or bitterness, implement the Supreme Court's decision of May 17, 1954.

In this junction of our nation's history there is an urgent need for dedicated and courageous leadership. If we are to solve the problems ahead and make racial justice a reality, this leadership must be fourfold.

First, there is need for a strong, aggressive leadership from the federal government. So far, only the judicial branch of the government has evinced this quality of leadership. If the executive and legislative branches of the government were as concerned about the protection of our citizenship rights as the federal courts have been, then the transition from a segregated to an integrated society would be infinitely smoother. But we so often look to Washington in vain for this concern.

In the midst of the tragic breakdown of law and order, the executive branch of the government is all too silent and apathetic. In the midst of the desperate need for civil rights legislation, the legislative branch of the government is all too stagnant and hypocritical.

This dearth of positive leadership from the federal government is not confined to one particular political party. Both parties have betrayed the cause of justice. The Democrats have betrayed it by capitulating to the prejudices and undemocratic practices of the southern dixiecrats. The Republicans have betrayed it by capitulating to the blatant hypocrisy of right-wing, reactionary northerners. These men so often have a high blood pressure of words and an anemia of deeds.

In the midst of these prevailing conditions, we come to Washington today pleading with the president and the members of Congress to pro-

---

*In March, 1956, more than ninety southerners, led by Senator Walter George, presented in Congress their "Declaration of Constitutional Principles," commonly known as the "Southern Manifesto." The document condemned the Supreme Court decision on segregation in education as a usurpation of the powers of the states and encouraged the use of "every lawful means" to resist its implementation.

vide a strong, moral and courageous leadership for a situation that cannot permanently be evaded. We come humbly to say to the men in the forefront of our government that the civil rights issue is not an ephemeral, evanescent domestic issue that can be kicked about by reactionary guardians of the status quo; it is rather an eternal moral issue which may well determine the destiny of our nation in the ideological struggle with communism. The hour is late. The clock of destiny is ticking out. We must act now, before it is too late.

A second area in which there is need for strong leadership is from the white northern liberals. There is a dire need today for a liberalism which is truly liberal. What we are witnessing today in so many northern communities is a sort of quasi liberalism which is based on the principle of looking sympathetically at all sides. It is a liberalism so bent on seeing all sides that it fails to become committed to either side. It is a liberalism that is so objectively analytical that it is not subjectively committed. It is a liberalism which is neither hot nor cold, but lukewarm.

We call for a liberalism from the North which will be thoroughly committed to the ideal of racial justice and will not be deterred by the propaganda and subtle words of those who say, "Slow up for a while; you are pushing too fast."

A third area that we must look to for strong leadership is from the moderates of the white South. It is unfortunate, indeed, that at this time the leadership of the white South stems from the closed-minded reactionaries. These persons gain prominence and power by the dissemination of false ideas, and by deliberately appealing to the deepest hate responses within the human mind. It is my firm belief that this closed-minded, reactionary, recalcitrant group constitutes a numerical minority. There are in the white South more open-minded moderates than appear on the surface. These persons are silent today because of fear of social, political and economic reprisals. God grant that the white moderates of the South will rise up courageously, without fear, and take up the leadership in this tense period of transition.

I cannot close without stressing the urgent need for strong, courageous and intelligent leadership from the Negro community. We need leadership that is calm and yet positive. This is no day for the rabble-rouser, whether he be Negro or white. We must realize that we are grappling with such a complex problem there is no place for misguided emotionalism. We must work passionately and unrelentingly for the goal of freedom, but we must be sure that our hands are clean in the struggle. We must never struggle with falsehood, hate or malice. Let us never become bitter.

There is another warning signal. We talk a great deal about our rights, and rightly so. We proudly proclaim that three-fourths of the peoples of the world are colored. We have the privilege of noticing in our generation the great drama of freedom and independence as it unfolds in Asia and Africa. All of these things are in line with the unfolding work of providence.

But we must be sure that we accept them in the right spirit. We must not seek to use our emerging freedom and our growing power to do the same thing to the white minority that has been done to us for so many centuries. We must not become victimized with a philosophy of "black supremacy." Our aim must never be to defeat or to humiliate the white man, but to win his friendship and understanding, and thereby create a society in which all men will be able to live together as brothers.

We must also avoid the temptation of being victimized with a psychology of victors. In our nation, under the guidance of the superb legal staff of the NAACP, we have been able, through the courts, to remove the legal basis of segregation. This is by far one of the most marvelous achievements of our generation. Every person of good will is profoundly indebted to the NAACP for its noble work. We must not, however, remain satisfied with a court "victory" over our white brothers.

We must respond to every decision with an understanding of those who have opposed us and with an appreciation of the difficult adjustments that the court orders pose for them.

We must act in such a way as to make possible a coming-together of white people and colored people on the basis of a real harmony of interest and understanding. We must seek an integration based on mutual respect.

I conclude by saying that each of us must keep faith in the future. Let us realize that as we struggle alone, but God struggles with us. He is leading us out of a bewildering Egypt, through a bleak and desolate wilderness, toward a bright and glittering promised land. Let us go forth into the glorious future with the words of James Weldon Johnson resounding in our souls:

> God of our weary years,
> God of our silent tears,
> Thou who has brought us thus far on the way;
> Thou who has by thy might,
> Led us into the light,
> Keep us forever in the path, we pray.
> Lest our feet stray from the places, our God,
> where we met thee.
> Lest our hearts, drunk with the wine of the world
> we forget thee;
> Shadowed beneath thy hand, may we forever stand
> True to our God, true to our native land.*

---

*The verses quoted are from Johnson's famous poem set to music, "Lift Every Voice and Sing," which was also known as the Negro national anthem.
*Congressional Record* 103 (28 May 1957): 7822–24.

# 34

# If the Negro Wins, Labor Wins

*This is the full text of an address that Dr. King delivered in Bal Harbour, Florida, on 11 December 1961, before the Fourth Constitutional Convention of the American Federation of Labor-Congress of Industrial Organizations (AFL-CIO). George Meany, the acerbic ex-plumber who was the president of this powerful political and economic bloc, invited King to speak, in an effort to placate unionists and civil rights leaders as well, who deplored him and his executive council for censuring A. Philip Randolph. Randolph, a stalwart, senior civil rights leader, was one of the vice presidents of the AFL-CIO and chairman of the Negro American Labor Council (NALC). The NALC was an inhouse group that constantly pressed Meany and the AFL-CIO to deal with racism within the American labor movement. Dr. King deeply admired A. Philip Randolph. With Randolph's help, he constantly sought the support of powerful national labor unions, but had only succeeded in securing the support of local labor unions, especially Randolph's Brotherhood of Sleeping Car Porters, New York City's District 65 of the Distributive Workers of America, and Chicago's Packing House Workers. All of these unions had a large percentage of black members. King used this speech to support Randolph, heal wounds, and court organized labor.*

Less than a century ago the laborer had no rights, little or no respect, and led a life which was socially submerged and barren.

He was hired and fired by economic despots whose power over him decreed his life or death. The children of workers had no childhood and no future. They, too, worked for pennies an hour and by the time they reached their teens they were wornout old men, devoid of spirit, devoid of hope and devoid of self-respect. Jack London described a child worker in these words: "He did not walk like a man. He did not look like a man. He was a travesty of the human. It was a twisted and stunted and nameless piece of life that shambled like a sickly ape, arms loose-hanging, stoop-shouldered, narrow-chested, grotesque and terrible."

American industry organized misery into sweatshops and proclaimed the right of capital to act without restraints and without conscience.

Victor Hugo, literary genius of that day, commented bitterly that there was always more misery in the lower classes than there was humanity in the upper classes. The inspiring answer to this intolerable and dehumanizing existence was economic organization through trade unions. The worker became determined not to wait for charitable impulses to grow in his employer. He constructed the means by which a fairer sharing of the fruits of his toil had to be given to him or the wheels of industry, which he alone turned, would halt and wealth for no one would be available.

## HISTORY REMEMBERS

This revolution within industry was fought mercilessly by those who blindly believed their right to uncontrolled profits was a law of the universe, and that without the maintenance of the old order catastrophe faced the nation.

History is a great teacher. Now, every one knows that the labor movement did not diminish the strength of the nation but enlarged it. By raising the living standards of millions, labor miraculously created a market for industry and lifted the whole nation to undreamed levels of production. Those who today attack labor forget these simple truths, but history remembers them.

Labor's next monumental struggle emerged in the thirties when it wrote into federal law the right freely to organize and bargain collectively. It was now apparently emancipated. The days when workers were jailed for organizing, and when in the English Parliament Lord Macauley had to debate against a bill decreeing the death penalty for anyone engaging in a strike, were grim but almost forgotten memories.

Yet, the Wagner Act, like any other legislation, tended merely to declare rights but did not deliver them. Labor had to bring the law to life by exercising its rights in practice over stubborn, tenacious opposition. It was warned to go slow, to be moderate, not to stir up strife. But labor knew it was always the right time to do right, and it spread its organization over the nation and achieved equality organizationally with capital. The day of economic democracy was born.

Negroes in the United States read this history of labor and find it mirrors their own experience. We are confronted by powerful forces telling us to rely on the good will and understanding of those who profit by exploiting us. They deplore our discontent, they resent our will to organize, so that we may guarantee that humanity will prevail and equality will be exacted. They are shocked that action organizations, sit-ins, civil disobedience, and protests are becoming our everyday tools, just as strikes, demonstrations and union organization became yours to insure that bargaining power genuinely existed on both sides of the table.

We want to rely upon the good will of those who oppose us. Indeed, we have brought forward the method of nonviolence to give an example of unilateral good will in an effort to evoke it in those who have not yet felt it in their hearts. But we know that if we are not simultaneously organizing our strength we will have no means to move forward. If we do not advance, the crushing burden of centuries of neglect and economic deprivation will destroy our will, our spirits and our hopes. In this way labor's historic tradition of moving forward to create vital people as consumers and citizens has become our own tradition, and for the same reasons.

This unity of purpose is not an historical coincidence. Negroes are almost entirely a working people. There are pitifully few Negro millionaires and few Negro employers. Our needs are identical with labor's needs: decent wages, fair working conditions, livable housing, old age security, health and welfare measures, conditions in which families can grow, have education for their children and respect in the community. That is why Negroes support labor's demands and fight laws which curb labor. That is why the labor-hater and labor-baiter is virtually always a twin-headed creature spewing anti-Negro epithets from one mouth and anti-labor propaganda from the other mouth.

The duality of interests of labor and Negroes makes any crisis which lacerates you a crisis from which we bleed. As we stand on the threshold of the second half of the twentieth century, a crisis confronts us both. Those who in the second half of the nineteenth century could not tolerate organized labor have had a rebirth of power and seek to regain the despotism of that era while retaining the wealth and privileges of the twentieth century. Whether it be the ultra-right wing in the form of Birch societies or the alliance which former President Eisenhower denounced, the alliance between big military and big industry, or the coalition of southern dixiecrats and northern reactionaries, whatever the form, these menaces now threaten everything decent and fair in American life.

Their target is labor, liberals, and the Negro people, not scattered "reds" or even Justice Warren, former presidents Eisenhower and Truman and President Kennedy, who are in truth beyond the reach of their crude and vicious falsehoods.

Labor today faces a grave crisis, perhaps the most calamitous since it began its march from the shadows of want and insecurity. In the next ten to twenty years automation will grind jobs into dust as it grinds out unbelievable volumes of production. This period is made to order for those who would seek to drive labor into impotency by viciously attacking it at every point of weakness.

## LABOR'S TRUE FRIENDS

Hard-core unemployment is now an ugly and unavoidable fact of life. Like malignant cancer, it has grown year by year and continues its spread. But automation can be used to generate an abundance of wealth for people or an abundance of poverty for millions as its human-like machines turn out human scrap along with machine scrap as a by-product of production. Our society, with its ability to perform miracles with machinery, has the capacity to make some miracles for men—if it values men as highly as it values machines.

To find a great design to solve a grave problem labor will have to intervene in the political life of the nation to chart a course which distributes the abundance to all instead of concentrating it among a few. The strength to carry through such a program requires that labor know its friends and collaborate as a friend. If all that I have said is sound, labor has no firmer friend than the twenty million Negroes whose lives will be deeply affected by the new patterns of production.

To say that we are friends would be an empty platitude if we fail to behave as friends and honestly look to weaknesses in our relationship. Unfortunately there are weaknesses. Labor has not adequately used its great power, its vision and resources to advance Negro rights. Undeniably it has done more than other forces in American society to this end. Aid from real friends in labor has often come when the flames of struggle heighten. But Negroes are a solid component within the labor movement and a reliable bulwark for labor's whole program, and should expect more from it exactly as a member of a family expects more from his relatives than he expects from his neighbors.

Labor, which made impatience for long-delayed justice for itself a vital motive force, cannot lack understanding of the Negro's impatience. It cannot speak, with the reactionaries' calm indifference, of progress around some obscure corner not yet possible even to see. There is a maxim in the law—justice too long delayed, is justice denied. When a Negro leader who has a reputation of purity and honesty which has benefited the whole labor movement criticizes it, his motives should not be reviled nor his earnestness rebuked. Instead, the possibility that he is revealing a weakness in the labor movement which it can ill afford, should receive thoughtful examination. A man who has dedicated his long and faultless life to the labor movement cannot be raising questions harmful to it any more than a lifelong devoted parent can become the enemy of his child. The report of a committee may smother with legal constructions a list of complaints and dispose of it for the day. But if it buries a far larger truth it has disposed of nothing and made justice more elusive.

## BIAS EXISTS IN UNIONS

Discrimination does exist in the labor movement. It is true that organized labor has taken significant steps to remove the yoke of discrimination from its own body. But in spite of this, some unions, governed by the racist ethos, have contributed to the degraded economic status of the Negro. Negroes have been barred from membership in certain unions, and denied apprenticeship training and vocational education. In every section of the country one can find local unions existing as a serious and vicious obstacle when the Negro seeks jobs or upgrading in employment. Labor must honestly admit these shameful conditions, and design the battle plan which will defeat and eliminate them. In this way, labor would be unearthing the big truth and utilizing its strength against the bleakness of injustice in the spirit of its finest traditions.

How can labor rise to the heights of its potential statesmanship and cement its bonds with Negroes to their mutual advantage?

First: Labor should accept the logic of its special position with respect to Negroes and the struggle for equality. Although organized labor has taken actions to eliminate discrimination in its ranks, it has not raised high enough the standard for the general community. Your conduct should and can set an example for others, as you have done in other crusades for social justice. You should root out vigorously every manifestation of discrimination so that some internationals, central labor bodies or locals may not besmirch the positive accomplishments of labor. I am aware this is not easy nor popular—but the eight-hour day was not popular nor easy to achieve. Nor was outlawing anti-labor injunctions. But you accomplished all of these with a massive will and determination. Out of such struggle for democratic rights you won both economic gains and the respect of the country, and you will win both again if you make Negro rights a great crusade.

Second: The political strength you are going to need to prevent automation from becoming a Moloch, consuming jobs and contract gains, can be multiplied if you tap the vast reservoir of Negro political power. Negroes, given the vote, will vote liberal and labor because they need the same liberal legislation labor needs.

To give just an example of the importance of the Negro vote to labor, I might cite the arresting fact that the only state in the South which repealed the right-to-work law is Louisiana. This was achieved because the Negro vote in that state grew large enough to become a balance of power, and it went along with labor to wipe out anti-labor legislation. Thus, support to assist us in securing the vote can make the difference between success and defeat for us both. You have organizing experience we need and you have an apparatus unparalleled in the nation. You recognized five years ago a moral opportunity and responsibility when several of your leaders, including Mr. Meany, Mr. Dubinsky, Mr. Reuther and Mr. MacDonald and others, projected a two million dollar campaign to assist the struggling Negroes fighting bitterly in handicapped circumstances in the South. A ten-thousand-dollar contribution was voted by the ILGWU to begin the drive, but for reasons unknown to me, the drive was never begun. The cost to us in lack of resources during these turbulent, violent years, is hard to describe. We are mindful that many unions thought of as immorally rich, in truth have problems in meeting the budget to properly service their members. So we do not ask that you tax your treasuries. Instead, we ask that you appeal to your members for one dollar apiece to make democracy real for millions of deprived American citizens. For this you have the experience, the organization and most of all, the understanding.

If you would do these two things now in this convention—resolve to deal effectively with discrimination and provide financial aid for our struggle in the South—this convention will have a glorious moral deed to add to an illustrious history.

The two most dynamic and cohesive liberal forces in the country are the labor movement and the Negro freedom movement. Together we can be architects of democracy in a South now rapidly industrializing. Together we can retool the political structure of the South, sending to Congress steadfast liberals who, joining with those from northern industrial states, will extend the frontiers of democracy for the whole nation. Together we can bring about the day when there will be no separate identification of Negroes and labor.

There is no intrinsic difference, as I have tried to demonstrate. Differences have been contrived by outsiders who seek to impose disunity by dividing brothers because the color of their skin has a different shade. I look forward confidently to the day when all who work for a living will be one with no thought to their separateness as Negroes, Jews, Italians or any other distinctions.

This will be the day when we shall bring into full realization the American dream—a dream yet unfilled. A dream of equality of opportunity, of privilege and property widely distributed; a dream of a land where men will not take necessities from the many to give luxuries to the few; a dream of a land where men will not argue that the color of a man's skin determines the content of his character; a dream of a nation where all our gifts and resources are held not for ourselves alone but as instruments of service for the rest of humanity; the dream of a country where every man will respect the dignity and worth of human personality—that is the dream.

## WE SHALL OVERCOME

And as we struggle to make racial and economic justice a reality, let us maintain faith in the future. We will confront difficulties and frustrating moments in the struggle to make justice a reality, but we must believe somehow that these problems can be solved.

There is a little song that we sing in the movement taking place in the South. It goes like this, "We shall overcome. We shall overcome." Deep in my heart I do believe we shall overcome. And somehow all over America we must believe that we shall overcome and that these problems can be solved. They will be solved before the victory is won.

Some of us will have to get scarred up, but we shall overcome. Before the victory of justice is a a reality, some may even face physical death.

But if physical death is the price that some must pay to free their children and their brothers from a permanent life of psychological death, then nothing could be more moral. Before the victory is won more will have to go to jail. We must be willing to go to jail and transform the jails from dungeons of shame to havens of freedom and human dignity. Yes, before the victory is won, some will be misunderstood. Some will be dismissed as dangerous rabble-rousers and agitators. Some will be called reds and Communists merely because they believe in economic justice and the brotherhood of man. But we shall overcome.

## BROTHERHOOD OF MAN

I am convinced that we shall overcome because the arc of the universe is long but it bends toward justice. We shall overcome because Carlyle is right when he says, "No lie can live forever." We shall overcome because William Cullen Bryant is right when he says, "Truth crushed to earth will rise again." We shall overcome because James Russell Lowell was right when he proclaimed: "Truth forever on the scaffold, wrong forever on the throne, yet that scaffold sways the future."

And so if we will go out with this faith and with this determination to solve these problems, we will bring into being that new day and that new America. When that day comes, the fears of insecurity and the doubts clouding our future will be transformed into radiant confidence, into glowing excitement to reach creative goals and into an abiding moral balance where the brotherhood of man will be undergirded by a secure and expanding prosperity for all.

Yes, this will be the day when all of God's children, black men and white men, Jews and Gentiles, Protestants and Catholics, will be able to join hands all over this nation and sing in the words of the old Negro spiritual: "Free At Last, Free At Last. Thank God Almighty, We Are Free At Last."

*Hotel* (12 February 1962): 4, 6.

# 35

# The American Dream

*Dr. King gave the commencement address at Lincoln University in Pennsylvania on 6 June 1961. This is a transcription of that address.*

. . . Today you bid farewell to the friendly security of this academic environment, a setting that will remain dear to you as long as the cords of memory shall lengthen. As you go out today to enter the clamorous highways of life, I should like to discuss with you some aspects of the American dream. For in a real sense, America is essentially a dream, a dream as yet unfulfilled. It is a dream of a land where men of all races, of all nationalities and of all creeds can live together as brothers. The substance of the dream is expressed in these sublime words, words lifted to cosmic proportions: "We hold these truths to be self-evident, that all men are created equal, that they are endowed by their Creator with certain unalienable rights, that among these are life, liberty, and the pursuit of happiness." This is the dream.

One of the first things we notice in this dream is an amazing universalism. It does not say some men, but it says all men. It does not say all white men, but it says all men, which includes black men. It does not say all Gentiles, but it says all men, which includes Jews. It does not say all Protestants, but it says all men, which includes Catholics.

And there is another thing we see in this dream that ultimately distinguishes democracy and our form of government from all of the totalitarian regimes that emerge in history. It says that each individual has certain basic rights that are neither conferred by nor derived from the state. To discover where they came from it is necessary to move back behind the dim mist of eternity, for they are God-given. Very seldom if ever in the history of the world has a sociopolitical document expressed in such profoundly eloquent and unequivocal language the dignity and the worth of human personality. The American dream reminds us that every man is heir to the legacy of worthiness.

Ever since the Founding Fathers of our nation dreamed this noble dream, America has been something of a schizophrenic personality, tragically divided against herself. On the one hand we have proudly professed the principles of democracy, and on the other hand we have sadly practiced the very antithesis of those principles. Indeed slavery and segregation have been strange paradoxes in a nation founded on the principle that all men are created equal. This is what the Swedish sociologist, Gunnar Myrdal, referred to as the American dilemma.

But the shape of the world today does not permit us the luxury of an anemic democracy. The price America must pay for the continued exploitation of the Negro and other minority groups is the price of its own destruction. The hour is late; the clock of destiny is ticking out. It is trite, but urgently true, that if America is to remain a first-class nation she can no longer have second-class citizens. Now, more than ever before, America is challenged to bring her noble dream into reality, and those who are working to implement the American dream are the true saviors of democracy.

Now may I suggest some of the things we must do if we are to make the American dream a reality. First I think all of us must develop a world perspective if we are to survive. The American dream will not become a reality devoid of the larger dream of a world of brotherhood and peace and good will. The world in which we live is a world of geographical oneness and we are challenged now to make it spiritually one.

Man's scientific genius and technological ingenuity has dwarfed distance and placed time in chains. Jet planes have compressed into minutes distances that once took days and months to cover. It is not common for a preacher to be quoting Bob Hope, but I think he has aptly described this jet age in which we live. If, on taking off on a nonstop flight from Los Angeles to New York City, you develop hiccups, he said, you will hic in Los Angeles and cup in New York City. That is really *moving.* If you take a flight from Tokyo, Japan, on Sunday morning, you will arrive in Seattle, Washington, on the preceding Saturday night. When your friends meet you at the airport and ask you when you left Tokyo, you will have to say, "I left tomorrow." This is the kind of world in which we live. Now this is a bit humorous but I am trying to laugh a basic fact into all of us: the world in which we live has become a single neighborhood.

Through our scientific genius we have made of this world a neighborhood; now through our moral and spiritual development we must make of it a brotherhood. In a real sense, we must all learn to live together as brothers, or we will all perish together as fools. We must come to see that no individual can live alone; no nation can live alone. We must all live together; we must all be concerned about each other.

Some months ago, Mrs. King and I journeyed to that great country in the Far East known as India. I will never forget the experiences that came to us as we moved around that great country, or the opportunity of meeting and talking with the great leaders of India and with people all over in the cities and the villages throughout India. Certainly this was an experience that I will always remember, but there were depressing moments. How can one avoid being depressed when he sees with his own eyes millions of people going to bed hungry at night? How can one avoid being depressed when he sees with his own eyes millions of people sleeping on the sidewalk at night?

In Calcutta alone, more than a million people sleep on the sidewalks every night; in Bombay, more than six hundred thousand people sleep on the sidewalks every night. They have no beds to sleep in; they have no houses to go into. How can one avoid being depressed when he discovers that of India's four hundred million people, more than 365 million make an annual income of less than sixty dollars a year? Most of these people have never seen a doctor or a dentist.

As I looked at these conditions, I found myself saying that we in America cannot stand idly by and not be concerned. Then something within me cried out, "Oh, no, because the destiny of the United States is tied up with the destiny of India—with the destiny of every other nation." And I remembered that we spend more than a million dollars a day to store surplus food in this country. I said to myself, 'I know where we can store that food free of charge—in the wrinkled stomachs of the millions of people who go to bed hungry at night." Maybe we spend too much of our national budget building military bases around the world, rather than bases of genuine concern and understanding.

All this is simply to say that all life is interrelated. We are caught in an inescapable network of mutuality; tied in a single garment of destiny. Whatever affects one directly, affects all indirectly. As long as there is poverty in this world, no man can be totally rich even if he has a billion dollars. As long as diseases are rampant and millions of people cannot expect to live more than twenty or thirty years, no man can be totally healthy, even if he just got a clean bill of health from the finest clinic in America. Strangely enough, I can never be what I ought to be until you are what you ought to be. You can never be what you ought to be until I am what I ought to be. This is the way the world is made. I didn't make it that way, but this is the interrelated structure of reality. John Donne caught it a few centuries ago and could cry out, "No man is an island entire of itself; every man is a piece of the continent, a part of the main . . . any man's death diminishes me, because I am involved in mankind, and therefore never send to know for whom the bell tolls; it tolls for thee." If we are to realize the American dream we must cultivate this world perspective.

There is another thing quite closely related to this. We must keep our moral and spiritual progress abreast with our scientific and technological advances. This poses another dilemma of modern man. We have allowed our civilization to outdistance our culture. Professor MacIver follows the German sociologist, Alfred Weber, in pointing out the distinction between culture and civilization. Civilization refers to what we use; culture refers to what we are. Civilization is that complex of devices, instrumentalities, mechanisms and techniques by means of which we live. Culture is that realm of ends expressed in art, literature, religion and morals for which at best we live.

The great problem confronting us today is that we have allowed the means by which we live to outdistance the ends for which we live. We have allowed our civilization to outrun our culture, and so we are in danger now of ending up with guided missiles in the hands of misguided men. This is what the poet Thoreau meant when he said, "Improved means to an unimproved end." If we are to survive today and realize the dream of our mission and the dream of the world, we must bridge the gulf and somehow keep the means by which we live abreast with the ends for which we live.

Another thing we must do is to get rid of the notion once and for all that there are superior and inferior races. Now we know that this view still lags around in spite of the fact that many great anthropologists, Margaret Mead and Ruth Benedict and Melville Herskovits and others have pointed out and made it clear through scientific evidence that there are no superior races and there are no inferior races. There may be intellectually superior individuals within all races. In spite of all this evidence, however, the view still gets around somehow that there are superior and inferior races. The whole concept of white supremacy rests on this fallacy.

You know, there was a time when some people used to argue the inferiority of the Negro and the colored races generally on the basis of the Bible and religion. They would say the Negro was inferior by nature because of Noah's curse upon the children of Ham. And then another brother had probably read the logic of Aristotle. You know Aristotle brought into being the syllogism which had a major premise and a minor premise and a conclusion, and one brother had probably read Aristotle and he put his argument in the framework of an Aristotelian syllogism. He could say that all men are made in the image of God. This was a major premise. Then came his minor premise: God, as everybody knows, is not a Negro; therefore the Negro is not a man. And that was called logic!

But we don't often hear these arguments today. Segregation is now based on "sociological and cultural" grounds. "The Negro is not culturally ready for integration, and if integration comes into being it will pull the white race back a generation. It will take fifty or seventy-five years to raise these standards." And then we hear that the Negro is a criminal, and there are those who would almost say he is a criminal by nature. But they never point out that these things are environmental and not racial; these problems are problems of urban dislocation. They fail to see that poverty, and disease, and ignorance breed crime whatever the racial group may be. And it is a tortuous logic that views the tragic results of segregation and discrimination as an argument for the continuation of it.

If we are to implement the American dream we must get rid of the notion once and for all that there are superior and inferior races. This means that members of minority groups must make it clear that they can use their resources even under adverse circumstances. We must make full and constructive use of the freedom we already possess. We must not use our oppression as an excuse for mediocrity and laziness. For history has proven that inner determination can often break through the outer shackles of circumstance. Take the Jews, for example, and the years they have been forced to walk through the long and desolate night of oppression. This did not keep them from rising up to plunge against cloud-filled nights of oppression, new and blazing stars of inspiration. Being a Jew did not keep Einstein from using his genius-packed mind to prove his theory of relativity.

And so, being a Negro does not have to keep any individual from rising up to make a contribution as so many Negroes have done within our own lifetime. Human nature cannot be catalogued, and we need not wait until the day of full emancipation. So from an old clay cabin in Virginia's hills, Booker T. Washington rose up to be one of the nation's great leaders. He lit a torch in Alabama; then darkness fled.

From the red hills of Gordon County, Georgia, from an iron foundry at Chattanooga, Tennessee, from the arms of a mother who could neither read nor write, Roland Hayes rose up to be one of the nation's and the world's greatest singers. He carried his melodious voice to the mansion of the Queen Mother of Spain and the palace of King George V. From the poverty-stricken areas of Philadelphia, Pennsylvania, Marian Anderson rose up to be the world's greatest contralto, so that Toscanini could say that a voice like this comes only once in a century. Sibelius of Finland could say, "My roof is too low for such a voice."

From humble, crippling circumstances, George Washington Carver rose up and carved for himself an inperishable niche in the annals of science. There was a star in the sky of female leadership. Then came Mary McLeod Bethune to let it shine in her life. There was a star in the diplomatic sky. Then came Ralph Bunche, the grandson of a slave preacher, and allowed it to shine in his life with all of its radiant beauty. There were stars in the athletic sky. Then came Joe Louis with his educated fists, Jesse Owens with his fleet and dashing feet, Jackie Robinson with his powerful bat and calm spirit. All of these people have come to remind us that we need not wait until the day of full emancipation. They have justified the conviction of the poet that:

> Fleecy locks and dark complexion
> Cannot forfeit nature's claim.
> Skin may differ but affection
> Dwells in black and white the same.
> Were I so tall as to reach the pole
> Or to grasp the ocean at a span,
> I must be measured by my soul,
> The mind is standard of the man.

Finally, if we are to implement the American dream, we must continue to engage in creative protest in order to break down all of those barriers that make it impossible for the dream to be realized. Now I know there are those people who will argue that we must wait on something. They fail to see the necessity for creative protest, but I say to you that I can see no way to break loose from an old order and to move into a new order without standing up and resisting the unjust dogma of the old order.

To do this, we must get rid of two strange illusions that have been held by the so-called moderates in race relations. First is the myth of time advanced by those who say that you must wait on time; if you "just wait and be patient," time will work the situation out. They will say this even about freedom rides.* They will say this about sit-ins: that you're pushing things too fast—cool off—time will work these problems out. Well, evolution may hold in the biological realm, and in that area Darwin was right. But when a Herbert Spencer seeks to apply "evoluation" to the whole fabric of society, there is no truth in it.† Even a superficial look at history shows that social progress never rolls in on the wheels of inevitability. It comes through the tireless effort and the persistent work of dedicated individuals. Without this hard work, time itself becomes an ally of the primitive forces of irrational emotionalism and social stagnation. And we must get rid of the myth of time.

There is another myth, that bases itself on a species of educational determinism. It leads one to think that you can't solve this problem through legislation; you can't solve this problem through judicial decree; you can't solve this problem through executive orders on the part of the president of the United States. It must be solved by education. Now I agree that education plays a great role, and it must continue to play a great role in changing attitudes, in getting people ready for the new order. And we must also see the importance of legislation.

It is not a question either of education or of legislation. Both legislation and education are required. Now, people will say, "You can't legislate morals." Well, that may be true. Even though morality may not be legislated, behavior can be regulated. And this is very important. We need religion and education to change attitudes and to change the hearts of men. We need legislation and federal action to control behavior. It may be true that the law can't make a man love me, but it can keep him from lynching me, and I think that's pretty important also.

And so we must get rid of these illusions and move on with determina-

---

*In May, 1961, the Congress of Racial Equality, an interracial direct-action group founded in 1942, sent buses of "Freedom Riders" into the South to test segregation laws and practices in interstate transportation. In Alabama and Mississippi the Freedom Riders were attacked by white racist mobs and arrested, but on September 22, 1961, the Interstate Commerce Commission ruled that passengers on interstate carriers would be seated without regard to race and that such carriers could not use segregated terminals.

†Herbert Spencer (1820–1903) was the formulator of "social Darwinism," an effort to apply Darwinism to society; he stressed, among other points, that Anglo-Saxon civilization was a superior development out of previous civilizations and the result of competition.

tion and with zeal to break down the unjust systems we find in our society, so that it will be possible to realize the American dream. As I have said so often, if we seek to break down discrimination, we must use the proper methods. I am convinced more than ever before that, as the powerful, creative way opens, men and women who are eager to break the barriers of oppression and of segregation and discrimination need not fall down to the levels of violence. They need not sink into the quicksands of hatred. Standing on the high ground of noninjury, love and soul force, they can turn this nation upside down and right side up.

I believe, more than ever before, in the power of nonviolent resistance. It has a moral aspect tied to it. It makes it possible for the individual to secure moral ends through moral means. This has been one of the great debates of history. People have felt that it is impossible to achieve moral ends through moral means. And so a Machiavelli could come into being and so force a sort of duality within the moral structure of the universe. Even communism could come into being and say that anything justifies the end of a classless society—lying, deceit, hate, violence—anything. And this is where nonviolent resistance breaks with communism and with all of those systems which argue that the end justifies the means, because we realize that the end is preexistent in the means. In the long run of history, destructive means cannot bring about constructive ends.

The practical aspect of nonviolent resistance is that it exposes the moral defenses of the opponent. Not only that, it somehow arouses his conscience at the same time, and it breaks down his morale. He has no answer for it. If he puts you in jail, that's all right; if he lets you out, that's all right too. If he beats you, you accept that; if he doesn't beat you—fine. And so you go on, leaving him with no answer. But if you use violence, he does have an answer. He has the state militia; he has police brutality.

Nonviolent resistance is one of the most magnificent expressions going on today. We see it in the movement taking place among students in the South and their allies who have been willing to come in from the North and other sections. They have taken our deep groans and passionate yearnings, filtered them in their own souls, and fashioned them into the creative protest, which is an epic known all over our nation. They have moved in a uniquely meaningful orbit, imparting light and heat to a distant satellite. And people say, "Does this bring results?" Well, look at the record.

In less than a year, lunch counters have been integrated in more than 142 cities of the Deep South, and this was done without a single court suit; it was done without spending millions and millions of dollars. We think of the freedom rides, and remember that more than sixty people are now in jail in Jackson, Mississippi. What has this done? These people have been beaten; they have suffered to bring to the attention of this nation, the indignities and injustices Negro people still confront in interstate travel. It has, therefore, had an educational value. But not only that—signs have come down from bus stations in Montgomery, Alabama. They've never been down before. Not only that—the attorney general of this nation has called on ICC to issue new regulations making it positively clear that segregation in interstate travel is illegal and unconstitutional.

And so this method can bring results. Sometimes it can bring quick results. But even when it doesn't bring immediate results, it is constantly working on the conscience; it is at all times using moral means to bring about moral ends. And so I say we must continue on the way of creative protest. I believe also that this method will help us to enter the new age with the proper attitude.

As I have said in so many instances, it is not enough to struggle for the new society. We must make sure that we make the psychological adjustment required to live in that new society. This is true of white people, and it is true of Negro people. Psychological adjustment will save white people from going into the new age with old vestiges of prejudice and attitudes of white supremacy. It will save the Negro from seeking to substitute one tyranny for another.

I know sometimes we get discouraged and sometimes disappointed with the slow pace of things. At times we begin to talk about racial separation instead of racial integration, feeling that there is no other way out. My only answer is that the problem never will be solved by substituting one tyranny for another. Black supremacy is as dangerous as white supremacy, and God is not interested merely in the freedom of black men and brown men and yellow men. God is interested in the freedom of the whole human race and in the creation of a society where all men can live together as brothers, where every man will respect the dignity and the worth of human personality.

By following this method, we may also be able to teach our world something that it so desperately needs at this hour. In a day when Sputniks and Explorers are dashing through outer space, and guided ballistic missiles are carving highways of death through the stratosphere, no nation can win a war. The choice is no longer between violence and nonviolence; it is either nonviolence or nonexistence. Unless we find some alternatve to war, we will destroy ourselves by the misuse of our own instruments. And so, with all of these attitudes and principles working together, I believe we will be able to make a contribution as men of good will to the ongoing structure of our society and toward the realization of the American dream. And so, as you go out today, I call upon you not to be detached spectators, but involved participants, in this great drama that is taking place in our nation and around the world.

Every academic discipline has its technical nomenclature, and modern psychology has a word that is used, probably, more than any other.

It is the word *maladjusted*. This word is the ringing cry of modern child psychology. Certainly all of us want to live a well-adjusted life in order to avoid the neurotic personality. But I say to you, there are certain things within our social order to which I am proud to be maladjusted and to which I call upon all men of good will to be maladjusted.

If you will allow the preacher in me to come out now, let me say to you that I never did intend to adjust to the evils of segregation and discrimination. I never did intend to adjust myself to religious bigotry. I never did intend to adjust myself to economic conditions that will take necessities from the many to give luxuries to the few. I never did intend to adjust myself to the madness of militarism, and the self-defeating effects of physical violence. And I call upon all men of good will to be maladjusted because it may well be that the salvation of our world lies in the hands of the maladjusted.

So let us be maladjusted, as maladjusted as the prophet Amos, who in the midst of the injustices of his day could cry out in words that echo across the centuries, "Let justice run down like waters and righteousness like a mighty stream." Let us be as maladjusted as Abraham Lincoln, who had the vision to see that this nation could not exist half slave and half free. Let us be maladjusted as Jesus of Nazareth, who could look into the eyes of the men and women of his generation and cry out, "Love your enemies. Bless them that curse you. Pray for them that despitefully use you."

I believe that it is through such maladjustment that we will be able to emerge from the bleak and desolate midnight of man's inhumanity to man into the bright and glittering daybreak of freedom and justice. That will be the day when all of God's children, black men and white men, Jews and Gentiles, Catholics and Protestants, will be able to join hands and sing in the words of the old Negro spiritual, "Free at last! Free at last! Thank God almighty, we are free at last!"

*The Negro History Bulletin* 31 (May 1968): 10–15.

# 36

# I Have a Dream

*This is perhaps the most well-known and most quoted address Dr. King deliv-
ered. He delivered this speech before the Lincoln Memorial on 28 August 1963
as the keynote address of the March on Washington, D.C., for Civil Rights. The
television cameras allowed the entire nation to hear and see him plead for justice
and freedom. Mrs. Coretta King once commented, "At that moment it seemed as
if the Kingdom of God appeared. But it only lasted for a moment."*

I am happy to join with you today in what will go down in history as the
greatest demonstration for freedom in the history of our nation.

Fivescore years ago, a great American, in whose symbolic shadow we
stand today, signed the Emancipation Proclamation. This momentous
decree came as a great beacon light of hope to millions of Negro slaves
who had been seared in the flames of withering injustice. It came as a
joyous daybreak to end the long night of their captivity.

But one hundred years later, the Negro still is not free; one hundred
years later, the life of the Negro is still sadly crippled by the manacles of
segregation and the chains of discrimination; one hundred years later,
the Negro lives on a lonely island of poverty in the midst of a vast ocean
of material prosperity; one hundred years later, the Negro is still languished in the corners of American society and finds himself in exile in
his own land.

So we've come here today to dramatize a shameful condition. In a
sense we've come to our nation's capital to cash a check. When the architects of our republic wrote the magnificent words of the Constitution
and the Declaration of Independence, they were signing a promissory
note to which every American was to fall heir. This note was the promise that all men, yes, black men as well as white men, would be guaranteed the unalienable rights of life, liberty, and the pursuit of happiness.

It is obvious today that America has defaulted on this promissory note
in so far as her citizens of color are concerned. Instead of honoring this
sacred obligation, America has given the Negro people a bad check; a
check which has come back marked "insufficient funds." We refuse to
believe that there are insufficient funds in the great vaults of opportunity of this nation. And so we've come to cash this check, a check that will
give us upon demand the riches of freedom and the security of justice.

We have also come to this hallowed spot to remind America of the fierce urgency of now. This is no time to engage in the luxury of cooling off or to take the tranquilizing drug of gradualism. Now is the time to make real the promises of democracy; now is the time to rise from the dark and desolate valley of segregation to the sunlit path of racial justice; now is the time to lift our nation from the quicksands of racial injustice to the solid rock of brotherhood; now is the time to make justice a reality for all God's children. It would be fatal for the nation to overlook the urgency of the moment. This sweltering summer of the Negro's legitimate discontent will not pass until there is an invigorating autumn of freedom and equality.

Nineteen sixty-three is not an end, but a beginning. And those who hope that the Negro needed to blow off steam and will now be content, will have a rude awakening if the nation returns to business as usual.

There will be neither rest nor tranquility in America until the Negro is granted his citizenship rights. The whirlwinds of revolt will continue to shake the foundations of our nation until the bright day of justice emerges.

But there is something that I must say to my people who stand on the warm threshold which leads into the palace of justice. In the process of gaining our rightful place we must not be guilty of wrongful deeds.

Let us not seek to satisfy our thirst for freedom by drinking from the cup of bitterness and hatred. We must forever conduct our struggle on the high plane of dignity and discipline. We must not allow our creative protest to degenerate into physical violence. Again and again we must rise to the majestic heights of meeting physical force with soul force.

The marvelous new militancy which has engulfed the Negro community must not lead us to a distrust of all white people, for many of our white brothers, as evidenced by their presence here today, have come to realize that their destiny is tied up with our destiny and they have come to realize that their freedom is inextricably bound to our freedom. This offense we share mounted to storm the battlements of injustice must be carried forth by a biracial army. We cannot walk alone.

And as we walk, we must make the pledge that we shall always march ahead. We cannot turn back. There are those who are asking the devotees of civil rights, "When will you be satisfied?" We can never be satisfied as long as the Negro is the victim of the unspeakable horrors of police brutality.

We can never be satisfied as long as our bodies, heavy with fatigue of travel, cannot gain lodging in the motels of the highways and the hotels of the cities. We cannot be satisfied as long as the Negro's basic mobility is from a smaller ghetto to a larger one.

We can never be satisfied as long as our children are stripped of their selfhood and robbed of their dignity by signs stating "for whites only." We cannot be satisfied as long as a Negro in Mississippi cannot vote and a Negro in New York believes he has nothing for which to vote. No, we are not satisfied, and we will not be satisfied until justice rolls down like waters and righteousness like a mighty stream.

I am not unmindful that some of you have come here out of excessive trials and tribulation. Some of you have come fresh from narrow jail cells. Some of you have come from areas where your quest for freedom left you battered by the storms of persecution and staggered by the winds of police brutality. You have been the veterans of creative suffering. Continue to work with the faith that unearned suffering is redemptive.

Go back to Mississippi; go back to Alabama; go back to South Carolina; go back to Georgia; go back to Louisiana; go back to the slums and ghettos of the northern cities, knowing that somehow this situation can, and will be changed. Let us not wallow in the valley of despair.

So I say to you, my friends, that even though we must face the difficulties of today and tomorrow, I still have a dream. It is a dream deeply rooted in the American dream that one day this nation will rise up and live out the true meaning of its creed—we hold these truths to be self-evident, that all men are created equal.

I have a dream that one day on the red hills of Georgia, sons of former slaves and sons of former slave-owners will be able to sit down together at the table of brotherhood.

I have a dream that one day, even the state of Mississippi, a state sweltering with the heat of injustice, sweltering with the heat of oppression, will be transformed into an oasis of freedom and justice.

I have a dream my four little children will one day live in a nation where they will not be judged by the color of their skin but by content of their character. I have a dream today!

I have a dream that one day, down in Alabama, with its vicious racists, with its governor having his lips dripping with the words of interposition and nullification, that one day, right there in Alabama, little black boys and black girls will be able to join hands with little white boys and white girls as sisters and brothers. I have a dream today!

I have a dream that one day every valley shall be exalted, every hill and mountain shall be made low, the rough places shall be made plain, and the crooked places shall be made straight and the glory of the Lord will be revealed and all flesh shall see it together.

This is our hope. This is the faith that I go back to the South with.

With this faith we will be able to hew out of the mountain of despair a stone of hope. With this faith we will be able to transform the jangling discords of our nation into a beautiful symphony of brotherhood.

With this faith we will be able to work together, to pray together, to struggle together, to go to jail together, to stand up for freedom together, knowing that we will be free one day. This will be the day when all of God's children will be able to sing with new meaning—"my country 'tis of thee; sweet land of liberty; of thee I sing; land where my fathers died, land of the pilgrim's pride; from every mountain side, let freedom ring"—and if America is to be a great nation, this must become true.

So let freedom ring from the prodigious hilltops of New Hampshire.

Let freedom ring from the mighty mountains of New York.

Let freedom ring from the heightening Alleghenies of Pennsylvania.

Let freedom ring from the snow-capped Rockies of Colorado.

Let freedom ring from the curvaceous slopes of California.

But not only that.

Let freedom ring from Stone Mountain of Georgia.

Let freedom ring from Lookout Mountain of Tennessee.

Let freedom ring from every hill and molehill of Mississippi, from every mountainside, let freedom ring.

And when we allow freedom to ring, when we let it ring from every village and hamlet, from every state and city, we will be able to speed up that day when all of God's children—black men and white men, Jews and Gentiles, Catholics and Protestants—will be able to join hands and to sing in the words of the old Negro spiritual, "Free at last, free at last; thank God Almighty, we are free at last."

*Negro History Bulletin* 21 (May 1968): 16–17.

# 37

# Eulogy for
# the Martyred Children

*The Reverend Dr. King delivered this sermon at the funeral of the little girls
who were killed on 15 September 1963 by a bomb as they attended the Sunday
school of the 16th Street Baptist Church in Birmingham, Alabama.*

This afternoon we gather in the quiet of this sanctuary to pay our last
tribute of respect to these beautiful children of God. They entered the
stage of history just a few years ago, and in the brief years that they were
privileged to act on this mortal stage, they played their parts exceedingly well. Now the curtain falls; they move through the exit; the drama of
their earthly life comes to a close. They are now committed back to that
eternity from which they came.

These children—unoffending; innocent and beautiful—were the victims of one of the most vicious, heinous crimes ever perpetrated against
humanity.

Yet they died nobly. They are the martyred heroines of a holy crusade
for freedom and human dignity. So they have something to say to us in
their death. They have something to say to every minister of the gospel
who has remained silent behind the safe security of stained-glass windows. They have something to say to every politician who has fed his
constituents the stale bread of hatred and the spoiled meat of racism.
They have something to say to a federal government that has compromised with the undemocratic practices of southern dixiecrats and the
blatant hypocrisy of right-wing northern Republicans. They have something to say to every Negro who passively accepts the evil system of segregation, and stands on the sidelines in the midst of a mighty struggle
for justice. They say to each of us, black and white alike, that we must
substitute courage for caution. They say to us that we must be concerned not merely about WHO murdered them, but about the system,
the way of life and the philosophy which PRODUCED the murderers.
Their death says to us that we must work passionately and unrelentingly
to make the American dream a reality.

So they did not die in vain. God still has a way of wringing good out of
evil. History has proven over and over again that unmerited suffering is

redemptive. The innocent blood of these little girls may well serve as the redemptive force that will bring new light to this dark city. The holy Scripture says, "A little child shall lead them." The death of these little children may lead our whole Southland from the low road of man's inhumanity to man to the high road of peace and brotherhood. These tragic deaths may lead our nation to substitute an aristocracy of character for an aristocracy of color. The spilt blood of these innocent girls may cause the whole citizenry of Birmingham to transform the negative extremes of a dark past into the positive extremes of a bright future. Indeed, this tragic event may cause the white South to come to terms with its conscience.

So in spite of the darkness of this hour we must not despair. We must not become bitter; nor must we harbor the desire to retaliate with violence. We must not lose faith in our white brothers. Somehow we must believe that the most misguided among them can learn to respect the dignity and worth of all human personality.

May I now say a word to you, the members of the bereaved families. It is almost impossible to say anything that can console you at this difficult hour and remove the deep clouds of disappointment which are floating in your mental skies. But I hope you can find a little consolation from the universality of this experience. Death comes to every individual. There is an amazing democracy about death. It is not aristocracy for some of the people, but a democracy for all of the people. Kings die and beggars die; rich men die and poor men die; old people die and young people die; death comes to the innocent and it comes to the guilty. Death is the irreducible common denominator of all men.

I hope you can find some consolation from Christianity's affirmation that death is not the end. Death is not a period that ends the great sentence of life, but a comma that punctuates it to more lofty significance. Death is not a blind alley that leads the human race into a state of nothingness, but an open door which leads man into life eternal. Let this daring faith, this great invincible surmise, be your sustaining power during these trying days.

At times, life is hard, as hard as crucible steel. It has its bleak and painful moments. Like the ever-flowing waters of a river, life has its moments of drought and its moments of flood. Like the ever-changing cycle of the seasons, life has the soothing warmth of the summers and the piercing chill of its winters. But through it all, God walks with us. Never forget that God is able to lift you from fatigue of despair to the buoyancy of hope, and transform dark and desolate valleys into sunlit paths of inner peace.

Your children did not live long, but they lived well. The quantity of their lives was disturbingly small, but the quality of their lives was magnificently big. Where they died and what they were doing when death came will remain a marvelous tribute to each of you and an eternal epitaph to each of them. They died not in a den or dive nor were they hearing and telling filthy jokes at the time of their death. They died within the sacred walls of the church after discussing a principle as eternal as love.

Shakespeare had Horatio utter some beautiful words over the dead body of Hamlet. I paraphrase these words today as I stand over the last remains of these lovely girls.

"Good-night sweet princesses; may the flight of angels take thee to thy eternal rest."

Epilogue: The doors of the Sixteenth Street Baptist Church reopened on Sunday, June 7, 1964.

The "reentry" sermon was preached by a white clergyman, the Reverend H. O. Hester, secretary of the Department of Missions, Alabama Baptist Convention.

Offprint in the Library of the Martin Luther King, Jr., Center for Nonviolent Social Change, Atlanta, Georgia.

# 38

# Nobel Prize
# Acceptance Speech

*This is the full text of Dr. King's acceptance speech on the occasion of receiving the Nobel Peace Prize in Oslo, Norway, on 10 December 1964. When once asked by an interviewer what was the significance for him of receiving this much coveted award, Dr. King replied, "The Nobel award recognizes the amazing discipline of the Negro. Though we have had riots, the bloodshed we would have known without the discipline of nonviolence would have been frightening."*

Your Majesty, your Royal Highness, Mr. President, excellencies, ladies and gentlemen:

I accept the Nobel Prize for Peace at a moment when twenty-two million Negroes of the United States of America are engaged in a creative battle to end the long night of racial injustice. I accept this award in behalf of a civil rights movement which is moving with determination and a majestic scorn for risk and danger to establish a reign of freedom and a rule of justice.

I am mindful that only yesterday in Birmingham, Alabama, our children, crying out for brotherhood, were answered with fire hoses, snarling dogs and even death. I am mindful that only yesterday in Philadelphia, Mississippi, young people seeking to secure the right to vote were brutalized and murdered.

I am mindful that debilitating and grinding poverty afflicts my people and chains·them to the lowest rung of the economic ladder.

Therefore, I must ask why this prize is awarded to a movement which is beleaguered and committed to unrelenting struggle: to a movement which has not won the very peace and brotherhood which is the essence of the Nobel Prize.

After contemplation, I conclude that this award which I receive on behalf of that movement is profound recognition that nonviolence is the answer to the crucial political and moral question of our time—the need for man to overcome oppression and violence without resorting to violence and oppression.

Civilization and violence are antithetical concepts. Negroes of the United States, following the people of India, have demonstrated that nonviolence is not sterile passivity, but a powerful moral force which makes for social transformation. Sooner or later, all the people of the world will have to discover a way to live together in peace, and thereby transform this pending cosmic elegy into a creative psalm of brotherhood.

If this is to be achieved, man must evolve for all human conflict a method which rejects revenge, aggression and retaliation. The foundation of such a method is love.

From the depths of my heart I am aware that this prize is much more than an honor to me personally.

Every time I take a flight I am always mindful of the many people who make a successful journey possible, the known pilots and the unknown ground crew.

So you honor the dedicated pilots of our struggle who have sat at the controls as the freedom movement soared into orbit. You honor, once again, Chief (Albert) Luthuli of South Africa, whose struggles with and for his people, are still met with the most brutal expression of man's inhumanity to man.

You honor the ground crew without whose labor and sacrifices the jet flights to freedom could never have left the earth.

Most of these people will never make the headlines and their names will not appear in *Who's Who*. Yet the years have rolled past and when the blazing light of truth is focused on this marvelous age in which we live—men and women will know and children will be taught that we have a finer land, a better people, a more noble civilization—because these humble children of God were willing to suffer for righteousness' sake.

I think Alfred Nobel would know what I mean when I say that I accept this award in the spirit of the curator of some precious heirloom which he holds in trust for its true owners—all those to whom beauty is truth and truth beauty—and in whose eyes the beauty of genuine brotherhood and peace is more precious than diamonds or silver or gold.

The tortuous road which has lead from Montgomery, Alabama, to Oslo bears witness to this truth. This is a road over which millions of Negroes are travelling to find a new sense of dignity. This same road has opened for all Americans a new era of progress and hope. It has led to a new civil rights bill, and it will, I am convinced, be widened and lengthened into a superhighway of justice as Negro and white men in increasing number create alliances to overcome their common problems.

I accept this award today with an abiding faith in America and an audacious faith in the future of mankind. I refuse to accept the idea that the "isness" of man's present nature makes him morally incapable of reaching up for the eternal "oughtness" that forever confronts him.

I refuse to accept the idea that man is mere flotsam and jetsam in the river of life which surrounds him. I refuse to accept the view that mankind is so tragically bound to the starless midnight of racism and war that the bright daybreak of peace and brotherhood can never become a reality.

I refuse to accept the cynical notion that nation after nation must spiral down a militaristic stairway into hell of thermonuclear destruction. I believe that unarmed truth and unconditional love will have the final word in reality. That is why right temporarily defeated is stronger than evil triumphant.

I believe that even amid today's mortar bursts and whining bullets, there is still hope for a brighter tomorrow. I believe that wounded justice, lying prostrate on the blood-flowing streets of our nations, can be lifted from this dust of shame to reign supreme among the children of men.

I have the audacity to believe that peoples everywhere can have three meals a day for their bodies, education and culture for their minds, and dignity, equality and freedom for their spirits. I believe that what self-centered men have torn down men other-centered can build up. I still believe that one day mankind will bow before the altars of God and be crowned triumphant over war and bloodshed, and nonviolent redemptive good will will proclaim the rule of the land. "And the lion and the lamb shall lie down together and every man shall sit under his own vine and fig tree and none shall be afraid." I still believe that we shall overcome.

This faith can give us courage to face the uncertainties of the future. It will give our tired feet new strength as we continue our forward stride toward the city of freedom. When our days become dreary with low-hovering clouds and our nights become darker than a thousand midnights, we will know that we are living in the creative turmoil of a genuine civilization struggling to be born.

Today I come to Oslo as a trustee, inspired and with renewed dedication to humanity. I accept this prize on behalf of all men who love peace and brotherhood.

*Liberation* 10 (January 1965): 28–29. The quotation comes from his *Playboy* interview (1965). The complete text of this interview appears on page 341.

# 39

# Our God Is Marching On!

*Like Jonah in the belly of the whale, Dr. King spoke triumphantly before the state capitol building in Montgomery, often called "the Cradle of the Confederacy." He defended the march from Selma's bloody Edmund Pettus Bridge to the state capital. The march finally began in earnest on 21 March and ended with this speech on 25 March 1965.*

My dear and abiding friends, Ralph Albernathy, and to all the distinguished Americans seated here on the rostrum, my friends and co-workers of the state of Alabama and to all of the freedom-loving people who have assembled here this afternoon, from all over our nation and from all over the world.

Last Sunday, more than eight thousand of us started on a mighty walk from Selma, Alabama. We have walked on meandering highways and rested our bodies on rocky byways. Some of our faces are burned from the outpourings of the sweltering sun. Some have literally slept in the mud. We have been drenched by the rains.

Our bodies are tired, and our feet are somewhat sore, but today as I stand before you and think back over that great march, I can say as Sister Pollard said, a seventy-year-old Negro woman who lived in this community during the bus boycott and one day she was asked while walking if she wanted a ride and when she answered, "No," the person said, "Well, aren't you tired?" And with her ungrammatical profundity, she said, "My feets is tired, but my soul is rested."

And in a real sense this afternoon, we can say that our feet are tired, but our souls are rested.

## "WE ARE HERE"

They told us we wouldn't get here. And there were those who said that we would get here only over their dead bodies, but all the world today knows that we are here and that we are standing before the forces of power in the state of Alabama saying, "We ain't goin' let nobody turn us around."

The Civil Rights Act of 1964 gave Negroes some part of their rightful dignity, but without the vote it was dignity without strength.

Once more the method of nonviolent resistance was unsheathed from its scabbard and once again an entire community was mobilized to confront the adversary. And again the brutality of a dying order shrieks across the land. Yet Selma, Alabama, became a shining moment in the conscience of man.

There never was a moment in American history more honorable and more inspiring than the pilgrimage of clergymen and laymen of every race and faith pouring into Selma to face danger at the side of its embattled Negroes.

Confrontation of good and evil compressed in the tiny community of Selma generated the massive power to turn the whole nation to a new course. A president born in the South had the sensitivity to feel the will of the country, and in an address that will live in history as one of the most passionate pleas for human rights ever made by a president of our nation, he pledged the might of the federal government to cast off the centuries-old blight. President Johnson rightly praised the courage of the Negro for awakening the conscience of the nation.

On our part we must pay our profound respects to the white Americans who cherish their democratic traditions over the ugly customs and privileges of generations and come forth boldly to join hands with us. From Montgomery to Birmingham, from Birmingham to Selma, from Selma back to Montgomery, a trail wound in a circle and often bloody, yet it has become a highway up from darkness. Alabama has tried to nurture and defend evil, but the evil is choking to death in the dusty roads and streets of this state.

So I stand before you this afternoon with the conviction that segregation is on its deathbed in Alabama and the only thing uncertain about it is how costly the segregationists and Wallace will make the funeral.

Our whole campaign in Alabama has been centered around the right to vote. In focusing the attention of the nation and the world today on the flagrant denial of the right to vote, we are exposing the very origin, the root cause, of racial segregation in the Southland.

The threat of the free exercise of the ballot by the Negro and the white masses alike resulted in the establishing of a segregated society. They segregated southern money from the poor whites; they segregated southern mores from the rich whites; they segregated southern churches from Christianity; they segregated southern minds from honest thinking, and they segregated the Negro from everything.

We have come a long way since that travesty of justice was prepetrated upon the American mind. Today I want to tell the city of Selma, today I want to say to the state of Alabama, today I want to say to the people of America and the nations of the world: We are not about to turn around. We are on the move now. Yes, we are on the move and no wave of racism can stop us.

## "WE ARE ON THE MOVE"

We are on the move now. The burning of our churches will not deter us. We are on the move now. The bombing of our homes will not dissuade us. We are on the move now. The beating and killing of our clergymen and young people will not divert us. We are on the move now. The arrest and release of known murderers will not discourage us. We are on the move now.

Like an idea whose time has come, not even the marching of mighty armies can halt us. We are moving to the land of freedom.

Let us therefore continue our triumph and march to the realization of the American dream. Let us march on segregated housing, until every ghetto of social and economic depression dissolves and Negroes and whites live side by side in decent, safe and sanitary housing.

Let us march on segregated schools until every vestige of segregated and inferior education becomes a thing of the past and Negroes and whites study side by side in the socially healing context of the classroom.

Let us march on poverty, until no American parent has to skip a meal so that their children may march on poverty, until no starved man walks the streets of our cities and towns in search of jobs that do not exist.

Let us march on ballot boxes, march on ballot boxes until race baiters disappear from the political arena. Let us march on ballot boxes until the Wallaces of our nation tremble away in silence.

Let us march on ballot boxes, until we send to our city councils, state legislatures, and the United States Congress men who will not fear to do justice, love mercy, and walk humbly with their God. Let us march on ballot boxes until all over Alabama God's children will be able to walk the earth in decency and honor.

For all of us today the battle is in our hands. The road ahead is not altogether a smooth one. There are no broad highways to lead us easily and inevitably to quick solutions. We must keep going.

## "MY PEOPLE, LISTEN!"

My people, my people, listen! The battle is in our hands. The battle is in our hands in Mississippi and Alabama, and all over the United States.

So as we go away this afternoon, let us go away more than ever before committed to the struggle and committed to nonviolence. I must admit to you there are still some difficulties ahead. We are still in for a season of suffering in many of the black belt counties of Alabama, many areas of Mississippi, many areas of Louisiana.

I must admit to you there are still jail cells waiting for us, dark and difficult moments. We will go on with the faith that nonviolence and its power transformed dark yesterdays into bright tomorrows. We will be able to change all of these conditions.

230 / FAMOUS SERMONS AND PUBLIC ADDRESSES

Our aim must never be to defeat or humiliate the white man but to win his friendship and understanding. We must come to see that the end we seek is a society at peace with itself, a society that can live with its conscience. That will be a day not of the white man, not of the black man. That will be the day of man as man.

I know you are asking today, "How long will it take?" I come to say to you this afternoon however difficult the moment, however frustrating the hour, it will not be long, because truth pressed to earth will rise again.

How long? Not long, because no lie can live forever.

How long? Not long, because you still reap what you sow.

How long? Not long. Because the arm of the moral universe is long but it bends toward justice.

How long? Not long, 'cause mine eyes have seen the glory of the coming of the Lord, trampling out the vintage where the grapes of wrath are stored. He has loosed the fateful lightning of his terrible swift sword. His truth is marching on.

He has sounded forth the trumpets that shall never call retreat. He is lifting up the hearts of man before His judgment seat. Oh, be swift, my soul, to answer Him. Be jubilant, my feet. Our God is marching on.

# 40

# A Time to Break Silence

*Dr. King delivered this historic address at a meeting of Clergy and Laity Concerned. The meeting was held at the Riverside Church in New York City on 4 April 1967, exactly a year before he was assassinated. Although this was not the first time he had expressed opposition to the Vietnam War, it was the first time he linked it to the civil rights movement. And it was the first time that he directly attacked the Johnson administration's war policy.*

I come to this magnificent house of worship tonight because my conscience leaves me no other choice. I join with you in this meeting because I am in deepest agreement with the aims and work of the organization which has brought us together: Clergy and Laymen Concerned about Vietnam. The recent statement of your executive committee are the sentiments of my own heart and I found myself in full accord when I read its opening lines: "A time comes when silence is betrayal." That time has come for us in relation to Vietnam.

The truth of these words is beyond doubt but the mission to which they call us is a most difficult one. Even when pressed by the demands of inner truth, men do not easily assume the task of opposing their government's policy, especially in time of war. Nor does the human spirit move without great difficulty against all the apathy of conformist thought within one's own bosom and in the surrounding world. Moreover when the issues at hand seem as perplexed as they often do in the case of this dreadful conflict we are always on the verge of being mesmerized by uncertainty; but we must move on.

Some of us who have already begun to break the silence of the night have found that the calling to speak is often a vocation of agony, but we must speak. We must speak with all the humility that is appropriate to our limited vision, but we must speak. And we must rejoice as well, for surely this is the first time in our nation's history that a significant number of its religious leaders have chosen to move beyond the prophesying of smooth patriotism to the high grounds of a firm dissent based upon the mandates of conscience and the reading of history. Perhaps a new spirit is rising among us. If it is, let us trace its movement well and pray that our own inner being may be sensitive to its guidance, for we are deeply in need of a new way beyond the darkness that seems so close around us.

Over the past two years, as I have moved to break the betrayal of my own silences and to speak from the burnings of my own heart, as I have called for radical departures from the destruction of Vietnam, many persons have questioned me about the wisdom of my path. At the heart of their concerns this query has often loomed large and loud: Why are *you* speaking about war, Dr. King? Why are *you* joining the voices of dissent? Peace and civil rights don't mix, they say. Aren't you hurting the cause of your people, they ask? And when I hear them, though I often understand the source of their concern, I am nevertheless greatly saddened, for such questions mean that the inquirers have not really known me, my commitment or my calling. Indeed, their questions suggest that they do not know the world in which they live.

In the light of such tragic misunderstandings, I deem it of signal importance to try to state clearly, and I trust concisely, why I believe that the path from Dexter Avenue Baptist Church—the church in Montgomery, Alabama, where I began my pastorate—leads clearly to this sanctuary tonight.

I come to this platform tonight to make a passionate plea to my beloved nation. This speech is not addressed to Hanoi or to the National Liberation Front. It is not addressed to China or to Russia.

Nor is it an attempt to overlook the ambiguity of the total situation and the need for a collective solution to the tragedy of Vietnam. Neither is it an attempt to make North Vietnam or the National Liberation Front paragons of virtue, nor to overlook the role they can play in a successful resolution of the problem. While they both may have justifiable reason to be suspicious of the good faith of the United States, life and history give eloquent testimony to the fact that conflicts are never resolved without trustful give and take on both sides.

Tonight, however, I wish not to speak with Hanoi and the NLF, but rather to my fellow Americans who, with me, bear the greatest responsibility in ending a conflict that has exacted a heavy price on both continents.

## IMPORTANCE OF VIETNAM

Since I am a preacher by trade, I suppose it is not surprising that I have seven major reasons for bringing Vietnam into the field of my moral vision. There is at the outset a very obvious and almost facile connection between the war in Vietnam and the struggle I, and others, have been waging in America. A few years ago there was a shining moment in that struggle. It seemed as if there was a real promise of hope for the poor—both black and white—through the poverty program. There were experiments, hopes, new beginnings. Then came the buildup in Vietnam and I watched the program broken and eviscerated as if it were some idle political plaything of a society gone mad on war, and I knew that America would never invest the necessary funds or energies in re-habilitation of its poor so long as adventures like Vietnam continued to draw men and skills and money like some demonic destructive suction tube. So I was increasingly compelled to see the war as an enemy of the poor and to attack it as such.

Perhaps the more tragic recognition of reality took place when it became clear to me that the war was doing far more than devastating the hopes of the poor at home. It was sending their sons and their brothers and their husbands to fight and to die in extraordinarily high proportions relative to the rest of the population. We were taking the black young men who had been crippled by our society and sending them eight thousand miles away to guarantee liberties in Southeast Asia which they had not found in southwest Georgia and East Harlem. So we have been repeatedly faced with the cruel irony of watching Negro and white boys on TV screens as they kill and die together for a nation that has been unable to seat them together in the same schools. So we watch them in brutal solidarity burning the huts of a poor village, but we realize that they would never live on the same block in Detroit. I could not be silent in the face of such cruel manipulation of the poor.

My third reason moves to an even deeper level of awareness, for it grows out of my experience in the ghettos of the North over the last three years—especially the last three summers. As I have walked among the desperate, rejected and angry young men I have told them that Molotov cocktails and rifles would not solve their problems. I have tried to offer them my deepest compassion while maintaining my conviction that social change comes most meaningfully through nonviolent action. But they asked—and rightly so—what about Vietnam? They asked if our own nation wasn't using massive doses of violence to solve its problems, to bring about the changes it wanted. Their questions hit home, and I knew that I could never again raise my voice against the violence of the oppressed in the ghettos without having first spoken clearly to the greatst purveyor of violence in the world today—my own government. For the sake of those boys, for the sake of this government, for the sake of the hundreds of thousands trembling under our violence, I cannot be silent.

For those who ask the question, "Aren't you a civil rights leader?" and thereby mean to exclude me from the movement for peace, I have this further answer. In 1957 when a group of us formed the Southern Christian Leadership Conference, we chose as our motto: "To save the soul of America." We were convinced that we could not limit our vision to certain rights for black people, but instead affirmed the conviction that America would never be free or saved from itself unless the descendants of its slaves were loosed completely from the shackles they still wear. In a way we were agreeing with Langston Hughes, that black bard of Harlem, who had written earlier:

O, yes,
I say it plain,
America never was America to me,
And yet I swear this oath—
America will be!

Now, it should be incandescently clear that no one who has any concern for the integrity and life of America today can ignore the present war. If America's soul becomes totally poisoned, part of the autopsy must read Vietnam. It can never be saved so long as it destroys the deepest hopes of men the world over. So it is that those of us who are yet determined that America *will* be are led down the path of protest and dissent, working for the health of our land.

As if the weight of such a commitment to the life and health of America were not enough, another burden of responsibility was placed upon me in 1964; and I cannot forget that the Nobel Prize for Peace was also a commission—a commission to work harder than I had ever worked before "the brotherhood of man." This is a calling that takes me beyond national allegiances, but even if it were not present I would yet have to live with the meaning of my commitment to the ministry of Jesus Christ. To me the relationship of this ministry to the making of peace is so obvious that I sometimes marvel at those who ask me why I am speaking against the war. Could it be that they do not know that the good news was meant for all men—for Communist and capitalist, for their children and ours, for black and for white, for revolutionary and conservative? Have they forgotten that my ministry is in obedience to the one who loved his enemies so fully that he died for them? What then can I say to the "Vietcong" or to Castro or to Mao as a faithful minister of this one? Can I threaten them with death or must I not share with them my life?

Finally, as I try to delineate for you and for myself the road that leads from Montgomery to this place I would have offered all that was most valid if I simply said that I must be true to my conviction that I share with all men the calling to be a son of the living God. Beyond the calling of race or nation or creed is this vocation of sonship and brotherhood, and because I believe that the Father is deeply concerned especially for his suffering and helpless and outcast children, I come tonight to speak for them.

This I believe to be the privilege and the burden of all of us who deem ourselves bound by allegiances and loyalties which are broader and deeper than nationalism and which go beyond our nation's self-defined goals and positions. We are called to speak for the weak, for the voiceless, for victims of our nation and for those it calls enemy, for no document from human hands can make these humans any less our brothers.

## STRANGE LIBERATORS

And as I ponder the madness of Vietnam and search within myself for ways to understand and respond to compassion my mind goes constantly to the people of that peninsula. I speak now not of the soldiers of each side, not of the junta in Saigon, but simply of the people who have been living under the curse of war for almost three continuous decades now. I think of them too because it is clear to me that there will be no meaningful solution there until some attempt is made to know them and hear their broken cries.

They must see Americans as strange liberators. The Vietnamese people proclaimed their own independence in 1945 after a combined French and Japanese occupation, and before the Communist revolution in China. They were led by Ho Chi Minh. Even though they quoted the American Declaration of Independence in their own document of freedom, we refused to recognize them. Instead, we decided to support France in its reconquest of her former colony.

Our government felt then that the Vietnamese people were not "ready" for independence, and we again fell victim to the deadly Western arrogance that has poisoned the international atmosphere for so long. With that tragic decision we rejected a revolutionary government seeking self-determination, and a government that had been established not by China (for whom the Vietnamese have no great love) but by clearly indigenous forces that included some Communists. For the peasants this new government meant real land reform, one of the most important needs in their lives.

For nine years following 1945 we denied the people of Vietnam the right of independence. For nine years we vigorously supported the French in their abortive effort to recolonize Vietnam.

Before the end of the war we were meeting eighty per cent of the French war costs. Even before the French were defeated at Dien Bien Phu, they began to despair of the reckless action, but we did not. We encouraged them with our huge financial and military supplies to continue the war even after they had lost the will. Soon we would be paying almost the full costs of this tragic attempt at recolonization.

After the French were defeated it looked as if independence and land reform would come again through the Geneva agreements. But instead there came the United States, determined that Ho should not unify the temporarily divided nation, and the peasants watched again as we supported one of the most vicious modern dictators—our chosen man, Premier Diem. The peasants watched and cringed as Diem ruthlessly routed out all opposition, supported their extortionist landlords and refused even to discuss reunification with the north. The peasants watched as all this was presided over by U.S. influence and then by increasing numbers of U.S. troops who came to help quell the insurgency that Diem's methods had aroused. When Diem was overthrown they may have been happy, but the long line of military dictatorships seemed to offer no real change—especially in terms of their need for land and peace.

The only change came from America as we increased our troop commitments in support of governments which were singularly corrupt, inept and without popular support. All the while the people read our leaflets and received regular promises of peace and democracy—and land reform. Now they languish under our bombs and consider us—not their fellow Vietnamese—the real enemy. They move sadly and apathetically as we herd them off the land of their fathers into concentration camps where minimal social needs are rarely met. They know they must move or be destroyed by our bombs. So they go—primarily women and children and the aged.

They watch as we poison their water, as we kill a million acres of their crops. They must weep as the bulldozers roar through their areas preparing to destroy the precious trees. They wander into the hospitals, with at least twenty casualties from American firepower for one "Vietcong"-inflicted injury. So far we may have killed a million of them—mostly children. They wander into the towns and see thousands of the children, homelss, without clothes, running in packs on the streets like animals. They see the children degraded by our soldiers as they beg for food. They see the children selling their sisters to our soldiers, soliciting for their mothers.

What do the peasants think as we ally ourselves with the landlords and as we refuse to put any action into our many words concerning land reform? What do they think as we test out our latest weapons on them, just as the Germans tested out new medicine and new tortures in the concentration camps of Europe? Where are the roots of the independent Vietnam we claim to be building? Is it among these voiceless ones?

We have destroyed their two most cherished institutions: the family and the village. We have destroyed their land and their crops. We have cooperated in the crushing of the nation's only non-Communist revolutionary political force—the unified Buddhist church. We have supported the enemies of the peasants of Saigon. We have corrupted their women and children and killed their men. What liberators!

Now there is little left to build on—save bitterness. Soon the only solid physical foundations remaining will be found at our military bases and in the concrete of the concentration camps we call fortified hamlets. The peasants may well wonder if we plan to build our new Vietnam on such grounds as these? Could we blame them for such thoughts? We must speak for them and raise the questions they cannot raise. These too are our brothers.

Perhaps the more difficult but no less necessary task is to speak for those who have been designated as our enemies. What of the National Liberation Front—that strangely anonymous group we call VC or Communists? What must they think of us in America when they realize that we permitted the repression and cruelty of Diem which helped to bring them into being as a resistance group in the south? What do they think of our condoning the violence which led to their own taking up of arms?

How can they believe in our integrity when now we speak of "aggression from the north" as if there were nothing more essential to the war? How can they trust us when now we charge them with violence after the murderous reign of Diem and charge them with violence while we pour every new weapon of death into their land? Surely we must understand their feelings even if we do not condone their actions. Surely we must see that the men we supported pressed them to their violence. Surely we must see that our own computerized plans of destruction simply dwarf their greatest acts.

How do they judge us when our officials know that their membership is less than twenty-five percent Communist and yet insist on giving them the blanket name? What must they be thinking when they know that we are aware of their control of major sections of Vietnam and yet we appear ready to allow national elections in which this highly organized political parallel government will have no part? They ask how we can speak of free elections when the Saigon press is censored and controlled by the military junta. And they are surely right to wonder what kind of new government we plan to help form without them—the only party in real touch with the peasants. They question our political goals and they deny the reality of a peace settlement from which they will be excluded. Their questions are frighteningly relevant. Is our nation planning to build on political myth again and then shore it up with the power of new violence?

Here is the true meaning and value of compassion and nonviolence when it helps us to see the enemy's point of view, to hear his questions, to know his assessment of ourselves. For from his view we may indeed see the basic weaknesses of our own condition, and if we are mature, we may learn and grow and profit from the wisdom of the brothers who are called the opposition.

So, too, with Hanoi. In the north, where our bombs now pummel the land, and our mines endanger the waterways, we are met by a deep but understandable mistrust. To speak for them is to explain this lack of confidence in Western words, and especially their distrust of American intentions now. In Hanoi are the men who led the nation to independence against the Japanese and the French, the men who sought membership in the French commonwealth and were betrayed by the weakness of Paris and the willfulness of the colonial armies. It was they who led a second struggle against French domination at tremendous costs, and then were persuaded to give up the land they controlled between the thirteenth and seventeenth parallel as a temporary measure at Geneva. After 1954 they watched us conspire with Diem to prevent elections which would have surely brought Ho Chi Minh to power over a united Vietnam, and they realized they had been betrayed again.

When we ask why they do not leap to negotiate, these things must be remembered. Also it must be clear that the leaders of Hanoi considered the presence of American troops in support of the Diem regime to have been the initial military breach of the Geneva agreements concerning foreign troops, and they remind us that they did not begin to send in any large number of supplies or men until American forces had moved into the tens of thousands.

Hanoi remembers how our leaders refused to tell us the truth about the earlier North Vietnamese overtures for peace, how the president claimed that none existed when they had clearly been made. Ho Chi Minh has watched as America has spoken of peace and built up its forces, and now he has surely heard of the increasing international rumors of American plans for an invasion of the north. He knows the bombing and shelling and mining we are doing are part of traditional pre-invasion strategy. Perhaps only his sense of humor and of irony can save him when he hears the most powerful nation of the world speaking of aggression as its drops thousands of bombs on a poor weak nation more than eight thousand miles away from its shores.

At this point I should make it clear that while I have tried in these last few minutes to give a voice to the voiceless on Vietnam and to understand the arguments of those who are called enemy, I am as deeply concerned about our troops there as anything else. For it occurs to me that what we are submitting them to in Vietnam is not simply the brutalizing process that goes on in any war where armies face each other and seek to destroy. We are adding cynicism to the process of death, for they must know after a short period there that none of the things we claim to be fighting for are really involved. Before long they must know that their government has sent them into a struggle among Vietnamese, and the more sophisticated surely realize that we are on the side of the wealthy and the secure while we create a hell for the poor.

*Somehow this madness must cease. We must stop now. I speak as a child of God and brother to the suffering poor of Vietnam. I speak for those whose land is being laid waste, whose homes are being destroyed, whose culture is being subverted. I speak for the poor of America who are paying the double price of smashed hopes at home and death and corruption in Vietnam. I speak as a citizen of the world, for the world as it stands aghast at the path we have taken. I speak as an American to the leaders of my own nation. The great initiative in this war is ours. The initiative to stop it must be ours.*

This is the message of the great Buddhist leaders of Vietnam. Recently one of them wrote these words: *Each day the war goes on the hatred increases in the heart of the Vietnamese and in the hearts of those of humanitarian instinct. The Americans are forcing even their friends into becoming their enemies. It is curious that the Americans, who calculate so carefully on the possibilities of military victory, do not realize that in the process they are incurring deep psychological and political defeat. The image of America will never again be the image of revolution, freedom and democracy, but the image of violence and militarism.*

If we continue there will be no doubt in my mind and in the mind of the world that we have no honorable intentions in Vietnam. It will become clear that our minimal expectation is to occupy it as an American colony and men will not refrain from thinking that our maximum hope is to goad China into a war so that we may bomb her nuclear installations. If we do not stop our war against the people of Vietnam immediately the world will be left with no other alternative than to see this as some horribly clumsy and deadly game we have decided to play.

The world now demands a maturity of America that we may not be able to achieve. It demands that we admit that we have been wrong from the beginning of our adventure in Vietnam, that we have been detrimental to the life of the Vietnamese people. The situation is one in which we must be ready to turn sharply from our present ways.

In order to atone for our sins and errors in Vietnam, we should take the initiative in bringing a halt to this tragic war. I would like to suggest five concrete things that our government should do immediately to begin the long and difficult process of extricating ourselves from this nightmarish conflict:

1. *End all bombing in North and South Vietnam.*
2. *Declare a unilateral cease-fire in the hope that such action will create the atmosphere for negotiation.*
3. *Take immediate steps to prevent other battlegrounds in Southeast Asia by curtailing our military buildup in Thailand and our interference in Laos.*
4. *Realistically accept the fact that the National Liberation Front has substantial support in South Vietnam and must thereby play a role in any meaningful negotiations and in any future Vietnam government.*
5. *Set a date that we will remove all foreign troops from Vietnam in accordance with the 1954 Geneva agreement.*

Part of our ongoing commitment might well express itself in an offer to grant asylum to any Vietnamese who fears for his life under a new regime which included the Liberation Front. Then we must make what reparations we can for the damage we have done. We must provide the medical aid that is badly needed, making it available in this country if necessary.

## PROTESTING THE WAR

Meanwhile we in the churches and synagogues have a continuing task while we urge our government to disengage itself from a disgraceful commitment. We must continue to raise our voices if our nation persists in its perverse ways in Vietnam. We must be prepared to match actions with words by seeking out every creative means of protest possible.

As we counsel young men concerning military service we must clarify for them our nation's role in Vietnam and challenge them with the alternative of conscientious objection. I am pleased to say that this is the path now being chosen by more than seventy students at my own alma mater, Morehouse College, and I recommend it to all who find the American course in Vietnam a dishonorable and unjust one. Moreover I would encourage all ministers of draft age to give up their ministerial exemptions and seek status as conscientious objectors. These are the times for real choices and not false ones. We are at the moment when our lives must be placed on the line if our nation is to survive its own folly. Every man of humane convictions must decide on the protest that best suits his convictions, but we must all protest.

There is something seductively tempting about stopping there and sending us all off on what in some circles has become a popular crusade against the war in Vietnam. I say we must enter the struggle, but I wish to go on now to say something even more disturbing. The war in Vietnam is but a symptom of a far deeper malady within the American spirit, and if we ignore this sobering reality we will find ourselves organizing clergy- and laymen-concerned committees for the next generation. They will be concerned about Guatemala and Peru. They will be concerned about Thailand and Cambodia. They will be concerned about Mozambique and South Africa. We will be marching for these and a dozen other names and attending rallies without end unless there is a significant and pro-found change in American life and policy. Such thoughts take us beyond Vietnam, but not beyond our calling as sons of the living God.

In 1957 a sensitive American official overseas said that it seemed to him that our nation was on the wrong side of a world revolution. During the past ten years we have seen emerge a pattern of suppression which now has justified the presence of U.S. military "advisors" in Venezuela. This need to maintain social stability for our investments accounts for the counter-revolutionary action of American forces in Guatemala. It tells why American helicopters are being used against guerrillas in Co-lombia and why American napalm and green beret forces have already been active against rebels in Peru. It is with such activity in mind that the words of the late John F. Kennedy come back to haunt us. Five years ago he said, "Those who make peaceful revolution impossible will make violent revolution inevitable."

Increasingly, by choice or by accident, this is the role our nation has taken—the role of those who make peaceful revolution impossible by refusing to give up the privileges and the pleasures that come from the immense profits of overseas investment.

I am convinced that if we are to get on the right side of the world revolution, we as a nation must undergo a radical revolution of values. We must rapidly begin the shift from a "thing-oriented" society to a "person-oriented" society. When machines and computers, profit mo-tives and property rights are considered more important than people, the giant triplets of racism, materialism, and militarism are incapable of being conquered.

A true revolution of values will soon cause us to question the fairness and justice of many of our past and present policies. On the one hand we are called to play the good Samaritan on life's roadside; but that will be only an initial act. One day we must come to see that the whole Jericho road must be transformed so that men and women will not be constantly beaten and robbed as they make their journey on life's highway. True compassion is more than flinging a coin to a beggar; it is not haphazard and superficial. It comes to see that an edifice which produces beggars needs restructuring. A true revolution of values will soon look uneasily on the glaring contrast of poverty and wealth. With righteous indignation, it will look across the seas and see individual capitalists of the West investing huge sums of money in Asia, Africa and South America, only to take the profits out with no concern for the social betterment of the countries, and say: "This is not just." It will look at our alliance with the landed gentry of Latin America and say: "This is not just." The Western arrogance of feeling that it has everything to teach others and nothing to learn from them is not just. A true revolution of values will lay hands on the world order and say of war: "This way of settling differences is not just." This business of burning human beings with napalm, of filling our nation's homes with orphans and widows, of injecting poisonous drugs of hate into veins of peoples normally humane, of sending men home from dark and bloody battlefields physically handicapped and psychologically deranged, cannot be reconciled with wisdom, justice and love. A nation that continues year after year to spend more money on military defense than on programs of social uplift is approaching spiritual death.

America, the richest and most powerful nation in the world, can well lead the way in this revolution of values. There is nothing, except a tragic death wish, to prevent us from reordering our priorities, so that the pursuit of peace will take precedence over the pursuit of war. There is nothing to keep us from molding a recalcitrant status quo with bruised hands until we have fashioned it into a brotherhood.

This kind of positive revolution of values is our best defense against communism. War is not the answer. Communism will never be defeated by the use of atomic bombs or nuclear weapons. Let us not join those who shout war and through their misguided passions urge the United States to relinquish its participation in the United Nations. These are days which demand wise restraint and calm reasonableness. We must not call everyone a Communist or an appeaser who advocates the seating of Red China in the United Nations and who recognizes that hate and hysteria are not the final answers to the problem of these turbulent days. We must not engage in a negative anti-communism, but rather in a positive thrust for democracy, realizing that our greatest defense against communism is to take offensive action in behalf of justice. We must with positive action seek to remove those conditions of poverty, insecurity and injustice which are the fertile soil in which the seed of communism grows and develops.

## THE PEOPLE ARE IMPORTANT

These are revolutionary times. All over the globe men are revolting against old systems of exploitation and oppression and out of the wombs of a frail world new systems of justice and equality are being born. The shirtless and barefoot people of the land are rising up as never before. "The people who sat in darkness have seen a great light." We in the West must support these revolutions. It is a sad fact that, because of comfort, complacency, a morbid fear of communism, and our proneness to adjust to injustice, the Western nations that initiated so much of the revolutionary spirit of the modern world have now become the arch anti-revolutionaries. This has driven many to feel that only Marxism has the revolutionary spirit. Therefore, communism is a judgment against our failure to make democracy real and follow through on the revolutions that we initiated. Our only hope today lies in our ability to recapture the revolutionary spirit and go out into a sometimes hostile world declaring eternal hostility to poverty, racism, and militarism. With this powerful commitment we shall boldly challenge the status quo and unjust mores and thereby speed the day when "every valley shall be exalted, and every mountain and hill shall be made low, and the crooked shall be made straight and the rough places plain."

A genuine revolution of values means in the final analysis that our loyalties must become ecumenical rather than sectional. Every nation must now develop an overriding loyalty to mankind as a whole in order to preserve the best in their individual societies.

This call for a world-wide fellowship that lifts neighborly concern beyond one's tribe, race, class and nation is in reality a call for an all-embracing and unconditional love for all men. Ths oft misunderstood and misinterpreted concept—so readily dismissed by the Nietzsches of the world as a weak and cowardly force—has now become an absolute necessity for the survival of man. When I speak of love I am not speaking of some sentimental and weak response. I am speaking of that force which all of the great religions have seen as the supreme unifying principle of life. Love is somehow the key that unlocks the door which leads to ultimate reality. This Hindu-Moslem-Christian-Jewish-Buddhist belief about ultimate reality is beautifully summed up in the first epistle of Saint John:

Let us love one another; for love is God and everyone that loveth is born of God and knoweth God. He that loveth not knoweth not God; for God is love. If we love one another God dwelleth in us, and his love is perfected in us.

Let us hope that this spirit will become the order of the day. We can no longer afford to worship the god of hate or bow before the altar of retaliation. The oceans of history are made turbulent by the ever-rising tides of hate. History is cluttered with the wreckage of nations and individuals that pursued this self-defeating path of hate. As Arnold Toynbee says: "Love is the ultimate force that makes for the saving choice of life and good against the damning choice of death and evil. Therefore the first hope in our inventory must be the hope that love is going to have the last word."

We are now faced with the fact that tomorrow is today. We are confronted with the fierce urgency of now. In this unfolding conundrum of life and history there is such a thing as being too late. Procrastination is still the thief of time. Life often leaves us standing bare, naked and dejected with a lost opportunity. The "tide in the affairs of men" does not remain at the flood; it ebbs. We may cry out desperately for time to pause in her passage, but time is deaf to every plea and rushes on. Over the bleached bones and jumbled residue of numerous civilizations are written the pathetic words: "Too late." There is an invisible book of life that faithfully records our vigilance or our neglect. "The moving finger writes, and having writ moves on. . . ." We still have a choice today; nonviolent coexistence or violent co-annihilation.

We must move past indecision to action. We must find new ways to speak for peace in Vietnam and justice throughout the developing world—a world that borders on our doors. If we do not act we shall surely be dragged down the long dark and shameful corridors of time reserved for those who possess power without compassion, might without morality, and strength without sight.

Now let us begin. Now let us rededicate ourselves to the long and bitter—but beautiful—struggle for a new world. This is the calling of the sons of God, and our brothers wait eagerly for our response. Shall we say the odds are too great? Shall we tell them the struggle is too hard? Will our message be that the forces of American life militate against their arrival as full men, and we send our deepest regrets? Or will there be another message, of longing, of hope, of solidarity with their yearnings, of commitment to their cause, whatever the cost? The choice is ours, and though we might prefer it otherwise we *must* choose in this crucial moment of human history.

As that noble bard of yesterday, James Russell Lowell, eloquently stated:

*Once to every man and nation,*
*Comes the moment to decide*
*In the strife of truth and falsehood*
*For the good or evil side;*
*Some great cause God's new Messiah*
*Offering each the gloom or blight*
*And the choice goes by forever*
*Twixt that darkness and that light.*

*Though the cause of evil prosper*
*Yet 'tis truth along is strong*

*Though her portion be the scaffold*
*And upon the throne be wrong*
*Yet that scaffold sways the future*
*And behind the dim unknown*
*Standeth God within the shadow*
*Keeping watch above his own.*

# 41

# Where Do We Go from Here?

*This was Dr. King's last, and most radical, SCLC presidential address.*

Now, in order to answer the question, "Where do we go from here?" which is our theme, we must first honestly recognize where we are now. When the Constitution was written, a strange formula to determine taxes and representation declared that the Negro was sixty percent of a person. Today another curious formula seems to declare that he is fifty percent of a person. Of the good things in life, the Negro has approximately one half those of whites. Of the bad things of life, he has twice those of whites. Thus half of all Negroes live in substandard housing. And Negroes have half the income of whites. When we view the negative experiences of life, the Negro has a double share. There are twice as many unemployed. The rate of infant mortality among Negroes is double that of whites and there are twice as many Negroes dying in Vietnam as whites in proportion to their size in the population.

In other spheres, the figures are equally alarming. In elementary schools, Negroes lag one to three years behind whites, and their segregated schools receive substantially less money per student than the white schools. One-twentieth as many Negroes as whites attend college. Of employed Negroes, seventy-five percent hold menial jobs.

This is where we are. Where do we go from here? First, we must massively assert our dignity and worth. We must stand up amidst a system that still oppresses us and develop an unassailable and majestic sense of values. We must no longer be ashamed of being black. The job of arousing manhood within a people that have been taught for so many centuries that they are nobody is not easy.

Even semantics have conspired to make that which is black seem ugly and degrading. In Roget's *Thesaurus* there are 120 synonyms for blackness and at least sixty of them are offensive, as for example, blot, soot, grim, devil and foul. And there are some 134 synonyms for whiteness and all are favorable, expressed in such words as purity, cleanliness, chastity and innocence. A white lie is better than a black lie. The most degenerate member of a family is a "black sheep." Ossie Davis has suggested that maybe the English language should be reconstructed so that teachers will not be forced to teach the Negro child sixty ways to despise himself, and thereby perpetuate his false sense of inferiority, and the white child 134 ways to adore himself, and thereby perpetuate his false sense of superiority.

The tendency to ignore the Negro's contribution to American life and to strip him of his personhood is as old as the earliest history books and as contemporary as the morning's newspaper. To upset this cultural homicide, the Negro must rise up with an affirmation of his own Olympian manhood. Any movement for the Negro's freedom that overlooks this necessity is only waiting to be buried. As long as the mind is enslaved, the body can never be free. Psychological freedom, a firm sense of self-esteem, is the most powerful weapon against the long night of physical slavery. No Lincolnian emancipation proclamation or Johnsonian civil rights bill can totally bring this kind of freedom. The Negro will only be free when he reaches down to the inner depths of his own being and signs with the pen and ink of assertive manhood his own emancipation proclamation. And, with a spirit straining toward true self-esteem, the Negro must boldly throw off the manacles of self-abegnation and say to himself and to the world, "I am somebody. I am a person. I am a man with dignity and honor. I have a rich and noble history. How painful and exploited that history has been. Yes, I was a slave through my foreparents and I am not ashamed of that. I'm ashamed of the people who were so sinful to make me a slave." Yes, we must stand up and say, "I'm black and I'm beautiful," and this self-affirmation is the black man's need, made compelling by the white man's crimes against him.

Another basic challenge is to discover how to organize our strength in terms of economic and political power. No one can deny that the Negro is in dire need of this kind of legitimate power. Indeed, one of the great problems that the Negro confronts is his lack of power. From old plantations of the South to newer ghettos of the North, the Negro has been confined to a life of voicelessness and powerlessness. Stripped of the right to make decisions concerning his life and destiny he has been subject to the authoritarian and sometimes whimsical decisions of this white power structure. The plantation and ghetto were created by those who had power, both to confine those who had no power and to perpetuate their powerlessness. The problem of transforming the ghetto, therefore, is a problem of power—confrontation of the forces of power demanding change and the forces of power dedicated to the preserving of the status quo. Now power properly understood is nothing but the ability to achieve purpose. It is the strength required to bring about social, political and economic change. Walter Reuther defined power one day. He said, "Power is the ability of a labor union like the UAW to make the most powerful corporation in the world, General Motors, say, 'Yes' when it wants to say 'No.' That's power."

Now a lot of us are preachers, and all of us have our moral convictions and concerns, and so often have problems with power. There is nothing wrong with power if power is used correctly. You see, what happened is that some of our philosophers got off base. And one of the great problems of history is that the concepts of love and power have usually been contrasted as opposites—polar opposites—so that love is identified with a resignation of power, and power with a denial of love.

It was this misinterpretation that caused Nietzsche, who was a philosopher of the will to power, to reject the Christian concept of love. It was this same misinterpretation which induced Christian theologians to reject the Nietzschean philosophy of the will to power in the name of the Christian idea of love. Now, we've got to get this thing right. What is needed is a realization that power without love is reckless and abusive, and love without power is sentimental and anemic. Power at its best is love implementing the demands of justice, and justice at its best is power correcting everything that stands against love. And this is what we must see as we move on. What has happened is that we have had it wrong and confused in our own country, and this has led Negro Americans in the past to seek their goals through power devoid of love and conscience.

This is leading a few extremists today to advocate for Negroes the same destructive and conscienceless power that they have justly abhorred in whites. It is precisely this collision of immoral power with powerless morality which constitutes the major crisis of our times.

We must develop a program that will drive the nation to a guaranteed annual income. Now, early in this century this proposal would have been greeted with ridicule and denunciation, as destructive of initiative and responsibility. At that time economic status was considered the measure of the individual's ability and talents. And, in the thinking of that day, the absence of worldly goods indicated a want of industrious habits and moral fiber. We've come a long way in our understanding of human motivation and of the blind operation of our economic system. Now we realize that dislocations in the market operations of our economy and the prevalence of discrimination thrust people into idleness and bind them in constant or frequent unemployment against their will. Today the poor are less often dismissed, I hope, from our consciences by being branded as inferior or incompetent. We also know that no matter how dynamically the economy develops and expands, it does not eliminate all poverty.

The problem indicates that our emphasis must be twofold. We must create full employment or we must create incomes. People must be made consumers by one method or the other. Once they are placed in this position we need to be concerned that the potential of the individual is not wasted. New forms of work that enhance the social good will have to be devised for those for whom traditional jobs are not available.

In 1879 Henry George anticipated this state of affairs when he wrote in *Progress and Poverty*:*

The fact is that the work which improves the condition of mankind, the work which extends knowledge and increases power and enriches literature and elevates thought, is not done to secure a living. It is not the work of slaves driven to their tasks either by the task, by the taskmaster, or by animal necessity. It is the work of men who somehow find a form of work that brings a security for its own sake and a state of society where want is abolished.

Work of this sort could be enormously increased, and we are likely to find that the problems of housing and education, instead of preceding the elimination of poverty, will themselves be affected if poverty is first abolished. The poor transformed into purchasers will do a great deal on their own to alter housing decay. Negroes who have a double disability will have a greater effect on discrimination when they have the additional weapon of cash to use in their struggle.

Beyond these advantages, a host of positive psychological changes inevitably will result from widespread economic security. The dignity of the individual will flourish when the decisions conerning his life are in his own hands, when he has the means to seek self-improvement. Personal conflicts among husbands, wives and children will diminish when the unjust measurement of human worth on the scale of dollars is eliminated.

Now our country can do this. John Kenneth Galbraith said that a guaranteed annual income could be done for about twenty billion dollars a year. And I say to you today, that if our nation can spend thirty-five billion dollars a year to fight an unjust, evil war in Vietnam, and twenty billion dollars to put a man on the moon, it can spend billions of dollars to put God's children on their own two feet right here on earth.

Now, let me say briefly that we must reaffirm our commitment to nonviolence. I want to stress this. The futility of violence in the struggle for racial justice has been tragically etched in all the recent Negro riots. Yesterday, I tried to analyze the riots and deal with their causes. Today I want to give the other side. There is certainly something painfully sad about a riot. One sees screaming youngsters and angry adults fighting hopelessly and aimlessly against impossible odds. And deep down within them, you can see a desire for self-destruction, a kind of suicidal longing.

Occasionally Negroes contend that the 1965 Watts riot and the other riots in various cities represented effective civil rights action. But those who express this view always end up with stumbling words when asked

---

*Henry George (1839–1897) was the father of the single-tax system, which he set forth in his *Progress and Poverty*, published in 1879. The book argued that the land belonged to society, which created its value and properly taxed that value, not improvements on the land.

what concrete gains have been won as a result. At best, the riots have produced a little additional antipoverty money allotted by frightened government officials, and a few water-sprinklers to cool the children of the ghettos. It is something like improving the food in the prison while the people remain securely incarcerated behind bars. Nowhere have the riots won any concrete improvement such as have the organized protest demonstrations. When one tries to pin down advocates of violence as to what acts would be effective, the answers are blatantly illogical. Sometimes they talk of overthrowing racist state and local governments and they talk about guerrilla warfare. They fail to see that no internal revolution has ever succeeded in overthrowing a government by violence unless the government had already lost the allegiance and effective control of its armed forces. Anyone in his right mind knows that this will not happen in the United States. In a violent racial situation, the power structure has the local police, the state troopers, the National Guard and, finally, the army to call on—all of which are predominantly white. Furthermore, few if any violent revolutions have been successful unless the violent minority had the sympathy and support of the nonresistant majority. Castro may have had only a few Cubans actually fighting with him up in the hills, but he could never have overthrown the Batista regime unless he had the sympathy of the vast majority of Cuban people.†

It is perfectly clear that a violent revolution on the part of American blacks would find no sympathy and support from the white population and very little from the majority of the Negroes themselves. This is no time for romantic illusions and empty philosophical debates about freedom. This is a time for action. What is needed is a strategy for change, a tactical program that will bring the Negro into the mainstream of American life as quickly as possible. So far, this has only been offered by the nonviolent movement. Without recognizing this we will end up with solutions that don't solve, answers that don't answer and explanations that don't explain.

And so I say to you today that I still stand by nonviolence. And I am still convinced that it is the most potent weapon available to the Negro in his struggle for justice in this country. And the other thing is that I am concerned about a better world. I'm concerned about justice. I'm concerned about brotherhood. I'm concerned about truth. And when one is concerned about these, he can never advocate violence. For through violence you may murder a murderer but you can't murder murder. Through violence you may murder a liar but you can't establish truth. Through violence you may murder a hater, but you can't murder hate. Darkness cannot put out darkness. Only light can do that.

---

†In 1956 Fidel Castro landed on the coast of Cuba in the vessel, *Gramma*, to overthrow the despot Fulgencio Batista. Twelve men survived the counterattack and went on to lead the Cuban people to victory over Batista, who fled the island on New Year's Day, 1959, which ushered in the Cuban revolutionary victory.

And I say to you, I have also decided to stick to love. For I know that love is ultimately the only answer to mankind's problems. And I'm going to talk about it everywhere I go. I know it isn't popular to talk about it in some circles today. I'm not talking about emotional bosh when I talk about love, I'm talking about a strong, demanding love. And I have seen too much hate. I've seen too much hate on the faces of sheriffs in the South. I've seen hate on the faces of too many Klansmen and too many White Citizens Councilors in the South to want to hate myself, because every time I see it, I know that it does something to their faces and their personalities and I say to myself that hate is too great a burden to bear. I have decided to love. If you are seeking the highest good, I think you can find it through love. And the beautiful thing is that we are moving against wrong when we do it, because John was right, God is love. He who hates does not know God, but he who has love has the key that unlocks the door to the meaning of ultimate reality.

I want to say to you as I move to my conclusion, as we talk about "Where do we go from here," that we honestly face the fact that the movement must address itself to the question of restructuring the whole of American society. There are forty million poor people here. And one day we must ask the question, "Why are there forty million poor people in America?" And when you begin to ask that question, you are raising questions about the economic system, about a broader distribution of wealth. When you ask that question, you begin to question the capitalistic economy. And I'm simply saying that more and more, we've got to begin to ask questions about the whole society. We are called upon to help the discouraged beggars in life's marketplace. But one day we must come to see that an edifice which produces beggars needs restructuring. It means that questions must be raised. You see, my friends, when you deal with this, you begin to ask the question, "Who owns the oil?" You begin to ask the question, "Who owns the iron ore?" You begin to ask the question, "Why is it that people have to pay water bills in a world that is two-thirds water?" These are questions that must be asked.

Now, don't think that you have me in a "bind" today. I'm not talking about communism.

What I'm saying to you this morning is that communism forgets that life is individual. Capitalism forgets that life is social, and the kingdom of brotherhood is found neither in the thesis of communism nor the antithesis of capitalism but in a higher synthesis. It is found in a higher synthesis that combines the truths of both. Now, when I say question the whole society, it means ultimately coming to see that the problem of racism, the problem of economic exploitation, and the problem of war are all tied together. These are the triple evils that are interrelated.

If you will let me be a preacher just a little bit—One night, a juror came to Jesus and he wanted to know what he could do to be saved. Jesus didn't get bogged down in the kind of isolated approach of what he shouldn't do. Jesus didn't say, "Now Nicodemus, you must stop lying."

He didn't say, "Nicodemus, you must stop cheating if you are doing that." He didn't say, "Nicodemus, you must not commit adultery." He didn't say, "Nicodemus, now you must stop drinking liquor if you are doing that excessively." He said something altogether different, because Jesus realized something basic—that if a man will lie, he will steal. And if a man will steal, he will kill. So instead of just getting bogged down in one thing, Jesus looked at him and said, "Nicodemus, you must be born again."

He said, in other words, "Your whole structure must be changed." A nation that will keep people in slavery for 244 years will "thingify" them—make them things. Therefore they will exploit them, and poor people generally, economically. And a nation that will exploit economically will have to have foreign investments and everything else, and will have to use its military might to protect them. All of these problems are tied together. What I am saying today is that we must go from this convention and say, "America, you must be born again!"

So, I conclude by saying again today that we have a task and let us go out with a "divine dissatisfaction." Let us be dissatisfied until America will no longer have a high blood pressure of creeds and an anemia of deeds. Let us be dissatisfied until the tragic walls that separate the outer city of wealth and comfort and the inner city of poverty and despair shall be crushed by the battering rams of the forces of justice. Let us be dissatisfied until those that live on the outskirts of hope are brought into the metropolis of daily security. Let us be dissatisfied until slums are cast into the junk heaps of history, and every family is living in a decent sanitary home. Let us be dissatisfied until the dark yesterdays of segregated schools will be transformed into bright tomorrows of quality, integrated education. Let us be dissatisfied until integration is not seen as a problem but as an opportunity to participate in the beauty of diversity. Let us be dissatisfied until men and women, however black they may be, will be judged on the basis of the content of their character and not on the basis of the color of their skin. Let us be dissatisfied. Let us be dissatisfied until every state capitol houses a governor who will do justly, who will love mercy and who will walk humbly with his God. Let us be dissatisfied until from every city hall, justice will roll, down like waters and righteousness like a mighty stream. Let us be dissatisfied until that day when the lion and the lamb shall lie down together, and every man will sit under his own vine and fig tree and none shall be afraid. Let us be dissatisfied. And men will recognize that out of one blood God made all men to dwell upon the face of the earth. Let us be dissatisfied until that day when nobody will shout "White Power!"—when nobody will shout "Black Power!"—but everybody will talk about God's power and human power.

I must confess, my friends, the road ahead will not always be smooth. There will be still rocky places of frustration and meandering points of bewilderment. There will be inevitable setbacks here and there. There will be those moments when the buoyancy of hope will be transformed into the fatigue of despair. Our dreams will sometimes be shattered and our ethereal hopes blasted. We may again with tear-drenched eyes have to stand before the bier of some courageous civil rights worker whose life will be snuffed out by the dastardly acts of bloodthirsty mobs. Difficult and painful as it is, we must walk on in the days ahead with an audacious faith in the future. And as we continue our charted course, we may gain consolation in the words so nobly left by that great black bard who was also a great freedom fighter of yesterday, James Weldon Johnson:

> Stony the road we trod,
> Bitter the chastening rod
> Felt in the days
> When hope unborn had died.
>
> Yet with a steady beat,
> Have not our weary feet
> Come to the place
> For which our fathers sighed?
>
> We have come over the way
> That with tears hath been watered.
> We have come treading our paths
> Through the blood of the slaughtered,
>
> Out from the gloomy past,
> Till now we stand at last
> Where the bright gleam
> Of our bright star is cast.

Let this affirmation be our ringing cry. It will give us the courage to face the uncertainties of the future. It will give our tired feet new strength as we continue our forward stride toward the city of freedom. When our days become dreary with low-hovering clouds of despair, and when our nights become darker than a thousand midnights, let us remember that there is a creative force in this universe, working to pull down the gigantic mountains of evil, a power that is able to make a way out of no way and transform dark yesterdays into bright tomorrows. Let us realize the arc of the moral universe is long but it bends toward justice.

Let us realize that William Cullen Bryant is right: "Truth crushed to earth will rise again." Let us go out realizing that the Bible is right: "Be not deceived, God is not mocked. Whatsoever a man soweth, that shall he also reap." This is for hope for the future, and with this faith we will be able to sing in some not too distant tomorrow with a cosmic past tense, "We have overcome, we have overcome, deep in my heart, I did believe we would overcome."

---

This speech was published under the title "New Sense of Direction" in *Worldview* 15 (April 1972): 5ff.

# 42

# A Christmas Sermon on Peace

*Dr. King first delivered this sermon at Ebenezer Baptist Church, where he served as co-pastor. On Christmas Eve, 1967, the Canadian Broadcasting Corporation aired this sermon as part of the seventh annual Massey Lectures.*

Peace on Earth. . . .

This Christmas season finds us a rather bewildered human race. We have neither peace within nor peace without. Everywhere paralyzing fears harrow people by day and haunt them by night. Our world is sick with war; everywhere we turn we see its ominous possibilities. And yet, my friends, the Christmas hope for peace and good will toward all men can no longer be dismissed as a kind of pious dream of some utopian. If we don't have good will toward men in this world, we will destroy ourselves by the misuse of our own instruments and our own power. Wisdom born of experience should tell us that war is obsolete. There may have been a time when war served as a negative good by preventing the spread and growth of an evil force, but the very destructive power of modern weapons of warfare eliminates even the possibility that war may any longer serve as a negative good. And so, if we assume that life is worth living, if we assume that mankind has a right to survive, then we must find an alternative to war—and so let us this morning explore the conditions for peace. Let us this morning think anew on the meaning of that Christmas hope: "Peace on Earth, Good Will toward Men." And as we explore these conditions, I would like to suggest that modern man really go all out to study the meaning of nonviolence, its philosophy and its strategy.

We have experimented with the meaning of nonviolence in our struggle for racial justice in the United States, but now the time has come for man to experiment with nonviolence in all areas of human conflict, and that means nonviolence on an international scale.

Now let me suggest first that if we are to have peace on earth, our loyalties must become ecumenical rather than sectional. Our loyalties must transcend our race, our tribe, our class, and our nation; and this means we must develop a world perspective. No individual can live alone; no nation can live alone, and as long as we try, the more we are going to have war in this world. Now the judgment of God is upon us, and we must either learn to live together as brothers or we are all going to perish together as fools.

Yes, as nations and individuals, we are interdependent. I have spoken to you before of our visit to India some years ago. It was a marvelous experience; but I say to you this morning that there were those depressing moments. How can one avoid being depressed when one sees with one's own eyes evidences of millions of people going to bed hungry at night? How can one avoid being depressed when one sees with one's own eyes thousands of people sleeping on the sidewalks at night? More than a million people sleep on the sidewalks of Bombay every night; more than half a million sleep on the sidewalks of Calcutta every night. They have no houses to go into. They have no beds to sleep in. As I beheld these conditions, something within me cried out: "Can we in America stand idly by and not be concerned?" And an answer came: "Oh, no!" And I started thinking about the fact that right here in our country we spend millions of dollars every day to store surplus food; and I said to myself: "I know where we can store that food free of charge—in the wrinkled stomachs of the millions of God's children in Asia, Africa, Latin America, and even in our own nation, who go to bed hungry at night."

It really boils down to this: that all life is interrelated. We are all caught in an inescapable network of mutuality, tied into a single garment of destiny. Whatever affects one directly, affects all indirectly. We are made to live together because of the interrelated structure of reality. Did you ever stop to think that you can't leave for your job in the morning without being dependent on most of the world? You get up in the morning and go to the bathroom and reach over for the sponge, and that's handed to you by a Pacific islander. You reach for a bar of soap, and that's given to you at the hands of a Frenchman. And then you go into the kitchen to drink your coffee for the morning, and that's poured into your cup by a South American. And maybe you want tea: that's poured into your cup by a Chinese. Or maybe you're desirous of having cocoa for breakfast, and that's poured into your cup by a West African. And then you reach over for your toast, and that's given to you at the hands of an English-speaking farmer, not to mention the baker. And before you finish eating breakfast in the morning, you've depended on more than half of the world. This is the way our universe is structured, this is its interrelated quality. We aren't going to have peace on earth until we recognize this basic fact of the interrelated structure of all reality.

Now let me say, secondly, that if we are to have peace in the world, men and nations must embrace the nonviolent affirmation that ends and means must cohere. One of the great philosophical debates of history has been over the whole question of means and ends. And there have always been those who argued that the end justifies the means, that the means really aren't important. The important thing is to get to the end, you see.

So, if you're seeking to develop a just society, they say, the important thing is to get there, and the means are really unimportant; any means will do so long as they get you there—they may be violent, they may be untruthful means; they may even be unjust means to a just end. There have been those who have argued this throughout history. But we will never have peace in the world until men everywhere recognize that ends are not cut off from means, because the means represent the ideal in the making, and the end in process, and ultimately you can't reach good ends through evil means, because the means represent the seed and the end represents the tree.

It's one of the strangest things that all the great military geniuses of the world have talked about peace. The conquerors of old who came killing in pursuit of peace, Alexander, Julius Caesar, Charlemagne, and Napoleon, were akin in seeking a peaceful world order. If you will read *Mein Kampf* closely enough, you will discover that Hitler contended that everything he did in Germany was for peace. And the leaders of the world today talk eloquently about peace. Every time we drop our bombs in North Vietnam, President Johnson talks eloquently about peace. What is the problem? They are talking about peace as a distant goal, as an end we seek, but one day we must come to see that peace is not merely a distant goal we seek, but that it is a means by which we arrive at that goal. We must pursue peaceful ends through peaceful means. All of this is saying that, in the final analysis, means and ends must cohere because the end is preexistent in the means, and ultimately destructive means cannot bring about constructive ends.

Now let me say that the next thing we must be concerned about if we are to have peace on earth and good will toward men is the nonviolent affirmation of the sacredness of all human life. Every man is somebody because he is a child of God. And so when we say "Thou shalt not kill," we're really saying that human life is too sacred to be taken on the battlefields of the world. Man is more than a tiny vagary of whirling electrons or a wisp of smoke from a limitless smoldering. Man is a child of God, made in His image, and therefore must be respected as such. Until men see this everywhere, until nations see this everywhere, we will be fighting wars. One day somebody should remind us that, even though there may be political and ideological differences between us, the Vietnamese are our brothers, the Russians are our brothers, the Chinese are our brothers; and one day we've got to sit down together at the table of brotherhood. But in Christ there is neither Jew nor Gentile. In Christ there is neither male nor female. In Christ there is neither Communist nor capitalist. In Christ, somehow, there is neither bound nor free. We are all one in Christ Jesus. And when we truly believe in the sacredness of human personality, we won't exploit people, we won't trample over people with the iron feet of oppression, we won't kill anybody.

There are three words for "love" in the Greek New Testament; one is the word "*eros.*" *Eros* is a sort of esthetic, romantic love. Plato used to talk about it a great deal in his dialogues, the yearning of the soul for the realm of the divine. And there is and can always be something beautiful about *eros*, even in its expressions of romance. Some of the most beautiful love in all of the world has been expressed this way.

Then the Greek language talks about "*philia*," which is another word for love, and *philia* is a kind of intimate love between personal friends. This is the kind of love you have for those people that you get along with well, and those whom you like on this level you love because you are loved.

Then the Greek language has another word for love, and that is the word "*agape.*" *Agape* is more than romantic love, it is more than friendship. *Agape* is understanding, creative, redemptive good will toward all men. *Agape* is an overflowing love which seeks nothing in return. Theologians would say that it is the love of God operating in the human heart. When you rise to love on this level, you love all men not because you like them, not because their ways appeal to you, but you love them because God loves them. This is what Jesus meant when he said, "Love your enemies." And I'm happy that he didn't say, "Like your enemies," because there are some people that I find it pretty difficult to like. Liking is an affectionate emotion, and I can't like anybody who would bomb my home. I can't like anybody who would exploit me. I can't like anybody who would trample over me with injustices. I can't like them. I can't like anybody who threatens to kill me day in and day out. But Jesus reminds us that love is greater than liking. Love is understanding, creative, redemptive good will toward all men. And I think this is where we are, as a people, in our struggle for racial justice. We can't ever give up. We must work passionately and unrelentingly for first-class citizenship. We must never let up in our determination to remove every vestige of segregation and discrimination from our nation, but we shall not in the process relinquish our privilege to love.

I've seen too much hate to want to hate, myself, and I've seen hate on the faces of too many sheriffs, too many white citizens' councilors, and too many Klansmen of the South to want to hate, myself; and every time I see it, I say to myself, hate is too great a burden to bear. Somehow we must be able to stand up before our most bitter opponents and say: "We shall match your capacity to inflict suffering by our capacity to endure suffering. We will meet your physical force with soul force. Do to us what you will and we will still love you. We cannot in all good conscience obey your unjust laws and abide by the unjust system, because noncooperation with evil is as much a moral obligation as is cooperation with good, and so throw us in jail and we will still love you. Bomb our homes and threaten our children, and, as difficult as it is, we will still love you. Send your hooded perpetrators of violence into our communities at the midnight hour and drag us out on some wayside road and leave us half-dead as you beat us, and we will still love you. Send your propaganda agents around the country, and make it appear that we are not fit, culturally and otherwise, for integration, and we'll still love you. But be assured that we'll wear you down by our capacity to suffer, and one day we will win our freedom. We will not only win freedom for ourselves; we will so appeal to your heart and conscience that we will win you in the process, and our victory will be a double victory."

If there is to be peace on earth and good will toward men, we must finally believe in the ultimate morality of the universe, and believe that all reality hinges on moral foundations. Something must remind us of this as we once again stand in the Christmas season and think of the Easter season simultaneously, for the two somehow go together. Christ came to show us the way. Men love darkness rather than the light, and they crucified him, and there on Good Friday on the cross it was still dark, but then Easter came, and Easter is an eternal reminder of the fact that the truth-crushed earth will rise again. Easter justifies Carlyle in saying, "No lie can live forever." And so this is our faith, as we continue to hope for peace on earth and good will toward men: let us know that in the process we have cosmic companionship.

In 1963, on a sweltering August afternoon, we stood in Washington, D.C., and talked to the nation about many things. Toward the end of that afternoon, I tried to talk to the nation about a dream that I had had, and I must confess to you today that not long after talking about that dream I started seeing it turn into a nightmare. I remember the first time I saw that dream turn into a nightmare, just a few weeks after I had talked about it. It was when four beautiful, unoffending, innocent Negro girls were murdered in a church in Birmingham, Alabama. I watched that dream turn into a nightmare as I moved through the ghettos of the nation and saw my black brothers and sisters perishing on a lonely island of poverty in the midst of a vast ocean of material prosperity, and saw the nation doing nothing to grapple with the Negroes' problem of poverty. I saw that dream turn into a nightmare as I watched my black brothers and sisters in the midst of anger and understandable outrage, in the midst of their hurt, in the midst of their disappointment, turn to misguided riots to try to solve that problem. I saw that dream turn into a nightmare as I watched the war in Vietnam escalating, and as I saw so-called military advisors, sixteen thousand strong, turn into fighting soldiers until today over five hundred thousand American boys are fighting on Asian soil. Yes, I am personally the victim of deferred dreams, of blasted hopes, but in spite of that I close today by saying I still have a dream, because, you know, you can't give up in life. If you lose hope, somehow you lose that vitality that keeps life moving, you lose that courage to be, that quality that helps you go on in spite of all. And so today I still have a dream.

I have a dream that one day men will rise up and come to see that they are made to live together as brothers. I still have a dream this morning that one day every Negro in this country, every colored person in the world, will be judged on the basis of the content of his character rather than the color of his skin, and every man will respect the dignity and worth of human personality. I still have a dream that one day the idle industries of Appalachia will be revitalized, and the empty stomachs of Mississippi will be filled, and brotherhood will be more than a few words at the end of a prayer, but rather the first order of business on every legislative agenda. I still have a dream today that one day justice will roll down like water, and righteousness like a mighty stream. I still have a dream today that in all of our state houses and city halls men will be elected to go there who will do justly and love mercy and walk humbly with their God. I still have a dream today that one day war will come to an end, that men will beat their swords into plowshares and their spears into pruning hooks, that nations will no longer rise up against nations, neither will they study war any more. I still have a dream today that one day the lamb and the lion will lie down together and every man will sit under his own vine and fig tree and none shall be afraid. I still have a dream today that one day every valley shall be exalted and every mountain and hill will be made low, the rough places will be made smooth and the crooked places straight, and the glory of the Lord shall be revealed, and all flesh shall see it together. I still have a dream that with this faith we will be able to adjourn the councils of despair and bring new light into the dark chambers of pessimism. With this faith we will be able to speed up the day when there will be peace on earth and good will toward men. It will be a glorious day, the morning stars will sing together, and the sons of God will shout for joy.

Martin Luther King, Jr., *The Trumpet of Conscience* (New York and London: Harper & Row, 1967), 67–78.

# 43

# The Drum Major Instinct

*Dr. King preached this sermon from the pulpit of Ebenezer Baptist Church, 4
February 1968. Famous excerpts from it were played at his nationally televised
funeral service held at Ebenezer Baptist Church on 9 April 1968, five days after
his assassination.*

This morning I would like to use as a subject from which to preach
"The Drum Major Instinct." And our text for the morning is taken
from a very familiar passage in the tenth chapter as recorded by Saint
Mark; beginning with the thirty-fifth verse of that chapter, we read
these words: "And James and John the sons of Zebedee came unto him
saying, 'Master, we would that thou shouldest do for us whatsoever we
shall desire.' And he said unto them, 'What would ye that I should do
for you?' And they said unto him, 'Grant unto us that we may sit one on
thy right hand, and the other on thy left hand in thy glory.' But Jesus
said unto them, 'Ye know not what ye ask. Can ye drink of the cup that I
drink of, and be baptized with the baptism that I am baptized with?'
And they said unto him, 'We can.' And Jesus said unto them, 'Ye shall
indeed drink of the cup that I drink of, and with the baptism that I am
baptized with all shall ye be baptized. But to sit on my right hand and on
my left hand is not mine to give, but it shall be given to them for whom
it is prepared.' "

And then, Jesus goes on toward the end of that passage to say, "But so
shall it not be among you, but whosoever will be great among you, shall
be your servant; and whosoever of you will be the chiefest, shall be servant of all." The setting is clear. James and John are making a specific
request of the master. They had dreamed, as most Hebrews dreamed, of
a coming king of Israel who would set Jerusalem free. And establish his
kingdom on Mount Zion, and in righteousness rule the world. And they
thought of Jesus as this kind of king, and they were thinking of that day
when Jesus would reign supreme as this new king of Israel. And they
were saying now, 'when you establish your kingdom, let one of us sit on
the right hand, and the other on the left hand of your throne.'

Now very quickly, we would automatically condemn James and John,
and we would say they were selfish. Why would they make such a selfish
request? But before we condemn them too quickly, let us look calmly
and honestly at ourselves, and we will discover that we too have those

same basic desires for recognition, for importance, that same desire for attention, that same desire to be first. Of course the other disciples got mad with James and John, and you could understand why, but we must understand that we have some of the same James and John qualities. And there is, deep down within all of us, an instinct. It's a kind of drum major instinct—a desire to be out front, a desire to lead the parade, a desire to be first. And it is something that runs a whole gamut of life.

And so before we condemn them, let us see that we all have the drum major instinct. We all want to be important, to surpass others, to achieve distinction, to lead the parade. Alfred Adler, the great psychoanalyst, contends that this is the dominant impulse. Sigmund Freud used to contend that sex was the dominant impulse, and Adler came with a new argument saying that this quest for recognition, this desire for attention, this desire for distinction is the basic impulse, the basic drive of human life—this drum major instinct.

And you know, we begin early to ask life to put us first. Our first cry as a baby was a bid for attention. And all through childhood the drum major impulse or instinct is a major obsession. Children ask life to grant them first place. They are a little bundle of ego. And they have innately the drum major impulse, or the drum major instinct.

Now in adult life, we still have it, and we really never get by it. We like to do something good. And you know, we like to be praised for it. Now if you don't believe that, you just go on living life, and you will discover very soon that you like to be praised. Everybody likes it, as a matter of fact. And somehow this warm glow we feel when we are praised, or when our name is in print, is something of the vitamin A to our ego. Nobody is unhappy when they are praised, even if they know they don't deserve it, and even if they don't believe it. The only unhappy people about praise is when that praise is going too much toward somebody else. But everybody likes to be praised, because of this real drum major instinct.

Now the presence of the drum major instinct is why so many people are joiners. You know there are some people who just join everything. And it's really a quest for attention, and recognition, and importance. And they get names that give them that impression. So you get your groups, and they become the grand patron, and the little fellow who is henpecked at home needs a chance to be the most worthy of the most worthy of something. It is the drum major impulse and longing that runs the gamut of human life. And so we see it everywhere, this quest for recognition. And we join things, over-join really, that we think that we will find that recognition in.

Now the presence of this instinct explains why we are so often taken by advertisers. You know those gentlemen of massive verbal persuasion. And they have a way of saying things to you that kind of gets you into buying. In order to be a man of distinction, you must drink this whiskey.

In order to make your neighbors envious, you must drive this type of car. In order to be lovely to love you must wear this kind of lipstick or this kind of perfume. And you know, before you know it you're just buying that stuff. That's the way the advertisers do it.

I got a letter the other day. It was a new magazine coming out. And it opened up, "Dear Dr. King. As you know, you are on many mailing lists. And you are categorized as highly intelligent, progressive, a lover of the arts, and the sciences, and I know you will want to read what I have to say." Of course I did. After you said all of that and explained me so exactly, of course I wanted to read it.

But very seriously, it goes through life, the drum major instinct is real. And you know what else it causes to happen? It often causes us to live above our means. It's nothing but the drum major instinct. Do you ever see people buy cars that they can't even begin to buy in terms of their income? You've seen people riding around in Cadillacs and Chryslers who don't earn enough to have a good Model-T Ford. But it feeds a repressed ego.

You know economists tell us that your automobiles should not cost more than half of your annual income. So if you're making an income of five thousand dollars, your car shouldn't cost more than about twenty-five hundred. That's just good economics. And if it's a family of two, and both members of the family make ten thousand dollars, they would have to make out with one car. That would be good economics, although it's often inconvenient. But so often . . . haven't you seen people making five thousand dollars a year and driving a car that costs six thousand. And they wonder why their ends never meet. That's a fact.

Now the economists also say that your house shouldn't cost, if you're buying a house, it shouldn't cost more than twice your income. That's based on the economy, and how you would make ends meet. So, if you have an income of five thousand dollars, it's kind of difficult in this society. But say it's a family with an income of ten thousand dollars, the house shouldn't cost more than twenty thousand. But I've seen folk making ten thousand dollars, living in a forty- and fifty-thousand-dollar house. And you know they just barely make it. They get a check every month somewhere, and they owe all of that out before it comes in; never have anything to put away for rainy days.

But now the problem is, it is the drum major instinct. And you know, you see people over and over again with the drum major instinct taking them over. And they just live their lives trying to outdo the Joneses. They got to get this coat because this particular coat is a little better, and a little better-looking than Mary's coat. And I got to drive this car because it's something about this car that makes my car a little better than my neighbor's car. I know a man who used to live in a thirty-five-thousand-dollar house. And other people started building thirty-five-thousand-dollar houses, so he built a seventy-thousand-dollar house, and he built a hundred-thousand-dollar house. And I don't know where he's going to end up if he's going to live his life trying to keep up with the Joneses.

There comes a time that the drum major instinct can become destructive. And that's where I want to move now. I want to move to the point of saying that if this instinct is not harnessed, ti becomes a very dangerous, pernicious instinct. For instance, if it isn't harnessed, it causes one's personality to become distorted. I guess that's the most damaging aspect of it—what it does to the personality. If it isn't harnessed, you will end up day in and day out trying to deal with your ego problem by boasting.

Have you ever heard people that—you know, and I'm sure you've met them—that really become sickening because they just sit up all the time talking about themselves. And they just boast, and boast, and boast, and that's the person who has not harnessed the drum major instinct.

And then it does other things to the personality. It causes you to lie about who you know sometimes. There are some people who are influence peddlers. And in their attempt to deal with the drum major instinct, they have to try to identify with the so-called big name people. And if you're not careful, they will make you think they know somebody that they don't really know. They know them well, they sip tea with them. And they . . . this and that. That . . . that happens to people.

And the other thing is that it causes one to engage ultimately in activities that are merely used to get attention. Criminologists tell us that some people are driven to crime because of this drum major instinct. They don't feel that they are getting enough attention through the normal channels of social behavior, and others turn to anti-social behavior in order to get attention, in order to feel important. And so they get that gun. And before they know it they rob the bank in a quest for recognition, in a quest for importance.

And then the final great tragedy of the distorted personality is the fact that when one fails to harness this instinct, he ends by trying to push others down in order to push himself up. And whenever you do that, you engage in some of the most vicious activities. You will spread evil, vicious, lying gossip on people, because you are trying to pull them down in order to push yourself up.

And the great issue of life is to harness the drum major instinct.

Now the other problem is when you don't harness the drum major instinct, this uncontrolled aspect of it, is that it leads to snobbish exclusivism. Now you know, this is the danger of social clubs, and fraternities. I'm in a fraternity; I'm in two or three. For sororities, and all of these, I'm not talking against them, I'm saying it's the danger. The danger is that they can become forces of classism and exclusivism where somehow you get a degree of satisfaction because you are in something exclusive, and that's fulfilling something, you know. And I'm in this fraternity, and it's the best fraternity in the world and everybody can't get in this fraternity. So it ends up, you know, a very exclusive kind of thing.

And you know, that can happen with the church. I've known churches get in that bind sometimes. I've been to churches you know, and they say, "We have so many doctors and so many school teachers, and so many lawyers, and so many businessmen in our church." And that's fine, because doctors need to go to church, and lawyers, and businessmen, teachers—they ought to be in church. But they say that, even the preacher sometime will go on through it, they say that as if the other people don't count. And the church is the one place where a doctor ought to forget that he's a doctor. The church is the one place where a Ph.D. ought to forget that he's a Ph.D. The church is the one place that a schoolteacher ought to forget the degree she has behind her name. The church is the one place where the lawyer ought to forget that he's a lawyer. And any church that violates the 'whosoever will, let him come' doctrine is a dead, cold church, and nothing but a little social club with a thin veneer of religiosity.

When the church is true to its nature, it says, "Whosoever will, let him come." And it does not propose to satisfy the perverted uses of the drum major instinct. It's the one place where everybody should be the same standing before a common master and savior. And a recognition grows out of this—that all men are brothers because they are children of a common father.

The drum major instinct can lead to exclusivism in one's thinking, and can lead one to feel that because he has some training, he's a little better than that person that doesn't have it, or because he has some economic security, that he's a little better than the person who doesn't have it. And that's the uncontrolled, perverted use of the drum major instinct.

Now the other thing is that it leads to tragic—and we've seen it happen so often—tragic race prejudice. Many have written about this problem—Lillian Smith used to say it beautifully in some of her books. And she would say it to the point of getting men and women to see the source of the problem. Do you know that a lot of the race problem grows out of the drum major instinct? A need that some people have to feel superior. A need that some people have to feel that they are first, and to feel that their white skin ordained them to be first. And they have said it over and over again in ways that we see with our own eyes. In fact, not too long ago, a man down in Mississippi said that God was a charter member of the White Citizens Council. And so God being the charter member means that everybody who's in that has a kind of divinity, a kind of superiority.

And think of what has happened in history as a result of this perverted use of the drum major instinct. It has led to the most tragic prejudice, the most tragic expressions of man's inhumanity to man.

I always try to do a little converting when I'm in jail. And when we were in jail in Birmingham the other day, the white wardens all enjoyed coming around to the cell to talk about the race problem. And they were showing us where we were so wrong demonstrating. And they were showing us where segregation was so right. And they were showing us where intermarriage was so wrong. So I would get to preaching, and we would get to talking—calmly, because they wanted to talk about it. And then we got down one day to the point—that was the second or third day—to talk about where they lived, and how much they were earning. And when those brothers told me what they were earning, I said, now "You know what? You ought to be marching with us. You're just as poor as Negroes." And I said, "You are put in the position of supporting your oppressor. Because through prejudice and blindness, you fail to see that the same forces that oppress Negroes in American society oppress poor white people. And all you are living on is the satisfaction of your skin being white, and the drum major instinct of thinking that you are somebody big because you are white. And you're so poor you can't send your children to school. You ought to be out here marching with every one of us every time we have a march."

Now that's a fact. That the poor white has been put into this position—where through blindness and prejudice, he is forced to support his oppressors, and the only thing he has going for him is the false feeling that he is superior because his skin is whtie. And can't hardly eat and make his ends meet week in and week out.

And not only does this thing go into the racial struggle, it goes into the struggle between nations. And I would submit to you this morning that what is wrong in the world today is that the nations of the world are engaged in a bitter, colossal contest for supremacy. And if something doesn't happen to stop this trend I'm sorely afraid that we won't be here to talk about Jesus Christ and about God and about brotherhood too many more years. If somebody doesn't bring an end to this suicidal thrust that we see in the world today, none of us are going to be around, because somebody's going to make the mistake through our senseless blundering of dropping a nuclear bomb somewhere, and then another one is going to drop. And don't let anybody fool you, this can happen within a matter of seconds. They have twenty-megaton bombs in Russia right now that can destroy a city as big as New York in three seconds with everybody wiped away, and every building. And we can do the same thing to Russia and China.

But this is where we are drifting, and we are drifting there, because nations are caught up with the drum major instinct. I must be first. I must be supreme. Our nation must rule the world. And I am sad to say that the nation in which we live is the supreme culprit. And I'm going to continue to say it to America, because I love this country too much to see the drift that it has taken.

God didn't call America to do what she's doing in the world now. God didn't call America to engage in a senseless, unjust war, [such] as the war in Vietnam. And we are criminals in that war. We have committed more war crimes almost than any nation in the world, and I'm going to continue to say it. And we won't stop it because of our pride, and our arrogance as a nation.

But God has a way of even putting nations in their place. The God that I worship has a way of saying, "Don't play with me." He has a way of saying, as the God of the Old Testament used to say to the Hebrews, "Don't play with me, Israel. Don't play with me, Babylon. Be still and know that I'm God. And if you don't stop your reckless course, I'll rise up and break the backbone of your power." And that can happen to America. Every now and then I go back and read Gibbons' *Decline and Fall of the Roman Empire*. And when I come and look at America, I say to myself, the parallels are frightening.

And we have perverted the drum major instinct. But let me rush on to my conclusion, because I want you to see what Jesus was really saying. What was the answer that Jesus gave these men? It's very interesting. One would have thought that Jesus would have said, "You are out of your place. You are selfish. Why would you raise such a question?"

But that isn't what Jesus did. He did something altogether different. He said in substance, "Oh, I see, you want to be first. You want to be great. You want to be important. You want to be significant. Well you ought to be. If you're going to be my disciple, you must be." But he re-ordered priorities. And he said, "Yes, don't give up this instinct. It's a good instinct if you use it right. It's a good instinct if you don't distort it and pervert it. Don't give it up. Keep feeling the need for being important. Keep feeling the need for being first. But I want you to be first in love. I want you to be first in moral excellence. I want you to be first in generosity. That is what I want you to do."

And he transformed the situation by giving a new definition of greatness. And you know how he said it? He said now, "Brethren, I can't give you greatness. And really, I can't make you first." This is what Jesus said to James and John. You must earn it. True greatness comes not by favoritism, but by fitness. And the right hand and the left are not mine to give, they belong to those who are prepared.

And so Jesus gave us a new norm of greatness. If you want to be important—wonderful. If you want to be recognized—wonderful. If you want to be great—wonderful. But recognize that he who is greatest among you shall be your servant. That's your new definition of greatness. And this morning, the thing that I like about it . . . by giving that definition of greatness, it means that everybody can be great. Because everybody can serve. You don't have to have a college degree to serve. You don't have to make your subject and your verb agree to serve. You don't have to know about Plato and Aristotle to serve. You don't have to know Einstein's theory of relativity to serve. You don't have to know the second theory of thermodynamics in physics to serve. You only need a heart full of grace. A soul generated by love. And you can be that servant.

I know a man, and I just want to talk about him a minute, and maybe you will discover who I'm talking about as I go down the way, because he was a great one. And he just went about serving. He was born in an obscure village, the child of a poor peasant woman. And then he grew up in still another obscure village, where he worked as a carpenter until he was thirty years old. Then for three years, he just got on his feet, and he was an itinerant preacher. And then he went about doing some things. He didn't have much. He never wrote a book. He never held an office. He never had a family. He never owned a house. He never went to college. He never visited a big city. He never went two hundred miles from where he was born. He did none of the usual things that the world would associate with greatness. He had no credentials but himself.

He was thirty-three when the tide of public opinion turned against him. They called him a rabble-rouser. They called him a troublemaker. They said he was an agitator. He practiced civil disobedience; he broke injunctions. And so he was turned over to his enemies, and went through the mockery of a trial. And the irony of it all is that his friends turned him over to them. One of his closest friends denied him. Another of his friends turned him over to his enemies. And while he was dying, the people who killed him gambled for his clothing, the only possession that he had in the world. When he was dead, he was buried in a borrowed tomb, through the pity of a friend.

Nineteen centuries have come and gone, and today, he stands as the most influential figure that ever entered human history. All of the armies that ever marched, all the navies that ever sailed, all the parliaments that ever sat, and all the kings that ever reigned put together have not affected the life of man on this earth as much as that one solitary life. His name may be a familiar one. But today I can hear them talking about him. Every now and then somebody says, "He's king of kings." And again I can hear somebody saying, "He's lord of lords." Somewhere else I can hear somebody saying, "In Christ there is no east nor west." And they go on and talk about. . . . "In him there's no north and south, but one great fellowship of love throughout the whole wide world." He didn't have anything. He just went around serving, and doing good.

This morning, you can be on his right hand and his left hand if you serve. It's the only way in.

Every now and then I guess we all think realistically about that day when we will be victimized with what is life's final common denominator—that something we call death. We all think about it. And every now and then I think about my own death, and I think about my own funeral.

And I don't think of it in a morbid sense. Every now and then I ask myself, "What is it that I would want said?" And I leave the word to you this morning.

If any of you are around when I have to meet my day, I don't want a long funeral. And if you get somebody to deliver the eulogy, tell them not to talk too long. Every now and then I wonder what I want them to say. Tell them not to mention that I have a Nobel Peace Prize, that isn't important. Tell them not to mention that I have three or four hundred other awards, that's not important. Tell him not to mention where I went to school.

I'd like somebody to mention that day, that Martin Luther King, Jr., tried to give his life serving others. I'd like for somebody to say that day, that Martin Luther King, Jr., tried to love somebody. I want you to say that day, that I tried to be right on the war question. I want you to be able to say that day, that I did try to feed the hungry. And I want you to be able to say that day, that I did try, in my life, to clothe those who were naked. I want you to say, on that day, that I did try, in my life, to visit those who were in prison. I want you to say that I tried to love and serve humanity.

Yes, if you want to say that I was a drum major, say that I was a drum major for justice; say that I was a drum major for peace; I was a drum major for righteousness. And all of the other shallow things will not matter. I won't have any money to leave behind. I won't have the fine and luxurious things of life to leave behind. But I just want to leave a committed life behind.

And that's all I want to say . . . if I can help somebody as I pass along, if I can cheer somebody with a word or song, if I can show somebody he's traveling wrong, then my living will not be in vain. If I can do my duty as a Christian ought, if I can bring salvation to a world once wrought, if I can spread the message as the master taught, then my living will not be in vain.

Yes, Jesus, I want to be on your right side or your left side, not for any selfish reason. I want to be on your right or your best side, not in terms of some political kingdom or ambition, but I just want to be there in love and in justice and in truth and in commitment to others, so that we can make of this old world a new world.

Flip Schulke, ed. *Martin Luther King, Jr.: A Documentary . . . Montgomery to Memphis* (New York and London: Norton, 1976), 220–22.

# 44

# Remaining Awake Through a Great Revolution

*At Dean Francis Sayre's invitation, Dr. King delivered this Passion Sunday sermon at the National Cathedral (Episcopal) in Washington, D.C., on 31 March 1968. It was his last Sunday morning sermon.*

I need not pause to say how very delighted I am to be here this morning . . . to have the opportunity of standing in this very great and significant pulpit . . . and I do want to express my deep personal appreciation to Dean Sayre and all of the Cathedral clergy for extending the invitation.

It is always a rich and rewarding experience to take a brief break from our day to day demands and the struggle for freedom and human dignity . . . and discuss the issues involved in that struggle with concerned friends of good will all over our nation. And certainly it is always a deep and meaningful experience to be in a worship service. And so for many reasons, I'm happy to be here today.

I would like to use as a subject from which to preach this morning: "Remaining awake through a great revolution." The text for the morning is found in the book of Revelation. There are two passages there, that I would like to quote, in the sixteenth chapter of that book—"Behold I make all things new, former things are passed away."

I am sure that most of you have read that arresting little story from the pen of Washington Irving, entitled "Rip Van Winkle." The one thing that we usually remember about the story is that Rip Van Winkle slept twenty years. But there is another point in that little story that is almost completely overlooked. It was the sign in the end, from which Rip went up in the mountain for his long sleep.

When Rip Van Winkle went up into the mountain, the sign had a picture of King George III of England. When he came down twenty years later the sign had a picture of George Washington, the first president of the United States. When Rip Van Winkle looked up at the picture of George Washington, and looking at the picture he was amazed . . . he was completely lost—he knew not who he was. And this reveals to us that the most striking thing about the story of Rip Van Winkle is not merely that Rip slept twenty years, but that he slept through a revolution. While he was peacefully snoring up in the mountain a revolution was taking place that at points would change the course of history—and Rip knew nothing about it: he was asleep. Yes, he slept through a revolution. And one of the great liabilities of life is that all too many people find themselves living amid a great period of social change and yet they fail to develop the new attitudes, the new mental responses—that the new situation demands. They end up sleeping through a revolution.

There can be no gainsaying of the fact that a great revolution is taking place in the world today. In a sense it is a triple revolution; that is a technological revolution, with the impact of automation and cybernation; then there is a revolution in weaponry, with the emergence of atomic and nuclear weapons of warfare. Then there is a human rights revolution, with the freedom explosion that is taking place all over the world. Yes, we do live in a period where changes are taking place and there is still the voice crying through the vista of time saying, "Behold, I make all things new, former things are passed away."

Now whenever anything new comes into history it brings with it new challenges . . . and new opportunities.

And I would like to deal with the challenges that we face today as a result of this triple revolution, that is taking place in the world today.

First, we are challenged to develop a world perspective. No individual can live alone, no nation can live alone, and anyone who feels that he can live alone is sleeping through a revolution. The world in which we live is geographically one. The challenge that we face today is to make it one in terms of brotherhood.

Now it is true that the geographical oneness of this age has come into being to a large extent through modern man's scientific ingenuity. Modern man through his scientific genius has been able to dwarf distance and place time in chains. And our jet planes have compressed into minutes distances that once took weeks and even months. All of this tells us that our world is a neighborhood.

Through our scientific and technological genius, we have made of this world a neighborhood and yet . . . we have not had the ethical commitment to make of it a brotherhood. But somehow, and in some way, we have got to do this. We must all learn to live together as brothers. Or we will all perish together as fools. We are tied together in the single garment of destiny, caught in an inescapable network of mutuality. And whatever affects one directly affects all indirectly. For some strange reason I can never be what I ought to be until you are what you ought to be. And you can never be what you ought to be until I am what I ought to be. This is the way God's universe is made; this is the way it is structured.

John Donne caught it years ago and placed it in graphic terms—"No man is an island entire of itself. Every man is a piece of the continent—a part of the main." And he goes on toward the end to say, "Any man's death diminishes me because I am involved in mankind. Therefore never send to know for whom the bell tolls; it tolls for thee." We must see this, believe this, and live by it . . . if we are to remain awake through a great revolution.

Secondly, we are challenged to eradicate the last vestiges of racial injustice from our nation. I must say this morning that racial injustice is still the black man's burden and the white man's shame.

It is an unhappy truth that racism is a way of life for the vast majority of white Americans, spoken and unspoken, acknowledged and denied, subtle and sometimes not so subtle—the disease of racism permeates and poisons a whole body politic. And I can see nothing more urgent than for America to work passionately and unrelentingly—to get rid of the disease of racism.

Something positive must be done, everyone must share in the guilt as individuals and as institutions. The government must certainly share the guilt, individuals must share the guilt, even the church must share the guilt.

We must face the sad fact that at eleven o'clock on Sunday morning when we stand to sing, "In Christ there is no East or West," we stand in the most segregated hour of America.

The hour has come for everybody, for all institutions of the public sector and the private sector to work to get rid of racism. And now if we are to do it we must honestly admit certain things and get rid of certain myths that have constantly been disseminated all over our nation.

One is the myth of time. It is the notion that only time can solve the problem of racial injustice. And there are those who often sincerely say to the Negro and his allies in the white community, "Why don't you slow up? Stop pushing things so fast. Only time can solve the problem. And if you will just be nice and patient and continue to pray, in a hundred or two hundred years the problem will work itself out."

There is an answer to that myth. It is that time is neutral. It can be used either constructively or destructively. And I am sorry to say this morning that I am absolutely convinced that the forces of ill will in our nation, the extreme rightists of our nation—the people on the wrong side—have used time much more effectively than the forces of good will. And it may well be that we will have to repent in this generation. Not merely for the vitriolic words and the violent actions of the bad people, but for the appalling silence and indifference of the good people who sit around and say, "Wait on time."

Somewhere we must come to see that human progress never rolls in on the wheels of inevitablity. It comes through the tireless efforts and the persistent work of dedicated individuals who are willing to be co-workers with God. And without this hard work, time itself becomes an ally of the primitive forces of social stagnation. So we must help time and realize that the time is always ripe to do right.

Now there is another myth that still gets around; it is a kind of overreliance on the bootstrap philosophy. There are those who still feel that if the Negro is to rise out of poverty, if the Negro is to rise out of slum conditions, if he is to rise out of discrimination and segregation, he must do it all by himself. And so they say the Negro must lift himself by his own bootstraps.

They never stop to realize that no other ethnic group has been a slave on American soil. The people who say this never stop to realize that the nation made the black man's color a stigma; but beyond this they never stop to realize the debt that they owe a people who were kept in slavery 244 years.

In 1863 the Negro was told that he was free as a result of the Emancipation Proclamation being signed by Abraham Lincoln. But he was not given any land to make that freedom meaningful. It was something like keeping a person in prison for a number of years and suddenly discovering that that person is not guilty of the crime for which he was convicted. And you just go up to him and say, "Now you are free," but you don't give him any bus fare to get to town. You don't give him any money to get some clothes to put on his back or to get on his feet again in life.

Every court of jurisprudence would rise up against this, and yet this is the very thing that our nation did to the black man. It simply said, "You're free," and it left him there penniless, illiterate, not knowing what to do. And the irony of it all is that at the same time the nation failed to do anything for the black man—through an act of Congress it was giving away millions of acres of land in the West and the Midwest—which meant that it was willing to undergird its white peasants from Europe with an economic floor.

But not only did it give the land, it built land-grant colleges to teach them how to farm. Not only that, it provided county agents to further their expertise in farming: not only that, as the years unfolded it provided low interest rates so that they could mechanize their farms. And to this day thousands of these very persons are receiving millions of dollars in federal subsidies every year not to farm. And these are so often the very people who tell Negroes that they must lift themselves by their own bootstraps. It's all right to tell a man to lift himself by his own bootstraps, but it is a cruel jest to say to a bootless man that he ought to lift himself by his own bootstraps.

We must come to see that the roots of racism are very deep in our country, and there must be something positive and massive in order to get rid of all the effects of racism and the tragedies of racial injustice.

There is another thing closely related to racism that I would like to mention as another challenge. We are challenged to rid our nation and the world of poverty. Like a monstrous octopus, poverty spreads its nagging, prehensile tentacles into hamlets and villages all over our world. They are ill-housed, they are ill-nourished, they are shabbily clad. I have seen it in Latin America; I have seen it in Africa; I have seen this poverty in Asia.

I remember some years ago Mrs. King and I journeyed to that great country known as India. And I never will forget the experience; it was a marvelous experience to meet and talk with the great leaders of India; to meet and talk with and speak to thousands and thousands of people all over that vast country. These experiences will remain dear to me as long as the cords of memory shall let them.

But I say to you this morning, my friends, there were those depressing moments—how can one avoid being depressed?—when he sees with his own eyes evidences of millions of people going to bed hungry at night? How can one avoid being depressed when he sees with his own eyes God's children sleeping on the sidewalks at night?

In Bombay more than a million people sleep on the sidewalks every night. In Calcutta more than six hundred thousand sleep on the sidewalks every night. They have no beds to sleep in; they have no houses to go in. How can one avoid being depressed when he discovers that out of India's population of more than five hundred million people—some 480,000,000 make an annual income of less than ninety dollars. And most of them have never seen a doctor or a dentist.

As I noticed these things, something within me cried out, "Can we in America stand idly by and not be concerned?" And an answer came— "Oh, no!" Because the destiny of the United States is tied up with the destiny of India and every other nation. And I started thinking of the fact that we spend in America millions of dollars a day to store surplus food, and I said to myself, "I know where we can store that food free of charge—in the wrinkled stomachs of millions of God's children all over the world who go to bed hungry at night." Maybe we spend far too much of our national budget establishing military bases around the world rather than bases of genuine concern and understanding.

Not only do we see poverty abroad, I would remind you that in our own nation there are about forty million people who are poverty-stricken. I have seen them here and there. I have seen them in the ghettos of the North; I have seen them in the rural areas of the South; I have seen them in Appalachia. I have just been in the process of touring many areas of our country and I must confess that in some situations I have literally found myself crying.

I was in Marks, Mississippi, the other day, which is in Whitman County, the poorest county in the United States. I tell you I saw hundreds of little black boys and black girls walking the streets with no shoes to wear. I saw their mothers and their fathers trying to carry on a little head-start program, but they had no money. The federal government hadn't funded them but they were trying to carry on. They raised a little money here and there; trying to get a little food to feed the children; trying to teach them a little something.

And I saw mothers and fathers who said to me not only were they unemployed, they didn't get any kind of income—no old-age pension, no welfare check, nor anything. I said, "How do you live?" And they say, "Well, we go around—go around to the neighbors and ask them for a little something. When the berry season comes, we pick berries; when the rabbit season comes, we hunt and catch a few rabbits, and that's about it."

And I was in Newark and Harlem just this week. And I walked into the homes of welfare mothers; I saw them in conditions—no, not with wall-to-wall carpet, but wall-to-wall rats and roaches. I stood in an apartment and this welfare mother said to me "The landlord will not repair this place. I've been here two years and he hasn't made a single repair." She pointed out the walls with all of the ceiling falling through. She showed me the holes where the rats came in. She said night after night we have to stay awake to keep the rats and roaches from getting to the children. I said, "How much do you pay for this apartment?" She said, "$125." I looked and I thought and said to myself, "It isn't worth sixty dollars." Poor people are forced to pay more for less. Living in conditions day in and day out where the whole area is constantly drained without being replenished. It becomes a kind of domestic colony. And the tragedy is so often—these forty million people are invisible because America is so affluent, so rich; becaues our expressways carry us away from the ghetto, we don't see the poor.

Jesus told a parable one day, and he reminded us that a man went to hell because he didn't see the poor. His name was Dives. He was a rich man. And there was a man by the name of Lazarus who was a poor man, but not only was he poor, he was sick. Sores were all over his body, and he was so weak that he could hardly move. But he managed to get to the gate of Dives every day, wanting just to have the crumbs that would fall from his table. And Dives did nothing about it. And the parable ends saying, "Dives went to hell, and there were a fixed gulf now between Lazarus and Dives."

There is nothing in that parable that said Dives went to hell because he was rich. Jesus never made a universal indictment against all wealth. It is true that one day a rich young ruler came to him, and he advised him to sell all, but in that instance Jesus was prescribing individual surgery and not setting forth a universal diagnosis. And if you will look at that parable with all of its symbolism, you will remember that a conversation took place between heaven and hell and on the other end of that long-distance call between heaven and hell was Abraham in heaven talking to Dives in hell.

Now Abraham was a very rich man. If you go back to the Old Testament, you see that he was the richest man of his day, so it was not a rich man in hell talking with a poor man in heaven, it was a little millionaire in hell talking with a multimillionaire in heaven. Dives didn't go to hell because he was rich; Dives didn't realize that his wealth was his opportunity. It was his opportunity to bridge the gulf that separated him from his brother, Lazarus. Dives went to hell because he was passed by Lazarus every day and he never really saw him. He went to hell because he allowed his brother to become invisible. Dives went to hell because he maximized the minimum and minimized the maximum. Indeed, Dives went to hell because he sought to be a conscientious objector in the war against poverty.

And this can happen to America, the richest nation in the world—and nothing's wrong with that—this is America's opportunity to help bridge the gulf between the haves and the have-nots. The question is whether America will do it. There is nothing new about poverty. What is new is that we now have the techniques and the resources to get rid of poverty. The real question is whether we have the will.

In a few weeks some of us are coming to Washington to see if the will is still alive or if it is alive in this nation. We are coming to Washington in a poor people's campaign. Yes, we are going to bring the tired, the poor, the huddled masses. We are going to bring those who have known long years of hurt and neglect. We are going to bring those who have come to feel that life is a long and desolate corridor with no exit signs. We are going to bring children and adults and old people; people who have never seen a doctor or a dentist in their lives.

We are not coming to engage in any histrionic gesture. We are not coming to tear up Washington. We are coming to demand that the government address itself to the problem of poverty. We read one day—We hold these truths to be self-evident, that all men are created equal, that they are endowed by their creator with certain inalienable rights. That among these are life, liberty and the pursuit of happiness. But if a man doesn't have a job or an income, he has neither life nor liberty nor the possibility for the pursuit of happiness. He merely exists.

We are coming to ask America to be true to the huge promissory note that it signed years ago. And we are coming to engage in dramatic non-violent action, to call attention to the gulf between promise and fulfillment; to make the invisible visible.

Why do we do it this way? We do it this way because it is our experience that the nation doesn't move around questions of genuine equality for the poor and for black people until it is confronted massively, dramatically in terms of direct action.

Great documents are here to tell us something should be done. We met here some years ago in the White House conference on civil rights, and we came out with the same recommendations that we will be demanding in our campaign here, but nothing has been done. The president's commission on technology, automation and economic progress recommended these things some time ago. Nothing has been done. Even the urban coalition of mayors of most of the cities of our country and the leading businessmen have said these things should be done. Nothing has been done. The Kerner commission came out with its report just a few days ago and then made specific recommendations. Nothing has been done.

And I submit that nothing will be done until people of good will put their bodies and their souls in motion. And it will be the kind of soul force brought into being as a result of this confrontation that I believe will make the difference. Yes, it will be a poor people's campaign. This is the question facing America. Ultimately a great nation is a compassionate nation. America has not met its obligations and its responsibilities to the poor.

One day we will have to stand before the God of history and we will talk in terms of things we've done. Yes, we will be able to say we built gargantuan bridges to span the seas, we built gigantic buildings to kiss the skies. Yes, we made our submarines to penetrate oceanic depths. We brought into being many other things with our scientific and technological power.

It seems that I can hear the God of history saying, "That was not enough! But I was hungry and ye fed me not. I was naked and ye clothed me not. I was devoid of a decent sanitary house to live in, and ye provided no shelter for me. And consequently, you cannot enter the kingdom of greatness. If ye do it unto the least of these, my brethren, ye do it unto me." That's the question facing America today.

I want to say one other challenge that we face is simply that we must find an alternative to war and bloodshed. Anyone who feels, and there are still a lot of people who feel that way, that war can solve the social problems facing mankind is sleeping through a revolution. President Kennedy said on one occasion, "Mankind must put an end to war or war will put an end to mankind." The world must hear this. I pray God that America will hear this before it is too late because today we're fighting a war.

I am convinced that it is one of the most unjust wars that has ever been fought in the history of the world. Our involvement in the war in Vietnam has torn up the Geneva accord. It has strengthened the military-industrial complex; it has strengthened the forces of reaction in our nation; it has put us against the self-determination of a vast majority of the Vietnamese people, and put us in the position of protecting a corrupt regime that is stacked against the poor.

It has played havoc with our domestic destinies. This day we are spending five hundred thousand dollars to kill every Vietcong soldier— every time we kill one we spend about five hundred thousand dollars while we spend only fifty-three dollars a year for every person characterized as poverty-stricken in the so-called poverty program; which is not even a good skirmish against poverty.

Not only that, it has put us in a position of appearing to the world as an arrogant nation. And here we are ten thousand miles away from home fighting for the so-called freedom of the Vietnamese people when we have not even put our own house in order. And we force young black men and young white men to fight and kill in brutal solidarity. Yet when they come back home that can't hardly live on the same block together.

The judgment of God is upon us today, and we could go right down the line and see that something must be done . . . and something must be done quickly. We have alienated ourselves from other nations so we end up morally and politically isolated in the world. There is not a single major ally of the United States of America that would dare send a troop to Vietnam and so the only friends that we have now are a few client-nations like Taiwan, Thailand, South Korea and a few others.

This is where we are. Mankind must put an end to war or war will put an end to mankind, and the best way to start is to put an end to war in Vietnam because if it continues, we will inevitably come to the point of confronting China which could lead the whole world to nuclear annihilation.

It is no longer a choice, my friends, between violence and nonviolence. It is either nonviolence or nonexistence, and the alternative to disarmament, the alternative to a greater suspension of nuclear tests, the alternative to strengthening the United Nations and thereby disarming the whole world may well be a civilization plunged into the abyss of annihilation, and our earthly habitat would be transformed into an inferno that even the mind of Dante could not imagine.

This is why I felt the need of raising my voice against that war and working wherever I can to arouse the conscience of our nation on it. I remember so well when I first took a stand against the war in Vietnam, the critics took me on and they had their say in the most negative and sometimes most vicious way.

One day a newsman came to me and said, "Dr. King, don't you think you're going to have to stop, now, opposing the war and move more in line with the administration's policy? As I understand it, it has hurt the budget of your organization and people who once respected you, have lost respect for you. Don't you feel that you've really got to change your position?" I looked at him and I had to say, "Sir, I'm sorry you don't know me. I'm not a consensus leader. I do not determine what is right and wrong by looking at the budget of the Southern Christian Leadership Conference. I've not taken a sort of Gallup poll of the majority opinion. Ultimately a genuine leader is not a searcher for consensus, but a molder of consensus."

On some positions, cowardice asks the question, is it expedient? And then expedience comes along and asks the question—is it politic? Vanity asks the question—is it popular? Conscience asks the question—is it right?

There comes a time when one must take the position that it is neither safe nor politic nor popular, but he must do it because conscience tells him it is right. I believe today that there is a need for all people of good will to come with a massive act of conscience and say in the words of the old Negro spiritual, "We ain't goin' study war no more." This is the challenge facing modern man.

Let me close by saying that we have difficult days ahead in the struggle for justice and peace, but I will not yield to a politic of despair. I'm going to maintain hope as we come to Washington in this campaign, the cards are stacked against us. This time we will really confront a Goliath. God grant that we will be that David of truth set out against the Goliath of injustice, the Goliath of neglect, the Goliath of refusing to deal with the problems, and go on with the determination to make America the truly great America that it is called to be.

I say to you that our goal is freedom, and I believe we are going to get there because however much she strays away from it, the goal of America is freedom. Abused and scorned though we may be as a people, our destiny is tied up in the destiny of America.

Before the Pilgrim Fathers landed at Plymouth, we were here. Before Jefferson etched across the pages of history, the majestic words of the Declaration of Independence, we were here. Before the beautiful words of the Star Spangled Banner were written, we were here.

For more than two centuries our forebears labored here without wages. They made cotton king, and they built the homes of their masters in the midst of the most humiliating and oppressive conditions. And yet out of a bottomless vitality they continued to grow and develop. If the inexpressible cruelties of slavery couldn't stop us, the opposition that we now face will surely fail.

We're going to win our freedom because both the sacred heritage of our nation and the eternal will of the almighty God are embodied in our echoing demands. And so, however dark it is, however deep the angry feelings are, and however violent explosions are, I can still sing "We Shall Overcome."

We shall overcome because the arc of a moral universe is long, but it bends toward justice. We shall overcome because Carlyle is right—no lie can live forever. We shall overcome because William Cullen Bryant is right—truth crushed to earth will rise again. We shall overcome because James Russell Lowell is right—as we were singing earlier today, "Truth forever on the scaffold, wrong forever on the throne, yet that scaffold sways the future, and behind the demon known, stands a God within the shadow, keeping watch above his own."

With this faith we will be able to hew out of the mountain of despair the stone of hope. With this faith we will be able to transform the jangling discords of our nation into a beautiful symphony of brotherhood.

Thank God for John, who centuries ago out on a lonely, obscure island called Patmos caught vision of a new Jerusalem descending out of heaven from God, who heard a voice saying, "Behold, I make all things new—former things are passed away."

God grant that we will be participants in this newness and this magnificent development. If we will but do it, we will bring about a new day of justice and brotherhood and peace. And that day the morning stars will sing together and the sons of God will shout for joy. God bless you.

# 45

# I See the Promised Land

*This was Dr. King's last, and most apocalyptic, sermon. He delivered it, on the eve of his assassination, at [the Bishop Charles] Mason Temple in Memphis, Tennessee, on 3 April 1968. Mason Temple is the headquarters of the Church of God in Christ, the largest African American pentecostal denomination in the United States.*

Thank you very kindly, my friends. As I listened to Ralph Abernathy in his eloquent and generous introduction and then thought about myself, I wondered who he was talking about. It's always good to have your closest friend and associate say something good about you. And Ralph is the best friend that I have in the world.

I'm delighted to see each of you here tonight in spite of a storm warning. You reveal that you are determined to go on anyhow. Something is happening in Memphis, something is happening in our world.

As you know, if I were standing at the beginning of time, with the possibility of general and panoramic view of the whole human history up to now, and the Almighty said to me, "Martin Luther King, which age would you like to live in?"—I would take my mental flight by Egypt through, or rather across the Red Sea, through the wilderness on toward the promised land. And in spite of its magnificence, I wouldn't stop there. I would move on by Greece, and take my mind to Mount Olympus. And I would see Plato, Aristotle, Socrates, Euripides and Aristophanes assembled around the Parthenon as they discussed the great and eternal issues of reality.

But I wouldn't stop there. I would go on, even to the great heyday of the Roman Empire. And I would see developments around there, through various emperors and leaders. But I wouldn't stop there. I would even come up to the day of the Renaissance, and get a quick picture of all that the Renaissance did for the cultural and esthetic life of man. But I wouldn't stop there. I would even go by the way that the man for whom I'm named had his habitat. And I would watch Martin Luther as he tacked his ninety-five theses on the door at the church in Wittenberg.

But I wouldn't stop there. I would come on up even to 1863, and watch a vacillating president by the name of Abraham Lincoln finally come to the conclusion that he had to sign the Emancipation Proclamation. But I wouldn't stop there. I would even come up to the early thirties, and see a man grappling with the problems of the bankruptcy of his nation. And come with an eloquent cry that we have nothing to fear but fear itself.

But I wouldn't stop there. Strangely enough, I would turn to the Almighty, and say, "If you allow me to live just a few years in the second half of the twentieth century, I will be happy." Now that's a strange statement to make, because the world is all messed up. The nation is sick. Trouble is in the land. Confusion all around. That's a strange statement. But I know, somehow, that only when it is dark enough, can you see the stars. And I see God working in this period of the twentieth century in a way that men, in some strange way, are responding—something is happening in our world. The masses of people are rising up. And wherever they are assembled today, whether they are in Johannesburg, South Africa; Nairobi, Kenya; Accra, Ghana; New York City; Atlanta, Georgia; Jackson, Mississippi; or Memphis, Tennessee—the cry is always the same—"We want to be free."

And another reason that I'm happy to live in this period is that we have been forced to a point where we're going to have to grapple with the problems that men have been trying to grapple with through history, but the demands didn't force them to do it. Survival demands that we grapple with them. Men, for years now, have been talking about war and peace. But now, no longer can they just talk about it. It is no longer a choice between violence and nonviolence in this world; it's nonviolence or nonexistence.

That is where we are today. And also in the human rights revolution, if something isn't done, and in a hurry, to bring the colored peoples of the world out of their long years of poverty, their long years of hurt and neglect, the whole world is doomed. Now, I'm just happy that God has allowed me to live in this period, to see what is unfolding. And I'm happy that he's allowed me to be in Memphis.

I can remember, I can remember when Negroes were just going around as Ralph has said, so often, scratching where they didn't itch, and laughing when they were not tickled. But that day is all over. We mean business now, and we are determined to gain our rightful place in God's world.

And that's all this whole thing is about. We aren't engaged in any negative protest and in any negative arguments with anybody. We are saying that we are determined to be men. We are determined to be people. We are saying that we are God's children. And that we don't have to live like we are forced to live.

Now, what does all of this mean in this great period of history? It means that we've got to stay together. We've got to stay together and maintain unity. You know, whenever Pharaoh wanted to prolong the period of slavery in Egypt, he had a favorite, favorite formula for doing it.

What was that? He kept the slaves fighting among themselves. But whenever the slaves get together, something happens in Pharaoh's court, and he cannot hold the slaves in slavery. When the slaves get together, that's the beginning of getting out of slavery. Now let us maintain unity.

Secondly, let us keep the issues where they are. The issue is injustice. The issue is the refusal of Memphis to be fair and honest in its dealings with its public servants, who happen to be sanitation workers. Now, we've got to keep attention on that. That's always the problem with a little violence. You know what happened the other day, and the press dealt only with the window-breaking. I read the articles. They very seldom got around to mentioning the fact that one thousand, three hundred sanitation workers were on strike, and that Memphis is not being fair to them, and that Mayor Loeb is in dire need of a doctor. They didn't get around to that.

Now we're going to march again, and we've got to march again, in order to put the issue where it is supposed to be. And force everybody to see that there are thirteen hundred of God's children here suffering, sometimes going hungry, going through dark and dreary nights wondering how this thing is going to come out. That's the issue. And we've got to say to the nation: we know it's coming out. For when people get caught up with that which is right and they are willing to sacrifice for it, there is no stopping point short of victory.

We aren't going to let any mace stop us. We are masters in our nonviolent movement in disarming police forces; they don't know what to do. I've seen them so often. I remember in Birmingham, Alabama, when we were in that majestic struggle there we would move out of the 16th Street Baptist Church day after day; by the hundreds we would move out. And Bull Connor would tell them to send the dogs forth and they did come; but we just went before the dogs singing, "Ain't gonna let nobody turn me round." Bull Connor next would say, "Turn the fire hoses on." And as I said to you the other night, Bull Connor didn't know history. He knew a kind of physics that somehow didn't relate to the transphysics that we knew about. And that was the fact that there was a certain kind of fire that no water could put out. And we went before the fire hoses; we had known water. If we were Baptist or some other denomination, we had been immersed. If we were Methodist, and some others, we had been sprinkled, but we knew water.

That couldn't stop us. And we just went on before the dogs and we would look at them; and we'd go on before the water hoses and we would look at it, and we'd just go on singing "Over my head I see freedom in the air." And then we would be thrown in the paddy wagons, and sometimes we were stacked in there like sardines in a can. And they would throw us in, and old Bull would say, "Take them off," and they did; and we would just go in the paddy wagon singing, "We Shall Overcome." And every now and then we'd get in the jail, and we'd see the jailers looking through the windows being moved by our prayers, and being moved by our words and our songs. And there was a power there which Bull Connor couldn't adjust to; and so we ended up transforming Bull into a steer, and we won our struggle in Birmingham.

Now we've got to go on to Memphis just like that. I call upon you to be with us Monday. Now about injunctions: We have an injunction and we're going into court tomorrow morning to fight this illegal, unconstitutional injunction. All we say to America is, "Be true to what you said on paper." If I lived in China or even Russia, or any totalitarian country, maybe I could understand the denial of certain basic First Amendment privileges, because they hadn't committed themselves to that over there. But somewhere I read of the freedom of assembly. Somewhere I read of the freedom of speech. Somewhere I read of the freedom of the press. Somewhere I read that the greatness of America is the right to protest for right. And so just as I say, we aren't going to let any injunction turn us around. We are going on.

We need all of you. And you know what's beautiful to me, is to see all of these ministers of the Gospel. It's a marvelous picture. Who is it that is supposed to articulate the longings and aspirations of the people more than the preacher? Somehow the preacher must be an Amos, and say, "Let justice roll down like waters and righteousness like a mighty stream." Somehow, the preacher must say with Jesus, "The spirit of the Lord is upon me, because he hath anointed me to deal with the problems of the poor."

And I want to commend the preachers, under the leadership of these noble men: James Lawson, one who has been in this struggle for many years; he's been to jail for struggling; but he's still going on, fighting for the rights of his people. Rev. Ralph Jackson, Billy Kiles; I could just go right on down the list, but time will not permit. But I want to thank them all. And I want you to thank them, because so often, preachers aren't concerned about anything but themselves. And I'm always happy to see a relevant ministry.

It's alright to talk about "long white robes over yonder," in all of its symbolism. But ultimately people want some suits and dresses and shoes to wear down here. It's alright to talk about "streets flowing with milk and honey," but God has commanded us to be concerned about the slums down here, and his children who can't eat three square meals a day. It's alright to talk about the new Jerusalem, but one day, God's preacher must talk about the New York, the new Atlanta, the new Philadelphia, the new Los Angeles, the new Memphis, Tennessee. This is what we have to do.

Now the other thing we'll have to do is this: Always anchor our external direct action with the power of economic withdrawal. Now, we are poor people, individually, we are poor when you compare us with white society in America. We are poor. Never stop and forget that collectively, that means all of us together, collectively we are richer than all the nations in the world, with the exception of nine. Did you ever think about that? After you leave the United States, Soviet Russia, Great Britain, West Germany, France, and I could name the others, the Negro collectively is richer than most nations of the world. We have an annual income of more than thirty billion dollars a year, which is more than all of the exports of the United States, and more than the national budget of Canada. Did you know that? That's power right there, if we know how to pool it.

We don't have to argue with anybody. We don't have to curse and go around acting bad with our words. We don't need any bricks and bottles, we don't need any Molotov cocktails, we just need to go around to these stores, and to these massive industries in our country, and say, "God sent us by here, to say to you that you're not treating his children right. And we've come by here to ask you to make the first item on your agenda—fair treatment, where God's children are concerned. Now, if you are not prepared to do that, we do have an agenda that we must follow. And our agenda calls for withdrawing economic support from you."

And so, as a result of this, we are asking you tonight, to go out and tell your neighbors not to buy Coca-Cola in Memphis. Go by and tell them not to buy Sealtest milk. Tell them not to buy—what is the other bread?—Wonder Bread. And what is the other bread company, Jesse? Tell them not to buy Hart's bread. As Jesse Jackson has said, up to now, only the garbage men have been feeling pain; now we must kind of redistribute the pain. We are choosing these companies because they haven't been fair in their hiring policies; and we are choosing them because they can begin the process of saying, they are going to support the needs and the rights of these men who are on strike. And then they can move on downtown and tell Mayor Loeb to do what is right.

But not only that, we've got to strengthen black institutions. I call upon you to take your money out of the banks downtown and deposit your money in Tri-State Bank—we want a "bank-in" movement in Memphis. So go by the savings and loan association. I'm not asking you something that we don't do ourselves at SCLC. Judge Hooks and others will tell you that we have an account here in the savings and loan association from the Southern Christian Leadership Conference. We're just telling you to follow what we're doing. Put your money there. You have six or seven black insurance companies in Memphis. Take out your insurance there. We want to have an "insurance-in."

Now these are some practical things we can do. We begin the process of building a greater economic base. And at the same time, we are putting pressure where it really hurts. I ask you to follow through here.

Now, let me say as I move to my conclusion that we've got to give ourselves to this struggle until the end. Nothing would be more tragic than to stop at this point, in Memphis. We've got to see it through. And when we have our march, you need to be there. Be concerned about your brother. You may not be on strike. But either we go up together, or we go down together.

Let us develop a kind of dangerous unselfishness. One day a man came to Jesus; and he wanted to raise some questions about some vital matters in life. At points, he wanted to trick Jesus, and show him that he knew a litle more than Jesus knew, and through this, throw him off base. Now that question could have easily ended up in a philosophical and theological debate. But Jesus immediately pulled that question from mid-air, and placed it on a dangerous curve between Jerusalem and Jericho. And he talked about a certain man, who fell among thieves. You remember that a Levite and a priest passed by on the other side. They didn't stop to help him. And finally a man of another race came by. He got down from his beast, decided not to be compassionate by proxy. But with him, administered first aid, and helped the man in need. Jesus ended up saying, this was the good man, this was the great man, because he had the capacity to project the "I" into the "thou," and to be concerned about his brother. Now you know, we use our imagination a great deal to try to determine why the priest and the Levite didn't stop. At times we say they were busy going to church meetings—an ecclesiastical gathering—and they had to get on down to Jerusalem so they wouldn't be late for their meeting. At other times we would speculate that there was a religious law that "One who was engaged in religious ceremonials was not to touch a human body twenty-four hours before the ceremony." And every now and then we begin to wonder whether maybe they were not going down to Jerusalem, or down to Jericho, rather to organize a "Jericho Road Improvement Association." That's a possibility. Maybe they felt that it was better to deal with the problem from the casual root, rather than to get bogged down with an individual effort.

But I'm going to tell you what my imagination tells me. It's possible that these men were afraid. You see, the Jericho road is a dangerous road. I remember when Mrs. King and I were first in Jerusalem. We rented a car and drove from Jerusalem down to Jericho. And as soon as we got on that road, I said to my wife, "I can see why Jesus used this as a setting for his parable." It's a winding, meandering road. It's really conducive for ambushing. You start out in Jerusalem, which is about 1200 miles, or rather 1200 feet above sea level. And by the time you get down to Jericho, fifteen or twenty minutes later, you're about 2200 feet below sea level. That's a dangerous road. In the days of Jesus it came to be known as the "Bloody Pass." And you know, it's possible that the priest and the Levite looked over that man on the ground and wondered if the robbers were still around. Or it's possible that they felt that the man on the ground was merely faking. And he was acting like he had been robbed and hurt, in order to seize them over there, lure them there for quick and easy seizure. And so the first question that the Levite asked was, "If I stop to help this man, what will happen to me?" But then the Good Samaritan came by. And he reversed the question: "If I do not stop to help this man, what will happen to him?"

That's the question before you tonight. Not, "If I stop to help the sanitation workers, what will happen to all of the hours that I usually spend in my office every day and every week as a pastor?" The question is not, "If I stop to help this man in need, what will happen to me?" "If I do not stop to help the sanitation workers, what will happen to them?" That's the question.

Let us rise up tonight with a greater readiness. Let us stand with a greater determination. And let us move on in these powerful days, these days of challenge to make America what it ought to be. We have an opportunity to make America a better nation. And I want to thank God, once more, for allowing me to be here with you.

You know, several years ago, I was in New York City autographing the first book that I had written. And while sitting there autographing books, a demented black woman came up. The only question I heard from her was, "Are you Martin Luther King?"

And I was looking down writing, and I said yes. And the next minute I felt something beating on my chest. Before I knew it I had been stabbed by this demented woman. I was rushed to Harlem Hospital. It was a dark Saturday afternoon. And that blade had gone through, and the X-rays revealed that the tip of the blade was on the edge of my aorta, the main artery. And once that's punctured, you drown in your own blood—that's the end of you.

It came out in the *New York Times* the next morning, that if I had sneezed, I would have died. Well, about four days later, they allowed me, after the operation, after my chest had been opened, and the blade had been taken out, to move around in the wheel chair in the hospital. They allowed me to read some of the mail that came in, and from all over the states, and the world, kind letters came in. I read a few, but one of them I will never forget. I had received one from the President and the Vice-President. I've forgotten what those telegrams said. I'd received a visit and a letter from the Governor of New York, but I've forgotten what the letter said. But there was another letter that came from a little girl, a young girl who was a student at the White Plains High School. And I looked at that letter, and I'll never forget it. It said simply, "Dear Dr. King: I am a ninth-grade student at the White Plains High School." She said, "While it should not matter, I would like to mention that I am a white girl. I read in the paper of your misfortune, and of your suffering. And I read that if you had sneezed, you would have died. And I'm simply writing you to say that I'm so happy that you didn't sneeze."

And I want to say tonight, I want to say that I am happy that I didn't sneeze. Because if I had sneezed, I wouldn't have been around here in 1960, when students all over the South started sitting-in at lunch counters. And I knew that as they were sitting in, they were really standing up for the best in the American dream. And taking the whole nation back to those great wells of democracy which were dug deep by the Founding Fathers in the Declaration of Independence and the Constitution. If I had sneezed, I wouldn't have been around in 1962, when Negroes in Albany, Georgia, decided to straighten their backs up. And whenever men and women straighten their backs up, they are going somewhere, because a man can't ride your back unless it is bent. If I had sneezed, I wouldn't have been here in 1963, when the black people of Birmingham, Alabama, aroused the conscience of this nation, and brought into being the Civil Rights Bill. If I had sneezed, I wouldn't have had a chance later that year, in August, to try to tell American about a dream that I had had. If I had sneezed, I wouldn't have been down in Selma, Alabama, to see the great movement there. If I had sneezed, I wouldn't have been in Memphis to see a community rally around those brothers and sisters who are suffering. I'm so happy that I didn't sneeze.

And they were telling me, now it doesn't matter now. It really doesn't matter what happens now. I left Atlanta this morning, and as we got started on the plane, there were six of us, the pilot said over the public address system, "We are sorry for the delay, but we have Dr. Martin Luther King on the plane. And to be sure that all of the bags were checked, and to be sure that nothing would be wrong with the plane, we had to check out everything carefully. And we've had the plane protected and guarded all night."

And then I got into Memphis. And some began to say the threats, or talk about the threats that were out. What would happen to me from some of our sick white brothers?

Well, I don't know what will happen now. We've got some difficult days ahead. But it doesn't matter with me now. Because I've been to the mountaintop. And I don't mind. Like anybody, I would like to live a long life. Longevity has its place. But I'm not concerned about that now. I just want to do God's will. And He's allowed me to go up to the mountain. And I've looked over. And I've seen the promised land. I may not get there with you. But I want you to know tonight, that we, as a people will get to the promised land. And I'm happy, tonight. I'm not worried about anything. I'm not fearing any man. Mine eyes have seen the glory of the coming of the Lord.

---

Flip Schulke, ed., *Martin Luther King, Jr: A Documentary . . . Montgomery to Memphis* (New York and London: Norton, 1976), 222–23. The "Judge Hooks" referred to on page 283 is the Reverend Dr. Benjamin Hooks, then a local justice in Memphis, now executive director of the NAACP.

# PART III: HISTORIC ESSAYS

# 46

# Letter from
# Birmingham City Jail

*Dr. King wrote this famous essay (written in the form of an open letter) on 16 April 1963 while in jail. He was serving a sentence for participating in civil rights demonstrations in Birmingham, Alabama. He rarely took time to defend himself against his opponents. But eight prominent "liberal" Alabama clergymen, all white, published an open letter earlier in January that called on King to allow the battle for integration to continue in the local and federal courts, and warned that King's nonviolent resistance would have the effect of inciting civil disturbances. Dr. King wanted Christian ministers to see that the meaning of Christian discipleship was at the heart of the African American struggle for freedom, justice, and equality.*

My dear Fellow Clergymen,

While confined here in the Birmingham city jail, I came across your recent statement calling our present activities "unwise and untimely." Seldom, if ever, do I pause to answer criticism of my work and ideas. If I sought to answer all of the criticisms that cross my desk, my secretaries would be engaged in little else in the course of the day, and I would have no time for constructive work. But since I feel that you are men of genuine good will and your criticisms are sincerely set forth, I would like to answer your statement in what I hope will be patient and reasonable terms.

I think I should give the reason for my being in Birmingham, since you have been influenced by the argument of "outsiders coming in." I have the honor of serving as president of the Southern Christian Leadership Conference, an organization operating in every southern state, with headquarters in Atlanta, Georgia. We have some eighty-five affiliate organizations all across the South—one being the Alabama Christian Movement for Human Rights. Whenever necessary and possible we share staff, educational and financial resources with our affiliates. Several months ago our local affiliate here in Birmingham invited us to be on call to engage in a nonviolent direct-action program if such were deemed necessary. We readily consented and when the hour came we lived up to our promises. So I am here, along with several members of my staff, because we were invited here. I am here because I have basic organizational ties here.

Beyond this, I am in Birmingham because injustice is here. Just as the eighth century prophets left their little villages and carried their "thus saith the Lord" far beyond the boundaries of their hometowns; and just as the Apostle Paul left his little village of Tarsus and carried the gospel of Jesus Christ to practically every hamlet and city of the Graeco-Roman world, I too am compelled to carry the gospel of freedom beyond my particular hometown. Like Paul, I must constantly respond to the Macedonian call for aid.

Moreover, I am cognizant of the interrelatedness of all communities and states. I cannot sit idly by in Atlanta and not be concerned about what happens in Birmingham. Injustice anywhere is a threat to justice everywhere. We are caught in an inescapable network of mutuality, tied in a single garment of destiny. Whatever affects one directly affects all indirectly. Never again can we afford to live with the narrow, provincial "outside agitator" idea. Anyone who lives in the United States can never be considered an outsider anywhere in this country.

You deplore the demonstrations that are presently taking place in Birmingham. But I am sorry that your statement did not express a similar concern for the conditions that brought the demonstrations into being. I am sure that each of you would want to go beyond the superficial social analyst who looks merely at effects, and does not grapple with underlying causes. I would not hesitate to say that it is unfortunate that so-called demonstrations are taking place in Birmingham at this time, but I would say in more emphatic terms that it is even more unfortunate that the white power structure of this city left the Negro community with no other alternative.

In any nonviolent campaign there are four basic steps: (1) collection of the facts to determine whether injustices are alive, (2) negotiation, (3) self-purification, and (4) direct action. We have gone through all of these steps in Birmingham. There can be no gainsaying of the fact that racial injustice engulfs this community.

Birmingham is probably the most thoroughly segregated city in the United States. Its ugly record of police brutality is known in every section of this country. Its injust treatment of Negroes in the courts is a notorious reality. There have been more unsolved bombings of Negro homes and churches in Birmingham than any city in this nation. These are the hard, brutal and unbelievable facts. On the basis of these conditions Negro leaders sought to negotiate with the city fathers. But the political leaders consistently refused to engage in good faith negotiation.

Then came the opportunity last September to talk with some of the leaders of the economic community. In these negotiating sessions certain promises were made by the merchants—such as the promise to remove the humiliating racial signs from the stores. On the basis of these promises Rev. Shuttlesworth and the leaders of the Alabama Christian Movement for Human Rights agreed to call a moratorium on any type of demonstrations. As the weeks and months unfolded we realized that we were the victims of a broken promise. The signs remained. Like so many experiences of the past we were confronted with blasted hopes, and the dark shadow of a deep disappointment settled upon us. So we had no alternative except that of preparing for direct action, whereby we would present our very bodies as a means of laying our case before the conscience of the local and national community. We were not unmindful of the difficulties involved. So we decided to go through a process of self-purification. We started having workshops on nonviolence and repeatedly asked ourselves the questions, "Are you able to accept blows without retaliating?" "Are you able to endure the ordeals of jail?" We decided to set our direct-action program around the Easter season, realizing that with the exception of Christmas, this was the largest shopping period of the year. Knowing that a strong economic withdrawal program would be the by-product of direct action, we felt that this was the best time to bring pressure on the merchants for the needed changes. Then it occurred to us that the March election was ahead and so we speedily decided to postpone action until after election day. When we discovered that Mr. Connor was in the run-off, we decided again to postpone action so that the demonstrations could not be used to cloud the issues. At this time we agreed to begin our nonviolent witness the day after the run-off.

This reveals that we did not move irresponsibly into direct action. We too wanted to see Mr. Connor defeated; so we went through postponement after postponement to aid in this community need. After this we felt that direct action could be delayed no longer.

You may well ask, "Why direct action? Why sit-ins, marches, etc.? Isn't negotiation a better path?" You are exactly right in your call for negotiation. Indeed, this is the purpose of direct action. Nonviolent direct action seeks to create such a crisis and establish such creative tension that a community that has constantly refused to negotiate is forced to confront the issue. It seeks so to dramatize the issue that it can no longer be ignored. I just referred to the creation of tension as a part of the work of the nonviolent resister. This may sound rather shocking. But I must confess that I am not afraid of the word tension. I have earnestly worked and preached against violent tension, but there is a type of constructive nonviolent tension that is necessary for growth. Just as Socrates felt that it was necessary to create a tension in the mind so that individuals could rise from the bondage of myths and half-truths to the unfettered realm of creative analysis and objective appraisal, we must see the need of having nonviolent gadflies to create the kind of tension in society that will help men to rise from the dark depths of prejudice and racism to the majestic heights of understanding and brotherhood.

So the purpose of the direct action is to create a situation so crisis-packed that it will inevitably open the door to negotiation. We, therefore, concur with you in your call for negotiation. Too long has our beloved Southland been bogged down in the tragic attempt to live in monologue rather than dialogue.

One of the basic points in your statement is that our acts are untimely. Some have asked, "Why didn't you give the new administration time to act?" The only answer that I can give to this inquiry is that the new administration must be prodded about as much as the outgoing one before it acts. We will be sadly mistaken if we feel that the election of Mr. Boutwell will bring the millennium to Birmingham. While Mr. Boutwell is much more articulate and gentle than Mr. Connor, they are both segregationists, dedicated to the task of maintaining the status quo. The hope I see in Mr. Boutwell is that he will be reasonable enough to see the futility of massive resistance to desegregation. But he will not see this without pressure from the devotees of civil rights. My friends, I must say to you that we have not made a single gain in civil rights without determined legal and nonviolent pressure. History is the long and tragic story of the fact that privileged groups seldom give up their privileges voluntarily. Individuals may see the moral light and voluntarily give up their unjust posture; but as Reinhold Niebuhr has reminded us, groups are more immoral than individuals.

We know through painful experience that freedom is never voluntarily given by the oppressor; it must be demanded by the oppressed. Frankly, I have never yet engaged in a direct action movement that was "well-timed," according to the timetable of those who have not suffered unduly from the disease of segregation. For years now I have heard the words "Wait!" It rings in the ear of every Negro with a piercing familiarity. This "Wait" has almost always meant "Never." It has been a tranquilizing thalidomide, relieving the emotional stress for a moment, only to give birth to an ill-formed infant of frustration. We must come to see with the distinguished jurist of yesterday that "justice too long delayed is justice denied." We have waited for more than 340 years for our constitutional and God-given rights. The nations of Asia and Africa are moving with jetlike speed toward the goal of political independence, and we still creep at horse and buggy pace toward the gaining of a cup of coffee at a lunch counter. I guess it is easy for those who have never felt the stinging darts of segregation to say, "Wait." But when you have seen vicious mobs lynch your mothers and fathers at will and drown your sisters and brothers at whim; when you have seen hate-filled policemen curse, kick, brutalize and even kill your black brothers and sisters with impunity; when you see the vast majority of your twenty million Negro brothers smothering in an airtight cage of poverty in the midst of an affluent society; when you suddenly find your tongue twisted and your speech stammering as you seek to explain to your six-year-old daughter why she can't go to the public amusement park that has just been advertised on television, and see tears welling up in her little eyes when she is told that Funtown is closed to colored children, and see the depressing clouds of inferiority begin to form in her little mental sky, and see her begin to distort her little personality by unconsciously developing a bitterness toward white people; when you have to concoct an answer for a five-year-old son asking in agonizing pathos: "Daddy, why do white people treat colored people so mean?"; when you take a cross-country drive and find it necessary to sleep night after night in the uncomfortable corners of your automobile because no motel will accept you; when you are humiliated day in and day out by nagging signs reading "white" and "colored"; when your first name becomes "nigger" and your middle name becomes "boy" (however old you are) and your last name becomes "John," and when your wife and mother are never given the respected title "Mrs."; when you are harried by day and haunted by night by the fact that you are a Negro, living constantly at tiptoe stance never quite knowing what to expect next, and plagued with inner fears and outer resentments; when you are forever fighting a degenerating sense of "nobodiness"; then you will understand why we find it difficult to wait. There comes a time when the cup of endurance runs over, and men are no longer willing to be plunged into an abyss of injustice where they experience the blackness of corroding despair. I hope, sirs, you can understand our legitimate and unavoidable impatience.

You express a great deal of anxiety over our willingness to break laws. This is certainly a legitimate concern. Since we so diligently urge people to obey the Supreme Court's decision of 1954 outlawing segregation in the public schools, it is rather strange and paradoxical to find us consciously breaking laws. One may well ask, "How can you advocate breaking some laws and obeying others?" The answer is found in the fact that there are two types of laws: there are *just* and there are *unjust* laws. I would agree with Saint Augustine that "An unjust law is no law at all."

Now what is the difference between the two? How does one determine when a law is just or unjust? A just law is a man-made code that squares with the moral law or the law of God. An unjust law is a code that is out of harmony with the moral law. To put it in the terms of Saint Thomas Aquinas, an unjust law is a human law that is not rooted in eternal and natural law. Any law that uplifts human personality is just. Any law that degrades human personality is unjust. All segregation statutes are unjust because segregation distorts the soul and damages the personality. It gives the segregator a false sense of superiority, and the segregated a false sense of inferiority. To use the words of Martin Buber, the great Jewish philosopher, segregation substitutes an "I-it" relationship for the "I-thou" relationship, and ends up relegating persons to the status of things. So segregation is not only politically, economically and sociologically unsound, but it is morally wrong and sinful. Paul Tillich has said that sin is separation. Isn't segregation an existential expression of man's tragic separation, an expression of his awful estrangement, his terrible sinfulness? So I can urge men to disobey segregation ordinances becuase they are morally wrong.

Let us turn to a more concrete example of just and unjust laws. An unjust law is a code that a majority inflicts on a minority that is not binding on itself. This is difference made legal. On the other hand a just law is a code that a majority compels a minority to follow that it is willing to follow itself. This is sameness made legal.

Let me give another explanation. An unjust law is a code inflicted upon a minority which that minority had no part in enacting or creating because they did not have the unhampered right to vote. Who can say that the legislature of Alabama which set up the segregation laws was democratically elected? Throughout the state of Alabama all types of conniving methods are used to prevent Negroes from becoming registered voters and there are some counties without a single Negro registered to vote despite the fact that the Negro constitutes a majority of the population. Can any law set up in such a state be considered democratically structured?

These are just a few examples of unjust and just laws. There are some instances when a law is just on its face and unjust in its application. For instance, I was arrested Friday on a change of parading without a permit. Now there is nothing wrong with an ordinance which requires a permit for a parade, but when the ordinance is used to preserve segregation and to deny citizens the First Amendment privilege of peaceful assembly and peaceful protest, then it becomes unjust.

I hope you can see the distinction I am trying to point out. In no sense do I advocate evading or defying the law as the rabid segregationist would do. This would lead to anarchy. One who breaks an unjust law must do it *openly*, *lovingly* (not hatefully as the white mothers did in New Orleans when they were seen on television screaming, "nigger, nigger, nigger"), and with a willingness to accept the penalty. I submit that an individual who breaks a law that conscience tells him is unjust, and willingly accepts the penalty by staying in jail to arouse the conscience of the community over its injustice, is in reality expressing the very highest respect for law.

Of course, there is nothing new about this kind of civil disobedience. It was seen sublimely in the refusal of Shadrach, Meshach and Abednego to obey the laws of Nebuchadnezzar because a higher moral law was involved. It was practiced superbly by the early Christians who were willing to face hungry lions and the excruciating pain of chopping blocks, before submitting to certain unjust laws of the Roman Empire. To a degree academic freedom is a reality today because Socrates practiced civil disobedience.

We can never forget that everything Hitler did in Germany was "legal" and everything the Hungarian freedom fighters did in Hungary was "illegal." It was "illegal" to aid and comfort a Jew in Hitler's Germany. But I am sure that if I had lived in Germany during that time I would have aided and comforted my Jewish brothers even though it was illegal. If I lived in a Communist country today where certain principles dear to the Christian faith are suppressed, I believe I would openly advocate disobeying these anti-religious laws. I must make two honest confessions to you, my Christian and Jewish brothers. First, I must confess that over the last few years I have been gravely disappointed with the white moderate. I have almost reached the regrettable conclusion that the Negro's great stumbling block in the stride toward freedom is not the White Citizen's Counciler or the Ku Klux Klanner, but the white moderate who is more devoted to "order" than to justice; who prefers a negative peace which is the absence of tension to a positive peace which is the presence of justice; who constantly says, "I agree with you in the goal you seek, but I can't agree with your methods of direct action"; who paternalistically feels that he can set the timetable for another man's freedom; who lives by the myth of time and who constantly advised the Negro to wait until a "more convenient season." Shallow understanding from people of good will is more frustrating than absolute misunderstanding from people of ill will. Lukewarm acceptance is much more bewildering than outright rejection.

I had hoped that the white moderate would understand that law and order exist for the purpose of establishing justice, and that when they fail to do this they become dangerously structured dams that block the flow of social progress. I had hoped that the white moderate would understand that the present tension of the South is merely a necessary phase of the transition from an obnoxious negative peace, where the Negro passively accepted his unjust plight, to a substance-filled positive peace, where all men will respect the dignity and worth of human personality. Actually, we who engage in nonviolent direct action are not the creators of tension. We merely bring to the surface the hidden tension that is already alive. We bring it out in the open where it can be seen and dealt with. Like a boil that can never be cured as long as it is covered up but must be opened with all its pus-flowing ugliness to the natural medicines of air and light, injustice must likewise be exposed, with all of the tension its exposing creates, to the light of human conscience and the air of national opinion before it can be cured.

In your statement you asserted that our actions, even though peaceful, must be condemned because they precipitate violence. But can this assertion be logically made? Isn't this like condemning the robbed man because his possession of money precipitated the evil act of robbery? Isn't this like condemning Socrates because his unswerving commitment to truth and his philosophical delvings precipitated the misguided popular mind to make him drink the hemlock? Isn't this like condemning Jesus because His unique God-consciousness and never-ceasing devotion to his will precipitated the evil act of crucifixion? We must come to see, as federal courts have consistently affirmed, that it is immoral to urge an individual to withdraw his efforts to gain his basic constitutional rights because the quest precipitates violence. Society must protect the robbed and punish the robber.

I had also hoped that the white moderate would reject the myth of time. I received a letter this morning from a white brother in Texas which said: "All Christians know that the colored people will receive equal rights eventually, but it is possible that you are in too great of a religious hurry. It has taken Christianity almost two thousand years to accomplish what it has. The teachings of Christ take time to come to earth." All that is said here grows out of a tragic misconception of time. It is the strangely irrational notion that there is something in the very flow of time that will inevitably cure all ills. Actually time is neutral. It can be used either destructively or constructively. I am coming to feel that the people of ill will have used time much more effectively than the people of good will. We will have to repent in this generation not merely for the vitriolic words and actions of the bad people, but for the appalling silence of the good people. We must come to see that human progress never rolls in on wheels of inevitability. It comes through the tireless efforts and persistent work of men willing to be co-workers with God, and without this hard word time itself becomes an ally of the forces of social stagnation. We must use time creatively, and forever realize that the time is always ripe to do right. Now is the time to make real the promise of democracy, and transform our pending national elegy into a creative psalm of brotherhood. Now is the time to lift our national policy from the quicksand of racial injustice to the solid rock of human dignity.

You spoke of our activity in Birmingham as extreme. At first I was rather disappointed that fellow clergymen would see my nonviolent efforts as those of the extremist. I started thinking about the fact that I stand in the middle of two opposing forces in the Negro community. One is a force of complacency made up of Negroes who, as a result of long years of oppression, have been so completely drained of self-respect and a sense of "somebodiness" that they have adjusted to segregation, and, of a few Negroes in the middle class who, because of a degree of academic and economic security, and because at points they profit by segregation, have unconsciously become insensitive to the problems of the masses. The other force is one of bitterness and hatred, and comes perilously close to advocating violence. It is expressed in the various black nationalist groups that are springing up over the nation, the largest and best known being Elijah Muhammad's Muslim movement. This movement is nourished by the contemporary frustration over the continued existence of racial discrimination. It is made up of people who have lost faith in America, who have absolutely repudiated Christianity, and who have concluded that the white man is an incurable "devil." I have tried to stand between these two forces, saying that we need not follow the "do-nothingism" of the complacent or the hatred and despair of the black nationalist. There is the more excellent way of love and nonviolent protest. I'm grateful to God that, through the Negro church, the dimension of nonviolence entered our struggle. If this philosophy had not emerged, I am convinced that by now many streets of the South would be flowing with floods of blood. And I am further convinced that if our white brothers dismiss us as "rabble-rousers" and "outside agitators" those of us who are working through the channels of nonviolent direct action and refuse to support our nonviolent efforts, millions of Negroes, out of frustration and despair, will seek solace and security in black nationalist ideologies, a development that will lead inevitably to a frightening racial nightmare.

Oppressed people cannot remain oppressed forever. The urge for freedom will eventually come. This is what happened to the American Negro. Something within has reminded him of his birthright of freedom; something without has reminded him that he can gain it. Consciously and unconsciously, he has been swept in by what the Germans call the *Zeitgeist*, and with his black brothers of Africa, and his brown and yellow brothers of Asia, South America and the Caribbean, he is moving with a sense of cosmic urgency toward the promised land of racial justice. Recognizing this vital urge that has engulfed the Negro community, one should readily understand public demonstrations. The Negro has many pent-up resentments and latent frustrations. He has to get them out. So let him march sometime; let him have his prayer pilgrimages to the city hall; understand why he must have sit-ins and freedom rides. If his repressed emotions do not come out in these nonviolent ways, they will come out in ominous expressions of violence. This is not a threat; it is a fact of history. So I have not said to my people "get rid of your discontent." But I have tried to say that this normal and healthy discontent can be channelized through the creative outlet of nonviolent direct action. Now this approach is being dismissed as extremist. I must admit that I was initially disappointed in being so categorized.

But as I continued to think about the matter I gradually gained a bit of satisfaction from being considered an extremist. Was not Jesus an extremist in love—"Love your enemies, bless them that curse you, pray for them that despitefully use you." Was not Amos an extremist for justice—"Let justice roll down like waters and righteousness like a mighty stream." Was not Paul an extremist for the gospel of Jesus Christ—"I bear in my body the marks of the Lord Jesus." Was not Martin Luther an extremist—"Here I stand; I can do none other so help me God." Was not John Bunyan an extremist—"I will stay in jail to the end of my days before I make a butchery of my conscience." Was not Abraham Lincoln an extremist—"This nation cannot survive half slave and half free." Was not Thomas Jefferson an extremist—"We hold these truths to be self-evident, that all men are created equal." So the question is not whether we will be extremist but what kind of extremist will we be. Will we be extremists for hate or will we be extremists for love? Will we be extremists for the preservation of injustice—or will we be extremists for the cause of justice? In that dramatic scene on Calvary's hill, three men were crucified. We must not forget that all three were crucified for the same crime—the crime of extremism. Two were extremists for immorality, and thusly fell below their environment. The other, Jesus Christ, was an extremist for love, truth and goodness, and thereby rose above his environment. So, after all, maybe the South, the nation and the world are in dire need of creative extremists.

I had hoped that the white moderate would see this. Maybe I was too optimistic. Maybe I expected too much. I guess I should have realized that few members of a race that has oppressed another race can understand or appreciate the deep groans and passionate yearnings of those that have been oppressed and still fewer have the vision to see that injustice must be rooted out by strong, persistent and determined action. I am thankful, however, that some of our white brothers have grasped the meaning of this social revolution and committed themselves to it. They are still all too small in quantity, but they are big in quality. Some like Ralph McGill, Lillian Smith, Harry Golden and James Dabbs have written about our struggle in eloquent, prophetic and understanding terms. Others have marched with us down nameless streets of the South. They have languished in filthy roach-infested jails, suffering the abuse and brutality of angry policemen who see them as "dirty nigger-lovers." They, unlike so many of their moderate brothers and sisters, have recognized the urgency of the moment and sensed the need for powerful "action" antidotes to combat the disease of segregation.

Let me rush on to mention my other disappointment. I have been so greatly disappointed with the white church and its leadership. Of course, there are some notable exceptions. I am not unmindful of the fact that each of you has taken some significant stands on this issue. I commend you, Rev. Stallings, for your Christian stance on this past Sunday, in welcoming Negroes to your worship service on a non-segregated basis. I commend the Catholic leaders of this state for integrating Springhill College several years ago.

But despite these notable exceptions I must honestly reiterate that I have been disappointed with the church. I do not say that as one of the negative critics who can always find something wrong with the church. I say it as a minister of the gospel, who loves the church; who was nurtured in its bosom; who has been sustained by its spiritual blessings and who will remain true to it as long as the cord of life shall lengthen.

I had the strange feeling when I was suddenly catapulted into the leadership of the bus protest in Montgomery several years ago that we would have the support of the white church. I felt that the white ministers, priests and rabbis of the South would be some of our strongest allies. Instead, some have been outright opponents, refusing to understand the freedom movement and misrepresenting its leaders; all too many others have been more cautious than courageous and have remained silent behind the anesthetizing security of the stained-glass windows.

In spite of my shattered dreams of the past, I came to Birmingham with the hope that the white religious leadership of this community would see the justice of our cause, and with deep moral concern, serve as the channel through which our just grievances would get to the power structure. I had hoped that each of you would understand. But again I have been disappointed. I have heard numerous religious leaders of the South call upon their worshippers to comply with a desegregation decision because it is the *law*, but I have longed to hear white ministers say, "Follow this decree because integration is morally *right* and the Negro is your brother." In the midst of blatant injustices inflicted upon the Negro, I have watched white churches stand on the sideline and merely mouth pious irrelevancies and sanctimonious trivialities. In the midst of a mighty struggle to rid our nation of racial and economic injustice, I have heard so many ministers say, "Those are social issues with which the gospel has no real concern," and I have watched so many churches commit themselves to a completely otherworldly religion which made a strange distinction between body and soul, the sacred and the secular.

So here we are moving toward the exit of the twentieth century with a religious community largely adjusted to the status quo, standing as a taillight behind other community agencies rather than a headlight leading men to higher levels of justice.

I have traveled the length and breadth of Alabama, Mississippi and all the other southern states. On sweltering summer days and crisp autumn mornings I have looked at her beautiful churches with their lofty spires pointing heavenward. I have beheld the impressive outlay of her massive religious education buildings. Over and over again I have found myself asking: "What kind of people worship here? Who is their God? Where were their voices when the lips of Governor Barnett dripped with words of interposition and nullification? Where were they when Governor Wallace gave the clarion call for defiance and hatred? Where were their voices of support when tired, bruised and weary Negro men and women decided to rise from the dark dungeons of complacency to the bright hills of creative protest?"

Yes, these questions are still in my mind. In deep disappointment, I have wept over the laxity of the church. But be assured that my tears have been tears of love. There can be no deep disappointment where there is not deep love. Yes, I love the church; I love her sacred walls. How could I do otherwise? I am in the rather unique position of being the son, the grandson and the great-grandson of preachers. Yes, I see the church as the body of Christ. But, oh! How we have blemished and scarred that body through social neglect and fear of being nonconformists.

There was a time when the church was very powerful. It was during that period when the early Christians rejoiced when they were deemed worthy to suffer for what they believed. In those days the church was not merely a thermometer that recorded the ideas and principles of popular opinion; it was a thermostat that transformed the mores of society. Wherever the early Christians entered a town the power structure got disturbed and immediately sought to convict them for being "disturbers of the peace" and "outside agitators." But they went on with the conviction that they were "a colony of heaven," and had to obey God rather than man. They were small in number but big in commitment. They were too God-intoxicated to be "astronomically intimidated." They brought an end to such ancient evils as infanticide and gladiatorial contest.

Things are different now. The contemporary church is often a weak, ineffectual voice with an uncertain sound. It is so often the arch-supporter of the status quo. Far from being disturbed by the presence of the church, the power structure of the average community is consoled by the church's silent and often vocal sanction of things as they are.

But the judgment of God is upon the church as never before. If the church of today does not recapture the sacrificial spirit of the early church, it will lose its authentic ring, forfeit the loyalty of millions, and be dismissed as an irrelevant social club with no meaning for the twentieth century. I am meeting young people every day whose disappointment with the church has risen to outright disgust.

Maybe again, I have been too optimistic. Is organized religion too inextricably bound to the status quo to save our nation and the world? Maybe I must turn my faith to the inner spiritual church, the church within the church, as the true *ecclesia* and the hope of the world. But again I am thankful to God that some noble souls from the ranks of organized religion have broken loose from the paralyzing chains of conformity and joined us as active partners in the struggle for freedom. They have left their secure congregations and walked the streets of Albany, Georgia, with us. They have gone through the highways of the South on tortuous rides for freedom. Yes, they have gone to jail with us. Some have been kicked out of their churches, and lost support of their bishops and fellow ministers. But they have gone with the faith that right defeated is stronger than evil triumphant. These men have been the leaven in the lump of the race. Their witness has been the spiritual salt that has preserved the true meaning of the gospel in these troubled times. They have carved a tunnel of hope through the dark mountain of disappointment.

I hope the church as a whole will meet the challenge of this decisive hour. But even if the church does not come to the aid of justice, I have no despair about the future. I have no fear about the outcome of our struggle in Birmingham, even if our motives are presently misunderstood. We will reach the goal of freedom in Birmingham and all over the nation, because the goal of America is freedom. Abused and scorned though we may be, our destiny is tied up with the destiny of America. Before the Pilgrims landed at Plymouth we were here. Before the pen of Jefferson etched across the pages of history the majestic words of the Declaration of Independence, we were here. For more than two centuries our foreparents labored in this country without wages; they made cotton king; and they built the homes of their masters in the midst of brutal injustice and shameful humiliation—and yet out of a bottomless vitality they continued to thrive and develop. If the inexpressible cruelties of slavery could not stop us, the opposition we now face will surely fail. We will win our freedom because the sacred heritage of our nation and the eternal will of God are embodied in our echoing demands.

I must close now. But before closing I am impelled to mention one other point in your statement that troubled me profoundly. You warmly commended the Birmingham police force for keeping "order" and "preventing violence." I don't believe you would have so warmly commended the police force if you had seen its angry violent dogs literally biting six unarmed, nonviolent Negroes. I don't believe you would so quickly commend the policemen if you would observe their ugly and inhuman treatment of Negroes here in the city jail; if you would watch them push and curse old Negro women and young Negro girls; if you would see them slap and kick old Negro men and young boys; if you will observe them, as they did on two occasions, refuse to give us food because we wanted to sing our grace together. I'm sorry that I can't join you in your praise for the police department.

It is true that they have been rather disciplined in their public handling of the demonstrators. In this sense they have been rather publicly "nonviolent." But for what purpose? To preserve the evil system of segregation. Over the last few years I have consistently preached that nonviolence demands that the means we use must be as pure as the ends we seek. So I have tried to make it clear that it is wrong to use immoral means to attain moral ends. But now I must affirm that it is just as wrong, or even more so, to use moral means to preserve immoral ends. Maybe Mr. Connor and his policemen have been rather publicly nonviolent, as Chief Pritchett was in Albany, Georgia, but they have used the moral means of nonviolence to maintain the immoral end of flagrant racial injustice. T. S. Eliot has said that there is no greater treason than to do the right deed for the wrong reason.

I wish you had commended the Negro sit-inners and demonstrators of Birmingham for their sublime courage, their willingness to suffer and their amazing discipline in the midst of the most inhuman provocation.

One day the South will recognize its real heroes. They wil be the James Merediths, courageously and with a majestic sense of purpose facing jeering and hostile mobs and the agonizing loneliness that characterizes the life of the pioneer. They will be old, oppressed, battered Negro women, symbolized in a seventy-two-year-old woman of Montgomery, Alabama, who rose up with a sense of dignity and with her people decided not to ride the segregated buses, and responded to one who inquired about her tiredness with ungrammatical profundity: "My feet is tired, but my soul is rested." They will be the young high school and college students, young ministers of the gospel and a host of their elders courageously and nonviolently sitting-in at lunch counters and willingly going to jail for conscience's sake. One day the South will know that when these disinherited children of God sat down at lunch counters they were in reality standing up for the best in the American dream and the most sacred values in our Judeo-Christian heritage, and thusly, carrying our whole nation back to those great wells of democracy which were dug deep by the Founding Fathers in the formulation of the Constitution and the Declaration of Independence.

Never before have I written a letter this long (or should I say a book?). I'm afraid that it is much too long to take your precious time. I can assure you that it would have been much shorter if I had been writing from a comfortable desk, but what else is there to do when you are alone for days in the dull monotony of a narrow jail cell other than write long letters, think strange thoughts, and pray long prayers?

If I have said anything in this letter that is an overstatement of the truth and is indicative of an unreasonable impatience, I beg you to forgive me. If I have said anything in this letter that is an understatement of the truth and is indicative of my having a patience that makes me patient with anything less than brotherhood, I beg God to forgive me.

I hope this letter finds you strong in the faith. I also hope that circumstances will soon make it possible for me to meet each of you, not as an integrationist or a civil rights leader, but as a fellow clergyman and a Christian brother. Let us all hope that the dark clouds of racial prejudice will soon pass away and the deep fog of misunderstanding will be lifted from our fear-drenched communities and in some not too distant tomorrow the radiant stars of love and brotherhood will shine over our great nation with all of their scintillating beauty.

Yours for the cause of Peace and Brotherhood,

Martin Luther King, Jr.

---

Martin Luther King, Jr., *Why We Can't Wait* (New York: Harper & Row, 1963, 1964). The American Friends Committee first published this essay as a pamphlet. It has probably been reprinted more than anything else Dr. King wrote.

# 47

# Black Power Defined

*The following article is a synopsis of King's understanding of the new wave of African American nationalism then being embraced by many within the black community. His book* **Where Do We Go from Here: Chaos or Community?** *(New York: Harper & Row, 1967) contains a more expanded discussion of this movement. Dr. King embraced the basic political and social agenda of black power advocates, but strongly condemned their endorsement of revolutionary violence and black separatism.*

When a people are mired in oppression, they realize deliverance only when they have accumulated the power to enforce change. The powerful never lose opportunities—they remain available to them. The powerless, on the other hand, never experience opportunity—it is always arriving at a later time.

The nettlesome task of Negroes today is to discover how to organize our strength into compelling power so that government cannot elude our demands. We must develop, from strength, a situation in which the government finds it wise and prudent to collaborate with us. It would be the height of naiveté to wait passively until the administration had somehow been infused with such blessings of good will that it implored us for our programs.

We must frankly acknowledge that in past years our creativity and imagination were not employed in learning how to develop power. We found a method in nonviolent protest that worked, and we employed it enthusiastically. We did not have leisure to probe for a deeper understanding of its laws and lines of development. Although our actions were bold and crowned with successes, they were substantially improvised and spontaneous. They attained the goals set for them but carried the blemishes of our inexperience.

This is where the civil rights movement stands today. Now we must take the next major step of examining the levers of power which Negroes must grasp to influence the course of events.

In our society power sources can always finally be traced to ideological, economic and political forces.

In the area of *ideology*, despite the impact of the works of a few Negro writers on a limited number of white intellectuals, all too few Negro thinkers have exerted an influence on the main currents of American thought. Nevertheless, Negroes have illuminated imperfections in the democratic structure that were formerly only dimly perceived, and have forced a concerned reexamination of the true meaning of American democracy. As a consequence of the vigorous Negro protest, the whole nation has for a decade probed more searchingly the essential nature of democracy, both economic and political. By taking to the streets and there giving practical lessons in democracy and its defaults, Negroes have decisively influenced white thought.

Lacking sufficient access to television, publications and broad forums, Negroes have had to write their most persuasive essays with the blunt pen of marching ranks. The many white political leaders and well-meaning friends who ask Negro leadership to leave the streets may not realize that they are asking us effectively to silence ourselves. More white people learned more about the shame of America, and finally faced some aspects of it, during the years of nonviolent protest than during the century before. Nonviolent direct action will continue to be a significant source of power until it is made irrelevant by the presence of justice.

The *economic* highway to power has few entry lanes for Negroes. Nothing so vividly reveals the crushing impact of discrimination and the heritage of exclusion as the limited dimensions of Negro business in the most powerful economy in the world. America's industrial production is half of the world's total, and within it the production of Negro business is so small that it can scarcely be measured on any definable scale.

Yet in relation to the Negro community the value of Negro business should not be underestimated. In the internal life of the Negro society it provides a degree of stability. Despite formidable obstacles it has developed a corps of men of competence and organizational discipline who constitute a talented leadership reserve, who furnish inspiration and who are a resource for the development of programs and planning. They are a strength among the weak though they are weak among the mighty.

There exist two other areas, however, where Negroes can exert substantial influence on the broader economy. As employees and consumers, Negro numbers and their strategic disposition endow them with a certain bargaining strength.

Within the ranks of organized labor there are nearly two million Negroes, and they are concentrated in key industries. In the truck transportation, steel, auto and food industries, which are the backbone of the nation's economic life, Negroes make up nearly twenty percent of the organized work force, although they are only ten percent of the general population. This potential strength is magnified further by the fact of their unity with millions of white workers in these occupations. As co-workers there is a basic community of interest that transcends many of the ugly divisive elements of traditional prejudice. There are undeniably points of friction, for example, in certain housing and education questions. But the severity of the abrasions is minimized by the more commanding need for cohesion in union organizations.

The union record in relation to Negro workers is exceedingly uneven, but potential for influencing union decisions still exists. In many of the larger unions the white leadership contains some men of ideals and many more who are pragmatists. Both groups find they are benefited by a constructive relationship to their Negro membership. For those compelling reasons, Negroes, who are almost wholly a working people, cannot be casual toward the union movement. This is true even though some unions remain uncontestably hostile.

In days to come, organized labor will increase its importance in the destinies of Negroes. Negroes pressed into the proliferating service occupations—traditionally unorganized and with low wages and long hours—need union protection, and the union movement needs their membership to maintain its relative strength in the whole society. On this new frontier Negroes may well become the pioneers that they were in the early organizing days of the thirties.

To play our role fully as Negroes we will also have to strive for enhanced representation and influence in the labor movement. Our young people need to think of union careers as earnestly as they do of business careers and professions. They could do worse than emulate A. Philip Randolph, who rose to the executive council of the AFL-CIO and became a symbol of the courage, compassion and integrity of an enlightened labor leader.

Indeed, the question may be asked why we have produced only one Randolph in nearly half a century. Discrimination is not the whole answer. We allowed ourselves to accept middle-class prejudices against the labor movement. Yet this is one of those fields in which higher education is not a requirement for high office. In shunning it, we have lost an opportunity. Let us try to regain it now, at a time when the joint forces of Negroes and labor may be facing a historic task of social reform.

The other economic lever available to the Negro is as a consumer. The Southern Christian Leadership Council has pioneered in developing mass boycott movements in a frontal attack on discrimination. In Birmingham it was not the marching alone that brought about integration of public facilities in 1963. The downtown business establishments suffered for weeks under our almost unbelievably effective boycott. The significant percentage of their sales that vanished, the ninety-eight percent of their Negro customers who stayed home, educated them forcefully to the dignity of the Negro as a consumer.

Later we crystallized our experiences in Birmingham and elsewhere and developed a department in SCLC called Operation Breadbasket. This has as its primary aim the securing of more and better jobs for the Negro people. It calls on the Negro community to support those businesses that will give a fair share of jobs to Negroes and to withdraw its support from those businesses that have discriminatory policies.

Operation Breadbasket is carried out mainly by clergymen. First, a team of ministers calls on the management of a business in the community to request basic facts on the company's total number of employees, the number of Negro employees, the departments or job classifications in which all employees are located, and the salary ranges for each category. The team then returns to the steering committee to evaluate the data and to make a recommendation concerning the number of new and upgraded jobs that should be requested. Then the team transmits the request to the management to hire or upgrade a specified number of "qualifiable" Negroes within a reasonable period of time. If negotiations on this request break down, the step of real power and pressure is taken: a massive call for economic withdrawal from the company's product and accompanying demonstrations if necessary.

At present SCLC has Operation Breadbasket functioning in some twelve cities, and the results have been remarkable. In Atlanta, for instance, the Negroes' earning power has been increased by more than twenty million dollars annually over the past three years through a carefully disciplined program of selective buying and negotiation by the Negro ministers. During the last eight months in Chicago, Operation Breadbasket successfully completed negotiations with three major industries: milk, soft drinks and chain grocery stores. Four of the companies involved concluded reasonable agreements only after short "don't buy" campaigns. Seven other companies were able to make the requested changes across the conference table, without necessitating a boycott. Two other companies, after providing their employment information to the ministers, were sent letters of commendation for their healthy equal-employment practices. The net results add up to approximately eight hundred new and upgraded jobs for Negro employees, worth a little over seven million dollars in new annual income for Negro families. In Chicago we have recently added a new dimension to Operation Breadbasket. Along with requesting new job opportunities, we are now requesting that businesses with stores in the ghetto deposit the income for those establishments in Negro-owned banks, and that Negro-owned products be placed on the counters of all their stores. In this way we seek to stop the drain of resources out of the ghetto with nothing remaining there for its rehabilitation.

The final major area of untapped power for the Negro is in the *political* arena. Higher Negro birth rates and increasing Negro migration, along with the exodus of the white population to the suburbs, are producing fast-gathering Negro majorities in the large cities. This changing composition of the cities has political significance. Particularly in the North, the large cities substantially determine the political destiny of the state. These states, in turn, hold the dominating electoral votes in presidential contests. The future of the Democratic party, which rests so heavily on its coalition of urban minorities, cannot be assessed without taking into account which way the Negro vote turns. The wistful hopes of the Republican party for large-city influence will also be decided not in the boardrooms of great corporations but in the teeming ghettos.

The growing Negro vote in the South is another source of power. As it weakness and enfeebles the dixiecrats, by concentrating its blows against them, it undermines the congressional coalition of southern reactionaries and their northern Republican colleagues. That coalition, which has always exercised a disproportionate power in Congress by controlling its major committees, will lose its ability to frustrate measures of social advancement and to impose its perverted definition of democracy on the political thought of the nation.

The Negro vote at present is only a partially realized strength. It can still be doubled in the South. In the North even where Negroes are registered in equal proportion to whites, they do not vote in the same proportions. Assailed by a sense of futility, Negroes resist participating in empty ritual. However, when the Negro citizen learns that united and organized pressure can achieve measurable results, he will make his influence felt. Out of this conscious act, the political power of the aroused minority will be enhanced and consolidated.

We have many assets to facilitate organization. Negroes are almost instinctively cohesive. We band together readily, and against white hostility we have an intense and wholesome loyalty to each other. We are acutely conscious of the need, and sharply sensitive to the importance, of defending our own. Solidarity is a reality in Negro life, as it always has been among the oppressed.

On the other hand, Negroes are capable of becoming competitive, carping and, in an expression of self-hate, suspicious and intolerant of each other. A glaring weakness in Negro life is lack of sufficient mutual confidence and trust.

Negro leaders suffer from this interplay of solidarity and divisiveness, being either exalted excessively or grossly abused. Some of these leaders suffer from an aloofness and absence of faith in their people. The white establishment is skilled in flattering and cultivating emerging leaders. It presses its own image on them and finally, from imitation of manners, dress and style of living, a deeper strain of corruption develops. This kind of Negro leader acquires the white man's contempt for the ordinary Negro. He is often more at home with the middle-class white than he is among his own people. His language changes, his location changes, his income changes, and ultimately he changes from the representative of the Negro to the white man into the white man's representative to the Negro. The tragedy is that too often he does not recognize what has happened to him.

I learned a lesson many years ago from a report of two men who flew to Atlanta to confer with a Negro civil rights leader at the airport. Before they could begin to talk, the porter sweeping the floor drew the local leader aside to talk about a matter that troubled him. After fifteen minutes had passed, one of the visitors said bitterly to his companion, "I am just too busy for this kind of nonsense. I haven't come a thousand miles to sit and wait while he talks to a porter."

The other replied, "When the day comes that he stops having time to talk to a porter, on that day I will not have the time to come one mile to see him."

We need organizations that are permeated with mutual trust, incorruptibility and militancy. Without this spirit we may have numbers but they will add up to zero. We need organizations that are responsible, efficient and alert. We lack experience because ours is a history of disorganization. But we will prevail because our need for progress is stronger than the ignorance forced upon us. If we realize how indispensable is responsible militant organization to our struggle, we will create it as we managed to create underground railroads, protest groups, self-help societies and the churches that have always been our refuge, our source of hope and our source of action.

Negroes have been slow to organize because they have been traditionally manipulated. The political powers take advantage of three major weaknesses: the manner in which our political leaders emerge; our failure so far to achieve effective political alliances; and the Negro's general reluctance to participate fully in political life.

The majority of Negro political leaders do not ascend to prominence on the shoulders of mass support. Although genuinely popular leaders are now emerging, most are still selected by white leadership, elevated to position, supplied with resources and inevitably subjected to white control. The mass of Negroes nurtures a healthy suspicion toward this manufactured leader, who spends little time in persuading them that he embodies personal integrity, commitment and ability and offers few programs and less service. Tragically, he is in too many respects not a fighter for a new life but a figurehead of the old one. Hence, very few Negro political leaders are impressive or illustrious to their constituents. They enjoy only limited loyalty and qualified support.

This relationship in turn hampers the Negro leader in bargaining with genuine strength and independent firmness with white party leaders. The whites are all too well aware of his impotence and his remoteness from his constituents, and they deal with him as a powerless subordinate. He is accorded a measure of dignity and personal respect but not political power.

The Negro politician therefore finds himself in a vacuum. He has no base in either direction on which to build influence and attain leverage.

In two national polls among Negroes to name their most respected leaders, out of the highest fifteen, only a single political figure, Congressman Adam Clayton Powell, was included and he was in the lower half of both lists. This is in marked contrast to polls in which white people choose their most popular leaders; political personalities are always high on the lists and are represented in goodly numbers. There is no Negro personality evoking affection, respect and emulation to correspond to John F. Kennedy, Eleanor Roosevelt, Herbert Lehman, Earl Warren and Adlai Stevenson, to name but a few.

The circumstances in which Congressman Powell emerged into leadership and the experiences of his career are unique. It would not shed light on the larger picture to attempt to study the very individual factors that apply to him. It is fair to say no other Negro political leader is similar, either in the strengths he possesses, the power he attained or the errors he has committed.

And so we shall have to create leaders who embody virtues we can respect, who have moral and ethical principles we can applaud with an enthusiasm that enables us to rally support for them based on confidence and trust. We will have to demand high standards and give consistent, loyal support to those who merit it. We will have to be a reliable constituency for those who prove themselves to be committed political warriors in our behalf. When our movement has partisan political personalities whose unity with their people is unshakable and whose independence is genuine, they will be treated in white political councils with the respect those who embody such power deserve.

In addition to the development of genuinely independent and representative political leaders, we shall have to master the art of political alliances. Negroes should be natural allies of many white reform and independent political groups, yet they are more commonly organized by old-line machine politicians. We will have to learn to refuse crumbs from the big-city machines and steadfastly demand a fair share of the loaf. When the machine politicians demur, we must be prepared to act in unity and throw our support to such independent parties or reform wings of the major parties as are prepared to take our demands seriously and fight for them vigorously.

The art of alliance politics is more complex and more intricate than it is generally pictured. It is easy to put exciting combinations on paper. It evokes happy memories to recall that our victories in the past decade were won with a broad coalition of organizations representing a wide variety of interests. But we deceive ourselves if we envision the same combination backing structural changes in the society. It did not come together for such a program and will not reassemble for it.

A true alliance is based upon some self-interest of each component group and a common interest into which they merge. For an alliance to have permanence and loyal commitment from its various elements, each of them must have a goal from which it benefits and none must have an outlook in basic conflict with the others.

If we employ the principle of selectivity along these lines, we will find millions of allies who in serving themselves also support us, and on such sound foundations unity and mutual trust and tangible accomplishment will flourish.

In the changing conditions of the South, we will find alliances increasingly instrumental in political progress. For a number of years there were de facto alliances in some states in which Negroes voted for the same candidate as whites because he had shifted from a racist to a moderate position, even though he did not articulate an appeal for Negro votes. In recent years the transformation has accelerated, and many white candidates have entered alliances publicly. As they perceived that the Negro vote was becoming a substantial and permanent factor, they could not remain aloof from it. More and more, competition will develop among white political forces for such a significant bloc of votes, and a monolithic white unity based on racism will no longer be possible.

Racism is a tenacious evil, but it is not immutable. Millions of underprivileged whites are in the process of considering the contradiction between segregation and economic progress. White supremacy can feed their egos but not their stomachs. They will not go hungry or forgo the affluent society to remain racially ascendant.

Governors Wallace and Maddox whose credentials as racists are impeccable, understand this, and for that reason they represent themselves as liberal populists as well. Temporarily they can carry water on both shoulders, but the ground is becoming unsteady beneath their feet. Each of them was faced in the primary last year with a new breed of white southerner who for the first time in history met with Negro organizations to solicit support and championed economic reform without racial demagogy. These new figures won significant numbers of white votes, insufficient for victory but sufficient to point the future directions of the South.

It is true that the Negro vote has not transformed the North; but the fact that northern alliances and political action generally have been poorly executed is no reason to predict that the negative experiences will be automatically extended in the North or duplicated in the South. The northern Negro has never used direct action on a mass scale for reforms, and anyone who predicted ten years ago that the southern Negro would also neglect it would have dramatically been proved in error.

Everything Negroes need will not like magic materialize from the use of the ballot. Yet as a lever of power, if it is given studious attention and employed with the creativity we have proved through our protest activities we possess, it will help to achieve many far-reaching changes during our lifetimes.

The final reason for our dearth of political strength, particularly in the North, arises from the grip of an old tradition on many individual Negroes. They tend to hold themselves aloof from politics as a serious concern. They sense that they are manipulated, and their defense is a cynical disinterest. To safeguard themselves on this front from the exploitation that torments them in so many areas, they shut the door to political activity and retreat into the dark shadows of passivity. Their sense of futility is deep, and in terms of their bitter experiences it is justified. They cannot perceive political action as a source of power. It will take patient and persistent effort to eradicate this mood, but the new consciousness of strength developed in a decade of stirring agitation can be utilized to channel constructive Negro activity into political life and eliminate the stagnation produced by an outdated and defensive paralysis.

In the future we must become intensive political activists. We must be guided in this direction because we need political strength, more desperately than any other group in American society. Most of us are too poor to have adequate economic power, and many of us are too rejected by the culture to be part of any tradition of power. Necessity will draw us toward the power inherent in the creative uses of politics.

Negroes nurture a persisting myth that the Jews of America attained social mobility and status solely because they had money. It is unwise to ignore the error for many reasons. In a negative sense it encourages anti-Semitism and overestimates money as a value. In a positive sense, the full truth reveals a useful lesson.

Jews progressed because they possessed a tradition of education combined wtih social and political action. The Jewish family enthroned education and sacrificed to get it. The result was far more than abstract learning. Uniting social action with educational competence, Jews became enormously effective in political life. Those Jews who became lawyers, businessmen, writers, entertainers, union leaders and medical men did not vanish into the pursuits of their trade exclusively. They lived an active life in political circles, learning the techniques and arts of politics.

Nor was it only the rich who were involved in social and political action. Millions of Jews for half a century remained relatively poor, but they were far from passive in social and political areas. They lived in homes in which politics was a household word. They were deeply involved in radical parties, liberal parties and conservative parties—they formed many of them. Very few Jews sank into despair and escapism even when discrimination assailed the spirit and corroded initiative. Their life raft in the sea of discouragement was social action.

Without overlooking the towering differences between the Negro and Jewish experiences, the lesson of Jewish mass involvement in social and political action and education is worthy of emulation. Negroes have already started on this road in creating the protest movement, but this is only a beginning. We must involve everyone we can reach, even those with inadequate education, and together acquire political sophistication by discussion, practice and reading.

The many thousands of Negroes who have already found intellectual growth and spiritual fulfillment on this path know its creative possibilities. They are not among the legions of the lost, they are not crushed by the weight of centuries. Most heartening, among the young the spirit of challenge and determination for change is becoming an unquenchable force.

But the scope of struggle is still too narrow and too restricted. We must turn more of our energies and focus our creativity on the useful things that translate into power. We in this generation must do the work and in doing it stimulate our children to learn and acquire higher levels of skill and technique.

It must become a crusade so vital that civil rights organizers do not repeatedly have to make personal calls to summon support. There must be a climate of social pressure in the Negro community that scorns the Negro who will not pick up his citizenship rights and add his strength enthusiastically and voluntarily to the accumulation of power for himself and his people. The past years have blown fresh winds through ghetto stagnation, but we are on the threshold of a significant change that demands a hundredfold acceleration. By 1970 ten of our larger cities will have Negro majorities if present trends continue. We can shrug off this opportunity or use it for a new vitality to deepen and enrich our family and community life.

We must utilize the community action groups and training centers now proliferating in some slum areas to create not merely an electorate, but a conscious, alert and informed people who know their direction and whose collective wisdom and vitality commands respect. The slave heritage can be cast into the dim past by our consciousness of our strengths and a resolute determination to use them in our daily experiences.

Power is not the white man's birthright; it will not be legislated for us and delivered in neat government packages. It is a social force any group can utilize by accumulating its elements in a planned, deliberate campaign to organize it under its own control.

New York Times Magazine (11 June 1967).

# 48

# A Testament of Hope

*This essay was published posthumously.*

Whenever I am asked my opinion of the current state of the civil rights movement, I am forced to pause; it is not easy to describe a crisis so profound that it has caused the most powerful nation in the world to stagger in confusion and bewilderment. Today's problems are so acute because the tragic evasions and defaults of several centuries have accumulated to disaster proportions. The luxury of a leisurely approach to urgent solutions—the ease of gradualism—was forfeited by ignoring the issues for too long. The nation waited until the black man was explosive with fury before stirring itself even to partial concern. Confronted now with the interrelated problems of war, inflation, urban decay, white backlash and a climate of violence, it is now *forced* to address itself to race relations and poverty, and it is tragically unprepared. What might once have been a series of separate problems now merge into a social crisis of almost stupefying complexity.

I am not sad that black Americans are rebelling; this was not only inevitable but eminently desirable. Without this magnificent ferment among Negroes, the old evasions and procrastinations would have continued indefinitely. Black men have slammed the door shut on a past of deadening passivity. Except for the Reconstruction years, they have never in their long history on American soil struggled with such creativity and courage for their freedom. These are our bright years of emergence; though they are painful ones, they cannot be avoided.

Yet despite the widening of our stride, history is racing forward so rapidly that the Negro's inherited and imposed disadvantages slow him down to an infuriating crawl. Lack of education, the dislocations of recent urbanization and the hardening of white resistance loom as such tormenting roadblocks that the goal sometimes appears not as a fixed point in the future but as a receding point never to be reached. Still, when doubts emerge, we can remember that only yesterday Negroes were not only grossly exploited but negated as human beings. They were invisible in their misery. But the sullen and silent slave of 110 years ago, an object of scorn at worst or of pity at best, is today's angry man. He is vibrantly on the move; he is forcing change, rather than waiting for it in pathetic futility. In less than two decades, he has roared out of slumber to change so many of his life's conditions that he may yet find the means to accelerate his march forward and overtake the racing locomotive of history.

These words may have an unexpectedly optimistic ring at a time when pessimism is the prevailing mood. People are often surprised to learn that I am an optimist. They know how often I have been jailed, how frequently the days and nights have been filled with frustration and sorrow, how bitter and dangerous are my adversaries. They expect these experiences to harden me into a grim and desperate man. They fail, however, to perceive the sense of affirmation generated by the challenge of embracing struggle and surmounting obstacles. They have no comprehension of the strength that comes from faith in God and man. It is possible for me to falter, but I am profoundly secure in my knowledge that God loves us; he has not worked out a design for our failure. Man has the capacity to do right as well as wrong, and his history is a path upward, not downward. The past is strewn with the ruins of the empires of tyranny, and each is a monument not merely to man's blunders but to his capacity to overcome them. While it is a bitter fact that in America in 1968, I am denied equality solely because I am black, yet I am not a chattel slave. Millions of people have fought thousands of battles to enlarge my freedom; restricted as it still is, progress has been made. This is why I remain an optimist, though I am also a realist, about the barriers before us. Why is the issue of equality still so far from solution in America, a nation that professes itself to be democratic, inventive, hospitable to new ideas, rich, productive and awesomely powerful? The problem is so tenacious because, despite its virtues and attributes, America is deeply racist and its democracy is flawed both economically and socially. All too many Americans believe justice will unfold painlessly or that its absence for black people will be tolerated tranquilly.

Justice for black people will not flow into society merely from court decisions nor from fountains of political oratory. Nor will a few token changes quell all the tempestuous yearnings of millions of disadvantaged black people. White America must recognize that justice for black people cannot be achieved without radical changes in the structure of our society. The comfortable, the entrenched, the privileged cannot continue to tremble at the prospect of change in the status quo.

Stephen Vincent Benét had a message for both white and black Americans in the title of a story, *Freedom Is a Hard Bought Thing*. When millions of people have been cheated for centuries, restitution is a costly process. Inferior education, poor housing, unemployment, inadequate health care—each is a bitter component of the oppression that has been our heritage. Each will require billions of dollars to correct. Justice so long deferred has accumulated interest and its cost for this society will be substantial in financial as well as human terms. This fact has not been fully grasped, because most of the gains of the past decade were obtained at bargain prices. The desegregation of public facilities cost nothing; neither did the election and appointment of a few black public officials.

The price of progress would have been high enough at the best of times, but we are in an agonizing national crisis because a complex of profound problems has intersected in an explosive mixture. The black surge toward freedom has raised justifiable demands for racial justice in our major cities at a time when all the problems of city life have simultaneously erupted.. Schools, transportation, water supply, traffic and crime would have been municipal agonies whether or not Negroes lived in our cities. The anarchy of unplanned city growth was destined to confound our confidence. What is unique to this period is our inability to arrange an order of priorities that promises solutions that are decent and just.

Millions of Americans are coming to see that we are fighting an immoral war that costs nearly thirty billion dollars a year, that we are perpetuating racism, that we are tolerating almost forty million poor during an overflowing material abundance. Yet they remain helpless to end the war, to feed the hungry, to make brotherhood a reality; this has to shake our faith in ourselves. If we look honestly at the realities of our national life, it is clear that we are not marching forward; we are groping and stumbling; we are divided and confused. Our moral values and our spiritual confidence sink, even as our material wealth ascends. In these trying circumstances, the black revolution is much more than a struggle for the rights of Negroes. It is forcing America to face all its interrelated flaws—racism, poverty, militarism and materialism. It is exposing evils that are rooted deeply in the whole structure of our society. It reveals systemic rather than superficial flaws and suggests that radical reconstruction of society itself is the real issue to be faced.

It is time that we stopped our blithe lip service to the guarantees of life, liberty and pursuit of happiness. These fine sentiments are embodied in the Declaration of Independence, but that document was always a declaration of intent rather than of reality. There were slaves when it was written; there were still slaves when it was adopted; and to this day, black Americans have not life, liberty nor the privilege of pursuing happiness, and millions of poor white Americans are in economic bondage that is scarcely less oppressive. Americans who genuinely treasure our national ideals, who know they are still elusive dreams for all too many, should welcome the stirring of Negro demands. They are shattering the complacency that allowed a multitude of social evils to accumulate. Negro agitation is requiring America to reexamine its comforting myths and may yet catalyze the drastic reforms that will save us from social catastrophe.

In indicting white America for its ingrained and tenacious racism, I am using the term "white" to describe the majority, not *all* who are

white. We have found that there are many white people who clearly perceive the justice of the Negro struggle for human dignity. Many of them
joined our struggle and displayed heroism no less inspiring than that of
black people. More than a few died by our side; their memories are
cherished and are undimmed by time.

Yet the largest portion of white America is still poisoned by racism,
which is as native to our soil as pine trees, sagebrush and buffalo grass.
Equally native to us is the concept that gross exploitation of the Negro is
acceptable, if not commendable. Many whites who concede that Negroes should have equal access to public facilities and the untrammeled
right to vote cannot understand that we do not intend to remain in the
basement of the economic structure; they cannot understand why a porter or a housemaid would dare dream of a day when his work will be
more useful, more remunerative and a pathway to rising opportunity.
This incomprehension is a heavy burden in our efforts to win white allies for the long struggle.

But the American Negro has in his nature the spiritual and worldly
fortitude to eventually win his struggle for justice and freedom. It is a
moral fortitude that has been forged by centuries of oppression. In
their sorrow and their hardship, Negroes have become almost instinctively cohesive. We band together readily; and against white hostility, we
have an intense and wholesome loyalty to one another. But we cannot
win our struggle for justice all alone, nor do I think that most Negroes
want to exclude well-intentioned whites from participation in the black
revolution. I believe there is an important place in our struggle for
white liberals and I hope that their present estrangement from our
movement is only temporary. But many white people in the past joined
our movement with a kind of messianic faith that they were going to
save the Negro and solve all of his problems very quickly. They tended,
in some instances, to be rather aggressive and insensitive to the opinions
and abilities of the black people with whom they were working; this has
been especially true of students. In many cases, they simply did not
know how to work in a supporting, secondary role. I think this problem
became most evident when young men and women from elite northern
universities came down to Mississippi to work with the black students at
Tougaloo and Rust colleges, who were not quite as articulate, didn't
type quite as fast and were not as sophisticated. Inevitably, feeling of
white paternalism and black inferiority became exaggerated. The Negroes who rebelled against white liberals were trying to assert their own
equality and to cast off the mantle of paternalism.

Fortunately, we haven't had this problem in the Southern Christian
Leadership Conference. Most of the white people who were working
with us in 1962 and 1963 are still with us. We have always enjoyed a
relationship of mutual respect. But I think a great many white liberals
outside SCLC also have learned this basic lesson in human relations,

thanks largely to Jimmy Baldwin and others who have articulated some of the problems of being black in a multiracial society. And I am happy to report that relationships between whites and Negroes in the human rights movement are now on a much healthier basis.

In society at large, abrasion between the races is far more evident—but the hostility was always there. Relations today are different only in the sense that Negroes are expressing the feelings that were so long muted. The constructive achievements of the decade 1955 to 1965 deceived us. Everyone underestimated the amount of violence and rage Negroes were suppressing and the vast amount of bigotry the white majority was disguising. All-black organizations are a reflection of that alienation—but they are only a comtemporary way station on the road to freedom. They are a product of this period of identity crisis and directionless confusion. As the human rights movement becomes more confident and aggressive, more nonviolently active, many of these emotional and intellectual problems will be resolved in the heat of battle, and we will not ask what is our neighbor's color but whether he is a brother in the pursuit of racial justice. For much of the fervent idealism of the white liberals has been supplemented recently by a dispassionate recognition of some of the cold realities of the struggle for that justice.

One of the most basic of these realities was pointed out by the President's Riot Commission, which observed that the nature of the American economy in the late nineteenth and early twentieth centuries made is possible for the European immigrants of that time to escape from poverty. It was an economy that had room for—even a great need for—unskilled manual labor. Jobs were available for willing workers, even those with the educational and language liabilities they had brought with them. But the American economy today is radically different. There are fewer and fewer jobs for the culturally and educationally deprived; thus does present-day poverty feed upon and perpetuate itself. The Negro today cannot escape from his ghetto in the way that Irish, Italian, Jewish and Polish immigrants escaped from their ghettos fifty years ago. New methods of escape must be found. And one of these roads to escape will be a more equitable sharing of political power between Negroes and whites. Integration is meaningless without the sharing of power. When I speak of integration, I don't mean a romantic mixing of colors, I mean a real sharing of power and responsibility. We will eventually achieve this, but it is going to be much more difficult for us than for any other minority. After all, no other minority has been so constantly, brutally and deliberately exploited. But because of this very exploitation, Negroes bring a special spiritual and moral contribution to American life—a contribution without which America could not survive.

The implications of true racial integration are more than just national in scope. I don't believe we can have world peace until America has an "integrated" foreign policy. Our disastrous experiences in Vietnam and the Dominican Republic have been, in one sense, a result of racist decision-making. Men of the white West, whether or not they like it, have grown up in a racist culture, and their thinking is colored by that fact. They have been fed on a false mythology and tradition that blinds them to the aspirations and talents of other men. They don't really respect anyone who is not white. But we simply cannot have peace in the world without mutual respect. I honestly feel that a man without racial blinders—or, even better, a man with personal experience of racial discrimination—would be in a much better position to make policy decisions and to conduct negotiations with the underprivileged and emerging nations of the world (or even with Castro, for that matter) than would an Eisenhower or a Dulles.

The American marines might not even have been needed in Santo Domingo, had the American ambassador there been a man who was sensitive to the color dynamics that pervade the national life of the Dominican Republic. Black men in positions of power in the business world would not be so unconscionable as to trade or traffic with the Union of South Africa, nor would they be so insensitive to the problems and needs of Latin America that they would continue the patterns of American exploitation that now prevail there. When we replace the rabidly segregationist chairman of the Armed Services Committee with a man of good will, when our ambassadors reflect a creative and wholesome interracial background, rather than a cultural heritage that is a conglomeration of Texas and Georgia politics, then we will be able to bring about a qualitative difference in the nature of American foreign policy. This is what we mean when we talk about redeeming the soul of America. Let me make it clear that I don't think white men have a monopoly on sin or greed. But I think there has been a kind of collective experience—a kind of shared misery in the black community—that makes it a little harder for us to exploit other people.

I have come to hope that American Negroes can be a bridge between white civilization and the nonwhite nations of the world, because we have roots in both. Spiritually, Negroes identify understandably with Africa, an identification that is rooted largely in our color; but all of us are a part of the white American world, too. Our education has been Western and our language, our attitudes—though we sometimes tend to deny it—are very much influenced by Western civilization. Even our emotional life has been disciplined and sometimes stifled and inhibited by an essentially European upbringing. So, although in one sense we are neither, in another sense we are both Americans and Africans. Our very bloodlines are a mixture. I hope and feel that out of the universality of our experience, we can help make peace and harmony in this world more possible.

Although American Negroes could, if they were in decision-making positions, give and encouragement to the underprivileged and disenfranchised people in other lands, I don't think it can work the other way around. I don't think the nonwhites in other parts of the world can really be of any concrete help to us, given their own problems of development and self-determination. In fact, American Negroes have greater collective buying power than Canada, greater than all four of the Scandinavian countries combined. American Negroes have greater economic potential than most of the nations—perhaps even more than *all* of the nations—of Africa. We don't *need* to look for help from some power outside the boundaries of our country, except in the sense of sympathy and identification. Our challenge, rather, is to organize the power we already have in our midst. The Newark riots, for example, could certainly have been prevented by a more aggressive political involvement on the part of that city's Negroes. There is utterly no reason Addonizio should be the mayor of Newark, with the Negro majority that exists in that city. Gary, Indiana, is another tinderbox city; but its black mayor, Richard Hatcher, has given Negroes a new faith in the effectiveness of the political process.

One of the most basic weapons in the fight for social justice will be the cumulative political power of the Negro. I can foresee the Negro vote becoming consistently the decisive vote in national elections. It is already decisive in states that have large numbers of electoral votes. Even today, the Negroes in New York City strongly influence how New York State will go in national elections, and the Negroes of Chicago have a similar leverage in Illinois. Negroes are even the decisive balance of power in the elections in Georgia, South Carolina and Virginia. So the party and the candidate that get the support of the Negro voter in national elections have a very definite edge, and we intend to use this fact to win advances in the struggle for human rights. I have every confidence that the black vote will ultimately help unseat the diehard opponents of equal rights in Congress—who are, incidentally, reactionary on all issues. But the Negro community cannot win this victory alone; indeed, it would be an empty victory even if the Negroes *could* win it alone. Intelligent men of good will everywhere must see this as their task and contribute to its support.

The election of Negro mayors, such as Hatcher, in some of the nation's larger cities has also had a tremendous psychological impact upon the Negro. It has shown him that he has the potential to participate in the determination of his own destiny—and that of society. We will see more Negro mayors in major cities in the next ten years, but this is not the ultimate answer. Mayors are relatively impotent figures in the scheme of national politics. Even a white mayor such as John Lindsay of New York simply does not have the money and resources to deal with the problems of his city. The necessary money to deal with urban problems must come from the federal government, and this money is ultimately controlled by the Congress of the United States. The success of these enlightened mayors is entirely dependent upon the financial support made available by Washington.

The past record of the federal government, however, has not been encouraging. No president has really done very much for the American Negro, though the past two presidents have received much undeserved credit for helping us. This credit has accrued to Lyndon Johnson and John Kennedy only because it was during their administrations that Negroes began doing more for themselves. Kennedy didn't voluntarily submit a civil rights bill, nor did Lyndon Johnson. In fact, both told us at one time that such legislation was impossible. President Johnson did respond realistically to the signs of the times and used his skills as a legislator to get bills through Congress that other men might not have gotten through. I must point out, in all honesty, however, that President Johnson has not been nearly so diligent in *implementing* the bills he has helped shepherd through Congress.

Of the ten titles of the 1964 Civil Rights Act, probably only the one concerning public accommodations—the most bitterly contested section—has been meaningfully enforced and implemented. Most of the other sections have been deliberately ignored. The same is true of the 1965 Voting Rights Act, which provides for federal referees to monitor the registration of voters in counties where Negroes have systematically been denied the right to vote. Yet of the some nine hundred counties that are eligible for federal referees, only fifty-eight counties to date have had them. The 842 other counties remain essentially just as they were before the march on Selma. Look at the pattern of federal referees in Mississippi, for example. They are dispersed in a manner that gives the appearance of change without any real prospect of actually shifting political power or giving Negroes a genuine opportunity to be represented in the government of their state. There is a similar pattern in Alabama, even though that state is currently at odds with the Democratic administration in Washington because of George Wallace. Georgia, until just recently, had no federal referees at all, not even in the hard-core black belt counties. I think it is significant that there are no federal referees at all in the home districts of the most powerful southern senators—particularly Senators Russell, Eastland and Talmadge. The power and moral corruption of these senators remain unchallenged, despite the weapon for change the legislation promised to be. Reform was thwarted when the legislation was inadequately enforced.

But not all is bad in the South, by any means. Though the fruits of our struggle have sometimes been nothing more than bitter despair, I must admit there have been some hopeful signs, some meaningful successes. One of the most hopeful of these changes is the attitude of the southern Negro himself. Benign acceptance of second-class citizenship has been displaced by vigorous demands for full citizenship rights and opportunities. In fact, most of our concrete accomplishments have been limited largely to the South. We have put an end to racial segregation in the South; we have brought about the beginnings of reform in the political system; and, as incongruous as it may seem, a Negro is probably safer in most southern cities than he is in the cities of the North. We have confronted the racist policemen of the South and demanded reforms in the police departments. We have confronted the southern racist power structure and we have elected Negro and liberal white candidates through much of the South in the past ten years. George Wallace is certainly an exception, and Lester Maddox is a sociological fossil. But despite these anachronisms, at the city and county level, there is a new respect for black votes and black citizenship that just did not exist ten years ago. Though school integration has moved at a depressingly slow rate in the South, it *has* moved. Of far more significance is the fact that we have learned that the integration of schools does not necessarily solve the inadequacy of schools. White schools are often just about as bad as black schools, and integrated schools sometimes tend to merge the problems of the two without solving either of them.

There *is* progress in the South, however—progress expressed by the presence of Negroes in the Georgia House of Representatives, in the election of a Negro to the Mississippi House of Representatives, in the election of a black sheriff in Tuskegee, Alabama, and, most especially, in the integration of police forces throughout the southern states. There are now even Negro deputy sheriffs in such black belt areas as Dallas County, Alabama. Just three years ago, a Negro could be beaten for going into the county courthouse in Dallas County; now Negroes share in running it. So there *are* some changes. But the changes are basically in the social and political areas; the problems we now face—providing jobs, better housing and better education for the poor throughout the country—will require money for their solution, a fact that makes those solutions all the more difficult.

The need for solutions, meanwhile, becomes more urgent every day, because these problems are far more serious now than they were just a few years ago. Before 1964, things were getting better economically for the Negro; but after that year, things began to take a turn for the worse. In particular, automation began to cut into our jobs very badly, and this snuffed out the few sparks of hope the black people had begun to nurture. As long as there was some measurable and steady economic progress, Negroes were willing and able to press harder and work harder and hope for something better. But when the door began to close on the few avenues of progress, then hopeless despair began to set in.

The fact that most white people do not comprehend this situation—which prevails in the North as well as in the South—is due largely to the press, which molds the opinions of the white community. Many whites hasten to congratulate themselves on what little progress we Negroes have made. I'm sure that most whites felt that with the passage of the

1964 Civil Rights Act, all race problems were automatically solved. Because most white people are so far removed from the life of the average Negro, there has been little to challenge this assumption. Yet Negroes continue to live with racism every day. It doesn't matter where we are individually in the scheme of things, how near we may be either to the top or to the bottom of society; the cold facts of racism slap each one of us in the face. A friend of mine is a lawyer, one of the most brilliant young men I know. Were he a white lawyer, I have no doubt that he would be in a hundred-thousand-dollar job with a major corporation or heading his own independent firm. As it is, he makes a mere twenty thousand dollars a year. This may seem like a lot of money and, to most of us, it is; but the point is that this young man's background and abilities would, if his skin color were different, entitle him to an income many times that amount.

I don't think there is a single major insurance company that hires Negro lawyers. Even within the agencies of the federal government, most Negro employees are in the lower echelons; only a handful of Negroes in federal employment are in upper-income brackets. This is a situation that cuts across this country's economic spectrum. The Chicago Urban League recently conducted a research project in the Kenwood community on the South Side. They discovered that the average educational grade level of Negroes in that community was 10.6 years and the median income was about forty-two hundred dollars a year. In nearby Gage Park, the medial educational grade level of the whites was 8.6 years, but the median income was ninety-six hundred dollars per year. In fact, the average white high school dropout makes as much as, if not more than, the average Negro college graduate.

Solutions for these problems, urgent as they are, must be constructive and rational. Rioting and violence provide no solutions for economic problems. Much of the justification for rioting has come from the thesis—originally set forth by Franz Fanon—that violence has a certain cleansing effect. Perhaps, in a special psychological sense, he may have had a point. But we have seen a better and more constructive cleansing process in our nonviolent demonstrations. Another theory to justify violent revolution is that rioting enables Negroes to overcome their fear of the white man. But they are just as afraid of the power structure after a riot as before. I remember that was true when our staff went into Rochester, New York, after the riot of 1964. When we discussed the possibility of going down to talk with the police, the people who had been most aggressive in the violence were afraid to talk. They still had a sense of inferiority; and not until they were bolstered by the presence of our staff and given reassurance of their political power and the rightness of their cause and the justness of their grievances were they able and willing to sit down and talk to the police chief and the city manager about the conditions that had produced the riot.

As a matter of fact, I think the aura of paramilitarism among the black militant groups speaks much more of fear than it does of confidence. I know, in my own experience, that I was much more afraid in Montgomery when I had a gun in my house. When I decided that, as a teacher of the philosophy of nonviolence, I couldn't keep a gun, I came face to face with the question of death and I dealt with it. And from that point on, I no longer needed a gun nor have I been afraid. Ultimately, one's sense of manhood must come from within him.

The riots in Negro ghettos have been, in one sense, merely another expression of the growing climate of violence in America. When a culture begins to feel threatened by its own inadequacies, the majority of men tend to prop themselves up by artificial means, rather than dig down deep into their spiritual and cultural wellsprings. America seems to have reached this point. Americans as a whole feel threatened by communism on one hand and, on the other, by the rising tide of aspirations among the undeveloped nations. I think most Americans know in their hearts that their country has been terribly wrong in its dealings with other peoples around the world. When Rome began to disintegrate from within, it turned to a strengthening of the military establishment, rather than to a correction of the corruption within the society. We are doing the same thing in this country and the result will probably be the same—unless, and here I admit to a bit of chauvinism, the black man in America can provide a new soul force for all Americans, a new expression of the American dream that need not be realized at the expense of other men around the world, but a dream of opportunity and life that can be shared with the rest of the world.

It seems glaringly obvious to me that the development of a humanitarian means of dealing with some of the social problems of the world—and the correlative revolution in American values that this will entail—is a much better way of protecting ourselves against the threat of violence than the military means we have chosen. On these grounds, I must indict the Johnson administration. It has seemed amazingly devoid of statesmanship; and when creative statesmanship wanes, irrational militarism increases. In this sense, President Kennedy was far more of a statesman than President Johnson. He was a man who was big enough to admit when he was wrong—as he did after the Bay of Pigs incident. But Lyndon Johnson seems to be unable to make this kind of statesmanlike gesture in connection with Vietnam. And I think that this has led, as Senator Fulbright has said, to such a strengthening of the military-industrial complex of this country that the president now finds himself almost totally trapped by it. Even at this point, when he can readily summon popular support to end the bombing in Vietnam, he persists. Yet bombs in Vietnam also explode at home; they destroy the hopes and possibilities for a decent America.

In our efforts to dispel this atmosphere of violence in this country, we cannot afford to overlook the root cause of the riots. The President's Riot Commission concluded that most violence-prone Negroes are teen-agers or young adults who, almost invariably, are underemployed ("underemployed" means working every day but earning an income below the poverty level) or who are employed in menial jobs. And according to a recent Department of Labor statistical report, 24.8 percent of Negro youth are currently unemployed, a statistic that does not include the drifters who avoid the census takers. Actually, it's my guess that the statistics are very, very conservative in this area. The Bureau of the Census has admitted a ten-percent error in this age group, and the unemployment statistics are based on those who are actually applying for jobs.

But it isn't just a lack of work; it's also a lack of *meaningful* work. In Cleveland, fifty-eight percent of the young men between the ages of six-teen and twenty-five were estimated to be either unemployed or under-employed. This appalling situation is probably ninety percent of the root cause of the Negro riots. A Negro who has finished high school often watches his white classmates go out into the job market and earn one hundred dollars a week, while he, because he is black, is expected to work for forty dollars a week. Hence, there is a tremendous hostility and resentment that only a difference in race keeps him out of an ade-quate job. This situation is social dynamite. When you add the lack of recreational facilities and adequate job counseling, and the continu-ation of an aggressively hostile police environment, you have a truly ex-plosive situation. Any night on any street corner in any Negro ghetto of the country, a nervous policeman can start a riot simply by being impo-lite or by expressing racial prejudice. And white people are sadly un-aware how routinely and frequently this occurs.

It hardly needs to be said that solutions to these critical problems are overwhelmingly urgent. The President's Riot Commission recommend-ed that funds for summer programs aimed at young Negroes should be increased. New York is already spending more on its special summer programs than on its year-round poverty efforts, but these are only ten-tative and emergency steps toward a truly meaningful and permanent solution. And the negative thinking in this area voiced by many whites does not help the situation. Unfortunately, many white people think that we merely "reward" a rioter by taking positive action to better his situation. What these white people do not realize is that the Negroes who riot have given up on America. When nothing is done to alleviate their plight, this merely confirms the Negroes' conviction that America is a hopelessly decadent society. When something positive is done, how-ever, when constructive action follows a riot, a rioter's despair is allayed and he is forced to reevaluate America and to consider whether some good might eventually come from our society after all.

But, I repeat, the recent curative steps that have been taken are, at best, inadequate. The summer poverty programs, like most other government projects, function well in some places and are totally ineffective in others. The difference, in large measure, is one of citizen participation; that is the key to success or failure. In cases such as the Farmers' Marketing Cooperative Association in the black belt of Alabama and the Child Development Group in Mississippi, where the people were really involved in the planning and action of the program, it was one of the best experiences in self-help and grass roots initiative. But in places like Chicago, where poverty programs are used strictly as a tool of the political machinery and for dispensing party patronage, the very concept of helping the poor is defiled and the poverty program becomes just another form of enslavement. I still wouldn't want to do away with it, though, even in Chicago. We must simply fight at both the local and the national levels to gain as much community control as possible over the poverty program.

But there is no single answer to the plight of the American Negro. Conditions and needs vary greatly in different sections of the country. I think that the place to start, however, is in the area of human relations, and especially in the area of community-police relations. This is a sensitive and touchy problem that has rarely been adequately emphasized. Virtually every riot has begun from some police action. If you try to tell the people in most Negro communities that the police are their friends, they just laugh at you. Obviously, something desperately needs to be done to correct this. I have been particularly impressed by the fact that even in the state of Mississippi, where the FBI did a significant training job with the Mississippi police, the police are much more courteous to Negroes than they are in Chicago or New York. Our police forces simply must develop an attitude of courtesy and respect for the ordinary citizen. If we can just stop policemen from using profanity in their encounters with black people, we will have accomplished a lot. In the larger sense, police must cease being occupation troops in the ghetto and start protecting its residents. Yet very few cities have really faced up to this problem and tried to do something about it. It is the most abrasive element in Negro-white relations, but it is the last to be scientifically and objectively appraised.

When you go beyond a relatively simple though serious problem such as police racism, however, you begin to get into all the complexities of the modern American economy. Urban transit systems in most American cities, for example, have become a genuine civil rights issue—and a valid one—because the layout of rapid-transit systems determines the accessibility of jobs to the black community. If transportation systems in American cities could be laid out so as to provide an opportunity for poor people to get meaningful employment, then they could begin to move into the mainstream of American life. A good example of this problem is my home city of Atlanta, where the rapid-transit system has been laid out for the convenience of the white upper-middle-class sub-

urbanites who commute to their jobs downtown. The system has virtually no consideration for connecting the poor people with their jobs.
There is only one possible explanation for this situation, and that is the
racist blindness of city planners.

The same problems are to be found in the areas of rent supplement
and low-income housing. The relevance of these issues to human relations and human rights cannot be overemphasized. The kind of house a
man lives in, along with the quality of his employment, determines, to a
large degree, the quality of his family life. I have known too many people in my own parish in Atlanta who, because they were living in overcrowded apartments, were constantly bickering with other members of
their families—a situation that produced many kinds of severe dysfunc-
tions in family relations. And yet I have seen these same families achieve
harmony when they were able to afford a house allowing for a little personal privacy and freedom of movement.

All these human-relations problems are complex and related, and it's
very difficult to assign priorities—especially as long as the Vietnam war
continues. The Great Society has become a victim of the war. I think
there was a sincere desire in this country four or five years ago to move
toward a genuinely great society, and I have little doubt that there
would have been a gradual increase in federal expenditures in this direction, rather than the gradual decline that has occurred, if the war in
Vietnam had been avoided.

One of the incongruities of this situation is the fact that such a large
number of the soldiers in the armed forces in Vietnam—especially the
front-line soldiers who are actually doing the fighting—are Negroes.
Negroes have always held the hope that if they really demonstrate that
they are great soldiers and if they really fight for America and help save
American democracy, then when they come back home, America will
treat them better. This has not been the case. Negro soldiers returning
from World War I were met with race riots, job discrimination and continuation of the bigotry that they had experienced before. After World
War II the GI Bill did offer some hope for a better life to those who had
the educational background to take advantage of it, and there was proportionately less turmoil. But for the Negro GI, military service still represents a means of escape from the oppressive ghettos of the rural
South and the urban North. He often sees the army as an avenue for
educational opportunities and job training. He sees in the military uniform a symbol of dignity that has long been denied him by society. The
tragedy in this is that military service is probably the only possible escape for most young Negro men. Many of them go into the army, risking death, in order that they might have a few of the human possibilities
of life. They know that life in the city ghetto of life in the rural South
almost certainly means jail or death or humiliation. And so, by comparison, military service is really the lesser risk.

One young man on our staff, Hosea Williams, returned from the fox-holes of Germany a sixty-percent-disabled veteran. After thirteen months in a veterans' hospital, he went back to his home town of Atta-pulgus, Georgia. On his way home, he went into a bus station at Ameri-cus, Georgia, to get a drink of water while waiting for his next bus. And while he stood there on his crutches, drinking from the fountain, he was beaten savagely by white hoodlums. This pathetic incident is all too typical of the treatment received by Negroes in this country—not only physical brutality but brutal discrimination when a Negro tries to buy a house, and brutal violence against the Negro's soul when he finds him-self denied a job that he knows he is qualified for.

There is also the violence of having to live in a community and pay higher consumer prices for goods or higher rent for equivalent housing than are charged in the white areas of the city. Do you know that a can of beans almost always costs a few cents more in grocery chain stores located in the Negro ghetto than in a store of that same chain located in the upper-middle-class suburbs, where the median income is five times as high? The Negro knows it, because he works in the white man's house as a cook or a gardener. And what do you think this knowledge does to his soul? How do you think it affects his view of the society he lives in? How can you expect anything but disillusionment and bitterness? The question that now faces us is whether we can turn the Negro's disillu-sionment and bitterness into hope and faith in the essential goodness of the American system. If we don't, our society will crumble.

It is a paradox that those Negroes who have given up on America are doing more to improve it than are its professional patriots. They are stirring the mass of smug, somnolent citizens, who are neither evil nor good, to an awareness of crisis. The confrontation involves not only their morality but their self-interest, and that combination promises to evoke positive action. This is not a nation of venal people. It is a land of individuals who, in the majority, have not cared, who have been heart-less about their black neighbors because their ears are blocked and their eyes blinded by the tragic myth that Negroes endure abuse without pain or complaint. Even when protest flared and denied the myth, they were fed new doctrines of inhumanity that argued that Negroes were arro-gant, lawless and ungrateful. Habitual white discrimination was trans-formed into white backlash. But for some, the lies had lost their grip and an internal disquiet grew. Poverty and discrimination were undeni-ably real; they scarred the nation; they dirtied our honor and diminish-ed our pride. An insistent question defied evasion: Was security for some being purchased at the price of degradation for others? Every-thing in our traditions said this kind of injustice was the system of the past or of other nations. And yet there it was, abroad in our own land.

Thus was born—particularly in the young generation—a spirit of dis-sent that ranged from superficial disavowal of the old values to total commitment to wholesale, drastic and immediate social reform. Yet all of it was dissent. Their voice is still a minority; but united with millions of black protesting voices, it has become a sound of distant thunder increasing in volume with the gathering of storm clouds. This dissent is America's hope. It shines in the long tradition of American ideals that began with courageous minutemen in New England, that continued in the abolitionist movement, that re-emerged in the populist revolt and, decades later, that burst forth to elect Franklin Roosevelt and John F. Kennedy. Today's dissenters tell the complacent majority that the time has come when further evasion of social responsibility in a turbulent world will court disaster and death. America has not yet changed because so many think it need not change, but this is the illusion of the damned. America must change because twenty-three million black citizens will no longer live supinely in a wretched past. They have left the valley of despair; they have found strength in struggle; and whether they live or die, they shall never crawl nor retreat again. Joined by white allies, they will shake the prison walls until they fall. America must change.

A voice out of Bethlehem two thousand years ago said that all men are equal. It said right would triumph. Jesus of Nazareth wrote no books; he owned no property to endow him with influence. He had no friends in the courts of the powerful. But he changed the course of mankind with only the poor and the despised. Naïve and unsophisticated though we may be, the poor and despised of the twentieth century will revolutionize this era. In our "arrogance, lawlessness and ingratitude," we will fight for human justice, brotherhood, secure peace and abundance for all. When we have won these—in a spirit of unshakable nonviolence—then, in luminous splendor, the Christian era will truly begin.

*Playboy* 16 (January 1969): 175ff.

# PART IV: INTERVIEWS

# 49

# Kenneth B. Clark Interview

*Kenneth Clark was himself deeply involved in Dr. King's struggle. As a noted black child psychologist and educator, he used his skills to provide psychological data to support the civil rights activists' claim that segregated education was psychologically debilitating for black youth, and made white youth culturally parochial and socially isolated. His own headnote to his interview with Dr. King provides a helpful insight into the setting for this conversation. Dr. Clark was quite adept in this interview at getting Dr. King to talk about his own feelings about facing death-threatening situations. He unfortunately did not state when this interview took place. But it appears to have been prior to the 28 August 1963 March on Washington.*

Martin Luther King was interviewed on a day when he had already spent three hours taping another television program. When we called for him at his hotel, he seemed weary, but desirous of hiding this fact. On the way to the studio, we talked generally about developments on the various civil rights fronts. He seemed particularly optimistic that a solid and workable agreement was going to be implemented in Birmingham. His tone before the interview was the same as his tone during the interview—a calm, quiet, confident belief in the future.

This observer has no doubts that Martin Luther King's philosophy of love for the oppressor is a genuine aspect of his being. He personally does not differentiate between this philosophy and the effectiveness of the nonviolent direct-action approach to the attainment of racial justice, which he personifies and leads. For him, the philosophy is not just a strategy; it is a truth, it is his assertion of the philosophical position that one cannot differentiate means from ends. The quiet, contemplative, at times exasperatingly academic style is truly King. He is the paradox of the scholar and the effective man of social action.

Martin Luther King is a quietly pleasant young man. There is little about his personal appearance that suggests the firm, courageous leader of public demonstrations. There is no way that one could tell by looking at him that he has exposed himself repeatedly to death, and that by sheer force of his personality and the depth of his convictions, has moved the South and the North. He is the embodiment of that dignity which is essential for every man.

CLARK: In December of 1955 an event in Montgomery, Alabama, catapulted a young man into national and international prominence. The Reverend Martin Luther King, Jr., led the effective Montgomery bus boycott wherein the Negro people of that city stated for the entire world the fact that they were no longer content with second-class citizenship. Since that time Dr. King has personified that dignity, that discipline, and that insistence upon the rights of an American citizen which the present thrust of the Negro people represents. Dr. King, I know that people throughout America have watched your leadership in the Birmingham situation. Before we talk about those problems which have gotten the headlines and coverage in all our mass media, I'd like to know a little about you as a person. Where were you born? Something about your family, brothers and sisters, and things of that sort.

KING: Yes. Well, I was born in the South, in Atlanta, Georgia, and I lived there all of my early years. In fact, I went to the public schools of Atlanta and I went to college in Atlanta. I left after college to attend theological school.

CLARK: What college did you go to?

KING: Morehouse College in Atlanta.

CLARK: Part of the Atlanta University system.

KING: That's right. And I was raised in the home of a minister; my father pastors the Ebenezer Church in Atlanta and has pastored this church for thirty-three years. I am now co-pastor of the same church with him. And we have—I mean there's a family of three children in the immediate family; I have one brother and one sister.

CLARK: Is your brother a pastor also?

KING: Yes, he is. He's the pastor of the First Baptist Church of Birmingham, Alabama.

CLARK: And you have a sister?

KING: Yes, she's in Atlanta, teaching at Spellman College.

CLARK: Now, about your own immediate family: I remember the last time we were together in Montgomery you had a son who had just been born before the Montgomery disturbances.

KING: Well, that was a daughter. The second child was a son, but our first child was a daughter. Since that time we've had two more, so we have four children now, two sons and two daughters, the most recent one being the daughter that came nine weeks ago.

CLARK: How wonderful. It seems as if you have children at times of major crises.

KING: Yes, that's right, and that brings new life to life.

CLARK: Very good. You went from Morehouse to Boston University to study philosophy, am I correct?

KING: Well, no, I went from Morehouse to Crozer Theological Seminary in Pennsylvania and then I went from Crozer to Boston University.

CLARK: In Boston you studied philosophy and, if I remember correctly, you have a Ph.D. in philosophy.

KING: Well, the actual field is philosophical theology.

CLARK: Now, if we could shift a little from the education within the academic halls to your education in the community. I look at our newspapers and see that you have not only engaged in and led many of these demonstrations, but have paid for this by seeing the inside of many jails. I've wondered—how many jails have you been to as a result of your involvement in this direct-action, nonviolent insistence upon the rights of Negroes?

KING: Well, I've been arrested fourteen times since we started out in Montgomery. Some have been in the same jail, that is, I've been in some jails more than once. I haven't calculated the number of different jails. I would say about eight of them were different jails. I remember once within eight days I transferred to three different jails within the state of Georgia. I think I've been to about eight different jails and I've been arrested about fourteen times.

CLARK: Have you attempted to make a study of these jails, for example, the type of jail, the type of individuals you've met in these jails as keepers, say, or wardens? What type of human beings are these or are they different types of human beings?

KING: Well, I have gone through the process of comparing the various jails. I guess this is one of those inevitable things that you find yourself doing to kind of lift yourself from the dull monotony of sameness when you're in jail and I find that they do differ. I've been in some new jails and I've been in some mighty old ones. In the recent jail experience in Birmingham I was in the new jail. The city jail is about a year old, I think, and in Albany, Georgia, last year I was in a very old jail. In Fulton County, Georgia, I was in a very new one.

CLARK: What about the human beings who are the jailkeepers? What about their attitude toward you as a person?

KING: Well, they vary also. I have been in jails where the jailers were exceptionally courteous and they went out of their way to see that everything went all right where I was concerned. On the other hand, I have been in jails where the jailers were extremely harsh and vitriolic in their words and in their manners. I haven't had any experience of physical violence from jailers, but I have had violence of words from them. Even in Birmingham, for the first few days, some of the jailers were extremely harsh in their statements.

CLARK: Have you ever been in an integrated jail? In the South?

KING: No, that's one experience I haven't had yet.

CLARK: Well, maybe after we get through integrating public accommodations the last thing will be to integrate the jailhouses.

KING: Yes.

CLARK: I am very much interested in the philosophy of nonviolence and particularly I would like to understand more clearly for myself the relationship between the direct-action nonviolence technique which you have used so effectively and your philosophy of, for want of better words I'll use, "love of the oppressor."

KING: All right.

CLARK: Dr. King, what do you see as the relationship between these two things, which could be seen as separate?

KING: Yes, I think so. One is a method of action: nonviolent direct action is a method of acting to rectify a social situation that is unjust and it involves in engaging in a practical technique that nullifies the use of violence or calls for nonviolence at every point. That is, you don't use physical violence against the opponent. Now, the love ethic is another dimension which goes into the realm of accepting nonviolence as a way of life. There are many people who will accept nonviolence as the most practical technique to be used in a social situation, but they would not go to the point of seeing the necessity of accepting nonviolence as a way of life. Now, I accept both. I think that nonviolent resistance is the most potent weapon available to oppressed people in their struggle for freedom and human dignity. It has a way of disarming the opponent. It exposes his moral defenses. It weakens his morale and at the same time it works on his conscience. He just doesn't know how to handle it and I have seen this over and over again in our struggle in the South. Now on the question of love or the love ethic, I think this is so important because hate is injurious to the hater as well as the hated. Many of the psychiatrists are telling us now that many of the strange things that happen in the subconscious and many of the inner conflicts are rooted in hate and so they are now saying "love or perish." Erich Fromm can write a book like *The Art of Loving* and make it very clear that love is the supreme unifying principle of life and I'm trying to say in this movement that it is necessary to follow the technique of nonviolence as the most potent weapon available to us, but it is necessary also to follow the love ethic which becomes a force of personality integration.

CLARK: But is it not too much to expect that a group of human beings who have been the victims of cruelty and flagrant injustice could actually love those who have been associated with the perpetrators, if not the perpetrators themselves? How could you expect, for example, the Negroes in Birmingham who know Bull Connor to really love him in any meaningful sense?

KING: Well, I think one has to understand the meaning of "love" at this point. I'm certainly not speaking of an affectionate response. I think it is really nonsense to urge oppressed peoples to love their oppressors in an affectionate sense. And I often call on the Greek language to aid me at this point because there are three words in the Greek for "love." One is "*eros*," which is sort of an aesthetic or a romantic love. Another is "*philia*," which is sort of an intimate affection between personal friends; this is friendship, it is a reciprocal love and on this level, you love those people that you like. And then the Greek language comes out with the word "*agape*," which is understanding, creative, redemptive good will for all men. It goes far beyond an affectionate response. Now when I say to you—

CLARK: That form means really understanding.

KING: Yes, that's right. And you come to the point of being able to love the person that does an evil deed in the sense of understanding and you can hate the deed that the person does. And I'm certainly not talking about "*eros*"; I'm not talking about friendship. I find it pretty difficult to like people like Bull Connor. I find it difficult to like Senator Eastman, but I think you can love where you can't like the person because life is an affectionate quality.

CLARK: Yes, I have admired your ability to feel this, and I must say to you also that as I read your expounding of the philosophy of love I found myself often feeling personally quite inadequate. Malcolm X, one of the most articulate exponents of the Black Muslim philosophy, has said of your movement and your philosophy that it plays into the hands of the white oppressors, that they are happy to hear you talk about love for the oppressor because this disarms the Negro and fits into the stereotype of the Negro as a meek, turning-the-other-cheek sort of creature. Would you care to comment on Mr. X's beliefs?

KING: Well, I don't think of love, as in this context, as emotional bosh. I don't think of it as a weak force, but I think of love as something strong and that organizes itself into powerful direct action. Now, this is what I try to teach in this struggle in the South: that we are not engaged in a struggle that means we sit down and do nothing; that there is a great deal of difference between nonresistance to evil and nonviolent resistance. Nonresistance leaves you in a state of stagnant passivity and deadly complacency where nonviolent resistance means that you do resist in a very strong and determined manner and I think some of the criticisms of nonviolence or some of the critics fail to realize that we are talking about something very strong and they confuse nonresistance with nonviolent resistance.

CLARK: He goes beyond that in some of the things I've heard him say—to say that this is deliberately your philosophy of love of the oppressor which he identifies completely with the nonviolent movement. He says this philosophy and this movement are actually encouraged by whites because it makes them comfortable. It makes them believe that Negroes are meek, supine creatures.

KING: Well, I don't think that's true. If anyone has ever lived with a nonviolent movement in the South, from Montgomery on through the freedom rides and through the sit-in movement and the recent Birmingham movement and seen the reactions of many of the extremists and reactionaries in the white community, he wouldn't say that this movement makes—this philosophy makes them comfortable. I think it arouses a sense of shame within them often—in many instances. I think it does something to touch the conscience and establish a sense of guilt. Now so often people respond to guilt by engaging more in the guilt-evoking act in an attempt to drown the sense of guilt, but this approach doesn't make the white man feel comfortable. I think it does the other thing. It disturbs his conscience and it disturbs this sense of contentment that he's had.

CLARK: James Baldwin raises still another point of the whole nonviolent position, an approach. He does not reject it in the ways that Malcolm X does, but he raises the question of whether it will be possible to contain the Negro people within this framework of nonviolence if we continue to have more of the kinds of demonstrations that we had in Birmingham, wherein police brought dogs to attack human beings. What is your reaction to Mr. Baldwin's anxiety?

KING: Well, I think these brutal methods used by the Birmingham police force and other police forces will naturally arouse the ire of Negroes and I think there is the danger that some will be so aroused that they will retaliate with violence. I think though that we can be sure that the vast majority of Negroes who engage in the demonstrations and who understand the nonviolent philosophy will be able to face dogs and all of the other brutal methods that are used without retaliating with violence because they understand that one of the first principles of nonviolence is the willingness to be the recipient of violence while never inflicting violence upon another. And none of the demonstrators in Birmingham engaged in aggressive or retaliatory violence. It was always someone on the sideline who had never been in the demonstrations and probably not in the mass meetings and had never been in a nonviolent workshop. So I think it will depend on the extent to which we can extend the teaching of the philosophy of nonviolence to the larger community rather than those who are engaged in the demonstrations.

CLARK: Well, how do you maintain this type of discipline, control and dignity in your followers who do participate in the demonstrations? You don't have police force, you have no uniform, you're not an authoritarian organization, you're a group of people who are voluntarily associated. How do you account for this, I would say, beautiful dignity and discipline?

KING: Well, we do a great deal in terms of teaching both the theoretical aspects of nonviolence as well as the practical application. We even have courses where we go through the experience of being roughed up and this kind of sociodrama has proved very helpful in preparing those who are engaged in demonstrations. The other thing is—

CLARK: Does this even include the children?

KING: Yes, it includes the children. In Birmingham where we had several young—we had some as young as seven years old to participate in the demonstrations, and they were in the workshops. In fact, none of them went out for a march, none of them engaged in any of the demonstrations before going through this kind of teaching session. So that through this method we are able to get the meaning of nonviolence over, and I think there is a contagious quality in a movement like this when everybody talks about nonviolence and being faithful to it and being dignified in your resistance. It tends to get over to the larger group because this becomes a part of the vocabulary of the movement.

CLARK: What is the relationship between your movement and such organizations as the NAACP, CORE and the Student Nonviolent Coordinating Committee? They're separate organizations, but do you work together?

KING: Yes, we do. As you say, each of these organizations is autonomous, but we work together in many, many ways. Last year we started a voter-registration drive, an intensified voter-registration drive. And all of the organizations are working together, sometimes two or three are working together in the same community. The same thing is true with our direct-action programs. In Birmingham we had the support of Snick [SNCC,

Student Nonviolent Coordinating Committee] and CORE and the NAACP. CORE sent some of its staff members in to assist us and Snick sent some of its staff members. Roy Wilkins came down to speak in one of the mass meetings and to make it clear that even though the NAACP cannot operate in Alabama, we had the support of the NAACP. So we are all working together in a very significant way, and we are doing even more in the days ahead to coordinate our efforts.

CLARK: Is there any machinery—does machinery for coordination actually exist now?

KING: Well, we have had a sort of coordinating council where we get together as often as possible. Of course, we get involved in many of our programs in the various areas and can't make as many of these meetings as we would like but we often come together (I mean, the heads of all these organizations) to try to coordinate our various efforts.

CLARK: What about the federal government? Have you made any direct appeal either in your own right or as part of this leadership group to have a more active involvement in the federal government in the rights of Negroes?

KING: Yes, I have. I've made appeals and other members of the Southern Christian Leadership Conference have appealed to the president and the new administration generally to do more in dealing with the problem of racial injustice. I think Mr. Kennedy has done some significant things in civil rights, but I do not feel that he has yet given the leadership that the enormity of the problem demands.

CLARK: By Mr. Kennedy, now, do you mean the president?

KING: Yes, I'm speaking now of the president, mainly. And I would include the attorney general. I think both of these men are men of genuine good will, but I think they must understand more about the depths and dimensions of the problem and I think there is a necessity now to see the urgency of the moment. There isn't a lot of time; time is running out, and the Negro is making it palpably clear that he wants all of his rights, that he wants them here, and that he wants them now.

CLARK: Is this not considered by some people an extremist position, that is, not really practical?

KING: Yes, I'm sure many people feel this, but I think they must see the truth of the situation. The shape of the world today does not afford us the luxury of slow movement and the Negro's quest for dignity and self-respect doesn't afford the nation this kind of slow movement.

CLARK: Dr. King, what do you think will be the outcome of the present confrontation, the present insistence of the Negroes for their rights as American citizens without equivocation and without qualification? Do you think this will be obtained?

KING: I do. Realism impels me to admit that there will be difficult days ahead. In some of the hard-core states in the South we will confront resistance. There will still be resistance and there will still be very real problems in the North as a result of the twin evils of employment and housing discrimination, but I think there are forces at work now that will somehow ward off all of these ominous possibilities. The rolling tide of world opinion will play a great part in this. I think the aroused conscience of many, many white people all over the country, the growing awareness of religious institutions that they have not done their job, and the determination of the Negro himself, and the growing industrialization in the South—all of these things, I believe—will conjoin to make it possible for us to move on toward the goal of integration.

CLARK: So you are hopeful?

KING: Yes, I am.

CLARK: And I thank you for your hope and I thank you for your actions.

KING: Thank you.

---

Interview in Kenneth B. Clark, ed., *The Negro Protest* (Boston: Beacon Press, 1963), 35–46.

# 50

# *Playboy* Interview:
# Martin Luther King, Jr.

*This interview with Dr. King is one of the finest that we have in print. He discusses a wide range of topics, but was especially insightful about his own religious and philosophical motivations for engaging in the struggle for racial justice. The headnote written by the* Playboy *interviewers provides helpful insights into Dr. King's daily routine and gargantuan responsibilities.*

On 5 December 1955, to the amused annoyance of the white citizens of Montgomery, Alabama, an obscure young Baptist minister named Martin Luther King, Jr., called a citywide Negro boycott of its segregated bus system. To their consternation, however, it was almost one hundred percent successful; it lasted for 381 days and nearly bankrupted the bus line. When King's home was bombed during the siege, thousands of enraged Negroes were ready to riot, but the soft-spoken clergyman prevailed on them to channel their anger into nonviolent protest—and became world-renowned as a champion of Gandhi's philosophy of passive resistance. Within a year the Supreme Court had ruled Jim Crow seating unlawful on Montgomery's buses, and King found himself, at twenty-seven, on the front lines of a nonviolent Negro revolution against racial injustice.

Moving to Atlanta, he formed the Southern Christian Leadership Conference, an alliance of church-affiliated civil rights organizations which joined such activist groups as CORE and SNCC in a widening campaign of sit-in demonstrations and freedom rides throughout the South. Dissatisfied with the slow pace of the protest movement, King decided to create a crisis in 1963 that would "dramatize the Negro plight and galvanize the national conscience." He was abundantly successful, for his mass nonviolent demonstration in arch-segregationist Birmingham resulted in the arrest of more than thirty-three hundred Negroes, including King himself; and millions were outraged by front-page pictures of Negro demonstrators being brutalized by the billy sticks, police dogs and fire hoses of police chief Bull Connor.

In the months that followed, mass sit-ins and demonstrations erupted in eight hundred southern cities; President Kennedy proposed a civil rights bill aimed at the enforcement of voting rights, equal employment opportunities, and the desegregation of public facilities; and the now-famous march on Washington, two hundred thousand strong, was eloquently addressed by King on the steps of the Lincoln Memorial. By the end of that "long hot summer," America's Negroes had won more tangible gains than in any year since 1865—and Martin Luther King had become their acknowledged leader and most respected spokesman.

He earned it the hard way: In the course of his civil rights work he has been jailed fourteen times and stabbed once in the chest; his home has been bombed three times; and his daily mail brings a steady flow of death threats and obscenities. Undeterred, he works twenty hours a day, travels 325,000 miles and makes 450 speeches a year throughout the country on behalf of the Negro cause. Inundated by calls, callers and correspondence at his SCLC office in Atlanta, he also finds time somehow to preach, visit the sick and help the poor among his congregation at the city's Ebenezer Baptist Church, of which he and his father are the pastors.

So heavy, in fact, were his commitments when we called him last summer for an interview, that two months elapsed before he was able to accept our request for an appointment. We kept it—only to spend a week in Atlanta waiting vainly for him to find a moment for more than an apology and a hurried handshake. A bit less pressed when we returned for a second visit, King was finally able to sandwich in a series of hour and half-hour conversations with us among the other demands of a grueling week. The resultant interview is the longest he has ever granted to any publication.

Though he spoke with heartfelt and often eloquent sincerity, his tone was one of businesslike detachment. And his mood, except for one or two flickering smiles of irony, was gravely serious—never more so than the moment, during a rare evening with his family on our first night in town, when his four children chided him affectionately for "not being home enough." After dinner, we began the interview on this personal note.

PLAYBOY: Dr. King, are your children old enough to be aware of the issues at stake in the civil rights movement, and of your role in it?

KING: Yes, they are—especially my oldest child, Yolanda. Two years ago, I remember, I returned home after serving one of my terms in the Albany, Georgia, jail, and she asked me, "Daddy, why do you have to go to jail so much?" I told her that I was involved in a struggle to make conditions better for the colored people, and thus for *all* people. I explained that because things are as they are, someone has to take a stand, that it is necessary for someone to go to jail, because many southern officials seek to maintain the barriers that have historically been erected to exclude the colored people. I tried to make her understand that someone had to do this to make the world better—for *all* children. She was only six at that time, but she was already aware of segregation because of an experience that we had had.

PLAYBOY: Would you mind telling us about it?

KING: Not at all. The family often used to ride with me to the Atlanta airport, and on our way, we always passed Funtown, a sort of miniature Disneyland with mechanical rides and that sort of thing. Yolanda would inevitably say, "I want to go to Funtown," and I would always evade a direct reply. I really didn't know how to explain to her why she couldn't go. Then one day at home, she ran downstairs exclaiming that a TV commercial was urging people to come to Funtown. Then my wife and I had to sit down with her between us and try to explain it. I have won some applause as a speaker, but my tongue twisted and my speech stammered seeking to explain to my six-year-old daughter why the public invitation on television didn't include her, and others like her. One of the most painful experiences I have ever faced was to see her tears when I told her that Funtown was closed to colored children, for I realized that at that moment the first dark cloud of inferiority had floated into her little mental sky, that at that moment her personality had begun to warp with that first unconscious bitterness toward white people. It was the first time that prejudice based upon skin color had been explained to her. But it was of paramount importance to me that she not grow up bitter. So I told her that although many white people were against her going to Funtown, there were many others who *did* want colored children to go. It helped somewhat. Pleasantly, word came to me later that Funtown had quietly desegregated, so I took Yolanda. A number of white persons there asked, "Aren't you Dr. King, and isn't this your daughter?" I said we were, and she heard them say how glad they were to see us there.

PLAYBOY: As one who grew up in the economically comfortable, socially insulated environment of a middle-income home in Atlanta, can you recall when it was that you yourself first became painfully and personally aware of racial prejudice?

KING: Very clearly. When I was fourteen, I had traveled from Atlanta to Dublin, Georgia, with a dear teacher of mine, Mrs. Bradley; she's dead now. I had participated there in an oratorical contest sponsored by the Negro Elks. It turned out to be a memorable day, for I had succeeded in winning the contest. My subject, I recall, ironically enough, was "The

Negro and the Constitution." Anyway, that night, Mrs. Bradley and I were on a bus returning to Atlanta, and at a small town along the way, some white passengers boarded the bus, and the white driver ordered us to get up and give the whites our seats. We didn't move quickly enough to suit him, so he began cursing us, calling us "black sons of bitches." I intended to stay right in that seat, but Mrs. Bradley finally urged me up, saying we had to obey the law. And so we stood up in the aisle for the ninety miles to Atlanta. That night will never leave my memory. It was the angriest I have ever been in my life.

PLAYBOY: Wasn't it another such incident on a bus, years later, that thrust you into your present role as a civil rights leader?

KING: Yes, it was—in Montgomery, Alabama, in 1955. E. D. Nixon, a Pullman porter long identified with the NAACP, telephoned me late one night to tell me that Mrs. Rosa Parks had been arrested around seven-thirty that evening when a bus driver demanded that she give up her seat, and she refused—because her feet hurt. Nixon had already bonded Mrs. Parks out of prison. He said, "It's time this stops; we ought to boycott the buses." I agreed and said, "Now." The next night we called a meeting of Negro community leaders to discuss it, and on Saturday and Sunday we appealed to the Negro community, with leaflets and from the pulpits, to boycott the buses on Monday. We had in mind a one-day boycott, and we were banking on sixty percent success. But the boycott saw instantaneous ninety-nine percent success. We were so pleasantly surprised and impressed that we continued, and for the next 381 days the boycott of Montgomery's buses by Negroes was ninety-nine and nine-tenths percent successful.

PLAYBOY: Were you sure you'd win?

KING: There was one dark moment when we doubted it. We had been struggling to make the boycott a success when the city of Montgomery successfully obtained an injunction from the court to stop our car pool. I didn't know what to say to our people. They had backed us up, and we had let them down. It was a desolate moment. I saw, all of us saw, that the court was leaning against us. I remember telling a group of those working closest with me to spread in the Negro community the message, "We must have the faith that things will work out somehow, that God will make a way for us when there seems no way." It was about noontime, I remember, when Rex Thomas of the Associated Press rushed over to where I was sitting and told me of the news flash that the U.S. Supreme Court had declared that bus segregation in Montgomery was unconstitutional. It had literally been the darkest hour before the dawn.

PLAYBOY: You and your followers were criticized, after your arrest for participating in the boycott, for accepting bail and leaving jail. Do you feel, in retrospect, that you did the right thing?

KING: No; I think it was a mistake, a tactical error for me to have left jail, by accepting bail, after being indicted along with 125 others, mainly drivers of our car pool, under an old law of doubtful constitutionality, an "antiboycott" ordinance. I should have stayed in prison. It would have nationally dramatized and deepened our movement even earlier, and it would have more quickly aroused and keened America's conscience.

PLAYBOY: Do you feel you've been guilty of any comparable errors in judgment since then?

KING: Yes, I do—in Albany, Georgia, in 1962. If I had that to do again, I would guide the community's Negro leadership differently than I did. The mistake I made there was to protest against segregation generally rather than against a single and distinct facet of it. Our protest was so vague that we got nothing, and the people were left very depressed and in despair. It would have been much better to have concentrated upon integrating the buses or the lunch counters. One victory of this kind would have been symbolic, would have galvanized support and boosted morale. But I don't mean that our work in Albany ended in failure. The Negro people there straightened up their bent backs; you can't ride a man's back unless it's bent. Also, thousands of Negroes registered to vote who never had voted before, and because of the expanded Negro vote in the next election for governor of Georgia—which pitted a moderate candidate against a rabid segregationist—Georgia elected its first governor who had pledged to respect and enforce the law impartially. And what we learned from our mistakes in Albany helped our later campaigns in other cities to be more effective. We have never since scattered our efforts in a general attack on segregation, but have focused upon specific, symbolic objectives.

PLAYBOY: Can you recall any other mistakes you've made in leading the movement?

KING: Well, the most pervasive mistake I have made was in believing that because our cause was just, we could be sure that the white ministers of the South, once their Christian consciences were challenged, would rise to our aid. I felt that white ministers would take our cause to the white power structures. I ended up, of course, chastened and disillusioned. As our movement unfolded, and direct appeals were made to white ministers, most folded their hands—and some even took stands *against* us.

PLAYBOY: Their stated reason for refusing to help was that it was not the proper role of the church to "intervene in secular affairs." Do you disagree with this view?

KING: Most emphatically. The essence of the Epistles of Paul is that Christians should *rejoice* at being deemed worthy to suffer for what they believe. The projection of a social gospel, in my opinion, is the true witness of a Christian life. This is the meaning of the true *ekklēsia*—the inner, spiritual church. The church once changed society. It was then a thermostat of society. But today I feel that too much of the church is merely a thermometer, which measures rather than molds popular opinion.

PLAYBOY: Are you speaking of the church in general—or the white church in particular?

KING: The white church, I'm sorry to say. Its leadership has greatly disappointed me. Let me hasten to say there are some outstanding exceptions. As one whose Christian roots go back through three generations of ministers—my father, grandfather and great-grandfather—I will remain true to the church as long as I live. But the laxity of the white church collectively has caused me to weep tears of love. There cannot be deep disappointment without deep love. Time and again in my travels, as I have seen the outward beauty of white churches, I have had to ask myself, "What kind of people worship there? Who is their God? Is their God the God of Abraham, Isaac and Jacob, and is their Savior the Savior who hung on the cross at Golgotha? Where were their voices when a black race took upon itself the cross of protest against man's injustice to man? Where were their voices when defiance and hatred were called for by white men who sat in these very churches?"

As the Negro struggles against grave injustice, most white churchmen offer pious irrelevancies and sanctimonious trivialities. As you say, they claim that the gospel of Christ should have no concern with social issues. Yet white churchgoers, who insist that they are Christians, practice segregation as rigidly in the house of God as they do in movie houses. Too much of the white church is timid and ineffectual, and some of it is shrill in its defense of bigotry and prejudice. In most communities, the spirit of status quo is endorsed by the churches.

My personal disillusionment with the church began when I was thrust into the leadership of the bus protest in Montgomery. I was confident that the white ministers, priests and rabbis of the South would prove strong allies in our just cause. But some became open adversaries, some cautiously shrank from the issue, and others hid behind silence. My optimism about help from the white church was shattered; and on too many occasions since, my hopes for the white church have been dashed. There are many signs that the judgment of God is upon the church as never before. Unless the early sacrificial spirit is recaptured, I am very much afraid that today's Christian church will lose its authenticity, forfeit the loyalty of millions, and we will see the Christian church dismissed as a social club with no meaning or effectiveness for our time, as a form without substance, as salt without savor. The real tragedy, though, is not Martin Luther King's disillusionment with the church—for I am sustained by its spiritual blessings as a minister of the gospel with a lifelong commitment; the tragedy is that in my travels, I meet young people of all races whose disenchantment with the church has soured into outright disgust.

PLAYBOY: Do you feel that the Negro church has come any closer to "the projection of a social gospel" in its commitment to the cause?

KING: I must say that when my Southern Christian Leadership Conference began its work in Birmingham, we encountered numerous Negro church reactions that had to be overcome. Negro ministers were among other Negro leaders who felt they were being pulled into something that they had not helped to organize. This is almost always a problem. Negro community unity was the first requisite if our goals were to be realized. I talked with many groups, including one group of two hundred ministers, my theme to them being that a minister cannot preach the glories of heaven while ignoring social conditions in his own community that cause men an earthly hell. I stressed that the Negro minister had particular freedom and independence to provide strong, firm leadership, and I asked how the Negro would ever gain freedom without his minister's guidance, support and inspiration. These ministers finally decided to entrust our movement with their support, and as a result, the role of the Negro church today, by and large, is a glorious example in the history of Christendom. For never in Christian history, within a Christian country, have Christian churches been on the receiving end of such naked brutality and violence as we are witnessing here in America today. Not since the days of the Christians in the catacombs has God's house, as a symbol, weathered such attack as the Negro churches.

I shall never forget the grief and bitterness I felt on that terrible September morning when a bomb blew out the lives of those four little, innocent girls sitting in their Sunday-school class in the 16th Street Baptist Church in Birmingham. I think of how a woman cried out, crunching through broken glass, "My God, we're not even safe in church!" I think of how that explosion blew the face of Jesus Christ from a stained-glass window. It was symbolic of how sin and evil had blotted out the life of Christ. I can remember thinking that if men were this bestial, was it all worth it? Was there any hope? Was there any way out?

PLAYBOY:    Do you still feel this way?

KING:    No, time has healed the wounds—and buoyed me with the inspiration of another moment which I shall never forget: when I saw with my own eyes over three thousand young Negro boys and girls, totally unarmed, leave Birmingham's 16th Street Baptist Church to march to a prayer meeting— ready to pit nothing but the power of their bodies and souls against Bull Connor's police dogs, clubs and fire hoses. When they refused Connor's bellowed order to turn back, he whirled and shouted to his men to turn on the hoses. It was one of the most fantastic events of the Birmingham story that these Negroes, many of them on their knees, stared, unafraid and unmoving, at Connor's men with the hose nozzles in their hands. Then, slowly the Negroes stood up and advanced, and Connor's men fell back as though hypnotized, as the Negroes marched on past to hold their prayer meeting. I saw there, I felt there, for the first time, the pride and the *power* of nonviolence.

Another time I will never forget was one Saturday night, late, when my brother telephoned me in Atlanta from Birmingham—that city which some call "Bombingham"— which I had just left. He told me that a bomb had wrecked his home, and that another bomb, positioned to exert its maximum force upon the motel room in which I had been staying, had injured several people. My brother described the terror in the streets as Negroes, furious at the bombings, fought whites. Then, behind his voice, I heard a rising chorus of beautiful singing: "We shall overcome." Tears came into my eyes that at such a tragic moment, my race still could sing its hope and faith.

PLAYBOY: *We Shall Overcome* has become the unofficial song and slogan of the civil rights movement. Do you consider such inspirational anthems important to morale?

KING: In a sense, songs are the *soul* of a movement. Consider, in World War II, *Praise the Lord and Pass the Ammunition*, and in World War I, *Over There* and *Tipperary*, and during the Civil War, *Battle Hymn of the Republic* and *John Brown's Body*. A Negro song anthology would include sorrow songs, shouts for joy, battle hymns, anthems. Since slavery, the Negro has sung throughout his struggle in America. *Steal Away* and *Go Down, Moses* were the songs of faith and inspiration which were sung on the plantations. For the same reasons the slaves sang, Negroes today sing freedom songs, for we, too, are in bondage. We sing out our determination that "We shall overcome, black and white together, we shall overcome someday." I should also mention a song parody that I enjoyed very much which the Negroes sang during our campaign in Albany, Georgia. It goes: "I'm coming', I'm comin'/And my head *ain't* bendin' low/I'm walkin' tall, I'm talking strong/I'm America's *New* Black Joe."

PLAYBOY: Your detractors in the Negro community often refer to you snidely as "De Lawd" and "Booker T. King." What's your reaction to this sort of Uncle Tom label?

KING: I hear some of those names, but my reaction to them is never emotional. I don't think you can be in public life without being called bad names. As Lincoln said, "If I answered all criticism, I'd have time for nothing else." But with regard to both of the names you mentioned, I've always tried to be what I call militantly nonviolent. I don't believe that anyone could seriously accuse me of not being totally committed to the breakdown of segregation.

PLAYBOY: What do you mean by "militantly nonviolent"?

KING: I mean to say that a strong man must be militant as well as moderate. He must be a realist as well as an idealist. If I am to merit the trust invested in me by some of my race, I must be both of these things. This is why nonviolence is a powerful as well as a *just* weapon. If you confront a man who has long been cruelly misusing you, and say, "Punish me, if you will; I do not deserve it, but I will accept it, so that the world will know I am right and you are wrong," then you wield a powerful and a just weapon. This man, your oppressor, is automatically morally defeated, and if he has any conscience, he is ashamed. Wherever this weapon is used in a manner that stirs a community's, or a nation's, anguished conscience, then the pressure of public opinion becomes an ally in your just cause.

Another of the major strengths of the nonviolent weapon is its strange power to transform and transmute the individuals who subordinate themselves to its disciplines, investing them with a cause that is larger than themselves. They become, for the first time, *somebody*, and they have, for the first time, the courage to be free. When the Negro finds the courage to be free, he faces dogs and guns and clubs and fire hoses totally unafraid, and the white men with those dogs, guns, clubs and fire hoses see that the Negro they have traditionally called "boy" has become a man.

We should not forget that, although nonviolent direct action did not originate in America, it found a natural home where it has been a revered tradition to rebel against injustice. This great weapon, which we first tried out in Montgomery during the bus boycott, has been further developed throughout the South over the past decade, until by today it has become instrumental in the greatest mass-action crusade for freedom that has occurred in America since the Revolutionary War. The effectiveness of this weapon's ability to dramatize, in the world's eyes, an oppressed peoples' struggle for justice is evident in the fact that of 1963's top ten news stories after the assassination of President Kennedy and the events immediately connected with it, nine stories dealt with one aspect or another of the Negro struggle.

PLAYBOY: Several of those stories dealt with your own nonviolent campaigns against segregation in various southern cities, where you and your followers have been branded "rabble-rousers" and "outside agitators." Do you feel you've earned these labels?

KING: Wherever the early Christians, spreading Christ's doctrine of love, the resident power structure accused them of being "disturbers of the peace" and "outside agitators." But the small Christian band continued to teach and exemplify love, convinced that they were "a colony of heaven" on this earth who were missioned to obey not man but God. If those of us who employ nonviolent direct action today are dismissed by our white brothers as "rabble-rousers" and "outside agitators," if they refuse to support our nonviolent efforts and goals, we can be assured that the summer of 1965 will be no less long and hot than the summer of 1964.

Our white brothers must be made to understand that nonviolence is a weapon fabricated of love. It is a sword that heals. Our nonviolent direct-action program has as its objective not the creation of tensions, but the *surfacing* of tensions already present. We set out to precipitate a crisis situation that must open the door to negotiation. I am not afraid of the words "crisis" and "tension." I deeply oppose violence, but constructive crisis and tension are necessary for growth. Innate in all life, and all growth, is tension. Only in death is there an absence of tension. To cure injustices, you must expose them before the light of human conscience and the bar of public opinion, regardless of whatever tensions that exposure generates. Injustices to the Negro must be brought out into the open where they cannot be evaded.

PLAYBOY: Is this the sole aim of your Southern Christian Leadership Conference?

KING: We have five aims: first, to stimulate nonviolent, direct, mass action to expose and remove the barriers of segregation and discrimination: second, to disseminate the creative philosophy and techniques of nonviolence through local and area workshops; third, to secure the right and unhampered use of the ballot for every citizen; fourth, to achieve full citizenship rights, and the total integration of the Negro into American life; and fifth, to reduce the cultural lag through our citizenship training program.

PLAYBOY: How does SCLC select the cities where nonviolent campaigns and demonstrations are to be staged?

KING: The operational area of SCLC is the entire South, where we have affiliated organizations in some eighty-five cities. Our major campaigns have been conducted only in cities where a request for our help comes from one of these affiliate organizations, and only when we feel that intolerable conditions in that community might be ameliorated with our help. I will give you an example. In Birmingham, one of our affiliate organizations is the Alabama Christian Movement for Human Rights, which was organized by the Reverend Fred Shuttlesworth, a most energetic and indomitable man. It was he who set out to end Birmingham's racism, challenging the terrorist reign of Bull Connor. SCLC watched admiringly as the small Shuttlesworth-led organization fought in the Birmingham courts and with boycotts. Shuttlesworth was jailed several times, his home and church were bombed, and still he did not back down. His defiance of Birmingham's racism inspired and encouraged Negroes throughout the South. Then, at a May 1962 board meeting of the SCLC in Chattanooga, the first discussions began that later led to our joining Shuttlesworth's organization in a massive direct-action campaign to attack Birmingham's segregation.

PLAYBOY: One of the highlights of that campaign was your celebrated "Letter from a Birmingham Jail"—written during one of your jail terms for civil disobedience—an eloquent reply to eight Protestant, Catholic and Jewish clergymen who had criticized your activities in Birmingham. Do you feel that subsequent events have justified the sentiments expressed in your letter?

KING: I would say yes. Two or three important and constructive things have happened which can be at least partially attributed to that letter. By now, nearly a million copies of the letter have been widely circulated in churches of most of the major denominations. It helped to focus greater international attention upon what was happening in Birmingham. And I am sure that without Birmingham, the march on Washington wouldn't have been called—which in my mind was one of the most creative steps the Negro struggle has taken. The march on Washington spurred and galvanized the consciences of millions. It gave the American Negro a new national and international stature. The press of the world recorded the story as nearly a quarter of a million Americans, white and black, assembled in grandeur as a testimonial to the Negro's determination to achieve freedom in this generation.

It was also the image of Birmingham which, to a great extent, helped to bring the Civil Rights Bill into being in 1963. Previously, President Kennedy had decided not to propose it that year, feeling that it would so arouse the South that it would meet a bottleneck. But Birmingham, and subsequent developments, caused him to reorder his legislative priorities.

One of these decisive developments was our last major campaign before the enactment of the Civil Rights Act—in St. Augustine, Florida. We received a plea for help from Dr. Robert Hayling, the leader of the St. Augustine movement. St. Augustine, America's oldest city, and one of the most segregated cities in America, was a stronghold of the Ku Klux Klan and the John Birch Society. Such things had happened as Klansmen abducting four Negroes and beating them unconscious with clubs, brass knuckles, ax handles and pistol butts. Dr. Hayling's home had been shot up with buckshot, three Negro homes had been bombed and several Negro night clubs shotgunned. A Negro's car had been destroyed by fire because his child was one of the six Negro children permitted to attend white schools. And the homes of two of the Negro children in the white schools had been burned down. Many Negroes had been fired from jobs that some had worked on for twenty-eight years because they were somehow connected with the demonstrations. Police had beaten and arrested Negroes for picketing, marching and singing freedom songs. Many Negroes had served up to ninety days in jail for demonstrating against segregation, and four teenagers had spent six months in jail for picketing. Then, on February 7 of last year, Dr. Hayling's home was shotgunned a second time, with his pregnant wife and two children barely escaping death; the family dog was killed while standing behind the living-room door. So SCLC decided to join in last year's celebration of St. Augustine's gala four hundredth birthday as America's oldest city—by converting it into a nonviolent battleground. This is just what we did.

PLAYBOY: But isn't it true, Dr. King, that during this and other "nonviolent" demonstrations, violence has occurred—sometimes resulting in hundreds of casualties on both sides?

KING: Yes, in part that is true. But what is always overlooked is how few people, in ratio to the numbers involved, have been casualties. An army on maneuvers, against no enemy, suffers casualties, even fatalities. A minimum of whites have been casualties in demonstrations solely because our teaching of nonviolence disciplines our followers not to fight even if attacked. A minimum of Negroes are casualties for two reasons: Their white oppressors know that the world watches their actions, and for the first time they are being faced by Negroes who display no fear.

PLAYBOY: It was shortly after your St. Augustine campaign last summer, as you mentioned, that the Civil Rights Bill was passed—outlawing many of the injustices against which you had been demonstrating. Throughout the South, predictably, it was promptly anathematized as unconstitutional and excessive in its concessions to Negro demands. How do you feel about it?

KING: I don't feel that the Civil Rights Act has gone far *enough* in some of its coverage. In the first place, it needs a stronger voting section. You will never have a true democracy until you can eliminate *all* restrictions. We need to do away with restrictive literacy tests. I've seen too much of native intelligence to accept the validity of these tests as a criterion for voting qualifications. Our nation needs a universal method of voter registration—one man, one vote, literally. Second, there is a pressing, urgent need to give the attorney general the right to initiate federal suits in any area of civil rights denial. Third, we need a strong and strongly enforced fair-housing section such as many states already have. President Kennedy initiated the present housing law, but it is not broad enough. Fourth, we need an extension of FEPC to grapple more effectively with the problems of poverty. Not only are millions of Negroes caught in the clutches of poverty, but millions of poor whites as well. And fifth, conclusive and effective measures must be taken immediately at the federal level to curb the worsening reign of terror in the South—which is aided and abetted, as everyone knows, by state and local law-enforcement agencies. It's getting so that anybody can kill a Negro and get away with it in the South, as long as they go through the motions of a jury trial. There is very little chance of conviction from lily-white southern jurors. It must be fixed so that in the case of inter-racial murder, the federal government can prosecute.

PLAYBOY:  Your dissatisfaction with the Civil Rights Act reflects that of most other Negro spokesmen. According to recent polls, however, many whites resent this attitude, calling the Negro "ungrateful" and "unrealistic" to press his demands for more.

KING:  This is a litany to those of us in this field. "What more will the Negro want?" "What will it take to make these demonstrations end?" Well, I would like to reply with another rhetorical question: Why do white people seem to find it so difficult to understand that the Negro is sick and tired of having reluctantly parceled out to him those rights and privileges which all others receive upon birth or entry in America? I never cease to wonder at the amazing presumption of much of white society, assuming that they have the right to bargain with the Negro for his freedom. This continued arrogant ladling out of pieces of the rights of citizenship has begun to generate a *fury* in the Negro. Even so, he is not pressing for revenge or for conquest, or to gain spoils, or to enslave, or even to marry the sisters of those who have injured him. What the Negro wants—and will not stop until he gets—is absolute and unqualified freedom and equality here in this land of his birth, and not in Africa or in some imaginary state. The Negro no longer will be tolerant of anything less than his due right and heritage. He is pursuing only that which he knows is honorably his. He knows that he is right.

But every Negro leader since the turn of the century has been saying this in one form or another. It is because we have been so long and so conscientiously ignored by the dominant white society that the situation has now reached such crisis proportions. Few white people, even today, will face the clear fact that the very future and destiny of this country are tied up in what answer will be given to the Negro. And that answer must be given soon.

PLAYBOY: Relatively few dispute the justness of the struggle to eradicate racial injustice, but many whites feel that the Negro should be more patient, that only the passage of time—perhaps generations—will bring about the sweeping changes he demands in traditional attitudes and customs. Do you think this is true?

KING: No, I do not. I feel that the time is always right to do what is right. Where progress for the Negro in America is concerned, there is a tragic misconception of time among whites. They seem to cherish a strange, irrational notion that something in the very flow of time will cure all ills. In truth, time itself is only neutral. Increasingly, I feel that time has been used destructively by people of ill will much more than it has been used constructively by those of good will.

If I were to select a timetable for the equalization of human rights, it would be the *intent* of the "all deliberate speed" specified in the historic 1954 Supreme Court decision. But what has happened? A Supreme Court decision was met, and balked, with utter defiance. Ten years later, in most areas of the South, less than one percent of the Negro children have been integrated in schools, and in some of the deepest South, not even one tenth of one percent. Approximately twenty-five percent of employable Negro youth, for another example, are presently unemployed. Though many would prefer not to, we must face the fact that progress for the Negro—to which white "moderates" like to point in justifying gradualism—has been relatively insignificant, particularly in terms of the Negro masses. What little progress has been made—and that includes the Civil Rights Act—has applied primarily to the middle-class Negro. Among the masses, especially in the northern ghettos, the situation remains about the same, and for some it is worse.

PLAYBOY: It would seem that much could be done at the local, state and federal levels to remedy these inequities. In your own contact with them, have you found government officials—in the North, if not in the South—to be generally sympathetic, understanding, and receptive to appeals for reform?

KING: On the contrary, I have been dismayed at the degree to which abysmal ignorance seems to prevail among many state, city and even federal officials on the whole question of racial justice and injustice. Particularly, I have found that these men seriously—and dangerously—underestimate the explosive mood of the Negro and the gravity of the crisis. Even among those whom I would consider to be both sympathetic and sincerely intellectually committed, there is a lamentable lack of understanding. But this white failure to comprehend the depth and dimension of the Negro problem is far from being peculiar to Government officials. Apart from bigots and backlashers, it seems to be a malady even among those whites who like to regard themselves as "enlightened." I would especially refer to those who counsel, "Wait!" and to those who say that they sympathize with our goals but cannot condone our methods of direct-action pursuit of these goals. I wonder at men who dare to feel that they have some paternalistic right to set the timetable for another man's liberation. Over the past several years, I must say, I have been gravely disappointed with such white "moderates." I am often inclined to think that they are more of a stumbling block to the Negro's progress than the White Citizen's Counciler or the Ku Klux Klanner.

PLAYBOY: Haven't both of these segregationist societies been implicated in connection with plots against your life?

KING: It's difficult to trace the authorship of these death threats. I seldom go through a day without one. Some are telephoned anonymously to my office; others are sent—unsigned, of course—through the mails. Drew Pearson wrote not long ago about one group of unknown affiliation that was committed to assassinate not only me but also Chief Justice Warren and President Johnson. And not long ago, when I was about to visit in Mississippi, I received some very urgent calls from Negro leaders in Mobile, who had been told by a very reliable source that a sort of guerrilla group led by a retired major in the area of Lucyville, Mississippi, was plotting to take my life during the visit. I was strongly urged to cancel the trip, but when I thought about it, I decided that I had no alternative but to go on into Mississippi.

PLAYBOY: Why?

KING: Because I have a job to do. If I were constantly worried about death, I couldn't function. After a while, if your life is more or less constantly in peril, you come to a point where you accept the possibility philosophically. I must face the fact, as all others in positions of leadership must do, that America today is an extremely sick nation, and that something could well happen to me at any time. I feel, though, that my cause is so right, so moral, that if I should lose my life, in some way it would aid the cause.

PLAYBOY: That statement exemplifies the total dedication to the civil rights movement for which you are so widely admired—but also denounced as an "extremist" by such segregationist spokesmen as Alabama's Governor Wallace. Do you accept this identification?

KING: It disturbed me when I first heard it. But when I began to consider the true meaning of the word, I decided that perhaps I would *like* to think of myself as an extremist—in the light of the spirit which made Jesus an extremist for love. If it sounds as though I am comparing myself to the Savior, let me remind you that all who honor themselves with the claim of being "Christians" *should* compare themselves to Jesus. Thus I consider myself an extremist for that brotherhood of man which Paul so nobly expressed: "There is neither Jew nor Greek, there is neither bond nor free, there is neither male nor female: for ye are all one in Christ Jesus." Love is the only force on earth that can be dispensed or received in an extreme manner, without any qualifications, without any harm to the giver or to the receiver.

PLAYBOY: Perhaps. But the kind of extremism for which you've been criticized has to do not with love, but with your advocacy of willful disobedience of what you consider to be "unjust laws." Do you feel you have the right to pass judgment on and defy the law—nonviolently or otherwise?

KING: Yes—morally, if not legally. For there are two kinds of laws: man's and God's. A man-made code that squares with the moral law, or the law of God, is a just law. But a man-made code that is inharmonious with the moral law is an unjust law. And an unjust law, as St. Augustine said, is no law at all. Thus a law that is unjust is morally null and void, and must be defied until it is legally null and void as well. Let us not forget, in the memories of six million who died, that everything Adolf Hitler did in Germany was "legal," and that everything the Freedom Fighters in Hungary did was "illegal." In spite of that, I am sure that I would have aided and comforted my Jewish brothers if I had lived in Germany during Hitler's reign, as some Christian priests and ministers did do, often at the cost of their lives. And if I lived now in a Communist country where principles dear to the Christian's faith are suppressed, I know that I would openly advocate defiance of that country's anti-religious laws—again, just as some Christian priests and ministers are doing today behind the iron curtain. Right here in America today there are white ministers, priests and rabbis who have shed blood in the support of our struggle against a web of human injustice, much of which is supported by immoral man-made laws.

PLAYBOY: Segregation laws?

KING: Specifically, court injunctions. Though the rights of the First Amendment guarantee that any citizen or group of citizens may engage in peaceable assembly, the South has seized upon the device of invoking injunctions to block our direct-action civil rights demonstrations. When you get set to stage a nonviolent demonstration, the city simply secures an injunction to cease and desist. Southern courts are well known for "sitting on" this type of case; conceivably a two- or three-year delay could be incurred. At first we found this to be a highly effective subterfuge against us. We first experienced it in Montgomery when, during the bus boycott, our car pool was outlawed by an injunction. An injunction also destroyed the protest movement in Talladega, Alabama. Another injunction outlawed the oldest civil rights organization, the NAACP, from the whole state of Alabama. Still another injunction thwarted our organization's efforts in Albany, Georgia. Then in Birmingham, we felt that we had to take a stand and disobey a court injunction against demonstrations, knowing the consequences and being prepared to meet them—or the unjust law would break our movement.

We did not take this step hastily or rashly. We gave the matter intense thought and prayer before deciding that the right thing was being done. And when we made our decision, I announced our plan to the press, making it clear that we were not anarchists advocating lawlessness, but that in good conscience we could not comply with a misuse of the judicial process in order to perpetuate injustice and segregation. When our plan was made known, it bewildered and immobilized our segregationist opponents. We felt that our decision had been morally as well as tactically right—in keeping with God's law as well as with the spirit of our nonviolent direct-action program.

PLAYBOY: If it's morally right for supporters of civil rights to violate segregation laws which they consider unjust, why is it wrong for segregationists to resist the enforcement of integration laws which *they* consider unjust?

KING: Because segregation, as even the segregationists know in their hearts, is morally wrong and sinful. If it weren't, the

PLAYBOY:          

KING:

white South would not be haunted as it is by a deep sense of guilt for what it has done to the Negro—guilt for patronizing him, degrading him, brutalizing him, depersonalizing him, thingifying him; guilt for lying to itself. This is the source of the schizophrenia that the South will suffer until it goes through its crisis of conscience.

PLAYBOY: Is this crisis imminent?

KING: It may not come next week or next year, but it is certainly more imminent in the South than in the North. If the South is honest with itself, it may well outdistance the North in the improvement of race relations.

PLAYBOY: Why?

KING: Well, the northern white, having had little actual contact with the Negro, is devoted to an abstract principle of cordial interracial relations. The North has long considered, in a theoretical way, that it supported brotherhood and the equality of man, but the truth is that deep prejudices and discriminations exist in hidden and subtle and covert disguises. The South's prejudice and discrimination, on the other hand, has been applied against the Negro in obvious, open, overt and glaring forms—which make the problem easier to get at. The southern white man has the advantage of far more actual contact with Negroes than the northerner. A major problem is that this contact has been paternalistic and poisoned by the myth of racial superiority.

PLAYBOY: Many southern whites, supported by the "research" of several southern anthropologists, vow that white racial superiority—and Negro inferiority—are a biological fact.

KING: You may remember that during the rise of Nazi Germany, a rash of books by respected German scientists appeared, supporting the master-race theory. This utterly ignorant fallacy has been so thoroughly refuted by the social scientists, as well as by medical science, that any individual who goes on believing it is standing in an absolutely misguided and diminishing circle. The American Anthropological Association has unanimously adopted a resolution repudiating statements that Negroes are biologically, in innate mental ability or in any other way inferior to whites. The collective weight and authority of world scientists are embodied in a UNESCO report on races which flatly refutes the theory of innate superiority among any ethnic group. And as far as Negro "blood" is concerned, medical science finds the same four blood types in all race groups.

When the southern white finally accepts this simple fact—as he eventually must—beautiful results will follow, for we will have come a long way toward transforming his master-servant perspective into a person-to-person perspective. The southern white man, discovering the "nonmyth" Negro, exhibits all the passion of the new convert, seeing the black man as a man among men for the first time. The South, if it is to survive economically, must make dramatic changes, and these must include the Negro. People of good will in the South, who are the vast majority, have the challenge to be open and honest, and to turn a deaf ear to the shrill cries of the irresponsible few on the lunatic fringe. I think and pray they will.

PLAYBOY: Whom do you include among "the irresponsible few"?

KING: I include those who preach racism and commit violence; and those who, in various cities where we have sought to peacefully demonstrate, have sought to goad Negroes into violence as an excuse for violent mass reprisal. In Birmingham, for example, on the day it was flashed about the world that a "peace pact" had been signed between the moderate whites and the Negroes, Birmingham's segregationist forces reacted with fury, swearing vengeance against the white businessmen who had "betrayed" them by negotiating with Negroes. On Saturday night, just outside of Birmingham, a Ku Klux Klan meeting was held, and that same night, as I mentioned earlier, a bomb ripped the home of my brother, the Reverend A. D. King, and another bomb was planted where it would have killed or seriously wounded anyone in the motel room which I had been occupying. Both bombings had been timed just as Birmingham's bars closed on Saturday midnight, as the streets filled with thousands of Negroes who were not trained in nonviolence, and who had been drinking. Just as whoever planted the bombs had *wanted* to happen, fighting began, policemen were stoned by Negroes, cars were overturned and fires started.

PLAYBOY: Were none of your SCLC workers involved?

KING: If they had been, there would have been no riot, for we believe that only just means may be used in seeking a just end. We believe that lasting gains can be made—and they *have* been made—only by practicing what we preach: a policy of nonviolent, peaceful protest. The riots, North and South, have involved mobs—not the disciplined, nonviolent, direct-action demonstrators with whom I identify. We do not condone lawlessness, looting and violence committed by the racist or the reckless of *any* color.

I must say, however, that riots such as have occurred do achieve at least one partially positive effect: They dramatically focus national attention upon the Negro's discontent. Unfortunately, they also give the white majority an excuse, a provocation, to look away from the cause of the riots—the poverty and the deprivation and the degradation of the Negro, especially in the slums and ghettos where the riots occur—and to talk instead of looting, and of the breakdown of law and order. It is never circulated that some of the looters have been white people, similarly motivated by their own poverty. In one riot in a northern city, aside from the Negroes and Puerto Ricans who were arrested, there were also 150 white people—including mothers stealing food, children's shoes and other necessity items. The poor, white and black, were rebelling together against the establishment.

PLAYBOY: Whom do you mean by "the establishment"?

KING: I mean the white leadership—which I hold as responsible as anyone for the riots, for not removing the conditions that cause them. The deep frustration, the seething desperation of the Negro today is a product of slum housing, chronic poverty, woefully inadequate education and substandard schools. The Negro is trapped in a long and desolate corridor with no exit sign, caught in a vicious socioeconomic vise. And he is ostracized as is no other minority group in America by the evil of oppressive and constricting prejudice based solely upon his color. A righteous man has no alternative but to resist such an evil system. If he does not have the courage to resist nonviolently, then he runs the risk of a violent emotional explosion. As much as I deplore violence, there is one evil that is *worse* than violence, and that's cowardice. It is still my basic article of faith that social justice can be achieved and democracy advanced only to the degree that there is firm adherence to *nonviolent* action and resistance in the pursuit of social justice. But America will be faced with the ever-present threat of violence, rioting and senseless crime as long as Negroes by the hundreds of thousands are packed into malodorous, rat-plagued ghettos; as long as Negroes remain smothered by poverty in the midst of an affluent society; as long as Negroes see their freedom endlessly delayed and diminished by the head winds of tokenism and small handouts from the white power structure. No nation can suffer any greater tragedy than to cause millions of its citizens to feel that they have no stake in their own society.

Understand that I am trying only to explain the *reasons* for violence and the threat of violence. Let me say again that by no means and under no circumstance do I condone outbreaks of looting and lawlessness. I feel that every responsible Negro leader must point out, with all possible vigor, that anyone who perpetrates and participates in a riot is immoral as well as impractical—that the use of immoral means will not achieve the moral end of racial justice.

PLAYBOY: Whom do you consider the most responsible Negro leaders?

KING: Well, I would say that Roy Wilkins of the NAACP has proved time and again to be a very articulate spokesman for the rights of Negroes. He is a most able administrator and a dedicated organization man with personal resources that have helped the whole struggle. Another outstanding man is Whitney Young, Jr., of the National Urban League, an extremely able social scientist. He has developed a meaningful balance between militancy and moderation. James Farmer of CORE is another courageous, dedicated and thoughtful civil rights spokesman. I have always been impressed by how he maintains a freshness in his awareness of the meaning of the whole quest for freedom. And John Lewis of SNCC symbolizes the kind of strong militancy, courage and creativity that our youth have brought to the civil rights struggle. But I feel that the greatest leader of these times that the Negro has produced is A. Philip Randolph, president of the Brotherhood of Sleeping Car Porters, whose total integrity, depth of dedication and caliber of statesmanship set an example for us all.

PLAYBOY: Many whites feel that last summer's riots occurred because leadership is no longer being offered by the men you named.

KING: The riots we have had are *minute* compared to what would have happened *without* their effective and restraining leadership. I am convinced that unless the nonviolent philosophy had emerged and taken hold among Negroes, North and South, by today the streets of dozens of American communities would have flowed with blood. Hundreds of cities might now be mourning countless dead, of both races, were it not for the nonviolent influence which has given political surgeons the time and opportunity to boldly and safely excise some aspects of the peril of violence that faced this nation in the summers of 1963 and 1964. The whole world has seen what happened in communities such as Harlem, Brooklyn, Rochester, Philadelphia, Newark, St. Petersburg and Birmingham, where this emergency operation was either botched or not performed at all.

PLAYBOY: Still, doesn't the very fact that riots have occurred tend to indicate that many Negroes are no longer heeding the counsels of nonviolence?

KING:  Not the majority, by any means. But it *is* true that some Negroes subscribe to a deep feeling that the tactic of nonviolence is not producing enough concrete victories. We have seen, in our experience, that nonviolence thrives best in a climate of justice. Violence grows to the degree that injustice prevails; the more injustice in a given community, the more violence, or potential violence, smolders in that community. I can give you a clear example. If you will notice, there have been fewer riots in the South. The reason for this is that the Negro in the South can see some visible, concrete victories in civil rights. Last year, the police would have been called if he sat down at a community lunch counter. This year, if he chooses to sit at that counter, he is served. More riots have occurred in the North because the fellow in Harlem, to name one northern ghetto, can't see any victories. He remains throttled, as he has always been, by vague, intangible economic and social deprivations. Until the concerned power structures begin to grapple creatively with these fundamental inequities, it will be difficult for violence to be eliminated. The longer our people see no progress, or halting progress, the easier it will be for them to yield to the counsels of hatred and demagoguery.

PLAYBOY:  The literature of the John Birch Society, accusing you of just such counsels, has branded you "a conscious agent of the Communist conspiracy."

KING:  As you know, they have sought to link many people with communism, including the chief justice of the Supreme Court and a former president of the United States. So I'm in good company, at least. The Birchers thrive on sneer and smear, on the dissemination of half-truths and outright lies. It would be comfortable to dismiss them as the lunatic fringe—which, by and large, they are; but some priests and ministers have also shown themselves to be among them. They are a very dangerous group—and they could become even more dangerous if the public doesn't reject the un-American travesty of patriotism that they espouse.

PLAYBOY:  Was there any basis in fact for the rumors, still circulating in some quarters, that last summer's riots were fomented and stage-directed by Communist agitators?

KING:  I'm getting sick and tired of people saying that this movement has been infiltrated by Communists. There are as many Communists in this freedom movement as there are Eskimos in Florida. The FBI provided the best answer to this absurd rumor in its report to the president after a special investigation which he had requested. It stated that the riots were not caused or directed by any such groups, although they did try to capitalize upon and prolong the riots. All Negro leaders, including myself, were most happy with the publication of these findings, for the public whisperings had troubled us. We knew that it could prove vitally harmful to the Negro struggle if the riots had been catalyzed or manipulated by the Communists or some other extremist group. It would have sown the seed of doubt in the public's mind that the Negro revolution is a genuine revolution, born from the same womb that produces all massive social upheavals—the womb of intolerable conditions and unendurable situations.

PLAYBOY: Is it destined to be a violent revolution?

KING: God willing, no. But white Americans must be made to understand the basic motives underlying Negro demonstrations. Many pent-up resentments and latent frustrations are boiling inside the Negro, and he must release them. It is not a threat but a fact of history that if an oppressed people's pent-up emotions are not nonviolently released, they will be violently released. So let the Negro march. Let him make pilgrimages to city hall. Let him go on freedom rides. And above all, make an effort to understand why he must do this. For if his frustration and despair are allowed to continue piling up, millions of Negroes will seek solace and security in black-nationalist ideologies. And this, inevitably, would lead to a frightening racial nightmare.

PLAYBOY: Among whites, the best-known and most feared of these militantly racist Negro sects is the Black Muslims. What is your estimation of its power and influence among the Negro masses?

KING: Except in a few metropolitan ghettos, my experience has been that few Negroes have any interest at all in this organization, much less give any allegiance to its pessimistic doctrines. The Black Muslims are a quasi-religious, sociopolitical movement that has appealed to some Negroes who formerly were Christians. For the first time, the Negro was presented with a choice of a religion other than Christianity. What this appeal actually represented was an indictment of Christian failures to live up to Christianity's precepts; for there is nothing in Christianity, nor in the Bible, that justifies racial segregation. But when the Negroes' genuine fighting spirit rose during 1963, the appeal of the Muslims began to diminish.

PLAYBOY: One of the basic precepts of black nationalism has been the attempt to engender a sense of communion between the

American Negro and his African "brother," a sense of identity between the emergence of black Africa and the Negro's struggle for freedom in America. Do you feel that this is a constructive effort?

KING: Yes, I do, in many ways. There is a distinct, significant and inevitable correlation. The Negro across America, looking at his television set, sees black statesmen voting in the United Nations on vital world issues, knowing that in many of America's cities, he himself is not yet permitted to place hs ballot. The Negro hears of black kings and potentates ruling in palaces, while he remains ghettoized in urban slums. It is only natural that Negroes would react to this extreme irony. Consciously or unconsciously, the American Negro has been caught up by the black *Zeitgeist*. He feels a deepening sense of identification with his black African brothers, and with his brown and yellow brothers of Asia, South America and the Caribbean. With them he is moving with a sense of increasing urgency toward the promised land of racial justice.

PLAYBOY: Do you feel that the African nations, in turn, should involve themselves more actively in American Negro affairs?

KING: I do indeed. The world is now so small in terms of geographic proximity and mutual problems that no nation should stand idly by and watch another's plight. I think that in every possible instance Africans should use the influence of their governments to make it clear that the struggle of their brothers in the U.S. is part of a worldwide struggle. In short, injustice anywhere is a threat to justice everywhere, for we are tied together in a garment of mutuality. What happens in Johannesburg affects Birmingham, however indirectly. We are descendants of the Africans. Our heritage is Africa. We should never seek to break the ties, nor should the Africans.

PLAYBOY: One of the most articulate champions of black Afro-American brotherhood has been Malcolm X, the former Black Muslim leader who recently renounced his racist past and converted to orthodox Mohammedanism. What is your opinion of him and his career?

KING: I met Malcolm X once in Washington, but circumstances didn't enable me to talk with him for more than a minute. He is very articulate, as you say, but I totally disagree with many of his political and philosophical views—at least insofar as I understand where he now stands. I don't want to seem to sound self-righteous, or absolutist, or that I think I have the only truth, the only way. Maybe he *does* have some of the answers. I don't know how he feels now, but I know that I have often wished that he would talk less of violence, because violence is not going to solve our problem. And in his litany of articulating the despair of the Negro without offering any positive, creative alternative, I feel that Malcolm has done himself and our people a great disservice. Fiery, demagogic oratory in the black ghettos, urging Negroes to arm themselves and prepare to engage in violence, as he has done, can reap nothing but grief.

PLAYBOY: For them or for whites?

KING: For everyone, but mostly for them. Even the extremist leaders who preach revolution are invariably unwilling to lead what they know would certainly end in bloody, chaotic and total defeat; for in the event of a violent revolution, we would be sorely outnumbered. And when it was all over, the Negro would face the same unchanged conditions, the same squalor and deprivation—the only difference being that his bitterness would be even more intense, his disenchantment even more abject. Thus, in purely practical as well as moral terms, the American Negro has no rational alternative to nonviolence.

PLAYBOY: You categorically reject violence as a tactical technique for social change. Can it not be argued, however, that violence, historically, has effected massive and sometimes constructive social change in some countries?

KING: I'd be the first to say that some historical victories have been won by violence; the U.S. Revolution is certainly one of the foremost. But the Negro revolution is seeking integration, not independence. Those fighting for independence have the purpose to *drive out* the oppressors. But here in America, we've got to live together. We've got to find a way to reconcile ourselves to living in community, one group with the other. The struggle of the Negro in America, to be successful, must be waged with resolute efforts, but efforts that are kept strictly within the framework of our democratic society. This means reaching, educating and moving large enough groups of people of both races to stir the conscience of the nation.

PLAYBOY: How do you propose to go about it?

KING: Before we can make any progress, we must avoid retrogression—by doing everything in our power to avert further racial violence. To this end, there are three immediate steps that I would recommend. Firstly, it is mandatory that people of good will across America, particularly those who are in positions to wield influence and power, conduct honest, soul-searching analyses and evaluations of the environmental causes that spawn riots. All major industrial and ghetto areas should establish serious biracial discussions of community problems, and of ways to begin solving them. Instead of ambulance service, municipal leaders need to provide preventive medicine. Secondly, these communities should make serious efforts to provide work and training for unemployed youth, through job-and-training programs such as the HARYOU-ACT program in New York City. Thirdly, all cities concerned should make first-priority efforts to provide immediate quality education for Negro youth—instead of conducting studies for the next five years. Young boys and girls now in the ghettos must be enabled to feel that they count, that somebody cares about them; they must be able to feel *hope*. And on a longer-range basis, the physical ghetto itself must be eliminated, because these are the environmental conditions that germinate riots. It is both socially and morally suicidal to continue a pattern of deploring effects while failing to come to grips with the *causes*. Ultimately, law and order will be maintained only when justice and dignity are accorded impartially to all.

PLAYBOY: Along with the other civil rights leaders, you have often proposed a massive program of economic aid, financed by the federal government, to improve the lot of the nation's twenty million Negroes. Just one of the projects you've mentioned, however—the HARYOU-ACT program to provide jobs for Negro youths—is expected to cost 141 million dollars over the next ten years, and that includes only Harlem. A nationwide program such as you propose would undoubtedly run into the billions.

KING: About fifty billion, actually—which is less than one year of our present defense spending. It is my belief that with the expenditure of this amount, over a ten-year period, a genuine and dramatic transformation could be achieved in the conditions of Negro life in America. I am positive, moreover, that the money spent would be more than amply justified by the benefits that would accrue to the nation through a spectacular decline in school dropouts, family breakups, crime rates, illegitimacy, swollen relief rolls, rioting and other social evils.

PLAYBOY: Do you think it's realistic to hope that the government would consider an appropriation of such magnitude other than for national defense?

KING: I certainly do. This country has the resources to solve any problem once that problem is accepted as national policy.

An example is aid to Appalachia, which has been made a policy of the federal government's much-touted war on poverty; one billion was proposed for its relief—without making the slightest dent in the defense budget. Another example is the fact that after World War II, during the years when it became policy to build and maintain the largest military machine the world has ever known, America also took upon itself, through the Marshall Plan and other measures, the financial relief and rehabilitation of millions of European people. If America can afford to underwrite its allies and ex-enemies, it can certainly afford—and has a much greater obligation, as I see it—to do at least as well by its own no less needy countrymen.

PLAYBOY: Do you feel it's fair to request a multibillion-dollar program of preferential treatment for the Negro, or for any other minority group?

KING: I do indeed. Can any fair-minded citizen deny that the Negro has been deprived? Few people reflect that for two centuries the Negro was enslaved, and robbed of any wages— potential accrued wealth which would have been the legacy of his descendants. *All* of America's wealth today could not adequately compensate its Negroes for his centuries of exploitation and humiliation. It is an economic fact that a program such as I propose would certainly cost far less than any computaton of two centuries of unpaid wages plus accumulated interest. In any case, I do not intend that this program of economic aid should apply only to the Negro; it should benefit the disadvantaged of *all* races.

Within common law, we have ample precedents for special compensatory programs, which are regarded as settlements. American Indians are still being paid for land in a settlement manner. Is not two centuries of labor, which helped to build this country, as real a commodity? Many other easily applicable precedents are readily at hand: our child labor laws, social security, unemployment compensation, manpower retraining programs. And you will remember that America adopted a policy of special treatment for her millions of veterans after the war—a program which cost far more than a policy of preferential treatment to rehabilitate the traditionally disadvantaged Negro would cost today.

The closest analogy is the GI Bill of Rights. Negro rehabilitation in America would require approximately the same breadth of program—which would not place an undue burden on our economy. Just as was the case with the returning soldier, such a bill for the disadvantaged and impoverished could enable them to buy homes without cash, at lower and easier repayment terms. They could negotiate loans from banks to launch businesses. They could receive, as did ex-GIs, special points to place them ahead in competition for civil service jobs. Under certain circumstances of physical disability, medical care and long-term financial grants could be made available. And together with these rights, a favorable social climate could be created to encourage the preferential employment of the disadvantaged, as was the case for so many years with veterans. During those years, it might be noted, there was no appreciable resentment of the preferential treatment being given to the special group. America was only compensating her veterans for their time lost from school or from business.

PLAYBOY: If a nationwide program of preferential employment for Negroes were to be adopted, how would you propose to assuage the resentment of whites who already feel that their jobs are being jeopardized by the influx of Negroes resulting from desegregation?

KING: We must develop a federal program of public works, retraining and jobs for all—so that none, white or black, will have cause to feel threatened. At the present time, thousands of jobs a week are disappearing in the wake of automation and other production efficiency techniques. Black and white, we will *all* be harmed unless something grand and imaginative is done. The unemployed, poverty-stricken white man must be made to realize that he is in the very same boat with the Negro. Together, they could exert massive pressure on the government to get jobs for all. Together, they could form a grand alliance. Together, they could merge all people for the good of all.

PLAYBOY: If Negroes are also granted preferential treatment in housing, as you propose, how would you allay the alarm with which many white homeowners, fearing property devaluation, greet the arrival of Negroes in hitherto all-white neighborhoods?

KING: We must expunge from our society the myths and half-truths that engender such groundless fears as these. In the first place, there is no truth to the myth that Negroes depreciate property. The fact is that most Negroes are kept out of residential neighborhoods so long that when one of us is finally sold a home, it's *already* depreciated. In the second place, we must dispel the negative and harmful atmosphere that has been created by avaricious and unprincipled realtors who engage in "blockbusting." If we had in America really serious efforts to break down discrimination in housing, and at the same time a concerted program of government aid to improve housing for Negroes, I think that many white people would be surprised at how many Negroes would choose to live among themselves, exactly as Poles and Jews and other ethnic groups do.

PLAYBOY: The B'nai B'rith, a prominent social-action organization which undertakes on behalf of the Jewish people many of the activities that you ask the government to perform for Negroes, is generously financed by Jewish charities and private donations. All of the Negro civil rights groups, on the other hand—including your own—are perennially in financial straits and must rely heavily on white philanthropy in order to remain solvent. Why do they receive so little support from Negroes?

KING: We have to face and live with the fact that the Negro has not developed a sense of stewardship. Slavery was so divisive and brutal, so molded to break up unity, that we never developed a sense of oneness, as in Judaism. Starting with the individual family unit, the Jewish people are closely knit into what is, in effect, one big family. But with the Negro, slavery separated families from families, and the pattern of disunity that we see among Negroes today derives directly from this cruel fact of history. It is also a cruel fact that the Negro, generally speaking, has not developed a responsible sense of financial values. The best economists say that your automobile shouldn't cost more than half of your annual income, but we see many Negroes earning seven thousand dollars a year paying five thousand dollars for a car. The home, it is said, should not cost more than twice the annual income, but we see many Negroes earning, say, eight thousand dollars a year living in a thirty-thousand-dollar home. Negroes, who amount to about eleven percent of the American population, are reported to consume over forty percent of the Scotch whisky imported into the U.S., and to spend over seventy-two million dollars a year in jewelry stores. So when we come asking for civil rights donations, or help for the United Negro College Fund, most Negroes are trying to make ends meet.

PLAYBOY: The widespread looting that took place during last summer's riots would seem to prove your point. Do you agree with those who feel that this looting—much of which was directed against Jewish-owned stores—was anti-Semitic in motivation?

KING: No, I do not believe that the riots could in any way be considered expressions of anti-Semitism. It's true, as I was particularly pained to learn, that a large percentage of the looted stores were owned by our Jewish friends, but I do no feel that anti-Semitism was involved. A high percentage of the merchants serving most Negro communities simply happen to be Jewish. How could there be anti-Semitism among Negroes when our Jewish friends have demonstrated their commitment to the principle of tolerance and brotherhood not only in the form of sizable contributions, but in many other tangible ways, and often at great personal sacrifice? Can we ever express our appreciation to the rabbis who chose to give moral witness with us in St. Augustine during our recent protest against segregation in that unhappy city? Need I remind anyone of the awful beating suffered by Rabbi Arthur Lelyveld of Cleveland when he joined the civil rights workers there in Hattiesburg, Mississippi? And who can ever forget the sacrifice of two Jewish lives, Andrew Goodman and Michael Schwerner, in the swamps of Mississippi? It would be impossible to record the contribution that the Jewish people have made toward the Negro's struggle for freedom—it has been so great.

PLAYBOY: In conspicuous contrast, according to a recent poll conducted by *Ebony*, only one Negro in ten has ever participated physically in any form of social protest. Why?

KING: It is not always sheer numbers that are the measure of public support. As I see it, every Negro who does participate represents the sympathy and the moral backing of thousands of others. Let us never forget how one photograph, of those Birmingham policemen with their knees on that Negro woman on the ground, touched something emotionally deep in most Negroes in America, no matter who they were. In city after city, where SCLC has helped to achieve sweeping social changes, it has been not only because of the quality of its members' dedication and discipline, but because of the moral support of many Negroes who never took an active part. It's significant, I think that during each of our city struggles, the usual average of crimes committed by Negroes has dropped to almost nothing.

But it is true, undeniably, that there are many Negroes who will *never* fight for freedom—yet who will be eager enough to accept it when it comes. And there are millions of Negroes who have never known anything but oppression, who are so devoid of pride and self-respect that they have resigned themselves to segregation. Other Negroes, comfortable and complacent, consider that they are *above* the struggle of the masses. And still others seek personal profit from segregation.

PLAYBOY: Many southern whites have accused *you* of being among those who exploit the race problem for private gain. You are widely believed throughout the South, in fact, to have amassed a vast personal fortune in the course of your civil rights activities.

KING: *Me* wealthy? This is so utterly fallacious and erroneous that I often wonder where it got started. For the sixth straight year since I have been SCLC's president, I have rejected our board's insistent recommendation that I accept some salary beyond the one dollar a year which I receive, which entitles me to participate in our employees' group insurance plan. I have rejected also our board's offer of financial gifts as a measure and expression of appreciation. My only salary is from my church, four thousand dollars a year, plus two thousand dollars more a year for what is known as "pastoral care." To earn a grand total of about ten thousand dollars a year, I keep about four to five thousand dollars a year for myself from the honorariums that I receive from various speaking engagements. About ninety percent of my speaking is for SCLC, and it brings into our treasury something around two hundred thousand dollars a year. Additionally, I get a fairly sizable but fluctuating income in the form of royalties from my writings. But all of this, too, I give to my church, or to my alma mater, Morehouse College, here in Atlanta.

I believe as sincerely as I believe anything that the struggle for freedom in which SCLC is engaged is not one that should reward any participant with individual wealth and gain. I think I'd rise up in my grave if I died leaving two or three hundred thousand dollars. But people just don't seem to believe that this is the way I feel about it. If I have any weaknesses, they are not in the area of coveting wealth. My wife knows this well; in fact, she feels that I overdo it. But the Internal Revenue people, they stay on me; they feel sure that one day they are going to find a fortune stashed in a mattress. To give you some idea of my reputed affluence, just last week I came in from a trip and learned that a television program had announced I was going to purchase an expensive home in an all-white neighborhood here in Atlanta. It was news to me!

PLAYBOY: Your schedule of speaking engagements and civil rights commitments throughout the country is a punishing one—

often twenty hours a day, seven days a week, according to reports. How much time do you get to spend at home?

KING: Very little, indeed. I've averaged not more than two days a week at home here in Atlanta over the past year—or since Birmingham, actually. I'm away two and three weeks at a time, mostly working in communities across the South. Wherever I am, I try to be in a pulpit as many Sundays as possible. But every day when I'm at home, I break from the office for dinner and try to spend a few hours with the children before I return to the office for some night work. And on Tuesdays when I'm not out of town, I don't go to the office. I keep this for my quiet day of reading and silence and meditation, and an entire evening with Mrs. King and the children.

PLAYBOY: If you could have a week's uninterrupted rest, with no commitments whatever, how would you spend it?

KING: It's difficult to imagine such a thing, but if I had the luxury of an entire week, I would spend it meditating and reading, refreshing myself spiritually and intellectually. I have a deep nostalgia for the periods in the past that I was able to devote in this manner. Amidst the struggle, amidst the frustrations, amidst the endless work, I often reflect that I am forever *giving*—never pausing to take in. I feel urgently the need for even an hour of time to get away, to withdraw, to refuel. I need more time to think through what is being done, to take time out from the mechanics of the movement, to reflect on the *meaning* of the movement.

PLAYBOY: If you were marooned on the proverbial desert island, and could have with you only one book—apart from the Bible— what would it be?

KING: That's tough. Let me think about it—one book, not the Bible. Well, I think I would have to pick Plato's *Republic*. I feel that it brings together more of the insights of history than any other book. There is not a creative idea extant that is not discussed, in some way, in this work. Whatever realm of theology or philosophy is one's interest—and I am deeply interested in both—somewhere along the way, in this book you will find the matter explored.

PLAYBOY: If you could send someone—anyone—to that desert island in your stead, who would it be?

KING: That's another tough one. Let me see, I guess I wouldn't mind seeing Mr. Goldwater dispatched to a desert island. I hope they'd *feed* him and everything, of course. I *am* nonviolent, you know. Politically, though, he's already on a desert island, so it may be unnecessary to send him there.

PLAYBOY: We take it you weren't overly distressed by his defeat in the presidential race.

KING: Until that defeat, Goldwater was the most dangerous man in America. He talked soft and nice, but he gave aid and comfort to the most vicious racists and the most extreme rightists in America. He gave respectability to views totally alien to the democratic process. Had he won, he would have led us down a fantastic path that would have totally destroyed America as we know it.

PLAYBOY: Until his withdrawal from the race following Goldwater's nomination, Alabama's Governor Wallace was another candidate for the presidency. What's your opinion of *his* qualifications for that office?

KING: Governor Wallace is a demagogue with a capital D. He symbolizes in this country many of the evils that were alive in Hitler's Germany. He is a merchant of racism, peddling hate under the guise of states' rights. He wants to turn back the clock, for his own personal aggrandizement, and he will do literally *anything* to accomplish this. He represents the misuse, the corruption, the destruction of leadership. I am not sure that he believes all the poison that he preaches, but he is artful enough to convince others that he does. Instead of guiding people to new peaks of reasonableness, he intensifies misunderstanding, deepens suspicion and prejudice. He is perhaps the most dangerous racist in America today.

PLAYBOY: One of the most controversial issues of the past year, apart from civil rights, was the question of school prayer, which has been ruled unlawful by the Supreme Court. Governor Wallace, among others, has denounced the decision. How do you feel about it?

KING: I endorse it. I think it was correct. Contrary to what many have said, it sought to outlaw neither prayer nor belief in God. In a pluralistic society such as ours, who is to determine what prayer shall be spoken, and by whom? Legally, constitutionally or otherwise, the state certainly has no such right. I am strongly opposed to the efforts that have been made to nullify the decision. They have been motivated, I think, by little more than the wish to harrass the Supreme Court. When I saw brother Wallace going up to Washington to testify against the decision at the congressional hearings, it only strengthened my conviction that the decision was right.

PLAYBOY: Governor Wallace has intimated that President Johnson, in championing the cause of civil rights only since he became vice-president, may be guilty of "insincerity."

KING:    How President Johnson may or may not have felt about or voted on civil rights during his years in Congress is less relevant, at this point, than what he has said and done about it during his tenure as president of the United States. In my opinion, he has done a good job up to now. He is an extremely keen political man, and he has demonstrated his wisdom and his commitment in forthrightly coming to grips with the problem. He does not tire of reminding the nation of the moral issues involved. My impression is that he will remain a strong president for civil rights.

PLAYBOY:    Late in 1963, you wrote: "As I look toward 1964, one fact is unmistakably clear: The thrust of the Negro toward full emancipation will *increase* rather than decrease." As last summer's riots testified, these words were unhappily prophetic. Do you foresee more violence in the year ahead?

KING:    To the degree that the Negro is not thwarted in his thrust forward, I believe that one can predict *less* violence. I am not saying that there will be no demonstrations. There assuredly will, for the Negro in America has not made one civil rights gain without tense legal and extralegal pressure. If the Constitution were today applied equally and impartially to all of America's citizens, in every section of the country, in every court and code of law, there would be no need for any group of citizens to seek extra-legal redress.

Our task has been a difficult one, and will continue to be, for privileged groups, historically, have not volunteered to give up their privileges. As Reinhold Niebuhr has written, individuals may see the moral light and voluntarily abandon their unjust posture, but groups tend to be more immoral, and more intransigent, than individuals. Our nonviolent direct-action program, therefore—which has proved its strength and effectiveness in more than a thousand American cities where some baptism of fire has taken place—will continue to dramatize and demonstrate against local injustices to the Negro until the last of those who impose those injustices are forced to negotiate; until, finally, the Negro wins the protections of the Constitution that have been denied to him; until society, at long last, is stricken gloriously and incurably color-blind.

PLAYBOY:    In well-earned recognition of your dedication to and leadership of the struggle to achieve these goals, you became, in October of last year, the youngest man to receive the Nobel Peace Prize. What was your reaction to the news?

KING:    It made me feel very humble indeed. But I would like to think that the award is not a personal tribute, but a tribute to the entire freedom movement, and to the gallant people of both races who surround me in the drive for civil rights which will make the American dream a reality. I think that this internationally known award will call even more attention to our struggle, gain even greater sympathy and understanding for our cause, from people all over the world. I like to think that the award recognizes symbolically the gallantry, the courage and the amazing discipline of the Negro in America, for these things are to his eternal credit. Though we have had riots, the bloodshed that we would have known without the discipline of nonviolence would have been truly frightening. I know that many whites feel the civil rights movement is getting out of hand; this may reassure them. It may let them see that basically this is a disciplined struggle, let them appreciate the *meaning* of our struggle, let them see that a great struggle for human freedom can occur within the framework of a democratic society.

PLAYBOY: Do you feel that this goal will be achieved within your lifetime?

KING: I confess that I do not believe this day is around the corner. The concept of supremacy is so imbedded in the white society that it will take many years for color to cease to be a judgmental factor. But it is certainly my hope and dream. Indeed, it is the keystone of my faith in the future that we will someday achieve a thoroughly integrated society. I believe that before the turn of the century, if trends continue to move and develop as presently, we will have moved a long, long way toward such a society.

PLAYBOY: Do you intend to dedicate the rest of your life, then, to the Negro cause?

KING: If need be, yes. But I dream of the day when the demands presently cast upon me will be greatly diminished. I would say that in the next five years, though, I can't hope for much letup—either in the South or in the North. After that time, it is my hope that things will taper off a bit.

PLAYBOY: If they do, what are your plans?

KING: Well, at one time I dreamed of pastoring for a few years, and then of going to a university to teach theology. But I gave that up when I became deeply involved in the civil rights struggle. Perhaps, in five years or so, I will have the chance to make that dream come true.

PLAYBOY: In the meanwhile, you are now the universally acknowledged leader of the American civil rights movement, and chief spokesman for the nation's twenty million Negroes.

Are there ever moments when you feel awed by this burden of responsibility, or inadequate to its demands?

KING: One cannot be in my position, looked to by some for guidance, without being constantly reminded of the awesomeness of its responsibility. I live with one deep concern: Am I making the right decisions? Sometimes I am uncertain, and I must look to God for guidance. There was one morning I recall, when I was in Birmingham jail, in solitary, with not even my lawyers permitted to visit, and I was in a nightmare of despair. The very future of our movement hung in the balance, depending upon capricious turns of events over which I could have no control there, incommunicado, in an utterly dark dungeon. This was about ten days after our Birmingham demonstrations began. Over four hundred of our followers had gone to jail; some had been bailed out, but we had used up all of our money for bail, and about three hundred remained in jail, and I felt personally responsible. It was then that President Kennedy telephoned my wife, Coretta. After that, my jail conditions were relaxed, and the following Sunday afternoon—it was Easter Sunday—two SCLC attorneys were permitted to visit me. The next day, word came to me from New York that Harry Belafonte had raised fifty thousand dollars that was available immediately for bail bonds, and if more was needed, he would raise that. I cannot express what I felt, but I knew at that moment that God's presence had never left me, that He had been with me there in solitary.

I subject myself to self-purification and to endless self-analysis; I question and soul-search constantly into myself to be as certain as I can that I am fulfilling the true meaning of my work, that I am maintaining my sense of purpose, that I am holding fast to my ideals, that I am guiding my people in the right direction. But whatever my doubts, however heavy the burden, I feel that I must accept the task of helping to make this nation and this world a better place to live in—for *all* men, black and white alike.

I never will forget a moment in Birmingham when a white policeman accosted a little Negro girl, seven or eight years old, who was walking in a demonstration with her mother. "What do you want?" the policeman asked her gruffly, and the little girl looked him straight in the eye and answered, "Fee-dom." She couldn't even pronounce it, but she knew. It was beautiful! Many times when I have been in sorely trying situations, the memory of that little one has come into my mind, and has buoyed me.

Similarly, not long ago, I toured in eight communities of the state of Mississippi. And I have carried with me ever since a visual image of the penniless and the unlettered, and of the expressions on their faces—of deep and courageous determination to cast off the imprint of the past and become free people. I welcome the opportunity to be a part of this great drama, for it is a drama that will determine America's destiny. If the problem is not solved, America will be on the road to its self-destruction. But if it *is* solved, America will just as surely be on the high road to the fulfillment of the Founding Fathers' dream, when they wrote: "We hold these truths to be self-evident. . . ."

*Playboy* (January 1965): 117ff.

# 51

# "Meet the Press"
# Television News Interview

*In this historic interview with the major leaders of the civil rights movement, we see clearly the power of August Meier's description of Dr. King as a "militant conservative." Meier and many other interpreters consistently see Martin Luther King, Jr., outside the context of the black church movement. Unless we begin to see that the so-called paradoxes that seemingly plagued Dr. King's public career were really the paradoxes of a Christian leader trying to be righteous in an unrighteous world, we shall continue to minimize his intellectual and organizational brilliance, reflected in how he skillfully maintained a consistent Christian position throughout his public ministry. This skill is evident in this interview. He left the interview early because of a prior commitment to lead a demonstration in Chicago. In the remainder of the interview, the absence of his centrist leadership led to subtle* ad hominem *attacks traded between the "old guard" civil rights leaders, represented by Roy Wilkins and Whitney Young, and the black power advocates, represented by James H. Meredith, Floyd McKissick, and Stokely Carmichael. Reporters Rowland Evans and Lawrence E. Spivak were particularly adept at accenting these schisms, despite the attempts of Stokely Carmichael and Roy Wilkins to mask the differences. Civil rights leaders in general tried to present a united front, and tried to adhere to the principle outlined at one point by Carmichael: "Privately we have a right to analyze other civil rights groups, but we never do it publicly." This principle of unity and civility was often violated by all the leaders of the civil rights movement in the heat of public debate and at the divisive prodding of the news media. But none of them adhered to this principle as religiously as Dr. King. In* Where Do We Go from Here *(1967), Dr. King spoke poignantly to this issue: "Too many Negro organizations are warring against each other with a claim to absolute truth. The Pharaohs had a favorite and effective strategy to keep their slaves in bondage: keep them fighting among themselves. The divide-and-conquer technique has been a potent weapon in the arsenal of oppression. But when slaves unite, the Red Sea of history opens, and the Egypts of slavery crumble." He added later that "Negroes can differ and still unite around common goals." The differences between the old guard and the new militant leadership were quite evident just a few weeks before this interview took place. On 6 June 1966, there was an attempted assassination of James Meredith, who was leading a "March Against Fear" between Memphis, Tennessee, and Jackson, Mississippi. Shortly thereafter, Carmichael, King, McKissick, Wilkins, and Young met in Memphis in order to plan how to resume the march.*

*A vehement dispute took place between these factions. Wilkins and Young returned to their headquarters in New York, and Carmichael and McKissick remained under the condition that Dr. King would leave the march if they persisted in their advocacy of violence. Carmichael broke the pact before the march was concluded, remarking that "Black Power"—a slogan used by Adam Clayton Powell, Jr., in his 1965 commencement address at Howard University—had become a national mood, if not a national movement, among many black people. Meredith was released from the hospital later, and was therefore able to participate in this nationally televised interview.*

Mr. Byrd of West Virginia. Mr. President, on Sunday, August 21, 1966, Dr. Martin Luther King, Jr., SCLC; Mr. Roy Wilkins, NAACP; Mr. Whitney Young, National Urban League; Stokely Carmichael, SNCC; Mr. Floyd B. McKissick, CORE; and Mr. James H. Meredith appeared on "Meet the Press," an NBC television and radio production. The moderator was Mr. Edwin Newman. The panel consisted of Mr. Lawrence E. Spivak; Mr. Rowland Evans, *Chicago Sun-Times & Publishers' Syndicate*; Mr. Carl Rowan, *Chicago Daily News*; Mr. James J. Kilpatrick, Richmond, Virginia, *News Leader*; and Mr. Richard Valeriani, NBC News.

I ask unanimous consent to include the transcript of this special ninety-minute edition of "Meet the Press" in the Record at this point.

There being no objection the transcript was ordered to be printed in the Record, as follows:

Moderator: Edwin Newman.

Guests: Dr. Martin Luther King, Jr., SCLC; Roy Wilkins, NAACP; Whitney Young, National Urban League; Stokely Carmichael, SNCC; Floyd B. McKissick, CORE; James H. Meredith.

Panel: Lawrence E. Spivak; Rowland Evans, *Chicago Sun-Times & Publishers' Syndicate*; Carl Rowan, *Chicago Daily News*; James J. Kilpatrick, Richmond (Virginia) *News Leader*; Richard Valeriani, NBC News.

NEWMAN: This is Edwin Newman inviting you to a special ninety-minute edition of "Meet the Press". [Announcement] Today in this special hour-and-a-half program of "Meet the Press" focuses on the country's number one domestic problem: civil rights. Our guests today are six of the nation's top Negro leaders in their first joint live broadcast. With us today in Chicago is the Reverend Martin Luther King, Jr., president and one of the founders of the Southern Christian Leadership Conference. Dr. King, winner of the Nobel Peace Prize, is a leading proponent of the principle of nonviolence. He's recognized throughout the world as the spiritual leader of the civil rights movement in the United States. Because of the march he is heading today in Chicago Dr. King finds it necessary to leave the studio before the end of our program. For this reason we will direct more questions to him than to our other guests in the first part of our broadcast.

And in our Washington studio Roy Wilkins, a former newspaper man and the executive director of the National Association for the Advancement of Colored People since 1950. The NAACP which he heads is the oldest and largest civil rights organization in the country. Founded in 1909, it now claims a national membership of over five hundred thousand. The first organization to use the picket line, it has been involved in many demonstrations and has played a major role in the fight for civil rights laws.

Whitney M. Young, Jr., executive director of the National Urban League since 1961, a former dean of the Atlanta University School of Social Work, he heads one of the most important biracial service organizations. Its policy has been to lead Negroes into the American mainstream through job training programs, and through housing, welfare, and education projects.

Floyd B. McKissick, national director of the Congress of Racial Equality. He is a lawyer who gave up his practice early this year to become head of the twenty-two-year-old CORE. Mr. McKissick's official biography describes him as a dynamic civil rights activist. He has played a leading role in picketings, sit-ins and other civil rights demonstrations. His organization, CORE, claims a membership of eighty thousand and is considered one of the most militant of the civil rights groups.

Stokely Carmichael, chairman of the Student Nonviolent Coordinating Committee. A graduate of Howard University and the youngest of the civil rights leaders, Mr. Carmichael heads the newest and most militant of the national organizations. His use of the slogan "black power" during the recent Mississippi march stirred up a storm in and out of the civil rights movement and brought him to front-page prominence.

And James H. Meredith who occupies a special position in the American Negro movement because of his leadership in desegregating the University of Mississippi, and in the recent march through Mississippi. He is now a student at the Columbia University Law School.

[Panel Intro.]

We will begin the questions now with Mr. Spivak.

SPIVAK: Dr. King, despite all of your marches and demonstrations, and despite major civil rights laws, the civil rights crisis is getting worse rather than better. Or at least it seems so. Do you think it is growing worse, and if so, why?

KING: Well, I think at points it is growing worse. This does not mean that we have not made significant progress. But I think the real problem today is there is still a tragic gulf between promise and fulfillment, and that the rising expectations of freedom and equality, the rising expectations of improvement have met with little results, so the problem today is that we have laws on the books but they have not been thoroughly implemented and there are still pockets of resistance that are seeking to hold the civil rights movement back in our just and legal and moral aspirations for a democratic society, are still being met with these forces of resistance.

SPIVAK: Mr. Wilkins, do you think the crisis is getting better or worse?

WILKINS: I think only outwardly worse. We're having some manifestations of abrasive resistance. But actually progress is being made, we are going forward, and this despite the fact that great masses of people cannot count the difference in today's living between that they had, say a year ago or two years ago. But the forces are in motion. I agree with Dr. King that they're not moving fast enough, not on a broad enough scale.

SPIVAK: Mr. Young, for many years we had no civil rights laws of any importance; very little was being done by the white community for the Negro population or with the Negro population, and yet we had relatively quiet. What is your explanation for the riots that are taking place at the present time?

YOUNG: Well, I think it reflects this high aspiration of the Negro. I never felt that social progress could be a painless process. I don't think that the good race relations is purely the absence of conflict. In fact, we probably have less disruption in South Africa today where we have the greatest segregation and discrimination. I think what we are really facing today, and I think it's positive, and that is that the white community is now coming to find out that it takes more than the passage of laws which relieve their guilt, and it takes actual determination to live with and to work with and to cooperate with Negro citizens, and it's this final confrontation that people find most difficult to make.

SPIVAK: Mr. McKissick, what do you think? Do you think things are getting better or worse?

MCKISSICK: I'm of the opinion that things have not progressed tremendously for the masses of the people. I would not dispute the statement that some progress has not been made. But I would say, by and large, the average black man in the ghetto has not profited within the last ten years. I think the last statistics showed, and I think even last week at the hearing in Washington here at the— Ribicoff, when he made the statement we'll find that we've got more discrimination in education, more segregated school systems; we find the unemployment rate is higher now than ever before. I think we could just go down the line and we could find that the situation has not improved as far as the masses are concerned, and that's what the Congress of Racial Equality is concerned with.

SPIVAK: Mr. Carmichael, from your experience are things getting better or worse?

CARMICHAEL: Well, I don't know if you can make a comparison like that. I believe that what is happening is that black people across the country are becoming politically aware of their position, of their strength, and of their ability to move and based on that feeling, the masses of people are beginning to now move, and the question is whether or not this country is going to be able to meet their needs peacefully or whether they will have to move to disrupt this country in order to force the country to speak to their needs.

SPIVAK: Mr. Meredith, may I hear from you on that? Do you think things are getting better or worse?

MEREDITH: Well, I think we've just reached a point in our history where we are really beginning to face the issue in question. And the question in this country is what is the basis or what is going to be the basis of our society? Up until now it's based on the theory of white superiority, and now this nation has to make decision whether we will continue to use this base of white supremacy or whether we will live up to our ideals of equality and equal justice before the law.

SPIVAK: Dr. King, I'd like to come back to you now. The superintendent of police of Chicago, Mr. O. W. Wilson, said the other day that your civil rights tactics have aroused hatred among Chicago white residents and are hampering the Negro's progress. What's your answer to that?

KING: Well, my answer is that this is totally erroneous. Our civil rights efforts have not aroused hatred, they have revealed a hatred that already existed. There is no doubt about the fact that there are many latent hostilities existing within certain white groups in the North, and what has happened now is that these latent hostilities have come out in the open, and I don't think you can blame the civil rights movement for that. Certainly no one would blame the physician for using his instruments and his skills and his knowhow to reveal to a patient that he has cancer. Indeed, one would praise a physician for having the wisdom and the judgment and the power to do that.

Now we have only revealed in Chicago that there is a blatant social, hate-filled cancer, and we haven't said even that it's an eternal state. We feel that it's curable, that it can be cured. But there is no doubt about the fact that the hate is here. We didn't create it, we merely exposed it and brought it to the surface.

SPIVAK: Dr. King, I'm sure you either heard or read President Johnson's speech yesterday when he warned that violence and discord would destroy Negroes' hopes for racial progress. Now isn't it time to stop demonstrations that create violence and discord?

KING: Well, I absolutely disagree with that, and I hope the president didn't mean to equate nonviolent demonstrations with a riot, and I think it is time for this country to see the distinction between the two. There is a great distinction between individuals who are nonviolently engaged in pursuit of basic constitutional rights and who in the process face violence and face hatred perpetrated against them, and individuals who aggressively throw Molotov cocktails and engage in riots. So that there can be no equation or there can be no identity between riots and demonstrations, I think demonstrations must continue, but I think riots must end because they are socially disruptive, I think they are self-defeating, and I think they can destroy the many creative steps that we have made in a forward sense over the last few years.

ROWAN: Mr. Wilkins, despite the fact that you gentlemen sit here together there is a feeling around the country that there's a crisis of leadership in the civil rights movement. Do you agree that the movement toward Negro equality is jeopardized by what now seems to be a host of warring civil rights groups, each pursuing its own special interests.

WILKINS: No, Mr. Rowan, I don't think it's quite that serious. We tend to feel that unity should be exhibited at all times, no matter what kind of organizations or what kind of personalities or what kind of tactics are involved. I think we have to grow up to the idea that there will be differences of opinion and that these will manifest themselves from time to time. I don't see as yet any great split in the civil rights movement.

ROWAN: Well, I've noticed in the *New York Times*, Mr. Wilkins, a quotation from a so-called SNCC position paper saying we are now aware that the NAACP has grown reactionary, is controlled by the black power structure itself, and stands as one of the main roadblocks to black freedom. I note also that an NAACP official was referring to the Urban League as an Uncle Tom organization. Now this you don't think is serious division, or anything to be worried about?

WILKINS: No, no. I call your attention, first of all, to the fact that the SNCC person said that we were, the NAACP, was controlled by the black power structure.

ROWAN: I wondered if that was a typo.

WILKINS: No, it wasn't a typographical error. And for that we moved up on the scale because there was a time when the spokesman would have said that we were controlled by the white power structure. But the NAACP official you referred to as calling the Urban League Uncle Tom was only a local official, an extremely individualistic one at that and in no sense can be said to represent the sentiment of the NAACP.

ROWAN: Well now I note, Mr. Wilkins, that your organization lost some fifteen thousand members between 1964 and 1965. Now you don't think the NAACP and the country are in trouble today because the NAACP put its faith in the law and court decisions but that when the crunch came the decisions were not enforced and the laws became just so much paper?

WILKINS: No, I don't think we're in trouble because we lost fifteen thousand members out of a half million; I don't consider that serious or beyond accounting for in the normal course of events. Nor do I believe that the adherence to law and order is a penalty that we suffer. I think we all have to come back to law and order. I understand Dr. King out in Chicago has a lawyer now working on his injunction business, and I see where SNCC is engaging lawyers up in Philadelphia; so we all come to the courtroom and to the law eventually. We find we can't solve it with rhetoric.

KILPATRICK: Dr. King, you have been quoted as saying that you have encountered more hatred among white opponents in Chicago than you have encountered in the Deep South. How do you account for this?

KING: Well, I think for years the hatred existed beneath the surface in northern communities, and as I said earlier, it's coming out now. I think also we have to see that this is something of a dislike for the unlike, and you see it a great deal among the lower-income ethnic enclaves who have basic fears about Negroes. They have grown up believing in certain stereotypes, whether it's the stereotype of the Negroes are lazy or inherently inferior, or whether it is a myth that Negroes depreciate property values when they move in a community. There is another fear, the fear that the Negro is an economic threat. Now I think all of these things have contributed to, and in a sense have conjoined to bring about this massive outpouring of hatred in Chicago and I'm sure in other communities.

KILPATRICK: But why should these factors carry greater weight in Chicago or in some other northern city than they would in the Deep South?

KING: Well, I'm not saying, and I haven't said they exist more than they do in the Deep South, because I must make one distinction, and that is in the South we have had the hatred, the violence, the vitriolic and vituperative words of the mobs on one hand; but often these mobs have been aided and abetted by the law and by law enforcement agents. I think the difference is here that we have the violence of the mobs but at least the law enforcement agents are trying to preserve a degree of law and order. In the South we've had a double blow; we've had the mob against us, as well as, in some instances, law enforcement agents actually and literally supporting the mob; in the North it's often the mob and the support on the other hand of the policemen trying to restrain the mob. But I don't say that the hatred is worse. I think it's equal, and I think we've got to see now that the problem is a national problem and that we must

|  | work passionately and unrelentingly to remove these conditions and the kind of hatred that we see, both North and South today. |
|---|---|
| KILPATRICK: | Let me ask you about your march today, Dr. King. You have decided, as I understand it, to obey the injunction that was laid down limiting the number of demonstrators? |
| KING: | Yes. |
| KILPATRICK: | Even though you have described that twice yesterday I believe as an unjust order? |
| KING: | Yes. It's an injunction which I feel is unjust and totally unconstitutional, but because we are engaged in negotiations now with the city, with the real estate agents and with labor and industry and other forces of power and good will in the community we decided that we would abide by this injunction until we have our negotiating session next Friday and determine on the basis of that whether we would continue to comply with what we consider a blatantly unjust, unconstitutional and I might say, immoral injunction. |
| EVANS: | Mr. Young, you had to contend with a new sort of militancy at your national convention in Philadelphia. What exactly did the younger Urban Leaguers want that is new? And let me ask you also, did they feel that the Urban League has become too identified today with the middle class? |
| YOUNG: | No, I think that that reflected more an impatience with the pace. Urban League staff people are probably in the best position of any to recognize how slowly the gap is closing, if at all, in economics, in education, in housing, in health and welfare. And I think it recognizes also that we can do all we want to in terms of getting parents motivated into getting their children into school and keeping them there; but unless there are school boards that are so politically structured and politically sensitive enough to provide the resources then our efforts to provide the motivation is of no value. And what they're really saying is we need these other activities: we need the other organizations who are doing the political activity. The Urban Leaguers know that we are not middle class in the sense of our services. Last year, for example, over fifty thousand Negroes were placed through the Urban League, and these were poor people who were placed, unemployed people. |
| EVANS: | But didn't it shock you when at your convention you were picketed by another organization? |

YOUNG:     No. I think, as Mr. Wilkins said, this was the act of an individual and not the act of an organization. Even there the executive committee of the Philadelphia NAACP totally discredited this and disowned it, and the individual himself apologized; he had made a mistake.

EVANS:     But surely Cecil Moore represents the NAACP in Philadelphia, and surely this represented a dissatisfaction with the work that the Urban League is doing in Philadelphia. Is that not a fair statement?

YOUNG:     No, it's not a fair statement. This was a personal thing, and the local board disowned the activity. Cecil Moore himself later apologized. I think what we are witnessing here, and I think it's a healthy thing, is that we do have in the Urban League at the moment of time when there is a great turmoil and when there is a great gulf, that we do have healthy dissent, we do have impatience, we do have people who want to push faster; but I think what we finally ended up with was saying the Urban League cannot do all of these things, that it's good to have other organizations who are suppposed to do some things and that what we need to do is to go back home and do all we can to help the other civil rights groups to do the job they're supposed to do so that the Urban League can do what it's supposed to do and do it better.

VALERIANI:     Dr. King, to follow up Mr. Spivak's question, recent polls suggest that in terms of national reaction, demonstrations are now counter-productive. By continuing them don't you run the risk of doing more harm than good?

KING:     Again I contend that we are not doing more harm than good in demonstrations because I think demonstrations serve the purpose of bringing the issues out in the open. I have never felt that demonstrations could actually solve the problem. They call attention to the problem, they dramatize the existence of social ills that could be very easily ignored if you did not have demonstrations, and I think the initial reaction to demonstrations is always negative. When we had them in the South initially there was a negative outpouring of disagreement. Now that they have started on a massive scale in the North it is only natural that we would have this reaction; but in spite of the reaction the demonstrations in Chicago, for instance, have not only brought the issues out but they have brought us to the conference table. And I don't believe that we would be in Chicago where we are today without demonstrations. And let me say, secondly, that it is very important to see the difference between nonviolent demonstrations and riots. It may be true that in a demonstration people react with violence toward nonviolent demonstrators. But you don't blame the demonstrators. This would be like blaming the robbed man because his possession of money precipitated the evil act of the robber. Ultimately society must condemn the robber and not the robbed. It must protect the robbed, and this is where we are in these demonstrations; and I'm still convinced that there is nothing more powerful to dramatize a social evil than the tramp, tramp of marching feet.

VALERIANI: In regard to your present movement in regard to housing, is it not conceivable to you that a majority of white Americans does not want a Negro for a neighbor, and if that's so as it was demonstrated in a vote in California, should the majority preference be respected?

KING: It's quite true that there are many people who are against open housing and who are against having Negroes as their neighbor. This does not mean that we don't go all out to end housing discrimination. It may be true that in the South many white people do not want Negroes to eat at lunch counters, do not want Negroes to have access to hotels and motels and restaurants. But this did not stop the nation from having its conscience so aroused that it brought into being a civil rights law as a result of our movement to end this. Now I think the same thing must happen in housing. The people have these fears, they have these prejudices and we are only saying that through legislation and a vigorous fair housing bill we will be able to change certain conditions. It doesn't mean that we will change the hearts of people, but we will change the laws and habits of people, and once their habits are changed pretty soon people will adjust to them just as in the South they've adjusted to integrated public accommodations. I think in the North and all over the country people will adjust to living next door to a Negro once they know that it has to be done, once realtors stop all of the block busting and the panic peddling and all of that. When the law makes it clear and it's vigorously enforced we will see that people will not only adjust but they will finally come to the point that even their attitudes are changed.

SPIVAK: Mr. McKissick, you've been quoted as saying, and these are the words: "The civil rights movement in 1966 has reached the moment of truth. And Negro leaders are not telling it to us like it is." Now most of the Negro leaders are here today. Will you tell us how you see the moment of truth that we're not being told?

MCKISSICK: I don't know whether I'm being quoted accurately, but in substance that's what I said, and I'll certainly explain it. First of all, I believe that the moment of truth is here for the simple reason that, one, nonviolence is something of the past. I don't believe nonviolence can be taught the way nonviolence could be taught years ago. At our recent convention in Baltimore the question of self-defense came up and the convention went on record favoring self-defense; not abolishing nonviolence but certainly favoring self-defense. And their attitude was that, one, we are an organization fighting for constitutional rights, and in fighting for constitutional rights one of those rights is the right to defend the home and the person, and no longer could we advocate that a person give up that right to self-defense. I think, too, the climate which prevailed in 1960 or the earlier years has changed, and I think it is difficult now to harness and to have the control over demonstrations at many points for the simple reason that most of the black people in communities do not and will not agree to be nonviolent. They will agree to participate in demonstrations but they will not agree to be hit and to passively stand there and not return blow for blow.

SPIVAK: Mr. McKissick, in your literature as late as 1965 you said nonviolence is effective, it has worked in hundreds of cases. This method attacks the practice of discrimination but respects the person who discriminates. Do you still stand by that or have you changed your definition of nonviolence? Everybody believes in self-defense.

MCKISSICK: Oh, no, let me get one point very clear. If we make a mistake we're going to be the first to say an error has been made. Now we are saying right today we have had CORE rules for action for a number of years at which we advocated a policy of nonviolence, and we still advocate nonviolence in a demonstration. We say that we can march down the street, if nobody hits us, okay, you've got nonviolence. But if somebody hits us well then you better have an ambulance on the side to pick up whoever hits somebody.

| | |
|---|---|
| SPIVAK: | Am I to understand then that you and Dr. Martin Luther King really are not in disagreement on the principle and philosophy of nonviolence? |
| MCKISSICK: | Well, first of all I'd like to answer by saying this, despite the fact that, as already has been said, that Dr. King believes in one thing and Mr. Wilkins believes in another and Stokely Carmichael believes in another— |
| SPIVAK: | I'm just talking about nonviolence. |
| MCKISSICK: | The fact of the injustices are so heaped and they weave us so closely together that I dare say that we would ever divorce ourselves from each other regardless to any point which we come. |
| SPIVAK: | You haven't answered my question on nonviolence. Are you in agreement or in disagreement with Dr. King on the matter of nonviolence? |
| MCKISSICK: | Well, my answer cannot be a positive yes and no answer. The Congress of Racial Equality adopts its position for the Southern Christian Leadership Conference. As far as we're concerned, as I said before, we believe in nonviolence, providing nobody hits us; when somebody hits us we believe in self-defense. |
| SPIVAK: | There's a difference between self-defense and nonviolence. |
| MCKISSICK: | Well, self-defense and nonviolence are not incompatible. |
| ROWAN: | Dr. King, you've heard what Mr. McKissick said. Are you in disagreement or not? |
| KING: | I believe firmly in nonviolence. I still believe that it is the most potent weapon available to oppressed people in their struggle for freedom and human dignity. I think a turn to violence on the part of the Negro at this time would be both impractical and immoral. Now if Mr. McKissick believes in that I certainly agree with him. |

Now on the question of defensive violence, I have made it clear that I don't think we need programmatic action around defensive violence. People are going to defend themselves anyway. I think that the minute you have programmatic action around defensive violence and pronouncements about it the line of demarcation between defense violence and aggressive violence becomes very thin. The minute the nomenclature of violence gets in the atmosphere people begin to respond violently, and in their unsophisticated minds they cannot quite make the distinction between defensive and aggressive violence.

I think that we must still stand on the premise of non-violence and I choose to do that not only because I think it is morally right, but I think it is practically sound.

NEWMAN: Mr. Kilpatrick.

KILPATRICK: Mr. Carmichael, in a recent speech in Cleveland you reportedly ridiculed as Uncle Toms those Negro spokesmen who counsel nonviolence and patience in the civil rights struggle. Did you mean thus to label such spokesmen as Kr. King and Mr. Wilkins?

CARMICHAEL: Let me first say that the Student Nonviolent Coordinating Committee will never publicly denounce any black leader in this country so that I couldn't have possibly said that.

KILPATRICK: The quote was simply a false quote. You didn't say anything of that sort?

CARMICHAEL: No, I never critically criticized any black leader in this country.

KILPATRICK: In the same story you were quoted by the United Press International as saying that, "When you talk of 'Black Power' you talk of bringing this country to its knees." You weren't correctly quoted on that?

CARMICHAEL: The rest of it was not there. The other half of it said that when you talk about Black Power you talk about bringing this country to its knees any time it messes with the black man.

KILPATRICK: "Any time it messes with the black man." By that you mean violence against the Negro?

CARMICHAEL: By that I mean messes with the black man.

KILPATRICK: You just stop it right there.

EVANS: Dr. King, a couple of political questions. You said recently that the "extravagant promises made a year ago in connection with the voting rights bills have now become a shattered mockery." What exactly did you mean by that, Dr. King?

KING: Well, I mean that this voting rights bill came into being to end not only discrimination in its overt expressions, and voter registration, but also to remove the atmosphere what intimidation for economic reprisals and for the creation of fear that cause people not to vote, and one of the things we have found is that when you have federal registrars in communities, many more Negroes go out to register because they see a different atmosphere, and they are not over-arched, under-girded with the fear of intimidation and economic reprisals as much as they do in dealing with some of the local registrars that they have dealt with so long.

Now, the problem is that after that bill came into being very few registrars were sent into the South, I mean federal registrars, and even today all too few have been sent, and this is even true in some communities where we know that there are outright patterns of discrimination.

EVANS: That's what I wanted to get to next, Dr. King. Who do you blame for the failure of, as you call it, enough federal registrars to have been sent South, is that President Johnson's responsibility, is it the Department of Justice? Where do you lay the blame?

KING: Well, I think it is both, and I think it is ultimately the responsibility of the president through the attorney general, and I would say that it is not either or, it is a both and give, the president and the attorney general have the responsibility to implement and to enforce it. I know that the ultimate enforcement of the law is with the president, but certainly he follows the advice of the attorney general so I said both ends.

EVANS: Dr. King, why do you think the president has not moved as forcefully on voting in the South as you think he should have, what reason do you give to his not having sent more registrars into the South?

KING: Well, there are probably many reasons and I must confess that I don't know all of the reasons. I think on the one hand some are sincere feelings that if you can get volun—I mean if you can move into certain areas forcefully with federal registrars that other areas will follow through inevitably in the realm of voluntary compliance.

I believe that that is a sincere analysis, although I think it is a wrong analysis of the situation. I think on the other hand there are certain political forces that have sought desperately to keep the administration from sending federal registrars in their areas. For instance, in southwest Georgia we need federal registrars right now, and I am convinced that the political leaders of Georgia in the Senate have used pressure to keep the federal government from sending federal registrars into Georgia.

VALERIANI: Mr. Meredith, looking back what do you feel your march on Mississippi accomplished?

MEREDITH: Well, if you recall I didn't march through Mississippi. I was shot the first day, and, of course, all of these other gentlemen carried on the march in Mississippi. I only returned for the last two days.

Now, I think that probably the biggest accomplishment was to place in focus the problems in this country, and as again I say the question is whether or not white supremacy and the rest of the theory of white superiority is going to be the rule in this country or if we are in fact going to follow the rule of equality and equal justice before the law as our ideals say.

VALERIANI: How is the philosophy of white supremacy going to be changed in your opinion?

MEREDITH: Well, it can only be changed by two ways and one more important than the other, that is, the white in this country decides that, and I think he must make this decision for his own survival, that this country will be one of equality and equal justice before the law, and, of course, the Negro must develop himself, make himself whole so that he can assert his twenty-five-million-manpower strength toward making sure that this nation becomes what it should be.

NEWMAN: Gentlemen, I must interrupt briefly here. Our thanks for being with us to Dr. King who is leaving us now.

Excerpts courtesy of National Broadcasting Co., Inc. Copyright © 1986 National Broadcasting Co., Inc. All rights reserved. This excerpt first appeared in *Congressional Record* 112 (29 August 1966): 21095–102. *See also* August Meier, "The Conservative Militant," in C. Eric Lincoln, ed., *Martin Luther King, Jr.: A Profile* (New York: Hill and Wang, 1970), 144–56; and Martin Luther King, Jr., *Where Do We Go From Here: Chaos or Community?* (New York: Harper & Row, 1967), 124.

# 52

# "Face to Face"
# Television News Interview

*The International Platform Association sponsored this interview with Mayor Ivan Allen of Atlanta; Dick Gregory, the famous black comedian and civil rights activist; Dr. King; and Roy Wilkins of the NAACP, in Washington, D.C., on 28 July 1967. President Lyndon Baines Johnson had made a nationally televised announcement of his appointments to the Special Advisory Committee on Civil Disorders on 27 July. Johnson appointed Governor Otto Kerner of Illinois as its chairman, and Mayor John Lindsay of New York as its vice-chairman. President Johnson charged this Kerner Commission with the responsibility of investigating the tidal wave of racial disorders that disrupted cities during the summer of 1967, such as Atlanta, Chicago, New York, New Haven, Tampa, Winston-Salem, Cleveland, Cincinnati, Toledo, Newark, Boston, Plainsfield, Cairo, Minneapolis, Buffalo, East St. Louis, and Detroit. The commission issued its report in February 1968, and concluded that the United States was "moving toward two separate societies, one black, one white—separate and unequal." It contended that racial and economic injustice were the chief causes of the riots. Dr. King was deeply grieved by the eruption of the racial violence, but he had been warning for years that the "triple ghetto of race, poverty, and human misery" in U.S. cities was certain to produce a huge conflagration. It came in the summer of 1967. This interview was an attempt to assess the damage in the midst of the fire, for the disorders continued throughout most of the month of August.*

Mr. Byrd of West Virginia. Mr. President, the International Platform Association recently held its sixty-fifth annual convention at the Sheraton Park Hotel here in Washington, D.C. At that convention there was a discussion between Dr. Martin Luther King, Mayor Ivan Allen, Mr. Roy Wilkins, and Mr. Dick Gregory on the subject of race riots. The discussion was moderated by Mr. Mark Evans, and Mr. Drew Pearson was a special guest. The discussion took place on WTTG 5, Metromedia Television.

I ask unanimous consent that the transcript of the entire discussion be inserted in the Record.

There being no objection, the transcript was ordered to be printed in the Record, as follows:

(A discussion between Dr. Martin Luther King, Mayor Ivan Allen, Mr. Roy Wilkins, Mr. Dick Gregory; moderated by Mark Evans; special guest, Mr. Drew Pearson)

KING:      I am Martin Luther King, president of the Southern Christian Leadership Conference.

ALLEN:      I am Ivan Allen, Jr., mayor of the city of Atlanta, Georgia.

WILKINS:      My name is Roy Wilkins, and I'm executive director of the National Association for the Advancement of Colored People.

GREGORY:      I am Dick Gregory, and I feel that I'm a passive revolutionist.

EVANS:      My name is Mark Evans. The gentlemen you have just met, and you, are about to meet face to face.

Welcome to a special edition of "Face to Face." The long, hot summer has been marked by race riots of such violence and unprecedented number tha every citizen among us must consider the cause and the cure his personal concern. Thanks to the cooperation of the International Platform Association, meeting here in convention in the Sheraton Park Hotel in Washington, D.C. "Face to Face" is bringing you an exploration of this explosive problem.

Drew Pearson, nationally syndicated columnist, is responsible for bringing to this platform the distinguished men you've just met. Now, let's meet Drew Pearson.

Drew, would you give us a little bit of the background of the association? First, I understand you've been its president, you are now its program chairman. Just a word about its history and its purpose.

PEARSON:      Well, the International Platform Association was founded approximately seventy-five years ago by my father, William Jennings Bryan, and other speakers of that era.

EVANS:      I thought you said your father was William Jennings Bryan there for a few moments.

PEARSON:      No, they were friends.

EVANS:      Oh, I see.

PEARSON:      This was in a day before the microphone, before television, when platform was the symbol of free discussion, and the members—it was a trade association, still is to some extent. The members believe in free discussion. They used the platform for speaking, for music, entertainment, and this is still the case, and we believe in discussion of all kinds.

EVANS:    The audience here primarily is made up of professional lecturers, amateur lecturers, and those who appear on platforms all over the nation.

PEARSON:    For the most part.

EVANS:    Thank you very much, Mr. Drew Pearson.

We're going to have some discussion now between some of these members of the panel, and each will make a brief summation of that which they have said in a short talk prior to our having gone on the air, and we'll have that right after I share this message with you.

EVANS:    At a most appropriate time this distinguished panel are appearing before a large gathering here at the Sheraton Park Hotel in Washington. All America, and all the world, is concerned about the riots that have taken place in our cities. As has been stated previously, these gentlemen have made some brief talks prior to our having gone on the air, and we're going to ask them in summation to point out the major points they wish to emphasize, and I'll turn first to Dr. King.

KING:    The problems of our cities today are very great, and the problems of Negroes living in these cities are equally great and extensive. Some ninety-two percent of the Negroes of the United States find themselves living in cities, and they find themselves living in a triple ghetto in these cities on the whole: a ghetto of race, a ghetto of poverty, and a ghetto of human misery, and by the thousands and even millions Negroes find themselves unemployed and underemployed. The young people find themselves attending segregated schools that are so often devoid of quality and thousands and thousands of Negroes in these cities are forced to live in rat-infested, vermin-filled slums. All of these conditions have made for great despair and so many of the people who find themselves caught up in the agony of their daily lives end up with the view that life is a long and desolate corridor with no exit sign, and these are the people who in moments of desperation find themselves engaging in riots that we have seen taking place in our country, and even though most of the people who are in these hopeless situations do not riot, it is now necessary for all to see that a destructive minority can poison the wellsprings from which the majority must drink, and so it is necessary for the nation as a whole to rise up now and find answers to the deep social problem. They must be answers that are real and honest, and they must be answers that will lead to positive and massive action programs, programs that will spend the necessary money, the billions of dollars to get rid of the blight of our cities, to get rid of the slums, to eradicate the poverty, to make integrated quality education a reality, and I believe that with this kind of commitment we can solve the problem. There can be no gainsaying of the fact that we're in a moment of crisis, but every crisis has not only its danger points, but it has its opportunities and it is my great hope that America at this hour will see the opportunities and meet them head on and stand up and make the American dream a reality.

EVANS: Thank you, Dr. King. Now, Mayor Ivan Allen of Atlanta, Georgia.

ALLEN: I support the position of the president of the United States, as stated last evening, that in a democratic society law and order must be maintained at all costs. Locally, I will attempt to do this through the protective forces of the city of Atlanta. Lacking the capabilities I'll have no hesitation to call for the national guard or in a rare instance to ask for—if necessary for federal troops and intervention.

I will not, however, hide behind just a facade of law and order. We must recognize that the deep problems that have created these unlawful acts must be solved. I would propose that in order to solve them that we mount a massive attack on the slums of America, that we provide the necessary funds over a three- to five-year period to build the necessary number of low-income housing units that would eliminate the slums. I would qualify that by saying that incorporated in the program we should provide for hiring people that are now unemployed in the slums in this building program. The units should be widely dispersed and we should provide a decent place for people in this country to live on a minimum standard that would make it possible to qualify them for good jobs and to receive the opportunities of education.

EVANS: Thank you very much. Now Mr. Roy Wilkins.

WILKINS: The primary necessity, as I see it, is for us to resurrect a phrase from the report on the Watts riots of 1965, a phrase that unfortunately has been ignored. The commission there recommended that the problems be attacked with a revolutionary attitude. That meant, if I understand the language, that our approach to the problems of the slums and of the minorities must not be business as usual, must not be routine, must not be bound by tradition, must take into account the cost only in the light of the results to be obtained. If we can spend twenty billion dollars for war, if we can revive a whole continent of Europe, underwrite the economies of Germany, France, Italy, England, and see that these people recover their equilibrium, then we can underwrite the cost of recovering the equilibrium of our own native black people now.

[Applause.]

This is not easy, and it will not yield to impatience or tantrums or foot stamping or accusations, but it must yield to a revolutionary attitude in schools, in housing, as Mayor Allen has suggested, and in employment. We have got to recognize that we have twenty million black deprived people here, we have several more millions of white deprived people, poor people, and if the richest nation in the history of the world cannot solve the problem of living for its own people, then we deserve to go down the drain. We won't, of course, because we will solve it.

EVANS: Thank you, Dr. Wilkins. Now Dick Gregory, please.

[Applause.]

GREGORY: I'm going to have to talk very fast because I have to fly out of here shortly to Kansas City, Missouri, to help out a friend of mine, a white cat that just moved into an all colored neighborhood.

[General laughter.]

And some colored bigot burned a watermelon on his front lawn.

[General laughter.]

You know, when you look at the amount of humor some times this gets very frightening. When you stop and think that I said it and Congress did not pass an anti-rat bill, but they passed an anti-riot bill, which means that our Senate and Congress might be more anti-Negro than anti-rat. I'm sitting here with some gentlemen that I've met in very strange position, Mr. Drew Pearson, who helped me feed people in Mississippi with $150,000 worth of turkeys on Christmas, and I would say—and I say this with qualified authority because I've spent over three hundred thousand dollars doing research of this problem, and I would say that offset violence in this country six months. Dr. Martin Luther King and I met in jail under strange circumstances. It's funny the night we got arrested on Good Friday morning and when I checked the cell block Easter Sunday, he was gone.

[General laughter. Applause.]

I had the good fortune of being in Mayor Allen's jails in Atlanta, and I say this in all sincerity, that I'm very thrilled when I heard that they picked brother Jenkins to serve on the board with you because out of all the jails I've been in, this was the only jail, through his police commissioner there, that you didn't feel like fighting when you come out, and I'm glad that he's on the board.

[Applause.]

Mr. Wilkins here, we met. We was trying to feed some people in Mississippi, and in one day's time, my introduction to him, is he helped me sell sixteen thousand dollars worth of records in one day's time, and I am very nervous sitting here for the first time in my life because you are sitting here looking at two men that are the most powerful people in this country today, because what they will come up on this commission will decide if America will survive or not, and this is how important this is. Our faith and destiny of this country surviving lies in these two gentlemen's hands. This is how important this commission is, and if they do not do the job, this country is in trouble. I listened to the president's speech last night. I felt that we should have had a Negro cochairman because I know what's going on out there, and I know what—how that ghetto brother feels. We have Roy Wilkins sitting here who has one of the most brilliant minds, one of most ethical, moral men in the world. Mayor Allen, to me, is not a politician. He is a statesman. I feel we should have had—

[Applause.]

I feel we should have had a militant Negro on there, whether you like it or not, because we're fighting for survival now. I also feel that we have too many politicians on there, that we're in a time of crisis—and I don't say this to belittle—and we need more statesmen. Statesmen flex their minds, and polticians flex their muscles, and I feel that we should have had more psychiatrists, more philosophers, more sociologists because we are in trouble in this country. Believe me.

[Applause.]

And in summing up what I want to say, that the first thing this commission should do—the first thing—is to get a national document, signed by the president, to apologize for the South, that we in this country blame the South for this filthy race problem for one hundred years, and now the whole world knows it was America's problem, and as the South was blamed wrongly they reacted by lynchings and bombing. The Negro have been blamed wrongly. We've been blamed for all of the ignorance, all of the wrong doings, and we're acting just like the southerner. We're tearing up buildings and doing everything. Follow the parallel please. The South needs to be apologized to because this is a national problem, and I hope you will see to it that they will do that. If we treat this problem the way we treat a slum building that burns down—when the fire commissioner shows up, the first thing he says, "We're going to check into it and see what caused it." If we check into these explosions and see what caused them instead of talking about looters and hoodlums, check and find out what caused it, because you're aware of a theory called spontaneous combustion. When you put dirty, oily, greasy rags in a closet, you close the door so air can't circulate, nature's going to take care of the rest. You can call those rags ignorant. You can call them nigger, you can call them fool. If you don't have enough wisdom to open up that door, it's spontaneous combustion. The black ghettos in America today is America's oily, dirty, greasy rags, and—

EVANS: I think we'll have to call a halt there. Thanks very much, Dick Gregory.

[Applause.]

We'll have plenty of opportunity as the program progresses. We hope that the audience will participate later in this program as we're going to ask them to do, and we hope that they will be abrasive with their questions because I think that's the best way to get information from these talented people.

From the convention of the International Platform Association, met in convention here in Washington, D.C., at the Sheraton Park Hotel, we have a distinguished panel from whom you've already heard in their summation statements. I'd like very much to throw this question out for you. I find that you agree more than you disagree, and I would like to ask this question, inasmuch as you have placed much of the blame on poverty in the nation, and I'd like to quote a man—I haven't got permission from the copyright owners, but he's within my arm's length here, and I'm going to ask a question which he proposed in a column recently, where he said, "No one thought it could have happened in America because we are directing our thoughts to what caused the race riots, but it did happen in a city completely integrated, in a city where Negroes had lucrative jobs in the auto plants, the only city in the United States sending two Negroes to Congress; in Detroit Negroes and whites for many years have lived side by side.

Most of then owned their own homes. Walter Reuther years ago had welcomed Negroes into the United Auto Workers, making it one of the most completely integrated unions in the nation. The state of Michigan has probably—is the leader in the civil rights movement as far as legislation is concerned." So the question now comes up, why the riots? Here it seems a city has taken the lead in the model city situation, poverty programs, name it. Would you care to answer that, any one of you?

GREGORY: I think riots are—again we just can't say why in one city. I think Abraham Lincoln told us in 1857, when he made a speech and said, when you have succeeded in dehumanizing the Negro, when you have put him down and placed him where the ray of hope is blown out as in the darkness of the damned, when you have extinguished his soul in this world and placed him where the ray of hope is blown out, are you quite sure the demon you have aroused will not turn and rend you? We was warned in 12—

EVANS: Well, my question is: the arguments that you have used as a reason for the race riots seemingly were on their way to being taken care of or had been taken care of in Detroit, and yet this has been probably the worst example of a riot in our American history.

GREGORY: Well, when we say—

EVANS: Dr. King?

KING: Well, I was about to say I would question whether the problem has been taken care of in Detroit in a thorough, massive sense. Now certainly, Detroit has made some significant progress, and I would be the first to say that some of the conditions that I've seen in some other cities are not as great or in as intensified form as in Detroit, but I think we would have to admit that Detroit has the same problems that we find in other cities; in other words, there is still a great gulf between Negro income and white income. That's true in Detroit; it's true in all of our major cities. The unemployment rate, as I said, is twice as high. Now, that's true in Detroit; I didn't know the figures on it, but it's about the same as we find across the nation. Negroes are twice—there are more Negroes unemployed than whites. Now these conditions—even though the gulf may not be as wide in Detroit as in some other cities, the gulf is there.

EVANS: Why should the violence be so much greater than in a city that's made more progress than any other?

KING: Well, this is always one of the facts of history that we must face. Progress whets the appetite for greater progress, and the nearer you get to the goal, often, the more determined you are to get there. And I think we must recognize this as a sociological fact; that often progress itself whets the appetite for greater progress, and if it isn't fast enough, then the despair sets in and this can lead to the kind of violence that we've seen there.

EVANS: May I ask this question: anybody else want to handle that? Dr. Wilkins?

WILKINS: I think that's what this commission was appointed to find out—why it happened in Detroit, and I'd rather display my ignorance before a smaller audience than a large one.
    [Laughter—applause.]

EVANS: Because this year has been such a dramatic year, and because it was predicted to be such a dramatic year, is there, in your opinion, any outside influence that has whetted this?

WILKINS: I think on that question, I, for one, will have to accept the judgment of the attorney general of the United States. He has more investigators than I have, and he has a bigger payroll than I have, and he has access to more information than I have. And he says there is no evidence of a conspiracy, so that it seems to me we have to proceed on the assumption that the causes lie within the cities themselves, and that nobody from outside came in, nobody underwrote it, nobody conspired to do it. Now, if the attorney general isn't telling us the truth, then we'll find that out sooner or later and then we can decide what to do about the attorney general.

EVANS: Mayor Allen?

ALLEN: I do not think that these are outside forces, except within the United States itself; I do not think that they're communistic inspired, or that there's a plot on the part of Russia to create a revolution in this country. I don't think so at all. From the limited experience that I have seen of minor incidents in the city of Atlanta, they usually come about from some act of provocation when there's a difference of opinion between someone who's probably had a little too much to drink and a police officer who may not handle the thing judiciously all the way through, and then with a few of the normal agitators that have come out of SNCC, they can build these things up into a fire, and this apparently got started in Detroit. Perhaps certain forces did not move rapidly enough; perhaps it was not met strongly enough, but by the time it builds up and gets going, why then it takes massive forces. I do not feel that these are outside

influences that have come into America to create these
situations.

EVANS:        Do you find any significance in the fact that one of the
most militant has now shown up at Castro's right elbow?
Or maybe I should say his left elbow?
[General laughter.]

ALLEN:        Well, he's now gone to Cuba; that's all right.

GREGORY:      Well, I think that there is an outside influence, and I think
in America we'd better see it, and that outside influence is
the Declaration of Independence, which says: "We hold
these truths to be self-evident; that all men are created
equal, and endowed by the Creator with certain inalienable rights" and when these rights are destroyed over long
periods of time it is your duty to destroy or abolish that
government, and if people follow that to the letter, then
that could be the influence.

EVANS:        Are you satisfied with this question? Do you have any comment on Mr. Carmichael's action, in connection with the
previous question?
Dr. Wilkins—Mr. Wilkins?

WILKINS:      No.

EVANS:        Mr. King?

KING:         No.

EVANS:        May I ask this further question? It's interesting to me, and
Dick Gregory may have answered it; it's interesting to me
that the violence in the North has been far in excess to the
violence in the South, and yet we have always been told
that the southerner has been the most antipathetic towards the Negro. To what do you attribute this? Mayor
Allen?

ALLEN:        I think that, basically, there are two causes for that. Perhaps one is that there's more of an inhibitory respect or
force of the police department in the South, that this is
still an inherited quality that's come down through the
years, and the second thing is that probably the most dissatisfied and the most misused citizens, or half-citizens of
the rural areas have moved into the East, and this has been
more of a transient population, the South has had Negro
citizens for years, many of whom have acquired good
homes and own them themselves. Atlanta has a major Negro business community; we have a certain stability that
perhaps does not exist in the East in these ghettos that
have developed over the past twenty years.

EVANS:        Any further comments? Dr. King?

KING:         Yes, I think there is another important point to be added to that, and that is in the realm of explaining the legislative and judicial advances that we've seen over the last few years, from the Supreme Court's decision of '54 right on through the civil rights bill of '64 and the voting rights bill. Now these legislative and judicial developments gave a great deal of hope to the Negro, and it is very important to see that they rectified long-standing evils of the South but they did very little to improve conditions for the millions of Negroes in the teeming ghettos of the North. In other words, it did very little to penetrate the lower depths of Negro deprivation, and I think that we must see that the North finds itself in that position now, of seeing retrogress and not progress. At least in the South, the Negro can see pockets of progress, but this isn't true of the Negro in the northern ghetto. He sees retrogress in the sense that the masses of Negroes find themselves in a worse economic situation now, and the progress that we've made economically has been mainly on the professional level, middle-class Negroes, so I think we have to see that these things did not apply in the northern ghetto, and this makes for a great deal of despair.

EVANS:      Mr. Wilkins? You have something to add?

WILKINS:    I think the reason we've had—one of the reasons that's not frequently cited, and perhaps I'll get in trouble by citing this, because it goes to a very touchy subject that arose last year—in the South we still have a great deal of Negro family stability and control, and community control of families, and the imposition of standards of conduct. In the North, with its great anonymous cities, Negro families come there, sometimes they're disintegrated—but even where they're not, they are lost in a huge population, the minister doesn't keep tabs on them like the minister did in the small town back home; they don't know the police chief, and they don't care, and they don't know the judge and they don't know the things and the controls that operated in their home community. And when they come to Harlem, they're just "John Smith," and they can do as they please. They don't have to pay any attention to Mom and Pop, and the minister and the neighbor, or anybody who knows about them and helps to control them. So they run wild, some of them; others busy themselves going to night school and doing all the things that other people do. I think this is one of the reasons we haven't had as much— whatever trouble we've had in the South has been in the struggle to get the rights; in the North, it's been the struggle to—to make the North give us what they say we're supposed to have, you see.

[General applause.]

EVANS: Dick Gregory would like to add a comment, but Dick, before you—you understand this language better than the rest of them.

Ladies and gentlemen, we're now going to turn to the audience. We're not on the air right now, but may I urge you to be orderly as you come forward, and we will designate either side to ask questions. However, Mr. Gregory has one final comment on the previous question.

Again, if you have compliments you want to pay by way of applause, don't hesitate and don't be afraid to make your questions as abrasive as you want, because I think that's the way we make for more enlightenment.

All right, we're ready. Name, the state from which you come, and again, we urge you, no speeches, just questions. And short questions. And if you'll listen carefully to the previous question, we won't have any repetitions. Thank you.

If "Face to Face," the program to which you are now listening and viewing has one purpose, it is to stimulate your thought, to excite your curiosity. This distinguished panel meeting here before the International Platform Association at the Sheraton Park in Washington, are about now to ask questions of our panel. However, in courtesy to Mr. Gregory, he had a final comment on the last question.

GREGORY: Yes, I think the last question will be the most important question the commission will deal with. With all of the southern white man's viciousness, he was always honest with the Negro, which has affected me physically in the knowledge he was never honest with me, which affected me mentally. And a man that has been affected mentally will tear up a town, that is the answer.

EVANS: Fine. Thanks very much.

Now, to our audience. We turn to the gentleman on my left, please. Your name and the state from which you come, sir?

ALLEN: I'm Henry G. Allen from the State of Mississippi, by way of Louisiana, and I hope I'm potato patch kin to the mayor up there. He sounded good. My question is to Mr. Wilkins. He's been an honest man through Louisiana, and got LSU integrated. And he came to Jackson last year, and they wouldn't let him march because he rode in a car, that's what Jackson Davis said, and he said we were here before the parade and we'll be here after.

EVANS: We remind you, no speeches sir, just the question.

ALLEN: Yes, the question is, have you got back to Mississippi yet? You were doing a good job.

WILKINS: Yes, sir, I've been back to Mississippi and I'm going back there very shortly.

EVANS: Thank you, very much. Now to the right, the lady?

AULICH: Joan Aulich, from New York state. And my question is directed to Mr. Wilkins. Earlier you said that Negro children require special teachers. What kind of teachers do you think can effectively teach them, maintain order in the classroom, and where do you get those teachers?

EVANS: Are you a teacher?

AULICH: I have done some teaching, yes.

EVANS: I suspected as much. Thank you.

WILKINS: In Harlem we have a school which is rather an exhibit school. It wasn't designed that way. These teachers have a simple requirement, and that is to believe that the children they are teaching are educable. We find throughout the United States, and this is not confined to Harlem, that so many teachers do not believe their Negro children can learn, so they give up trying to teach them. They also ought to learn that they can't teach them out of *Time* and the *Saturday Review of Literature* which they never heard of, and which they can't subscribe to in their homes. They have to explore ways of reaching them, arousing their interests. And I'm not a teacher and I'm not an educator or professional. We need to explore new methods with a revolutionary attitude. Get rid of all the old cobwebs.

EVANS: Thank you, very much. The gentleman on my left?
[Applause.]

MANUS: My name is Arthur Tate Manus, and I am the senior minister of the First Community Church, Columbus, Ohio. My question is to Dr. Martin Luther King. We are churchmen and concerned with the institution especially, and so I ask the question, what are the few important steps that the church should be taking now to prevent racial conflict?

KING: Well, I think there are two or three things that the church should be doing. First, we must recognize all over that this issue that we are dealing with is basically a moral issue. It's a question of the dignity of man and the church being the chief moral guardian of the community should be in the forefront, taking a stand.

Number one, the church should make it crystal clear

that segregation and discrimination are morally wrong. Secondly, the church through its channels of religious education can do a great deal to remove the fears and the half-truths that are disseminated concerning Negroes. The fact is that a lot of people are prejudiced because of these basic fears and because they've heard so many half-truths and outright lies concerning Negroes. And I think the church has failed to do a job through its channels of religious education in getting rid or seeking to get rid, of these fears that people have about housing and all of the other things. The third thing is the church must support meaningful legislation. Just as we got a number of churchmen to support the civil rights bill in '64, we must continue to do that. There's a civil rights bill before Congress right now, and we're all afraid that it won't get through. Churchmen ought to be here in Washington, lobbying creatively for that kind of thing.

And the tragedy is that the church has too often been a taillight rather than a headlight, and it's time for the church to be a headlight on all these problems that we face.

EVANS: Thank you, very much. The gentleman on my right.

[Applause.]

You, sir, are who?

MCCRAY: I'm Vance McCray, from Mesa, Arizona. I have one son back from Vietnam and another son in the army, and we have more sons to send over, and I want to ask Dr. King, he says that Negroes in Vietnam who are fighting and who are being killed are double that of the white man. I want to ask him, is that not true because the Negro reenlists. Neither one of my boys would care to reenlist, but I understand that the Negroes do, and I believe that's because they like it better there than they do at home.

EVANS: Thank you. Dr. King?

KING: Well, let me answer that by saying I don't think Negro soldiers like it being in Vietnam better than they like being at home, if home is all right. Now, I would say that you are right in saying we have reenlistments, and this probably doubles the number, but the fact is the Negroes are in combat in disproportionate numbers because they don't have the adequate education so often. In many instances they reenlist because of a lack of economic opportunities at home, because of the life they have to live as a result of not having a job or nice home. So Negroes do end up going in the army so often to get away from the terrible conditions that they face at home.

EVANS:    All right.

KING:    And it seems to me that this is the tragedy of it, and it's a great tragedy that Negroes have to go in the army because they face these terrible conditions at home. And this is why I take a stand against the conditions at home and against the war situation which they are forced to get is as a result of that.

EVANS:    Do we have some other questions for Mayor Allen or Dick Gregory so we can spread it out?

Would you step up a little closer then? Young lady, you go first.

VOICE:    I'm addressing my question to Dr. King. I'd like to ask him why he is spending more time today speaking out against the war in Vietnam than raising funds for job training and scholarships for Negroes which they so desperately need?

[Applause.]

KING:    Well, I think you have one or two misconceptions. I don't spend that much of my time on the peace question or on Vietnam. Because ninety-five percent of my time is still spent in the civil rights struggle. So that on the time question you have a misconception there.

On the other hand, I'm a clergyman. I was a clergyman before I was a civil rights leader, and when I was ordained to the Christian ministry, I accepted that as a commission to constantly and forever bring the ethical insights of our Judeo-Christian heritage to bear on the social evils of our day. And I happen to think war is one of the major evils facing mankind.

Secondly—

[Applause.]

Secondly, it would be foolhardy for me to work for integrated schools or integrated lunch counters and not be concerned about the survival of the world in which to be integrated.

Third, I have worked too long—

[Applause.]

Third, I have worked too long now, and too hard to get rid of segregation in public accommodations to turn back to the point of segregating my moral concern. Justice is indivisible. Injustice anywhere is a threat to justice everywhere. And wherever I see injustice, I'm going to take a stand against it whether it's in Mississippi or whether it's in Vietnam.

EVANS:    Thank you, very much.

[Applause.]

We have other distinguished people who would like to ask questions and there's another party from whom we'd like to hear and he also has priority.

We continue now, as the ladies and gentlemen of the International Platform Association gathered here in convention at the Sheraton Park Hotel in Washington are meeting face to face men who have answers, and they have questions.

POLK: My name is Roy E. Polk, Jr., from Nashville, Tennessee. I would like to ask a question of Dr. King, who has proposed a guaranteed annual wage. I would like to know what yardstick Dr. King would propose for this guaranteed wage, and to ask if that will not tend to deprive the recipients of the human dignity that he seeks to give them?

EVANS: Thank you, very much, Dr. King?

[Applause.]

KING: Let me say this: that I'm not guaranteeing—I mean calling for a guaranteed annual wage as a substitute for a guaranteed job. I think that ought to be the first thing, that we guarantee every person capable of working a job. And this can be done in many, many ways. There are many things that we need to be done that could be done that's not being done now. And this could provide the jobs.

I'm speaking of a guaranteed annual wage as a minimum income for every American family, so that there is an economic floor, and nobody falls beneath that. And of course, there are definitely going to be people all along, people who are unemployable, as a result of age, as a result of lack of something that failed to develop here or there, and as a result of physical disability. Now these are the people who just couldn't work. Certainly they have a right to have an income. If one has a right to life, liberty and the pursuit of happiness, then he has a right to have an income.

Now, this may mean a radical, in a sense, redefinition of work. Maybe we've got to come to see that a mother who's at home as a housekeeper or as a housewife is working. Maybe we've got to see now that the fellow who drops out of school and later needs to go back to school is working when he's studying and he couldn't get back to school, maybe, if he didn't get some money. So maybe we need to redefine work.

EVANS: I think his question, Dr. King, was will this rob him of his dignity, which you made reference to earlier.

KING: Yes, all right; that's the thing. I think it will give him more dignity and I think the problem, I think the question you're asking is whether I'm advocating that you just give people money and not seek to have a situation develop where everybody can work if they're capable of working.

I feel first that we ought to talk about guaranteed jobs; then guaranteed annual income would be the minimum wage, which ought to be beyond the poverty level, that everybody would get in this country.

EVANS: Thank you, very much. The lady here now, a very lovely lady in the front row.

PANCOES: I'm Wilma Pancoes, from Maryland. My question is addressed to Mayor Allen. Do we have the administrative structure, the business planning and structure to enable us to undertake and to carry out the massive house building program which you propose in from three to five years? Have we got the economic know-how and speed to do it, and to use the untrained, unskilled workers which it's been proposed should be hired for that purpose?

ALLEN: Obviously, an economy that can supply a war effort like we did in World War II, and has the vigor of the American economy today, certainly has the capabilities in a three- or five-year period of time to build the necessary number of low-income housing units in this country that would eliminate the slums. The problem of using the unskilled worker out of the slums is a more difficult one, but I personally feel that with a minimum of job training this could be accomplished and they could be taken off of the unemployment rolls and put into gainful employment. Yes, ma'am, we do have the capabilities and at the present time we have the timing to do it. It's merely a matter of the appropriation of dollars.

EVANS: Thank you, Mayor. Now the gentleman on my right.

SHRIVER: I am Dr. Ed Shriver from Alexandria, Virginia. I have a question about revolution. We know the old forms of revolution, of violence. That's the oldest one. The mayor of Atlanta has described a modified revolutionary form of unprecedented massive effort on housing. I'm curious about anyone on the panel saying what they might about what are the new forms of revolution.

EVANS: Alright, Dick, you handle that.

GREGORY: I think revolution follows the form of evolution, which is a naturalistic, gradualistic change that after long periods of time leads into revolution, which is quick change. When a pregnant woman goes through nine months gestation period, that's evolution; and when the water bag breaks, that's revolution, and all the soldiers on the face of this earth couldn't cross one woman's legs after that water bag breaks and keep the baby in, and I think we have moved this country's personal shame from evolution to revolution, and this again is why I say this commission is so important, and our faith and destiny depends on these gentlemen.

EVANS: Any other comments from the panel? Alright, the lady on my left.

BAILEY: I am Mrs. George R. Bailey, Jr., from Roxbury, Massachusetts, president of the Roxbury-Dorchester Community Beautification Program. I would like to direct my question to Mayor Allen. What can be done about planning massive type programs? We are now working on this type program from a local level on community beautification program, a program that is working—

EVANS: We'd like you not to make a speech. Just a question.

BAILEY: People on a local level, we have to have a medium to meet all people. Gardening is one of the answers. What can we do to bring this to our nation?

ALLEN: Well, obviously there are major programs being advocated with federal help for urban beautification, and I think if your local officials will cooperate with the federal programs, that they can develop a program and apply for the necessary funds that will certainly help beautify the town in which you live.

EVANS: Thank you very much. The gentleman on my right now.

ZED: My name is D. E. Zed from Baltimore, Maryland. All the talk so far about urban renewal will take three to five years. Is there any way of a stopgap measure where a fast remodeling job can be done? For instance, they tried in New York; they built an apartment, a completely new apartment in four days. The United States Gypsum Corporation did that. Can anything be done now, where it can be worked faster until real urban renewal can take over?

EVANS: Are you directing that to any specific panelist?

ZED: To Mr. Wilkins.

WILKINS: I think we can do certain things that we've done in New York with prefabricated and arranged furniture and a concentrated crew to get it all in in ten or twelve hours, but of course this depends, and on a great scale, on the cooperation of many, many areas, and you'd have to get the cooperation of the building trades and the politicians and the budget makers and the people who live there and all that sort of thing. I think it's the kind of thinking we need if we're going to do something and not wait five years for it.

EVANS:     Alright, one more question here.

POLAND:    Blanken N. Poland of West Virginia. I think that Mr. Wilkins touched on this question, but I'd like to ask Rev. King. In relation to the irrationality—or the question of irrationality of why Detroit, is it possible that the important point of social suicide is being neglected? It is known that when individuals are freed of destructive influences that they will suicide. Is Detroit an example of social community suicide because destructive forces have been relieved?

EVANS:     We have time for a short answer, Dr. Wilkins—or Dr. King, if you can.

KING:      Well, I think there is no doubt about it from a psychological point of view that there can be a suicidal tendency in all riots. When one commits suicide, often he's trying to get attention or to communicate a message that has not been communicated, and I do see in some of the riots a kind of saying, "I would be rather dead than ignored." It's this final mad quest for attention, trying to find voice for the voiceless, so that from that point of view, I think there may be a suicidal quality, but it's a purely psychological explanation.

EVANS:     Thank you very much. We have a few more questions. I think we stopped on this gentleman to my left. You, sir. Your name and from whence you come.

BESSAMARA: My name is Auriel Bessamara. I'm from Columbia, South Carolina, and I would like to ask Mayor Allen of Atlanta if he doesn't think that in making a massive attack on this problem that the nation faces we also must make a massive attack on education.

EVANS:     Alright, is that your question?

ALLEN:     Well, I heartily agree with you. We have a three-fold problem in simple terms, and that's housing, jobs, and education, and—but what I say is, if you correct the housing problem, at the same time that gives you the capabilities of better educating people. I don't think that you can give quality education while people are living in slums.

EVANS:     Alright, thank you. We have so many questions, my friend, that we'll have to ask somebody—

VOICE:     I wanted to ask, if we do not need to make a massive attack on the problem of educating the people how to live in these new apartments and housing units. This is most important because—
           [Applause.]

VOICE:     I have seen units put up and turned to slums; these very brand new units are put up and the people moved in and four months later they have turned them into slums because their consciousness has not been raised to the right level.

[Applause.]

EVANS: Thank you. Are any of you eager to answer that question?

ALLEN: Well, I'm delighted to come in on it. I heartily agree with you.

EVANS: I'd rather—I think I'd rather have the answer from one of the other fellows.

VOICE: I have not had my question answered.

EVANS: Alright.

GREGORY: I think when you stop and look at the housing projects, I think that's the education. They build these skyscrapers for poor people, and they don't put doorbells in them. Dogs bark. People ring. You have eighty percent of the people living in the projects are little kids. They got nineteen floors to go. They got a play yard downstairs. When they have to go to the washroom, they have to go eighteen floors. You would tear up a building too if you had to live under the same conditions that they build—they build the buildings for poor people, and that's why they get so tore up.

[Boos.]

EVANS: Mr. Wilkins.

WILKINS: Obviously, we have a lot of landlords here.

[General laughter.]

I went to visit a friend of mine who lives in a brand new apartment house in the Riverdale section of the Bronx, and the rental is about five hundred dollars a month, and when my wife and I got on the elevator we saw words scrawled on the walls, and I said, "I didn't know Harlem lived up here." And I spoke to my friends, and they said, "Oh, the kids in the building are most like the kids in Harlem; they write over everything, even in a five hundred dollar a month apartment." But of course, we always hear about Negroes creating slums, but we don't hear about what white people do to slums.

[Applause.]

EVANS: Obviously time is our worst enemy, and time has run out. "Face to Face" has attempted to explore and explain the terrifying phenomenon of summer, 1967. We're grateful to the International Platform Association, very grateful to you, Drew Pearson, for making this program possible, and we most sincerely thank our distinguished guests for their effective participation: Dr. Martin Luther King, of the

Southern Christian Leadership Conference; Mayor Ivan Allen of Atlanta, Georgia; Mr. Roy Wilkins, of the National Association for the Advancement of Colored People; and Mr. Dick Gregory, citizen.

This is Mark Evans. Thank you for joining us on "Face to Face."

[Applause.]

# PART V: BOOKS

# 53

# Stride Toward Freedom

*With the help of scholars such as George D. Kelsey and Lawrence D. Reddick,
the able editorial assistance of Hermine Popper, and the assistance of his staff,
Dr. King was finally able to share and to reflect on the meaning of the Montgomery story with the American reading public. His book* **Stride Toward Freedom**
*became the handbook of the movement. Scholars such as August Meier are cer-
tainly correct to point out that the Congress on Racial Equality (CORE) as early
as 1942 preceded Dr. King and SCLC in embracing nonviolent direct action as
a tool to oppose segregation. Moreover, Dr. King himself indicated that he
learned much from prior nonviolent resisters such as the Reverend Theodore J.
Jemison of Baton Rouge, Louisiana, who had led a successful boycott against
that city's public bus system as early as 1953, and from the earlier attempts of
the Reverend Vernon Johns, who preceded King as pastor of the Dexter Avenue
Baptist Church in Montgomery.* **Stride Toward Freedom** *served many purposes both for Dr. King and for the civil rights movement. It was one of the first
summaries of the motivations and objectives of a new, and more militant, generation of black leaders, who saw no contradiction in aggressively pursuing
black freedom. They were mainly young African Americans who were not impressed with the civic virtue and race loyalty of what E. Franklin Frazier called
the "old Negro middle class," and who did not feel called to sacrificial service to
racial uplift for the sake of both race and their country. Frazier's rather polemi-
cal attack on the "new Negro middle class" sounded a powerful warning that
something noble and historic was being subverted by a rising commitment to materialism and parochialism within middle-class black America. Frazier declared
in 1957 that the separation of black people had produced a lack of responsibility
among middle-class blacks. King himself complained about the political and social cynicism that gripped black ministers in particular. In his famous "Letter
from Birmingham City Jail," he pinpointed where he stood in this struggle to
capture the mind and heart of the black middle class: "I stand in the middle of
two opposing forces in the Negro community. One is a force of complacency, made
up in part of Negroes who, as a result of long years of oppression, are so drained
of self-respect and a sense of 'somebodiness' that they have adjusted to segregation; and in part of a few middle-class Negroes who, because of a degree of academic and economic security and because in some ways they profit by segregation,
have become insensitive to the problems of the masses. The other force is one of
bitterness and hatred, and it comes perilously close to advocating violence." He
saw the Montgomery story, and every triumph on his "highroad to destiny," as a
victory against these extremes.*

## RETURN TO THE SOUTH (CHAPTER 1)

On a cool Saturday afternoon in January 1954, I set out to drive from Atlanta, Georgia, to Montgomery, Alabama. It was a clear wintry day. The Metropolitan Opera was on the radio with a performance of one of my favorite operas—Donizetti's *Lucia di Lammermoor*. So with the beauty of the countryside, the inspiration of Donizetti's inimitable music, and the splendor of the skies, the usual monotony that accompanies a relatively long drive—especially when one is alone—was dispelled in pleasant diversions.

After a few hours I drove through rich and fertile farmlands to the sharp bend in the Alabama River on whose shores Montgomery stands. Although I had passed through the city before, I had never been there on a real visit. Now I would have the opportunity to spend a few days in this beautiful little city, one of the oldest in the United States.

Not long after I arrived a friend took me to see the Dexter Avenue Baptist Church where I was to preach the following morning. A solid brick structure erected in Reconstruction days, it stood at one corner of a handsome square not far from the center of town. As we drove up to the church I noticed diagonally across the square a stately white building of impressive proportions and arresting beauty, the state capitol. The present building was erected in 1851, and its high-domed central portion is one of the finest examples of classical Georgian architecture in America. Here on 7 January 1861, Alabama voted to secede from the Union, and on 18 February on the steps of the portico, Jefferson Davis took his oath of office as president of the Confederate States. It is for this reason that Montgomery has been known across the years as the Cradle of the Confederacy. Here the first Confederate flag was made and unfurled. One could see many of the patterns of the old Confederacy and the ante-bellum tradition persisting in Montgomery today, alongside the lively evidence of modern economic development.

I was to see this imposing reminder of the Confederacy from the steps of the Dexter Avenue Baptist Church many times in the following years; for my visit in January proved to be a prelude to my coming to live in Montgomery.

The previous August of 1953, after being in school twenty-one years without a break, I had reached the satisfying moment of completing the residential requirements for the Ph.D. degree. The major job that remained was to write my doctoral thesis. In the meantime I had felt that it would be wise to start considering a job so that I could be placed at least by September 1954. Two churches in the East—one in Massachusetts and one in New York—had expressed an interest in calling me. Three colleges had offered me attractive and challenging posts—one a teaching post, one a deanship, and the other an administrative position. In the midst of thinking about each of these positions, I had recived a letter form the officers of the Dexter Avenue Baptist Church of Montgomery, saying that they were without a pastor and that they would be glad to have me preach when I was again in that section of the country. The officers who extended the invitation had heard of me through my father in Atlanta and other ministerial friends. I had written immediately saying that I would be home in Atlanta for the Christmas holidays, and that I would be happy to come to Montgomery to preach one Sunday in January.

The church was comparatively small, with a membership of around three hundred people, but it occupied a central place in the community. Many influential and respected citizens—professional people with substantial incomes—were among its members. Moreover it had a long tradition of an educated ministry. Some of the nation's best-trained Negro ministers had held pastorates there.

That Saturday evening as I began going over my sermon, I was aware of a certain anxiety. Although I had preached many times before—having served as associate pastor of my father's church in Atlanta for four years, and having done all of the preaching there for three successive summers—I was very conscious this time that I was on trial. How could I best impress the congregation? Since the membership was educated and intelligent, should I attempt to interest it with a display of scholarship? Or should I preach just as I had always done, depending finally on the inspiration of the spirit of God? I decided to follow the latter course. I said to myself, "Keep Martin Luther King in the background and God in the foreground and everything will be all right. Remember you are a channel of the gospel and not the source."

At eleven o'clock on Sunday I was in the pulpit, delivering my sermon before a large congregation. My topic was: "The Three Dimensions of a Complete Life." The congregation was receptive, and I left with the feeling that God had used me well, and that here was a fine church with challenging possibilities. Later in the day the pulpit committee talked to me concerning many business details of the church, and asked me if I would accept the pastorate in the event they saw fit to call me. After answering that I would give such a call my most prayerful and serious consideration, I left Montgomery for Atlanta, and then took a flight back to Boston.

About a month later I received an air-mail, special-delivery letter from Montgomery, telling me that I had been unanimously called to the pastorate of the Dexter Avenue Baptist Church. I was very happy to have this offer, but I did not answer immediately; for I was to fly to Detroit the next morning for a preaching engagement the following Sunday.

It was one of those turbulent days in which the clouds hovered low, but as the plane lifted itself above the weather, the choppiness of the flight soon passed. As I watched the silvery sheets of clouds below and the deep dark shadow of the blue above, I faced up to the problem of what to do about the several offers that had come my way. At this time I was torn in two directions. On the one hand I was inclined toward the pastorate; on the other hand, toward educational work. Which way should I go? And if I accepted a church, should it be one in the South, with all the tragic implicaitons of segregation, or one of the two available pulpits in the North?

As far back as I could remember, I had resented segregation, and had asked my parents urgent and pointed questions about it. While I was still too young for school I had already learned something about discrimination. For three or four years my inseparable playmates had been two white boys whose parents ran a store across the street from our home in Atlanta. Then something began to happen. When I went across the street to get them, their parents would say that they couldn't play. They weren't hostile; they just made excuses. Finally I asked my mother about it.

Every parent at some time faces the problem of explaining the facts of life to his child. Just as inevitably, for the Negro parent, the moment comes when he must explain to his offspring the facts of segregation. My mother took me on her lap and began by telling me about slavery and how it had ended with the Civil War. She tried to explain the divided system of the South—the segregated schools, restaurants, theaters, housing; the white and colored signs on drinking fountains, waiting rooms, lavatories—as a social condition rather than a natural order. Then she said the words that almost every Negro hears before he can yet understand the injustice that makes them necessary: "You are as good as anyone."

My mother, as the daughter of a successful minister, had grown up in comparative comfort. She had been sent to the best available school and college and had, in general, been protected from the worst blights of discrimination. But my father, a sharecropper's son, had met its brutalities at first hand, and had begun to strike back at an early age. With his fearless honesty and his robust, dynamic presence, his words commanded attention.

I remembered a trip to a downtown shoestore with Father when I was still small. We had sat down in the first empty seats at the front of the store. A young white clerk came up and murmured politely:

"I'll be happy to wait on you if you'll just move to those seats in the rear."

My father answered, "There's nothing wrong with these seats. We're quite comfortable here."

"Sorry," said the clerk, "but you'll have to move."

"We'll either buy shoes sitting here," my father retorted, "or we won't buy shoes at all." Whereupon he took me by the hand and walked out of the store. This was the first time I had ever seen my father so angry. I still remember walking down the street beside him as he muttered, "I don't care how long I have to live with this system, I will never accept it."

And he never has. I remember riding with him another day when he accidentally drove past a stop sign. A policeman pulled up to the car and said:

"All right, boy, pull over and let me see your license."

My father replied indignantly, "I'm no boy." Then, pointing to me, "This is a boy. I'm a man, and until you call me one, I will not listen to you."

The policeman was so shocked that he wrote the ticket up nervously, and left the scene as quickly as possible.

From before I was born, my father had refused to ride the city buses, after witnessing a brutal atatck on a load of Negro passengers. He had led the fight in Atlanta to equalize teachers' salaries, and had been instrumental in the elimination of jim-crow elevators in the courthouse. As pastor of the Ebenezer Baptist Church, where he still presides over a congregation of four thousand, he had wielded great influence in the Negro community, and had perhaps won the grudging respect of the whites. At any rate, they had never attacked him physically, a fact that filled my brother and sister and me with wonder as we grew up in this tension-packed atmosphere.

With this heritage, it is not surprising that I had also learned to abhor segregation, considering it both rationally inexplicable and morally unjustifiable. As a teenager I had never been able to accept the fact of having to go to the back of a bus or sit in the segregated section of a train. The first time that I had been seated behind a curtain in a dining car, I felt as if the curtain had been dropped on my selfhood. Having the usual growing boy's pleasure in movies, I had yet gone to a downtown theater in Atlanta only once. The experience of having to enter a rear door and sit in a filthy peanut gallery was so obnoxious that I could not enjoy the picture. I could never adjust to the separate waiting rooms, separate eating places, separate rest rooms, partly because the separate was always unequal, and partly because the very idea of separation did something to my sense of dignity and self-respect.

Now, I thought, as the plane carried me toward Detroit, I have a chance to escape from the long night of segregation. Can I return to a society that condones a system I have abhorred since childhood?

These questions were still unanswered when I returned to Boston. I discussed them with my wife, Coretta (we had been married less than a year), to find that she too was hesitant about returning South. We discussed the all-important question of raising children in the bonds of segregation. We reviewed our own growth in the South, and the many advantages that we had been deprived of as a result of segregation. The question of my wife's musical career came up. She was certain that a northern city would afford a greater opportunity for continued study than any city in the deep South. For several days we talked and thought and prayed over each of these matters. Finally we agreed that, in spite of the disadvantages and inevitable sacrifices, our greatest service could be rendered in our native South. We came to the conclusion that we had something of a moral obligation to return—at least for a few years.

The South, after all, was our home. Despite its shortcomings we loved it as home, and had a real desire to do something about the problems that we had felt so keenly as youngsters. We never wanted to be considered detached spectators. Since racial discrimination was most intense in the South, we felt that some of the Negroes who had received a portion of their training in other sections of the country should return to share their broader contacts and educational experience in its solution. Moreover, despite having to sacrifice much of the cultural life we loved, despite the existence of Jim Crow which kept reminding us at all times of the color of our skin, we had the feeling that something remarkable was unfolding in the South, and we wanted to be on hand to witness it. The region had marvelous possibilities, and once it came to itself and removed the blight of racial segregation, it would experience a moral, political, and economic boom hardly paralleled by any other section of the country.

With this decision my inclination toward the pastorate temporarily won out over my desire to teach, and I decided to accept the call to Dexter for a few years and satisfy my fondness for scholarship later by turning to the teaching field. I sent a telegram to Montgomery that I would be down in three weeks to discuss details.

So I went back to Montgomery. After exploring arrangements with the officers, I accepted the pastorate. Because of my desire to spend at least four more months of intensive work on my doctoral thesis, I asked for and was granted the condition that I would not be required to take up the full-time pastorate until 1 September 1954. I agreed, however, to come down to Montgomery at least once a month to keep things running smoothly during this interim period. On a Sunday in May 1954 I preached my first sermon as minister of the Dexter Avenue Baptist Church, and for the next four months I commuted by plane between Boston and Montgomery.

On my July trip I was accompanied by Coretta. Montgomery was not unfamiliar to her, for her home was just eighty miles away, in the little town of Marion, Alabama. There her father, Obie Scott, though born on a farm, had made a success in business, operating a trucking concern, a combination filling station and grocery store, and a chicken farm. Despite the reprisals and physical threats of his white competitors, he had dared to make a decent living for his family, and to maintain an abiding faith in the future. Coretta had lived in Marion until she left to attend Antioch College in Yellow Springs, Ohio. Having inherited a talent for music from her mother, Bernice Scott, as well as the strength of quiet determination, she had then gone on with the aid of a scholarship to work her way through the New England Conservatory in Boston. It was in Boston that I had met and fallen in love with the attractive young singer whose gentle manner and air of repose did not disguise her lively spirit. And although we had returned to Marion on 18 June 1953, to be married by my father on the Scotts' spacious lawn, it was in Boston that we had begun our married life together.

So on the July visit Coretta looked at Montgomery with fresh eyes. Since her teens she had breathed the free air of unsegregated colleges, and stayed as a welcome guest in white homes. Now in preparation for our long-term return to the South, she visited the Negro section of town where we would be living without choice. She saw the Negroes crowded into the backs of segregated buses and knew that she would be riding there too. But on the same visit she was introduced to the church and cordially received by its fine congregation. And with her sense of optimism and balance, which were to be my constant support in the days to come, she placed her faith on the side of the opportunities and the challenge for Christian service that were offered by Dexter and the Montgomery community.

On 1 September 1954, we moved into the parsonage and I began my full-time pastorate. The first months were busy with the usual chores of getting to know a new house, a new job, a new city. There were old friendships to pick up and new ones to be made, and little time to look beyond our private lives to the general community around us. And although we had come back to the South with the hope of playing a part in the changes we knew were on the horizon, we had no notion yet of how the changes would come about, and no inkling that in little more than a year we would be involved in a movement that was to alter Montgomery forever and to have repercussions throughout the world.

## THE DECISIVE ARREST (CHAPTER 3)

On 1 December 1955, an attractive Negro seamstress, Mrs. Rosa Parks, boarded the Cleveland Avenue bus in downtown Montgomery. She was returning home after her regular day's work in the Montgomery Fair—a leading department store. Tired from long hours on her feet, Mrs. Parks sat down in the first seat behind the section reserved for whites. Not long after she took her seat, the bus operator ordered her, along with three other Negro passengers, to move back in order to accommodate boarding white passengers. By this time every seat in the bus was taken. This meant that if Mrs. Parks followed the driver's command she would have to stand while a white male passenger, who had just boarded the bus, would sit. The other three Negro passengers immediately complied with the driver's request. But Mrs. Parks quietly refused. The result was her arrest.

There was to be much speculation about why Mrs. Parks did not obey the driver. Many people in the white commnity argued that she had been "planted" by the NAACP in order to lay the groundwork for a test case, and at first glance that explanation seemed plausible, since she was a former secretary of the local branch of the NAACP. So persistent and persuasive was this argument that it convinced many reporters from all over the country. Later on, when I was having press conferences three times a week—in order to accommodate the reporters and journalists who came to Montgomery from all over the world—the invariable first question was: "Did the NAACP start the bus boycott?"

But the accusation was totally unwarranted, as the testimony of both Mrs. Parks and the officials of the NAACP revealed. Actually, no one can understand the action of Mrs. Parks unless he realizes that eventually the cup of endurance runs over, and the human personality cries out, "I can take it no longer." Mrs. Parks's refusal to move back was her intrepid affirmation that she had had enough. It was an individual expression of a timeless longing for human dignity and freedom. She was not "planted" there by the NAACP, or any other organization; she was planted there by her personal sense of dignity and self-respect. She was anchored to that seat by the accumulated indignities of days gone by and the boundless aspirations of generations yet unborn. She was a victim of both the forces of history and the forces of destiny. She had been tracked down by the *Zeitgeist*—the spirit of the time.

Fortunately, Mrs. Parks was ideal for the role assigned to her by history. She was a charming person with a radiant personality, soft spoken and calm in all situations. Her character was impeccable and her dedication deep-rooted. All of these traits together made her one of the most respected people in the Negro community.

Only E. D. Nixon—the signer of Mrs. Parks's bond—and one or two other persons were aware of the arrest when it occurred early Thursday evening. Later in the evening the word got around to a few influential women of the community, mostly members of the Women's Political Council. After a series of telephone calls back and forth they agreed that the Negroes should boycott the buses. They immediately suggested the idea to Nixon, and he readily concurred. In his usual courageous manner he agreed to spearhead the idea.

Early Friday morning, 2 December Nixon called me. He was so caught up in what he was about to say that he forgot to greet me with the usual "hello" but plunged immediately into the story of what had happened to Mrs. Parks the night before. I listened, deeply shocked, as he described the humiliating incident. "We have taken this type of thing too long already," Nixon concluded, his voice trembling. "I feel that the time has come to boycott the buses. Only through a boycott can we make it clear to the white folks that we will not accept this type of treatment any longer."

I agreed at once that some protest was necessary, and that the boycott method would be an effective one.

Just before calling me Nixon had discussed the idea with Rev. Ralph Abernathy, the young minister of Montgomery's First Baptist Church who was to become one of the central figures in the protest, and one of my closest associates. Abernathy also felt a bus boycott was our best course of action. So for thirty or forty minutes the three of us telephoned back and forth concerning plans and strategy. Nixon suggested that we call a meeting of all the ministers and civic leaders the same evening in order to get their thinking on the proposal, and I offered my church as the meeting place. The three of us got busy immediately. With the sanction of the Rev. H. H. Hubbard—president of the Baptist Ministerial Alliance—Abernathy and I began calling all of the Baptist ministers. Since most of the Methodist ministers were attending a denominational meeting in one of the local churches that afternoon, it was possible for Abernathy to get the announcement to all of them simultaneously. Nixon reached Mrs. A. W. West—the widow of a prominent dentist—and enlisted her assistance in getting word to the civic leaders.

By early afternoon the arrest of Mrs. Parks was becoming public knowledge. Word of it spread around the community like uncontrolled fire. Telephones began to ring in almost rhythmic succession. By two o'clock an enthusiastic group had mimeographed leaflets concerning the arrest and the proposed boycott, and by evening these had been widely circulated.

As the hour for the evening meeting arrived, I approached the doors of the church with some apprehension, wondering how many of the leaders would respond to our call. Fortunately, it was one of those pleasant winter nights of unseasonable warmth, and to our relief, almost everybody who had been invited was on hand. More than forty people, from every segment of Negro life, were crowded into the large church meeting room. I saw physicians, schoolteachers, lawyers, businessmen, postal workers, union leaders, and clergymen. Virtually every organization of the Negro community was represented.

The largest number there was from the Christian ministry. Having left so many civic meetings in the past sadly disappointed by the dearth of ministers participating, I was filled with joy when I entered the church and found so many of them there; for then I knew that something unusual was about to happen.

Had E. D. Nixon been present, he would probably have been automatically selected to preside, but he had had to leave town earlier in the afternoon for his regular run on the railroad. In his absence, we concluded that Rev. L. Roy Bennett—as president of the Interdenominational Ministerial Alliance—was the logical person to take the chair. He agreed and was seated, his tall, erect figure dominating the room.

The meeting opened around seven-thirty with H. H. Hubbard leading a brief devotional period. Then Bennett moved into action, explaining the purpose of the gathering. With excited gestures he reported on Mrs. Parks's resistance and her arrest. He presented the proposal that the Negro citizens of Montgomery should boycott the buses on Monday in protest. "Now is the time to move," he concluded. "This is no time to talk; it is time to act."

So seriously did Bennett take his "no time to talk" admonition that for quite a while he refused to allow anyone to make a suggestion or even raise a question, insisting that we should move on and appoint committees to implement the proposal. This approach aroused the opposition of most of those present, and created a temporary uproar. For almost forty-five minutes the confusion persisted. Voices rose high, and many people threatened to leave if they could not raise questions and offer suggestions. It looked for a time as though the movement had come to an end before it began. But finally, in the face of this blistering protest, Bennett agreed to open the meeting to discussion.

Immediately questions began to spring up from the floor. Several people wanted further clarification of Mrs. Parks's actions and arrest. Then came the more practical questions. How long would the protest last? How would the idea be further disseminated throughout the community? How would the people be transported to and from their jobs?

As we listened to the lively discussion, we were heartened to notice that, despite the lack of coherence in the meeting, not once did anyone question the validity or desirability of the boycott itself. It seemed to be the unanimous sense of the group that the boycott should take place.

The ministers endorsed the plan with enthusiasm, and promised to go to their congregations on Sunday morning and drive home their approval of the projected one-day protest. Their cooperation was significant, since virtually all of the influential Negro ministers of the city were present. It was decided that we should hold a city-wide mass meeting on Monday night, 5 December, to determine how long we would abstain from riding the buses. Rev. A. W. Wilson—minister of the Holt Street Baptist Church—offered his church, which was ideal as a meeting place because of its size and central location. The group agreed that additional leaflets should be distributed on Saturday, and the chairman appointed a committee, including myself, to prepare the statement.

Our committee went to work while the meeting was still in progress. The final message was shorter than the one that had appeared on the first leaflets, but the substance was the same. It read as follows:

Don't ride the bus to work, to town, to school, or any place Monday, December 5.

Another Negro woman has been arrested and put in jail because she refused to give up her bus seat.

Don't ride the buses to work, to town, to school, or anywhere on Monday. If you work, take a cab, or share a ride, or walk.

Come to a mass meeting, Monday at 7:00 P.M., at the Holt Street Baptist Church for further instruction.

After finishing the statement the committee began to mimeograph it on the church machine; but since it was late, I volunteered to have the job completed early Saturday morning.

The final question before the meeting concerned transportation. It was agreed that we should try to get the Negro taxi companies of the city—eighteen in number, with approximately two hundred and ten taxis—to transport the people for the same price that they were currently paying on the bus. A committee was appointed to make this contact, with Rev. W. J. Powell, minister of the Old Ship A.M.E. Zion Church, as chairman.

With these responsibilities before us the meeting closed. We left with our hearts caught up in a great idea. The hours were moving fast. The clock on the wall read almost midnight, but the clock in our souls revealed that it was daybreak.

I was so excited that I slept very little that night, and early the next morning I was on my way to the church to get the leaflets out. By nine o'clock the church secretary had finished mimeographing the seven thousand leaflets and by eleven o'clock an army of women and young people had taken them off to distribute by hand.

Those on the committee that was to contact the taxi companies got to work early Saturday afternoon. They worked assiduously, and by evening they had reached practically all of the companies, and triumphantly reported that every one of them so far had agreed to cooperate with the proposed boycott by transporting the passengers to and from work for the regular ten-cent bus fare.

Meanwhile our efforts to get the word across to the Negro community were abetted in an unexpected way. A maid who could not read very well came into possession of one of the unsigned appeals that had been distributed Friday afternoon. Apparently not knowing what the leaflet said, she gave it to her employer. As soon as the white employer received the notice she turned it over to the local newspaper, and the *Montgomery Advertiser* made the contents of the leaflet a front-page story on Saturday morning. It appears that the *Advertiser* printed the story in order to let the white community know what the Negroes were up to; but the whole thing turned out to the Negroes' advantage, since it served to bring the information to hundreds who had not previously heard of the plan. By Sunday afternoon word had spread to practically every Negro citizen of Montgomery. Only a few people who lived in remote areas had not heard of it.

After a heavy day of work, I went home late Sunday afternoon and sat down to read the morning paper. There was a long article on the proposed boycott. Implicit throughout the article, I noticed, was the idea that the Negroes were preparing to use the same approach to their problem as the white citizens councils used. This suggested parallel had serious implications. The white citizens councils, which had had their birth in Mississippi a few months after the Supreme Court's school decision, had come into being to preserve segregation. The councils had multiplied rapidly throughout the South, purporting to achieve their ends by the legal maneuvers of "interposition" and "nullification." Unfortunately, however, the actions of some of these councils extended far beyond the bounds of the law. Their methods were the methods of open and covert terror, brutal intimidation, and threats of starvation to Negro men, women, and children. They took open economic reprisals against whites who dared to protest their defiance of the law, and the aim of their boycotts was not merely to impress their victims but to destroy them if possible.

Disturbed by the fact that our pending action was being equated with the boycott methods of the white citizens councils, I was forced for the first time to think seriously on the nature of the boycott. Up to this time I had uncritically accepted this method as our best course of action. Now certain doubts began to bother me. Were we following an ethical course of action? Is the boycott method basically unchristian? Isn't it a negative approach to the solution of a problem? Is it true that we would be following the course of some of the white citizens councils? Even if lasting practical results came from such a boycott, would immoral means justify moral ends? Each of these questions demanded honest answers.

I had to recognize that the boycott method could be used to unethical and unchristian ends. I had to concede, further, that this was the method used so often by the white citizens councils to deprive many Negroes, as well as white persons of good will, of the basic necessities of life. But certainly, I said to myself, our pending actions could not be interpreted in this light. Our purposes were altogether different. We would use this method to give birth to justice and freedom, and also to urge men to comply with the law of the land; the white citizens councils used it to perpetuate the reign of injustice and human servitude, and urged men to defy the law of the land. I reasoned, therefore, that the word "boycott" was really a misnomer for our proposed action. A boycott suggests an economic squeeze, leaving one bogged down in a negative. But we were concerned with the positive. Our concern would not be to put the bus company out of business, but to put justice in business.

As I thought further I came to see that what we were really doing was withdrawing our cooperation from an evil system, rather than merely withdrawing our economic support from the bus company. The bus company, being an external expression of the system, would naturally suffer, but the basic aim was to refuse to cooperate with evil. At this point I began to think about Thoreau's *Essay on Civil Disobedience*. I remembered how, as a college student, I had been moved when I first read this work. I became convinced that what we were preparing to do in Montgomery was related to what Thoreau had expressed. We were simply saying to the white community, "We can no longer lend our cooperation to an evil system."

Something began to say to me, "He who passively accepts evil is as much involved in it as he who helps to perpetrate it. He who accepts evil without protesting against it is really cooperating with it." When oppressed people willingly accept their oppression they only serve to give the oppressor a convenient justification for his acts. Often the oppressor goes along unaware of the evil involved in his oppression so long as the oppressed accepts it. So in order to be true to one's conscience and true to God, a righteous man has no alternative but to refuse to cooperate with an evil system. This I felt was the nature of our action. From this moment on I conceived of our movement as an act of massive noncooperation. From then on I rarely used the word "boycott."

Wearied, but no longer doubtful about the morality of our proposed protest, I saw that the evening had arrived unnoticed. After several telephone calls I prepared to retire early. But soon after I was in bed our two-week-old daughter—Yolanda Denise—began crying; and shortly after that the telephone started ringing again. Clearly condemned to stay awake for some time longer, I used the time to think about other things. My wife and I discussed the possible success of the protest. Frankly, I still had doubts. Even though the word had gotten around amazingly well and the ministers had given the plan such crucial support, I still wondered whether the people had enough courage to follow through. I had seen so many admirable ventures fall through in Montgomery. Why should this be an exception? Coretta and I finally agreed that if we could get 60 percent cooperation the protest would be a success.

Around midnight a call from one of the committee members informed me that every Negro taxi company in Montgomery had agreed to support the protest on Monday morning. Whatever our prospects of success, I was deeply encouraged by the untiring work that had been done by the ministers and civic leaders. This in itself was a unique accomplishemnt.

After the midnight call the phone stopped ringing. Just a few minutes earlier "Yoki" had stopped crying. Wearily I said good night to Coretta, and with a strange mixture of hope and anxiety, I fell asleep.

## THE DAY OF DAYS, 5 DECEMBER (CHAPTER 4)

My wife and I awoke earlier than usual on Monday morning. We were up and fully dressed by five-thirty. The day for the protest had arrived, and we were determined to see the first act of this unfolding drama. I was still saying that if we could get 60 percent cooperation the venture would be a success.

Fortunately, a bus stop was just five feet from our house. This meant that we could observe the opening stages from our front window. The first bus was to pass around six o'clock. And so we waited through an interminable half hour. I was in the kitchen drinking my coffee when I heard Coretta cry, "Martin, Martin, come quickly!" I put down my cup and ran toward the living room. As I approached the front window Coretta pointed joyfully to a slowly moving bus: "Darling, it's empty!" I could hardly believe what I saw. I knew that the South Jackson line, which ran past our house, carried more Negro passengers than any other line in Montgomery, and that this first bus was usually filled with domestic workers going to their jobs. Would all of the other buses follow the pattern that had been set by the first? Eagerly we waited for the next bus. In fifteen minutes it rolled down the street, and, like the first, it was empty. A third bus appeared, and it too was empty of all but two white passengers.

I jumped in my car and for almost an hour I cruised down every major street and examined every passing bus. During this hour, at the peak of the morning traffic, I saw no more than eight Negro passengers riding the buses. By this time I was jubilant. Instead of the 60 percent cooperation we had hoped for, it was becoming apparent that we had reached almost 100 percent. A miracle had taken place. The once dormant and quiescent Negro community was now fully awake.

All day long it continued. At the afternoon peak the buses were still as empty of Negro passengers as they had been in the morning. Students of Alabama State College, who usually kept the South Jackson bus crowded, were cheerfully walking or thumbing rides. Job holders had either found other means of transportation or made their way on foot. While some rode in cabs or private cars, others used less conventional means. Men were seen riding mules to work, and more than one horse-drawn buggy drove the streets of Montgomery that day.

During the rush hours the sidewalks were crowded with laborers and domestic workers, many of them well past middle age, trudging patiently to their jobs and home again, sometimes as much as twelve miles. They knew why they walked, and the knowledge was evident in the way they carried themselves. And as I watched them I knew that there is nothing more majestic than the determined courage of individuals willing to suffer and sacrifice for their freedom and dignity.

Many spectators had gathered at the bus stops to watch what was happening. At first they stood quietly, but as the day progressed they began to cheer the empty buses and laugh and make jokes. Noisy youngsters could be heard singing out, "No riders today." Trailing each bus through the Negro section were two policemen on motorcycles, assigned by the city commissioners, who claimed that Negro "goon squads" had been organized to keep other Negroes from riding the buses. In the course of the day the police succeeded in making one arrest. A college student who was helping an elderly woman across the street was charged with "intimidating passengers." But the "goon squads" existed only in the commission's imagination. No one was threatened or intimidated for riding the buses; the only harassment anyone faced was that of his own conscience.

Around nine-thirty in the morning I tore myself from the action of the city streets and headed for the crowded police court. Here Mrs. Parks was being tried for disobeying the city segregation ordinance. Her attorney, Fred D. Gray—the brilliant young Negro who later became the chief counsel for the protest movement—was on hand to defend her. After the judge heard the arguments, he found Mrs. Parks guilty and fined her ten dollars and court costs (a total of fourteen dollars). She appealed the case. This was one of the first clear-cut instances in which a Negro had been convicted for disobeying the segregation law. In the past, either cases like this had been dismissed or the people involved had been charged with disorderly conduct. So in a real sense the arrest and conviction of Mrs. Parks had a twofold impact: it was a precipitating factor to arouse the Negroes to positive action; and it was a test of the validity of the segregation law itself. I am sure that supporters of such prosecutions would have acted otherwise if they had had the prescience to look beyond the moment.

Leaving Mrs. Parks's trial, Ralph Abernathy, E. D. Nixon, and Rev. E. N. French—then minister of the Hilliard Chapel A.M.E. Zion Church—discussed the need for some organization to guide and direct the protest. Up to this time things had moved forward more or less spontaneously. These men were wise enough to see that the moment had now come for a clearer order and direction.

Meanwhile Roy Bennett had called several people together at three o'clock to make plans for the evening mass meeting. Everyone present was elated by the tremendous success that had already attended the protest. But beneath this feeling was the question, where do we go from here? When E. D. Nixon reported on his discussion with Abernathy and French earlier in the day, and their suggestions for an ad hoc organization, the group responded enthusiastically. The next job was to elect the officers for the new organization.

As soon as Bennett had opened the nominations for president, Rufus Lewis spoke from the far corner of the room: "Mr. Chairman, I would like to nominate Reverend M. L. King for president." The motion was seconded and carried, and in a matter of minutes I was unanimously elected.

The action had caught me unawares. It had happened so quickly that I did not even have time to think it through. It is probable that if I had, I would have declined the nomination. Just three weeks before, several members of the local chapter of the NAACP had urged me to run for the presidency of that organization, assuring me that I was certain of election. After my wife and I had discussed the matter, we agreed that I should not then take on any heavy community responsibilities, since I had so recently finished my thesis, and needed to give more attention to my church work. But on this occasion events had moved too fast.

The election of the remaining officers was speedily completed: Rev. L. Roy Bennett, vice-president; Rev. U. J. Fields, recording secretary; Rev. E. N. French, corresponding secretary; Mrs. Erna A. Dungee, financial secretary; Mr. E. D. Nixon, treasurer. It was then agreed that all those present would constitute the executive board of the new organization. This board would serve as the coordinating agency of the whole movement. It was a well-balanced group, including ministers of all denominations, schoolteachers, businessmen, and two lawyers.

The new organization needed a name, and several were suggested. Someone proposed the Negro Citizens Committee; but this was rejected because it resembled too closely the White Citizens Council. Other suggestions were made and dismissed until finally Ralph Abernathy offered a name that was agreeable to all—the Montgomery Improvement Association (MIA).

With these organizational matters behind us, we turned to a discussion of the evening meeting. Several people, not wanting the reporters to know our future moves, suggested that we just sing and pray; if there were specific recommendations to be made to the people, these could be mimeographed and passed out secretly during the meeting. This, they felt, would leave the reporters in the dark. Others urged that something should be done to conceal the true identity of the leaders, feeling that if no particular name was revealed it would be safer for all involved. After a rather lengthy discussion, E. D. Nixon rose impatiently:

"We are acting like little boys," he said. "Somebody's name will have to be known, and if we are afraid we might just as well fold up right now. We must also be men enough to discuss our recommendations in the open; this idea of secretly passing something around on paper is a lot of bunk. The white folks are eventually going to find out anyway. We'd better decide now if we are going to be fearless men or scared boys."

With this forthright statement the air was cleared. Nobody would again suggest that we try to conceal our identity or avoid facing the issue head on. Nixon's courageous affirmation had given new heart to those who were about to be crippled by fear.

It was unanimously agreed that the protest should continue until certain demands were met, and that a committee under the chairmanship of Ralph Abernathy would draw up those demands in the form of a resolution and present them to the evening mass meeting for approval. We worked out the remainder of the program quickly. Bennett would preside and I would make the main address. Remarks by a few other speakers, along with Scripture reading, prayer, hymns, and collection, would round out the program.

Immediately the resolution committee set to drafting its statement. Despite our satisfaction at the success of the protest so far, we were still concerned. Would the evening meeting be well attended? Could we hope that the fortitude and enthusiasm of the Negro community would survive more than one such day of hardship? Someone suggested that perhaps we should reconsider our decision to continue the protest. "Would it not be better," said the speaker, "to call off the protest while it is still a success rather than let it go on a few more days and fizzle out? We have already proved our united strength to the white community. If we stop now we can get anything we want from the bus company, simply because they will have the feeling that we can do it again. But if we continue, and most of the people return to the buses tomorrow or the next day, the white people will laugh at us, and we will end up getting nothing." This argument was so convincing that we almost resolved to end the protest. But we finally agreed to let the mass meeting—which was only about an hour off—be our guide. If the meeting was well attended and the people were enthusiastic, we would continue; otherwise we would call off the protest that night.

I went home for the first time since seven that morning, and found Coretta relaxing from a long day of telephone calls and general excitement. After we had brought each other up to date on the day's developments, I told her, somewhat hesitantly—not knowing what her reaction would be—that I had been elected president of the new association. I need not have worried. Naturally surprised, she still saw that since the responsiblity had fallen on me, I had no alternative but to accept it. She did not need to be told that we would now have even less time together, and she seemed undisturbed at the possible danger to all of us in my new position. "You know," she said quietly, "that whatever you do, you have my backing."

Reassured, I went to my study and closed the door. The minutes were passing fast. It was now six-thirty, and I had to leave no later than six-fifty to get to the meeting. This meant that I had only twenty minutes to prepare the most decisive speech of my life. As I thought of the limited time before me and the possible implications of this speech, I became possessed by fear. Each week I needed at least fifteen hours to prepare my Sunday sermon. Now I was faced with the inescapable task of preparing, in almost no time at all, a speech that was expected to give a sense of direction to a people imbued with a new and still unplumbed passion for justice. I was also conscious that reporters and television men would be there with their pencils and sound cameras poised to record my words and send them across the nation.

I was now almost overcome, obsessed by a feeling of inadequacy. In this state of anxiety, I had already wasted five minutes of the original twenty. With nothing left but faith in a power whose matchless strength stands over against the frailties and inadequacies of human nature, I turned to God in prayer. My words were brief and simple, asking God to restore my balance and to be with me in a time when I needed His guidance more than ever.

With less than fifteen minutes left, I began preparing an outline. In the midst of this, however, I faced a new and sobering dilemma: How could I make a speech that would be militant enough to keep my people aroused to positive action and yet moderate enough to keep this fervor within controllable and Christian bounds? I knew that many of the Negro people were victims of bitterness that could easily rise to flood proportions. What could I say to keep them courageous and prepared for positive action and yet devoid of hate and resentment? Could the militant and the moderate be combined in a single speech?

I decided that I had to face the challenge head on, and attempt to combine two apparent irreconcilables. I would seek to arouse the group to action by insisting that their self-respect was at stake and that if they accepted such injustices without protesting, they would betray their own sense of dignity and the eternal edicts of God Himself. But I would balance this with a strong affirmation of the Christian doctrine of love. By the time I had sketched an outline of the speech in my mind, my time was up. Without stopping to eat supper (I had not eaten since morning) I said goodbye to Coretta and drove to the Holt Street Church.

Within five blocks of the church I noticed a traffic jam. Cars were lined up as far as I could see on both sides of the street. It was a moment before it occurred to me that all of these cars were headed for the mass meeting. I had to park at least four blocks from the church, and as I started walking I noticed that hundreds of people were standing outside. In the dark night, police cars circled slowly around the area, surveying the orderly, patient, and good-humored crowd. The three or four thousand people who could not get into the church were to stand cheerfully throughout the evening listening to the proceedings on the loud-speakers that had been set up outside for their benefit. And when, near the end of the meeting, these speakers were silenced at the request of the white people in surrounding neighborhoods, the crowd would still remain quietly, content simply to be present.

It took fully fifteen minutes to push my way through to the pastor's study, where Dr. Wilson told me that the church had been packed since five o'clock. By now my doubts concerning the continued success of our venture were dispelled. The question of calling off the protest was now academic. The enthusiasm of these thousands of people swept everything along like an onrushing tidal wave.

It was some time before the remaining speakers could push their way to the rostrum through the tightly packed church. When the meeting began it was almost half an hour late. The opening hymn was the old familiar "Onward Christian Soldiers," and when that mammoth audience stood to sing, the voices outside swelling the chorus in the church, there was a mighty ring like the glad echo of heaven itself.

Rev. W. F. Alford, minister of the Beulah Baptist Church, led the congregation in prayer, followed by a reading of the Scripture by Rev. U. J. Fields, minister of the Bell Street Baptist Church. Then the chairman introduced me. As the audience applauded, I rose and stood before the pulpit. Television cameras began to shoot from all sides. The crowd grew quiet.

Without manuscript or notes, I told the story of what had happened to Mrs. Parks. Then I reviewed the long history of abuses and insults that Negro citizens had experienced on the city buses. "But there comes a time," I said, "that people get tired. We are here this evening to say to those who have mistreated us so long that we are tired—tired of being segregated and humiliated; tired of being kicked about by the brutal feet of oppression." The congregation met this statement with fervent applause. "We had no alternative but to protest," I continued. "For many years, we have shown amazing patience. We have sometimes given our white brothers the feeling that we liked the way we were being treated. But we come here tonight to be saved from that patience that makes us patient with anything less than freedom and justice." Again the audience interrupted with applause.

Briefly I justified our actions, both morally and legally. "One of the great glories of democracy is the right to protest for right." Comparing our methods with those of the white citizens councils and the Ku Klux Klan, I pointed out that while "these organizations are protesting for the perpetuation of injustice in the community, we are protesting for the birth of justice in the community. Their methods lead to violence and lawlessness. But in our protest there will be no cross burnings. No white person will be taken from his home by a hooded Negro mob and brutally murdered. There will be no threats and intimidation. We will be guided by the highest principle of law and order."

With this groundwork for militant action, I moved on to words of caution. I urged the people not to force anybody to refrain from riding the buses. "Our method will be that of persuasion, not coercion. We will only say to the people, 'Let your conscience be your guide.' " Emphasizing the Christian doctrine of love, "our actions must be guided by the deepest principles of our Christian faith. Love must be our regulating ideal. Once again we must hear the words of Jesus echoing across the centuries: 'Love your enemies, bless them that curse you, and pray for them that despitefully use you.' If we fail to do this our protest will end up as a meaningless drama on the stage of history, and its memory will be shrouded with the ugly garments of shame. In spite of the mistreatment that we have confronted we must not become bitter, and end up hating our white brothers. As Booker T. Washington said, 'Let no man pull you so low as to make you hate him.' '' Once more the audience responded enthusiastically.

Then came my closing statement. "If you will protest courageously, and yet with dignity and Christian love, when the history books are written in future generations, the historians will have to pause and say, ''There lived a great people—a black people—who injected new meaning and dignity into the veins of civilizaton.' This is our challenge and our overwhelming responsibility." As I took my seat the people rose to their feet and applauded. I was thankful to God that the message had gotten over and that the task of combining the militant and the moderate had been at least partially accomplished. The people had been as enthusiastic when I urged them to love as they were when I urged them to protest.

As I sat listening to the continued applause I realized that this speech had evoked more response than any speech or sermon I had ever delivered, and yet it was virtually unprepared. I came to see for the first time what the older preachers meant when they said, "Open your mouth and God will speak for you." While I would not let this experience tempt me to overlook the need for continued preparation, it would always remind me that God can transform man's weakness into his glorious opportunity.

When Mrs. Parks was introduced from the rostrum by E. N. French, the audience responded by giving her a standing ovation. She was their heroine. They saw in her courageous person the symbol of their hopes and aspirations.

Now the time had come for the all-important resolution. Ralph Abernathy read the words slowly and forcefully. The main substance of the resolution called upon the Negroes not to resume riding the buses until (1) courteous treatment by the bus operators was guaranteed; (2) passengers were seated on a first-come, first-served basis—Negroes seating from the back of the bus toward the front while whites seated from the front toward the back; (3) Negro bus operators were employed on predominantly Negro routes. At the words "All in favor of the motion stand," every person to a man stood up, and those who were already standing raised their hands. Cheers began to ring out from both inside and outside. The motion was carried unanimously. The people had expressed their determination not to ride the buses until conditions were changed.

At this point I had to leave the meeting and rush to the other side of town to speak at a YMCA banquet. As I drove away my heart was full. I had never seen such enthusiasm for freedom. And yet this enthusiasm was tempered by amazing self-discipline. The unity of purpose and esprit de corps of these people had been indescribably moving. No historian would ever be able fully to describe this meeting and no sociologist would ever be able to interpret it adequately. One had to be a part of the experience really to understand it.

At the Ben Moore Hotel, as the elevator slowly moved up to the roof garden where the banquet was being held, I said to myself, the victory is already won, no matter how long we struggle to attain the three points of the resolution. It is a victory infinitely larger than the bus situation. The real victory was in the mass meeting, where thousands of black people stood revealed with a new sense of dignity and destiny.

Many will inevitably raise the question, why did this event take place in Montgomery, Alabama, in 1955? Some have suggested that the Supreme Court decision on school desegregation, handed down less than two years before, had given new hope of eventual justice to Negroes everywhere, and fired them with the necessary spark of encouragement to rise against their oppression. But although this might help to explain why the protest occurred when it did, it cannot explain why it happened in Montgomery.

Certainly, there is a partial explanation in the long history of injustice on the buses of Montgomery. The bus protest did not spring into being full grown as Athena sprang from the head of Zeus; it was the culmination of a slowly developing process. Mrs. Parks's arrest was the precipitating factor rather than the cause of the protest. The cause lay deep in the record of similar injustices. Almost everybody could point to an unfortunate episode that he himself had experienced or seen.

But there comes a time when people get tired of being trampled by oppression. There comes a time when people get tired of being plunged into the abyss of exploitation and nagging injustice. The story of Montgomery is the story of fifty thousand such Negroes who were willing to substitute tired feet for tired souls, and walk the streets of Montgomery until the walls of segregation were finally battered by the forces of justice.

But neither is this the whole explanation. Negroes in other communities confronted conditions equally as bad, and often worse. So we cannot explain the Montgomery story merely in terms of the abuses that Negroes suffered there. Moreover, it cannot be explained by a preexistent unity among the leaders, since we have seen that the Montgomery Negro community prior to the protest was marked by divided leadership, indifference, and complacency. Nor can it be explained by the appearance upon the scene of new leadership. The Montgomery story would have taken place if the leaders of the protest had never been born.

So every rational explanation breaks down at some point. There is something about the protest that is suprarational; it cannot be explained without a divine dimension. Some may call it a principle of concretion, with Alfred N. Whitehead; or a process of integration, with Henry N. Wieman; or Being-itself, with Paul Tillich; or a personal God. Whatever the name, some extra-human force labors to create a harmony out of the discord of the universe. There is a creative power that works to pull down mountains of evil and level hilltops of injustice. God still works through history His wonders to perform. It seems as though God had decided to use Montgomery as the proving ground for the struggle and triumph of freedom and justice in America. And what better place for it than the leading symbol of the Old South? It is one of the splendid ironies of our day that Montgomery, the Cradle of the Confederacy, is being transformed into Montgomery, the cradle of freedom and justice.

The day of days, Monday, December 5, 1955, was drawing to a close. We all prepared to go to our homes, not yet fully aware of what had happened. The deliberations of that brisk, cool night in December will not be forgotten. That night we were starting a movement that would gain national recognition; whose echoes would ring in the ears of people of every nation; a movement that would astound the oppressor, and bring new hope to the oppressed. That night was Montgomery's moment in history.

## THE MOVEMENT GATHERS MOMENTUM (CHAPTER 5)

After ascending the mountain on Monday night, I woke up Tuesday morning urgently aware that I had to leave the heights and come back to earth. I was faced with a number of organizational decisions. The movement could no longer continue without careful planning.

I began to think of the various committees necessary to give the movement guidance and direction. First we needed a more permanent transportation committee, since the problem of getting the ex-bus riders about the city was paramount. I knew that we could not work out any system that would solve all the transportation problems of the nearly 17,500 Negroes who had formerly ridden the buses twice daily; even the most effective system that we could devise would still leave everyone walking a little more than he had done formerly. But a well-worked-out system could do a good deal to alleviate the problem.

We would also need to raise money to carry on the protest. Therefore, a finance committee was necessary. Since we would be having regular mass meetings, there must be a program committee for these occasions. And then, I reasoned, from time to time strategic decisions would have to be made; we needed the best minds of the association to think them through and then make recommendations to the executive board. So I felt that a strategy committee was essential.

With all of these things in mind I called a meeting of the executive board for Wednesday at ten o'clock in one of the larger rooms of the Alabama Negro Baptist Center. Every board member was present to applaud the report that after almost two and a half days the protest was still more than 99 percent effective. There followed the appointment of the various committees. Because of the relatively small number on the executive board, it was necessary to place several people on more than one committee. As in all organizations, the problem of conflicting egos was involved, and the selections were guided by the desire to assure that the people on each committee could work well together. Rufus Lewis agreed to be chairman of the transportation committee, and Rev. R. J. Glasco, our host for the morning, chairman of the finance committee. The executive board was expanded to make it a broad cross section of the Negro community.

The members of the strategy committee were appointed a few days later. This new committee brought together a dozen men and women who had already provided strong leadership in the early days of the protest, and whose clear thinking and courageous guidance were to be of inestimable help in the difficult decisions that still lay ahead. Besides the indispensable E. D. Nixon and our brilliant legal strategist, Fred Gray, the committee included Roy Bennett, who had chaired the first meeting to organize the protest and was to continue to give the movement his loyal support until he was transferred to a pastorate in California. H. H. Hubbard and A. W. Wilson, both Baptist ministers, represented the largest Negro congregations in Montgomery. Hubbard's stately presence brought a sense of security to every meeting that he attended; and his colleague, Wilson, who has held key positions in the Alabama Baptist State Convention, contributed his fine talent as an organizer and administrator.

Mrs. Euretta Adair, the wife of a prominent Montgomery physician, was a one-time faculty member of Tuskegee Institute who combined a rich academic background with a passion for social betterment. The current academic world was represented by Jo Ann Robinson and J. E. Pierce, both faculty members of Alabama State College, who had never allowed their secure positions to make them indifferent to the problems of the people. Rufus Lewis, a businessman who had also had a long interest in the Negroes' struggle for first-class citizenship, was to display his conscientiousness and cooperative spirit as first chairman of the transportation committee. When, after several months, the need for extending the MIA's activities into such areas as voting became apparent, he took the chairmanship of the new registration and voting committee, a responsibility which he still holds.

W. J. Powell and S. S. Seay, like Bennett, were ministers of the A.M.E. Zion Church. Powell brought a cool head and an even temper to the problems that confronted the strategy committee in these tempestuous days. S. S. Seay's was one of the few clerical voices that, in the years preceding the protest, had lashed out against the injustices heaped on the Negro, and urged his people to a greater appreciation of their own worth. A dynamic preacher, his addresses from time to time at the weekly mass meetings raised the spirits of all who heard him.

The final member of the strategy committee was already in the forefront of the forces of protest. Ralph Abernathy was another of the few Negro clergymen who had long been active in civic affairs. Although he was then only twenty-nine, his devotion to the cause of freedom was already beyond question. With his short, stocky frame and his thoughtful expression, he looked older than his years. But a boyish smile always lurked beneath the surface of his face. Ralph's slow movements and slow, easy talk were deceptive. For he was an indefatigable worker and a sound thinker, possessed of a fertile mind. As a speaker, he was persuasive and dynamic, with the gift of laughing people into positive action. When things became languid around the mass meetings, Ralph Abernathy infused his audiences with new life and ardor. The people loved and respected him as a symbol of courage and strength.

From the beginning of the protest Ralph Abernathy was my closest associate and most trusted friend. We prayed together and made important decisions together. His ready good humor lightened many tense moments. Whenever I went out of town I always left him in charge of the important business of the association, knowing that it was in safe hands. After Bennett left Montgomery, Ralph became first vice-president of the MIA, and has held that position ever since with dignity and efficiency.

These were the people with whom, from the beginning, I worked most closely. As time went on others were added. Among these, an early recruit to the executive committee was Rev. Robert Graetz, whom I had first met in the Council on Human Relations. This boyish-looking white minister of the Negro Trinity Lutheran Church was a constant reminder to us in the trying months of the protest that many white people as well as Negroes were applying the "love-thy-neighbor-as-thyself" teachings of Christianity in their daily lives. Other close associates who were later added to the board were Clarence W. Lee, a tall distinguished-looking mortician, whose sound business ability became a great asset to the organization, and Moses W. Jones, a prominent physician, who later became the second vice-president of the MIA.

We met at all hours, whenever a new emergency demanded attention. It was not unusual to find some of us talking things over in one of our homes at two-thirty in the morning. While our wives plied us with coffee, and joined the informal discussions, we laid plans and arrived at agreements on policy. No parliamentary rules were necessary in this small group; the rule of the majority was tacitly accepted.

In the early stages of the protest the problem of transportation demanded most of our attention. The labor and ingenuity that went into that task is one of the most interesting sides of the Montgomery story. For the first few days we had depended on the Negro taxi companies who had agreed to transport the people for the same ten-cent fare that they paid on the buses. Except for a few private cars that had been volunteered, these taxis had provided the only transportation. But during the first "negotiation meeting" that we were to hold with the city commission on Thursday, December 8, Police Commissioner Sellers mentioned in passing that there was a law that limited the taxis to a minimum fare. I caught this hint and realized that Commissioner Sellers would probably use this point to stop the taxis from assisting in the protest.

At that moment I remembered that some time previously my good friend Rev. Theodore Jemison had led a bus boycott in Baton Rouge, Louisiana. Knowing that Jemison and his associates had set up an effective private car pool, I put in a long-distance call to ask him for suggestions for a similar pool in Montgomery. As I expected, his painstaking description of the Baton Rouge experience was invaluable. I passed on word of Sellers' remark and Jemison's advice to the transportation committee and suggested that we immediately begin setting up a pool in order to offset the confusion which could come if the taxis were eliminated from service.

Fortunately, a mass meeting was being held that night. There I asked all those who were willing to offer their cars to give us their names, addresses, telephone numbers, and the hours that they could drive, before leaving the meeting. The response was tremendous. More than a hundred and fifty signed slips volunteering their automobiles. Some who were not working offered to drive in the car pool all day; others volunteered a few hours before and after work. Practically all of the ministers offered to drive whenever they were needed.

On Friday afternoon, as I had predicted, the police commissioner issued an order to all of the cab companies reminding them that by law they had to charge a minimum fare of forty-five cents, and saying that failure to comply would be a legal offense. This brought an end to the cheap taxi service.

Our answer was to call hastily on our volunteers, who responded immediately. They started out simply by cruising the streets of Montgomery with no particular system. On Saturday the ministers agreed to go to their pulpits the following day and seek additional recruits. Again the response was tremendous. With the new additions, the number of cars swelled to about three hundred.

The real job was just beginning—that of working out some system for these three hundred-odd automobiles, to replace their haphazard movement around the city. During the days that followed, the transportation committee worked every evening into the morning hours attempting to set up an adequate system. Several of Jemison's suggestions proved profitable. Finally, the decision was made to set up "dispatch" and "pick-up" stations, points at which passengers would assemble for transportation to their jobs and home again. The dispatch stations would be open from six to ten A.M., and the pick-up stations from three to seven P.M.

Next came the difficult task of selecting sites for the stations that would adequately cover the whole city. While most of us found it relatively easy to think of dispatch stations, since they would be in Negro sections of town, we discovered that we were at a loss in selecting pick-up stations. The problem was that the vast majority of those who had ridden the buses worked for white employers, and the pick-up stations would therefore have to be in white sections, of which we had little, if any, knowledge. Fortunately, however, we had two postal workers on the committee, who knew the city from end to end. With their assistance and the aid of a city map we began working with the new facility.

At this time, R. J. Glasco was prominent on the transportation committee along with the chairman, Rufus Lewis. These men, with the assistance of the whole committee, worked assiduously to lay out the plan. By Tuesday, December 13, the system had been worked out. Thousands of mimeographed leaflets were distributed throughout the Negro community with a list of the forty-eight dispatch and the forty-two pick-up stations. Most of the dispatch stations were located at the Negro churches. These churches cooperated by opening their doors early each morning so that the waiting passengers could be seated, and many of them provided heat on cold mornings. Each of the private cars was assigned to one of the dispatch and one of the pick-up stations, the number of cars assigned to each station determined by the number of persons using it. By far the most heavily used station was a Negro-owned parking lot located in the downtown section of Montgomery. It was a combination pick-up and dispatch point.

In a few days this system was working astonishingly well. The white opposition was so impressed at this miracle of quick organization that they had to admit in a White Citizens Council meeting that the pool moved with "military precision." The MIA had worked out in a few nights a transportation problem that the bus company had grappled with for many years.

Despite this success, so profoundly had the spirit of the protest become a part of the people's lives that sometimes they even preferred to walk when a ride was available. The act of walking, for many, had become of symbolic importance. Once a pool driver stopped beside an elderly woman who was trudging along with obvious difficulty.

"Jump in, grandmother," he said. "You don't need to walk."

She waved him on. "I'm not walking for myself," she explained. "I'm walking for my children and my grandchildren." And she continued toward home on foot.

While the largest number of drivers were ministers, their ranks were augmented by housewives, teachers, businessmen, and unskilled laborers. At least three white men from the air bases drove in the pool during their off-duty hours. One of the most faithful drivers was Mrs. A. W. West, who had early shown her enthusiasm for the protest idea by helping to call the civic leaders to the first organizing meeting. Every morning she drove her large green Cadillac to her assigned dispatch station, and for several hours in the morning and again in the afternoon one could see this distinguished and handsome gray-haired chauffeur driving people to work and home again.

Another loyal driver was Jo Ann Robinson. Attractive, fair-skinned, and still youthful, Jo Ann came by her goodness naturally. She did not need to learn her nonviolence from any book. Apparently indefatigable, she, perhaps more than any other person, was active on every level of the protest. She took part in both the executive board and the strategy committee meetings. When the MIA newsletter was inaugurated a few months after the protest began, she became its editor. She was sure to be present whenever negotiations were in progress. And although she carried a full teaching load at Alabama State, she still found time to drive both morning and afternoon.

The ranks of our drivers were further swelled from an unforeseen source. Many white housewives, whatever their commitment to segregation, had no intention of being without their maids. And so every day they drove to the Negro sections to pick up their servants and returned them at night. Certainly, if selfishness was a part of the motive, in many cases affection for a faithful servant also played its part. There was some humor in the tacit understandings—and sometimes mutually accepted misunderstandings—between these white employers and their Negro servants. One old domestic, an influential matriarch to many young relatives in Montgomery, was asked by her wealthy employer, "Isn't this bus boycott terrible?"

The old lady responded: "Yes, ma'am, it sure is. And I just told all my young'uns that this kind of thing is white folks' business and we just stay off the buses until they get this whole thing settled."

As time moved on the pool continued to grow and expand. Rev. B. J. Simms, college professor and pastor of a Baptist church in Tuskegee, took over the chairmanship of the committee, adding his own creative ideas to the good work of his predecessor, Rufus Lewis. Soon the transportation office had grown to a staff of six. More than twenty-five people were employed as all-day drivers, working six days a week. In most of the stations, dispatchers were employed to keep things running smoothly and divide the passengers on the basis of the direction in which they were going. A chief dispatcher—Rev. J. H. Cherry—stationed at the downtown parking lot proved to be of inestimable value. Richard Harris, a Negro pharmacist, was also a great asset to the transportation system. From the office of his drugstore he dispatched cars by telephone from early morning till late evening. Visitors were always astonished to see this young energetic businessman standing with a telephone at his ear dispatching cars and filling a prescription simultaneously.

Finally, a fleet of more than fifteen new station wagons was added. Each of these 1956 cars was registered as the property of a different church, and the name of the sponsoring church was emblazoned on the front and side of each vehicle. As these "rolling churches" carried their spirited loads of passengers along to work, an occasional sound of hymn-singing came from their windows. Pedestrians who could find no room in the crowded vehicles waved as their own "church" passed by, and walked on with new heart.

Altogether the operation of the motor pool represented organization and coordination at their best. Reporters and visitors from all over the country looked upon the system as a unique accomplishment. But the job took money. For a while the MIA had been able to carry on through local contributions. Week after week, wealthy or poor, the Negroes of Montgomery gave what they could, even though sometimes there was only a dime or a quarter to put into the collection box. But as the pool grew and other expenses mounted, it was evident that we needed additional funds to carry on. The cost of running the MIA had increased to five thousand dollars a month.

Fortunately the liberal coverage of the press had carried the word of our struggle across the world. Although we never made a public appeal for funds, contributions began to pour in from as far away as Tokyo. MIA leaders were invited to cities all over the country to appear in fund-raising meetings. Every day brought visitors bearing gifts, and every mail brought checks. Sometimes the gift was as large as five thousand dollars, sometimes only a single dollar bill, but altogether they added up to nearly $250,000.

The largest response came from church groups—particularly, though by no means only, Negro churches. Several ministerial associations contributed generously. It would be safe to say that churches in almost every city in the United States sent help. Labor, civic, and social groups were our staunch supporters, and in many communities new organizations were founded just to support the protest. Almost every branch of the NAACP responded generously to a letter from Roy Wilkins, the executive secretary, urging them to give moral and financial support to the movement; and this was only one of the many ways in which the NAACP was to lend its strength in the days ahead.

Contributions came from many individuals, too, both white and Negro, here and abroad. Often these were accompanied by letters that raised our spirits and helped to break the sense of isolation that surrounded us in our own community. From Pennsylvania came a check for one hundred dollars, along with a note in the spidery handwriting of an elderly gentlewoman: "Your work . . . is outstanding and unprecedented in the history of our country. Indeed, it is epoch-making and it should have a far-reaching effect. . . . 'Not by might, nor by power, but by my spirit, saith the Lord'—this might well be the motto of the Montgomery Improvement Association." A former federal judge wrote: "You have shown that decency and courage will eventually prevail. . . . The immediate issue has not been won as yet but such faith and determination is bound to be triumphant and the persecutors must themselves by this time come to realize that they are fighting a cruel but losing effort. The entire nation salutes you and prays for your early relief and victory."

From Singapore came the assurance that "what you are doing is a real inspiration to us here in the part of the world where the struggle between democracy and communism is raging." The crew of a ship at sea cabled: "We offer a prayer in sympathy in the fight for justice." And a Swiss woman whose "friends and husband do not understand" saved her own money to send us one of our largest individual contributions. "Since I have no possibility," she wrote, "to help you in an efficacious manner (this is such a bad feeling, believe me) and I burningly would like to do just something. I send you these $500. . . . You would make me a very great pleasure, if you accepted, because what else could I do?"

Truly the Montgomery movement had spoken to a responsive world. But while these letters brought us much-needed encouragement, they were also the source of persistent frustration for me. The MIA lacked proper office facilities and staff, and due to the shortage of secretarial help most of the early letters had to go unanswered. Even financial contributions were often unacknowledged. The more I thought of my inability to cope with these matters, the more disturbed I became.

My frustration was augmented by the fact that for several weeks after the protest began, people were calling me at every hour of the day and night. The phone would start ringing as early as five o'clock in the morning and seldom stopped before midnight. Sometimes it was an ex–bus rider asking me to arrange to get her to work and back home at a certain hour. Sometimes it was a driver complaining about uncooperative passengers or a passenger complaining about a temperamental driver. Sometimes a driver's car had broken down. Sometimes it was a maid who had been threatened with firing by her employer if she continued to stay off the buses, and sometimes a person who simply wanted to know where the nearest pick-up station was located. From time to time someone called to say that a certain driver was charging his passengers, and needed to be stopped before his acts jeopardized the legal status of the whole system.

We came to see the necessity of having a well-staffed office to face such problems as these. At first we attempted to run it with volunteer secretarial help. But this was not sufficient. So we hired a full-time secretary to do the regular work of the association, and set up a transportation office with a secretary to work directly in that area. As time went on the correspondence became so heavy and the transportation work so detailed that it was necessary to employ an office staff of ten persons. With the growth of the office staff and other administrative matters, the board finally supplied me with an executive asistant, Rev. R. J. Glasco. All of these steps—the hiring of office secretaries, setting up a transportation office, and the hiring of an executive assistant—served to lighten an almost unbearable load, and helped me to regain my bearings.

But the job of getting the movement going was not yet finished. There was still the task of finding permanent office space to house the MIA. This problem proved to be unexpectedly difficult, and we were forced to move no less than four times before we found a relatively permanent locaiton.

The first office was in the Alabama Negro Baptist Center. Here we had access to two large rooms and also an assembly room for board meetings. Both location and facilities met our needs. As soon as we were settled there, however, the white officials of the Montgomery Baptist Association—the organization which supplied the largest amount of money for the operation of the center—called the trustees of the center into a conference and suggested that "for the good of the center" and "the good of the community" the MIA headquarters should be moved. Although it was never explicitly stated, we could discern an implicit threat to withdraw financial assiatnce if the request were not complied with immediately.

Seeing that we were almost out of doors, Rufus Lewis offered the MIA the use of his club—the Citizens Club. He set at our disposal a large room, which was usually used for banquets, and a small room for the transportation committee. But after we had been in the Citizens Club for a few weeks Mr. Lewis got word from reliable sources that if the MIA remained there his license would be revoked on the grounds that the club was being used as an office building. In this emergency the First Baptist Church offered its limited office space as a temporary abode.

Finally, we discovered that the new building of the Bricklayers Union had available space which would serve our purposes well. Here the white community could not force us out, since most of the members and all of the offices of the union that owned the building were Negroes. With this consideration in mind we decided to rent space there.

By then the office staff was exhausted. They had moved back and forth all over the city. In this continuous moving process some important letters had almost certainly been lost and significant records misplaced. But at least we now had an office with an air of permanence. For the first time we had enough space to work with a modicum of peace and security.

The biggest job in getting any movement off the ground is to keep together the people who form it. This task requires more than a common aim: it demands a philosophy that wins and holds the people's allegiance; and it depends upon open channels of communication between the people and their leaders. All of these elements were present in Montgomery.

From the beginning a basic philosophy guided the movement. This guiding principle has since been referred to variously as nonviolent resistance, noncooperation, and passive resistance. But in the first days of the protest none of these expressions was mentioned; the phrase most often heard was "Christian love." It was the Sermon on the Mount, rather than a doctrine of passive resistance, that initially inspired the Negroes of Montgomery to dignified social action. It was Jesus of Nazareth that stirred the Negroes to protest with the creative weapon of love.

As the days unfolded, however, the inspiration of Mahatma Gandhi began to exert its influence. I had come to see early that the Christian doctrine of love operating through the Gandhian method of nonviolence was one of the most potent weapons available to the Negro in his struggle for freedom. About a week after the protest started, a white woman who understood and sympathized with the Negroes' efforts wrote a letter to the editor of the *Montgomery Advertiser* comparing the bus protest with the Gandhian movement in India. Miss Juliette Morgan, sensitive and frail, did not long survive the rejection and condemnation of the white community, but long before she died in the summer of 1957 the name of Mahatma Gandhi was well known in Montgomery. People who had never heard of the little brown saint of India were now saying his name with an air of familiarity. Nonviolent resistance had emerged as the technique of the movement, while love stood as the regulating ideal. In other words, Christ furnished the spirit and motivation, while Gandhi furnished the method.

This philosophy was disseminated mainly through the regular mass meetings which were held in the various Negro churches of the city. For the first several months the meetings occurred twice a week—on Mondays and Thursdays—but in the fall of 1956 the number was reduced to one a week, a schedule that continues to this day. At the beginning of the protest these twice-a-week get-togethers were indispensable channels of communication, since Montgomery had neither a Negro-owned radio station nor a widely read Negro newspaper.

The meetings rotated from church to church. The speakers represented the various denominations, thus removing any grounds for sectarian jealousy. One of the glories of the Montgomery movement was that Baptists, Methodists, Lutherans, Presbyterians, Episcopalians, and others all came together with a willingness to transcend denominational lines. Although no Catholic priests were actively involved in the protest, many of their parishioners took part. All joined hands in the bond of Christian love. Thus the mass meetings accomplished on Monday and Thursday nights what the Christian church had failed to accomplish on Sunday mornings.

The mass meetings also cut across class lines. The vast majority present were working people; yet there was always an appreciable number of professionals in the audience. Physicians, teachers, and lawyers sat or stood beside domestic workers and unskilled laborers. The Ph.D's and the no "D's" were bound together in a common venture. The so-called "big Negroes" who owned cars and had never ridden the buses came to know the maids and the laborers who rode the buses every day. Men and women who had been separated from each other by false standards of class were now singing and praying together in a common struggle for freedom and human dignity.

The meetings started at seven, but people came hours ahead of time to get a seat. It was not uncommon to find the churches completely filled by five in the afternoon. Some read papers and books while they waited; others joined in group singing. Usually the hymns preceding the meeting were unaccompanied lined tunes of low pitch and long meter. One could not help but be moved by these traditional songs, which brought to mind the long history of the Negro's suffering.

By the time the meeting started, virtually every space was taken, and hundreds often overflowed into the streets. Many late-comers learned to bring their own folding stools, and many others stayed away because they knew that it would be impossible to find a space. At first we tried to deal with this problem by having as many as five simultaneous meetings in different parts of the city, each with the same theme and pattern. For several weeks I made it a practice to appear at all five meetings, but this was a strenuous undertaking. Moreover, the people began to insist that they wanted to be together; so we soon went back to the one big meeting.

The evenings followed a simple pattern: songs, prayer, Scripture reading, opening remarks by the president, collection, reports from various committees, and a "pep talk." The latter was the main address of the evening, usually given by a different minister at each meeting. The "pep talk" acquired its rather undignified title during the early days of the protest, when the primary purpose was to give the people new "pep" and enthusiasm for the struggle ahead. Night after night the group was admonished to love rather than hate, and urged to be prepared to suffer violence if necessary but never to inflict it. Every "pep" speaker was asked to make nonviolence a central part of his theme.

Inevitably, a speaker would occasionally get out of hand. One minister, after lashing out against the whites in distinctly untheological terms, ended by referring to the extremists of the white community as "dirty crackers." After the meeting he was politely but firmly informed that his insulting phrases were out of place. But such instances of offensive language were surprisingly few.

In my weekly remarks as president, I stressed that the use of violence in our struggle would be both impractical and immoral. To meet hate with retaliatory hate would do nothing but intensify the existence of evil in the universe. Hate begets hate; violence begets violence; toughness begets a greater toughness. We must meet the forces of hate with the power of love; we must meet physical force with soul force. Our aim must never be to defeat or humiliate the white man, but to win his friendship and understanding.

From the beginning the people responded to this philosophy with amazing ardor. To be sure, there were some who were slow to concur. Occasionally members of the executive board would say to me in private that we needed a more militant approach. They looked upon nonviolence as weak and compromising. Others felt that at least a modicum of violence would convince the white people that the Negroes meant business and were not afraid. A member of my church came to me one day and solemnly suggested that it would be to our advantage to "kill off" eight or ten white people. "This is the only language these white folks will understand," he said. "If we fail to do this they will think we're afraid. We must show them we're not afraid any longer." Besides, he thought, if a few white persons were killed the federal government would inevitably intervene and this, he was certain, would benefit us.

Still others felt that they could be nonviolent only if they were not attacked personally. They would say: "If nobody bothers me, I will bother nobody. If nobody hits me, I will hit nobody. But if I am hit, I will hit back." They thus drew a moral line between aggressive and retaliatory violence. But in spite of these honest disagreements, the vast majority were willing to try the experiment.

The very spirit of the meetings revealed their nature. The songs, the prayers, the Scripture readings, and the speeches were by and large nonviolent in tone. A favorite scriptural passage was, "And now abideth faith, hope, love, these three; but the greatest of these is love." Another was the famous dialogue on forgiveness between Jesus and Peter: "Then came Peter to him, and said, Lord, how oft shall my brother sin against me, and I forgive him? til seven times? Jesus saith unto him, I say not unto thee, Until seven times: but, Until seventy times seven." For the mass-meeting audiences, these scriptural admonitions were not abstractions that came to them from a distance across the centuries; they had a personal and immediate meaning for them today.

Throughout, there was a surprising lack of bitterness, even when speakers referred to the latest white insult or act of terrorism. And when, later on, the MIA was to be faced with its only serious internal crisis, the people showed that they could handle dissension among themselves with equal restraint, refraining not only from physical violence but also from violence of spirit.

In a real sense, Montgomery's Negroes showed themselves willing to grapple with a new approach to the crisis in race relations. It is probably true that most of them did not believe in nonviolence as a philosophy of life, but because of their confidence in their leaders and because nonviolence was presented to them as a simple expression of Christianity in action, they were willing to use it as a technique. Admittedly, nonviolence in the truest sense is not a strategy that one uses simply because it is expedient at the moment; nonviolence is ultimately a way of life that men live by because of the sheer morality of its claim. But even granting this, the willingness to use nonviolence as a technique is a step forward. For he who goes this far is more likely to adopt nonviolence later as a way of life.

## DESEGREGATION AT LAST (CHAPTER 9)

From the beginning of the bus protest most of the Negro leaders lived with the hope that a settlement would soon be worked out. Our demands were limited, moderate enough to permit adjustment within the segregation laws. Even the most conservative white person could go along with them, we reasoned. But as the days and months unfolded we discovered that our optimism was misplaced. The intransigence of the city commission, the crudeness of the "get-tough" policy, and the viciousness of the recent bombings convinced us all that an attack must be made upon bus segregation itself. Accordingly a suit was filed in the United States Federal District Court, asking for an end of bus segregation on the grounds that it was contrary to the Fourteenth Amendment. The court was also asked to stop the city commissioners from violating the civil rights of Negro motorists and pedestrians.

The hearing was set for May 11, 1956, before a three-judge federal court panel. It was a great relief to be in a federal court. Here the atmosphere of justice prevailed. No one can understand the feeling that comes to a southern Negro on entering a federal court unless he sees with his own eyes and feels with his own soul the tragic sabotage of justice in the city and state courts of the South. The Negro goes into these courts knowing that the cards are stacked against him. Here he is virtually certain to face a prejudiced jury or a biased judge, and is openly robbed with little hope of redress. But the southern Negro goes into the federal court with the feeling that he has an honest chance of justice before the law.

Our suit was filed by the same attorneys who had acted for the defense before Judge Carter in the boycott case. This time they presented persuasive arguments against the constitutionality of segregation itself. Robert Carter of the legal staff of the NAACP argued against the validity of the old Plessy Doctrine. This doctrine, first promulgated by the United States Supreme Court in 1896, had given legal validity to the southern institution of separate-but-equal facilities for Negroes and whites. In the area of education, the Supreme Court had already reversed this position in its historic decision of May 1954; but the Plessy Doctrine still remained as the rationale of segregation in other areas. This injustice and inconsistency in the segregation laws was the object of Bob Carter's brilliant attack. Meanwhile the city attorneys, throughout their argument, dwelt on a single theme: if bus segregation ended, Montgomery would become a battleground of violence and bloodshed.

After listening to these arguments for several hours, Judge Rives addressed the city attorneys. "Is it fair," he asked, "to command one man to surrender his constitutional rights, if they are his constitutional rights, in order to prevent another man from committing a crime?" At this I touched Ralph Abernathy, who was sitting on one side of me, and Vernon Johns (he was on a brief visit to Montgomery at this time), on the other side, and whispered: "It looks as though we might get a favorable verdict."

The judges deliberated for about three weeks. On June 4, 1956, they declared in a two-to-one decision, Judge Lynn of Birmingham dissenting, that the city bus segregation laws of Alabama were unconstitutional. The city attorneys immediately announced that they would appeal the case to the United States Supreme Court.

The battle was not yet won. We would have to walk and sacrifice for several more months, while the city appealed the case. But at least we could walk with new hope. Now it was only a matter of time.

Or so we thought. But almost on the heels of the court's decision, disaster threatened the movement from a new quarter. On June 11, Rev. U. J. Fields made a statement to the press claiming that he was resigning as recording secretary of the MIA. In his announcement the youthful, goateed pastor of the Bell Street Baptist Church, who had been an officer of the association from the beginning, accused the members of "misusing money sent from all over the nation," and appropriating it "for their own purposes." Many of the leaders, he claimed, had taken on an air of "bigness" and had become "too egotistical and interested in perpetuating themselves." The association, he said, no longer represented what he had stood for, and he was severing his relations with a movement in which "the many are exploited by the few."

I was out of the city when Fields released his statement. Coretta and I had driven to California with Ralph and Juanita Abernathy to attend some conferences, and to enjoy our first vacation together away from the daily tensions of the protest. Rev. R. J. Glasco, then administrative assistant at the MIA office, telephoned the news. Earlier in the evening Fields had come to the mass meeting indignant because the executive board had failed to reelect him to office. When he brought the matter before the audience, he was further enraged by their almost unanimous approval of the board's action. He had left the meeting immediately to announce his "resignation" and prepare his attack on the MIA.

Although the news did not come entirely as a surprise, I realized the seriousness of the possible repercussions. While I was certain that there was no truth in Fields's charges, I knew that some people would believe them, and that many others would be left in a state of confusion. A charge of misappropriation of funds could cause a curtailment of contributions, thus hampering the car pool. Moreover, the white opposition would welcome this break as an opportunity to investigate our books with the ultimate aim of freezing our funds. I was also worried about how the Negroes of Montgomery might express their resentment against Fields.

My vacation had ended before it had well begun. I canceled the remainder of my engagements, promising to rejoin Coretta and the Abernathys later, and flew back to Montgomery. There I found, as I had expected, that emotions were running high. No one would speak in Fields's support, and so obviously distorted were his charges that even the local white press reported them with little enthusiasm. The Negroes were describing him as either a "fool" or a "black Judas." "I jest wish I could get my hands on him," said one indignant maid. The group of his own congregation had met and voted him out. (He was subsequently reinstated.) Everywhere in the Negro community sentiment mounted against him.

Fortunately by this time Fields had privately confessed to several people that he deeply regretted what he had done. Early on the morning of 18 June my telephone rang. Fields had learned that I was back in town, and wanted to see me. He arrived with a sober face, and went immediately to the point.

"I want you to know that I was not referring to you in my accusations. I have always had the greatest respect for your integrity and I still do. But there are some members of the MIA board that I don't care for at all. We never could get along."

I interrupted him. "You mean that your statements about the egotism of the leaders grew out of a personal conflict between you and one or two men on the board?"

"Yes," he admitted, "I guess that is true."

I asked him about the charge of misappropriation of funds, saying that if any such thing existed I wanted to know about it. With chagrin Fields answered:

"I confess that I don't know a single instance of misappropriation. All of those things I made up in a moment of anger. I felt that I had been mistreated by the board, and this was my way of retaliating."

By now it was clear that Fields was more to be pitied than scorned. I asked if he would be willing to make the same statements in the mass meeting that night. With some apprehension, he agreed.

People started assembling in front of the Beulah Baptist Church at three that afternoon. By five the church was filled. In the sweltering evening there was an unaccustomed atmosphere of bitterness. When Fields joined me on the rostrum at seven, the crowd muttered angrily, and I heard one voice call out, "Look at that devil sitting right next to Reverend King."

I had a double task ahead: one was to convince the people that there had been no misappropriation of funds and that the internal structure of the MIA was still stable; the other was to persuade them to forgive Fields for his errors and to give him a hearing. I plunged immediately into the first issue.

"I guess," I said, "that I know as much about the MIA as anyone in Montgomery, and I can truthfully say that I do not know of a single instance of misappropriation of funds. The finance committee of our association is composed of honest men and women—persons whose integrity has been established over the years and whose character is above reproach. I have implicit faith in the finance committee and the ministers who have spoken at fund-raising meetings all over the country."

I denied the accusaton of "bigness." "It is true," I said, "that some of the leaders have received national and international publicity, but only the shallow-minded are excited over publicity. Publicity is evanescent; it is here today and gone tomorrow. Today Autherine Lucy is showered with publicity; tomorrow it is Gus Courts. Today it is Emmet Till, tomorrow it is Martin Luther King. Then in another tomorrow it will be somebody else. Whoever falls in love with publicity is not fit to have it and will end up in misery.

"The honors and privileges," I continued, "that often come as a result of leadership constitute only one side of the picture. The greater the privileges, the greater the responsibilities and sacrifices."

So far the audience had listened sympathetically. But when I began to speak about Fields, they moved restlessly in their seats and I could hear a low murmur of disapproval. I expressed frank regret at Fields's statement. "Certainly it has created many unnecessary problems for us."

"You said it, Reverend," someone shouted.

"But," I continued, "we must meet this situation with the same dignity and discipline with which we have met so many difficult situations in the past. Let us never forget that we have committed ourselves to a way of nonviolence, and nonviolence means avoiding not only external physical violence but also internal violence of spirit. You not only refuse to shoot a man, but you refuse to hate him. Now in the spirit of our nonviolent movement I call upon you to forgive the Reverend Fields." I could see a few heads shaking in refusal, but I did not stop speaking. "We are all aware of the weaknesses of human nature. We have all made mistakes along the way of life, and we have all had moments when our emotions overpowered us. Now some of us are here this evening to stone one of our brothers because he has made a mistake." I paused a moment, and then spoke the words of Christ: "Let him who is without sin cast the first stone." With this a deep hush came across the audience.

In conclusion I recited the parable of the prodigal son. "Will we be like the unforgiving elder brother, or will we, in the spirit of Christ, follow the example of the loving and forgiving father?"

As Fields rose to speak, instead of the boos and catcalls he had expected he was met with respectful silence. He began to pray. "Lord, help us to live in such a way from day to day, that even when we kneel to pray, our prayers will be for others. . . ." A great amen came from the audience. Then he asked forgiveness for his mistake, and assured the group that he had no evidence that money had been misused or misplaced by the MIA. By the time he had finished the group was deeply moved. He left the platform to solid applause.

So nonviolence triumphed again, and a situation that many had predicted would be the end of the MIA left it more united than ever in the spirit of tolerance.

The summer days gave way to the shorter cooler days of an Alabama autumn. The Supreme Court decision on our appeal was still pending. Meanwhile we were facing continued attempts to block the car pool. Insurance agents decided, almost overnight, to refuse to insure our station wagons, contending that the risk was too high. The liability insurance on our station wagons was canceled no less than four times within four months. (We had no trouble with the collision insurance because it was with a Negro company.)

Finally the company that held our liability insurance notified us that all the policies would be canceled as of September 15. A northern friend who had read of our trouble wrote suggesting that we contact Lloyds of London. A few days later I talked to T. M. Alexander, an insurance broker in Atlanta, who approved of the idea and agreed to make the contact for us. In a few days he was able to tell us that Lloyds of London would take the insurance. From that moment on our insurance problems were solved.

But we were in for even greater difficulties. The city decided to take legal action against the car pool itself. On October 30, 1956, Mayor Gayle introduced a resolution instructing the city's legal department "to file such proceedings as it may deem proper to stop the operation of car pool or transportation systems growing out of the bus boycott." We tried to block this maneuver by filing a request in the federal court for an order restraining the city from interfering with the pool. But U.S. District Judge Frank M. Johnson refused to grant the request. Soon several of us received subpoenas; the city had filed the petition. The hearing was set for Tuesday, 13 November.

The night before the hearing I had to go before the mass meeting to warn the people that the car pool would probably be enjoined. I knew that they had willingly suffered for nearly twelve months, but how could they function at all with the car pool destroyed? Could we ask them to walk back and forth every day to their jobs? And if not, would we then be forced to admit that the protest had failed in the end? For the first time in our long struggle together, I almost shrank from appearing before them.

The evening came, and I mustered up enough courage to tell them the truth. I tried, however, to end on a note of hope. "This may well be," I said, "the darkest hour just before dawn. We have moved all of these months with the daring faith that God was with us in our struggle. The many experiences of days gone by have vindicated that faith in a most unexpected manner. We must go out with the same faith, the same conviction. We must believe that a way will be made out of no way." But in spite of these words, I could feel the cold breeze of pessimism passing through the audience. It was a dark night—darker than a thousand midnights. It was a night in which the light of hope was about to fade away and the lamp of faith about to flicker. We went home with nothing before us but a cloud of uncertainty.

Tuesday morning found us in court, once again before Judge Carter. The city's petition was directed against the MIA and several churches and individuals. It asked the court to grant the city compensation for damages growing out of the car pool operation. The city contended that it had lost more than fifteen thousand dollars as a result of the reduction in bus travel (the city receives 2 percent of the bus company revenues). It further alleged that the car pool was a "public nuisance" and a "private enterprise" operating without license fee or franchise. As the arguments unfolded the issue boiled down to this: Was the car pool a "private enterprise" operating without a franchise? Or was it a voluntary "share-a-ride" plan provided as a service by Negro churches without a profit?

As chief defendant I sat at the front table with the prosecuting and defense attorneys. Around twelve o'clock—during a brief recess—I noticed unusual commotion in the courtroom. Both Commissioner Sellers and Mayor Gayle were called to a back room, followed by two of the city attorneys. Several reporters moved excitedly in and out of the room.

I turned to Fred Gray and Peter Hall and said: "Something is wrong."

Before I could fully get these words out, Rex Thomas—a reporter for Associated Press—came up to me with a paper in his hand.

"Here is the decision that you have been waiting for. Read this release."

Quickly, with a mixture of anxiety and hope, I read these words: "The United States Supreme Court today affirmed a decision of a special three-judge U.S. District Court in declaring Alabama's state and local laws requiring segregation on buses unconstitutional. The Supreme Court acted without listening to any argument; it simply said 'the motion to affirm is granted and the Judgment is affirmed.' "

At this moment my heart began to throb with an inexpressible joy. The darkest hour of our struggle had indeed proved to be the first hour of victory. At once I told the news to the attorneys at the table. Then I rushed to the back of the room to tell my wife, Ralph Abernathy, and E. D. Nixon. Soon the word had spread to the whole courtroom. The faces of the Negroes showed that they had heard. "God Almighty has spoken from Washington, D.C.," said one joyful bystander.

After a few minutes Judge Carter called the court to order again, and we settled down to the case at hand for the remainder of the day. About five o'clock both sides rested, and the judge's decision came in a matter of minutes: As we had all expected, the city was granted a temporary injunction to halt the motor pool. But the decision was an anticlimax. Tuesday, 13 November 1956, will always remain an important and ironic date in the history of the Montgomery bus protest. On that day two historic decisions were rendered—one to do away with the pool; the other to remove the underlying conditions that made it necessary.

I rushed home and notified the press that I was calling the Negro citizens together on Wednesday night, 14 November, to decide whether to call off the protest. In order to accommodate as many people as possible, two simultaneous meetings were scheduled, one on each side of town, with the speakers traveling from one meeting to the other. In the meantime, the executive board decided, on the advice of counsel, to recommend that the official protest be ended immediately, but that the return to the buses be delayed until the mandatory order arrived from the Supreme Court in Washington. It was expected in a few days.

The eight thousand men and women who crowded in and around the two churches were in high spirits. At the first meeting it was clear that the news of the decision had spread fast, and the opening hymn had a special note of joy. Reading the Scripture that night was Bob Graetz, who had chosen Paul's famous letter to the Corinthians: "Though I have all faith, so that I could remove mountains, and have not love, I am nothing. . . . Love suffereth long, and is kind . . ."

When the slender blond minister came to the words: "When I was a child, I spoke as a child, I understood as a child, I thought as a child: but when I became a man, I put away childish things," the congregation burst into applause. Soon they were shouting and cheering and waving their handkerchiefs, as if to say that they knew they had come of age, had won new dignity. When Bob Graetz concluded: "And now abideth faith, hope, love, but the greatest of these is love," there was another spontaneous outburst. Only a people who had struggled to love in the midst of bitter conflict could have reacted in this fashion. I knew then that nonviolence, for all its difficulties, had won its way into our hearts.

Later Ralph Abernathy spoke. He told how a white newspaperman had reproached him for this outburst on the part of the congregation.

"Isn't it a little peculiar," the journalist had asked, "for people to interrupt the Scripture in that way?"

"Yes it is," Abernathy quoted himself in reply. "Just as it is peculiar for people to walk in the snow and rain when there are empty buses available; just as it is peculiar for people to pray for those who persecute them; just as it is peculiar for the southern Negro to stand up and look a white man in the face as an equal." At this his audience laughed and shouted and applauded.

Each of the meetings accepted the recommendations of the executive board to call off the protest but refrain from riding the buses until the mandate reached Alabama.

That night the Ku Klux Klan rode. The radio had announced their plan to demonstrate throughout the Negro community, and threats of violence and new bombings were in the air. My mail was warning that "if you allow the niggers to go back on the buses and sit in the front seats we're going to burn down fifty houses in one night, including yours." Another letter cursed the Supreme Court and threatened "that damn Hugo Black": "When he comes to Alabama we're going to hang you and him from the same tree."

Ordinarily, threats of Klan action were a signal to the Negroes to go into their houses, close the doors, pull the shades, or turn off the lights. Fearing death, they played dead. But this time they had prepared a surprise. When the Klan arrived—according to the newspapers "about forty carloads of robed and hooded members"—porch lights were on and doors open. As the Klan drove by, the Negroes behaved as though they were watching a circus parade. Concealing the effort it cost them, many walked about as usual; some simply watched from their steps; a few waved at the passing cars. After a few blocks, the Klan, nonplussed, turned off into a sidestreet and disappeared into the night.

Soon we discovered that it was going to take the mandate more than four or five days to reach Montgomery. A reporter in contact with the clerk of the Court in Washington revealed that it would be closer to a month. This created a serious problem since the car pool was still enjoined. To meet this crisis we suggested that each area and street work out a cooperative "share-a-ride" plan. With S. S. Seay as skillful coordinator, the plan succeeded. The buses remained empty.

Meanwhile we went to work to prepare the people for integrated buses. In mass meeting after mass meeting we stressed nonviolence. The prevailing theme was that "we must not take this as a victory over the white man, but as a victory for justice and democracy." We hammered away at the point that "we must not go back on the buses and push people around unnecessarily boasting of our rights. We must simply sit where there is a vacant seat."

In several meetings we ran teaching sessions to school the people in nonviolent techniques. We lined up chairs in front of the altar to resemble a bus, with a driver's seat out front. From the audience we selected a dozen or so "actors" and assigned each one a role in a hypothetical situation. One man was driver and the others were white and Negro passengers. Both groups contained some hostile and some courteous characters. As the audience watched, the actors played out a scene of insult or violence. At the end of each scene the actors returned to the audience and another group took their place; and at the end of each session a general discussion followed.

Sometimes the person playing a white man put so much zeal into his performance that he had to be gently reproved from the sidelines. Often a Negro forgot his nonviolent role and struck back with vigor; whenever this happened we worked to rechannel his words and deeds in a nonviolent direction.

As the day for the mandate drew near, several MIA leaders went into the schools and urged the high school and college students to adhere to the way of nonviolence. We also distributed throughout the city a mimeographed list of "Suggestions for Integrating Buses." In preparing this text we had the assistance of the Rev. Glenn Smiley, a southern-born white minister of the Fellowship of Reconciliation who was in Montgomery at the time.

INTEGRATED BUS SUGGESTIONS

This is a historic week because segregation on buses has now been declared unconstitutional. Within a few days the Supreme Court mandate will reach Montgomery and you will be reboarding *integrated* buses. This places upon us all a tremendous responsibility of maintaining, in the face of what could be some unpleasantness, a calm and loving dignity befitting good citizens and members of our race. If there is violence in word or deed it must not be our people who commit it.

For your help and convenience the following suggestions are made. Will you read, study, and memorize them so that our nonviolent determination may not be endangered. First, some general suggestions:

1. Not all white people are opposed to integrated buses. Accept goodwill on the part of many.
2. The *whole* bus is now for the use of *all* people. Take a vacant seat.
3. Pray for guidance and commit yourself to complete nonviolence in word and action as you enter the bus.
4. Demonstrate the calm dignity of our Montgomery people in your actions.
5. In all things observe ordinary rules of courtesy and good behavior.
6. Remember that this is not a victory for Negroes alone, but for all Montgomery and the South. Do not boast! Do not brag!

7. Be quiet but friendly; proud, but not arrogant; joyous, but not boisterous.

8. Be loving enough to absorb evil and understanding enough to turn an enemy into a friend.

Now for some specific suggestions:

1. The bus driver is in charge of the bus and has been instructed to obey the law. Assume that he will cooperate in helping you occupy any vacant seat.

2. Do not deliberately sit by a white person, unless there is no other seat.

3. In sitting down by a person, white or colored, say "May I" or "Pardon me" as you sit. This is a common courtesy.

4. If cursed, do not curse back. If pushed, do not push back. If struck, do not strike back, but evidence love and goodwill at all times.

5. In case of an incident, talk as little as possible, and always in a quiet tone. Do not get up from your seat! Report all serious incidents to the bus driver.

6. For the first few days try to get on the bus with a friend in whose nonviolence you have confidence. You can uphold one another by a glance or a prayer.

7. If another person is being molested, do not arise to go to his defense, but pray for the oppressor and use moral and spiritual force to carry on the struggle for justice.

8. According to your own ability and personality, do not be afraid to experiment with new and creative techniques for achieving reconciliation and social change.

9. If you feel you cannot take it, walk for another week or two. We have confidence in our people. GOD BLESS YOU ALL.

In spite of all of our efforts to prepare the Negroes for integrated buses, not a single white group would take the responsibility of preparing the white community. We tried to get the white ministerial alliance to make a simple statement calling for courtesy and Christian brotherhood, but in spite of the favorable response of a few ministers, Robert Graetz reported that the majority "dared not get involved in such a controversial issue." This was a deep disappointment. Although the white ministers as a group had been appallingly silent throughout the protest, I had still maintained the hope that they would take a stand once the decision was rendered. Yes, there were always a few; but they were far too rare.

The only white group that came near to making a positive statement was the Men of Montgomery, the businessmen who had already shown their good will in their earlier efforts to settle the protest. About ten days before the mandate came to Montgomery, a committee of the Men of Montgomery met with a group from the MIA and worked out a statement, calling for courtesy and nonviolence, to be issued jointly. When the statement was presented to the full membership of the Men of Montgomery, however, two or three members objected to it and, since unanimous approval was required, the release of the statement was blocked. Thus passed the one opportunity of the white community to take a positive stand for law and order.

Soon the reactionaries had taken over. A White Citizens Council leader threatened: "Any attempt to enforce this decision will lead to riot and bloodshed." One group suggested the establishment of a fleet of station wagons for a white pick-up service—an interesting proposal from those who had just succeeded in outlawing the Negro fleet! On 18 December, the city commissioners issued the following statement:

This decision in the bus case has had a tremendous impact on the customs of our people here in Montgomery. It is not an easy thing to live under a law recognized as constitutional for these many years and then have it suddenly overturned on the basis of psychology. . . . The city commission, and we know our people are with us in this determination, will not yield one inch, but will do all in its power to oppose the integration of the Negro race with the white race in Montgomery, and will forever stand like a rock against social equality, inter-marriage, and mixing of the races under God's creation and plan.

On 20 December, the bus integration order finally reached Montgomery. A mass meeting was immediately scheduled for that evening, to give the people final instructions before returning to the buses the following day. I called Mr. Bagley, manager of the bus company, and asked him to be sure to have service restored on all of the major lines. With evident relief, he agreed.

To the overflow crowd at the St. John A.M.E. Church I read the following message that I had carefully prepared in the afternoon:

For more than twelve months now, we, the Negro citizens of Montgomery, have been engaged in a nonviolent protest against injustices and indignities experienced on city buses. We came to see that, in the long run, it is more honorable to walk in dignity than ride in humiliation. So in a quiet dignified manner, we decided to substitute tired feet for tired souls, and walk the streets of Montgomery until the sagging walls of injustice had been crushed. . . .

These twelve months have not been easy. Our feet have often been tired. We have struggled against tremendous odds to maintain alternative transportation. We can remember days when unfavorable court decisions came upon us like tidal waves, leaving us treading the waters of despair. But amid all of this we have kept going with the faith that as we struggle, God struggles with us, and that the arc of the moral universe, although long, is bending toward justice. We have lived under the agony and darkness of Good Friday with the conviction that one day the heightened glow of Easter would emerge on the horizon. We have seen truth crucified and goodness buried, but we have kept going with the conviction that truth crushed to earth will rise again.

Now our faith seems to be vindicated. This morning the long awaited mandate from the U.S. Supreme Court concerning bus segregation came to Montgomery. This mandate expresses in terms that are crystal clear that segregation in public transportation is both legally and sociologically invalid. In the light of this mandate and the unanimous vote rendered by the Montgomery Improvement Association about a month ago, the year-old protest against city buses is officially called off, and the Negro citizens of Montgomery are urged to return to the buses tomorrow morning on a nonsegregated basis.

I cannot close without giving just a word of caution. Our experience and growth during this past year of nonviolent protest has been such that we cannot be satisfied with a court "victory" over our white brothers. We must respond to the decision with an understanding of those who have oppressed us and with an appreciation of the new adjustments that the court order poses for them. We must be able to face up honestly to our own shortcomings. We must act in such a way as to make possible a coming together of white people and colored people on the basis of a real harmony of interests and understanding. We seek an integration based on mutual respect.

This is the time that we must evince calm dignity and wise restraint. Emotions must not run wild. Violence must not come from any of us, for if we become victimized with violent intents, we will have walked in vain, and our twelve months of glorious dignity will be transformed into an eve of gloomy catastrophe. As we go back to the buses let us be loving enough to turn an enemy into a friend. We must now move from protest to reconciliation. It is my firm conviction that God is working in Montgomery. Let all men of goodwill, both Negro and white, continue to work with him. With this dedication we will be able to emerge from the bleak and desolate midnight of man's inhumanity to man to the bright and glittering daybreak of freedom and justice.

The audience stood and cheered loudly. This was the moment toward which they had pressed for more than a year. The return to the buses, on an integrated basis, was a new beginning. But it was a conclusion, too, the end of an effort that had drawn Montgomery's Negroes together as never before. To many of those present the joy was not unmixed. Some perhaps feared what might happen when they began to ride the buses again the next day. Others had found a spiritual strength in sacrifice to a cause; now the sacrifice was no longer necessary. Like many consummations, this one left a slight aftertaste of sadness.

At the close of the meeting I asked the ministers to stay over for a few minutes to urge them to ride the buses during the rush hours for the first few days. It was our feeling that their presence would give the Negro citizens courage and made them less likely to retaliate in case of insults. The ministers readily agreed. Accordingly, two were assigned to each bus line in the city, to ride mainly during the morning and afternoon rush. They were given suggestions as to how to handle situations of violence and urged to keep an accurate record of all incidents.

I had decided that after many months of struggling with my people for the goal of justice I should not sit back and watch, but should lead them back to the buses myself. I asked Ralph Abernathy, E. D. Nixon, and Glenn Smiley to join me in riding on the first integrated bus. They reached my house around 5:45 on Friday morning. Television cameras, photographers, and news reporters were hovering outside the door. At 5:55 we walked toward the bus stop, the cameras shooting, the reporters bombarding us with questions. Soon the bus appeared; the door opened, and I stepped on. The bus driver greeted me with a cordial smile. As I put my fare in the box he said:

"I believe you are Reverend King, aren't you?"

I answered: "Yes I am."

"We are glad to have you this morning," he said.

I thanked him and took my seat, smiling now too. Abernathy, Nixon, and Smiley followed, with several reporters and television men behind them. Glenn Smiley sat next to me. So I rode the first integrated bus in Montgomery with a white minister, and a native southerner, as my seatmate.

Downtown we transferred to one of the buses that serviced the white residential section. As the white people boarded, many took seats as if nothing were going on. Others looked amazed to see Negroes sitting in front, and some appeared peeved to know that they either had to sit behind Negroes or stand. One elderly man stood up by the conductor, despite the fact that there were several vacant seats in the rear. When someone suggested to him that he sit in back, he responded: "I would rather die and go to hell than sit behind a nigger." A white woman unknowingly took a seat by a Negro. When she noticed her neighbor, she jumped up and said in a tone of obvious anger: "What are these niggers gonna do next?"

But despite such signs of hostility there were no major incidents on the first day. Many of the whites responded to the new system calmly. Several deliberately and with friendly smiles took seats beside Negroes. True, one Negro woman was slapped by a white man as she alighted, but she refused to retaliate. Later she said: "I could have broken that little fellow's neck all by myself, but I left the mass meeting last night determined to do what Reverend King asked." The *Montgomery Advertiser* reported at the end of the first day: "The calm but cautious acceptance of this significant change in Montgomery's way of life came without any major disturbance."

But the reactionaries were not in retreat. Many of them had predicted violence, and such predictions are always a conscious or unconscious invitation to action. When people, especially in public office, talk about bloodshed as a concomitant of integration, they stir and arouse the hoodlums to acts of destruction, and often work under cover to bring them about. In Montgomery several public officials had predicted violence, and violence there had to be if they were to save face.

By 28 December the first few days of peaceful compliance had given way to a reign of terror. City buses were fired on throughout the city, especially in poorly lighted sections. A teenage girl was beaten by four or five white men as she alighted from a bus. A pregnant Negro woman was shot in the leg. Fearfully, many Negroes and whites refused to ride the buses. The city commission responded by suspending the night runs on city lines. No bus could begin a run after five o'clock, which meant that once again returning workers were without transportation. This was exactly what the violent elements wanted.

During this period a new effort was made to divide the Negroes. Handbills were distributed urging Negroes to rebel against me in particular and their leaders in general. These leaflets purported to come from "fed-up" Negroes, but virtually everyone knew that they were the work of white extremists. Referring to me as Luther, one leaflet said: "We get shot at while he rides. He is getting us in more trouble every day. Wake up. Run him out of town." Another one stated: "We have been doing OK in Montgomery before outside preachers were born! Ask Reverend King's papa & Mamma if they like his doings—ask him if they going to help in Atlanta. Better quit him before it is too late!"

The KKK was in its element. One day it descended upon Montgomery in full regalia. But it seemed to have lost its spell. A college student who saw the Klansmen swarming the streets in their white costumes with red insignia went cheerfully on about her business, thinking that they were collecting for the United Fund. And one cold night a small Negro boy was seen warming his hands at a burning cross.

On 9 January, Ralph Abernathy and I went to Atlanta to prepare for a meeting of Negro leaders that I had called for the following day. In the middle of the night we were awakened by a telephone call from Ralph's wife, Juanita. I knew that only some new disaster would make her rouse us at two in the morning. When Ralph came back, his sober face told part of the story. "My home has been bombed," he said, "and three or four other explosions have been heard in the city, but Juanita doesn't know where yet." I asked about Juanita and their daughter. "Thank God, they are safe." Before we could talk any more, the telephone rang a second time. It was Juanita again, saying that the First Baptist Church had been hit. I looked at Ralph as he sat down beside me, stunned. Both his home and his church bombed in one night, and I knew no words to comfort him. There in the early morning hours we prayed to God together, asking for the power of endurance, the strength to carry on.

Between three and seven we received no less than fifteen calls. We finally learned that besides Ralph's home and church, Bob Graetz's home and three other Baptist churches—Bell Street, Hutchinson Street, and Mt. Olive—had all been hit. Worrying that this time the people might be goaded into striking back, I called a few ministers in Montgomery and urged them to do what they could to keep control. In the meantime, Ralph and I arranged to fly back, leaving the meeting of southern leaders to begin without us.

From the Montgomery airport we drove directly to Ralph's house. The street was roped off, and hundreds of people stood staring at the ruins. The front porch had been almost completely destroyed, and things inside the house were scattered from top to bottom. Juanita, though shocked and pale, was fairly composed.

The rest of the morning was spent in a grim tour of the other bombings. The Bell Street and Mt. Olive Baptist churches had been almost completely destroyed. The other two churches were less severely damaged, but nevertheless faced great losses. The total damage to the four churches was estimated at $70,000. Bob Graetz's home had been a bomb target the previous summer, but had escaped serious damage. This time he was not so fortunate. The front of his house lay in ruins, and shattered glass throughout the interior showed the violence of the explosion. Assembled at each of the bombed sites was a large group of angry people; but with a restraint that I never ceased to wonder at, they held themselves under control.

The next morning, three important white agencies issued statements condemning the bombings. Grover Hall, editor of the *Montgomery Advertiser*, wrote a strong editorial entitled "Is is safe to live in Montgomery?" in which he insisted that the issue had gone beyond the question of segregation versus integration. As I read Hall's strong statement I could not help admiring this brilliant but complex man who claimed to be a supporter of segregation but could not stomach the excesses performed in its name. Several white ministers denounced the bombing as unchristian and uncivilized, and all through the day their statement was repeated over television by the distinguished minister of the First Presbyterian Church, Rev. Merle Patterson. The Men of Montgomery, too, made known their unalterable opposition to the bombings. For the first time since the protest began, these influential whites were on public record on the side of law and order. Their stands gave us new confidence in the basic decency of the vast majority of whites in the community. Despite their commitment to segregation, it was clear that they were still law-abiding, and would never sanction the use of violence to preserve the system.

That afternoon, I returned to Atlanta to make at least an appearance at the meeting of Negro leaders. There I found an enthusiastic group of almost a hundred men from all over the South, committed to the idea of a southern movement to implement the Supreme Court's decision against bus segregation through nonviolent means. Before adjourning they voted to form a permanent organization, the Southern Christian Leadership Conference, and elected me president, a position I still hold.

When I returned to Montgomery over the weekend I found the Negro community in low spirits. After the bombings the city commission had ordered all buses off the streets; and it now appeared that the city fathers would use this reign of violence as an excuse to cancel the bus company's franchise. As a result, many were coming to feel that all our gains had been lost; and I myself started to fear that we were in for another long struggle to get bus service renewed. I was also beginning to wonder whether the virulent leaflets that were bombarding the Negro community might be having their effect. Discouraged, and still revolted by the bombings, for some strange reason I began to feel a personal sense of guilt for everything that was happening.

In this mood I went to the mass meeting on Monday night. There for the first time, I broke down in public. I had invited the audience to join me in prayer, and had begun by asking God's guidance and direction in all our activities. Then, in the grip of an emotion I could not control, I said, "Lord, I hope no one will have to die as a result of our struggle for freedom in Montgomery. Certainly I don't want to die. But if anyone has to die, let it be me." The audience was in an uproar. Shouts and cries of "no, no" came from all sides. So intense was the reaction, that I could not go on with my prayer. Two of my fellow ministers came to the pulpit and suggested that I take a seat. For a few minutes I stood with their arms around me, unable to move. Finally, with the help of my friends, I sat down. It was this scene that caused the press to report mistakenly that I had collapsed.

Unexpectedly, this episode brought me great relief. Many people came up to me after the meeting and many called the following day to assure me that we were all together until the end. For the next few days, the city was fairly quiet. Bus service was soon resumed, though still on a daytime schedule only.

Then another wave of terror hit. Early in the morning of 28 January, the People's Service Station and Cab Stand was bombed, and another bomb fell at the home of Allen Robertson, a sixty-year-old Negro hospital worker. It was never discovered why these two victims had been singled out for attack. The same morning an unexploded bomb, crudely assembled from twelve sticks of dynamite, was found still smoldering on my porch.

I was staying with friends on the other side of town, and Coretta and "Yoki" were in Atlanta. So once more I heard the news first on the telephone. On my way home, I visited the other scenes of disaster nearby, and found to my relief that no one had been hurt. I noticed a police car driving away from the area with two Negroes on the rear seat. These men, I learned, were under arrest because they had challenged the police to their faces with having done nothing to catch the bombers. Both were later convicted of trying to "incite to riot." But there was no riot that day, although the crowds that had gathered around the damaged buildings were once again ready for violence. They were just waiting for a signal. Fortunately, the signal never came.

At home I addressed the crowd from my porch, where the mark of the bomb was clear. "We must not return violence under any condition. I know this is difficult advice to follow, especially since we have been the victims of no less than ten bombings. But this is the way of Christ; it is the way of the cross. We must somehow believe that unearned suffering is redemptive." Then since it was Sunday morning, I urged the people to go home and get ready for church. Gradually they dispersed.

With these bombings the community came to see that Montgomery was fast being plunged into anarchy. Finally, the city began to investigate in earnest. Rewards of $4000 were offered for information leading to the arrest and conviction of the bombers. On 31 January, the Negro community was surprised to hear that seven white men had been arrested in connection with the bombings. Detective J. D. Shows was given credit for apprehending them.

All of the men were released on bonds ranging from $250 to $13,000, and the city court passed the charges to the Montgomery County Grand Jury without testimony. The grand jury indicted five of the men and dropped charges against the other two.

The trial of the first two defendants, Raymond D. York and Sonny Kyle Livingston, came up in the Montgomery County Court, the same court where I had been tried in the antiboycott case a year before, and with the same solicitor, William F. Thetford, in charge of the prosecution. With the Emmet Till case in Mississippi still fresh in our memories, the Negroes held little hope of conviction.

Several of us were subpoenaed as witnesses. On the opening day, we found the courtroom jammed with spectators, most of them white. In fact there was scarcely room for the Negroes. One could tell from the dress and manner of the whites that most of them were poor and uneducated, the kind that would find security in the Ku Klux Klan. As we entered they looked at us with undisguised hate.

The defense attorneys spent two days attempting to prove the innocence of their clients, arguing that the bombings had been carried out by the MIA in order to inspire new outside donations for their dwindling treasury. At the end of the second day I was called to the witness stand by the defense. For more than an hour I was questioned on things which had no relevance to the bombing case. The lawyers lifted statements of mine out of context to give the impression that I was a perpetrator of hate and violence. At many points they invented derogatory statements concerning white people, and attributed them to me.

On the other hand Mr. Thetford fought as diligently for a conviction as he had fought for mine a year earlier. He had an excellent case. The men had signed confessions. But in spite of all the evidence, the jury returned a verdict of not guilty. With their friends crowding around them, Raymond D. York and Sonny Kyle Livingston walked grinning out of the courtroom.

Justice had once more miscarried. But the diehards had made their last stand. The disturbances ceased abruptly. Desegregation on the buses proceeded smoothly. In a few weeks transportation was back to normal, and people of both races rode together wherever they pleased. The skies did not fall when integrated buses finally traveled the streets of Montgomery.

## WHERE DO WE GO FROM HERE? (CHAPTER 11)

The bus struggle in Montgomery, Alabama, is now history. As the integrated buses roll daily through the city they carry, along with their passengers, a meaning-crowded symbolism. Accord among the great majority of passengers is evidence of the basic good will of man for man and a portent of peace in the desegregated society to come. Occasional instances of discord among passengers are a reminder that in other areas of Montgomery life segregation yet obtains with all of its potential for group strife and personal conflict. Indeed, segregation is still a reality throughout the South.

Where do we go from here? Since the problem in Montgomery is merely symptomatic of the larger national problem, where do we go not only in Montgomery but all over the South and the nation? Forces maturing for years have given rise to the present crisis in race relations. What are these forces that have brought the crisis about? What will be the conclusion? Are we caught in a social and political impasse, or do we have at our disposal the creative resources to achieve the ideals of brotherhood and harmonious living?

The last half century has seen crucial changes in the life of the American Negro. The social upheavals of the two world wars, the Great Depression, and the spread of the automobile have made it both possible and necessary for the Negro to move away from his former isolation on the rural plantation. The decline of agriculture and the parallel growth of industry have drawn large numbers of Negroes to urban centers and brought about a gradual improvement in their economic status. New contacts have led to a broadened outlook and new possibilities for educational advance. All of these factors have conjoined to cause the Negro to take a fresh look at himself. His expanding life experiences have created within him a consciousness that he is an equal element in a larger social compound and accordingly should be given rights and privileges commensurate with his new responsibilities. Once plagued with a tragic sense of inferiority resulting from the crippling effects of slavery and segregation, the Negro has now been driven to revaluate himself. He has come to feel that he is somebody. His religion reveals to him that God loves all His children and that the important thing about a man is not "his specificity but his fundamentum"—not the texture of his hair or the color of his skin but his eternal worth to God.

This growing self-respect has inspired the Negro with a new determination to struggle and sacrifice until first-class citizenship becomes a reality. This is the true meaning of the Montgomery story. One can never understand the bus protest in Montgomery without understanding that there is a new Negro in the South, with a new sense of dignity and destiny.

Along with the Negro's changing image of himself has come an awakening moral consciousness on the part of millions of white Americans concerning segregation. Ever since the signing of the Declaration of Independence, America has manifested a schizophrenic personality on the question of race. She has been torn between selves—a self in which she has proudly professed democracy and a self in which she has sadly practiced the antithesis of democracy. The reality of segregation, like slavery, has always had to confront the ideals of democracy and Christianity. Indeed, segregation and discrimination are strange paradoxes in a nation founded on the principle that all men are created equal. This contradiction has disturbed the consciences of whites both North and South, and has caused many of them to see that segregation is basically evil.

Climaxing this process was the Supreme Court's decision outlawing segregation in the public schools. For all men of good will 17 May 1954, marked a joyous end to the long night of enforced segregation. In unequivocal language the Court affirmed that "separate but equal" facilities are inherently unequal, and that to segregate a child on the basis of his race is to deny that child equal protection of the law. This decision brought hope to millions of disinherited Negroes who had formerly dared only to dream of freedom. It further enhanced the Negro's sense of dignity and gave him even greater determination to achieve justice.

This determination of Negro Americans to win freedom from all forms of oppression springs from the same deep longing that motivates oppressed peoples all over the world. The rumblings of discontent in Asia and Africa are expressions of a quest for freedom and human dignity by people who have long been the victims of colonialism and imperialism. So in a real sense the racial crisis in America is a part of the larger world crisis.

But the numerous changes which have culminated in a new sense of dignity on the part of the Negro are not of themselves responsible for the present crisis. If all men accepted these historical changes in good faith there would be no crisis. The crisis developed when the collective pressures to achieve fair goals for the Negro met with tenacious and determined resistance. Then the emerging new order, based on the principle of democratic equalitarianism, came face to face with the older order, based on the principles of paternalism and subordination. The crisis was not produced by outside agitators, NAACPers, Montgomery protesters, or even the Supreme Court. The crisis developed, paradoxically, when the most sublime principles of American democracy—imperfectly realized for almost two centuries,—began fulfilling themselves and met with the brutal resistance of forces seeking to contract and repress freedom's growth.

The resistance has risen at times to ominous proportions. Many states have reacted in open defiance. The legislative halls of the South still ring loud with such words as "interposition" and "nullification." Many public officials are using the power of their offices to defy the law of the land. Through their irresponsible actions, their inflammatory statements, and their dissemination of distortions and half-truths, they have succeeded in arousing abnormal fears and morbid antipathies within the minds of underprivileged and uneducated whites, leaving them in such a state of excitement and confusion that they are led to acts of meanness and violence that no normal person would commit.

This resistance to the emergence of the new order expresses itself in the resurgence of the Ku Klux Klan. Determined to preserve segregation at any cost, this organization employs methods that are crude and primitive. It draws its members from underprivileged groups who see in the Negro's rising status a political and economic threat. Although the Klan is impotent politically and openly denounced from all sides, it remains a dangerous force which thrives on racial and religious bigotry. Because of its past history, whenever the Klan moves there is fear of violence.

Then there are the white citizens councils. Since they occasionally recruit members from a higher social and economic level than the Klan, a halo of partial respectability hovers over them. But like the Klan they are determined to preserve segregation despite the law. Their weapons of threat, intimidation, and boycott are directed both against Negroes and against any whites who stand for justice. They demand absolute conformity from whites and abject submission from Negroes. The citizens councils often argue piously that they abhor violence, but their defiance of the law, their unethical methods, and their vitriolic public pronouncements inevitably create the atmosphere in which violence thrives.

As a result of the councils' activities most white moderates in the South no longer feel free to discuss in public the issues involved in desegregation for fear of social ostracism and economic reprisals. What channels of communication had once existed between whites and Negroes have thus now been largely closed.

The present crisis in race relations has characteristics that come to the forefront in any period of social transition. The guardians of the status quo lash out with denunciation against the person or organization that they consider most responsible for the emergence of the new order. Often this denunciation rises to major proportions. In the transition from slavery to restricted emancipation Abraham Lincoln was assassinated. In the present transition from segregation to desegregation the Supreme Court is castigated and the NAACP is maligned and subjected to extralegal reprisals.

As in other social crises the defenders of the status quo in the South argue that they were gradually solving their own problems until external pressure was brought to bear upon them. The unfamiliar complaint in the South today is that the Supreme Court's decision on education has set us back a generation in race relations, that people of different races who had long lived at peace have now been turned against one another. But this is a misinterpretation of what is taking place. When a subject people moves toward freedom, they are not creating a cleavage, but are revealing the cleavage which apologists of the old order have sought to conceal. It is not the movement for integration which is creating a cleavage in the United States today. The depth of the cleavage that existed, the true nature of which the moderates failed to see and make clear, is being revealed by the resistance to integration.

During a crisis period, a desperate attempt is made by the extremists to influence the minds of the liberal forces in the ruling majority. So, for example, in the present transition white southerners attempt to convince northern whites that the Negroes are inherently criminal. They seek instances of Negro crime and juvenile delinquency in northern communities and then say: "You see, the Negroes are problems to you. They create problems wherever they go." The accusation is made without reference to the true nature of the situation. Environmental problems of delinquency are interpreted as evidence of racial criminality. Crises arising in northern schools are interpreted as proofs that Negroes are inherently delinquent. The extremists do not recognize that these school problems are symptoms of urban dislocation, rather than expressions of racial deficiency. Criminality and delinquency are not racial; poverty and ignorance breed crime whatever the racial group may be.

In the attempt to influence the minds of northern and southern liberals, the segregationists are often subtle and skillful. Those who are too smart to argue for the validity of segregation and racial inferiority on the basis of the Bible set forth their arguments on cultural and sociological grounds. The Negro is not ready for integration, they say; because of academic and cultural lags on the part of the Negro, the integration of schools will pull the white race down. They are never honest enough to admit that the academic and cultural lags in the Negro community are themselves the result of segregation and discrimination. The best way to solve any problem is to remove its cause. It is both rationally unsound and sociologically untenable to use the tragic effects of segregation as an argument for its continuation.

All of these calculated patterns—the defiance of southern legislative bodies, the activities of white supremacy organizations, and the distortions and rationalizations of the segregationists—have mounted up to massive resistance. This resistance grows out of the desperate attempt of the white South to perpetuate a system of human values that came into being under a feudalistic plantation system and which cannot survive in a day of growing urbanization and industrial expansion. These are the rock-bottom elements of the present crisis.

The schools of the South are the present storm center. Here the forces that stand for the best in our national life have been tragically ineffectual. A year after the Supreme Court had declared school segregation unconstitutional, it handed down a decree outlining the details by which integration should proceed "with all deliberate speed." While the Court did not set a definite deadline for the termination of this process, it did set a time for the beginning. It was clear that the Court had chosen this reasonable approach with the expectation that the forces of good will would immediately get to work and prepare the communities for a smooth and peaceful transition.

But the forces of good will failed to come through. The office of the president was appallingly silent, though just an occasional word from this powerful source, counseling the nation on the moral aspects of integration and the need for complying with the law, might have saved the South from much of its present confusion and terror. Other forces of justice also failed to act. It is true that immediately after the first decision was rendered, leading church, labor, and social welfare leaders issued statements upholding the decision, and many supporting resolutions were adopted by their organizations. But hardly a single group set forth an action program wherein their members could actively work to bring about a peaceable transition. Neither did they develop a plan whereby individuals in southern communities who were willing to work for desegregation could receive organization support in the face of economic reprisals and physical violence.

As a result of the failure of the moral forces of the nation to mobilize behind school integration, the forces of defeat were given the chance to organize and crystallize their opposition. While the good people stood silently and complacently by, the misguided people acted. If every church and synagogue had developed an action program; if every civic and social welfare organization, every labor union and educational institution, had worked out concrete plans for implementing their righteous resolutions; if the press, radio, and television had turned their powerful instruments in the direction of educating and elevating the people on this issue; if the president and Congress had taken a forthright stand; if these things had happened, federal troops might not have been forced to walk the corridors of Central High School.

But it is still not too late to act. Every crisis has both its dangers and opportunities. It can spell either salvation or doom. In the present crisis America can achieve either racial justice or the ultimate social psychosis that can only lead to domestic suicide. The democratic ideal of freedom and equality will be fulfilled for all—or all human beings will share in the resulting social and spiritual doom. In short, this crisis has the potential for democracy's fulfillment or fascism's triumph; for social progress or retrogression. We can choose either to walk the high road of human brotherhood or to tread the low road of man's inhumanity to man.

History has thrust upon our generation an indescribably important destiny—to complete a process of democratization which our nation has too long developed too slowly, but which is our most powerful weapon for world respect and emulation. How we deal with this crucial situation will determine our moral health as individuals, our cultural health as a region, our political health as a nation, and our prestige as a leader of the free world. The future of America is bound up with the solution of the present crisis. The shape of the world today does not permit us the luxury of a faltering democracy. The United States cannot hope to attain the respect of the vital and growing colored nations of the world unless it remedies its racial problems at home. If America is to remain a first-class nation, it cannot have a second-class citizenship.

A solution for the present crisis will not take place unless men and women work for it. Human progress is neither automatic nor inevitable. Even a superficial look at history reveals that no social advance rolls in on the wheels of inevitability. Every step twoard the goal of justice requires sacrifice, suffering, and struggle; the tireless exertions and passionate concern of dedicated individuals. Without persistent effort, time itself becomes an ally of the insurgent and primitive forces of irrational emotionalism and social destruction. This is no time for apathy or complacency. This is a time for vigorous and positive action.

It is the shame of the sunshine patriots if the foregoing paragraphs have a hollow sound, like an echo of countless political speeches. These things must be repeated time and again, for men forget quickly; but once said, they must be followed with a dynamic program, or else they become a refuge for those who shy from any action. If America is to respond creatively to the present crisis, many groups and agencies must rise above the reiteration of generalities and begin to take an active part in changing the face of their nation.

First, there is need for strong and aggressive leadership from the federal government. If the executive and legislative branches were as concerned about the protection of the citizenship rights of all people as the federal courts have been, the transition from a segregated to an integrated society would be much further along than it is today. The dearth of positive leadership from Washington is not confined to one political party. Both major parties have lagged in the service of justice. Many Democrats have betrayed it by capitulating to the undemocratic practices of the southern dixiecrats. Many Republicans have betrayed it by capitulating to the hypocrisy of right-wing northerners.

In spite of the crucial role of the federal judiciary in this tense period of transition, the courts cannot do the job alone. The courts can clarify constitutional principles and remove the legal basis for segregation, but they cannot write laws, appoint administrators, or enforce justice on the local level.

The states and localities have the powers if they choose to exercise them. But the southern states have made their policy clear. States' rights, they say in effect, include the right to abrogate power when it involves distasteful responsibilities, even to the Constitution of the United States, its amendments, and its judicial interpretation. So the power and the responsibility return by default to the federal government. It is up to all branches of the central government to accept the challenge.

Government action is not the whole answer to the present crisis, but it is an important partial answer. Morals cannot be legislated, but behavior can be regulated. The law cannot make an employer love me, but it can keep him from refusing to hire me because of the color of my skin. We must depend on religion and education to alter the errors of the heart and mind; but meanwhile it is an immoral act to compel a man to accept injustice until another man's heart is set straight. As the experience of several northern states has shown, antidiscrimination laws can provide powerful sanctions against this kind of immorality.

Moreover, the law itself is a form of education. The words of the Supreme Court, of Congress, and of the Constitution are eloquent instructors. In fact, it would be a mistake to minimize the impact upon the South of the federal court orders and legislative and executive acts already in effect. Desegregation of the armed services, for instance, has already had an immense, incalculable impact. Federal court decrees have altered transportation patterns, teachers' salaries, the use of recreational facilities, and myriad other matters. The habits if not the hearts of people have been and are being altered every day by federal action.

Another group with a vital role to play in the present crisis is the white northern liberals. The racial issue that we confront in America is not a sectional but a national problem. The citizenship rights of Negroes cannot be flouted anywhere without impairing the rights of every other American. Injustice anywhere is a threat to justice everywhere. A breakdown of law in Alabama weakens the very foundations of lawful government in the other forty-seven states. The mere fact that we live in the United States means that we are caught in a network of inescapable mutuality. Therefore, no American can afford to be apathetic about the problem of racial justice. It is a problem that meets every man at his front door. The racial problems will be solved in America to the degree that every American considers himself personally confronted with it. Whether one lives in the heart of the Deep South or on the periphery of the North, the problem of injustice is his problem; it is his problem because it is America's problem.

There is a pressing need for a liberalism in the North which is truly liberal, a liberalism that firmly believes in integration in its own community as well as in the Deep South. It is one thing to agree that the goal of integration is morally and legally right; it is another thing to commit oneself positively and actively to the ideal of integration—the former is intellectual assent, the latter is actual belief. These are days that demand practices to match professions. This is no day to pay lip service to integration, we must pay *life* service to it.

Today in all too many northern communities a sort of quasi-liberalism prevails, so bent on seeing all sides that it fails to become dedicated to any side. It is so objectively analytical that it is not subjectively committed. A true liberal will not be deterred by the propaganda and subtle words of those who say, "Slow up for a while; you are pushing things too fast." I am not calling for an end to sympathetic understanding and abiding patience; but neither sympathy nor patience should be used as excuses for indecisiveness. They must be guiding principles for all of our actions, rather than substitutes for action itself.

A significant role, in this tense period of transition, is assigned to the moderates of the white South. Unfortunately today, the leadership of the white South is by and large in the hands of close-minded extremists. These persons gain prominence and power by the dissemination of false ideas, and by appealing to the deepest fears and hates within the human mind. But they do not speak for the South; of that I am convinced. They speak only for a willful and vocal minority.

Even the most casual observer can see that the South has marvelous possibilities. It is rich in natural resources, blessed with the beauties of nature, and endowed with a native warmth of spirit. Yet in spite of these assets, it is retarded by a blight that debilitates not only the Negro but also the white man. Poor white men, women, and children, bearing the scars of ignorance, deprivation, and poverty, are evidence of the fact that harm to one is injury to all. Segregation has placed the whole South socially, educationally, and economically behind the rest of the nation.

Yet actually, there is no single "solid" South; there are at least three, geographically speaking. There is the South of compliance—Oklahoma, Kentucky, Kansas, Missouri, West Virginia, Delaware, and the District of Columbia. There is the wait-and-see South—Tennessee, Texas, North Carolina, Arkansas, and Florida. And there is the South of resistance—Georgia, Alabama, Mississippi, Louisiana, South Carolina, and Virginia.

Just as there are three Souths geographically, there are several Souths in terms of attitudes. A minority in each of these states would use almost any means, including physical violence, to preserve segregation. A majority, through tradition and custom, sincerely believe in segregation, but at the same time stand on the side of law and order. Hence, they are willing to comply with the law not because they feel it is sound but because it is the law. A third group, a growing minority, is working courageously and conscientiously to implement the law of the land. These people believe in the morality as well as the constitutionality of integration. Their still small voices often go unheard among the louder shouts of defiance, but they are actively in the field.

Furthermore there are in the white South millions of people of good will whose voices are yet unheard, whose course is yet unclear, and whose courageous acts are yet unseen. These persons are often silent today because of fear—fear of social, political, and economic reprisals. In the name of God, in the interest of human dignity, and for the cause of democracy these millions are called upon to gird their courage, to speak out, to offer the leadership that is needed. Still another South calls upon them: The colored South, the South of millions of Negroes whose sweat and blood has also built Dixie, who yearn for brotherhood and respect, who want to join hands with their white fellow southerners to build a freer, happier land for all. If the moderates of the white South fail to act now, history will have to record that the greatest tragedy of this period of social transition was not the strident clamor of the bad people, but the appalling silence of the good people. Our generation will have to repent not only for the acts and words of the children of darkness but also for the fears and apathy of the children of light.

Who can best lead the South out of the social and economic quagmire? Her native sons. Those who were born and bred on her rich and fertile soil; those who love her because they were nurtured by her. Through love, patience, and understanding good will they can call their brothers to a way of noble living. This hour represents a great opportunity for the white moderates, if they will only speak the truth, obey the law, and suffer if necessary for what they know is right.

Still another agency of effective change today is the labor movement. Across the years the Negro has been a perpetual victim of economic exploitation. Prior to the Civil War the slaves worked under a system which offered neither compensation nor civil rights. Since emancipation the Negro American has continued to suffer under an essentially unreconstructed economy. He was freed without land or legal protection, and was made an outcast entitled only to the most menial jobs. Even the federal government that set him free failed to work out any long-range policy that would guarantee economic resources to a previously enslaved people—as much entitled to the land they had worked as were their former owners. The exploitation of the Negro population persisted through the Reconstruction period and continues down to the present day.

Labor unions can play a tremendous role in making economic justice a reality for the Negro. Trade unions are engaged in a struggle to advance the economic welfare of those American citizens whose wages are their livelihood. Since the American Negro is virtually nonexistent as the owner and manager of mass production industry, he must depend on the payment of wages for his economic survival.

There are in the United States 16.5 million members of approximately 150 bona fide trade unions. Of this number 142 are national and international affiliated organizations of the AFL-CIO. The unions forming the AFL-CIO include 1.3 million Negroes among their 13.4 million members. Only the combined religious institutions serving the Negro community can claim a greater membership of Negroes. The Negro then has the right to expect the resources of the American trade union movement to be used in assuring him—like all the rest of its members—of a proper place in American society. He has gained this right along with all the other workers whose mutual efforts have built this country's free and democratic trade unions.

Economic insecurity strangles the physical and cultural growth of its victims. Not only are millions deprived of formal education and proper health facilities but our most fundamental social unit—the family—is tortured, corrupted, and weakened by economic insufficiency. When a Negro man is inadequately paid, his wife must work to provide the simple necessities for the children. When a mother has to work she does violence to motherhood by depriving her children of her loving guidance and protection; often they are poorly cared for by others or by none—left to roam the streets unsupervised. It is not the Negro alone who is wronged by a disrupted society; many white families are in similar straits. The Negro mother leaves home to care for—and be a substitute mother for—white children, while the white mother works. In this strange irony lies the promise of future correction.

Both Negro and white workers are equally oppressed. For both, the living standards need to be raised to levels consistent with our national resources. Not logic but a hollow social distinction has separated the races. The economically depressed white accepts his poverty by telling himself that, if in no other respect, at least socially he is above the Negro. For this empty pride in a racial myth he has paid the crushing price of insecurity, hunger, ignorance, and hopelessness for himself and his children.

Strong ties must be made between those whites and Negroes who have problems in common. White and Negro workers have mutual aspirations for a fairer share of the products of industries and farms. Both seek job security, old-age security, health and welfare protection. The organized labor movement, which has contributed so much to the economic security and well-being of millions, must concentrate its powerful forces on bringing economic emancipation to white and Negro by organizing them together in social equality.

Certainly the labor movement has already made significant moves in this direction. Virtually every national or international union has clear policies of nondiscrimination, and the national leaders of AFL-CIO have proclaimed sincerely the ultimate objective of eliminating racial bias not only from the American labor movement but also from American society as a whole. But in spite of this stand, some unions, governed by the racist ethos, have contributed to the degraded economic status of the Negroes. Negroes have been barred from membership in certain unions, and denied apprenticeship training and vocational education. In every section of the country one can find local unions existing as a serious and vicious obstacle when the Negro seeks jobs or upgrading in employment. The AFL-CIO drive to organize the South has been virtually abandoned because of the massive resistance of a significant portion of the organized labor oligarchy, many of whom have been active in white citizens councils.

The existence of these conditions within the ranks of labor reveals that the job is a continuing one. The AFL-CIO must use all of the powerful forces at its command to enforce the principles it has professed. Labor leaders must continue to recognize that labor has a great stake in the struggle for civil rights, if only because the forces that are anti-Negro are usually antilabor too. The current attacks on organized labor because of the misdeeds of a few malefactors should not blind us to labor's essential role in the present crisis.

The church too must face its historic obligation in this crisis. In the final analysis the problem of race is not a political but a moral issue. Indeed, as the Swedish economist Gunnar Myrdal has pointed out, the problem of race is America's greatest moral dilemma. This tragic dilemma presents the church with a great challenge. The broad universalism standing at the center of the gospel makes segregation morally unjustifiable. Racial segregation is a blatant denial of the unity which we have in Christ; for in Christ there is neither Jew nor Gentile, bond nor free, Negro nor white. Segregation scars the soul of both the segregator and the segregated. The segregator looks upon the segregated as a thing to be used, not a person to be respected. Segregation substitutes an "I-it" relationship for the "I-thou" relationship. Thus it is utterly opposed to the noble teachings of our Judeo-Christian tradition.

It has always been the responsibility of the church to broaden horizons, challenge the status quo, and break the mores when necessary. The task of conquering segregation is an inescapable *must* confronting the church today.

There are several specific things that the church can do. First, it should try to get to the ideational roots of race hate, something that the law cannot accomplish. All race prejudice is based upon fears, suspicions, and misunderstandings, usually groundless. The church can be of immeasurable help in giving the popular mind direction here. Through its channels of religious education, the church can point out the irrationality of these beliefs. It can show that the idea of a superior or inferior race is a myth that has been completely refuted by anthropoligical evidence. It can show that Negroes are not innately inferior in academic, health, and moral standards. It can show that, when given equal opportunities, Negroes can demonstrate equal achievement.

The church can also do a great deal to reveal the true intentions of the Negro—that he is not seeking to dominate the nation, but simply wants the right to live as a first-class citizen, with all the responsibilities that good citizenship entails. The church can also help by mitigating the prevailing and irrational fears concerning intermarriage. It can say to men that marriage is an individual matter that must be decided on the merits of individual cases. Properly speaking, races do not marry; individuals marry. Marriage is a condition which requires the voluntary consent of two contracting parties, and either side can always say no. The church can reveal that the continual outcry concerning intermarriage is a distortion of the real issue. It can point out that the Negro's primary aim is to be the white man's brother, not his brother-in-law.

Another thing that the church can do to make the principle of brotherhood a reality is to keep men's minds and visions centered on God. Many of the problems America now confronts can be explained in terms of fear. There is not only the job of freeing the Negro from the bondage of segregation but also the responsibility of freeing his white brothers from the bondage of fears concerning integration. One of the best ways to rid oneself of fear is to center one's life in the will and purpose of God. "Perfect love casteth out fear."

When people think about race problems they are too often more concerned with men than with God. The question usually asked is: "What will my friends think if I am too friendly with Negroes or too liberal on the race question?" Men forget to ask: "What will God think?" And so they live in fear because they tend to seek social approval on the horizontal plane rather than spiritual devotion on the vertical plane.

The church must remind its worshipers that man finds greater security in devoting his life to the eternal demands of the Almighty God than in giving his ultimate allegiance to the transitory demands of man. The church must continually say to Christians, "Ye are a colony of heaven." True, man has a dual citizenry. He lives both in time and in eternity; both in heaven and on earth. But he owes his ultimate allegiance to God. It is this love for God and devotion to His will that casteth out fear.

A further effort that the church can make in attempting to solve the race problem is to take the lead in social reform. It is not enough for the church to be active in the realm of ideas; it must move out into the arena of social action. First, the church must remove the yoke of segregation from its own body. Only by doing this can it be effective in its attack on outside evils. Unfortunately, most of the major denominations still practice segregation in local churches, hospitals, schools, and other church institutions. It is appalling that the most segregated hour of Christian America is eleven o'clock on Sunday morning, the same hour when many are standing to sing, "In Christ there is no East nor West." Equally appalling is the fact that the most segregated school of the week is the Sunday School. How often the church has had a high blood count of creeds and an anemia of deeds! Dean Liston Pope of the Yale Divinity School rightly says in *The Kingdom beyond Caste*: "The church is the most segregated major institution in American society. It has lagged behind the Supreme Court as the conscience of the nation on questions of race, and it has fallen far behind trade unions, factories, schools, department stores, athletic gatherings and most other major areas of human association as far as the achievement of integration in its own life is concerned."

There has been some progress. Here and there churches are courageously making attacks on segregation, and actually integrating their congregations. The National Council of Churches has repeatedly condemned segregation and has requested constituent denominations to do likewise. Most of the major denominations have endorsed that action. The Roman Catholic church has declared, "Segregation is morally wrong and sinful." All this is admirable. But these stands are still too far too few, and they move all too slowly down to the local churches in actual practice. The church has a schism in its own soul that it must close. It will be one of the tragedies of Christian history if a future Gibbon is able to say that at the height of the twentieth century the church proved to be one of the greatest bulwarks of segregated power.

The church must also become increasingly active in social action outside its doors. It must seek to keep channels of communication open between the Negro and white community. It must take an active stand against the injustice that Negroes confront in housing, education, police protection, and in city and state courts. It must exert its influence in the area of economic justice. As guardian of the moral and spiritual life of the community the church cannot look with indifference upon these glaring evils.

It is impossible to speak of the role of the church without referring to the ministers. Every minister of the gospel has a mandate to stand up courageously for righteousness, to proclaim the eternal verities of the gospel, and to lead men from the darkness of falsehood and fear to the light of truth and love.

In the South this mandate presents white ministers with a difficult choice. Many who believe segregation to be directly opposed to the will of God and the spirit of Christ are faced with the painful alternative of taking a vocal stand and being fired or staying quiet in order to remain in the situation and do some good. Pastors who have adopted the latter course feel that if they were forced out of their churches their successors would in all probability be segregationist, thus setting the Christian cause back. Many ministers have kept their peace not merely to save a job but because they feel that restraint is the best way to serve the cause of Christ in the South. In quiet unpublicized ways many of these ministers are making for a better day and helpfully molding the minds of young people. These men should not be criticized.

In the final analysis every white minister in the South must decide for himself which course he will follow. There is no single right strategy. The important thing is for every minister to dedicate himself to the Christian ideal of brotherhood, and be sure that he is doing something positive to implement it. He must never allow the theory that it is better to remain quiet and help the cause to become a rationalization for doing nothing. Many ministers can do much more than they are doing and still hold their congregations. There is a great deal that ministers can achieve collectively. In every southern city there should be interracial ministerial associations in which Negro and white ministers can come together in Christian fellowship and discuss common community problems. One of the most disappointing experiences of the Montgomery struggle was the fact that we could not get the white ministerial association to sit down with us and discuss our problem. With individual exceptions the white ministers, from whom I had naively expected so much, gave little.

Ministers can also collectively call for compliance with the law and a cessation of violence. This has been done by white ministers of Atlanta, Richmond, Dallas, and other cities, and not a single one has, to my knowledge, lost his job. It is difficult for a denomination to fire all of its ministers in a city. If ever the white ministers of the South decide to declare in a united voice the truth of the gospel on the question of race, the transition from a segregated to an integrated society will be infinitely smoother.

Any discussion of the role of the Christian minister today must ultimately emphasize the need for prophecy. Not every minister can be a prophet, but some must be prepared for the ordeals of this high calling and be willing to suffer courageously for righteousness. May the problem of race in America soon make hearts burn so that prophets will rise up, saying, "Thus saith the Lord," and cry out as Amos did, ". . . let justice roll down like waters, and righteousness like an ever-flowing stream."

Fortunately, a few in the South have already been willing to follow this prophetic way. I have nothing but praise for these ministers of the gospel of Jesus Christ and rabbis of the Jewish faith who have stood unflinchingly before threats and intimidations, inconvenience and unpopularity, even at times in physical danger, to declare the doctrine of the Fatherhood of God and the brotherhood of man. For such noble servants of God there is the consolation of the words of Jesus: "Blessed are ye, when men shall revile you, and persecute you, and shall say all manner of evil against you falsely, for my sake. Rejoice, and be exceeding glad: for great is your reward in heaven: for so persecuted they the prophets which were before you."

Here, then, is the hard challenge and the sublime opportunity: to let the spirit of Christ work toward fashioning a truly great Christian nation. If the church accepts the challenge with devotion and valor, the day will be speeded when men everywhere will recognize that they "are all one in Christ Jesus."

Finally, the Negro himself has a decisive role to play if integration is to become a reality. Indeed, if first-class citizenship is to become a reality for the Negro he must assume the primary responsibility for making it so. Integration is not some lavish dish that the federal government or the white liberal will pass out on a silver platter while the Negro merely furnishes the appetite. One of the most damaging effects of past segregation on the personality of the Negro may well be that he has been victimized with the delusion that others should be more concerned than himself about his citizenship rights.

In this period of social change, the Negro must come to see that there is so much he himself can do about his plight. He may be uneducated or poverty-stricken, but these handicaps must not prevent him from seeing that he has within his being the power to alter his fate. The Negro can take direct action against injustice without waiting for the government to act or a majority to agree with him or a court to rule in his favor.

Oppressed people deal with their oppression in three characteristic ways. One way is acquiescence: the oppressed resign themselves to their doom. They tacitly adjust themselves to oppression, and thereby become conditioned to it. In every movement toward freedom some of the oppressed prefer to remain oppressed. Almost twenty-eight hundred years ago Moses set out to lead the children of Israel from the slavery of Egypt to the freedom of the promised land. He soon discovered that slaves do not always welcome their deliverers. They become accustomed to being slaves. They would rather bear those ills they have, as Shakespeare pointed out, than flee to others that they know not of. They prefer the "fleshpots of Egypt" to the ordeals of emancipation.

There is such a thing as the freedom from exhaustion. Some people are so worn down by the yoke of oppression that they give up. A few years ago in the slum areas of Atlanta, a Negro guitarist used to sing almost daily: "Ben down so long that down don't bother me." This is the type of negative freedom and resignation that often engulfs the life of the oppressed.

But this is not the way out. To accept passively an unjust system is to cooperate with that system; thereby the oppressed become as evil as the oppressor. Noncooperation with evil is as much a moral obligation as is cooperation with good. The oppressed must never allow the conscience of the oppressor to slumber. Religion reminds every man that he is his brother's keeper. To accept injustice or segregation passively is to say to the oppressor that his actions are morally right. It is a way of allowing his conscience to fall asleep. At this moment the oppressed fails to be his brother's keeper. So acquiescence—while often the easier way—is not the moral way. It is the way of the coward. The Negro cannot win the respect of his oppressor by acquiescing; he merely increases the oppressor's arrogance and contempt. Acquiescence is interpreted as proof of the Negro's inferiority. The Negro cannot win the respect of the white people of the South or the peoples of the world if he is willing to sell the future of his children for his personal and immediate comfort and safety.

A second way that oppressed people sometimes deal with oppression is to resort to physical violence and corroding hatred. Violence often brings about momentary results. Nations have frequently won their independence in battle. But in spite of temporary victories, violence never brings permanent peace. It solves no social problem; it merely creates new and more complicated ones.

Violence as a way of achieving racial justice is both impractical and immoral. It is impractical because it is a descending spiral ending in destruction for all. The old law of an eye for an eye leaves everybody blind. It is immoral because it seeks to humiliate the opponent rather than win his understanding; it seeks to annihilate rather than to convert. Violence is immoral because it thrives on hatred rather than love. It destroys community and makes brotherhood impossible. It leaves society in monologue rather than dialogue. Violence ends by defeating itself. It creates bitterness in the survivors and brutality in the destroyers.

A voice echoes through time saying to every potential Peter, "Put up your sword." History is cluttered with the wreckage of nations that failed to follow this command.

If the American Negro and other victims of oppression succumb to the temptation of using violence in the struggle for freedom, future generations will be the recipients of a desolate night of bitterness, and our chief legacy to them will be an endless reign of meaningless chaos. Violence is not the way.

The third way open to oppressed people in their quest for freedom is the way of nonviolent resistance. Like the synthesis in Hegelian philosophy, the principle of nonviolent resistance seeks to reconcile the truths of two opposites—acquiescence and violence—while avoiding the extremes and immoralities of both. The nonviolent resister agrees with the person who acquiesces that one should not be physically aggressive toward his opponent but he balances the equation by agreeing with the person of violence that evil must be resisted. He avoids the nonresistance of the former and the violent resistance of the latter. With nonviolent resistance, no individual or group need submit to any wrong, nor need anyone resort to violence in order to right a wrong.

It seems to me that this is the method that must guide the actions of the Negro in the present crisis in race relations. Through nonviolent resistance the Negro will be able to rise to the noble height of opposing the unjust system while loving the perpetrators of the system. The Negro must work passionately and unrelentingly for full stature as a citizen, but he must not use inferior methods to gain it. He must never come to terms with falsehood, malice, hate, or destruction.

Nonviolent resistance makes it possible for the Negro to remain in the South and struggle for his rights. The Negro's problem will not be solved by running away. He cannot listen to the glib suggestion of those who would urge him to migrate en masse to other sections of the country. By grasping his great opportunity in the South he can make a lasting contribution to the moral strength of the nation and set a sublime example of courage for generations yet unborn.

By nonviolent resistance, the Negro can also enlist all men of good will in his struggle for equality. The problem is not a purely racial one, with Negroes set against whites. In the end, it is not a struggle between people at all, but a tension between justice and injustice. Nonviolent resistance is not aimed against oppressors but against oppression. Under its banner consciences, not racial groups, are enlisted.

If the Negro is to achieve the goal of integration, he must organize himself into a militant and nonviolent mass movement. All three elements are indispensable. The movement for equality and justice can only be a success if it has both a mass and militant character; the barriers to be overcome require both. Nonviolence is an imperative in order to bring about ultimate community.

A mass movement of a militant quality that is not at the same time committed to nonviolence tends to generate conflict, which in turn breeds anarchy. The support of the participants and the sympathy of the uncommitted are both inhibited by the threat that bloodshed will engulf the community. This reaction in turn encourages the opposition to threaten and resort to force. When, however, the mass movement repudiates violence while moving resolutely toward its goal, its opponents are revealed as the instigators and practitioners of violence if it occurs. Then public support is magnetically attracted to the advocates of nonviolence, while those who employ violence are literally disarmed by overwhelming sentiment against their stand.

Only through a nonviolent approach can the fears of the white community be mitigated. A guilt-ridden white minority lives in fear that if the Negro should ever attain power, he would act without restraint or pity to revenge the injustices and brutality of the years. It is something like a parent who continually mistreats a son. One day that parent raises his hand to strike the son, only to discover that the son is now as tall as he is. The parent is suddenly afraid—fearful that the son will use his new physical power to repay his parent for all the blows of the past.

The Negro, once a helpless child, has now grown up politically, culturally, and economically. Many white men fear retaliation. The job of the Negro is to show them that they have nothing ot fear, that the Negro understands and forgives and is ready to forget the past. He must convince the white man that all he seeks is justice, *for both himself and the white man*. A mass movement exercising nonviolence is an object lesson in power under discipline, a demonstration to the white community that if such a movement attained a degree of strength, it would use its power creatively and not vengefully.

Nonviolence can touch men where the law cannot reach them. When the law regulates behavior it plays an indirect part in molding public sentiment. The enforcement of the law is itself a form of peaceful persuasion. But the law needs help. The courts can order desegregation of the public schools. But what can be done to mitigate the fears, to disperse the hatred, violence, and irrationality gathered around school integration, to take the initiative out of the hands of racial demagogues, to release respect for the law? In the end, for laws to be obeyed, men must believe they are right.

Here nonviolence comes in as the ultimate form of persuasion. It is the method which seeks to implement the just law by appealing to the conscience of the great decent majority who through blindness, fear, pride, or irrationality have allowed their consciences to sleep.

The nonviolent resisters can summarize their message in the following simple terms: We will take direct action against injustice without waiting for other agencies to act. We will not obey unjust laws or submit to unjust practices. We will do this peacefully, openly, cheerfully because our aim is to persuade. We adopt the means of nonviolence because our end is a community at peace with itself. We will try to persuade with our words, but if our words fail, we will try to persuade with our acts. We will always be willing to talk and seek fair compromise, but we are ready to suffer when necessary and even risk our lives to become witnesses to the truth as we see it.

The way of nonviolence means a willingness to suffer and sacrifice. It may mean going to jail. If such is the case the resister must be willing to fill the jail houses of the South. It may even mean physical death. But if physical death is the price that a man must pay to free his children and his white brethren from a permanent death of the spirit, then nothing could be more redemptive.

What is the Negro's best defense against acts of violence inflicted upon him? As Dr. Kenneth Clark has said so eloquently, "His only defense is to meet every act of barbarity, illegality, cruelty and injustice toward an individual Negro with the fact that one hundred more Negroes will present themselves in his place as potential victims." Every time one Negro school teacher is fired for believing in integration, a thousand others should be ready to take the same stand. If the oppressors bomb the home of one Negro for his protest, they must be made to realize that to press back the rising tide of the Negro's courage they will have to bomb hundreds more, and even then they will fail.

Faced with this dynamic unity, this amazing self-respect, this willingness to suffer, and this refusal to hit back, the oppressor will find, as oppressors have always found, that he is glutted with his own barbarity. Forced to stand before the world and his God splattered with the blood of his brother, he will call an end to his self-defeating massacre.

American Negroes must come to the point where they can say to their white brothers, paraphrasing the words of Gandhi: "We will match your capacity to inflict suffering with our capacity to endure suffering. We will meet your physical force with soul force. We will not hate you, but we cannot in all good conscience obey your unjust laws. Do to us what you will and we will still love you. Bomb our homes and threaten our children; send your hooded perpetrators of violence into our communities and drag us out on some wayside road, beating us and leaving us half dead, and we will still love you. But we will soon wear you down by our capacity to suffer. And in winning our freedom we will so appeal to your heart and conscience that we will win you in the process."

Realism impels me to admit that many Negroes will find it difficult to follow the path of nonviolence. Some will consider it senseless; some will argue that they have neither the strength nor the courage to join in such a mass demonstration of nonviolent action. As E. Franklin Frazier points out in *Black Bourgeoisie*, many Negroes are occupied in a middle-class struggle for status and prestige. They are more concerned about "conspicuous consumption" than about the cause of justice, and are probably not prepared for the ordeals and sacrifices involved in nonviolent action. Fortunately, however, the success of this method is not dependent on its unanimous acceptance. A few Negroes in every community, unswervingly committed to the nonviolent way, can persuade hundreds of others at least to use nonviolence as a technique and serve as the moral force to awaken the slumbering national conscience. Thoreau was thinking of such a creative minority when he said: "I know this well, that if one thousand, if one hundred, if ten men whom I could name—if ten honest men only—aye, if one honest man, in the state of Massachusetts, ceasing to hold slaves, were actually to withdraw from the copartnership, and be locked up in the county jail therefore, it would be the abolition of slavery in America. For it matters not how small the beginning may seem to be, what is once well done is done forever."

Mahatma Gandhi never had more than one hundred persons absolutely committed to his philosophy. But with this small group of devoted followers, he galvanized the whole of India, and through a magnificent feat of nonviolence challenged the might of the British Empire and won freedom for his people.

This method of nonviolence will not work miracles overnight. Men are not easily moved from their mental ruts, their prejudiced and irrational feelings. When the underprivileged demand freedom, the privileged first react with bitterness and resistance. Even when the demands are couched in nonviolent terms, the initial response is the same. Nehru once remarked that the British were never so angry as when the Indians resisted them with nonviolence, that he never saw eyes so full of hate as those of the British troops to whom he turned the other cheek when they beat him with lathis. But nonviolent resistance at least changed the minds and hearts of the Indians, however impervious the British may have appeared. "We cast away our fear," says Nehru. And in the end the British not only granted freedom to India but came to have a new respect for the Indians. Today a mutual friendship based on complete equality exists between these two peoples within the Commonwealth.

In the South too, the initial white reaction to Negro resistance has been bitter. I do not predict that a similar happy ending will come to Montgomery in a few months, because integration is more complicated than independence. But I know that the Negroes of Montgomery are already walking straighter because of the protest. And I expect that this generation of Negro children throughout the United States will grow up stronger and better because of the courage, the dignity, and the suffering of the nine children of Little Rock, and their counterparts in Nashville, Clinton, and Sturges. And I believe that the white people of this country are being affected too, that beneath the surface this nation's conscience is being stirred.

The nonviolent approach does not immediately change the heart of the oppressor. It first does something to the hearts and souls of those committed to it. It gives them new self-respect; it calls up resources of strength and courage that they did not know they had. Finally it reaches the opponent and so stirs his conscience that reconciliation becomes a reality.

I suggest this approach because I think it is the only way to reestablish the broken community. Court orders and federal enforcement agencies will be of inestimable value in achieving desegregation. But desegregation is only a partial, though necessary, step toward the ultimate goal which we seek to realize. Desegregation will break down the legal barriers, and bring men together physically. But something must happen so to touch the hearts and souls of men that they will come together, not because the law says it, but because it is natural and right. In other words, our ultimate goal is integration which is genuine intergroup and interpersonal living. Only through nonviolence can this goal be attained, for the aftermath of nonviolence is reconciliation and the creation of the beloved community.

It is becoming clear that the Negro is in for a season of suffering. As victories for civil rights mount in the federal courts, angry passions and deep prejudices are further aroused. The mountain of state and local segregation laws still stands. Negro leaders continue to be arrested and harassed under city ordinances, and their homes continue to be bombed. State laws continue to be enacted to circumvent integration. I pray that, recognizing the necessity of suffering, the Negro will make of it a virtue. To suffer in a righteous cause is to grow to our humanity's full stature. If only to save himself from bitterness, the Negro needs the vision to see the ordeals of this generation as the opportunity to transfigure himself and American society. If he has to go to jail for the cause of freedom, let him enter it in the fashion Gandhi urged his countrymen, "as the bridegroom enters the bride's chamber"—that is, with a little trepidation but with a great expectation.

Nonviolence is a way of humility and self-restraint. We Negroes talk a great deal about our rights, and rightly so. We proudly proclaim that three-fourths of the people of the world are colored. We have the privilege of watching in our generation the great drama of freedom and independence as it unfolds in Asia and Africa. All of these things are in line with the work of providence. We must be sure, however, that we accept them in the right spirit. In an effort to achieve freedom in America, Asia, and Africa we must not try to leap from a position of disadvantage to one of advantage, thus subverting justice. We must seek democracy and not the substitution of one tyranny for another. Our aim must never be to defeat or humiliate the white man. We must not become victimized with a philosophy of black supremacy. God is not interested merely in the freedom of black men, and brown men, and yellow men; God is interested in the freedom of the whole human race.

The nonviolent approach provides an answer to the long debated question of gradualism versus immediacy. On the one hand it prevents one from falling into the sort of patience which is an excuse for do-nothingism and escapism, ending up in standstillism. On the other hand it saves one from the irresponsible words which estrange without reconciling and the hasty judgment which is blind to the necessities of social process. It recognizes the need for moving toward the goal of justice with wise restraint and calm reasonableness. But it also recognizes the immorality of slowing up in the move toward justice and capitulating to the guardians of an unjust status quo. It recognizes that social change cannot come overnight. But it causes one to work as if it were a possibility the next morning.

Through nonviolence we avoid the temptation of taking on the psychology of victors. Thanks largely to the noble and invaluable work of the NAACP, we have won great victories in the federal courts. But we must not be self-satisfied. We must respond to every decision with an understanding of those who have opposed us, and with acceptance of the new adjustments that the court orders pose for them. We must act in such a way that our victories will be triumphs for good will in all men, white and Negro.

Nonviolence is essentially a positive concept. Its corollary must always be growth. On the one hand nonviolence requires noncooperation with evil; on the other hand it requires cooperation with the constructive forces of good. Without this constructive aspect noncooperation ends where it begins. Therefore, the Negro must get to work on a program with a broad range of positive goals.

One point in the Negro's program should be a plan to improve his own economic lot. Through the establishment of credit unions, savings and loan associations, and cooperative enterprises the Negro can greatly improve his economic status. He must develop habits of thrift and techniques of wise investment. He must not wait for the end of the segregation that lies at the basis of his economic deprivation; he must act now to lift himself up by his own bootstraps.

The constructive program ahead must include a campaign to get Negroes to register and vote. Certainly they face many external barriers. All types of underhand methods are still being used in the South to prevent the Negroes from voting, and the success of these efforts is not only unjust, it is a real embarrassment to the nation we love and must protect. The advocacy of free elections in Europe by American officials is hypocrisy when free elections are not held in great sections of America.

But external resistance is not the only present barrier to Negro voting. Apathy among the Negroes themselves is also a factor. Even where the polls are open to all, Negroes have shown themselves too slow to exercise their voting privileges. There must be a concerted effort on the part of Negro leaders to arouse their people from their apathetic indifference to this obligation of citizenship. In the past, apathy was a moral failure. Today, it is a form of moral and political suicide.

The constructive program ahead must include a vigorous attempt to improve the Negro's personal standards. It must be reiterated that the standards of the Negro as a group lag behind not because of an inherent inferiority, but because of the fact that segregation does exist. The "behavior deviants" within the Negro community stem from the economic deprivation, emotional frustration, and social isolation which are the inevitable concomitants of segregation. When the white man argues that segregation should continue because of the Negro's lagging standards, he fails to see that the standards lag because of segregation.

Yet Negroes must be honest enough to admit that our standards do often fall short. One of the sure signs of maturity is the ability to rise to the point of self-criticism. Whenever we are objects of criticism from white men, even though the criticisms are maliciously directed and mixed with half-truths, we must pick out the elements of truth and make them the basis of creative reconstruction. We must not let the fact that we are the victims of injustice lull us into abrogating responsibility for our own lives.

Our crime rate is far too high. Our level of cleanliness is frequently far too low. Too often those of us who are in the middle class live above our means, spend money on nonessentials and frivolities, and fail to give to serious causes, organizations, and educational institutions that so desperately need funds. We are too often loud and boisterous, and spend far too much on drink. Even the most poverty-stricken among us can purchase a ten-cent bar of soap; even the most uneducated among us can have high morals. Through community agencies and religious institutions Negro leaders must develop a positive program through which Negro youth can become adjusted to urban living and improve their general level of behavior. Since crime often grows out of a sense of futility and despair, Negro parents must be urged to give their children the love, attention, and sense of belonging that a segregated society deprives them of. By improving our standards here and now we will go a long way toward breaking down the arguments of the segregationist.

This then must be our present program: Nonviolent resistance to all forms of racial injustice, including state and local laws and practices, even when this means going to jail; and imaginative, bold, constructive action to end the demoralization caused by the legacy of slavery and segregation, inferior schools, slums, and second-class citizenship. The nonviolent struggle, if conducted with the dignity and courage already shown by the people of Montgomery and the children of Little Rock, will in itself help end the demoralization; but a new frontal assault on the poverty, disease, and ignorance of a people too long ignored by America's conscience will make victory more certain.

In short, we must work on two fronts. On the one hand, we must continue to resist the system of segregation which is the basic cause of our lagging standards; on the other hand we must work constructively to improve the standards themselves. There must be a rhythmic alternation between attacking the causes and healing the effects.

This is a great hour for the Negro. The challenge is here. To become the instruments of a great idea is a privilege that history gives only occasionally. Arnold Toynbee says in *A Study of History* that it may be the Negro who will give the new spiritual dynamic to Western civilization that it so desperately needs to survive. I hope this is possible. The spiritual power that the Negro can radiate to the world comes from love, understanding, good will, and nonviolence. It may even be possible for the Negro, through adherence to nonviolence, so to challenge the nations of the world that they will seriously seek an alternative to war and destruction. In a day when Sputniks and Explorers dash through outer space and guided ballistic missiles are carving highways of death through the stratosphere, nobody can win a war. Today the choice is no longer between violence and nonviolence. It is either nonviolence or nonexistence. The Negro may be God's appeal to this age—an age drifting rapidly to its doom. The eternal appeal takes the form of a warning: "All who take the sword will perish by the sword."

---

Martin Luther King, Jr., *Stride Toward Freedom: The Montgomery Story* (New York: Harper & Row, 1958). For a fuller account of the Baton Rouge bus boycott, and other movements that preceded the work of Dr. King and the Montgomery Improvement Association, see Aldon D. Morris, *The Origins of the Civil Rights Movement: Black Communities Organizing for Change* (New York and London: Free Press, 1984); and Frazier's essay titled, "The Negro Middle Class and Desegregation" (1957), in G. Franklin Edwards, ed., *E. Franklin Frazier on Race Relations* (Chicago and London: University of Chicago Press, 1968), 304–5, as well as Frazier's *Black Bourgeoisie*, also published in 1957.

# 54

# The Strength to Love

*Martin Luther King, Jr., was one of the great preachers of the twentieth century. He embellished his graceful cadence with a disciplined commitment to exegete grand themes. His mellow baritone voice could soar toward the sweet relief that only clarity and insight can provide, and then collapse in the often somber or sober embrace of finely woven metaphors. He refused to accept the false dichotomy between folk and intellectual preaching. One way he stayed in touch with common folk was to preach practically every week. In fact, he delivered some of his finest sermons in the pulpit of the Ebenezer Baptist Church in Atlanta. It was difficult. But he did find enough time to sometimes take care of his pastoral duties of visiting the sick and caring for the material needs of this congregation, which he served as co-pastor along with his father. Therefore, his sermons were often pastoral in nature, and reflected a broad range of deep personal and public concerns. The now classic sample of the numerous ones he delivered at Ebenezer and elsewhere were collected in* The Strength to Love. *The soul of a spiritual genius is revealed in this collection of sermons.*


## A TOUGH MIND AND A TENDER HEART (CHAPTER 1)

*Be ye therefore wise as serpents, and harmless as doves.*

Matthew 10:16


A French philosopher said, "No man is strong unless he bears within his character antitheses strongly marked." The strong man holds in a living blend strongly marked opposites. Not ordinarily do men achieve this balance of opposites. The idealists are not usually realistic, and the realists are not usually idealistic. The militant are not generally known to be passive, nor the passive to be militant. Seldom are the humble self-assertive, or the self-assertive humble. But life at its best is a creative synthesis of opposites in fruitful harmony. The philosopher Hegel said that truth is found neither in the thesis nor the antithesis, but in an emergent synthesis which reconciles the two.

Jesus recognized the need for blending opposites. He knew that his disciples would face a difficult and hostile world, where they would confront the recalcitrance of political officials and the intransigence of the protectors of the old order. He knew that they would meet cold and arrogant men whose hearts had been hardened by the long winter of traditionalism. So he said to them, "Behold, I send you forth as sheep in the midst of wolves." And he gave them a formula for action: "Be ye therefore wise as serpents, and harmless as doves." It is pretty difficult to imagine a single person having, simultaneously, the characteristics of the serpent and the dove, but this is what Jesus expects. We must combine the toughness of the serpent and the softness of the dove, a tough mind and a tender heart.

1

Let us consider, first, the need for a tough mind, characterized by incisive thinking, realistic appraisal, and decisive judgment. The tough mind is sharp and penetrating, breaking through the crust of legends and myths and sifting the true from the false. The tough-minded individual is astute and discerning. He has a strong, austere quality that makes for firmness of purpose and solidity of commitment.

Who doubts that this toughness of mind is one of man's greatest needs? Rarely do we find men who willingly engage in hard, solid thinking. There is an almost universal quest for easy answers and half-baked solutions. Nothing pains some people more than having to think.

This prevalent tendency toward softmindedness is found in man's unbelievable gullibility. Take our attitude toward advertisements. We are so easily led to purchase a product because a television or radio advertisement pronounces it better than any other. Advertisers have long since learned that most people are softminded, and they capitalize on this susceptibility with skillful and effective slogans.

This undue gullibility is also seen in the tendency of many readers to accept the printed word of the press as final truth. Few people realize that even our authentic channels of information—the press, the platform, and in many instances the pulpit—do not give us objective and unbiased truth. Few people have the toughness of mind to judge critically and to discern the true from the false, the fact from the fiction. Our minds are constantly being invaded by legions of half-truths, prejudices, and false facts. One of the great needs of mankind is to be lifted above the morass of false propaganda.

Softminded individuals are prone to embrace all kinds of superstitions. Their minds are constantly invaded by irrational fears, which range from fear of Friday the thirteenth to fear of a black cat crossing one's path. As the elevator made its upward climb in one of the large hotels of New York City, I noticed for the first time that there was no thirteenth floor—floor fourteen followed floor twelve. On inquiring from the elevator operator the reason for this omission, he said, "This practice is followed by most large hotels because of the fear of numerous people to stay on a thirteenth floor." Then he added, "The real foolishness of the fear is to be found in the fact that the fourteenth floor is actually the thirteenth." Such fears leave the soft mind haggard by day and haunted by night.

The softminded man always fears change. He feels security in the status quo, and he has an almost morbid fear of the new. For him, the greatest pain is the pain of a new idea. An elderly segregationist in the South is reported to have said, "I have come to see now that desegregation is inevitable. But I pray God it will not take place until after I die." The softminded person always wants to freeze the moment and hold life in the gripping yoke of sameness.

Softmindedness often invades religion. This is why religion has sometimes rejected new truth with a dogmatic passion. Through edicts and bulls, inquisitions and excommunications, the church has attempted to prorogue truth and place an impenetrable stone wall in the path of the truth-seeker. The historical-philological criticism of the Bible is considered by the softminded as blasphemous, and reason is often looked upon as the exercise of a corrupt faculty. Softminded persons have revised the Beatitudes to read, "Blessed are the pure in ignorance: for they shall see God."

This has also led to a widespread belief that there is a conflict between science and religion. But this is not true. There may be a conflict between softminded religionists and toughminded scientists, but not between science and religion. Their respective worlds are different and their methods are dissimilar. Science investigates; religion interprets. Science gives man knowledge which is power; religion gives man wisdom which is control. Science deals mainly with facts; religion deals mainly with values. The two are not rivals. They are complementary. Science keeps religion from sinking into the valley of crippling irrationalism and paralyzing obscurantism. Religion prevents science from falling into the marsh of obsolete materialism and moral nihilism.

We do not need to look far to detect the dangers of softmindedness. Dictators, capitalizing on softmindedness, have led men to acts of barbarity and terror that are unthinkable in civilized society. Adolf Hitler realized that softmindedness was so prevalent among his followers that he said, "I use emotion for the many and reserve reason for the few." In *Mein Kampf* he asserted:

> By means of shrewd lies, unremittingly repeated, it is possible to make people believe that heaven is hell—and hell, heaven. . . . The greater the lie, the more readily it will be believed.

Softmindedness is one of the basic causes of race prejudice. The toughminded person always examines the facts before he reaches conclusions; in short, he postjudges. The tenderminded person reaches a conclusion before he has examined the first fact; in short, he prejudges and is prejudiced. Race prejudice is based on groundless fears, suspicions, and misunderstandings. There are those who are sufficiently softminded to believe in the superiority of the white race and the inferiority of the Negro race in spite of the toughminded research of anthropologists who reveal the falsity of such a notion. There are softminded persons who argue that racial segregation should be perpetuated because Negroes lag behind in academic, health, and moral standards. They are not toughminded enough to realize that lagging standards are the result of segregation and discrimination. They do not recognize that it is rationally unsound and sociologically untenable to use the tragic effects of segregation as an argument for its continuation. Too many politicians in the South recognize this disease of softmindedness which engulfs their constituency. With insidious zeal, they make inflammatory statements and disseminate distortions and half-truths which arouse abnormal fears and morbid antipathies within the minds of uneducated and underprivileged whites, leaving them so confused that they are led to acts of meanness and violence which no normal person commits.

There is little hope for us until we become toughminded enough to break loose from the shackles of prejudice, half-truths, and downright ignorance. The shape of the world today does not permit us the luxury of softmindedness. A nation or a civilization that continues to produce softminded men purchases its own spiritual death on an installment plan.

II

But we must not stop with the cultivation of a tough mind. The gospel also demands a tender heart. Toughmindedness without tenderheartedness is cold and detached, leaving one's life in a perpetual winter devoid of the warmth of spring and the gentle heat of summer. What is more tragic than to see a person who has risen to the disciplined heights of toughmindedness but has at the same time sunk to the passionless depths of hardheartedness?

The hardhearted person never truly loves. He engages in a crass utilitarianism which values other people mainly according to their usefulness to him. He never experiences the beauty of friendship, because he is too cold to feel affection for another and is too self-centered to share another's joy and sorrow. He is an isolated island. No outpouring of love links him with the mainland of humanity.

The hardhearted person lacks the capacity for genuine compassion. He is unmoved by the pains and afflictions of his brothers. He passes unfortunate men every day, but he never really sees them. He gives dollars to a worthwhile charity, but he gives not of his spirit.

The hardhearted individual never sees people as people, but rather as mere objects or as impersonal cogs in an ever-turning wheel. In the vast wheel of industry, he sees men as hands. In the massive wheel of big city life, he sees men as digits in a multitude. In the deadly wheel of army life, he sees men as numbers in a regiment. He depersonalizes life.

Jesus frequently illustrated the characteristics of the hardhearted. The rich fool was condemned, not because he was not toughminded, but rather because he was not tenderhearted. Life for him was a mirror in which he saw only himself, and not a window through which he saw other selves. Dives went to hell, not because he was wealthy, but because he was not tenderhearted enough to see Lazarus and because he made no attempt to bridge the gulf between himself and his brother.

Jesus reminds us that the good life combines the toughness of the serpent and the tenderness of the dove. To have serpentlike qualities devoid of dovelike qualities is to be passionless, mean, and selfish. To have dovelike without serpentlike qualities is to be sentimental, anemic, and aimless. We must combine strongly marked antitheses.

We as Negroes must bring together toughmindedness and tenderheartedness, if we are to move creatively toward the goal of freedom and justice. Softminded individuals among us feel that the only was to deal with oppression is by adjusting to it. They acquiesce and resign themselves to segregation. They prefer to remain oppressed. When Moses led the children of Israel from the slavery of Egypt to the freedom of the Promised Land, he discovered that slaves do not always welcome their deliverers. They would rather bear those ills they have, as Shakespeare pointed out, than flee to others that they know not of. They prefer the "fleshpots of Egypt" to the ordeals of emancipation. But this is not the way out. Softminded acquiescence is cowardly. My friends, we cannot win the respect of the white people of the South or elsewhere if we are willing to trade the future of our children for our personal safety and comfort. Moreover, we must learn that passively to accept an unjust system is to co-operate with that system, and thereby to become a participant in its evil.

And there are hardhearted and bitter individuals among us who would combat the opponent with physical violence and corroding hatred. Violence brings only temporary victories; violence, by creating many more social problems than it solves, never brings permanent peace. I am convinced that if we succumb to the temptation to use violence in our struggle for freedom, unborn generations will be the recipients of a long and desolate night of bitterness, and our chief legacy to them will be a never-ending reign of chaos. A voice, echoing through the corridors of time, says to every intemperate Peter, "Put up thy sword." History is cluttered with the wreckage of nations that failed to follow Christ's command.

III

A third way is open in our quest for freedom, namely, nonviolent resistance, that combines toughmindedness and tenderheartedness and avoids the complacency and do-nothingness of the softminded and the violence and bitterness of the hardhearted. My belief is that this method must guide our action in the present crisis in race relations. Through nonviolent resistance we shall be able to oppose the unjust system and at the same time love the perpetrators of the system. We must work passionately and unrelentingly for full stature as citizens, but may it never be said, my friends, that to gain it we used the inferior methods of falsehood, malice, hate, and violence.

I would not conclude without applying the meaning of the text to the nature of God. The greatness of our God lies in the fact that he is both toughminded and tenderhearted. He has qualities both of austerity and of gentleness. The Bible, always clear in stressing both attributes of God, expresses his toughmindedness in his justice and wrath and his tenderheartedness in his love and grace. God has two outstretched arms. One is strong enough to surround us with justice, and one is gentle enough to embrace us with grace. On the one hand, God is a God of justice who punished Israel for her wayward deeds, and on the other hand, he is a forgiving father whose heart was filled with unutterable joy when the prodigal returned home.

I am thankful that we worship a God who is both toughminded and tenderhearted. If God were only toughminded, he would be a cold, passionless despot sitting in some far-off heaven "contemplating all," as Tennyson puts it in "The Palace of Art." He would be Aristotle's "unmoved mover," self-knowing, but not other-loving. But if God were only tenderhearted, he would be too soft and sentimental to function when things go wrong and incapable of controlling what he has made. He would be like H. G. Wells's lovable God in *God, the Invisible King*, who is strongly desirous of making a good world, but finds himself helpless before the surging powers of evil. God is neither hardhearted nor softminded. He is toughminded enough to transcend the world; he is tenderhearted enough to live in it. He does not leave us alone in our agonies and struggles. He seeks us in dark places and suffers with us and for us in our tragic prodigality.

At times we need to know that the Lord is a God of justice. When slumbering giants of injustice emerge in the earth, we need to know that there is a God of power who can cut them down like the grass and leave them withering like the green herb. When our most tireless efforts fail to stop the sweep of oppression, we need to know that in this universe is a God whose matchless strength is a fit contrast to the sordid weakness of man. But there are also times when we need to know that God possesses love and mercy. When we are staggered by the chilly winds of adversity and battered by the raging storms of disappointment and when through our folly and sin we stray into some destructive far country and are frustrated because of a strange feeling of homesickness, we need to know that there is someone who loves us, cares for us, understands us, and will give us another chance. When days grow dark and nights grow dreary, we can be thankful that our God combines in his nature a creative synthesis of love and justice which will lead us through life's dark valleys and into sunlit pathways of hope and fulfillment.

## A KNOCK AT MIDNIGHT (CHAPTER 6)

*Which of you who has a friend will go to him at midnight and say to him, "Friend, lend me three loaves; for a friend of mine has arrived on a journey, and I have nothing to set before him"?*

Luke 11:5–6, RSV

Although this parable is concerned with the power of persistent prayer, it may also serve as a basis for our thought concerning many contemporary problems and the role of the church in grappling with them. It is midnight in the parable; it is also midnight in our world, and the darkness is so deep that we can hardly see which way to turn.

I

It is midnight within the social order. On the international horizon nations are engaged in a colossal and bitter contest for supremacy. Two world wars have been fought within a generation, and the clouds of another war are dangerously low. Man now has atomic and nuclear weapons that could within seconds completely destroy the major cities of the world. Yet the arms race continues and nuclear tests still explode in the atmosphere, with the grim prospect that the very air we breathe will be poisoned by radioactive fallout. Will these circumstances and weapons bring the annihilation of the human race?

When confronted by midnight in the social order we have in the past turned to science for help. And little wonder! On so many occasions science has saved us. When we were in the midnight of physical limitation and material inconvenience, science lifted us to the bright morning of physical and material comfort. When we were in the midnight of crippling ignorance and superstition, science brought us to the daybreak of the free and open mind. When we were in the midnight of dread plagues and diseases, science, through surgery, sanitation, and the wonder drugs, ushered in the bright day of physical health, thereby prolonging our lives and making for greater security and physical well-being. How naturally we turn to science in a day when the problems of the world are so ghastly and ominous.

But alas! science cannot now rescue us, for even the scientist is lost in the terrible midnight of our age. Indeed, science gave us the very instruments that threaten to bring universal suicide. So modern man faces a dreary and frightening midnight in the social order.

This midnight in man's external collective life is paralleled by midnight in his internal individual life. It is midnight within the psychological orer. Everywhere paralyzing fears harrow people by day and haunt them by night. Deep clouds of anxiety and depression are suspended in our mental skies. More people are emotionally disturbed today than at any other time of human history. The psychopathic wards of our hospitals are crowded, and the most popular psychologists today are the psychoanalysts. Bestsellers in psychology are books such as *Man Against Himself, The Neurotic Personality of Our Times*, and *Modern Man in Search of a Soul*. Bestsellers in religion are such books as *Peace of Mind* and *Peace of Soul*. The popular clergyman preaches soothing sermons on "How to be Happy" and "How to Relax." Some have been tempted to revise Jesus' command to read, "Go ye into all the world, keep your blood pressure down, and, lo, I will make you a well-adjusted personality." All of this is indicative that it is midnight within the inner lives of men and women.

It is also midnight within the moral order. At midnight colors lose their distinctiveness and become a sullen shade of gray. Moral principles have lost their distinctiveness. For modern man, absolute right and absolute wrong is a matter of what the majority is doing. Right and wrong are relative to likes and dislikes and the customs of a particular community. We have unconsciously applied Einstein's theory of relativity, which properly described the physical universe, to the moral and ethical realm.

Midnight is the hour when men desperately seek to obey the eleventh commandment, "Thou shalt not get caught." According to the ethic of midnight, the cardinal sin is to be caught and the cardinal virtue is to get by. It is all right to lie, but one must lie with real finesse. It is all right to steal, if one is so dignified that, if caught, the charge becomes embezzlement, not robbery. It is permissible even to hate, if one so dresses his hating in the garments of love that hating appears to be loving. The Darwinian concept of the survival of the fittest has been substituted by a philosophy of the survival of the slickest. This mentality has brought a tragic breakdown of moral standards, and the midnight of moral degeneration deepens.

II

As in the parable, so in our world today, the deep darkness of midnight is interrupted by the sound of a knock. On the door of the church millions of people knock. In this country the roll of church members is longer than ever before. More than 115 million people are at least paper members of some church or synagogue. This represents an increase of 100 percent since 1929, although the population has increased by only 31 percent.

Visitors to Soviet Russia, whose official policy is atheistic, report that the churches in that nation are not only crowded, but that attendance continues to grow. Harrison Salisbury, in an article in *The New York Times*, states that Communist officials are disturbed that so many young people express a growing interest in the church and religion. After forty years of the most vigorous efforts to suppress religion, the hierarchy of the Communist party now faces the inescapable fact that millions of people are knocking on the door of the church.

This numerical growth should not be overemphasized. We must not be tempted to confuse spiritual power and large numbers. Jumboism, as someone has called it, is an utterly fallacious standard for measuring positive power. An increase in quantity does not automatically bring an increase in quality. A larger membership does not necessarily represent a correspondingly increased commitment to Christ. Almost always the creative, dedicated minority has made the world better. But although a numerical growth in church membership does not necessarily reflect a concomitant increase in ethical commitment, millions of people do feel that the church provides an answer to the deep confusion that encompasses their lives. It is still the one familiar landmark where the weary traveler by midnight comes. It is the one house which stands where it has always stood, the house to which the man traveling at midnight either comes or refuses to come. Some decide not to come. But the many who come and knock are desperately seeking a little bread to tide them over.

The traveler asks for three loaves of bread. He wants the bread of faith. In a generation of so many colossal disappointments, men have lost faith in God, faith in man, and faith in the future. Many feel as did William Wilberforce, who in 1801 said, "I dare not marry—the future is so unsettled," or as did William Pitt, who in 1806 said, "There is scarcely anything round us but ruin and despair." In the midst of staggering disillusionment, many cry for the bread of faith.

There is also a deep longing for the bread of hope. In the early years of this century many people did not hunger for this bread. The days of the first telephones, automobiles, and airplanes gave them a radiant optimism. They worshiped at the shrine of inevitable progress. They believed that every new scientific achievement lifted man to higher levels of perfection. But then a series of tragic developments, revealing the selfishness and corruption of man, illustrated with frightening clarity the truth of Lord Acton's dictum, "Power tends to corrupt and absolute power corrupts absolutely." This awful discovery led to one of the most colossal breakdowns of optimism in history. For so many people, young and old, the light of hope went out, and they roamed wearily in the dark chambers of pessimism. Many concluded that life has no meaning. Some agreed with the philosopher Schopenhauer that life is an endless pain with a painful end, and that life is a tragicomedy played over and over again with only slight changes in costume and scenery. Others cried out with Shakespeare's Macbeth that life

is a tale
Told by an idiot, full of sound and fury,
Signifying nothing.

But even in the inevitable moments when all seems hopeless, men know that without hope they cannot really live, and in agonizing desperation they cry for the bread of hope.

And there is the deep longing for the bread of love. Everybody wishes to love and to be loved. He who feels that he is not loved feels that he does not count. Much has happened in the modern world to make men feel that they do not belong. Living in a world which has become oppressively impersonal, many of us have come to feel that we are little more than numbers. Ralph Borsodi in an arresting picture of a world wherein numbers have replaced persons writes that the modern mother is often maternity case No. 8434 and her child, after being fingerprinted and footprinted, becomes No. 8003, and that a funeral in a large city is an event in Parlor B with Class B flowers and decorations at which Preacher No. 14 officiates and Musician No. 84 sings Selection No. 174. Bewildered by this tendency to reduce man to a card in a vast index, man desperately searches for the bread of love.

III

When the man in the parable knocked on his friend's door and asked for the three loaves of bread, he received the impatient retort, "Do not bother me; the door is now shut, and my children are with me in bed; I cannot get up and give you anything." How often have men experienced a similar disappointment when at midnight they knock on the door of the church. Millions of Africans, patiently knocking on the door of the Christian church where they seek the bread of social justice, have either been altogether ignored or told to wait until later, which almost always means never. Millions of American Negroes, starving for the want of the bread of freedom, have knocked again and again on the door of so-called white churches, but they have usually been greeted by a cold indifference or a blatant hypocrisy. Even the white religious leaders, who have a heartfelt desire to open the door and provide the bread, are often more cautious than courageous and more prone to follow the expedient than the ethical path. One of the shameful tragedies of history is that the very institution which should remove man from the midnight of racial segregation participates in creating and perpetuating the midnight.

In the terrible midnight of war men have knocked on the door of the church to ask for the bread of peace, but the church has often disappointed them. What more pathetically reveals the irrelevancy of the church in present-day world affairs than its witness regarding war? In a world gone mad with arms buildups, chauvinistic passions, and imperialistic exploitation, the church has either endorsed these activities or remained appallingly silent. During the last two world wars, national churches even functioned as the ready lackeys of the state, sprinkling holy water upon the battleships and joining the mighty armies in singing, "Praise the Lord and pass the ammunition." A weary world, pleading desperately for peace, has often found the church morally sanctioning war.

And those who have gone to the church to seek the bread of economic justice have been left in the frustrating midnight of economic deprivation. In many instances the church has so aligned itself with the priveleged classes and so defended the status quo that it has been unwilling to answer the knock at midnight. The Greek church in Russia allied itself with the status quo and became so inextricably bound to the despotic czarist regime that it became impossible to be rid of the corrupt political and social system without being rid of the church. Such is the fate of every ecclesiastical organization that allies itself with things-as-they-are.

The church must be reminded that it is not the master or the servant of the state, but rather the conscience of the state. It must be the guide and the critic of the state, and never its tool. If the church does not recapture its prophetic zeal, it will become an irrelevant social club without moral or spiritual authority. If the church does not participate actively in the struggle for peace and for economic and racial justice, it will forfeit the loyalty of millions and cause men everywhere to say that it has atrophied its will. But if the church will free itself from the shackles of a deadening status quo, and, recovering its great historic mission, will speak and act fearlessly and insistently in terms of justice and peace, it will enkindle the imagination of mankind and fire the souls of men, imbuing them with a glowing and ardent love for truth, justice, and peace. Men far and near will know the church as a great fellowship of love that provides light and bread for lonely travelers at midnight.

While speaking of the laxity of the church, I must not overlook the fact that the so-called Negro church has also left men disappointed at midnight. I say so-called Negro church because ideally there can be no Negro or white church. It is to their everlasting shame that white Christians developed a system of racial segregation within the church, and inflicted so many indignities upon its Negro worshipers that they had to organize their own churches.

Two types of Negro churches have failed to provide bread. One burns with emotionalism, and the other freezes with classism. The former, reducing worship to entertainment, places more emphasis on volume than on content and confuses spirituality with muscularity. The danger in such a church is that the members may have more religion in their hands and feet than in their hearts and souls. At midnight this type of church has neither the vitality nor the relevant gospel to feed hungry souls.

The other type of Negro church that feeds no midnight traveler has developed a class system and boasts of its dignity, its membership of professional people, and its exclusiveness. In such a church the worship service is cold and meaningless, the music dull and uninspiring, and the sermon little more than a homily on current events. If the pastor says too much about Jesus Christ, the members feel that he is robbing the pulpit of dignity. If the choir sings a Negro spiritual, the members claim an affront to their class status. This type of church tragically fails to recognize that worship at its best is a social experience in which people from all levels of life come together to affirm their oneness and unity under God. At midnight men are altogether ignored because of their limited education, or they are given bread that has been hardened by the winter of morbid class consciousness.

IV

In the parable we notice that after the man's initial disappointment, he continued to knock on his friend's door. Because of his importunity—his persistence—he finally persuaded his friend to open the door. Many men continue to knock on the door of the church at midnight, even after the church has so bitterly disappointed them, because they know the bread of life is there. The church today is challenged to proclaim God's Son, Jesus Christ, to be the hope of men in all of their complex personal and social problems. Many will continue to come in quest of answers to life's problems. Many young people who knock on the door are perplexed by the uncertainties of life, confused by daily disappointments, and disillusioned by the ambiguities of history. Some who come have been taken from their schools and careers and cast in the role of soldiers. We must provide them with the fresh bread of hope and imbue them with the conviction that God has the power to bring good out of evil. Some who come are tortured by a nagging guilt resulting from their wandering in the midnight of ethical relativism and their surrender to the doctrine of self-expression. We must lead them to Christ who will offer them the fresh bread of forgiveness. Some who knock are tormented by the fear of death as they move toward the evening of life. We must provide them with the bread of faith in immortality, so that they may realize that this earthly life is merely an embryonic prelude to a new awakening.

Midnight is a confusing hour when it is difficult to be faithful. The most inspiring word that the church may speak is that no midnight long remains. The weary traveler by midnight who asks for bread is really seeking the dawn. Our eternal message of hope is that dawn will come. Our slave foreparents realized this. They were never unmindful of the fact of midnight, for always there was the rawhide whip of the overseer and the auction block where families were torn asunder to remind them of its reality. When they thought of the agonizing darkness of midnight, they sang:

> Oh, nobody knows de trouble I've seen;
> Glory Hallelujah!
>
> Sometimes I'm up, sometimes I'm down,
> Oh, yes, Lord,

> Sometimes I'm almost to de groun',
> Oh, yes, Lord,
>
> Oh, nobody knows de trouble I've seen,
> Glory Hallelujah!

Encompassed by a staggering midnight but believing that morning would come, they sang:

> I'm so glad trouble don't last alway.
> O my Lord, O my Lord, what shall I do?

Their positive belief in the dawn was the growing edge of hope that kept the slaves faithful amid the most barren and tragic circumstances.

Faith in the dawn arises from the faith that God is good and just. When one believes this, he knows that the contradictions of life are neither final nor ultimate. He can walk through the dark night with the radiant conviction that all things work together for good for those that love God. Even the most starless midnight may herald the dawn of some great fulfillment.

At the beginning of the bus boycott in Montgomery, Alabama, we set up a voluntary car pool to get the people to and from their jobs. For eleven long months our car pool functioned extraordinarily well. Then Mayor Gayle introduced a resolution instructing the city's legal department to file such proceedings as it might deem proper to stop the operation of the car pool or any transportation system growing out of the bus boycott. A hearing was set for Tuesday, November 13, 1956.

At our regular weekly mass meeting, scheduled the night before the hearing, I had the responsibility of warning the people that the car pool would probably be enjoined. I knew that they had willingly suffered for nearly twelve months, but could we now ask them to walk back and forth to their jobs? And if not, would we be forced to admit that the protest had failed? For the first time I almost shrank from appearing before them.

When the evening came, I mustered sufficient courage to tell them the truth. I tried, however, to conclude on a note of hope. "We have moved all of these months," I said, "in the daring faith that God is with us in our struggle. The many experiences of days gone by have vindicated that faith in a marvelous way. Tonight we must believe that a way will be made out of no way." Yet I could feel the cold breeze of pessimism pass over the audience. The night was darker than a thousand midnights. The light of hope was about to fade and the lamp of faith to flicker.

A few hours later, before Judge Carter, the city argued that we were operating a "private enterprise" without a franchise. Our lawyers argued brilliantly that the car pool was a voluntary "share-a-ride" plan provided without profit as a service by Negro churches. It became obvious that Judge Carter would rule in favor of the city.

At noon, during a brief recess, I noticed an unusual commotion in the courtroom. Mayor Gayle was called to the back room. Several reporters moved excitedly in and out of the room. Momentarily a reporter came to the table where, as chief defendant, I sat with the lawyers. "Here is the decision that you have been waiting for," he said. "Read this release."

In anxiety and hope, I read these words: "The United States Supreme Court today unanimously ruled bus segregation unconstitutional in Montgomery, Alabama." My heart throbbed with an inexpressible joy. The darkest hour of our struggle had become the first hour of victory. Someone shouted from the back of the courtroom, "God Almighty has spoken from Washington!"

The dawn will come. Disappointment, sorrow, and despair are born at midnight, but morning follows. "Weeping may endure for a night," says the Psalmist, "but joy cometh in the morning." This faith adjourns the assemblies of hopelessness and brings new light into the dark chambers of pessimism.

## OUR GOD IS ABLE (CHAPTER 13)

*Now unto him that is able to keep you from falling.*

Jude 24

At the center of the Christian faith is the conviction that in the universe there is a God of power who is able to do exceedingly abundant things in nature and in history. This conviction is stressed over and over in the Old and the New Testaments. Theologically, this affirmation is expressed in the doctrine of the omnipotence of God. The God whom we worship is not a weak and incompetent God. He is able to beat back gigantic waves of opposition and to bring low prodigious mountains of evil. The ringing testimony of the Christian faith is that God is able.

There are those who seek to convince us that only man is able. Their attempt to substitute a man-centered universe for a God-centered universe is not new. It had its modern beginnings in the Renaissance and subsequently in the Age of Reason, when some men gradually came to feel that God was an unnecessary item on the agenda of life. In these periods and later in the industrial revolution in England, others questioned whether God was any longer relevant. The laboratory began to replace the church, and the scientist became a substitute for the prophet. Not a few joined Swinburne in singing a new anthem: "Glory to Man in the highest! for Man is the master of things."

The devotees of the new man-centered religion point to the spectacular advances of modern science as justification for their faith. Science and technology have enlarged man's body. The telescope and television have enlarged his eyes. The telephone, radio, and microphone have strengthened his voice and ears. The automobile and airplane have lengthened his legs. The wonder drugs have prolonged his life. Have not these amazing achievements assured us that man is able?

But alas! something has shaken the faith of those who have made the laboratory "the new cathedral of men's hopes." The instruments which yesterday were worshiped today contain cosmic death, threatening to plunge all of us into the abyss of annihilation. Man is not able to save himself or the world. Unless he is guided by God's spirit, his new-found scientific power will become a devastating Frankenstein monster that will bring to ashes his earthly life.

At times other forces cause us to question the ableness of God. The stark and colossal reality of evil in the world—what Keats calls "the giant agony of the world"; ruthless floods and tornadoes that wipe away people as though they were weeds in an open field; ills like insanity plaguing some individuals from birth and reducing their days to tragic cycles of meaninglessness; the madness of war and the barbarity of man's inhumanity to man—why, we ask, do these things occur if God is able to prevent them? This problem, namely, the problem of evil, has always plagued the mind of man. I would limit my response to an assertion that much of the evil which we experience is caused by man's folly and ignorance and also by the misuse of his freedom. Beyond this, I can say only that there is and always will be a penumbra of mystery surrounding God. What appears at the moment to be evil may have a purpose that our finite minds are incapable of comprehending. So in spite of the presence of evil and the doubts that lurk in our minds, we shall wish not to surrender the conviction that our God is able.

I

Let us notice, first, that God is able to sustain the vast scope of the physical universe. Here again, we are tempted to feel that man is the true master of the physical universe. Man-made jet planes compress into minutes distances that formerly required weeks of tortuous effort. Man-made space ships carry cosmonauts through outer space at fantastic speeds. Is not God being replaced in the mastery of the cosmic order?

But before we are consumed too greatly by our man-centered arrogance, let us take a broader look at the universe. Will we not soon discover that our man-made instruments seem barely to be moving in comparison to the movement of the God-created solar system? Think about the fact, for instance, that the earth is circling the sun so fast that the fastest jet would be left sixty-six thousand miles behind in the first hour of a space race. In the past seven minutes we have been hurtled more than eight thousand miles through space. Or consider the sun which scientists tell us is the center of the solar system. Our earth revolves around this cosmic ball of fire once each year, traveling 584,000,000 miles at the rate of 66,700 miles per hour or 1,600,000 miles per day. By this time tomorrow we shall be 1,600,000 miles from where we are at this hundredth of a second. The sun, which seems to be remarkably near, is 93,000,000 miles from the earth. Six months from now we shall be on the other side of the sun—93,000,000 miles beyond it—and in a year from now we shall have been swung completely around it and back to where we are right now. So when we behold the illimitable expanse of space, in which we are compelled to measure stellar distance in light years and in which heavenly bodies travel at incredible speeds, we are forced to look beyond man and affirm anew that God is able.

II

Let us notice also that God is able to subdue all the powers of evil. In affirming that God is able to conquer evil we admit the reality of evil. Christianity has never dismissed evil as illusory, or an error of the mortal mind. It reckons with evil as a force that has objective reality. But Christianity contends that evil contains the seed of its own destruction. History is the story of evil forces that advance with seemingly irresistible power only to be crushed by the battling rams of the forces of justice. There is a law in the moral world—a silent, invisible imperative, akin to the laws of the physical world—which reminds us that life will work only in a certain way. The Hitlers and the Mussolinis have their day, and for a period they may wield great power, spreading themselves like a green bay tree, but soon they are cut down like the grass and wither as the green herb.

In his graphic account of the Battle of Waterloo in *Les Misérables*, Victor Hugo wrote:

Was it possible that Napoleon should win this battle? We answer no. Why? Because of Wellington? Because of Blücher? No. Because of God. . . . Napoleon had been impeached before the Infinite, and his fall was decreed. He vexed God. Waterloo is not a battle; it is the change of front of the universe.

In a real sense, Waterloo symbolizes the doom of every Napoleon and is an eternal reminder to a generation drunk with military power that in the long run of history might does not make right and the power of the sword cannot conquer the power of the spirit.

An evil system, known as colonialism, swept across Africa and Asia. But then the quiet invisible law began to operate. Prime Minister Macmillan said, "The wind of change began to blow." The powerful colonial empires began to disintegrate like stacks of cards, and new, independent nations began to emerge like refreshing oases in deserts sweltering under the heat of injustice. In less than fifteen years independence has swept through Asia and Africa like an irresistible tidal wave, releasing more than 1,500,000 people from the crippling manacles of colonialism.

In our own nation another unjust and evil system, known as segregation, for nearly one hundred years inflicted the Negro with a sense of inferiority, deprived him of his personhood, and denied him his birthright of life, liberty, and the pursuit of happiness. Segregation has been the Negroes' burden and America's shame. But as on the world scale, so in our nation, the wind of change began to blow. One event has followed another to bring a gradual end to the system of segregation. Today we know with certainty that segregation is dead. The only question remaining is how costly will be the funeral.

These great changes are not mere political and sociological shifts. They represent the passing of systems that were born in injustice, nurtured in inequality, and reared in exploitation. They represent the inevitable decay of any system based on principles that are not in harmony with the moral laws of the universe. When in future generations men look back upon these turbulent, tension-packed days through which we are passing, they will see God working through history for the salvation of man. They will know that God was working through those men who had the vision to perceive that no nation could survive half slave and half free.

God is able to conquer the evils of history. His control is never usurped. If at times we despair because of the relatively slow progress being made in ending racial discrimination and if we become disappointed because of the undue cautiousness of the federal government, let us gain new heart in the fact that God is able. In our sometimes difficult and often lonesome walk up freedom's road, we do not walk alone. God walks with us. He has placed within the very structure of this universe certain absolute moral laws. We can neither defy nor break them. If we disobey them, they will break us. The forces of evil may temporarily conquer truth, but truth will ultimately conquer its conqueror. Our God is able. James Russell Lowell was right:

> Truth forever on the scaffold, Wrong forever on the throne,—
> Yet that scaffold sways the future, and, behind the dim unknown,
> Standeth God within the shadow, keeping watch above his own.

III

Let us notice, finally, that God is able to give us interior resources to confront the trials and difficulties of life. Each of us faces circumstances in life which compel us to carry heavy burdens of sorrow. Adversity assails us with hurricane force. Glowing sunrises are transformed into darkest nights. Our highest hopes are blasted and our noblest dreams are shattered.

Christianity has never overlooked these experiences. They come inevitably. Like the rhythmic alternation in the natural order, life has the glittering sunlight of its summers and the piercing chill of its winters. Days of unutterable joy are followed by days of overwhelming sorrow. Life brings periods of flooding and periods of drought. When these dark hours of life emerge, many cry out with Paul Laurence Dunbar:

> A crust of bread and a corner to sleep in,
> A minute to smile and an hour to weep in,
> A pint of joy to a peck of trouble,
> And never a laugh but the moans come double;
>     And that is life!

Admitting the weighty problems and staggering disappointments, Christianity affirms that God is able to give us the power to meet them. He is able to give us the inner equilibrium to stand tall amid the trials and burdens of life. He is able to provide inner peace amid outer storms. This inner stability of the man of faith is Christ's chief legacy to his disciples. He offers neither material resources nor a magical formula that exempts us from suffering and persecution, but he brings an imperishable gift: "Peace I leave with thee." This is that peace which passeth all understanding.

At times we may feel that we do not need God, but on the day when the storms of disappointment rage, the winds of disaster blow, and the tidal waves of grief beat against our lives, if we do not have a deep and patient faith our emotional lives will be ripped to shreds. There is so much frustration in the world because we have relied on gods rather than God. We have genuflected before the god of science only to find that it has given us the atomic bomb, producing fears and anxieties that science can never mitigate. We have worshiped the god of pleasure only to discover that thrills play out and sensations are short-lived. We have bowed before the god of money only to learn that there are such things as love and friendship that money cannot buy and that in a world of possible depressions, stock market crashes, and bad business investments, money is a rather uncertain deity. These transitory gods are not able to save us or bring happiness to the human heart.

Only God is able. It is faith in him that we must rediscover. With this faith we can transform bleak and desolate valleys into sunlit paths of joy and bring new light into the dark caverns of pessimism. Is someone here moving toward the twilight of life and fearful of that which we call death? Why be afraid? God is able. Is someone here on the brink of despair because of the death of a loved one, the breaking of a marriage, or the waywardness of a child? Why despair? God is able to give you the power to endure that which cannot be changed. Is someone here anxious because of bad health? Why be anxious? Come what may, God is able.

As I come to the conclusion of my message, I would wish you to permit a personal experience. The first twenty-four years of my life were years packed with fulfillment. I had no basic problems or burdens. Because of concerned and loving parents who provided for my every need, I sallied through high school, college, theological school, and graduate school without interruption. It was not until I became a part of the leadership of the Montgomery bus protest that I was actually confronted with the trials of life. Almost immediately after the protest had been undertaken, we began to receive threatening telephone calls and letters in our home. Sporadic in the beginning, they increased day after day. At first I took them in stride, feeling that they were the work of a few hotheads who would become discouraged after they discovered that we would not fight back. But as the weeks passed, I realized that many of the threats were in earnest. I felt myself faltering and growing in fear.

After a particularly strenuous day, I settled in bed at a late hour. My wife had already fallen asleep and I was about to doze off when the telephone rang. An angry voice said, "Listen, nigger, we've taken all we want from you. Before next week you'll be sorry you ever came to Montgomery." I hung up, but I could not sleep. It seemed that all of my fears had come down on me at once. I had reached the saturation point.

I got out of bed and began to walk the floor. Finally, I went to the kitchen and heated a pot of coffee. I was ready to give up. I tried to think of a way to move out of the picture without appearing to be a coward. In this state of exhaustion, when my courage had almost gone, I determined to take my problem to God. My head in my hands, I bowed over the kitchen table and prayed aloud. The words I spoke to God that midnight are still vivid in my memory. "I am here taking a stand for what I believe is right. But now I am afraid. The people are looking to me for leadership, and if I stand before them without strength and courage, they too will falter. I am at the end of my powers. I have nothing left. I've come to the point where I can't face it alone."

At that moment I experienced the presence of the Divine as I had never before experienced him. It seemed as though I could hear the quiet assurance of an inner voice, saying, "Stand up for righteousness, stand up for truth. God will be at your side forever." Almost at once my fears began to pass from me. My uncertainty disappeared. I was ready to face anything. The outer situation remained the same, but God had given me inner calm.

Three nights later, our home was bombed. Strangely enough, I accepted the word of the bombing calmly. My experience with God had given me a new strength and trust. I knew now that God is able to give us the interior resources to face the storms and problems of life.

Let this affirmation be our ringing cry. It will give us courage to face the uncertainties of the future. It will give our tired feet new strength as we continue our forward stride toward the city of freedom. When our days become dreary with low-hovering clouds and our nights become darker than a thousand midnights, let us remember that there is a great benign Power in the universe whose name is God, and he is able to make a way out of no way, and transform dark yesterdays into bright tomorrows. This is our hope for becoming better men. This is our mandate for seeking to make a better world.

## ANTIDOTES FOR FEAR (CHAPTER 14)

*There is no fear in love; but perfect love*
*casteth out fear: because fear hath torment.*
*He that feareth is not made perfect in love.*

1 John 4:18

In these days of catastrophic change and calamitous uncertainty, is there any man who does not experience the depression and bewilderment of crippling fear, which, like a nagging hound of hell, pursues our every footstep?

Everywhere men and women are confronted by fears that often appear in strange disguises and a variety of wardrobes. Haunted by the possibility of bad health, we detect in every meaningless symptom an evidence of disease. Troubled by the fact that days and years pass so quickly, we dose ourselves with drugs which promise eternal youth. If we are physically vigorous, we become so concerned by the prospect that our personalities may collapse that we develop an inferiority complex and stumble through life with a feeling of insecurity, a lack of self-confidence, and a sense of impending failure. A fear of what life may bring encourages some persons to wander aimlessly along the frittering road of excessive drink and sexual promiscuity. Almost without being aware of the change, many people have permitted fear to transform the sunrise of love and peace into a sunset of inner depression.

When unchecked, fear spawns a whole brood of phobias—fear of water, high places, closed rooms, darkness, loneliness, among others—and such an accumulation culminates in phobiaphobia or the fear of fear itself.

Especially common in our highly competitive society are economic fears, from which, Karen Horney says, come most of the psychological problems of our age. Captains of industry are tormented by the possible failure of their business and the capriciousness of the stock market. Employees are plagued by the prospect of unemployment and the consequences of an ever-increasing automation.

And consider, too, the multiplication in our day of religious and ontological fears, which include the fear of death and racial annihilation. The advent of the atomic age, which should have ushered in an era of plenty and of prosperity, has lifted the fear of death to morbid proportions. The terrifying spectacle of nuclear warfare has put Hamlet's words, "To be or not to be," on millions of trembling lips. Witness our frenzied efforts to construct fallout shelters. As though even these offer sanctuary from an H-bomb attack! Witness the agonizing desperation of our petitions that our government increase the nuclear stockpile. But our fanatical quest to maintain "a balance of terror" only increases our fear and leaves nations on tiptoes lest some diplomatic *faux pas* ignite a frightful holocaust.

Realizing that fear drains a man's energy and depletes his resources, Emerson wrote, "He has not learned the lesson of life who does not every day surmount a fear."

But I do not mean to suggest that we should seek to eliminate fear altogether from human life. Were this humanly possible, it would be practically undesirable. Fear is the elemental alarm system of the human organism which warns of approaching dangers and without which man could not have survived in either the primitive or modern worlds.

Fear, moreover, is a powerfully creative force. Every great invention and intellectual advance represents a desire to escape from some dreaded circumstance or condition. The fear of darkness led to the discovery of the secret of electricity. The fear of pain led to the marvelous advances of medical science. The fear of ignorance was one reason that man built great institutions of learning. The fear of war was one of the forces behind the birth of the United Nations. Angelo Patri has rightly said, "Education consists in being afraid at the right time." If man were to lose his capacity to fear, he would be deprived of his capacity to grow, invent, and create. So in a sense fear is normal, necessary, and creative.

But we must remember that abnormal fears are emotionally ruinous and psychologically destructive. To illustrate the difference between normal and abnormal fear, Sigmund Freud spoke of a person who was quite properly afraid of snakes in the heart of an African jungle and of another person who neurotically feared that snakes were under the carpet in his city apartment. Psychologists say that normal children are born with only two fears—the fear of falling and the fear of loud noises—and that all others are environmentally acquired. Most of these acquired fears are snakes under the carpet.

It is to such fears that we usually refer when we speak of getting rid of fear. But this is only a part of the story. Normal fear protects us; abnormal fear paralyzes us. Normal fear motivates us to improve our individual and collective welfare; abnormal fear constantly poisons and distorts our inner lives. Our problem is not to be rid of fear but rather to harness and master it. How may it be mastered?

I

First, we must unflinchingly face our fears and honestly ask ourselves why we are afraid. This confrontation will, to some measure, grant us power. We shall never be cured of fear by escapism or repression, for the more we attempt to ignore and repress our fears, the more we multiply our inner conflicts.

By looking squarely and honestly at our fears we learn that many of them are residues of some childhood need or apprehension. Here, for instance, is a person haunted by a fear of death or the thought of punishment in the afterlife, who discovers that he has unconsciously projected into the whole of reality the childhood experience of being punished by parents, locked in a room, and seemingly deserted. Or here is a man plagued by the fear of inferiority and social rejection, who discovers that rejection in childhood by a self-centered mother and a preoccupied father left him with a self-defeating sense of inadequacy and a repressed bitterness toward life.

By bringing our fears to the forefront of consciousness, we may find them to be more imaginary than real. Some of them will turn out to be snakes under the carpet.

And let us also remember that, more often than not, fear involves the misuse of the imagination. When we get our fears into the open, we may laugh at some of them, and this is good. One psychiatrist said, "Ridicule is the master cure for fear and anxiety."

II

Second, we can master fear through one of the supreme virtues known to man: courage. Plato considered courage to be an element of the soul which bridges the cleavage between reason and desire. Aristotle thought of courage as the affirmation of man's essential nature. Thomas Aquinas said that courage is the strength of mind capable of conquering whatever threatens the attainment of the highest good.

Courage, therefore, is the power of the mind to overcome fear. Unlike anxiety, fear has a definite object which may be faced, analyzed, attacked, and, if need be, endured. How often the object of our fear is fear itself! In his *Journal* Henry David Thoreau wrote, "Nothing is so much to be feared as fear." Centuries earlier, Epictetus wrote, "For it is not death or hardship that is a fearful thing, but the fear of hardship and death." Courage takes the fear produced by a definite object into itself and thereby conquers the fear involved. Paul Tillich has written, "Courage is self-affirmation 'in spite of' . . . that which tends to hinder the self from affirming itself." It is self-affirmation in spite of death and nonbeing, and he who is courageous takes the fear of death into his self-affirmation and acts upon it. This courageous self-affirmation, which is surely a remedy for fear, is not selfishness, for self-affirmation includes both a proper self-love and a properly propositioned love of others. Erich Fromm has shown in convincing terms that the right kind of self-love and the right kind of love of others are interdependent.

Courage, the determination not to be overwhelmed by any object, however frightful, enables us to stand up to any fear. Many of our fears are not mere snakes under the carpet. Trouble is a reality in this strange medley of life, dangers lurk within the circumference of every action, accidents do occur, bad health is an ever-threatening possibility, and death is a stark, grim, and inevitable fact of human experience. Evil and pain in this conundrum of life are close to each of us, and we do both ourselves and our neighbors a great disservice when we attempt to prove that there is nothing in this world of which we should be frightened. These forces that threaten to negate life must be challenged by courage, which is the power of life to affirm itself in spite of life's ambiguities. This requires the exercise of a creative will that enables us to hew out a stone of hope from a mountain of despair.

Courage and cowardice are antithetical. Courage is an inner resolution to go forward in spite of obstacles and frightening situations; cowardice is a submissive surrender to circumstance. Courage breeds creative self-affirmation; cowardice produces destructive self-abnegation.

Courage faces fear and thereby masters it; cowardice represses fear and is thereby mastered by it. Courageous men never lose the zest for living even though their life situation is zestless; cowardly men, overwhelmed by the uncertainties of life, lose the will to live. We must constantly build dykes of courage to hold back the flood of fear.

III

Third, fear is mastered through love. The New Testament affirms, "There is no fear in love; but perfect love casteth out fear." The kind of love which led Christ to a cross and kept Paul unembittered amid the angry torrents of persecution is not soft, anemic, and sentimental. Such love confronts evil without flinching and shows in our popular parlance an infinite capacity "to take it." Such love overcomes the world even from a rough-hewn cross against the skyline.

But does love have a relationship to our modern fear of war, economic displacement, and racial injustice? Hate is rooted in fear, and the only cure for fear-hate is love. Our deteriorating international situation is shot through with the lethal darts of fear. Russia fears America, and America fears Russia. Likewise China and India, and the Israelis and the Arabs. These fears include another nation's aggression, scientific and technological supremacy, and economic power, and our own loss of status and power. Is not fear one of the major causes of war? We say that war is a consequence of hate, but close scrutiny reveals this sequence: first fear, then hate, then war, and finally deeper hatred. Were a nightmarish nuclear war to engulf our world, the cause would be not so much that one nation hated another, but that both nations feared each other.

What method has the sophisticated ingenuity of modern man employed to deal with the fear of war? We have armed ourselves to the nth degree. The West and the East have engaged in a fever-pitched arms race. Expenditures for defense have risen to mountainous proportions, and weapons of destruction have been assigned priority over all other human endeavors. The nations have believed that greater armaments will cast out fear. But alas! they have produced greater fear. In these turbulent, panic-stricken days we are once more reminded of the judicious words of old, "Perfect love casteth out fear." Not arms, but love, understanding, and organized goodwill can cast out fear. Only disarmament, based on good faith, will make mutual trust a living reality.

Our own problem of racial injustice must be solved by the same formula. Racial segregation is buttressed by such irrational fears as loss of preferred economic privilege, altered social status, intermarriage, and adjustment to new situations. Through sleepless nights and haggard days numerous white people attempt to combat these corroding fears by diverse methods. By following the path of escape, some seek to ignore the question of race relations and to close their mind to the issues involved. Others placing their faith in such legal maneuvers as interposition and nullification, counsel massive resistance. Still others hope to drown their fear by engaging in acts of violence and meanness toward their Negro brethren. But how futile are all these remedies! Instead of eliminating fear, they instill deeper and more pathological fears that leave the victims inflicted with strange psychoses and peculiar cases of paranoia. Neither repression, massive resistance, nor aggressive violence will cast out the fear of integration; only love and goodwill can do that.

If our white brothers are to master fear, they must depend not only on their commitment to Christian love but also on the Christlike love which the Negro generates toward them. Only through our adherence to love and nonviolence will the fear in the white community be mitigated. A guilt-ridden white minority fears that if the Negro attains power, he will without restraint or pity act to revenge the accumulated injustices and brutality of the years. A parent, who has continually mistreated his son, suddenly realizes that he is now taller than the parent. Will the son use his new physical power to repay for all of the blows of the past?

Once a helpless child, the Negro has now grown politically, culturally, and economically. Many white men fear retaliation. The Negro must show them that they have nothing to fear, for the Negro forgives and is willing to forget the past. *The Negro must convince the white man that he seeks justice for both himself and the white man.* A mass movement exercising love and nonviolence and demonstrating power under discipline should convince the white community that were such a movement to attain strength its power would be used creatively and not vengefully.

What then is the cure of this morbid fear of integration? We know the cure. God help us to achieve it! Love casts out fear.

This truth is not without a bearing on our personal anxieties. We are afraid of the superiority of other people, of failure, and of the scorn or disapproval of those whose opinions we most value. Envy, jealousy, a lack of self-confidence, a feeling of insecurity, and a haunting sense of inferiority are all rooted in fear. We do not envy people and then fear them; first we fear them and subsequently we become jealous of them. Is there a cure for these annoying fears that pervert our personal lives? Yes, a deep and abiding commitment to the way of love. "Perfect love casteth out fear."

Hatred and bitterness can never cure the disease of fear; only love can do that. Hatred paralyzes life; love releases it. Hatred confuses life; love harmonizes it. Hatred darkens life; love illuminates it.

IV

Fourth, fear is mastered through faith. A common source of fear is an awareness of deficient resources and of a consequent inadequacy for life. All too many people attempt to face the tensions of life with inadequate spiritual resources. When vacationing in Mexico, Mrs. King and I wished to go deep-sea fishing. For reasons of economy, we rented an old and poorly equipped boat. We gave this little thought until, ten miles from shore, the clouds lowered and howling winds blew. Then we became paralyzed with fear, for we knew our boat was deficient. Multitudes of people are in a similar situation. Heavy winds and weak boats explain their fear.

Many of our abnormal fears can be dealt with by the skills of psychiatry, a relatively new discipline pioneered by Sigmund Freud, which investigates the subconscious drives of men and seeks to discover how and why fundamental energies are diverted into neurotic channels. Psychiatry helps us to look candidly at our inner selves and to search out the causes of our failures and fears. But much of our fearful living encompasses a realm where the service of psychiatry is ineffectual unless the psychiatrist is a man of religious faith. For our trouble is simply that we attempt to confront fear without faith; we sail through the stormy seas of life without adequate spiritual boats. One of the leading physicians and psychiatrists in America has said, "The only known cure for fear is faith."

Abnormal fears and phobias that are expressed in neurotic anxiety may be cured by psychiatry; but the fear of death, nonbeing, and nothingness, expressed in existential anxiety, may be cured only by a positive religious faith.

A positive religious faith does not offer an illusion that we shall be exempt from pain and suffering, nor does it imbue us with the idea that life is a drama of unalloyed comfort and untroubled ease. Rather, it instills us with the inner equilibrium needed to face strains, burdens, and fears that inevitably come, and assures us that the universe is trustworthy and that God is concerned.

Irreligion, on the other hand, would have us believe that we are orphans cast into the terrifying immensities of space in a universe that is without purpose or intelligence. Such a view drains courage and exhausts the energies of men. In his *Confession* Tolstoi wrote concerning the aloneness and emptiness he felt before his conversion:

> There was a period in my life when everything seemed to be crumbling, the very foundations of my convictions were beginning to give way, and I felt myself going to pieces. There was no sustaining influence in my life and there was no God there, and so every night before I went to sleep, I made sure that there was no rope in my room lest I be tempted during the night to hang myself from the rafters of my room; and I stopped from going out shooting lest I be tempted to put a quick end to my life and to my misery.

Like so many people, Tolstoi at that stage of his life lacked the sustaining influence which comes from the conviction that this universe is guided by a benign Intelligence whose infinite love embraces all mankind.

Religion endows us with the conviction that we are not alone in this vast, uncertain universe. Beneath and above the shifting sands of time, the uncertainties that darken our days, and the vicissitudes that cloud our nights is a wise and loving God. This universe is not a tragic expression of meaningless chaos but a marvelous display of orderly cosmos—"The Lord by wisdom hath founded the earth; by understanding hath he established the heavens." Man is not a wisp of smoke from a limitless smoldering, but a child of God created "a little lower than the angels." Above the manyness of time stands the one eternal God, with wisdom to guide us, strength to protect us, and love to keep us. His boundless love supports and contains us as a mighty ocean contains and supports the tiny drops of every wave. With a surging fullness he is forever moving toward us, seeking to fill the little creeks and bays of our lives with unlimited resources. This is religion's everlasting diapason, its eternal answer to the enigma of existence. Any man who finds this cosmic sustenance can walk the highways of life without the fatigue of pessimism and the weight of morbid fears.

Herein lies the answer to the neurotic fear of death that plagues so many of our lives. Let us face the fear that the atomic bomb has aroused with the faith that we can never travel beyond the arms of the Divine. Death is inevitable. It is a democracy for all of the people, not an aristocracy for some of the people—kings die and beggars die; young men die and old men die; learned men die and ignorant men die. We need not fear it. The God who brought our whirling planet from primal vapor and has led the human pilgrimage for lo these many centuries can most assuredly lead us through death's dark night into the bright daybreak of eternal life. His will is too perfect and his purposes are too extensive to be contained in the limited receptacle of time and the narrow walls of earth. Death is not the ultimate evil; the ultimate evil is to be outside God's love. We need not join the mad rush to purchase an earthly fallout shelter. God is our eternal fallout shelter.

Jesus knew that nothing could separate man from the love of God. Listen to his majestic words:

Fear them not therefore; for there is nothing covered, that shall not be revealed; and hid, that shall not be known. . . . And fear not them which kill the body, but are not able to kill the soul: but rather fear him which is able to destroy both soul and body in hell. Are not two sparrows sold for a farthing? and one of them shall not fall on the ground without your Father. But the very hairs of your head are all numbered. Fear ye not therefore, ye are of more value than many sparrows.

Man, for Jesus, is not mere flotsam and jetsam in the river of life, but he is a child of God. Is it not unreasonable to assume that God, whose creative activity is expressed in an awareness of a sparrow's fall and the number of hairs on a man's head, excludes from his encompassing love the life of man itself? The confidence that God is mindful of the individual is of tremendous value in dealing with the disease of fear, for it gives us a sense of worth, of belonging, and of at-homeness in the universe.

One of the most dedicated participants in the bus protest in Montgomery, Alabama, was an elderly Negro whom we affectionately called Mother Pollard. Although poverty-stricken and uneducated, she was amazingly intelligent and possessed a deep understanding of the meaning of the movement. After having walked for several weeks, she was asked if she were tired. With ungrammatical profundity, she answered, "My feets is tired, but my soul is rested."

On a particular Monday evening, following a tension-packed week which included being arrested and receiving numerous threatening telephone calls, I spoke at a mass meeting. I attempted to convey an overt impression of strength and courage, although I was inwardly depressed and fear-stricken. At the end of the meeting, Mother Pollard came to the front of the church and said, "Come here, son." I immediately went to her and hugged her affectionately. "Something is wrong with you," she said. "You didn't talk strong tonight." Seeking further to disguise my fears, I retorted, "Oh, no, Mother Pollard, nothing is wrong. I am feeling as fine as ever." But her insight was discerning. "Now you can't fool me," she said. "I knows something is wrong. Is it that we ain't doing things to please you? Or is it that the white folks is bothering you?" Before I could respond, she looked directly into my eyes and said, "I don told you we is with you all the way." Then her face became radiant and she said in words of quiet certainty, "But even if we ain't with you, God's gonna take care of you." As she spoke these consoling words, everything in me quivered and quickened with the pulsing tremor of raw energy.

Since that dreary night in 1956, Mother Pollard has passed on to glory and I have known very few quiet days. I have been tortured without and tormented within by the raging fires of tribulation. I have been forced to muster what strength and courage I have to withstand howling winds of pain and jostling storms of adversity. But as the years have unfolded the eloquently simple words of Mother Pollard have come back again and again to give light and peace and guidance to my troubled soul. "God's gonna take care of you."

This faith transforms the whirlwind of despair into a warm and reviving breeze of hope. The words of a motto which a generation ago were commonly found on the wall in the homes of devout persons need to be etched on our hearts:

> Fear knocked at the door.
> Faith answered.
> There was no one there.

Martin Luther King, Jr., *The Strength to Love* (New York: Harper & Row, 1963).

# 55

# Why We Can't Wait

*After the assassination of President John Fitzgerald Kennedy on 22 November 1963, King declared in* Why We Can't Wait *that "we were all involved in the death of John Kennedy. We tolerated hate; we tolerated the sick stimulation of violence in all walks of life; and we tolerated the differential application of law, which said that a man's life was sacred only if we agreed with his views. This may explain the cascading grief that flooded the country in late November. We mourned a man who had become the pride of the nation, but we grieved as well for ourselves because we knew we were sick." SCLC's successful campaign in Birmingham, Alabama, and the successful, nationally televised 28 August March on Washington seemed to be eclipsed by the hideous murder of four little black girls as they attended the Sunday school of the Sixteenth Street Baptist Church, which was bombed in September, as well as by the shocking assassination of the president. Dr. King's message of nonviolence sounded like the voice of a lonely prophet crying in a wilderness of hate and violence.* Why We Can't Wait *was an attempt to defend the potency of nonviolent direct action by showing how it had succeeded in Birmingham and other Southern cities.*

## THE NEGRO REVOLUTION (CHAPTER 1)

The bitterly cold winter of 1962 lingered throughout the opening months of 1963, touching the land with chill and frost, and then was replaced by a placid spring. Americans awaited a quiet summer. That is would be pleasant they had no doubt. The worst of it would be the nightmare created by 60 million cars, all apparently trying to reach the same destination at the same time. Fifty million families looked forward to the pleasure of 200 million vacations in the American tradition of the frenetic hunt for relaxation.

It would be a pleasant summer because, in the mind of the average man, there was little cause for concern. The blithe outlook about the state of the nation was reflected from as high up as the White House. The administration confidently readied a tax-reduction bill. Business and employment were at comfortable levels. Money was—for many Americans—plentiful.

Summer came, and the weather was beautiful. But the climate, the social climate of American life, erupted into lightning flashes, trembled with thunder and vibrated to the relentless, growing rain of protest come to life through the land. Explosively, America's third revolution—the Negro revolution—had begun.

For the first time in the long and turbulent history of the nation, almost one thousand cities were engulfed in civil turmoil, with violence trembling just below the surface. Reminiscent of the French Revolution of 1789, the streets had become a battleground, just as they had become the battleground, in the 1830s, of England's tumultuous Chartist movement. As in these two revolutions, a submerged social group, propelled by a burning need for justice, lifting itself with sudden swiftness, moving with determination and a majestic scorn for risk and danger, created an uprising so powerful that it shook a huge society from its comfortable base.

Never in American history had a group seized the streets, the squares, the sacrosanct business thoroughfares and the marbled halls of government to protest and proclaim the unendurability of their oppression. Had room-size machines turned human, burst from the plants that housed them and stalked the land in revolt, the nation could not have been more amazed. Undeniably, the Negro had been an object of sympathy and wore the scars of deep grievances, but the nation had come to count on him as a creature who could quietly endure, silently suffer and patiently wait. He was well trained in service and, whatever the provocation, he neither pushed back nor spoke back.

Just as lightning makes no sound until it strikes, the Negro revolution generated quietly. But when it struck, the revealing flash of its power and the impact of its sincerity and fervor displayed a force of a frightening intensity. Three hundred years of humiliation, abuse and deprivation cannot be expected to find voice in a whisper. The storm clouds did not release a "gentle rain from heaven," but a whirlwind, which has not yet spent its force or attained its full momentum.

Because there is more to come; because American society is bewildered by the spectacle of the Negro in revolt; because the dimensions are vast and the implications deep in a nation with 20 million Negroes, it is important to understand the history that is being made today.

II

Some years ago, I sat in a Harlem department store, surrounded by hundreds of people. I was autographing copies of *Stride Toward Freedom*, my book about the Montgomery bus boycott of 1955–56. As I signed my name to a page, I felt something sharp plunge forcefully into my chest. I had been stabbed with a letter opener, struck home by a woman who would later be judged insane. Rushed by ambulance to Harlem Hospital, I lay in a bed for hours while preparations were made to remove the keen-edged knife from my body. Days later, when I was well enough to talk with Dr. Aubrey Maynard, the chief of the surgeons who performed the delicate, dangerous operation, I learned the reason for the long delay that preceded surgery. He told me that the razor tip of the instrument had been touching my aorta and that my whole chest had to be opened to extract it.

"If you had sneezed during all those hours of waiting," Dr. Maynard said, "your aorta would have been punctured and you would have drowned in your own blood."

In the summer of 1963 the knife of violence was just that close to the nation's aorta. Hundreds of cities might now be mourning countless dead but for the operation of certain forces which gave political surgeons an opportunity to cut boldly and safely to remove the deadly peril.

What was it that gave us the second chance? To answer this we must answer another question. Why did this revolution occur in 1963? Negroes had for decades endured evil. In the words of the poet, they had long asked: "Why must the blackness of nighttime collect in our mouth; why must we always taste grief in our blood?" Any time would seem to have been the right time.. Why 1963?

Why did a thousand cities shudder almost simultaneously and why did the whole world—in gleaming capitals and mud-hut villages—hold its breath during those months? Why was it this year that the American Negro, so long ignored, so long written out of the pages of history books, tramped a declaration of freedom with his marching feet across the pages of newspapers, the television screens and the magazines? Sarah Turner closed the kitchen cupboard and went into the streets; John Wilkins shut down the elevator and enlisted in the nonviolent army; Bill Griggs slammed the brakes of his truck and slid to the sidewalk; the Reverend Arthur Jones led his flock into the streets and held church in jail. The words and actions of parliaments and statesmen, of kings and prime ministers, movie stars and athletes, were shifted from the front pages to make room for the history-making deeds of the servants, the drivers, the elevator operators and the ministers. Why in 1963, and what has this to do with why the dark threat of violence did not erupt in blood?

III

The Negro had been deeply disappointed over the slow pace of school desegregation. He knew that in 1954 the highest court in the land had handed down a decree calling for desegregation of schools "with all deliberate speed." He knew that this edict from the Supreme Court had been heeded with all deliberate delay. At the beginning of 1963, nine years after this historic decision, approximately 9 percent of southern Negro students were attending integrated schools. If this pace were maintained, it would be the year 2054 before integration in southern schools would be a reality.

In its wording the Supreme Court decision had revealed an awareness that attempts would be made to evade its intent. The phrase "all deliberate speed" did not mean that another century should be allowed to unfold before we released Negro children from the narrow pigeonhole of the segregated schools; it meant that, giving some courtesy and consideration to the need for softening old attitudes and outdated customs, democracy must press ahead, out of the past of ignorance and intolerance, and into the present of educational opportunity and moral freedom.

Yet the statistics make it abundantly clear that the segregationists of the South remained undefeated by the decision. From every section of Dixie, the announcement of the high court had been met with declarations of defiance. Once recovered from their initial outrage, these defenders of the status quo had seized the offensive to impose their own schedule of change. The progress that was supposed to have been achieved with deliberate speed had created change for less than 2 percent of Negro children in most areas of the South and not even one-tenth of one percent in some parts of the deepest South.

There was another factor in the slow pace of progress, a factor of which few are aware and even fewer understand. It is an unadvertised fact that soon after the 1954 decision the Supreme Court retreated from its own position by giving approval to the Pupil Placement Law. This law permitted the states themselves to determine where school children might be placed by virtue of family background, special ability and other subjective criteria. The Pupil Placement Law was almost as far-reaching in modifying and limiting the integration of schools as the original decision had been in attempting to eliminate segregation. Without technically reversing itself, the court had granted legal sanction to tokenism and thereby guaranteed that segregation, in substance, would last for an indefinite period, though formally it was illegal.

In order, then, to understand the deep disillusion of the Negro in 1963, one must examine his contrasting emotions at the time of the decision and during the nine years that followed. One must understand the pendulum swing between the elation that arose when the edict was handed down and the despair that followed the failure to bring it to life.

A second reason for the outburst in 1963 was rooted in disappointment with both political parties. From the city of Los Angeles in 1960, the Democratic party had written an historic and sweeping civil-rights pronouncement into its campaign platform. The Democratic standard bearer had repeated eloquently and often that the moral weight of the presidency must be applied to this burning issue. From Chicago, the Republican party had been generous in its convention vows on civil rights, although its candidate had made no great effort in his campaign to convince the nation that he would redeem his party's promises.

Then 1961 and 1962 arrived, with both parties marking time in the cause of justice. In the Congress, reactionary Republicans were still doing business with the dixiecrats. And the feeling was growing among

Negroes that the administration had oversimplified and underestimated the civil-rights issue. President Kennedy, if not backing down, had backed away from a key pledge of his campaign—to wipe out housing discrimination immediately "with the stroke of a pen." When he had finally signed the housing order, two years after taking office, its terms, though praiseworthy, had revealed a serious weakness in its failure to attack the key problem of discrimination in financing by banks and other institutions.

While Negroes were being appointed to some significant jobs, and social hospitality was being extended at the White House to Negro leaders, the dreams of the masses remained in tatters. The Negro felt that he recognized the same old bone that had been tossed to him in the past—only now it was being handed to him on a platter, with courtesy.

The administration had fashioned its primary approach to discrimination in the South around a series of lawsuits chiefly designed to protect the right to vote. Opposition toward action on other fronts had begun to harden. With each new Negro protest, we were advised, sometimes privately and sometimes in public, to call off our efforts and channel all of our energies into registering voters. On each occasion we would agree with the importance of voting rights, but would patiently seek to explain that Negroes did not want to neglect all other rights while one was selected for concentrated attention.

It was necessary to conclude that our argument was not persuading the administration any more than the government's logic was prevailing with us. Negroes had manifested their faith by racking up a substantial majority of their votes for President Kennedy. They had expected more of him than of the previous administration. In no sense had President Kennedy betrayed his promises. Yet his administration appeared to believe it was doing as much as was politically possible and had, by its positive deeds, earned enough credit to coast on civil rights. Politically, perhaps, this was not a surprising conclusion. How many people understood, during the first two years of the Kennedy administration, that the Negroes' "Now" was becoming as militant as the segregationists' "Never"? Eventually the president would set political considerations aside and rise to the level of his own unswerving moral commitment. But this was still in the future.

No discussion of the influences that bore on the thinking of the Negro in 1963 would be complete without some attention to the relationship of this revolution to international events. Throughout the upheavals of cold war politics, Negroes had seen their government go to the brink of nuclear conflict more than once. The justification for risking the annihilation of the human race was always expressed in terms of America's willingness to go to any lengths to preserve freedom. To the Negro that readiness for heroic measures in the defense of liberty disappeared or became tragically weak when the threat was within our own borders and was concerned with the Negro's liberty. While the Negro is not so selfish as to stand isolated in his concern for his own dilemma, ignoring the ebb and flow of events around the world, there is a certain bitter irony in the picture of his country championing freedom in foreign lands and failing to ensure that freedom to 20 million of its own.

From beyond the borders of his own land, the Negro had been inspired by another powerful force. He had watched the decolonization and liberation of nations in Africa and Asia since World War II. He knew that yellow, black and brown people had felt for years that the American Negro was too passive, unwilling to take strong measures to gain his freedom. He might have remembered the visit to this country of an African head of state, who was called upon by a delegation of prominent American Negroes. When they began reciting to him their long list of grievances, the visiting statesman had waved a weary hand and said:

"I am aware of current events. I know everything you are telling me about what the white man is doing to the Negro. Now tell me: What is the Negro doing for himself?"

The American Negro saw, in the land from which he had been snatched and thrown into slavery, a great pageant of political progress. He realized that just thirty years ago there were only three independent nations in the whole of Africa. He knew that by 1963 more than thirty-four African nations had risen from colonial bondage. The Negro saw black statesmen voting on vital issues in the United Nations—and knew that in many cities of his own land he was not permitted to take that significant walk to the ballot box. He saw black kings and potentates ruling from palaces—and knew he had been condemned to move from small ghettos to larger ones. Witnessing the drama of Negro progress elsewhere in the world, witnessing a level of conspicuous consumption at home exceeding anything in our history, it was natural that by 1963 Negroes would rise with resolution and demand a share of governing power, and living conditions measured by American standards rather than by the standards of colonial impoverishment.

An additional and decisive fact confronted the Negro and helped to bring him out of the houses, into the streets, out of the trenches and into the front lines. This was his recognition that one hundred years had passed since emancipation, with no profound effect on his plight.

With the dawn of 1963, plans were afoot all over the land to celebrate the Emancipation Proclamation, the one-hundredth birthday of the Negro's liberation from bondage. In Washington, a federal commission had been established to mark the event. Governors of states and mayors of cities had utilized the date to enhance their political image by naming commissions, receiving committees, issuing statements, planning state pageants, sponsoring dinners, endorsing social activities. Champagne, this year, would bubble on countless tables. Appropriately attired, over thick cuts of roast beef, legions would listen as luminous phrases were spun to salute the great democratic landmark which 1963 represented.

But alas! All the talk and publicity accompanying the centennial only served to remind the Negro that he still wasn't free, that he still lived a form of slavery disguised by certain niceties of complexity. As the then vice-president, Lyndon B. Johnson, phrased it: "Emancipation was a Proclamation but not a fact." The pen of the Great Emancipator had moved the Negro into the sunlight of physical freedom, but actual conditions had left him behind in the shadow of political, psychological, social, economic and intellectual bondage. In the South, discrimination faced the Negro in its obvious and glaring forms. In the North, it confronted him in hidden and subtle disguise.

The Negro also had to recognize that one hundred years after emancipation he lived on a lonely island of economic insecurity in the midst of a vast ocean of material prosperity. Negroes are still at the bottom of the economic ladder. They live within two concentric circles of segregation. One imprisons them on the basis of color, while the other confines them within a separate culture of poverty. The average Negro is born into want and deprivation. His struggle to escape his circumstances is hindered by color discrimination. He is deprived of normal education and normal social and economic opportunities. When he seeks opportunity, he is told, in effect, to lift himself by his own bootstraps, advice which does not take into account the fact that he is barefoot.

By 1963, most of America's working population had forgotten the Great Depression or had never known it. The slow and steady growth of unemployment had touched some of the white working force but the proportion was still not more than one in twenty. This was not true for the Negro. There were two and one-half times as many jobless Negroes as whites in 1963, and their median income was half that of the white man. Many white Americans of good will have never connected bigotry with economic exploitation. They have deplored prejudice, but tolerated or ignored economic injustice. But the Negro knows that these two evils have a malignant kinship. He knows this because he has worked in shops that employ him exclusively because the pay is below a living standard. He knows it is not an accident of geography that wage rates in the South are significantly lower than those in the North. He knows that the spotlight recently focused on the growth in the number of women who work is not a phenomenon in Negro life. The average Negro woman has always had to work to help keep her family in food and clothes.

To the Negro, as 1963 approached, the economic structure of society appeared to be so ordered that a precise sifting of jobs took place. The lowest-paid employment and the most tentative jobs were reserved for him. If he sought to change his position, he was walled in by the tall barrier of discrimination. As summer came, more than ever the spread of unemployment had visible and tangible dimensions to the colored

American. Equality meant dignity and dignity demanded a job that was secure and a pay check that lasted throughout the week.

The Negro's economic problem was compounded by the emergence and growth of automation. Since discrimination and lack of education confined him to unskilled and semi-skilled labor, the Negro was and remains the first to suffer in these days of great technological development. The Negro knew all too well that there was not in existence the kind of vigorous retraining program that could really help him to grapple with the magnitude of his problem.

The symbol of the job beyond the great wall was construction work. The Negro whose slave labor helped to build a nation was being told by employers on the one hand and unions on the other that there was no place for him in this industry. Billions were being spent on city, state and national building for which the Negro paid taxes but could draw no pay check. No one who saw the spanning bridges, the grand mansions, the sturdy docks and stout factories of the South could question the Negro's ability to build if he were given a chance for apprenticeship training. It was plain, hard, raw discrimination that shut him out of decent employment.

In 1963, the Negro, who had realized for many years that he was not truly free, awoke from a stupor of inaction with the cold dash of realization that 1963 meant one hundred years after Lincoln gave his autograph to the cause of freedom.

The milestone of the centennial of emancipation gave the Negro a reason to act—a reason so simple and obvious that he almost had to step back to see it.

Simple logic made it painfully clear that if this centennial were to be meaningful, it must be observed not as a celebration, but rather as a commemoration of the one moment in the country's history when a bold, brave *start* had been made, and a rededication to the obvious fact that urgent business was at hand—the resumption of that noble journey toward the goals reflected in the Preamble to the Constitution, the Constitution itself, the Bill of Rights and the Thirteenth, Fourteenth and Fifteenth Amendments.

Yet not all of these forces conjoined could have brought about the massive and largely bloodless revolution of 1963 if there had not been at hand a philosophy and a method worthy of its goals. Nonviolent direct action did not originate in America, but it found its natural home in this land, where refusal to cooperate with injustice was an ancient and honorable tradition and where Christian forgiveness was written into the minds and hearts of good men. Tested in Montgomery during the winter of 1955–56, and toughened throughout the South in the eight ensuing years, nonviolent resistance had become, by 1963, the logical force in the greatest mass-action crusade for freedom that has ever occurred in American history.

Nonviolence is a powerful and just weapon. It is a weapon unique in history, which cuts without wounding and ennobles the man who wields it. It is a sword that heals. Both a practical and a moral answer to the Negro's cry for justice, nonviolent direct action proved that it could win victories without losing wars, and so became the triumphant tactic of the Negro revolution of 1963.

## BULL CONNOR'S BIRMINGHAM (CHAPTER 3)

If you had visited Birmingham before the third of April in the one-hundredth-anniversary year of the Negro's emancipation, you might have come to a startling conclusion. You might have concluded that here was a city which had been trapped for decades in a Rip Van Winkle slumber; a city whose fathers had apparently never heard of Abraham Lincoln, Thomas Jefferson, the Bill of Rights, the Preamble to the Constitution, the Thirteenth, Fourteenth and Fifteenth Amendments, or the 1954 decision of the United States Supreme Court outlawing segregation in the public schools.

If your powers of imagination were great enough to enable you to place yourself in the position of a Negro baby born and brought up to physical maturity in Birmingham, you would have pictured your life in the following manner:

You would be born in a jim crow hospital to parents who probably lived in a ghetto. You would attend a jim crow school. It is not really true that the city fathers had never heard of the Supreme Court's school-desegregation order. They had heard of it and, since its passage, had consistently expressed their defiance, typified by the prediction of one official that blood would run in the streets before desegregation would be permitted to come to Birmingham.

You would spend your childhood playing mainly in the streets because the "colored" parks were abysmally inadequate. When a federal court order banned park segregation, you would find that Birmingham closed down its parks and gave up its baseball team rather than integrate them.

If you went shopping with your mother or father, you would trudge along as they purchased at every counter, except one, in the large or small stores. If you were hungry or thirsty you would have to forget about it until you got back to the Negro section of town, for in your city it was a violation of the law to serve food to Negroes at the same counter with whites.

If your family attended church, you would go to a Negro church. If you wanted to visit a church attended by white people, you would not be welcome. For although your white fellow citizens would insist that they were Christians, they practiced segregation as rigidly in the house of God as they did in the theatre.

If you loved music and yearned to hear the Metropolitan Opera on its tour of the South, you could not enjoy this privilege. Nor could your white fellow music-lovers; for the Metropolitan had discontinued scheduling Birmingham on its national tours after it had adopted a policy of not performing before segregated audiences.

If you wanted to contribute to and be a part of the work of the National Association for the Advancement of Colored People, you would not be able to join a local branch. In the state of Alabama, segregationist authorities had been successful in enjoining the NAACP from performing its civil rights work by declaring it a "foreign corporation" and rendering its activities illegal.

If you wanted a job in this city—one of the greatest iron- and steel-producing centers in the nation—you had better settle on doing menial work as a porter or laborer. If you were fortunate enough to get a job, you could expect that promotions to a better status or more pay would come, not to you, but to a white employee regardless of your comparative talents. On your job, you would eat in a separate place and use a water fountain and lavatory labeled "Colored" in conformity to citywide ordinances.

If you believed your history books and thought of America as a country whose governing officials—whether city, state or nation—are selected by the governed, you would be swiftly disillusioned when you tried to exercise your right to register and vote. You would be confronted with every conceivable obstacle to taking that most important walk a Negro American can take today—the walk to the ballot box. Of the eighty thousand voters in Birmingham, prior to January 1963, only ten thousand were Negroes. Your race, constituting two-thirds of the city's population, would make up one-eighth of its voting strength.

You would be living in a city where brutality directed against Negroes was an unquestioned and unchallenged reality. One of the city commissioners, a member of the body that ruled municipal affairs, would be Eugene "Bull" Connor, a racist who prided himself on knowing how to handle the Negro and keep him in his "place." As commissioner of public safety, Bull Connor, entrenched for many years in a key position in the Birmingham power structure, displayed as much contempt for the rights of the Negro as he did defiance for the authority of the federal government.

You would have found a general atmosphere of violence and brutality in Birmingham. Local racists have intimidated, mobbed, and even killed Negroes with impunity. One of the more vivid and recent examples of the terror of Birmingham was the castration of a Negro man, whose mutilated body had then been abandoned on a lonely road. No Negro home was protected from bombings and burnings. From the year 1957 through January of 1963, while Birmingham was still claiming that its Negroes were "satisfied," seventeen unsolved bombings of Negro churches and homes of civil rights leaders had occurred.

Negroes were not the only persons who suffered because of Bull Connor's rule. It was Birmingham's safety commissioner who, in 1961, arrested the manager of the local bus station when the latter sought to obey the law of the land by serving Negroes. Although a federal district judge condemned Connor in strong terms for this action and released the victim, the fact remained that in Birmingham, early in 1963, no places of public accommodation were integrated except the bus station, the train station and the airport.

In Bull Connor's Birmingham, you would be a resident of a city where a United States senator, visiting to deliver a speech, had been arrested because he walked through a door marked "Colored."

In Connor's Birmingham, the silent password was fear. It was a fear not only on the part of the black oppressed, but also in the hearts of the white oppressors. Guilt was a part of their fear. There was also the dread of change, that all too prevalent fear which hounds those whose attitudes have been hardened by the long winter of reaction. Many were apprehensive of social ostracism. Certainly Birmingham had its white moderates who disapproved of Bull Connor's tactics. Certainly Birmingham had its decent white citizens who privately deplored the maltreatment of Negroes. But they remained publicly silent. It was a silence born of fear—fear of social, political and economic reprisals. The ultimate tragedy of Birmingham was not the brutality of the bad people, but the silence of the good people.

In Birmingham, you would be living in a community where the white man's long-lived tyranny had cowed your people, led them to abandon hope, and developed in them a false sense of inferiority. You would be living in a city where the representatives of economic and political power refused to even discuss social justice with the leaders of your people.

You would be living in the largest city of a police state, presided over by a governor—George Wallace—whose inauguration vow had been a pledge of "segregation now, segregation tomorrow, segregation forever!" You would be living, in fact, in the most segregated city in America.

II

There was one threat to the reign of white supremacy in Birmingham. As an outgrowth of the Montgomery bus boycott, protest movements had sprung up in numerous cities across the South. In Birmingham, one of the nation's most courageous freedom fighters, the Reverend Fred Shuttlesworth, had organized the Alabama Christian Movement for Human Rights—ACHR—in the spring of 1956. Shuttlesworth, a wiry, energetic and indomitable man, had set out to change Birmingham and to end for all time the terrorist, racist rule of Bull Connor.

When Shuttlesworth first formed his organization—which soon became one of the eighty-five affiliates of our Southern Christian Leadership Conference—Bull Connor doubtless regarded the group as just another bunch of troublesome "niggers." It soon became obvious even to Connor, however, that Shuttlesworth was in dead earnest. ACHR grew, month by month, to become the acknowledged basic mass movement of the Birmingham Negro. Weekly mass meetings were held at various churches. The meetings were packed. ACHR began working through the courts to compel the city to relax its segregation policies. A suit was instituted to open Birmingham's public-recreation facilities to all of its citizens. It was when the city lost this case that the authorities responded by closing down the parks, rather than permit Negro youngsters to share facilities maintained by the taxes of black and white alike.

Early in 1962, students at Miles College initiated a staggered series of boycotts against downtown white merchants. Shuttlesworth and his fellow leaders of ACHR joined with the students and helped them to mobilize many of Birmingham's Negroes in a determined withdrawal of business from stores that displayed jim crow signs, refused to hire Negroes in other than menial capacities, refused to promote the few Negroes in their employ, and would not serve colored people at their lunch counters. As a result of the campaign, business fell off as much as 40 percent at some downtown stores. Fred was leading a militant crusade, but Birmingham and Bull Connor fought, tooth and nail, to keep things as they were.

As the parent organization of ACHR, the Southern Christian Leadership Conference in Atlanta had kept a close and admiring watch on Fred Shuttlesworth's uphill fight. We knew that he had paid the price in personal suffering for the battle he was waging. He had been jailed several times. His home and church had been badly damaged by bombs. Yet he had refused to back down. This courageous minister's audacious public defiance of Bull Connor had become a source of inspiration and encouragement to Negroes throughout the South.

In the May, 1962, board meeting of SCLC at Chattanooga, we decided to give serious consideration to joining Shuttlesworth and ACHR in a massive direct-action campaign to attack segregation in Birmingham. It happened that we had scheduled that city as the site of our forthcoming annual convention in September. Immediately after the board meeting, rumors began to circulate in Birmingham that SCLC had definitely decided to support Fred's fight by mounting a prolonged campaign in that city at the time of the convention. These rumors gained so much impetus that stories supporting them appeared in the daily press. For the first time, Birmingham businessmen, who had pursued a policy of ignoring demands for integration, become concerned and concluded that they would have to do something drastic to forestall large-scale protest.

Several weeks before our convention was scheduled, the business community began negotiating with ACHR Meeting with the white Senior Citizens Committee were Shuttlesworth; Dr. Lucius Pitts, president of Miles College; A. G. Gaston, wealthy businessman and owner of the Gaston Motel; Arthur Shores, an attorney with wide experience in civil rights cases; the Reverend Edward Gardner, vice-president of ACHR; and insurance broker John Drew. After several talks, the group came to some basic agreements. As a first step, some of the merchants agreed to remove the jim crow signs from their stores, and several actually did so. The businessmen further agreed to join in a suit with ACHR to seek nullification of city ordinances forbidding integration of lunch counters. It appeared that a small crack had opened in Birmingham.

Although wary of the permanence of these promises, the Negro group decided to give the merchants a chance to demonstrate their good faith. Shuttlesworth called a press conference to announce that a moratorium had been declared on boycotts and demonstrations. However, to protect the position of ACHR, he made it clear that his organization's parent body, SCLC, would be coming to Birmingham for its convention as planned, and informed the press that after the convention, SCLC would be asked to return to the Steel City to help launch an action campaign if the pledges of the business community were violated.

Bull Connor had been issuing ominous statements about our forthcoming meeting. When he realized that his threats were frightening to no one, he began to try to intimidate the press by announcing that the press cards of any "outside reporters" would be taken away from them. It was clear that Connor felt the bastions of segregation could be most securely maintained in Birmingham if national exposure could be avoided.

The SCLC convention took place in September 1962, as scheduled. Shortly thereafter, Fred Shuttlesworth's fears were justified: The jim-crow signs reappeared in the stores. The rumor was that Bull Connor had threatened some of the merchants with loss of their licenses if they did not restore the signs. It seemed obvious to Fred that the merchants had never intended to keep any of their promises; their token action had merely been calculated to stall off demonstrations while SCLC was in the city. During a series of lengthy telephone calls between Birmingham and Atlanta, we reached the conclusion that we had no alternative but to go through with our proposed combined-action campaign.

III

Along with Fred Shuttlesworth, we believed that while a campaign in Birmingham would surely be the toughest fight of our civil rights careers, it could, if successful, break the back of segregation all over the nation. This city had been the country's chief symbol of racial intolerance. A victory there might well set forces in motion to change the entire course of the drive for freedom and justice. Because we were convinced of the significance of the job to be done in Birmingham, we decided that the most thorough planning and prayerful preparation must go into the effort. We began to prepare a top-secret file which we called "Project C"—the "C" for Birmingham's *Confrontation* with the fight for justice and morality in race relations.

In preparation for our campaign, I called a three-day retreat and planning session with SCLC staff and board members at our training center near Savannah, Georgia. Here we sought to perfect a timetable and discuss every possible eventuality. In analyzing our campaign in Albany, Georgia, we decided that one of the principal mistakes we had made there was to scatter our efforts too widely. We had been so involved in attacking segregation in general that we had failed to direct our protest effectively to any one major facet. We concluded that in hardcore communities a more effective battle could be waged if it was concentrated against one aspect of the evil and intricate system of segregation. We decided, therefore, to center the Birmingham struggle on the business community, for we knew that the Negro population had sufficient buying power so that its withdrawal could make the difference between profit and loss for many businesses. Stores with lunch counters were our first target. There is a special humiliation for the Negro in having his money accepted at every department in a store except the lunch counter. Food is not only a necessity but a symbol, and our lunch-counter campaign had not only a practical but a symbolic importance.

Two weeks after the retreat at our training center, I went to Birmingham with my able executive assistant, the Reverend Wyatt Tee Walker, and my abiding friend and fellow campaigner from the days of Montgomery, the Reverend Ralph Abernathy, SCLC's treasurer. There we began to meet with the board of ACHR to assist in preparing the Negro community for what would surely be a difficult, prolonged and dangerous campaign.

We met in the now famous Room 30 of the Gaston Motel, situated on Fifth Avenue North, in the Negro ghetto. This room, which housed Ralph and myself, and served as the headquarters for all of the strategy sessions in subsequent months, would later be the target of one of the bombs on the fateful and violent Saturday night of 11 May, the eve of Mother's Day.

The first major decision we faced was setting the date for the launching of "Project C." Since it was our aim to bring pressure to bear on the merchants, we felt that our campaign should be mounted around the Easter season—the second biggest shopping period of the year. If we started the first week of March, we would have six weeks to mobilize the community before Easter, which fell on 14 April. But at this point we were reminded that a mayoralty election was to be held in Birmingham on 5 March.

The leading candidates were Albert Boutwell, Eugene "Bull" Connor and Tom King. All were segregationists, running on a platform to preserve the status quo. Yet both King and Boutwell were considered moderates in comparison to Connor. We were hopeful that Connor would be so thoroughly defeated that at least we would not have to deal with him. Since we did not want our campaign to be used as a political football, we decided to postpone it, planning to begin demonstrations two weeks after the election.

Meanwhile Wyatt Walker was detailed to return to Birmingham and begin work on the mechanics of the campaign. From then on, he visited Birmingham periodically, unannounced, organizing a transportation corps and laying the groundwork for an intensive boycott. He conferred with lawyers about the city code on picketing, demonstrations and so forth, gathered data on the probable bail-bond situation, and prepared for the injunction that was certain to come.

In addition to scheduling workshops on nonviolence and direct-action techniques for our recruits, Wyatt familiarized himself with downtown Birmingham, not only plotting the main streets and landmarks (target stores, city hall, post office, etc.), but meticulously surveying each store's eating facilities, and sketching the entrances and possible paths of ingress and egress. In fact, Walker detailed the number of stools, tables and chairs to determine how many demonstrators should go to each store. His survey of the downtown area also included suggested secondary targets in the event we were blocked from reaching our primary targets. By 1 March, the project was in high gear and the loose ends of organizational structure were being pulled together. Some two hundred and fifty people had volunteered to participate in the initial demonstrations and had pledged to remain in jail at least five days.

At this point the results of the 5 March election intervened to pose a serious new problem. No candidate had won a clear victory. There would have to be a run-off vote, to be held the first week in April. We had hoped that if a run-off resulted, it would have been between Boutwell and King. As it turned out, the competing candidates were to be Boutwell and Connor.

Again we had to remap strategy. Had we moved in while Connor and Boutwell were electioneering, Connor would undoubtedly have capitalized on our presence by using it as an emotion-charged issue for his own political advantage, waging a vigorous campaign to persuade the white community that he, and he alone, could defend the city's official policies of segregation. We might actually have had the effect of helping Connor win. Reluctantly, we decided to postpone the demonstrations until the day after the run-off. We would have to move promptly if we were still to have time to affect Easter shopping.

We left Birmingham sadly, realizing that after this second delay the intensive groundwork we had done in the Negro community might not bring the effective results we sought. We were leaving some two hundred and fifty volunteers who had been willing to join our ranks and to go to jail. Now we must lose contact with those recruits for several weeks. Yet we dared not remain. It was agreed that no member of the SCLC staff would return to Birmingham until after the run-off.

In the interim, I was busy on another preparatory measure. Realizing the difficulties that lay ahead, we felt it was vital to get the support of key people across the nation. We addressed confidential letters to the National Association for the Advancement of Colored People, the Congress of Racial Equality, the Student Nonviolent Coordinating Committee and the Southern Regional Council, telling them of our plans and advising them that we might be calling on them for aid. We corresponded in the same vein with the seventy-five religious leaders of all faiths who had joined us in the Albany Movement.

In New York City, Harry Belafonte, an old friend and supporter of SCLC, agreed to call a meeting at his apartment. Approximately seventy-five New Yorkers were present. They were a cross section of citizens, including newspapermen (who kept their promise not to publish stories about the meeting until the action was launched), clergymen, business and professional people, and unofficial representatives from the offices of Mayor Wagner and Governor Rockefeller.

Fred Shuttlesworth and I spoke of the problems then existing in Birmingham and those we anticipated. We explained why we had delayed taking action until after the run-off, and why we felt it necessary to proceed with our plans whether Connor or Boutwell was the eventual victor. Shuttlesworth, wearing the scars of earlier battles, brought a sense of the danger as well as the earnestness of our crusade into that peaceful New York living room. Although many of those present had worked with SCLC in the past, there was a silence almost like the shock of a fresh discovery when Shuttlesworth said, "You have to be prepared to die before you can begin to live."

When we had finished, the most frequent question was: "What can we do to help?"

We answered that we were certain to need tremendous sums of money for bail bonds. We might need public meetings to organize more support. On the spot, Harry Belafonte organized a committee, and money was pledged the same night. For the next three weeks, Belafonte, who never does anything without being totally involved, gave unlimited hours to organizing people and money. Throughout the subsequent campaign, he talked with me or my aides two or three times a day. It would be hard to overestimate the role this sensitive artist played in the success of the Birmingham crusade.

Similar meetings were held with two of our strongest affiliates, the Western Christian Leadership Conference in Los Angeles, and the Virginia Christian Leadership Conference in Richmond. Both pledged and gave their unswerving support to the campaign. Later on, with the NAACP and other local organizations, the Western Conference raised the largest amount of money—some $75,000—which has ever been raised in a single rally for SCLC Many of the men from these conferences would later join our ranks during the crisis.

With these contacts established, the time had come to return to Birmingham. The run-off election was April 2. We flew in the same night. By word of mouth, we set about trying to make contact with our two hundred and fifty volunteers for an unadvertised meeting. About sixty-five came out. The following day, with this modest task force, we launched the direct-action campaign in Birmingham.

## NEW DAY IN BIRMINGHAM (CHAPTER 4)

On Wednesday, 3 April 1963, the Birmingham *News* appeared on the stands, its front page bright with a color drawing showing a golden sun rising over the city. It was captioned: "New Day Dawns for Birmingham," and celebrated Albert Boutwell's victory in the run-off vote for mayor. The golden glow of racial harmony, the headline implied, could now be expected to descend on the city. As events were to show, it was indeed a new day for Birmingham, but not because Boutwell had won the election.

For all the optimism expressed in the press and elsewhere, we were convinced that Albert Boutwell was, in Fred Shuttlesworth's apt phrase, "just a dignified Bull Connor." We knew that the former state senator and lieutenant governor had been the principal author of Alabama's Pupil Placement Law, and was a consistent supporter of segregationist views. His statement a few days after the election that "we citizens of Birmingham respect and understand one another" showed that he understood nothing about two-fifths of Birmingham's citizens, to whom even polite segregation was no respect.

Meanwhile, despite the results of the run-off, the city commissioners, including Bull Connor, had taken the position that they could not legally be removed from office until 1965. They would go into the courts to defend their position, and refused in the interim to move out of their city hall offices. If they won in court (and conflict in the laws of Birmingham made this theoretically possible), they would remain in office for another two years. If they lost, their terms would still not expire until 15 April, the day after Easter. In either case, we were committed to enter the situation in a city which was operating literally under two governments.

We had decided to limit the first few days' efforts to sit-ins. Being prepared for a long struggle, we felt it best to begin modestly, with a limited number of arrests each day. By rationing our energies in this manner, we would help toward the buildup and drama of a growing campaign. The first demonstrations were, accordingly, not spectacular, but they were well organized. Operating on a precise timetable, small groups maintained a series of sit-ins at lunch counters in the downtown department stores and drugstores. When the demonstrators were asked to leave and refused, they were arrested under the local "trespass after warning" ordinance. By Friday night, there had been no disturbances worth note. Evidently neither Bull Connor nor the merchants expected this quiet beginning to blossom into a large-scale operation.

After the first day we held a mass meeting, the first of sixty-five nightly meetings conducted at various churches in the Negro community. Through these meetings we were able to generate the power and depth which finally galvanized the entire Negro community. The mass meetings had a definite pattern, shaped by some of the finest activists in the civil-rights movement. Ralph Abernathy, with his unique combination of humor and dedication, has a genuis for lifting an audience to heights of enthusiasm and holding it there. When he plants himself behind the lectern, squat and powerful, his round face breaking easily into laughter, his listeners both love and believe him. Wyatt Walker, youthful, lean and bespectacled, brought his energetic and untiring spirit to our meetings, whose members already knew and admired his dedicated work as a behind-the-scenes organizer of the campaign. There was a special adulation that went out to the fiery words and determined zeal of Fred Shuttlesworth, who had proved to his people that he would not ask anyone to go where he was not willing to lead. Although for the first week I was busy on matters that prevented my taking an active part in the demonstrations, I spoke at the mass meetings nightly on the philosophy of nonviolence and its methods. Besides these "regulars," local speakers appeared from time to time to describe the injustices and humiliation of being a Negro in Birmingham, and occasional visitors from elsewhere across the country brought us welcome messages of support.

An important part of the mass meetings was the freedom songs. In a sense the freedom songs are the soul of the movement. They are more than just incantations of clever phrases designed to invigorate a campaign; they are as old as the history of the Negro in America. They are adaptations of the songs the slaves sang—the sorrow songs, the shouts for joy, the battle hymns and the anthems of our movement. I have heard people talk of their beat and rhythm, but we in the movement are as inspired by their words. "Woke Up This Morning with My Mind Stayed on Freedom" is a sentence that needs no music to make its point. We sing the freedom songs today for the same reason the slaves sang them, because we too are in bondage and the songs add hope to our determination that "We shall overcome, Black and white together, We shall overcome someday."

I have stood in a meeting with hundreds of youngsters and joined in while they sang "Ain't Gonna Let Nobody Turn Me 'Round." It is not just a song; it is a resolve. A few minutes later, I have seen those same youngsters refuse to turn around from the onrush of a police dog, refuse to turn around before a pugnacious Bull Connor in command of men armed with power hoses. These songs bind us together, give us courage together, help us to march together.

Toward the end of the mass meetings, Abernathy or Shuttlesworth or I would extend an appeal for volunteers to serve in our nonviolent army. We made it clear that we would not send anyone out to demonstrate who had not convinced himself and us that he could accept and endure violence without retaliating. At the same time, we urged the volunteers to give up any possible weapons that they might have on their persons. Hundreds of people responded to this appeal. Some of those who carried penknives, Boy Scout knives—all kinds of knives—had them not because they wanted to use them against the police or other attackers, but because they wanted to defend themselves against Mr. Connor's dogs. We proved to them that they needed no weapons—not so much as a toothpick. We proved that we possessed the most formidable weapon of all—the conviction that we were right. We had the protection of our knowledge that we were more concerned about realizing our righteous aims than about saving our skins.

The invitational periods at the mass meetings, when we asked for volunteers, were much like those invitational periods that occur every Sunday morning in Negro churches, when the pastor projects the call to those present to join the church. By twenties and thirties and forties, people came forward to join our army. We did not hesitate to call our movement an army. But it was a special army, with no supplies but its sincerity, no uniform but its determination, no arsenal except its faith, no currency but its conscience. It was an army that would move but not maul. It was an army that would sing but not slay. It was an army that would flank but not falter. It was an army to storm bastions of hatred, to lay siege to the fortresses of discrimination. It was an army whose allegiance was to God and whose strategy and intelligence were the eloquently simple dictates of conscience.

As the meetings continued and as the battle for the soul of Birmingham quickened and caught the attention of the world, the meetings were more crowded and the volunteers more numerous. Men, women and children came forward to shake hands, and then proceeded to the back of the church, where the Leadership Training Committee made an appointment with them to come to our office the following day for screening and intensive training.

The focus of these training sessions was the sociodramas designed to prepare the demonstrators for some of the challenges they could expect to face. The harsh language and physical abuse of the police and the self-appointed guardians of the law were frankly presented, along with the nonviolent creed in action: to resist without bitterness; to be cursed and not reply; to be beaten and not hit back. The SCLC staff members who conducted these sessions played their roles with the conviction born of experience. They included the Reverend James Lawson, expelled from Vanderbilt University a few years back for his militant civil rights work, and one of the country's leading exponents of the nonviolent credo; the Reverend James Bevel, already an experienced leader in Nashville, Greenwood and other campaigns; his wife, Diane Nash Bevel, who as a student at Fisk had become an early symbol of the young Negroes' thrust toward freedom; the Reverend Bernard Lee, whose devotion to civil rights dated back to his leadership of the student movement at Alabama State College; the Reverend Andy Young, our able and dedicated program director; and Dorothy Cotton, director of our ongoing citizenship education program, who also brought her rich talent for song to the heart of the movement.

Not all who volunteered could pass our strict tests for service as demonstrators. But there was much to be done, over and above the dramatic act of presenting one's body in the marches. There were errands to be run, phone calls to be made, typing, so many things. If a volunteer wasn't suited to march, he was utilized in one of a dozen other ways to help the cause. Every volunteer was required to sign a commitment card that read:

I HEREBY PLEDGE MYSELF—MY PERSON AND BODY—TO THE NON-VIOLENT MOVEMENT. THEREFORE I WILL KEEP THE FOLLOWING TEN COMMANDMENTS:

1. MEDITATE daily on the teachings and life of Jesus.

2. REMEMBER always that the nonviolent movement in Birmingham seeks justice and reconciliation—not victory.
3. WALK and TALK in the manner of love, for God is love.
4. PRAY daily to be used by God in order that all men might be free.
5. SACRIFICE personal wishes in order that all men might be free.
6. OBSERVE with both friend and foe the ordinary rules of courtesy.
7. SEEK to perform regular service for others and for the world.
8. REFRAIN from the violence of fist, tongue, or heart.
9. STRIVE to be in good spiritual and bodily health.
10. FOLLOW the directions of the movement and of the captain of a demonstration.

I sign this pledge, having seriously considered what I do and with the determination and will to persevere.

Name _____

Address _____

Phone _____

Nearest Relative _____

Address _____

Besides demonstrations, I could also help the movement by: (Circle the proper items)

Run errands, Drive my car, Fix food for volunteers, Clerical work, Make phone calls, Answer phones, Mimeograph, Type, Print signs, Distribute leaflets.

ALABAMA CHRISTIAN MOVEMENT FOR HUMAN RIGHTS
BIRMINGHAM Affiliate of S.C.L.C.
505½ North 17th Street
F. L. Shuttlesworth, President

II

I had planned to submit myself to imprisonment two or three days after our demonstrations began. It didn't take long after returning to Birmingham, however, to recognize the existence of a problem that made it unwise and impractical for me to go to jail before something had been done to solve it.

We had been forced to change our timetable twice. We had had to make a strategic retreat until after the run-off and had lost contact with the community for several weeks. We had returned to find that our own people were not united. There was tremendous resistance to our program from some of the Negro ministers, businessmen and professionals in the city. This opposition did not exist because these Negroes did not want to be free. It existed for several other reasons.

The Negro in Birmingham, like the Negro elsewhere in this nation, had been skillfully brainwashed to the point where he had accepted the white man's theory that he, as a Negro, was inferior. He wanted to believe that he was the equal of any man; but he didn't know where to begin or how to resist the influences that had conditioned him to take the least line of resistance and go along with the white man's views. He knew that there were exceptions to the white man's evaluation: a Ralph Bunche, a Jackie Robinson, a Marian Anderson. But to the Negro, in Birmingham and in the nation, the exception did not prove the rule.

Another consideration had also affected the thinking of some of the Negro leaders in Birmingham. This was the widespread feeling that our action was ill-timed, and that we should have given the new Boutwell government a chance. Attorney General Robert Kennedy had been one of the first to voice this criticism. The *Washington Post*, which covered Birmingham from the first day of our demonstrations, had editorially attacked our "timing." In fact, virtually all the coverage in the national press at first had been negative, picturing us as irresponsible hotheads who had plunged into a situation just when Birmingham was getting ready to change overnight into paradise. The sudden emergence of our protest seemed to give the lie to this vision.

In Montgomery, during the bus boycott, and in the Albany, Georgia, campaign, we had had the advantage of a sympathetic and understanding national press from the outset. In Birmingham we did not. It is terribly difficult to wage such a battle without the moral support of the national press to counteract the hostility of local editors. The words "bad timing" came to be ghosts haunting our every move in Birmingham. Yet people who used this argument were ignorant of the background of our planning. They did not know we had postponed our campaign twice. They did not know our reason for attacking in time to affect Easter shopping. Above all they did not realize that it was ridiculous to speak of timing when the clock of history showed that the Negro had already suffered one hundred years of delay.

Not only were many of the Negro leaders affected by the administration's position, but they were themselves indulging in a false optimism about what would happen to Birmingham under the new government. The situation had been critical for so many years that, I suppose, these people felt that any change represented a giant step toward the good. Many truly believed that once the influence of Bull Connor had faded, everything was going to be all right.

Another reason for the opposition within the Negro community was resentment on the part of some groups and leaders because we had not kept them informed about the date we planned to begin or the strategy we would adopt. They felt that they were being pulled in on something they had no part in organizing. They did not realize that, because of the local political situation, we had been forced to keep our plans secret.

We were seeking to bring about a great social change which could only be achieved through unified effort. Yet our community was divided. Our goals could never be attained in such an atmosphere. It was decided that we would conduct a whirlwind campaign of meetings with organizations and leaders in the Negro community, to seek to mobilize every key person and group behind our movement.

Along with members of my staff, I began addressing numerous groups representing a cross section of our people in Birmingham. I spoke to one hundred and twenty five business and professional people at a call meeting in the Gaston Building. I talked to a gathering of two hundred ministers. I met with many smaller groups, during a hectic one-week schedule. In most cases, the atmosphere when I entered was tense and chilly, and I was aware that there was a great deal of work to be done.

I went immediately to the point, explaining to the business and professional men why we had been forced to proceed without letting them know the date in advance. I dealt with the argument of timing. To the ministers I stressed the need for a social gospel to supplement the gospel of individual salvation. I suggested that only a "dry as dust" religion prompts a minister to extol the glories of heaven while ignoring the social conditions that cause men an earthly hell. I pleaded for the projection of strong, firm leadership by the Negro minister, pointing out that he is freer, more independent, than any other person in the community. I asked how the Negro would ever gain his freedom without the guidance, support and inspiration of his spiritual leaders.

I challenged those who had been persuaded that I was an "outsider." I pointed out that Fred Shuttlesworth's Alabama Christian Movement for Human Rights was an affiliate of the Southern Christian Leadership Conference, and that the Shuttlesworth group had asked SCLC to come to Birmingham, and that as president of SCLC, I had come in the interests of aiding an SCLC affiliate.

I expanded further on the weary and worn "outsider" charge, which we have faced in every community where we have gone to try to help. No Negro, in fact, no American, is an outsider when he goes to any community to aid the cause of freedom and justice. No Negro anywhere, regardless of his social standing, his financial status, his prestige and position, is an outsider so long as dignity and decency are denied to the humblest black child in Mississippi, Alabama or Georgia.

The amazing aftermath of Birmingham, the sweeping Negro Revolution, revealed to people all over the land that there were no outsiders in all these fifty states of America. When a police dog buried his fangs in the ankle of a small child in Birmingham, he buried his fangs in the ankle of every American. The bell of man's inhumanity to man does not toll for any one man. It tolls for you, for me, for all of us.

Somehow God gave me the power to transform the resentments, the suspicions, the fears and the misunderstanding that I found that week into faith and enthusiasm. I spoke from my heart, and out of each meeting came firm endorsements and pledges of participation and support. With the new unity that developed and now poured fresh blood into our protest, the foundations of the old order were doomed. A new order was destined to be born, and not all the powers of bigotry or Bull Connor could abort it.

III

By the end of the first three days of lunch counter sit-ins, there had been thirty-five arrests. On Saturday, 6 April, we began the next stage of our crusade with a march on City Hall. Carefully selected and screened, the first waves of demonstrators conducted themselves exactly as they had been trained to do. They marched in orderly files of two, without banners or band or singing. When they reached a point, three blocks from their goal, where Bull Connor's officers loomed in their path, they stood silently by as their leaders politely but firmly refused to obey Connor's orders to disperse. Thereupon forty-two were arrested for "parading without a permit." They were escorted with amazing politeness into the paddy wagons, and they, in turn, allowed themselves to be led without resisting, singing freedom songs on the way to jail. The sidewalks were lined with cheering Negroes, singing and lustily applauding their jailbound heroes—for this is exactly what they were in the eyes of their neighbors and friends. Something was happening to the Negro in this city, just as something revolutionary was taking place in the mind, heart and soul of Negroes all over America.

From then on, the daily demonstrations grew stronger. Our boycott of the downtown merchants was proving amazingly effective. A few days before Easter, a careful check showed less than twenty Negroes entering all the stores in the downtown area. Meanwhile, with the number of volunteers increasing daily, we were able to launch campaigns against a variety of additional objectives: kneel-ins at churches; sit-ins at the library; a march on the county building to mark the opening of a voter-registration drive. And all the time the jails were slowly but steadily filling up.

Birmingham residents of both races were surprised at the restraint of Connor's men at the beginning of the campaign. True, police dogs and clubs made their debut on Palm Sunday, but their appearance that day was brief and they quickly disappeared. What observers probably did not realize was that the commissioner was trying to take a leaf from the book of Police Chief Laurie Pritchett of Albany. Chief Pritchett felt that by directing his police to be nonviolent, he had discovered a new way to defeat the demonstrations. Mr. Connor, as it developed, was not to adhere to nonviolence long; the dogs were baying in kennels not far away; the hoses were primed. But that is another part of the story.

A second reason Bull Connor had held off at first was that he thought he had found another way out. This became evident on April 10, when the city government obtained a court injunction directing us to cease our activities until our right to demonstrate had been argued in court. The time had now come for us to counter their legal maneuver with a strategy of our own. Two days later, we did an audacious thing, something we had never done in any other crusade. We disobeyed a court order.

We did not take this radical step without prolonged and prayerful consideration. Planned, deliberate civil disobedience had been discussed as far back as the meeting at Harry Belafonte's apartment in March. There, in consultation with some of the closest friends of the movement, we had decided that if an injunction was issued to thwart our demonstrators, it would be our duty to violate it. To some, this will sound contradictory and morally indefensible. We, who contend for justice, and who oppose those who will not honor the law of the Supreme Court and the rulings of federal agencies, were saying that we would overtly violate a court order. Yet we felt that there were persuasive reasons for our position.

When the Supreme Court decision on school desegregation was handed down, leading segregationists vowed to thwart it by invoking "a century of litigation." There was more significance to this threat than many Americans imagined. The injunction method has now become the leading instrument of the South to block the direct-action civil rights drive and to prevent Negro citizens and their white allies from engaging in peaceable assembly, a right guaranteed by the First Amendment. You initiate a nonviolent demonstration. The power structure secures an injunction against you. It can conceivably take two or three years before any disposition of the case is made. The Alabama courts are notorious for "sitting on" cases of this nature. This has been a maliciously effective, pseudo-legal way of breaking the back of legitimate moral protest.

We had anticipated that this procedure would be used in Birmingham. It had been invoked in Montgomery to outlaw our car pool during the bus boycott. It had destroyed the protest movement in Talladega, Alabama. It had torpedoed our effort in Albany, Georgia. It had routed the NAACP from the state of Alabama. We decided, therefore, knowing well what the consequences would be and prepared to accept them, that we had no choice but to violate such an injunction.

When the injunction was issued in Birmingham, our failure to obey it bewildered our opponents. They did not know what to do. We did not hide our intentions. In fact, I announced our plan to the press, pointing out that we were not anarchists advocating lawlessness, but that it was obvious to us that the courts of Alabama had misused the judicial process in order to perpetuate injustice and segregation. Consequently, we could not, in good conscience, obey their findings.

I intended to be one of the first to set the example of civil disobedience. Ten days after the demonstrations began, between four and five hundred people had gone to jail; some had been released on bail, but about three hundred remained. Now that the job of unifying the Negro community had been accomplished, my time had come. We decided that Good Friday, because of its symbolic significance, would be the day that Ralph Abernathy and I would present our bodies as personal witnesses in this crusade.

Soon after we announced our intention to lead a demonstration on April 12 and submit to arrest, we received a message so distressing that it threatened to ruin the movement. Late Thursday night, the bondsman who had been furnishing bail for the demonstrators notified us that he would be unable to continue. The city had notified him that his financial assets were insufficient. Obviously, this was another move on the part of the city to hurt our cause.

It was a serious blow. We had used up all the money we had on hand for cash bonds. There were our people in jail, for whom we had a moral responsibility. Fifty more were to go in with Ralph and me. This would be the largest single group to be arrested to date. Without bail facilities, how could we guarantee their eventual release?

Good Friday morning, early, I sat in Room 30 of the Gaston Motel discussing this crisis with twenty-four key people. As we talked, a sense of doom began to pervade the room. I looked about me and saw that, for the first time, our most dedicated and devoted leaders were overwhelmed by a feeling of hopelessness. No one knew what to say, for no one knew what to do. Finally someone spoke up and, as he spoke, I could see that he was giving voice to what was on everyone's mind.

"Martin," he said, "this means you can't go to jail. We need money. We need a lot of money. We need it now. You are the only one who has the contacts to get it. If you go to jail, we are lost. The battle of Birmingham is lost."

I sat there, conscious of twenty-four pairs of eyes. I thought about the people in jail. I thought about the Birmingham Negroes already lining the streets of the city, waiting to see me put into practice what I had so passionately preached. How could my failure now to submit to arrest be explained to the local community? What would be the verdict of the country about a man who had encouraged hundreds of people to make a stunning sacrifice and then excused himself?

Then my mind began to race in the opposite direction. Suppose I went to jail? What would happen to the three hundred? Where would the money come from to assure their release? What would happen to our campaign? Who would be willing to follow us into jail, not knowing when or whether he would ever walk out once more into the Birmingham sunshine?

I sat in the midst of the deepest quiet I have ever felt, with two dozen others in the room. There comes a time in the atmosphere of leadership when a man surrounded by loyal friends and allies realizes he has come face to face with himself. I was alone in that crowded room.

I walked to another room in the back of the suite, and stood in the center of the floor. I think I was standing also at the center of all that my life had brought me to be. I thought of the twenty-four people, waiting in the next room. I thought of the three hundred, waiting in prison. I thought of the Birmingham Negro community, waiting. Then my mind leaped beyond the Gaston Motel, past the city jail, past city lines and state lines, and I thought of 20 million black people who dreamed that someday they might be able to cross the Red Sea of injustice and find their way to the promised land of integration and freedom. There was no more room for doubt.

I pulled off my shirt and pants, got into work clothes and went back to the other room to tell them I had decided to go to jail.

"I don't know what will happen; I don't know where the money will come from. But I have to make a faith act."

I turned to Ralph Abernathy.

"I know you want to be in your pulpit on Easter Sunday, Ralph. But I am asking you to go with me."

As Ralph stood up without hesitation, we all linked hands, and twenty-five voices in Room 30 at the Gaston Motel in Birmingham, Alabama, chanted the battle hymn of our movement: "We Shall Overcome."

We rode from the motel to the Zion Hill Church, where the march would begin. Many hundreds of Negroes had turned out to see us, and great hope grew within me as I saw those faces smiling approval as we passed. It seemed that every Birmingham police officer had been sent into the area. Leaving the church, where we were joined by the rest of our group of fifty, we started down the forbidden streets that lead to the downtown sector. It was a beautiful march. We were allowed to walk farther than the police had ever permitted before. We walked for seven or eight blocks. All along the way Negroes lined the streets. We were singing, and they were joining in. Occasionally the singing from the sidewalks was interspersed with bursts of applause.

As we neared the downtown area, Bull Connor ordered his men to arrest us. Ralph and I were hauled off by two muscular policemen, clutching the backs of our shirts in handfuls. All the others were promptly arrested. In jail Ralph and I were separated from everyone else, and later from each other.

For more than twenty-four hours I was held incommunicado, in solitary confinement. No one was permitted to visit me, not even my lawyers. Those were the longest, most frustrating and bewildering hours I have lived. Having no contact of any kind, I was beseiged with worry. How was the movement faring? Where would Fred and the other leaders get the money to have our demonstrators released? What was happening to morale in the Negro community?

I suffered no physical brutality at the hands of my jailers. Some of the prison personnel were surly and abusive, but that was to be expected in southern prisons. Solitary confinement, however, was brutal enough. In the mornings the sun would rise, sending shafts of light through the window high in the narrow cell which was my home. You will never know the meaning of utter darkness until you have lain in such a dungeon, knowing that sunlight is streaming overhead and still seeing only darkness below. You might have thought I was in the grip of a fantasy brought on by worry. I did worry. But there was more to the blackness than a phenomenon conjured up by a worried mind. Whatever the cause, the fact remained that I could not see the light.

When I had left my Atlanta home some days before, my wife, Coretta, had just given birth to our fourth child. As happy as we were about the new little girl, Coretta was disappointed that her condition would not allow her to accompany me. She had been my strength and inspiration during the terror of Montgomery. She had been active in Albany, Georgia, and was preparing to go to jail with the wives of other civil rights leaders here, just before the campaign ended.

Now, not only was she confined to our home, but she was denied even the consolation of a telephone call from her husband. On the Monday following our jailing, she decided she must do something. Remembering the call that John Kennedy had made to her when I was jailed in Georgia during the 1960 election campaign, she placed a call to the president. Within a few minutes, his brother, Attorney General Robert Kennedy, phoned back. She told him that she had learned I was in solitary confinement and was afraid for my safety. The attorney general promised to do everything he could to have my situation eased. A few hours later President Kennedy himself called Coretta from Palm Beach, and assured her that he would look into the matter immediately. Apparently the president and his brother placed calls to officials in Birmingham; for immediately after Coretta heard from them, my jailers asked if I wanted to call her. After the President's intervention, conditions changed considerably.

Meanwhile, on Easter Sunday afternoon, two of our attorneys, Orzell Billingsley and Arthur Shores, had been allowed to visit me. They told me that Clarence B. Jones, my friend and lawyer, would be coming in from New York the following day. When they left, none of the questions tormenting me had been answered, but when Clarence Jones arrived the next day, before I could even tell him how happy I was to see him, he said a few words that lifted a thousand pounds from my heart:

"Harry Belafonte has been able to raise $50,000 for bail bonds. It is available immediately. And he says that whatever else you need, he will raise it."

I found it hard to say what I felt. Jones's message brought me more than relief from the immediate concern about money; more than gratitude for the loyalty of friends far away; more than confirmation that the life of the movement could not be snuffed out. What silenced me was a profound sense of awe. I was aware of a feeling that had been present all along below the surface of consciousness, pressed down under the weight of concern for the movement: I had never been truly in solitary confinement; God's companionship does not stop at the door of a jail cell. I don't know whether the sun was shining at that moment. But I know that once again I could see the light.

## BLACK AND WHITE TOGETHER (CHAPTER 6)

After eight days of imprisonment, Ralph Abernathy and I accepted bond to come out of jail for two purposes. It was necessary for me to regain communication with the SCLC officers and our lawyers in order to map the strategy for the contempt cases that would be coming up shortly in the circuit court. Also, I had decided to put into operation a new phase of our campaign, which I felt would speed victory.

I called my staff together and repeated a conviction I had been voicing ever since the campaign began. If our drive was to be successful, we must involve the students of the community. In most of the recent direct-action crusades, it had been the young people who sparked the movement. But in Birmingham, of the first four or five hundred people who had submitted themselves to arrest, two-thirds had been adults. We had considered this a good thing at the time, for a really effective campaign incorporates a cross section of the community. But now it was time to enlist the young people in larger numbers. Even though we realized that involving teen-agers and high-school students would bring down upon us a heavy fire of criticism, we felt that we needed this dramatic new dimension. Our people were demonstrating daily and going to jail in numbers, but we were still beating our heads against the brick wall of the city officials' stubborn resolve to maintain the status quo. Our fight, if won, would benefit people of all ages. But most of all we were inspired with a desire to give to our young a true sense of their own stake in freedom and justice. We believed they would have the courage to respond to our call.

James Bevel, Andy Young, Bernard Lee and Dorothy Cotton began visiting colleges and high schools in the area. They invited students to attend after-school meetings at churches. The word spread fast, and the response from Birmingham's youngsters exceeded our fondest dreams. By the fifties and by the hundreds, these youngsters attended mass meetings and training sessions. They listened eagerly as we talked of bringing freedom to Birmingham, not in some distant time, but right now. We taught them the philosophy of nonviolence. We challenged them to bring their exuberance, their youthful creativity, into the disciplined dedication of the movement. We found them eager to belong, hungry for participation in a significant social effort. Looking back, it is clear that the introduction of Birmingham's children into the campaign was one of the wisest moves we made. It brought a new impact to the crusade, and the impetus that we needed to win the struggle.

Immediately, of course, a cry of protest went up. Although by the end of April the attitude of the national press had changed considerably, so that the major media were according us symphathetic coverage, yet many deplored our "using" our children in this fashion. Where had these writers been, we wondered, during the centuries when our segregated social system had been misusing and abusing Negro children? Where had they been with their protective words when, down through the years, Negro infants were born into ghettos, taking their first breath of life in a social atmosphere where the fresh air of freedom was crowded out by the stench of discrimination?

The children themselves had the answer to the misguided sympathies of the press. One of the most ringing replies came from a child or no more than eight who walked with her mother one day in a demonstration. An amused policeman leaned down to her and said with mock gruffness: "What do you want?"

The child looked into his eyes, unafraid, and gave her answer.

"F'eedom," she said.

She could not even pronounce the word, but no Gabriel trumpet could have sounded a truer note.

Even children too young to march requested and earned a place in our ranks. Once when we sent out a call for volunteers, six tiny youngsters responded. Andy Young told them that they were not old enough to go to jail but that they could go to the library. "You won't get arrested there," he said, "but you might learn something." So these six small children marched off to the building in the white district, where, up to two weeks before, they would have been turned away at the door. Shyly but doggedly, they went to the children's room and sat down, and soon they were lost in their books. In their own way, they had struck a blow for freedom.

The children understood the stakes they were fighting for. I think of one teen-age boy whose father's devotion to the movement turned sour when he learned that his son had pledged himself to become a demonstrator. The father forbade his son to participate.

"Daddy," the boy said, "I don't want to disobey you, but I have made my pledge. If you try to keep me home, I will sneak off. If you think I deserve to be punished for that, I'll just have to take the punishment. For, you see, I'm not doing this only because I want to be free. I'm doing it also because I want freedom for you and Mama, and I want it to come before you die."

That father thought again, and gave his son his blessing.

The movement was blessed by the fire and excitement brought to it by young people such as these. And when Birmingham youngsters joined the march in numbers, an historic thing happened. For the first time in the civil rights movement, we were able to put into effect the Gandhian principle: "Fill up the jails."

Jim Bevel had the inspiration of setting a "D" Day, when the students would go to jail in historic numbers. When that day arrived, young people converged on the Sixteenth Street Baptist Church in wave after wave. Altogether on "D" Day, May 2, more than a thousand young people demonstrated and went to jail. At one school, the principal gave orders to lock the gates to keep the students in. The youngsters climbed over the gates and ran toward freedom. The Assistant Superintendent of Schools threatened them with expulsion, and still they came, day after day. At the height of the campaign, by conservative estimates, there were 2,500 demonstrators in jail at one time, a large proportion of them young people.

Serious as they were about what they were doing, these teen-agers had that marvelous humor that arms the unarmed in the face of danger. Under their leaders, they took delight in confusing the police. A small decoy group would gather at one exit of the church, bringing policemen streaming in cars and on motorcycles. Before the officers knew what was happening, other groups, by the scores, would pour out of other exits and move, two by two, toward our goal in the downtown section.

Many arrived at their destination before the police could confront and arrest them. They sang as they marched and as they were loaded into the paddy wagons. The police ran out of paddy wagons and had to press sheriff's cars and school buses into service.

Watching those youngsters in Birmingham, I could not help remembering an episode in Montgomery during the bus boycott. Someone had asked an elderly women why she was involved in our struggle.

"I'm doing it for my children and for my grandchildren," she had replied.

Seven years later, the children and grandchildren were doing it for themselves.

II

With the jails filling up and the scorching glare of national disapproval focused on Birmingham, Bull Connor abandoned his posture of nonviolence. The result was an ugliness too well known to Americans and to people all over the world. The newspapers of May 4 carried pictures of prostrate women, and policemen bending over them with raised clubs; of children marching up to the bared fangs of police dogs; of the terrible force of pressure hoses sweeping bodies into the streets.

This was the time of our greatest stress, and the courage and conviction of those students and adults made it our finest hour. We did not fight back, but we did not turn back. We did not give way to bitterness. Some few spectators, who had not been trained in the discipline of nonviolence, reacted to the brutality of the policemen by throwing rocks and bottles. But the demonstrators remained nonviolent. In the face of this resolution and bravery, the moral conscience of the nation was deeply stirred and, all over the country, our fight became the fight of decent Americans of all races and creeds.

The moral indignation which was spreading throughout the land; the sympathy created by the children; the growing involvement of the Negro community—all these factors were mingling to create a certain atmosphere inside our movement. It was a pride in progress and a conviction that we were going to win. It was a mounting optimism which gave us the feeling that the implacable barriers that confronted us were doomed and already beginning to crumble. We were advised, in the utmost confidence, that the white business structure was weakening under the adverse publicity, the pressure of our boycott, and a parallel falling-off of white buying.

Strangely enough, the masses of white citizens in Birmingham were not fighting us. This was one of the most amazing aspects of the Birmingham crusade. Only a year or so ago, had we begun such a campaign, Bull Connor would have had his job done for him by murderously angry white citizens. Now, however, the majority were maintaining a strictly hands-off policy. I do not mean to insinuate that they were in sympathy with our cause or that they boycotted stores because we did. I simply suggest that it is powerfully symbolic of shifting attitudes in the South that the majority of the white citizens of Birmingham remained neutral through our campaign. This neutrality added force to our feeling that we were on the road to victory.

On one dramatic occasion even Bull Connor's men were shaken. It was a Sunday afternoon, when several hundred Birmingham Negroes had determined to hold a prayer meeting near the city jail. They gathered at the New Pilgrim Baptist Church and began an orderly march. Bull Connor ordered out the police dogs and fire hoses. When the marchers approached the border between the white and Negro areas, Connor ordered them to turn back. The Reverend Charles Billups, who was leading the march, politely refused. Enraged, Bull Connor whirled on his men and shouted:

"Dammit. Turn on the hoses."

What happened in the next thirty seconds was one of the most fantastic events of the Birmingham story. Bull Connor's men, their deadly hoses poised for action, stood facing the marchers. The marchers, many of them on their knees, stared back, unafraid and unmoving. Slowly the Negroes stood up and began to advance. Connor's men, as though hypnotized, fell back, their hoses sagging uselessly in their hands while several hundred Negroes marched past them, without further interference, and held their prayer meeting as planned.

One more factor helped to encourage us in the belief that our goals were coming within reach. We had demonstrated in defiance of a civil injunction. For this act of disobedience, we had been cited for contempt. In Alabama, if you are cited for criminal contempt, you serve five days and that is the end of it. If you are cited for civil contempt, however, you figuratively hold the jailhouse keys in the palm of your hand. At any time, if you are willing to recant, you can earn release. If you do not recant, you can be held for the rest of your natural life.

Most of the demonstrators had been cited for criminal contempt. About ten of us, however, all leaders of the movement, had been cited for civil contempt. When we were first placed under this charge, I am certain that the Birmingham authorities believed we would back down rather than face the threat of indefinite imprisonment. But by the time we appeared in court late in April to answer the charges, all of Birmingham knew that we would never recant, even if we had to rot away in their jails. The city thus faced the prospect of putting us into jail for life. Confronted with the certain knowledge that we would not give in, the city attorney undoubtedly realized that he would be sentencing us to a martyrdom which must eventually turn the full force of national public opinion against Birmingham.

Abruptly the tactics were reversed. The civil-contempt charge was changed to the less stringent criminal-contempt charge, under which we were swiftly convicted on April 26. In addition, the judge announced that he would delay sentence and give us about twenty days to file an appeal. At this point there was little doubt in our minds that Birmingham's bastions of segregation were weakening.

### III

Throughout the campaign, we had been seeking to establish some dialogue with the city leaders in an effort to negotiate on four major issues:

1. The desegregation of lunch counters, rest rooms, fitting rooms and drinking fountains in variety and department stores.
2. The upgrading and hiring of Negroes on a nondiscriminatory basis throughout the business and industrial community of Birmingham.
3. The dropping of all charges against jailed demonstrators.
4. The creation of a biracial committee to work out a timetable for desegregation in other areas of Birmingham life.

Even though pressure on Birmingham's business community was intense, there were stubborn men in its midst who seemed to feel they would rather see their own enterprises fail than sit across the table and negotiate with our leadership. However, when national pressure began to pile up on the White House, climaxing with the infamous day of May 3, the administration was forced to act. On May 4, the attorney general dispatched Burke Marshall, his chief civil rights assistant, and Joseph F. Dolan, assistant deputy attorney general, to seek a truce in the tense racial situation. Though Marshall had no ultimate power to impose a solution, he had full authority to represent the president in the negotiations. It was one of the first times the federal government had taken so active a role in such circumstances.

I must confess that although I appreciated the fact that the administration had finally made a decisive move, I had some initial misgivings concerning Marshall's intentions. I was afraid that he had come to urge a "cooling off" period—to ask us to declare a one-sided truce as a condition to negotiations. To his credit, Marshall did not adopt such a position. Rather, he did an invaluable job of opening channels of communication between our leadership and the top people in the economic power structure. Said one staunch defender of segregation, after conferring with Marshall: "There is a man who listens. I had to listen back, and I guess I grew up a little."

With Burke Marshall as catalyst, we began to hold secret meetings with the Senior Citizens Committee. At these sessions, unpromising as they were at the outset, we laid the groundwork for the agreement that would eventually accord us all of our major demands.

Meanwhile, however, for several days violence swept through the streets of Birmingham. An armored car was added to Bull Connor's strange armament. And some Negroes, not trained in our nonviolent methods, again responded with bricks and bottles. On one of these days, when the pressure in Connor's hoses was so high that it peeled the bark off the trees, Fred Shuttlesworth was hurled by a blast of water against the side of a building. Suffering injuries in his chest, he was carried away in an ambulance. Connor, when told, responded in characteristic fashion. "I wish he'd been carried away in a hearse," he said. Fortunately, Shuttlesworth is resilient and though still in pain he was back at the conference table the next day.

Terrified by the very destructiveness brought on by their own acts, the city police appealed for state troopers to be brought into the area. Many of the white leaders now realized that something had to be done. Yet there were those among them who were still adamant. But one other incident was to occur that would transform recalcitrance into good faith. On Tuesday, May 7, the Senior Citizens Committee had assembled in a downtown building to discuss our demands. In the first hours of this meeting, they were so intransigent that Burke Marshall despaired of a pact. The atmosphere was charged with tension, and tempers were running high.

In this mood, these 125-odd business leaders adjourned for lunch. As they walked out on the street, an extraordinary sight met their eyes. On that day several thousand Negroes had marched on the town. The jails were so full that the police could only arrest a handful. There were Negroes on the sidewalks, in the streets, standing, sitting in the aisles of downtown stores. There were square blocks of Negroes, a veritable sea of black faces. They were committing no violence; they were just present and singing. Downtown Birmingham echoed to the strains of the freedom songs.

Astounded, these businessmen, key figures in a great city, suddenly realized that the movement could not be stopped. When they returned—from the lunch they were unable to get—one of the men who had been in the most determined opposition cleared his throat and said: "You know, I've been thinking this thing through. We ought to be able to work something out."

That admission marked the beginning of the end. Late that afternoon, Burke Marshall informed us that representatives from the business and industrial community wanted to meet with the movement leaders immediately to work out a settlement. After talking with these men for about three hours, we became convinced that they were negotiating in good faith. On the basis of this assurance we called a twenty-four-hour truce on Wednesday morning.

That day the president devoted the entire opening statement of his press conference to the Birmingham situation, emphasizing how vital it was that the problems be squarely faced and resolved and expressing encouragement that a dialogue now existed beetwen the opposing sides. Even while the president spoke, the truce was briefly threatened when

Ralph and I were suddenly clapped into jail on an old charge. Some of my associates, feeling that they had again been betrayed, put on their walking shoes and prepared to march. They were restrained, however; we were swiftly bailed out; and negotiations were resumed.

After talking all night Wednesday, and practically all day and night Thursday, we reached an accord. On Friday, May 10, this agreement was announced. In contained the following pledges:

1. The desegregation of lunch counters, rest rooms, fitting rooms and drinking fountains, in planned stages within ninety days after signing.
2. The upgrading and hiring of Negroes on a nondiscriminatory basis throughout the industrial community of Birmingham, to include hiring of Negroes as clerks and salesmen within sixty days after signing of the agreement—and the immediate appointment of a committee of business, industrial and professional leaders to implement an area-wide program for the acceleration of upgrading and employment of Negroes in job categories previously denied to them.
3. Official cooperation with the movement's legal representatives in working out the release of all jailed persons on bond or on their personal recognizance.
4. Through the Senior Citizens Committee or Chamber of Commerce, communications between Negro and white to be publicly established within two weeks after signing, in order to prevent the necessity of further demonstrations and protests.

Our troubles were not over. The announcement that a peace pact had been signed in Birmingham was flashed across the world by the hundred-odd foreign correspondents then covering the campaign on the crowded scene. It was headlined in the nation's press and heralded on network television. Segregationist forces within the city were consumed with fury. They vowed reprisals against the white businessmen who had "betrayed" them by capitulating to the cause of Negro equality. On Saturday night, they gave their brutal answer to the pact. Following a Ku Klux Klan meeting on the outskirts of town, the home of my brother, the Reverend A. D. King, was bombed. That same night a bomb was planted near the Gaston Motel, a bomb so placed as to kill or seriously wound anyone who might have been in Room 30—my room. Evidently the would-be assassins did not know I was in Atlanta that night.

The bombing had been well timed. The bars in the Negro district close at midnight, and the bombs exploded just as some of Birmingham's Saturday-night drinkers came out of the bars. Thousands of Negroes poured into the streets. Wyatt Walker, my brother and others urged them to go home, but they were not under the discipline of the movement and were in no mood to listen to counsels of peace. Fighting began. Stones were hurled at the police. Cars were wrecked and fires started. Whoever planted the bombs had *wanted* the Negroes to riot. They wanted the pact upset.

Governor George Wallace's state police and "conservation men" sealed off the Negro area and moved in with their bullies and pistols. They beat numerous innocent Negroes; among their acts of chivalry was the clubbing of the diminutive Anne Walker, Wyatt's wife, as she was about to enter her husband's quarters at the partially bombed-out Gaston Motel. They further distinguished themselves by beating Wyatt when he was attempting to drive back home after seeing his wife to the hospital.

I shall never forget the phone call my brother placed to me in Atlanta that violent Saturday night. His home had just been destroyed. Several people had been injured at the motel. I listened as he described the erupting tumult and catastrophe in the streets of the city. Then, in the background as he talked, I heard a swelling burst of beautiful song. Feet planted in the rubble of debris, threatened by criminal violence and hatred, followers of the movement were singing "We Shall Overcome." I marveled that in a moment of such tragedy the Negro could still express himself with hope and with faith.

The following evening, a thoroughly aroused president told the nation that the federal government would not allow extremists to sabotage a fair and just pact. He ordered three thousand federal troops into position near Birmingham and made preparations to federalize the Alabama National Guard. This firm action stopped the troublemakers in their tracks.

Yet the segregationist die-hards were to attempt still once more to destroy the peace. On 20 May the headlines announced that more than a thousand students who had participated in the demonstrations had been either suspended or expelled by the city's Board of Education. I am convinced that this was another attempt to drive the Negro community to an unwise and impulsive move. The plot might have worked; there were some people in our ranks who sincerely felt that, in retaliation, all the students of Birmingham should stay out of school and that demonstrations should be resumed.

I was out of the city at the time, but I rushed back to Birmingham to persuade the leaders that we must not fall into the trap. We decided to take the issue into the courts and did so, through the auspices of the NAACP Legal Defense and Educational Fund. On 22 May, the local federal district court judge upheld the Birmingham Board of Education. But that same day, Judge Elbert P. Tuttle, of the Fifth Circuit Court of Appeals, not only reversed the decision of the district judge but strongly condemned the Board of Education for its action. In a time when the nation is trying to solve the problem of school drop-outs, Judge Tuttle's ruling indicated, it is an act of irresponsibility to drive those youngsters from school in retaliation for having engaged in a legally permissible action to achieve their constitutional rights. The night this ruling was handed down, we had a great mass meeting. It was a jubilant moment, another victory in the titanic struggle.

The following day, in an appropriate postscript, the Alabama Supreme Court ruled Eugene "Bull" Connor and his fellow commissioners out of office, once and for all.

IV

I could not close an account of events in Birmingham without noting the tremendous moral and financial support which poured in upon us from all over the world during the six weeks of demonstrations and in the weeks and months to follow. Although we were so preoccupied with the day-to-day crises of the campaign that we did not have time to send out a formal plea for funds, letters of encouragement and donations ranging from pennies taken from piggy banks to checks of impressive size flowed into our besieged command post at the Gaston Motel and our Atlanta headquarters.

One of the most gratifying developments was the unprecedented show of unity that was displayed by the national Negro community in support of our crusade. From all over the country came Negro ministers, civil rights leaders, entertainers, star athletes and ordinary citizens, ready to speak at our meetings or join us in jail. The NAACP Legal Defense and Educational Fund came to our aid several times both with money and with resourceful legal talent. Many other organizations and individuals contributed invaluable gifts of time, money and moral support.

The signing of the agreement was the climax of a long struggle for justice, freedom and human dignity. The millennium still had not come, but Birmingham had made a fresh, bold step toward equality. Today Birmingham is by no means miraculously desegregated. There is still resistance and violence. The last-ditch struggle of a segregationist governor still soils the pages of current events and it is still necessary for a harried president to invoke his highest powers so that a Negro child may go to school with a white child in Birmingham. But these factors only serve to emphasize the truth that even the segregationists know: The system to which they have been committed lies on its deathbed. The only imponderable is the question of how costly they will make the funeral.

I like to believe that Birmingham will one day become a model in southern race relations. I like to believe that the negative extremes of Birmingham's past will resolve into the positive and utopian extreme of her future; that the sins of a dark yesterday will be redeemed in the achievements of a bright tomorrow. I have this hope because, once on a summer day, a dream came true. The city of Birmingham discovered a conscience.

---

Martin Luther King, Jr., *Why We Can't Wait* (New York: Harper & Row, 1963).

# 56

# Where Do We Go from Here: Chaos or Community?

*This book was perhaps the toughest writing project Dr. King ever pursued. He finally had to travel to Jamaica in order to find the time to finish it. His schedule was grueling. He worked twenty-hour days, traveled approximately 325,000 miles per year, and often gave as many as 450 speeches per year. When he wrote this book, it seemed that the civil rights leadership was being bypassed by the new advocates of black power. He tried to show that many objectives of the black power advocates were no different from his own. Moreover, he called for recognition of the importance of many strategies, and lamented the rise of logistical imperialists such as Floyd McKissick and Stokeley Carmichael, who argued for their own strategies and demeaned nonviolent direct action, which King felt was a more reasonable, practical, and moral strategy.*

## WHERE ARE WE? (CHAPTER 1)

On 6 August 1965, the president's room of the Capitol could scarcely hold the multitude of white and Negro leaders crowding it. President Lyndon Johnson's high spirits were marked as he circulated among the many guests whom he had invited to witness an event he confidently felt to be historic, the signing of the 1965 Voting Rights Act. The legislation was designed to put the ballot effectively into Negro hands in the south after a century of denial by terror and evasion.

The bill that lay on the polished mahogany desk was born in violence in Selma, Alabama, where a stubborn sheriff handling Negroes in the southern tradition had stumbled against the future. During a nonviolent demonstration for voting rights, the sheriff had directed his men in tear-gassing and beating the marchers to the ground. The nation had seen and heard, and exploded in indignation. In protest, Negroes and whites marched fifty miles through Alabama, and arrived at the state capital of Montgomery in a demonstration fifty thousand strong. President Johnson, describing Selma as a modern Concord, addressed a joint session of Congress before a television audience of millions. He pledged that "We shall overcome," and declared that the national government must by law insure to every Negro his full rights as a citizen. The Voting Rights Bill of 1965 was the result. In signing the measure, the president announced that "Today is a triumph for freedom as huge as any victory that's ever been won on any battlefield . . . today we strike away the last major shackle of . . . fierce and ancient bonds."

One year later, some of the people who had been brutalized in Selma and who were present at the Capitol ceremonies were leading marchers in the suburbs of Chicago amid a rain of rocks and bottles, among burning automobiles, to the thunder of jeering thousands, many of them waving Nazi flags.

A year later, some of the Negro leaders who had been present in Selma and at the Capitol ceremonies no longer held office in their organizations. They had been discarded to symbolize a radical change of tactics.

A year later, the white backlash had become an emotional electoral issue in California, Maryland and elsewhere. In several southern states men long regarded as political clowns had become governors or only narrowly missed election, their magic achieved with a witches' brew of bigotry, prejudice, half-truths and whole lies.

During the year, white and Negro civil rights workers had been murdered in several southern communities. The swift and easy acquittals that followed for the accused had shocked much of the nation but sent a wave of unabashed triumph through southern segregationist circles. Many of us wept at the funeral services for the dead and for democracy.

During the year, in several northern and western cities, most tragically in Watts, young Negroes had exploded in violence. In an irrational burst of rage they had sought to say something, but the flames had blackened both themselves and their oppressors.

A year later, *Ramparts* magazine was asserting, "After more than a decade of the Civil Rights Movement the black American in Harlem, Haynesville, Baltimore and Bogalousa is worse off today than he was ten years ago . . . the Movement's leaders know it and it is the source of their despair. . . . The Movement is in despair because it has been forced to recognize the Negro revolution as a myth."

Had Negroes fumbled the opportunities described by the president? Was the movement in despair? Why was widespread sympathy with the Negro revolution abruptly submerged in indifference in some quarters or banished by outright hostility in others? Why was there ideological disarray?

A simple explanation holds that Negroes rioted in Watts, the voice of Black Power was heard through the land and the white backlash was born; the public became infuriated and sympathy evaporated. This pat explanation founders, however, on the hard fact that the change in mood had preceded Watts and the Black Power slogan. Moreover, the white backlash had always existed underneath and sometimes on the surface of American life. No, the answers are both more complex and, for the long run, less pessimistic.

With Selma and the Voting Rights Act one phase of development in the civil rights revolution came to an end. A new phase opened, but few observers realized it or were prepared for its implications. For the vast majority of white Americans, the past decade—the first phase—had been a struggle to treat the Negro with a degree of decency, not of equality. White America was ready to demand that the Negro should be spared the lash of brutality and coarse degradation, but it had never been truly committed to helping him out of poverty, exploitation or all forms of discrimination. The outragd white citizen had been sincere when he snatched the whips from the southern sheriffs and forbade them more cruelties. But when this was to a degree accomplisehd, the emotions that had momentarily inflamed him melted away. White Americans left the Negro on the ground and in devastating numbers walked off with the aggressor. It appeared that the white segregationist and the ordinary white citizen had more in common with one another than either had with the Negro.

When Negroes looked for the second phase, the realization of equality, they found that many of their white allies had quietly disappeared. The Negroes of America had taken the president, the press and the pulpit at their word when they spoke in broad terms of freedom and justice. But the absence of brutality and unregenerate evil is not the presence of justice. To stay murder is not the same thing as to ordain brotherhood. The word was broken, and the free-running expectations of the Negro crashed into the stone walls of white resistance. The result was havoc. Negroes felt cheated, especially in the North, while many whites felt that the Negroes had gained so much it was virtually impudent and greedy to ask for more so soon.

The paths of Negro-white unity that had been converging crossed at Selma, and like a giant X began to diverge. Up to Selma there had been unity to eliminate barbaric conduct. Beyond it the unity had to be based on the fulfillment of equality, and in the absence of agreement the paths began inexorably to move apart.

II

Why is equality so assiduously avoided? Why does white America delude itself, and how does it rationalize the evil it retains?

The majority of white Americans consider themselves sincerely committed to justice for the Negro. They believe that American society is essentially hospitable to fair play and to steady growth toward a middle-class utopia embodying racial harmony. But unfortunately this is a fantasy of self-deception and comfortable vanity. Overwhelmingly America is still struggling with irresolution and contradictions. It has been sincere and even ardent in welcoming some change. But too quickly apathy and disinterest rise to the surface when the next logical steps are to be taken. Laws are passed in a crisis mood after a Birmingham or a Selma, but no substantial fervor survives the formal signing of legislation. The recording of the law in itself is treated as the reality of the reform.

This limited degree of concern is a reflection of an inner conflict which measures cautiously the impact of any change on the status quo. As the nation passes from opposing extremist behavior to the deeper and more pervasive elements of equality, white America reaffirms its bonds to the status quo. It had contemplated comfortably hugging the shoreline but now fears that the winds of change are blowing it out to sea.

The practical cost of change for the nation up to this point has been cheap. The limited reforms have been obtained at bargain rates. There are no expenses, and no taxes are required, for Negroes to share lunch counters, libraries, parks, hotels and other facilities with whites. Even the psychological adjustment is far from formidable. Having exaggerated the emotional difficulties for decades, when demands for new conduct became inescapable, white southerners may have trembled under the strain but they did not collapse.

Even more significant changes involved in voter registration required neither large monetary nor psychological sacrifice. Spectacular and turbulent events that dramatized the demand created an erroneous impression that a heavy burden was involved.

The real cost lies ahead. The stiffening of white resistance is a recognition of that fact. The discount education given Negroes will in the future have to be purchased at full price if quality education is to be realized. Jobs are harder and costlier to create than voting rolls. The eradication of slums housing millions is complex far beyond integrating buses and lunch counters.

The assistant director of the Office of Economic Opportunity, Hyman Bookbinder, in a frank statement on 29 December 1966, declared that the long-range costs of adequately implementing programs to fight poverty, ignorance and slums will reach one trillion dollars. He was not awed or dismayed by this prospect but instead pointed out that the growth of the gross national product during the same period makes this expenditure comfortably possible. It is, he said, as simple as this: "The poor can stop being poor if the rich are willing to become even richer at a slower rate." Furthermore, he predicted that unless a "substantial sacrifice is made by the American people," the nation can expect further deterioration of the cities, increased antagonisms between races and continued disorders in the streets. He asserted that people are not informed enough to give adequate support to antipoverty programs, and he leveled a share of the blame at the government because it "must do more to get people to understand the size of the problem."

Let us take a look at the size of the problem through the lens of the Negro's status in 1967. When the Constitution was written, a strange formula to determine taxes and representation declared that the Negro was 60 percent of a person.[1] Today another curious formula seems to declare he is 50 percent of a person. Of the good things in life he has approximately one-half those of whites; of the bad he has twice those of whites. Thus, half of all Negroes live in substandard housing, and Negroes have half the income of whites. When we turn to the negative experiences of life, the Negro has a double share. There are twice as many unemployed. The rate of infant mortality (widely accepted as an accurate index of general health) among Negroes is double that of whites.[2] The equation pursues Negroes even into war. There were twice as many Negroes as whites in combat in Vietnam at the beginning of 1967, and twice as many Negro soldiers died in action (20.6 percent) in proportion to their numbers in the population.[3]

In other spheres the figures are equally alarming. In elementary schools Negroes lag one to three years behind whites, and their segregated schools receive substantially less money per student than do the white schools. One-twentieth as many Negroes as whites attend college, and half of these are in ill-equipped Southern institutions.[4]

Of employed Negroes, 75 percent hold menial jobs.[5] Depressed living standards for Negroes are not simply the consequence of neglect. Nor can they be explained by the myth of the Negro's innate incapacities, or by the more sophisticated rationalization of his acquired infirmities (family disorganization, poor education, etc.). They are a structural part of the economic system in the United States. Certain industries and enterprises are based upon a supply of low-paid, underskilled and immobile nonwhite labor. Hand assembly factories, hospitals, service industries, housework, agricultural operations using itinerant labor would suffer economic trauma, if not disaster, with a rise in wage scales.

Economic discrimination is especially deeply rooted in the South. In industry after industry there is a significant differential in wage scales between North and South. The lower scale in the South is directly a consequence of cheap Negro labor (which ironically not only deprives the Negro but by its presence drives down the wages of the white worker). The new South, while undergoing certain marked changes as a result of industrialization, is adapting the forms of discrimination that keep the Negro in a subordinate role and hold his wage scales close to the bottom.

The personal torment of discrimination cannot be measured on a numerical scale, but the grim evidence of its hold on white Americans is revealed in polls that indicate that 88 percent of them would object if

1. Article I, section 2, paragraph 3.
2. *Vital Statistics, 1961,* New York City Department of Health.
3. *New York Times*, 14 February 1967.
4. 1960 Census.
5. *Ibid.*

their teen-age child dated a Negro. Almost 80 percent would mind it if a close friend or relative married a Negro, and 50 percent would not want a Negro as a neighbor.[6]

These brief facts disclose the magnitude of the gap between existing realities and the goal of equality. Yet they would be less disturbing if it were not for a greater difficulty. There is not even a common language when the term "equality" is used. Negro and white have a fundamentally different definition.

Negroes have proceeded from a premise that equality means what it says, and they have taken white Americans at their word when they talked of it as an objective. But most whites in America in 1967, including many persons of goodwill, proceed from a premise that equality is a loose expression for improvement. White America is not even psychologically organized to close the gap—essentially it seeks only to make it less painful and less obvious but in most respects to retain it. Most of the abrasions between Negroes and white liberals arise from this fact.

White America is uneasy with injustice and for ten years it believed it was righting wrongs. The struggles were often bravely fought by fine people. The conscience of man flamed high in hours of peril. The days can never be forgotten when the brutalities at Selma caused thousands all over the land to rush to our side, heedless of danger and of differences in race, class and religion.

After the march to Montgomery, there was a delay at the airport and several thousand demonstrators waited more than five hours, crowding together on the seats, the floors and stairways of the terminal building. As I stood with them and saw white and Negro, nuns and priests, ministers and rabbis, labor organizers, lawyers, doctors, housemaids and shopworkers brimming with vitality and enjoying a rare comradeship, I knew I was seeing a microcosm of the mankind of the future in this moment of luminous and genuine brotherhood.

But these were the best of America, not all of America. Elsewhere the commitment was shallower. Conscience burned only dimly, and when atrocious behavior was curbed, the spirit settled easily into well-padded pockets of complacency. Justice at the deepest level had but few stalwart champions.

A good many observers have remarked that if equality could come at once the Negro would not be ready for it. I submit that the white American is even more unprepared.

The Negro on a mass scale is working vigorously to overcome his deficiencies and his maladjustments. Wherever there are job-training programs Negroes are crowding them. Those who are employed are revealing an eagerness for advancement never before so widespread and persistent. In the average Negro home a new appreciation of culture is

---

6. *Newsweek* Survey–Harris Poll, 22 August 1966.

manifest. The circulation of periodicals and books written for Negroes is now in the multimillions while a decade ago it was scarcely past one hundred thousand. In the schools more Negro students are demanding courses that lead to college and beyond, refusing to settle for the crude vocational training that limited so many of them in the past.

Whites, it must frankly be said, are not putting in a similar mass effort to reeducate themselves out of their racial ignorance. It is an aspect of their sense of superiority that the white people of America believe they have so little to learn. The reality of substantial investment to assist Negroes into the twentieth century, adjusting to Negro neighbors and genuine school integration, is still a nightmare for all too many white Americans.

White America would have liked to believe that in the past ten years a mechanism had somehow been created that needed only orderly and smooth tending for the painless accomplishment of change. Yet this is precisely what has not been achieved. Every civil rights law is still substantially more dishonored than honored. School desegregatoin is still 90 percent unimplemented across the land; the free exercise of the franchise is the exception rather than the rule in the South; open-occupancy laws theoretically apply to population centers embracing tens of millions, but grim ghettos contradict the fine language of the legislation. Despite the mandates of law, equal employment still remains a distant dream.

The legal structures have in practice proved to be neither structures nor law. The sparse and insufficient collection of statutes is not a structure; it is barely a naked framework. Legislation that is evaded, substantially nullified and unenforced is a mockery of law. Significant progress has effectively been barred by equivocations and retreats of government—the same government that was exultant when it sought political credit for enacting the measures.

In this light, we are now able to see why the Supreme Court decisions on school desegregation, which we described at the time as historic, have not made history. After twelve years, barely 12 percent school integration existed in the whole South, and in the Deep South the figure hardly reached 2 percent.[7] And even these few schools were in many cases integrated only with a handful of Negroes. The decisions indeed mandated a profound degree of genuine equality; for that very reason, they failed of implementation. They were, in a sense, historical errors from the point of view of white America.

Even the Supreme Court, despite its original courage and integrity, curbed itself only a little over a year after the 1954 landmark cases, when it handed down its pupil placement decision, in effect returning to the states the power to determine the tempo of change. This subsequent decision became the keystone in the structure that slowed school de-

---

7. Southern Regional Council, 1966.

segregation down to a crawl. Thus America, with segregationist obstruction and majority indifference, silently nibbled away at a promise of true equality that had come before its time.

These are the deepest causes for contemporary abrasions between the races. Loose and easy language about equality, resonant resolutions about brotherhood fall pleasantly on the ear, but for the Negro there is a credibility gap he cannot overlook. He remembers that with each modest advance the white population promptly raises the argument that the Negro has come far enough. Each step forward accents an ever-present tendency to backlash.

This characterization is necessarily general. It would be grossly unfair to omit recognition of a minority of whites who genuinely want authentic equality. Their commitment is real, sincere, and is expressed in a thousand deeds. But they are balanced at the other end of the pole by the unregenerated segregationists who have declared that democracy is not worth having if it involves equality. The segregationist goal is the total reversal of all reforms, with reestablishment of naked oppression and if need be a native form of fascism. America had a master race in the ante bellum South. Reestablishing it with a resurgent Klan and a totally disenfranchised lower class would realize the dream of too many extremists on the right.

The great majority of Americans are suspended between these opposing attitudes. They are uneasy with injustice but unwilling yet to pay a significant price to eradicate it.

The persistence of racism in depth and the dawning awareness that Negro demands will necessitate structural changes in society have generated a new phase of white resistance in North and South. Based on the cruel judgment that Negroes have come far enough, there is a strong mood to bring the civil rights movement to a halt or reduce it to a crawl. Negro demands that yesterday evoked admiration and support, today—to many—have become tiresome, unwarranted and a disturbance to the enjoyment of life. Cries of Black Power and riots are not the causes of white resistance, they are consequences of it.

III

Meanwhile frustration and a loss of confidence in white power have engendered among many Negroes a response that is essentially a loss of confidence in themselves. They are failing to appreciate two important facts.

First, the line of progress is never straight. For a period a movement may follow a straight line and then it encounters obstacles and the path bends. It is like curving around a mountain when you are approaching a city. Often it feels as though you were moving backward, and you lose sight of your goal; but in fact you are moving ahead, and soon you will see the city again, closer by.

We are encountering just such an experience today. The inevitable counterrevolution that succeeds every period of progress is taking place. Failing to understand this as a normal process of development, some Negroes are falling into unjustified pessimism and despair. Focusing on the ultimate goal, and discovering it still distant, they declare no progress at all has been made.

This mood illustrates another fact that has been misinterpreted. A final victory is an accumulation of many short-term encounters. To lightly dismiss a success because it does not usher in a complete order of justice is to fail to comprehend the process of achieving full victory. It underestimates the value of confrontation and dissolves the confidence born of a partial victory by which new efforts are powered.

The argument that the Negro has made no progress in a decade of turbulent effort rests on demonstrable facts that paint an ugly picture of stagnation in many areas, including income levels, housing and schools. But from a deeper perspective a different conclusion emerges. The increases in segregated schools and the expanded slums are developments confined largely to the North. Substantial progress has been achieved in the South. The struggles of the past decade were not national in scope; they were southern; they were specifically designed to change life in the South; and the principal role of the North was supportive. It would be a serious error to misconstrue the movement's strategy by measuring northern accomplishments when virtually all programs were applied in the South and sought remedies applicable solely to it.

The historic achievement is found in the fact that the movement in the South has profoundly shaken the entire edifice of segregation. This is an accomplishment whose consequences are deeply felt by every southern Negro in his daily life. It is no longer possible to count the number of public establishments that are open to Negroes. The persistence of segregation is not the salient fact of southern experience; the proliferating areas in which the Negro moves freely is the new advancing truth.

The South was the stronghold of racism. In the white migrations through history from the South to the North and West, racism was carried to poison the rest of the nation. Prejudice, discrimination and bigotry had been intricately imbedded in all institutions of southern life, political, social and economic. There could be no possibility of life-transforming change anywhere so long as the vast and solid influence of southern segregation remained unchallenged and unhurt. The ten-year assault at the roots was fundamental to undermining the system. What distinguished this period from all preceding decades was that it constituted the first frontal attack on racism at its heart.

Since before the Civil War, the alliance of southern racism and northern reaction has been the major roadblock to all social advancement. The cohesive political structure of the South working through this alliance enabled a minority of the population to imprint its ideology on the nation's laws. This explains why the United States is still far behind European nations in all forms of social legislation. England, France, Germany, Sweden, all distinctly less wealthy than us, provide more security relatively for their people.

Hence in attacking southern racism the Negro has already benefited not only himself but the nation as a whole. Until the disproportionate political power of the reactionary South in Congress is ended, progress in the United States will always be fitful and uncertain.

Since the beginning of the civil rights revolution, Negro registration in almost every southern state has increased by at least 100 percent, and in Virginia and Alabama, by 300 and 600 percent, respectively.[8] There are no illusions among southern segregationists that these gains are unimportant. The old order has already lost ground; its retreats are symbolized by the departure from public life of sheriffs Clark and Bull Connor. Far more important, the racists have restructured old parties to cope with the emerging challenge. In some states, such as Georgia and Alabama, white supremacy temporarily holds the state house, but it would be a foolish and shortsighted politician who felt secure with this victory. In both of these states the most serious contender in recent elections was a white former governor who publicly welcomed the Negro vote, shaped his policies to it and worked with Negro political organizations in the campaign. This change is itself a revolutionary event. This amazing transformation took place in one decade of struggle after ten decades of virtually total disenfranchisement. The future shape of southern politics will never again operate without a strong Negro electorate as a significant force.

Even in Mississippi, where electoral advances are not yet marked, a different form of change is manifest. When Negroes decided to march for freedom across the state, they boldly advanced to the capital itself, in a demonstration of thirty thousand people. Ten years before, a Mississippi Negro would have submissively stepped to the gutter to leave the sidewalk for a white man. Ten years before, to plan a meeting, Negroes would have come together at night in the woods as conspirators.

A decade ago, not a single Negro entered the legislative chambers of the South except as a porter or a chauffeur. Today eleven Negroes are members of the Georgia House.

Ten years ago, Negroes seemed almost invisible to the larger society, and the facts of their harsh lives were unknown to the majority of the nation. Today civil rights is a dominating issue in every state, crowding the pages of the press and the daily conversation of white Americans.

In this decade of change the Negro stood up and confronted his

---

8. Donald R. Matthews and James W. Prothro, *Negroes and the New Southern Politics*, Harcourt, Brace and World, 1966, p. 148.

oppressor—he faced the bullies and the guns, the dogs and the tear gas, he put himself squarely before the vicious mobs and moved with strength and dignity toward them and decisively defeated them.

For more than a century of slavery and another century of segregation Negroes did not find mass unity nor could they mount mass actions. The American brand of servitude tore them apart and held them in paralyzed solitude. But in the last decade Negroes united and marched. And out of the new unity and action vast monuments of dignity were shaped, courage was forged and hope took concrete form.

For hundreds of years Negroes had fought to stay alive by developing an endurance to hardship and heartbreak. In this decade the Negro stepped into a new role. He no longer would endure; he would resist and win. He still had the age-old capacity to live in hunger and want, but now he banished these as his lifelong companions. He could tolerate humiliation and scorn, but now he armed himself with dignity and resistance and his adversary tasted the gall of defeat.

For the first time in his history the Negro did not have to use subterfuge as a defense, or solicit pity. His endurance was not employed for compromise with evil but to supply the strength to crush it.

He came out of his struggle integrated only slightly in the external society but powerfully integrated within. This was the victory that had to precede all other gains.

He made his government write new laws to alter some of the cruelest injustices that affected him. He made an indifferent and unconcerned nation rise from lethargy and recognize his oppression and struggle with a newly aroused conscience. He gained manhood in the nation that had always called him "boy."

These were the values he won that enlivened hope even while sluggish progress made no substantial changes in the quality or quantity of his daily bread.

The great deal the Negro has won in spiritual undergirding and the great deal he has not won in material progress indicate the strengths and weaknesses in the life of the Negro in 1967. They also reveal that no matter how many obstacles persist the Negro's forward march can no longer be stopped.

The fight is far from over, because it is neither won, as some assert, nor lost, as the calamity-ridden declare.

Negroes have irrevocably undermined the foundations of southern segregation; they have assembled the power through self-organization and coalition to place their demands on all significant national agendas. And beyond this, they have now accumulated the strength to change the quality and substance of their demands. From issues of personal dignity they are now advancing to programs that impinge upon the basic system of social and economic control. At this level Negro programs go beyond race and deal with economic inequality, wherever it exists. In the pursuit of these goals, the white poor become involved, and the potentiality emerges for a powerful new alliance.

Another momentous gain of the last decade is now being taken for granted. Negroes forged their own tactical theory of nonviolent direct action. It was born in Montgomery, Alabama, and for a time was considered of only limited application. But as it inspired and informed far-flung movements that included sit-ins, boycotts and mass marches, it became clear that a new method of protest action had been born.

When legal contests were the sole form of activity, the ordinary Negro was involved as a passive spectator. His interest was stirred, but his energies were unemployed. Mass marches transformed the common man into the star performer and engaged him in a total commitment. Yet nonviolent resistance caused no explosions of anger—it instigated no riots—it controlled anger and released it under discipline for maximum effect. What lobbying and imploring could not do in legislative halls, marching feet accomplished a thousand miles away. When the Southern Christian Leadership Conference went into Birmingham in 1963, it intended to change that city. But the effect of its campaign was so extensive that President Kennedy was forced to conclude that national legislation was indispensable, and the first civil rights bill with substance was enacted in 1964. Nonviolent direct action had proved to be the most effective generator of change that the movement had seen, and by 1965 all civil rights organizations had embraced it as theirs.

In the past year nonviolent direct action has been pronounced for the tenth time dead. New tactics have been proposed to replace it. The Black Power slogan was described as a doctrine that reached Negro hearts with so deep an appeal that no alternative method could withstand its magnetic force. Rioting was described as a new Negro form of action that evoked results when disciplined demonstration sputtered out against implacable opposition.

Yet Black Power has proved to be a slogan without a program, and with an uncertain following. If it is true that the controversy is not yet resolved, it is also true that no new alternatives to nonviolence within the movement have found viable expression. Confusion has been created, but extensive despair and dissipation of fighting strength have not occurred.

IV

By 1967 the resounding shout of the Negro's protest had shattered the myth of his contentment. The courage with which he confronted enraged mobs dissolved the stereotype of the grinning, submissive Uncle Tom. Indeed, by the end of a turbulent decade there was a new quality to Negro life. The Negro was no longer a subject of change; he was the active organ of change. He powered the drive. He set the pace.

At the same time it had become clear that though white opposition could be defeated it remained a formidable force capable of hardening its resistance when the cost of change was increased.

The daily life of the Negro is still lived in the basement of the Great Society. He is still at the bottom despite the few who have penetrated to slightly higher levels. Even where the door has been forced partially open, mobility for the Negro is still sharply restricted. There is often no bottom at which to start, and when there is, there is almost always no room at the top.

The northern ghetto dweller still lives in a schizophrenic social milieu. In the past decade he supported and derived pride from southern struggles and accomplishment. Yet the civil rights revolution appeared to drain energy from the North, energy that flowed South to transform life there while stagnation blanketed northern Negro communities.

This was a decade of role reversal. The North, heretofore vital, languished, while the traditionally passive South burst with dynamic vigor. The North at best stood still as the South caught up.

Civil rights leaders had long thought the North would benefit derivatively from the southern struggle. They assumed that without massive upheavals certain systemic changes were inevitable as the whole nation reexamined and searched its conscience. This was a miscalculaiton. It was founded on the belief that opposition in the North was not intransigent, that it was flexible and was, if not fully, at least partially hospitable to corrective influences. We forgot what we knew daily in the South: freedom is not given, it is won. Concentration of effort in the large northern cities can no longer be postponed in favor of southern campaigns. Both must now be sustained.

In assessing the results of the Negro revolution so far, it can be concluded that Negroes have established a foothold, no more. We have written a declaration of independence, itself an accomplishment, but the effort to transform the words into a life experience still lies ahead.

The hard truth is that neither Negro nor white has yet done enough to expect the dawn of a new day. While much has been done, it has been accomplished by too few and on a scale too limited for the breadth of the goal. Freedom is not won by a passive acceptance of suffering. Freedom is won by a struggle *against* suffering. By this measure, Negroes have not yet paid the full price for freedom. And whites have not yet faced the full cost of justice.

The brunt of the Negro's past battles was borne by a very small striking force. Though millions of Negroes were ardent and passionate supporters, only a modest number were actively engaged, and these were relatively too few for a broad war against racism, poverty and discrimination. Negroes fought and won, but our engagements were skirmishes, not climactic battles.

No great victories are won in a war for the transformation of a whole people without total participation. Less than this will not create a new society; it will only evoke more sophisticated token amelioration. The Negro has been wrong to toy with the optimistic thought that the breakdown of white resistance could be accomplished at small cost. He will have to do more before his pressure crystallizes new white principles and new responses. The two forces must continue to collide as Negro aspiratoins burst against the ancient fortresses of the status quo.

This should not be construed as a prediction of violence. On the one hand, there will certainly be new expressions of nonviolent direct action on an enlarged scale. If one hundred thousand Negroes march in a major city to a strategic location, they will make municipal operations difficult to conduct; they will exceed the capacity of even the most reckless local government to use force against them; and they will repeat this action daily if necessary. Without harming persons or property they can draw as much attention to their grievances as the outbreak at Watts, and they will have asserted their unwavering determination while retaining their dignity and discipline.

But on the other hand, it cannot be taken for granted that Negroes will adhere to nonviolence under any and all conditions. When there is rocklike intransigence or sophisticated manipulation that mocks the empty-handed petitioner, rage replaces reason. Nonviolence is a powerful demand for reason and justice. If it is rudely rebuked, it is not transformed into resignation and passivity. Southern segregationists in many places yielded to it because they realized that the alternatives could be intolerable. Northern white leadership has relied too much on tokens and substitutes, and on Negro patience. The end of this road is clearly in sight. The cohesive, potentially explosive Negro community in the North has a short fuse and a long train of abuses. Those who argue that it is hazardous to give warnings, lest the expression of apprehension lead to violence, are in error. Violence has already been practiced too often, and always because remedies were postponed.

It is understandable that the white community should fear the outbreak of riots. They are indefensible as weapons of struggle, and Negroes must sympathize with whites who feel menaced by them. Indeed, Negroes are themselves no less menaced, and those living in the ghetto always suffer most directly from the destructive turbulence of a riot.

Yet the average white person also has a responsiblity. He has to resist the impulse to seize upon the rioter as the exclusive villain. He has to rise up with indignation against his own municipal, state and national governments to demand that the necessary reforms be instituted which alone will protect him. If he reserves his resentment only for the Negro, he will be the victim by allowing those who have the greatest culpability to evade responsibility.

Social justice and progress are the absolute guarantors of riot prevention. There is no other answer. Constructive social change will bring certain tranquility; evasions will merely encourage turmoil.

Negroes hold only one key to the double lock of peaceful change. The other is in the hands of the white community.

## BLACK POWER (CHAPTER 2)

"James Meredith has been shot!"

It was about three o'clock in the afternoon on a Monday in June, 1966, and I was presiding over the regular staff meeting of the Southern Christian Leadership Conference in our Atlanta headquarters. When we heard that Meredith had been shot in the back only a day after he had begun his Freedom March through Mississippi, there was a momentary hush of anger and dismay throughout the room. Our horror was compounded by the fact that the early reports announced that Meredith was dead. Soon the silence was broken, and from every corner of the room came expressions of outrage. The business of the meeting was forgotten in the shock of this latest evidence that a Negro's life is still worthless in many parts of his own country.

When order was finally restored, our executive staff immediately agreed that the march must continue. After all, we reasoned, Meredith had begun his lonely journey as a pilgrimage against fear. Wouldn't failure to continue only intensify the fears of the oppressed and deprived Negroes of Mississippi? Would this not be a setback for the whole civil rights movement and a blow to nonviolent discipline?

After several calls between Atlanta and Memphis, we learned that the earlier reports of Meredith's death were false and that he would recover. This news brought relief, but it did not alter our feeling that the civil rights movement had a moral obligation to continue along the path the Meredith had begun.

The next morning I was off to Memphis along with several members of my staff. Floyd McKissick, national director of CORE, flew in from New York and joined us on the flight from Atlanta to Memphis. After landing we went directly to the Municipal Hospital to visit Meredith. We were happy to find him resting well. After expressing our sympathy and gratitude for his courageous witness, Floyd and I shared our conviction with him that the march should continue in order to demonstrate to the nation and the world that Negroes would never again be intimidated by the terror of the extremist white violence. Realizing that Meredith was often a loner and that he probably wanted to continue the march without a large group, we felt that it would take a great deal of persuasion to convince him that the issue involved the whole civil rights movement. Fortunately, he soon saw this and agreed that we should continue without him. We spent some time discussing the character and logistics of the march, and agreed that we would consult with him daily on every decision.

As we prepared to leave, the nurse came to the door and said, "Mr.

Meredith, there is a Mr. Carmichael in the lobby who would like to see you and Dr. King. Should I give him permission to come in?" Meredith consented. Stokely Carmichael entered with his associate, Cleveland Sellers, and immediately reached out for Meredith's hand. He expressed his concern and admiration and brought messages of sympathy from his colleagues in the Student Nonviolent Coordinating Committee. After a brief conversation we all agreed that James should get some rest and that we should not burden him with any additional talk. We left the room assuring him that we would conduct the march in his spirit and would seek as never before to expose the ugly racism that pervaded Mississippi and to arouse a new sense of dignity and manhood in every Negro who inhabited that bastion of man's inhumanity to man.

In a brief conference Floyd, Stokely and I agreed that the march would be jointly sponsored by CORE, SNCC and SCLC, with the understanding that all other civil rights organizations would be invited to join. It was also agreed that we would issue a national call for support and participation.

One hour later, after making staff assignments and setting up headquarters at the Rev. James Lawson's church in Memphis, a group of us packed into four automobiles and made our way to that desolate spot on Highway 51 where James Meredith had been shot the day before. So began the second stage of the Meredith Mississippi Freedom March.

As we walked down the meandering highway in the sweltering heat, there was much talk and many questions were raised.

"I'm not for that nonviolence stuff any more," shouted one of the younger activists.

"If one of these damn white Mississippi crackers touches me, I'm gonna knock the hell out of him," shouted another.

Later on a discussion of the composition of the march came up.

"This should be an all-black march," said one marcher. "We don't need any more white phonies and liberals invading our movement. This is our march."

Once during the afternoon we stopped to sing "We Shall Overcome." The voices rang out with all the traditional fervor, the glad thunder and gentle strength that had always characterized the singing of this noble song. But when we came to the stanza which speaks of "black and white together," the voices of a few of the marchers were muted. I asked them later why they refused to sing that verse. The retort was:

"This is a new day, we don't sing those words any more. In fact, the whole song should be discarded. Not 'We Shall Overcome,' but 'We Shall Overrun.' "

As I listened to all these comments, the words fell on my ears like strange music from a foreign land. My hearing was not attuned to the sound of such bitterness. I guess I should not have been surprised. I should have known that in an atmosphere where false promises are daily realities, where deferred dreams are nightly facts, where acts of unpunished violence toward Negroes are a way of life, nonviolence would eventually be seriously questioned. I should have been reminded that disappointment produces despair and despair produces bitterness, and that the one thing certain about bitterness is its blindness. Bitterness has not the capacity to make the distinction between some and *all*. When some members of the dominant group, particularly those in power, are racist in attitude and practice, bitterness accuses the whole group.

At the end of the march that first day we all went back to Memphis and spent the night in a Negro motel, since we had not yet secured the tents that would serve as shelter each of the following nights on our journey. The discussion continued at the motel. I decided that I would plead patiently with my brothers to remain true to the time-honored principles of our movement. I began with a plea for nonviolence. This immediately aroused some of our friends from the Deacons for Defense, who contended that self-defense was essential and that therefore nonviolence should not be a prerequisite for participation in the march. They were joined in this view by some of the activists from CORE and SNCC.

I tried to make it clear that besides opposing violence on principle, I could imagine nothing more impractical and disastrous than for any of us, through misguided judgment, to precipitate a violent confrontation in Mississippi. We had neither the resources nor the techniques to win. Furthermore, I asserted, many Mississippi whites, from the government on down, would enjoy nothing more than for us to turn to violence in order to use this as an excuse to wipe out scores of Negroes in and out of the march. Finally, I contended that the debate over the question of self-defense was unnecessary since few people suggested that Negroes should not defend themselves as individuals when attacked. The question was not whether one should use his gun when his home was attacked, but whether it was tactically wise to use a gun while participating in an organized demonstration. If they lowered the banner of nonviolence, I said, Mississippi injustice would not be exposed and the moral issues would be obscured.

Next the question of the participation of whites was raised. Stokely Carmichael contended that the inclusion of whites in the march should be de-emphasized and that the dominant appeal should be for black participation. Others in the room agreed. As I listened to Stokely, I thought about the years that we had worked together in communities all across the South, and how joyously we had then welcomed and accepted our white allies in the movement. What accounted for this reversal in Stokely's philosophy?

I surmised that much of the change had its psychological roots in the experience of SNCC in Mississippi during the summer of 1964, when a large number of northern white students had come down to help in that racially torn state. What the SNCC workers saw was the most articulate, powerful and self-assured young white people coming to work with the poorest of the Negro people—and simply overwhelming them. That summer Stokely and others in SNCC had probably unconsciously concluded that this was no good for Negroes, for it simply increased their sense of their own inadequacies. Of course, the answer to this dilemma was not to give up, not to conclude that blacks must work with blacks in order for Negroes to gain a sense of their own meaning. The answer was only to be found in persistent trying, perpetual experimentation, persevering togetherness.

Like life, racial understanding is not something that we find but something that we must create. What we find when we enter these mortal plains is existence; but existence is the raw material out of which all life must be created. A productive and happy life is not something that you find; it is something that you make. And so the ability of Negroes and whites to work together, to understand each other, will not be found ready made; it must be created by the fact of contact.

Along these lines, I implored everyone in the room to see the morality of making the march completely interracial. Consciences must be enlisted in our movement, I said, not merely racial groups. I reminded them of the dedicated whites who had suffered, bled and died in the cause of racial justice, and suggested that to reject white participation now would be a shameful repudiation of all for which they had sacrificed.

Finally, I said that the formidable foe we now faced demanded more unity than ever before and that I would stretch every point to maintain this unity, but that I could not in good conscience agree to continue my personal involvement and that of SCLC in the march if it were not publicly affirmed that it was based on nonviolence and the participation of both black and white. After a few more minutes of discussion Floyd and Stokely agreed that we could unite around these principles as far as the march was concerned. The next morning we had a joint press conference affirming that the march was nonviolent and that whites were welcomed.

As the days progressed, debates and discussions continued, but they were usually pushed to the background by the onrush of enthusiasm engendered by the large crowds that turned out to greet us in every town. We had been marching for about ten days when we pased through Grenada on the way to Greenwood. Stokely did not conceal his growing eagerness to reach Greenwood. This was SNCC territory, in the sense that the organization had worked courageously there during that turbulent summer of 1964.

As we approached the city, large crowds of old friends and new turned out to welcome us. At a huge mass meeting that night, which was held in a city park, Stokely mounted the platform and after arousing the audience with a powerful attack on Mississippi justice, he proclaimed:

"What we need is black power." Willie Ricks, the fiery orator of SNCC, leaped to the platform and shouted, "What do you want?" The crowd roared, "Black Power." Again and again Ricks cried, "What do you want?" and the response "Black Power" grew louder and louder, until it had reached fever pitch.

So Greenwood turned out to be the arena for the birth of the Black Power slogan in the civil rights movement. The phrase had been used long before by Richard Wright and others, but never until that night had it been used as a slogan in the civil rights movement. For people who had been crushed so long by white power and who had been taught that black was degrading, it had a ready appeal.

Immediately, however, I had reservations about its use. I had the deep feeling that it was an unfortunate choice of words for a slogan. Moreover, I saw it bringing about division within the ranks of the marchers. For a day or two there was fierce competition between those who were wedded to the Black Power slogan and those wedded to Freedom Now. Speakers on each side sought desperately to get the crowds to chant their slogan the loudest.

Sensing this widening split in our ranks, I asked Stokely and Floyd to join me in a frank discussion of the problem. We met the next morning, along with members of each of our staffs, in a small Catholic parish house in Yazoo City. For five long hours I pleaded with the group to abandon the Black Power slogan. It was my contention that a leader has to be concerned about the problem of semantics. Each word, I said, has a denotative meaning—its explicit and recognized sense—and a connotative meaning—its suggestive sense. While the concept of legitimate Black Power might be denotatively sound, the slogan "Black Power" carried the wrong connotations. I mentioned the implication of violence that the press had already attached to the phrase. And I went on to say that some of the rash statements on the part of a few marchers only reinforced this impression.

Stokely replied by saying that the question of violence versus nonviolence was irrelevant. The real question was the need for black people to consolidate their political and economic resources to achieve power. "Power," he said, "is the only thing respected in this world, and we must get it at any cost." Then he looked me squarely in the eye and said, "Martin, you know as well as I do that practically every other ethnic group in America has done just this. The Jews, the Irish and the Italians did it, why can't we?"

"That is just the point," I answered. "No one has ever heard the Jews publicly chant a slogan of Jewish power, but they have power. Through group unity, determination and creative endeavor, they have gained it. The same thing is true of the Irish and Italians. Neither group has used a slogan of Irish or Italian power, but they have worked hard to achieve it. This is exactly what we must do," I said. "We must use every constructive means to amass economic and political power. This is the kind of legitimate power we need. We must work to build racial pride and refute the notion that black is evil and ugly. But this must come through a program, not merely through a slogan."

Stokely and Floyd insisted that the slogan itself was important. "How can you arouse people to unite around a program without a slogan as a rallying cry? Didn't the labor movement have slogans? Haven't we had slogans all along in the freedom movement? What we need is a new slogan with 'black' in it."

I conceded the fact that we must have slogans. But why have one that would confuse our allies, isolate the Negro community and give many prejudiced whites, who might otherwise be ashamed of their anti-Negro feeling, a ready excuse for self-justification?

"Why not use the slogan 'black consciousness' or 'black equality'?" I suggested. "These phrases would be less vulnerable and would more accurately describe what we are about. The words 'black' and 'power' together give the impression that we are talking about black domination rather than black equality."

Stokely responded that neither would have the ready appeal and persuasive force of Black Power. Throughout the lengthy discussion, Stokely and Floyd remained adamant, and Stokely concluded by saying, with candor, "Martin, I deliberately decided to raise this issue on the march in order to give it a national forum, and force you to take a stand for Black Power."

I laughed. "I have been used before," I said to Stokely. "One more time won't hurt."

The meeting ended with the SCLC staff members still agreeing with me that the slogan was unfortunate and would only divert attention for the evils of Mississippi, while most CORE and SNCC staff members joined Stokely and Floyd in insisting that it should be projected nationally. In a final attempt to maintain unity I suggested that we compromise by not chanting either "Black Power" or "Freedom Now" for the rest of the march. In this way neither the people nor the press would be confused by the apparent conflict, and staff members would not appear to be at loggerheads. They all agreed with this compromise.

But while the chant died out, the press kept the debate going. News stories now centered, not on the injustices of Mississippi, but on the apparent ideological division in the civil rights movement. Every revolutionary movement has its peaks of united activity and its valleys of debate and internal confusion. This debate might well have been little more than a healthy internal difference of opinion, but the press loves the sensational and it could not allow the issue to remain within the private domain of the movement. In every drama there has to be an antagonist and a protagonist, and if the antagonist is not there the press will find and build one.

II

So Black Power is now a part of the nomenclature of the national community. To some it is abhorrent, to others dynamic; to some it is repugnant, to others exhilarating; to some it is destructive; to others it is useful. Since Black Power means different things to different people and indeed, being essentially an emotional concept, can mean different things to the same person on differing occasions, it is impossible to attribute its ultimate meaning to any single individual or organization. One must look beyond personal styles, verbal flourishes and the hysteria of the mass media to assess its values, its assets and liabilities honestly.

First, it is necessary to understand that Black Power is a cry of disappointment. The Black Power slogan did not spring full grown from the head of some philosophical Zeus. It was born from the wounds of despair and disappointment. It is a cry of daily hurt and persistent pain. For centuries the Negro has been caught in the tentacles of white power. Many Negroes have given up faith in the white majority because "white power" with total control has left them empty-handed. So in reality the call for Black Power is a reaction to the failure of white power.

It is no accident that the birth of this slogan in the civil rights movement took place in Mississippi—the state symbolizing the most blatant abuse of white power. In Mississippi the murder of civil rights workers is still a popular pastime. In that state more than forty Negroes and whites have either been lynched or murdered over the last three years, and not a single man has been punished for these crimes. More than fifty Negro churches have been burned or bombed in Mississippi in the last two years, yet the bombers still walk the streets surrounded by the halo of adoration.[1] This is white power in its most brutal, cold-blooded and vicious form.

Many of the young people proclaiming Black Power today were but yesterday the devotees of black-white cooperation and nonviolent direct action. With great sacrifice and dedication and a radiant faith in the future they labored courageously in the rural areas of the South; with idealism they accepted blows without retaliating; with dignity they allowed themselves to be plunged into filthy, stinking jail cells; with a majestic scorn for risk and danger they nonviolently confronted the Jim Clarks and the Bull Connors of the South, and exposed the disease of racism in the body politic. If they are America's angry children today, this anger is not congenital. It is a response to the feeling that a real solution is hopelessly distant because of the inconsistencies, resistance and faintheartedness of those in power. If Stokely Carmichael now says that nonviolence is irrelevant, it is because he, as a dedicated veteran of many battles, has seen with his own eyes the most brutal white violence against

---

Southern Regional Council, 1966.

Negroes and white civil rights workers, and he has seen it go unpunished.

Their frustration is further fed by the fact that even when blacks and whites die together in the cause of justice, the death of the white person gets more attention and concern than the death of the black person. Stokely and his colleagues from SNCC were with us in Alabama when Jimmy Lee Jackson, a brave young Negro man, was killed and when James Reeb, a committed Unitarian white minister, was fatally clubbed to the ground. They remembered how President Johnson sent flowers to the gallant Mrs. Reeb, and in his eloquent "We Shall Overcome" speech paused to mention that one person, James Reeb, had already died in the struggle. Somehow the president forgot to mention Jimmy, who died first. The parents and sister of Jimmy received no flowers from the president. The students felt this keenly. Not that they felt that the death of James Reeb was less than tragic, but because they felt that the failure to mention Jimmy Jackson only reinforced the impression that to white America the life of a Negro is insignificant and meaningless.

There is also great disappointment with the federal government and its timidity in implementing the civil rights laws on its statute books. The gap between promise and fulfillment is distressingly wide. Million of Negroes are frustrated and angered because extravagant promises made little more than a year ago are a mockery today. When the 1965 Voting Rights Law was signed, it was proclaimed as the dawn of freedom and the open door to opportunity. What was minimally required under the law was the appointment of hundreds of registrars and thousands of federal marshals to inhibit southern terror. Instead, fewer than sixty registrars were appointed and not a single federal law officer capable of making arrests was sent into the South. As a consequence the old way of life—economic coercion, terrorism, murder and inhuman contempt—has continued únabated. This gulf between the laws and their enforcement is one of the basic reasons why Black Power advocates express contempt for the legislative process.

The disappointment mounts as they turn their eyes to the North. In the northern ghettos, unemployment, housing discrimination and slum schools mock the Negro who tries to hope. There have been accomplishments and some material gain, but these beginnings have revealed how far we have yet to go. The economic plight of the masses of Negroes has worsened. The gap between the wages of the Negro worker and those of the white worker has widened. Slums are worse and Negroes attend more thoroughly segregated schools today than in 1954.

The Black Power advocates are disenchanted with the inconsistencies in the militaristic posture of our government. Over the last decade they have seen America applauding nonviolence whenever the Negroes have practiced it. They have watched it being praised in the sit-in movements of 1960, in the freedom rides of 1961, in the Albany movement of 1962, in the Birmingham movement of 1963 and in the Selma movement of 1965. But then these same black young men and women have watched as America sends black young men to burn Vietnamese with napalm, to slaughter men, women and children; and they wonder what kind of nation it is that applauds nonviolence whenever Negroes face white people in the streets of the United States but then applauds violence and burning and death when these same Negroes are sent to the fields of Vietnam.

All of this represents disappointment lifted to astronomical proportions. It is disappointment with timid white moderates who feel that they can set the timetable for the Negro's freedom. It is disappointment with a federal administration that seems to be more concerned about winning an ill-considered war in Vietnam than about winning the war against poverty here at home. It is disappointment with white legislators who pass laws in behalf of Negro rights that they never intended to implement. It is disappointment with the Christian church that appears to be more white than Christian, and with many white clergymen who prefer to remain silent behind the security of stained-glass windows. It is disappointment with some Negro clergymen who are more concerned about the size of the wheel base on their automobiles than about the quality of their service to the Negro community. It is disappointment with the Negro middle class that has sailed or struggled out of the muddy ponds into the relatively fresh-flowing waters of the mainstream, and in the process has forgotten the stench of the backwaters where their brothers are still drowning.

Second, Black Power, in its broad and positive meaning, is a call to black people to amass the political and economic strength to achieve their legitimate goals. No one can deny that the Negro is in dire need of this kind of legitimate power. Indeed, one of the great problems that the Negro confronts is his lack of power. From the old plantations of the South to the newer ghettos of the North, the Negro has been confined to a life of voicelessness and powerlessness. Stripped of the right to make decisions concerning his life and destiny, he has been subject to the authoritarian and sometimes whimsical decisions of the white power structure. The plantation and the ghetto were created by those who had power both to confine those who had no power and to perpetuate their powerlessness. The problem of transforming the ghetto is, therefore, a problem of power—a confrontation between the forces of power demanding change and the forces of power dedicated to preserving the status quo.

Power, properly understood, is the ability to achieve purpose. It is the strength required to bring about social, political or economic changes. In this sense power is not only desirable but necessary in order to implement the demands of love and justice. One of the greatest problems of history is that the concepts of love and power are usually contrasted as polar opposites. Love is identified with a resignation of power and power with a denial of love. It was this misinterpretation that caused Nietzsche, the philosopher of the "will to power," to reject the Christian concept of love. It was this same misinterpretation which induced Christian theologians to reject Nietzsche's philosophy of the "will to power" in the name of the Christian idea of love. What is needed is a realization that power without love is reckless and abusive and that love without power is sentimental and anemic. Power at its best is love implementing the demands of justice. Justice at its best is love correcting everything that stands against love.

There is nothing essentially wrong with power. The problem is that in America power is unequally distributed. This has led Negro Americans in the past to seek their goals through love and moral suasion devoid of power and white Americans to seek their goals through power devoid of love and conscience. It is leading a few extremists today to advocate for Negroes the same destructive and conscienceless power that they have justly abhorred in whites. It is precisely this collision of immoral power with powerless morality which constitutes the major crisis of our times.

In his struggle for racial justice, the Negro must seek to transform his condition of powerlessness into creative and positive power. One of the most obvious sources of this power is political. In *Why We Can't Wait*[2] I wrote at length of the need for Negroes to unite for political action in order to compel the majority to listen. I urged the development of political awareness and strength in the Negro community, the election of blacks to key positions, and the use of the bloc vote to liberalize the political climate and achieve our just aspirations for freedom and human dignity. To the extent that Black Power advocates these goals, it is a positive and legitimate call to action that we in the civil rights movement have sought to follow all along and which we must intensify in the future.

Black Power is also a call for the pooling of black financial resources to achieve economic security. While the ultimate answer to the Negroes' economic dilemma will be found in a massive federal program for all the poor along the lines of A. Philip Randolph's Freedom Budget, a kind of Marshall Plan for the disadvantaged, there is something that the Negro himself can do to throw off the shackles of poverty. Although the Negro is still at the bottom of the economic ladder, his collective annual income is upwards of $30 billion. This gives him a considerable buying power that can make the difference between profit and loss in many businesses.

---

2. Harper, 1964, pp. 162ff.

Through the pooling of such resources and the development of habits of thrift and techniques of wise investment, the Negro will be doing his share to grapple with his problem of economic deprivation. If Black Power means the development of this kind of strength within the Negro community, then it is a quest for basic, necessary, legitimate power.

Finally, Black Power is a psychological call to manhood. For years the Negro has been taught that he is nobody, that his color is a sign of his biological depravity, that his being has been stamped with an indelible imprint of inferiority, that his whole history has been soiled with the filth of worthlessness. All too few people realize how slavery and racial segregation have scarred the soul and wounded the spirit of the black man. The whole dirty business of slavery was based on the premise that the Negro was a thing to be used, not a person to be respected.

The historian Kenneth Stampp, in his remarkable book *The Peculiar Institution*[3], has a fascinating section on the psychological indoctrination that was necessary from the master's viewpoint to make a good slave. He gathered the material for this section primarily from the manuals and other documents which were produced by slaveowners on the subject of training slaves. Stampp notes five recurring aspects of this training.

First, those who managed the slaves had to maintain strict discipline. One master said, "Unconditional submission is the only footing upon which slavery should be placed." Another said, "The slave must know that his master is to govern absolutely and he is to obey implicitly, that he is never, for a moment, to exercise either his will or judgment in opposition to a positive order." Second, the masters felt that they had to implant in the bondsman a consciousness of personal inferiority. This sense of inferiority was deliberately extended to his past. The slaveowners were convinced that in order to control the Negroes, the slaves "had to feel that African ancestry tainted them, that their color was a badge of degradation." The third step in the training process was to awe the slaves with a sense of the masters' enormous power. It was necessary, various owners said, "to make them stand in fear." The fourth aspect was the attempt to "persuade the bondsman to take an interest in the master's enterprise and to accept his standards of good conduct." Thus the master's criteria of what was good and true and beautiful were to be accepted unquestioningly by the slaves. The final step, according to Stampp's documents, was "to impress Negroes with their helplessness: to create in them a habit of perfect dependence upon their masters."

Here, then, was the way to produce a perfect slave. Accustom him to rigid discipline, demand from him unconditional submission, impress

Knopf, 1956.

upon him a sense of his innate inferiority, develop in him a paralyzing fear of white men, train him to adopt the master's code of good behavior, and instill in him a sense of complete dependence.

Out of the soil of slavery came the psychological roots of the Black Power cry. Anyone familiar with the Black Power movement recognizes that defiance of white authority and white power is a constant theme; the defiance almost becomes a kind of taunt. Underneath it, however, there is a legitimate concern that the Negro break away from "unconditional submission" and thereby assert his own selfhood.

Another obvious reaction of Black Power to the American system of slavery is the determination to glory in blackness and to resurrect joyously the African past. In response to the emphasis on their masters' "enormous power," Black Power advocates contend that the Negro must develop his own sense of strength. No longer are "fear, awe and obedience" to rule. This accounts for, though it does not justify, some Black Power advocates who encourage contempt and even uncivil disobedience as alternatives to the old patterns of slavery. Black Power assumes that Negroes will be slaves unless there is a new power to counter the force of the men who are still determined to be masters rather than brothers.

It is in the context of the slave tradition that some of the ideologues of the Black Power movement call for the need to devleop new and indigenous codes of justice for the ghettos, so that blacks may move entirely away from their former masters' "standards of good conduct." Those in the Black Power movement who contend that blacks should cut themselves off from every level of dependence upon whites for advice, money or other help are obviously reacting against the slave pattern of "perfect dependence" upon the masters.

Black Power is a psychological reaction to the psychological indoctrination that led to the creation of the perfect slave. While this reaction has often led to negative and unrealistic responses and has frequently brought about intemperate words and actions, one must not overlook the positive value in calling the Negro to a new sense of manhood, to a deep feeling of racial pride and to an audacious appreciation of his heritage. The Negro must be grasped by a new realization of his dignity and worth. He must stand up amid a system that still oppressed him and develop an unassailable and majestic sense of his own value. He must no longer be ashamed of being black.

The job of arousing manhood within a people that have been taught for so many centuries that they are nobody is not easy. Even semantics have conspired to make that which is black seem ugly and degrading. In Roget's Thesaurus there are some 120 synonyms for "blackness" and at least sixty of them are offensive—such words as "blot," "soot," "grime," "devil," and "foul." There are some 134 synonyms for "whiteness," and all are favorable, expressed in such words as "purity," "cleanliness," "chastity," and "innocence." A white lie is better than a black lie. The most degenerate member of a family is the "black sheep," not the "white sheep." Ossie Davis has suggested that maybe the English language should be "reconstructed" so that teachers will not be forced to teach the Negro child sixty ways to despise himself and thereby perpetuate his false sense of inferiority and the white child 134 ways to adore himself and thereby perpetuate his false sense of superiority.

The history books, which have almost completely ignored the contribution of the Negro in American history, have only served to intensify the Negroes' sense of worthlessness and to augment the anachronistic doctrine of white supremacy. All too many Negroes and whites are unaware of the fact that the first American to shed blood in the revolution which freed this country from British oppression was a black seaman named Crispus Attucks. Negroes and whites are almost totally oblivious of the fact that it was a Negro physician, Dr. Daniel Hale Williams, who performed the first successful operation on the heart in America, and that another Negro physician, Dr. Charles Drew, was largely responsible for developing the method of separating blood plasma and storing it on a large scale, a process that saved thousands of lives in World War II and has made possible many of the important advances in postwar medicine. History books have virtually overlooked the many Negro scientists and inventors who have encircled American life. Although a few refer to George Washington Carver, whose research in agricultural products helped to revive the economy of the South when the throne of King Cotton began to totter, they ignore the contribution of Norbert Rillieux, whose invention of an evaporating pan revolutionized the process of sugar refining. How many people know that the mutimillion-dollar United Shoe Machinery Company developed from the shoe-lasting machine invented in the last century by a Negro from Dutch Guiana, Jan Matzeliger; or that Granville T. Woods, an expert in electric motors, whose many patents speeded the growth and improvement of the railroads at the beginning of this century, was a Negro?

Even the Negroes' contribution to the music of America is sometimes overlooked in astonishing ways. Two years ago my oldest son and daughter entered an integrated school in Atlanta. A few months later my wife and I were invited to attend a program entitled "music that has made America great." As the evening unfolded, we listened to the folk songs and melodies of the various immigrant groups. We were certain that the program would end with the most original of all American music, the Negro spiritual. But we were mistaken. Instead, all the students, including our children, ended the program by singing "Dixie."

As we rose to leave the hall, my wife and I looked at each other with a combination of indignation and amazement. All the students, black and white, all the parents present that night, and all the faculty members had been victimized by just another expression of America's penchant for ignoring the Negro, making him invisible and making his contributions insignificant. I wept within that night. I wept for my children and all black children who have been denied a knowledge of their heritage; I wept for all white children, who, through daily miseducation, are taught that the Negro is an irrelevant entity in American society; I wept for all the white parents and teachers who are forced to overlook the fact that the wealth of cultural and technological progress in America is a result of the commonwealth of inpouring contributions.

The tendency to ignore the Negro's contribution to American life and strip him of his personhood is as old as the earliest history books and as contemporary as the morning's newspaper. To offset this cultural homicide, the Negro must rise up with an affirmation of his own Olympian manhood. Any movement for the Negro's freedom that overlooks this necessity is only waiting to be buried. As long as the mind is enslaved the body can never be free. Psychological freedom, a firm sense of self-esteem, is the most powerful weapon against the long night of physical slavery. No Lincolnian emancipation proclamation or Kennedyan or Johnsonian civil rights bill can totally bring this kind of freedom. The Negro will only be truly free when he reaches down to the inner depths of his own being and signs with the pen and ink of assertive selfhood his own emancipation proclamation. With a spirit straining toward true self-esteem, the Negro must boldly throw off the manacles of self-abnegation and say to himself and the world: "I am somebody. I am a person. I am a man with dignity and honor. I have a rich and noble history, however painful and exploited that history has been. I am black *and* comely." This self-affirmation is the black man's need made compelling by the white man's crimes against him. This is positive and necessary power for black people.

III

Nevertheless, in spite of the positive aspects of Black Power, which are compatible with what we have sought to do in the civil rights movement all along without the slogan, its negative values, I believe, prevent it from having the substance and program to become the basic strategy for the civil rights movement in the days ahead.

Beneath all the satisfaction of a gratifying slogan, Black Power is a nihilistic philosophy born out of the conviction that the Negro can't win. It is, at bottom, the view that American society is so hopelessly corrupt and enmeshed in evil that there is no possibility of salvation from within. Although this thinking is understandable as a response to a white power structure that never completely committed itself to true equality for the Negro, and a die-hard mentality that sought to shut all windows and doors against the winds of change, it nonetheless carries the seeds of its own doom.

Before this century, virtually all revolutions had been based on hope and hate. The hope was expressed in the rising expectation of freedom and justice. The hate was an expression of bitterness toward the perpetrators of the old order. It was the hate that made revolutions bloody and violent. What was new about Mahatma Gandhi's movement in India was that he mounted a revolution on hope and love, hope and nonviolence. This same new emphasis characterized the civil rights movement in our country dating from the Montgomery bus boycott of 1956 to the Selma movement of 1965. We maintained the hope while transforming the hate of traditional revolutions into positive nonviolent power. As long as the hope was fulfilled there was little questioning of nonviolence. But when the hopes were blasted, when people came to see that in spite of progress their conditions were still insufferable, when they looked out and saw more poverty, more school segregaton and more slums, despair began to set in.

Unfortunately, when hope diminishes, the hate is often turned most bitterly toward those who originally built up the hope. In all the speaking that I have done in the United States before varied audiences, including some hostile whites, the only time that I have been booed was one night in a Chicago mass meeting by some young members of the Black Power movement. I went home that night with an ugly feeling. Selfishly I thought of my sufferings and sacrifices over the last twelve years. Why would they boo one so close to them? But as I lay awake thinking, I finally came to myself, and I could not for the life of me have less than patience and understanding for those young people. For twelve years I, and others like me, had held out radiant promises of progress. I had preached to them about my dream. I had lectured to them about the not too distant day when they would have freedom, "all, here and now." I had urged them to have faith in America and in white society. Their hopes had soared. They were now booing because they felt that we were unable to deliver on our promises. They were booing because we had urged them to have faith in people who had too often proved to be unfaithful. They were now hostile because they were watching the dream that they had so readily accepted turn into a frustrating nightmare.

But revolution, though born of despair, cannot long be sustained by despair. This is the ultimate contradiction of the Black Power movement. It claims to be the most revolutionary wing of the social revolution taking place in the United States. Yet it rejects the one thing that keeps the fire of revolutions burning: the ever-present flame of hope. When hope dies, a revolution degenerates into an undiscriminating catchall for evanescent and futile gestures. The Negro cannot entrust his destiny to a philosophy nourished solely on despair, to a slogan that cannot be implemented into a program.

The Negro's disappointment is real and a part of the daily menu of our lives. One of the most agonizing problems of human experience is how to deal with disappointment. In our individual lives we all too often distill our frustrations into an essence of bitterness, or drown ourselves in the deep waters of self-pity, or adopt a fatalistic philosophy that whatever happens must happen and all events are determined by necessity. These reactions poison the soul and scar the personality, always harming the person who harbors them more than anyone else. The only healthy answer lies in one's honest recognition of disappointment even as he still clings to hope, one's acceptance of finite disappointment even while clinging to infinite hope.

We Negroes, who have dreamed for so long of freedom, are still confined in a prison of segregation and discrimination. Must we respond with bitterness and cynicism? Certainly not, for this can lead to black anger so desperate that it ends in black suicide. Must we turn inward in self-pity? Of course not, for this can lead to a self-defeating black paranoia. Must we conclude that we cannot win? Certainly not, for this can lead to black nihilism that seeks disruption for disruption's sake. Must we, by fatalistically concluding that segregation is a foreordained pattern of the universe, resign ourselves to oppression? Of course not, for passively to cooperate with an unjust system makes the oppressed as evil as the oppressors. Our most fruitful course is to stand firm, move forward nonviolently, accept disappointments and cling to hope. Our determined refusal not to be stopped will eventually open the door to fulfillment. By recognizing the necessity of suffering in a righteous cause, we may achieve our humanity's full stature. To guard ourselves from bitterness, we need the vision to see in this generation's ordeals the opportunity to transfigure both ourselves and American society.

In 1956 I flew from New York to London in the propeller-type aircraft that required nine and a half hours for a flight now made in six hours by jet. Returning from London to the United States, the stewardess announced that the flying time would be twelve and a half hours. The distance was the same. Why an additional three hours? When the pilot entered the cabin to greet the passengers, I asked him to explain.

"You must understand about the winds," he said. "When we leave New York, a strong tail wind is in our favor, but when we return, a strong head wind is against us." Then he added, "Don't worry. These four engines are capable of battling the winds."

In any social revolution there are times when the tail winds of triumph and fulfillment favor us, and other times when strong head winds of disappointment and setbacks beat against us relentlessly. We must not permit adverse winds to overwhelm us as we journey across life's mighty Atlantic; we must be sustained by our engines of courage in spite of the winds. This refusal to be stopped, this "courage to be," this determination to go on "in spite of" is the hallmark of any great movement.

The Black Power movement of today, like the Garvey "Back to Africa" movement of the 1920s, represents a dashing of hope, a conviction of the inability of the Negro to win and a belief in the infinitude of the ghetto. While there is much grounding in past experience for all these feelings, a revolution cannot succumb to any of them. Today's despair is a poor chisel to carve out tomorrow's justice.

Black Power is an implicit and often explicit belief in black separatism. Notice that I do not call it black racism. It is inaccurate to refer to Black Power as racism in reverse, as some have recently done. Racism is a doctrine of the congenital inferiority and worthlessness of a people. While a few angry proponents of Black Power have, in moments of bitterness, made wild statements that come close to this kind of racism, the major proponents of Black Power have never contended that the white man is innately worthless.

Yet behind Black Power's legitimate and necessary concern for group unity and black identity lies the belief that there can be a separate black road to power and fulfillment. Few ideas are more unrealistic. There is no salvation for the Negro through isolation.

One of the chief affirmations of Black Power is the call for the mobilization of political strength for black people. But we do not have to look far to see that effective political power for Negroes cannot come through separatism. Granted that there are cities and counties in the country where the Negro is in a majority, there are so few that concentration on them alone would still leave the vast majority of Negroes outside the mainstream of American political life.

Out of the eighty-odd counties in Alabama, the state where SNCC sought to develop an all-black party, only nine have a majority of Negroes. Even if blacks could control each of these counties, they would have little influence in overall state politics and could do little to improve conditions in the major Negro population centers of Birmingham, Mobile and Montgomery. There are still relatively few congressional districts in the South that have such large black majorities that Negro candidates could be elected without the aid of whites. Is it a sounder program to concentrate on the election of two or three Negro congressmen from predominantly Negro districts or to concentrate on the election of fifteen or twenty Negro congressmen from southern districts where a coalition of Negro and white moderate voters is possible?

Moreover, any program that elects all black candidates simply because they are black and rejects all white candidates simply because they are white is politically unsound and morally unjustifiable. It is true that in many areas of the South Negroes still must elect Negroes in order to be effectively represented. SNCC staff members are eminently correct when they point out that in Lowndes County, Alabama, there are no white liberals or moderates and no possibility for cooperation between the races at the present time. But the Lowndes County experience cannot be made a measuring rod for the whole of America. The basic thing in determining the best candidate is not his color but his integrity.

Black Power alone is no more insurance against social injustice than white power. Negro politicians can be as opportunistic as their white counterparts if there is not an informed and determined constituency demanding social reform. What is most needed is a coalition of Negroes and liberal whites that will work to make both major parties truly responsive to the needs of the poor. Black Power does not envision or desire such a program.

Just as the Negro cannot achieve political power in isolation, neither can he gain economic power thorugh separatism. While there must be a continued emphasis on the need for blacks to pool their economic resources and withdraw consumer support from discriminating firms, we must not be oblivious to the fact that the larger economic problems confronting the Negro community will only be solved by federal programs involving billions of dollars. One unfortunate thing about Black Power is that it gives priority to race precisely at a time when the impact of automation and other forces have made the economic question fundamental for blacks and whites alike. In this context a slogan "Power for Poor People" would be much more appropriate than the slogan "Black Power."

However much we pool our resources and "buy black," this cannot create the multiplicity of new jobs and provide the number of low-cost houses that will lift the Negro out of the economic depression caused by centuries of deprivation. Neither can our resources supply quality integrated education. All of this requires billions of dollars which only an alliance of liberal-labor-civil-rights forces can stimulate. In short, the Negroes' problem cannot be solved unless the whole of American society takes a new turn toward greater economic justice.

In a multiracial society no group can make it alone. It is a myth to believe that the Irish, the Italians and the Jews—the ethnic groups that Black Power advocates cite as justification for their views—rose to power through separatism. It is true that they stuck together. But their group unity was always enlarged by joining in alliances with other groups such as political machines and trade unions. To succeed in a pluralistic society, and an often hostile one at that, the Negro obviously needs organized strength, but that strength will only be effective when it is consolidated through constructive alliances with the majority group.

Those proponents of Black Power who have urged Negroes to shun alliances with whites argue that whites as a group cannot have a genuine concern for Negro progress. Therefore, they claim, the white man's main interest in collaborative effort is to diminish Negro militancy and deflect it from constructive goals.

Undeniably there are white elements that cannot be trusted, and no militant movement can afford to relax its vigilance against halfhearted associates or conscious betrayers. Every alliance must be considered on its own merits. Negroes may embrace some and walk out on others where their interests are imperiled. Occasional betrayals, however, do not justify the rejection of the principle of Negro-white alliance.

The oppression of Negroes by whites has left an understandable residue of suspicion. Some of this suspicion is a healthy and appropriate safeguard. An excess of skepticism, however, becomes a fetter. It denies that there can be reliable white allies, even though some whites have died heroically at the side of Negroes in our struggle and others have risked economic and political peril to support our cause.

The history of the movement reveals that Negro-white alliances have played a powerfully constructive role, especially in recent years. While Negro initiative, courage and imagination precipitated the Birmingham and Selma confrontations and revealed the harrowing injustice of segregated life, the organized strength of Negroes alone would have been insufficient to move Congress and the administration without the weight of the aroused conscience of white America. In the period ahead Negroes will continue to need this support. Ten percent of the population cannot by tensions alone induce ninety percent to change a way of life.

Within the white majority there exists a substantial group who cherish democratic principles above privilege and who have demonstrated a will to fight side by side with the Negro against injustice. Another and more substantial group is composed of those having common needs with the Negro and who will benefit equally with him in the achievement of social progress. There are, in fact, more poor white Americans than there are Negro. Their need for a war on poverty is no less desperate than the Negro's. In the South they have been deluded by race prejudice and largely remained aloof from common action. Ironically, with this posture they were fighting not only the Negro but themselves. Yet there are already signs of change. Without formal alliances, Negroes and whites have supported the same candidates in many *de facto* electoral coalitions in the South because each sufficiently served his own needs.

The ability of Negroes to enter alliances is a mark of our growing strength, not of our weakness. In entering an alliance, the Negro is not relying on white leadership or ideology; he is taking his place as an equal partner in a common endeavor. His organized strength and his new independence pave the way for alliances. Far from losing independence in an alliance, he is using it for constructive and multiplied gains.

Negroes must shun the very narrow-mindedness that in others has so long been the source of our own afflictions. We have reached the stage of organized strength and independence to work securely in alliances. History has demonstrated with major victories the effectiveness, wisdom and moral soundness of Negro-white alliance. The cooperation of Negro and white based on the solid ground of honest conscience and proper self-interest can continue to grow in scope and influence. It can attain the strength to alter basic institutions by democratic means. Negro isolation can never approach this goal.

In the final analysis the weakness of Black Power is its failure to see that the black man needs the white man and the white man needs the black man. However much we may try to romanticize the slogan, there is no separate black path to power and fulfillment that does not intersect white paths, and there is no separate white path to power and fulfillment, short of social disaster, that does not share that power with black aspirations for freedom and human dignity. We are bound together in a single garment of destiny. The language, the cultural patterns, the music, the material prosperity and even the food of America are an amalgam of black and white.

James Baldwin once related how he returned home from school and his mother asked him whether his teacher was colored or white. After a pause he answered: "She is a little bit colored and a little bit white."[4] This is the dilemma of being a Negro in America. In physical as well as cultural terms every Negro is a little bit colored and a little bit white. In our search for identity we must recognize this dilemma.

Every man must ultimately confront the question "Who am I?" and seek to answer it honestly. One of the first principles of personal adjustment is the principle of self-acceptance. The Negro's greatest dilemma is that in order to be healthy he must accept his ambivalence. The Negro is the child of two cultures—Africa and America. The problem is that in the search for wholeness all too many Negroes seek to embrace only one side of their natures. Some, seeking to reject their heritage, are ashamed of their color, ashamed of black art and music, and determine what is beautiful and good by the standards of white society. They end up frustrated and without cultural roots. Others seek to reject everything American and to identify totally with Africa, even to the point of wearing African clothes. But this approach leads also to frustration because the American Negro is not an African. The old Hegelian synthesis still offers the best answer to many of life's dilemmas. The American Negro is neither totally African nor totally Western. He is Afro-American, a true hybrid, a combination of two cultures.

Who are we? We are the descendants of slaves. We are the offspring of noble men and women who were kidnapped from their native land and chained in ships like beasts. We are the heirs of a great and exploited continent known as Africa. We are the heirs of a past of rope, fire and murder. I for one am not ashamed of this past. My shame is for those who became so inhuman that they could inflict this torture upon us.

But we are also Americans. Abused and scorned though we may be, our destiny is tied up with the destiny of America. In spite of the psychological appeals of identification with Africa, the Negro must face the fact that America is now his home, a home that he helped to build through "blood, sweat and tears." Since we are Americans the solution

---

4. In *The Negro Protest*, Kenneth B. Clark (ed.), Beacon, 1963.

to our problem will not come through seeking to build a separate black nation within a nation, but by finding that creative minority of the concerned from the ofttimes apathetic majority, and together moving toward that colorless power that we all need for security and justice.

In the first century B.C., Cicero said: "Freedom is participation in power." Negroes should never want all power because they would deprive others of their freedom. By the same token, Negroes can never be content without participation in power. America must be a nation in which its multiracial people are partners in power. This is the essence of democracy toward which all Negro struggles have been directed since the distant past when he was transplanted here in chains.

Probably the most destructive feature of Black Power is its unconscious and often conscious call for retaliatory violence. Many well-meaning persons within the movement rationalize that Black Power does not really mean black violence, that those who shout the slogan don't really mean it that way, the the violent connotations are solely the distortions of a vicious press. That the press has fueled the fire is true. But as one who has worked and talked intimately with devotees of Black Power, I must admit that the slogan is mainly used by persons who have lost faith in the method and philosophy of nonviolence. I must make it clear that no guilt by association is intended. Both Floyd McKissick and Stokely Carmichael have declared themselves opponents of aggressive violence. This clarification is welcome and useful, despite the persistence of some of their followers in examining the uses of violence.

Over cups of coffee in my home in Atlanta and my apartment in Chicago, I have often talked late at night and over into the small hours of the morning with the proponents of Black Power who argued passionately about the validity of violence and riots. They don't quote Gandhi or Tolstoy. Their bible is Frantz Fanon's *The Wretched of the Earth*.[5] This black psychiatrist from Martinique, who went to Algeria to work with the National Liberation Front in its fight against the French, argues in his book—a well-written book, incidentally, with many penetrating insights—that violence is a psychologically healthy and tactically sound method for the oppressed. And so, realizing that they are a part of that vast company of the "wretched of the earth," these young American Negroes, who are predominantly involved in the Black Power movement, often quote Fanon's belief that violence is the only thing that will bring about liberation. As they say, "Sing us no songs of nonviolence, sing us no songs of progress, for nonviolence and progress belong to middle-class Negroes and whites and we are not interested in you."

As we have seen, the first public expression of disenchantment with nonviolence arose around the question of "self-defense." In a sense this

_____
5. Evergreen, 1966.

is a false issue, for the right to defend one's home and one's person when attacked has been guaranteed through the ages by common law. In a nonviolent demonstration, however, self-defense must be approached from another perspective.

The cause of a demonstration is the existence of some form of exploitation or oppression that has made it necessary for men of courage and good will to protest the evil. For example, a demonstration against *de facto* school segregation is based on the awareness that a child's mind is crippled by inadequate educational opportunities. The demonstrator agrees that it is better to suffer publicly for a short time to end the crippling evil of school segregation than to have generation after generation of children suffer in ignorance. In such a demonstration the point is made that the schools are inadequate. This is the evil one seeks to dramatize; anything else distracts from that point and interferes with the confrontation of the primary evil. Of course no one wants to suffer and be hurt. But it is more important to get at the cause than to be safe. It is better to shed a little blood from a blow on the head or a rock thrown by an angry mob than to have children by the thousands finishing high school who can only read at a sixth-grade level.

Furthermore, it is dangerous to organize a movement around self-defense. The line of demarcation between defensive violence and aggressive violence is very thin. The minute a program of violence is enunciated, even for self-defense, the atmosphere is filled with talk of violence, and the words falling on unsophisticated ears may be interpreted as an invitation to aggression.

One of the main questions that the Negro must confront in his pursuit of freedom is that of effectiveness. What is the most effective way to achieve the desired goal? If a method is not effective, no matter how much steam it releases, it is an expression of weakness, not of strength. Now the plain, inexorable fact is that any attempt of the American Negro to overthrow his oppressor with violence will not work. We do not need President Johnson to tell us this by reminding Negro rioters that they are outnumbered ten to one. The courageous efforts of our own insurrectionist brothers, such as Denmark Vesey and Nat Turner, should be eternal reminders to us that violent rebellion is doomed from the start. In violent warfare one must be prepared to face the fact that there will be casualties by the thousands. Anyone leading a violent rebellion must be willing to make an honest assessment regarding the possible casualties to a minority population confronting a well-armed, wealthy majority with a fanatical right wing that would delight in exterminating thousands of black men, women and children.

Arguments that the American Negro is a part of a world which is two-thirds colored and that there will come a day when the oppressed people of color will violently rise together to throw off the yoke of white oppression are beyond the realm of serious discussion. There is no colored nation, including China, that now shows even the potential of leading a violent revolution of color in any international proportions. Ghana, Zambia, Tanganyika and Nigeria are so busy fighting their own battles against povery, illiteracy and the subversive influence of neocolonialism that they offer little hope to Angola, Southern Rhodesia and South Africa, much less to the American Negro. The hard cold facts today indicate that the hope of the people of color in the world may well rest on the American Negro and his inability to reform the structure of racist imperialism from within and thereby turn the technology and wealth of the West to the task of liberating the world from want.

The futility of violence in the struggle for racial justice has been tragically etched in all the recent Negro riots. There is something painfully sad about a riot. One sees screaming youngsters and angry adults fighting hopelessly and aimlessly against impossible odds. Deep down within them you perceive a desire for self-destruction, a suicidal longing. Occasionally Negroes contend that the 1965 Watts riot and other riots in various cities represented effective civil rights action. But those who express this view always end up with stumbling words when asked what concrete gains have been won as a result. At best the riots have produced a little additional antipoverty money, alloted by frightened government officials, and a few water sprinklers to cool the children of the ghettos. It is something like improving the food in a prison while the people remain securely incarcerated behind bars. Nowhere have the riots won any concrete improvement such as have the organized protest demonstrations.

It is not overlooking the limitations of nonviolence and the distance we have yet to go to point out the remarkable record of achievements that have already come through nonviolent action. The 1960 sit-ins desegregated lunch counters in more than 150 cities within a year. The 1961 freedom rides put an end to segregation in interstate travel. The 1956 bus boycott in Montgomery, Alabama, ended segregation on the buses not only of that city but in practically every city of the South. The 1963 Birmingham movement and the climactic March on Washington won passage of the most powerful civil rights law in a century. The 1965 Selma movement brought enactment of the Voting Rights Law. Our nonviolent marches in Chicago last summer brought about a housing agreement which, if implemented, will be the strongest step toward open housing taken in any city in the nation. Most significant is the fact that this progress occurred with minimum human sacrifice and loss of life. Fewer people have been killed in ten years of nonviolent demonstrations across the South than were killed in one night of rioting in Watts.

When one tries to pin down advocates of violence as to what acts would be effective, the answers are blatantly illogical. Sometimes they talk of overthrowing racist state and local governments. They fail to see that no internal revolution has ever succeeded in overthrowing a government by violence unless the government has already lost the allegiance and effective control of its armed forces. Anyone in his right mind knows that this will not happen in the United States. In a violent racial situation, the power structure has the local police, the state troopers, the national guard and finally the army to call on, all of which are predominantly white.

Furthermore, few if any violent revolutions have been successful unless the violent minority had the sympathy and support of the nonresisting majority. Castro may have had only a few Cubans actually fighting with him, but he would never have overthrown the Batista regime unless he had had the sympathy of the vast majority of the Cuban people. It is perfectly clear that a violent revolution on the part of American blacks would find no sympathy and support from the white population and very little from the majority of the Negroes themselves.

This is no time for romantic illusions and empty philosophical debates about freedom. This is a time for action. What is needed is a strategy for change, a tactical program that will bring the Negro into the mainstream of American life as quickly as possible. So far, this has only been offered by the nonviolent movement. Without recognizing this we will end up with solutions that don't solve, answers that don't answer and explanations that don't explain.

Beyond the pragmatic invalidity of violence is its inability to appeal to conscience. Some Black Power advocates consider an appeal to conscience irrelevant. A Black Power exponent said to me not long ago: "To hell with conscience and morality. We want power." But power and morality must go together, implementing, fulfilling and ennobling each other. In the quest for power I cannot bypass the concern for morality. I refuse to be driven to a Machiavellian cynicism with respect to power. Power at its best is the right use of strength. The words of Alfred the Great are still true: "Power is never good unless he who has it is good."

Nonviolence is power, but it is the right and good use of power. Constructively it can save the white man as well as the Negro. Racial segregation is buttressed by such irrational fears as loss of preferred economic privilege, altered social status, intermarriage and adjustment to new situations. Through sleepless nights and haggard days numerous white people struggle pitifully to combat these fears. By following the path of escape, some seek to ignore the questions of race relations and to close their minds to the issues involved. Others, placing their faith in legal maneuvers, counsel massive resistance. Still others hope to drown their fears by engaging in acts of meanness and violence toward their Negro brethren. But how futile are all these remedies! Instead of eliminating fear, they instill deeper and more pathological fears. The white man, through his own efforts, through education and goodwill, through searching his conscience and through confronting the fact of integration, must do a great deal to free himself of these paralyzing fears. But to master fear he must also depend on the spirit the Negro generates toward him. Only through our adherence to nonviolence—which also means love in its strong and commanding sense—will the fear in the white community be mitigated.

A guilt-ridden white minority fears that if the Negro attains power, he will without restraint or pity act to revenge the accumulated injustices and brutality of the years. The Negro must show that the white man has nothing to fear, for the Negro is willing to forgive. A mass movement exercising nonviolence and demonstrating power under discipline should convince the white community that as such a movement attained strength, its power would be used creatively and not for revenge.

In a moving letter to his nephew on the one hundredth anniversary of emancipation, James Baldwin wrote concerning white people:

The really terrible thing, old buddy, is that *you* must accept *them*. And I mean that very seriously. You must accept them and accept them with love. For these innocent people have no other hope. They are, in effect, still trapped in a history which they do not understand; and until they understand it, they cannot be released from it. They have had to believe for many years, and for innumerable reasons, that black men are inferior to white men. Many of them, indeed, know better, but, as you will discover, people find it very difficult to act on what they know. To act is to be committed, and to be committed is to be in danger. In this case, the danger, in the minds of most white Americans, is the loss of their identity. . . . But these men are your brothers—your lost, younger brothers. And if the word *integration* means anything, this is what it means: that we, with love, shall force our brothers to see themselves as they are, to cease fleeing from reality and begin to change it. . . . [6]

The problem with hatred and violence is that they intensify the fears of the white majority, and leave them less ashamed of their prejudices toward Negroes. In the guilt and confusion confronting our society, violence only adds to the chaos. It deepens the brutality of the oppressor and increases the bitterness of the oppressed. Violence is the antithesis of creativity and wholeness. It destroys community and makes brotherhood impossible.

My friend John Killens recently wrote in the *Negro Digest*: "Integration comes after liberation. A slave cannot integrate with his master. In the whole history of revolts and revolutions, integration has never been the main slogan of the revolution. The oppressed fights to free himself

6. *The Fire Next Time*, Dial, 1963, pp. 22–23.

from his oppressor, not to integrate with him. Integration is the step after freedom when the freedman makes up his mind as to whether he wishes to integrate with his former master."[7]

At first glance this sounds very good. But after reflection one has to face some inescapable facts about the Negro and American life. This is a multiracial nation where all groups are dependent on each other, whether they want to recognize it or not. In this vast interdependent nation no racial group can retreat to an island entire of itself. The phenomena of integration and liberation cannot be as neatly divided as Killens would have it.

There is no theoretical or sociological divorce between liberation and integration. In our kind of society liberation cannot come without integration and integration cannot come without liberation. I speak here of integration in both the ethical and the political senses. On the one hand, integration is true intergroup, interpersonal living. On the other hand, it is the mutual sharing of power. I cannot see how the Negro will be totally liberated from the crushing weight of poor education, squalid housing and economic strangulation until he is integrated, with power, into every level of American life.

Mr. Killens's assertion might have some validity in a struggle for independence against a foreign invader. But the Negro's struggle in America is quite different from and more difficult than the struggle for independence. The American Negro will be living tomorrow with the very people against whom he is struggling today. The American Negro is not in a Congo where the Belgians will go back to Belgium after the battle is over, or in an India where the British will go back to England after independence is won. In the struggle for national independence one can talk about liberation now and integration later, but in the struggle for racial justice in a multiracial society where the oppressor and the oppressed are both "at home," liberation must come through integration.

Are we seeking power for power's sake? Or are we seeking to make the world and our nation better places to live. If we seek the latter, violence can never provide the answer. The ultimate weakness of violence is that it is a descending spiral, begetting the very thing it seeks to destroy. Instead of diminishing evil, it multiplies it. Through violence you may murder the liar, but you cannot murder the lie, nor establish the truth. Through violence you may murder the hater, but you do not murder hate. In fact, violence merely increases hate. So it goes. Returning violence for violence multiplies violence, adding deeper darkness to a night already devoid of stars. Darkness cannot drive out darkness: only light can do that. Hate cannot drive out hate: only love can do that.

The beauty of nonviolence is that in its own way and in its own time it seeks to break the chain reaction of evil. With a majestic sense of spiritu-

---

7. November 1966.

al power, it seeks to elevate truth, beauty and goodness to the throne. Therefore I will continue to follow this method because I think it is the most practically sound and morally excellent way for the Negro to achieve freedom.

IV

In recent months several people have said to me: "Since violence is the new cry, isn't there a danger that you will lose touch with the people in the ghetto and be out of step with the times if you don't change your views on nonviolence?"

My answer is always the same. While I am convinced the vast majority of Negroes reject violence, even if they did not I would not be interested in being a consensus leader. I refuse to determine what is right by taking a Gallup poll of the trends of the time. I imagine that there were leaders in Germany who sincerely opposed what Hitler was doing to the Jews. But they took their poll and discovered that anti-Semitism was the prevailing trend. In order to "be in step with the times," in order to "keep in touch," they yielded to one of the most ignominious evils that history has ever known.

Ultimately a genuine leader is not a searcher for consensus but a molder of consensus. I said on one occasion, "If every Negro in the United States turns to violence, I will choose to be that one lone voice preaching that this is the wrong way." Maybe this sounded like arrogance. But it was not intended that way. It was simply my way of saying that I would rather be a man of conviction than a man of conformity. Occasionally in life one develops a conviction so precious and meaningful that he will stand on it til the end. This is what I have found in nonviolence.

One of the greatest paradoxes of the Black Power movement is that it talks unceasingly about not imitating the values of white society, but in advocating violence it is imitating the worst, the most brutal and the most uncivilized value of American life. American Negroes have not been mass murderers. They have not murdered children in Sunday school, nor have they hung white men on trees bearing strange fruit. They have not been hooded perpetrators of violence, lynching human beings at will and drowning them at whim.

This is not to imply that the Negro is a saint who abhors violence. Unfortunately, a check of the hospitals in any Negro community on any Saturday night will make you painfully aware of the violence within the Negro community. By turning his hostility and frustration with the larger society inward, the Negro often inflicts terrible acts of violence on his own black brother. This tragic problem must be solved. But I would not advise Negroes to solve the problem by turning these inner hostilities outward through the murdering of whites. This would substitute one evil for another. Nonviolence provides a healthy way to deal with understandable anger.

I am concerned that Negroes achieve full status as citizens and as human beings here in the United States. But I am also concerned about our moral uprightness and the health of our souls. Therefore I must oppose any attempt to gain our freedom by the methods of malice, hate and violence that have characterized our oppressors. Hate is just as injurious to the hater as it is to the hated. Like an unchecked cancer, hate corrodes the personality and eats away its vital unity. Many of our inner conflicts are rooted in hate. This is why the psychiatrists say, "Love or perish." I have seen hate expressed in the countenances of too many Mississippi and Alabama sheriffs to advise the Negro to sink to this miserable level. Hate is too great a burden to bear.

Of course, you may say, this is not *practical*; life is a matter of getting even, of hitting back, of dog eat dog. Maybe in some distant utopia, you say, that idea will work, but not in the hard, cold world in which we live. My only answer is that mankind has followed the so-called practical way for a long time now, and it has led inexorably to deeper confusion and chaos. Time is cluttered with the wreckage of individuals and communities that surrendered to hatred and violence. For the salvation of our nation and the salvation of mankind, we must follow another way. This does not mean that we abandon our militant efforts. With every ounce of our energy we must continue to rid our nation of the incubus of racial injustice. But we need not in the process relinquish our privilege and obligation to love.

Fanon says at the end of *The Wretched of the Earth*:

So, comrades, let us not pay tribute to Europe by creating states, institutions and societies which draw their inspiration from her.

Humanity is waiting for something other from us than such an imitation, which would be almost an obscene caricature.

If we want to turn Africa into a new Europe, and America into a new Europe, then let us leave the destiny of our countries to Europeans. They will know how to do it better than the most gifted among us.

But if we want humanity to advance a step further, if we want to bring it up to a different level than that which Europe has shown it, then we must invent and we must make discoveries.

If we wish to live up to our peoples' expectations, we must seek the response elsewhere than in Europe.

Moreover, if we wish to reply to the expectations of the people of Europe, it is no good sending them back a reflection, even an ideal reflection, of their society and their thought with which from time to time they feel immeasurably sickened.

For Europe, for ourselves and for humanity, comrades, we must turn over a new leaf, we must work out new concepts, and try to set afoot a new man.[8]

These are brave and challenging words; I am happy that young black men and women are quoting them. But the problem is that Fanon and

8. *Op cit.*, p. 255.

those who quote his words are seeking "to work out new concepts" and
"set afoot a new man" with a willingness to imitate old copies of violence. Is there not a basic contradiction here? Violence has been the inseparable twin of materialism, the hallmark of its grandeur and misery.
This is the one thing about modern civilization that I do not care to
imitate.

Humanity is waiting for something other than blind imitation of the
past. If we want truly to advance a step further, if we want to turn over a
new leaf and really set a new man afoot, we must begin to turn mankind
away from the long and desolate night of violence. May it not be that
the new man the world needs is the nonviolent man? Longfellow said,
"In this world a man must either be an anvil or a hammer." We must be
hammers shaping a new society rather than anvils molded by the old.
This not only will make us new men, but will give us a new kind of power. It will not be Lord Acton's image of power that tends to corrupt or
absolute power that corrupts absolutely. It will be power infused with
love and justice, that will change dark yesterdays into bright tomorrows,
and lift us from the fatigue of despair to the buoyancy of hope. A dark,
desperate, confused and sin-sick world waits for this new kind of man
and this new kind of power.

## WHERE WE ARE GOING (CHAPTER 5)

As the administration has manifested a faltering and fluctuating interest in civil rights during the past year, a flood of words rather than deeds
has inundated the dry desert of expectations.

One curious explanation of the defaults of the government warrants
analysis, because it reveals, without intention, the disadvantages under
which the civil rights movement has labored. After describing the obvious—the president's overwhelming preoccupation with the war in Vietnam—it then argues that in 1965 the president was prepared to implement measures leading to full equality but waited in vain for the civil
rights movement to offer the programs. The movement is depicted as
absorbed in controversy, confused in direction, venal toward its friends
and in such turmoil it has tragically lost its golden opportunity to attain
change today.

This argument, by explaining everything in terms of the presence or
absence of programs, illuminates how the insistence on programs can be
used as a sophisticated device to evade action. Actually there was no
dearth of programs in 1965, ranging from my own proposal, published
in 1965, for a bill of rights for the disadvantaged, to elaborate and detailed programs in the published material of many agencies, organizations and individual social scientists. If there had been a sincere disposition seriously to entertain a program, its preparation in final form
would have taken but a few weeks. If the federal government had been

consumed with fervor to strike an effective blow for civil rights, it need only have begun implementing all the existing laws that are a nullity from one end of the country to the other.

Underneath the invitation to prepare programs is the premise that the government is inherently benevolent—it only awaits presentation of imaginative ideas. When these issue from fertile minds, they will be accepted, enacted and implemented. This premise shifts the burden of responsibility from the white majority, by pretending it is withholding nothing, and places it on the oppressed minority, by pretending the latter is asking for nothing. This is a fable, not a fact. Neither our government nor any government that has sanctioned a century of denial can be depicted as ardent and impatient to bestow gifts of freedom.

When a people are mired in oppression, they realize deliverance when they have accumulated the power to enforce change. When they have amassed such strength, the writing of a program becomes almost an administrative detail. It is immaterial who presents the program; what is material is the presence of an ability to make events happen. The powerful never lose opportunities—they remain available to them. The powerless, on the other hand, never experience opportunity—it is always arriving at a later time.

The deeper truth is that the call to prepare programs distracts us excessively from our basic and primary tasks. If we are seeking a home, there is not much value in discussing blueprints if we have no money and are barred from acquiring the land. We are, in fact, being counseled to put the cart before the horse. We have to put the horse (power) before the cart (programs).

Our nettlesome task is to discover how to organize our strength into compelling power so that government cannot elude our demands. We must develop, from strength, a situation in which the government finds it wise and prudent to collaborate with us. It would be the height of naivete to wait passively until the administration had somehow been infused with such blessings of good will that it implored us for our programs. The first course is grounded in mature realism; the other is childish fantasy.

We do need certain general programs for the movement, but not for use as supplicants. We require programs to hold up to our followers which mirror their aspirations. In this fashion our goals are dramatized and our supporters are inspired to action and to deeper moral commitment.

We must frankly acknowledge that in past years our creativity and imagination were not employed in learning how to develop power. We found a method in nonviolent protest that worked, and we employed it enthusiastically. We did not have leisure to probe for a deeper understanding of its laws and lines of development. Although our actions were bold and crowned with success, they were substantially improvised and spontaneous. They attained the goals set for them but carried the blemishes of our inexperience.

When a new dawn reveals a landscape dotted with obstacles, the time has come for sober reflection, for assessment of our methods and for anticipating pitfalls. Stumbling and groping through the wilderness finally must be replaced by a planned, organized and orderly march.

None of us can pretend that he knows all the answers. It is enormously difficult for any oppressed people even to arrive at an awareness of their latent strengths. They are not only buffeted by defeats, but they have been schooled assiduously to believe in their lack of capacity. People struggling from the depths of society have not been equipped with knowledge of the science of social change. Only when they break out of the fog of self-denigration can they begin to discover the forms of action that influence events. They can then embark on social experimentation with their own strengths to generate the kind of power that shapes basic decisions.

This is where the civil rights movement stands today. We will err and falter as we climb the unfamiliar slopes of steep mountains, but there is no alternative, well-trod, level path. There will be agonizing setbacks along with creative advances. Our consolation is that no one can know the true taste of victory if he has never swallowed defeat.

For the moment, therefore, we must subordinate programs to studying the levers of power Negroes must grasp to influence the course of events. In our society power sources are sometimes obscure and indistinct. Yet they can always finally be traced to those forces we describe as ideological, ecnomic and political.

In the area of ideology, despite the impact of the works of a few Negro writers on a limited number of white intellectuals, all too few Negro thinkers have exerted an influence on the main currents of American thought. Nevertheless Negroes have illuminated imperfections in the democratic structure that were formerly only dimly perceived, and have forced a concerned re-examination of the true meaning of American democracy. As a consequence of the vigorous Negro protest, the whole nation has for a decade probed more searchingly the essential nature of democracy, both economic and political. By taking to the streets and there giving practical lessons in democracy and its defaults, Negroes have decisively influenced white thought.

Lacking sufficient access to television, publications and broad forums, Negroes have had to write their most persuasive essays with the blunt pen of marching ranks. The many white political leaders and well-meaning friends who ask Negro leadership to leave the streets may not realize that they are asking us effectively to silence ourselves. The twice forgotten man in America has always been the Negro. His groans were not heard, his needs were unfelt, until he found the means to state his case in the public square. More white people learned more about the shame of America, and finally faced some aspects of it, during the years of nonviolent protest than during the century before. Nonviolent direct action will continue to be a significant source of power until it is made irrelevant by the presence of justice.

II

The economic highway to power has few entry lanes for Negroes. Nothing so vividly reveals the crushing impact of discrimination and the heritage of exclusion as the limited dimensions of Negro business in the most powerful economy in the world. America's industrial production is half of the world's total, and within it the production of Negro business is so small that it can scarcely be measured on any definable scale.

Yet in relation to the Negro community the value of Negro business should not be underestimated. In the internal life of the Negro society it provides a degree of stability. Despite formidable obstacles it has developed a corps of men of competence and organizational discipline who constitute a talented leadership reserve. Their cumulative strength may be feeble measured against the mammoth of white industry, but within the community they furnish inspiration and are a resource for the development of programs and planning. They are a strength among the weak though they are weak among the mighty.

There exist two other areas, however, where Negroes can exert substantial influence on the broader economy. As employees and consumers Negro numbers and their strategic disposition endow them with a certain bargaining strength.

Within the ranks of organized labor there are nearly 2 million Negroes. Not only are they found in large numbers as workers, but they are concentrated in key industries. In the truck transportation, steel, auto and food industries which are the backbone of the nation's economic life, Negroes make up nearly 20 percent of the organized work force, although they are only 10 percent of the general population. This potential strength is magnified further by the fact of their unity with millions of white workers in these occupations. As co-workers there is a basic community of interest that transcends many of the ugly divisive elements of traditional prejudice. There are undeniably points of friction, for example, in certain housing and education questions. But the severity of the abrasions is minimized by the more commanding need for cohesion in union organizations.

If manifestations of race prejudice were to erupt within an organized plant, it would set into motion many corrective forces. It would not flourish as it does in a neighborhood with nothing to inhibit it but morbid observers looking for thrills. In the shop the union officials from highest to lowest levels would be immediately involved, for internal discord is no academic matter; it weakens the union in its contests with the employers. Therefore an important self-interest motivates harmonious race relations. Here Negroes have a substantial weight to bring to bear on all measures of social concern.

The labor movement, especially in its earlier days, was one of the few great institutions where a degree of hospitality and mobility was available to Negroes. When the rest of the nation accepted rank discrimination and prejudice as ordinary and usual—like the rain, to be deplored but accepted as part of nature—trade unions, particularly the CIO, leveled all barriers to equal membership. In a number of instances Negroes rose to influential national office.

Today the union record in relation to Negro workers is exceedingly uneven, but the potentiality for influencing union decisions still exists. In many of the larger unions the white leadership contains some men of ideals and many more who are pragmatists. Both groups find they are benefited by a constructive relationship to their Negro membership. For those compelling reasons, Negroes, who are almost wholly a working people, cannot be casual toward the union movement. This is true even though some unions remain incontestably hostile.

In days to come, organized labor will increase its importance in the destinies of Negroes. Automation is imperceptibly but inexorably producing dislocations, skimming off unskilled labor from the industrial force. The displaced are flowing into proliferating service occupations. These enterprises are traditionally unorganized and provide low wage scales with longer hours. The Negroes pressed into these services need union protection, and the union movement needs their membership to maintain its relative strength in the whole society. On this new frontier Negroes may well become the pioneers that they were in the early organizing days of the thirties.

The trade union movement in the last two decades, despite its potential strength, has been an inarticulate giant with an unsteady gait, subjected to abuse and confused in its responses. Some circles of labor, after simmering discontent, are now allowing their challenge to vent itself.

The Teamsters Union, ousted some years ago from the AFL-CIO, instead of tottering or perishing, launched an expansion program that has increased its membership to nearly 2 million. It is not well known that the Teamsters have well over a quarter of a million Negroes in their ranks, with some of the highest rates of pay enjoyed by Negro workers anywhere in industry. In other mass unions new leaders have emerged with a deep commitment to broad social issues.

Recently, Walter Reuther and other leaders of 1.5 million auto workers have announced a new policy directed toward a restoration of the crusading spirit that characterized the unions of the past. They have fashioned a program for organizing the poor, Negro and white, in the South and the North. This will be no simple crusade, because the poor have many problems to overcome even to get into motion. Yet they are so many millions in number that the promise is stirring and its implications are vast.

The emergence of social initiatives by a revitalized labor movement would be taking place as Negroes are placing economic issues on the highest agenda. The coalition of an energized section of labor, Negroes, unemployed and welfare recipients may be the source of power that reshapes economic relationships and ushers in a breakthrough to a new level of social reform. The total elimination of poverty, now a practical responsibility, the reality of equality in race relations and other profound structural changes in society may well begin here.

To play our role fully as Negroes we will have to strive for enhanced representation and influence in the labor movement. Our young people need to think of union careers as earnestly as they do of business careers and professions. They could do worse than emulate A. Philip Randolph, who rose to the executive council of the AFL-CIO, and became a symbol of the courage, compassion and integrity of an enlightened labor leader. Indeed, the question may be asked why we have produced only one Randolph in nearly half a century. Discrimination is not the whole answer. We allowed ourselves to accept middle-class prejudices toward the labor movement. Yet this is one of those fields in which higher education is not a requirement for high office. In shunning it, we have lost an opportunity. Let us try to regain it now, at a time when the joint forces of Negro and labor may be facing an historic task of social reform.

The other economic lever available to the Negro is as a consumer. As long ago as 1932, in his book *Moral Man and Immoral Society*, Reinhold Niebuhr pointed out that "boycotts against banks which discriminate against Negroes in quantity credit, against stores which refuse to employ Negores while serving Negro trade, and against public service corporations which practice racial discrimination, would undoubtedly be crowned with some measure of success."[1] These words have proved to be prophetic, for we have been seeing the success of this approach in the last few years.

SCLC has pioneered in developing mass boycott movements in a frontal attack on discrimination. Our dramatic demonstrations tended to obscure the role of the boycott in cities such as Birminghan. It was not the marching alone that brought about integration of public facilities in 1963. The downtown business establishments suffered for weeks under our almost unbelievably effective boycott. The significant percentage of their sales that vanished, the 98 percent of their Negro customers who stayed home, educated them forcefully to the dignity of the Negro as a consumer.

---

Scribner's, p. 254.

Later we crystallized our experiences in Birmingham and elsewhere and developed a department in SCLC called Operation Breadbasket. This has as its primary aim the securing of more and better jobs for the Negro people. It calls on the Negro community to support those businesses that will give a fair share of jobs to Negroes and to withdraw its support from those businesses that have discriminatory policies. The key word in Operation Breadbasket is "respect"; it says in substance, "If you respect my dollars, you must respect my person. If you respect my quantitative support, then you must respect the quality of my job and my basic material needs."

Operation Breadbasket is carried out mainly by clergymen. First, a team of ministers calls on the management of a business in the community to request basic facts on the company's total number of employees, the number of Negro employees, the department or job classifications in which all employees are located, and the salary ranges for each category. The team then returns to the steering committee to evaluate the data and to make a recommendation concerning the number of new and upgraded jobs that should be requested. The decision on the number of jobs requested is usually based on population figures. For instance, if a city has a 30 percent Negro population, then it is logical to assume that Negroes should have at least 30 percent of the jobs in any particular company, and jobs in all categories rather than only in menial areas, as the case almost always happens to be.

The next step is negotiation. The team of clergymen returns to the management of the company and transmits the request to hire or upgrade a specified number of "qualifiable" Negroes within a reasonable period of time. The negotiating sessions are also educational, in that the clergymen seek to arouse within management an awareness of the devastating problems of the ghetto and point out the immorality of companies that make profits from Negro consumers while at the same time excluding them from jobs.

If negotiations break down, the step of real power and pressure is taken. This fourth step consists of a massive call for economic withdrawal from the company's product and accompanying demonstration if necessary. The ministers go to their pulpits and to other communications media and ask Negroes to stop buying the employer's product or patronizing his business. Clergy-led teams dramatize the dispute to the ghetto inhabitants by picketing the stores where the products in question are sold. The fall-off in trade and the concomitant silencing of the cash register as a result of this boycott is a powerful force in causing the company ultimately to meet the demands.

In most cases it is not necessary to go to step four, because most business executives are keenly aware of the Negro's buying power and the consequent effect of its withdrawal. At present SCLC has Operation Breadbasket functioning in some twelve cities, and the results have been remarkable. In Atlanta, Georgia, for instance, the Negroes' earning power has been increased by more than $20 million annually over the past three years through a carefully disciplined program of selective buying and negotiation by the Negro ministers. During the last eight months in Chicago, Operation Breadbasket successfully completed negotiations with three major industries: milk, soft drinks and chain grocery stores. Four of the companies involved concluded reasonable agreements only after short "don't buy" campaigns. Seven other companies were able to make the requested changes across the conference table, without necessitating a boycott. Two other companies, after providing their employment information to the ministers, were sent letters of commendation for their healthy equal-employment practices. The net results add up to approximately eight hundred new and upgraded jobs for Negro employees, worth a little over $7 million in new annual income for Negro families.

In Chicago we have recently added a new dimension to Operation Breadbasket. Along with requesting new job opportunities, we are now requesting that businesses with stores in the ghetto deposit the income for those establishments in Negro-owned banks, and that Negro-owned products be placed on the counters of all their stores. In this way we seek to stop the drain of resources out of the ghetto with nothing remaining there for its rehabilitation. The two chain grocery stores with which we have so far negotiated, Hi-Low and National Tea, have readily agreed. They have now opened accounts in the two Negro banks of Chicago, and their shelves display every Negro-owned product of the city. This has given new vibrancy and growth to Negro businesses in Chicago, and will contribute to the continued economic growth of the city.

III

The final major area of untapped power for the Negro is in the political arena. Negro population is burgeoning in major cities as tides of migrants flow into them in search of employment and opportunity. These new migrants have substantially higher birth rates than characterize the white population. The two trends, along with the exodus of the white population to the suburbs, are producing fast-gathering Negro majorities in the large cities.

The changing composition of the cities must be seen in the light of their politcial significance. Particularly in the North, the large cities substantially determine the political destiny of the state. These states, in turn, hold the dominating electoral votes in presidential contests. The future of the Democratic party, which rests so heavily on its coalition of urban minorities, cannot be assessed without taking into account which way the Negro vote turns. The wistful hopes of the Republican party for large city influence will also be decided not in the board rooms of great corporations but in the teeming ghettos. Its 1964 disaster with Goldwater, in which fewer than 6 percent of Negroes voted Republican, indicates that the illustrious ghost of Abraham Lincoln is not sufficient for winning Negro confidence, not so long as the party fails to shrink the influence of its ultra-right wing.

The growing Negro vote in the South is another source of power. As it weakens and enfeebles the dixiecrats, by concentrating its blows against them, it undermines the congressional coalition of southern reactionaries and their northern Republican colleagues. That coalition, which has always exercised a disproportionate power in Congress by controlling its major committees, will lose its ability to frustrate measures of social advancement and to impose its perverted definition of democracy on the political thought of the nation.

The Negro vote presently is only a partially realized strength. It can still be doubled in the South. In the North, even where Negroes are registered in equal proportion to whites, they do not vote in the same proportions. Assailed by a sense of futility, Negroes resist participating in empty ritual. However, when the Negro citizen learns that united and organized pressure can achieve measurable results, he will make his influence felt. Out of this consciousness the political power of the aroused minority will be enhanced and consolidated.

Up to now that power has been inconsequential because, paradoxically, although Negroes vote with great discernment and traditionally as a bloc, essentially we are unorganized, disunited and subordinated in the decision-making process. There is no correlation between the numerical importance of the urban Negro vote to the party it supports and the influence we wield in determining the party's program and policies, or its implementation of existing legislation. Our political leaders are bereft of influence in the councils of political power.

The new task of the liberation movement, therefore, is not merely to increase the Negro registration and vote; equally imperative is the development of a strong voice that is heard in the smoke-filled rooms where party debating and bargaining proceed. A black face that is mute in party councils is not political representation; the ability to be independent, assertive and respected when the final decisions are made is indispensable for an authentic expression of power.

Negroes are traditionally manipulated because the political powers take advantage of three major weaknesses. The first relates to the manner in which our political leaders emerge; the second is our failure so far to achieve effective political alliances; the third is the Negro's general reluctance to participate fully in political life.

The majority of Negro political leaders do not ascend to prominence on the shoulders of mass support. Although genuinely popular leaders are now emerging, most are selected by white leadership, elevated to position, supplied with resources and inevitably subjected to white control. The mass of Negroes nurtures a healthy suspicion toward these manufactured leaders. Experience tells them that color is the chief argument their leaders are offering to induce loyalty and solidarity. The Negro politician they know spends little time in persuading them that he embodies personal integrity, commitment and ability; he offers few programs and less service. Tragically, he is in too many respects not a fighter for a new life but a figurehead of the old one. Hence very few Negro political leaders are impressive or illustrious to their constituents. They enjoy only limited loyalty and qualified support.

This relationship in turn hampers the Negro leader in bargaining with genuine strength and independent firmness with white party leaders. The whites are all too well aware of his impotence and his remoteness from his constituents, and they deal with him as a powerless subordinate. He is accorded a measure of dignity and personal respect but not political power.

The Negro politician therefore finds himself in a vacuum. He has no base in either direction on which to build influence and attain leverage.

In Negro life there is a unique and unnatural dichotomy between community leaders who have the respect of the masses and professional political leaders who are held in polite disdain. Those who lead civil rights groups, churches, unions and other social organizations are actually hybrids; although they bargain for political programs, they generally operate outside of partisan poltics. In two national polls[2] to name the most respected Negro leaders, out of the highest fifteen, only a single political figure, Congressman Adam Clayton Powell, was included and he was in the lower half of both lists. This is in marked contrast to polls in which white people choose their most popular leaders; political personalities are always high on the lists and are represented in goodly numbers. There is no Negro political personality evoking affection, respect and emulation to correspond to John F. Kennedy, Eleanor Roosevelt, Herbert Lehman, Earl Warren and Adlai Stevenson, to name but a few.

The circumstances in which Congressman Powell emerged into leadership and the experiences of his career are unique. It would not shed light on the larger picture to attempt to study the very individual factors that apply to him. It is fair to say no other Negro political leader is similar, either in the strengths he possesses, the power he attained or the errors he has committed.

And so we shall have to do more than register and more than vote; we shall have to create leaders who embody virtues we can respect, who have moral and ethical principles we can applaud with an enthusiasm that enables us to rally support for them based on confidence and trust. We will have to demand high standards and give consistent, loyal support to those who merit it. We will have to be a reliable constituency for

---

2. *Newsweek* Survey–Harris Poll, 29 July 1963, and 22 August 1966.

those who prove themselves to be committed political warriors in our behalf. When our movement has partisan political personalities whose unity with their people is unshakable and whose independence is genuine, they will be treated in white political councils with the respect those who embody such power deserve.

In addition to the development of genuinely independent and representative political leaders, we shall have to master the art of political alliances. Negroes should be natural allies of many white reform and independent political groups, yet they are more commonly organized by old-line machine politicians. We will have to learn to refuse crumbs from the big-city machines and steadfastly demand a fair share of the loaf. When the machine politicians demur, we must be prepared to act in unity and throw our support to such independent parties or reform wings of the major parties as are prepared to take our demands seriously and fight for them vigorously. This is political freedom; this is political maturity expressing our aroused and determined new spirit to be treated as equals in all aspects of life.

The future of the deep structural changes we seek will not be found in the decaying political machines. It lies in new alliances of Negroes, Puerto Ricans, labor, liberals, certain church and middle-class elements. It is noteworthy that the largest single civil rights action ever conducted was the New York school boycott, when nearly half a million Negroes and Puerto Ricans united in a demonstration that emptied segregated schools.

The art of alliance politics is more complex and more intricate than it is generally pictured. It is easy to put exciting combinations on paper. It evokes happy memories to recall that our victories in the past decade were won with a broad coalition of organizations representing a wide variety of interests. But we deceive ourselves if we envision the same combination backing structural changes in the society. It did not come together for such a program and will not reassemble for it.

A true alliance is based upon some self-interest of each component group and a common interest into which they merge. For an alliance to have permanence and loyal commitment from its various elements, each of them must have a goal from which it benefits and none must have an outlook in basic conflict with the others. Thus we cannot talk loosely of an alliance with all labor. Most unions have mutual interests with us; both can profit in the relationship. Yet with some unions that persist in discrimination to retain their monopoly of jobs we have no common ground. To talk of alliances with them is to talk of mutual deception and mutual hypocrisy. The same test must be applied to churches and church bodies. Some churches recognize that to be relevant in moral life they must make equality an imperative. With them the basis for alliance is strong and enduring. But toward those churches that shun and evade the issue, that are mute or timorous on social and economic questions, we are no better than strangers even though we sing the same hymns in worship of the same God.

If we employ the principle of selectivity along these lines, we will find millions of allies who in serving themselves also support us, and on such sound foundations unity and mutual trust and tangible accomplishment will flourish.

It is no mere academic exercise to scrutinize alliance relationships. They are the keys to political progress. Of late some scholars have begun to question the usefulness of the Negro vote as a tool for social advancement. Matthews and Prothro put it "that the concrete benefits to be derived from the franchise—under the conditions that prevail in the South—have often been exaggerated. . . . The concrete, measurable payoffs from Negro voting in the South will *not* be revolutionary."[3] They point to the limited gains Negroes have attained in the North and apply them to the South. Their conclusion has some validity because they confine them to conditions that *prevail* in the South. But conditions in the South are not static; they are changing.

A primary Negro political goal in the South is the elimination of racism as an electoral issue. No objective observer can fail to see that even with a half-finished campaign to enfranchise Negroes some profound changes have already occurred. For a number of years there were de facto alliances in some states in which Negroes voted for the same candidate as whites because he had shifted from a racist to a moderate position, even though he did not articulate an appeal for Negro votes. In recent years the transformation has accelerated, and many white candidates have entered alliances publicly. As they perceived that the Negro vote was becoming a substantial and permanent factor, they could not remain aloof from it. More and more, competition will develop among white political forces for such a significant bloc of votes, and a monolithic white unity based on racism will no longer be possible.

Racism is a tenacious evil, but it is not immutable. Millions of underprivileged whites are in the process of considering the contradiction between segregation and economic progress. White supremacy can feed their egos but not their stomachs. They will not go hungry or forego the affluent society to remain racially ascendant. Governors Wallace and Maddox, whose credentials as racists are impeccable, understand this, and for that reason they present themselves as liberal populists as well. Their demagoguery is little known to northerners, who have no opportunity to hear the speeches they make in local communities. Temporarily they can carry water on both shoulders, but the ground is becoming unsteady beneath their feet. Each of them was faced in the primary with a new breed of white southerner. Their opponents were not inconse-

---

3. Op. cit., p. 481.

quential political figures. Former governors were in the race, making open public appeals for the Negro vote and for the first time in history meeting with Negro organizations to solicit support. They championed economic reform without racial demagoguery. They won significant numbers of white votes, insufficient for victory but sufficient to point the future directions of the South.

The time may not be far off when an awakened poor and backward white voter will heed and support the authentic economic liberalism of former Governor Arnall of Georgia and former Lieutenant Governor Flowers of Alabama. Then with the growing Negro vote they will develop an alliance that displaces the Wallaces and with them racism as a political issue.

It is true that the Negro vote has not transformed the North; but the fact that northern alliances and political action generally have been poorly executed is no reason to predict that the negative experiences will be automatically extended in the North or duplicated in the South. The northern Negro has never used direct action on a mass scale for reforms, and anyone who predicted ten years ago that the southern Negro would also neglect it would have dramatically been proved in error.

Everything Negroes need—and many of us need almost everything—will not like magic materialize from the use of the ballot. Yet as a lever of power, if it is given studious attention and employed with the creativity we have proved through our protest activities we possess, it will help to achieve many far-reaching changes during our lifetime.

The final reason for our dearth of political strength, particularly in the North, arise from the grip of an old tradition on many individual Negroes. They tend to hold themselves aloof from politics as a serious concern. They sense that they are manipulated, and their defense is a cynical disinterest. To safeguard themselves on this front from the exploitation that torments them in so many areas, they shut the door to political activity and retreat into the dark shadows of passivity. Their sense of futility is deep, and in terms of their bitter experiences it is justified. They cannot perceive political action as a source of power. It will take patient and persistent effort to eradicate this mood, but the new consciousness of strength developed in a decade of stirring agitation can be utilized to channel constructive Negro activity into political life and eliminate the stagnation produced by an outdated and defensive paralysis.

In the future we must become intensive political activists. We must be guided in this direction because we need political strength more desperately than any other group in American society. Most of us are too poor to have adequate economic power, and many of us are too rejected by the culture to be part of any tradition of power. Necessity will draw us toward the power inherent in the creative uses of politics.

Negroes nurture a persisting myth that the Jews of America attained social mobility and status solely because they had money. It is unwise to ignore the error for many reasons. In a negative sense it encourages anti-Semitism and overestimates money as a value. In a positive sense the full truth reveals a useful lesson.

Jews progressed because they possessed a tradition of education combined with social and political action. The Jewish family enthroned education and sacrificed to get it. The result was for more than abstract learning. Uniting social action with educational competence, Jews became enormously effective in political life. Those Jews who became lawyers, businessmen, writers, entertainers, union leaders and medical men did not vanish into the pursuits of their trade exclusively. They lived an active life in political circles, learning the techniques and arts of politics.

Nor was it only the rich who were involved in social and political action. Millions of Jews for half a century remained relatively poor, but they were far from passive in social and political areas. They lived in homes in which politics was a household word. They were deeply involved in radical parties, liberal parties and conservative parties—they formed many of them. Very few Jews sank into despair and escapism even when discrimination assailed the spirit and corroded initiative. Their life raft in the sea of discouragement was social action.

Without overlooking the towering differences between the Negro and Jewish experiences, the lesson of Jewish mass involvement in social and political action and education is worthy of emulation. Negroes have already started on this road in creating the protest movement, but this is only a beginning. We must involve everyone we can reach, even those with inadequate education, and together acquire political sophistication by discussion, practice and reading. Jews without education learned a great deal from political meetings, mass meetings and trade union activities. Informal discussions and reading at home or in the streets are educational; they challenge the mind and inform our actions.

Education without social action is a one-sided value because it has no true power potential. Social action without education is a weak expression of pure energy. Deeds uninformed by educated thought can take false directions. When we go into action and confront our adversaries, we must be as armed with knowledge as they. Our policies should have the strength of deep analysis beneath them to be able to challenge the clever sophistries of our opponents.

The many thousands of Negroes who have already found intellectual growth and spiritual fulfillment on this path know its creative possibilities. They are not among the legions of the lost, they are not crushed by the weight of centuries. Most heartening, among the young the spirit of challenge and determination for change is becoming an unquenchable force.

But the scope of struggle is still too narrow and too restricted. We must turn more of our energies and focus our creativity on the useful things that translate into power. This is not a program for a distant to-morrow, when our children will somehow have acquired enough education to do it for themselves. We in this generation must do the work and in doing it stimulate our children to learn and acquire higher levels of skill and technique.

It must become a crusade so vital that civil rights organizers do not repeatedly have to make personal calls to summon support. There must be a climate of social pressure in the Negro community that scorns the Negro who will not pick up his citizenship rights and add his strength enthusiastically and voluntarily to the accumulation of power for himself and his people. The past years have blown fresh winds through ghetto stagnation, but we are on the threshold of a significant change that demands a hundredfold acceleration. By 1970 ten of our larger cities will have Negro majorities if present trends continue. We can shrug off this opportunity or use it for a new vitality to deepen and enrich our family and community life.

How shall we turn the ghettos into a vast school? How shall we make every street corner a forum, not a lounging place for trivial gossip and petty gambling, where life is wasted and human experience withers to trivial sensations? How shall we make every houseworker and every laborer a demonstrator, a voter, a canvasser and a student? The dignity their jobs may deny them is waiting for them in political and social action.

We must utilize the community action groups and training centers now proliferating in some slum areas to create not merely an electorate, but a conscious, alert and informed people who know their direction and whose collective wisdom and vitality commands respect. The slave heritage can be cast into the dim past by our consciousness of our strengths and a resolute determination to use them in our daily experiences. Power is not the white man's birthright; it will not be legislated for us and delivered in neat government packages. It is a social force any group can utilize by accumulating its elements in a planned, deliberate campaign to organize it under its own control.

IV

While the existence of a militant morale is immensely important, a fighting spirit that is insufficiently organized can become useless and even hazardous. To attempt radical reform without adequate organization is like trying to sail a boat without a rudder. Yet any mature analysis of recent events cannot fail to recognize the frailties of Negro civil rights organizations.

Prominent among the significant weaknesses of our organizations is their disunity and petty competition. When false rumors are circulated that some leaders have "sold out" to the power structure or are making opportunistic alliances with one or another political party to gain individual advantage, the whole movement suffers. If the criticism is true, it is not destructive; it is a necessary attack on weakness. But often such criticisms is a reflex response to gain organizational advantage. Too often a genuine achievement has been falsely condemned as spurious and useless, and a victory has been turned into disheartening defeat for the less informed. Our enemies will adequately deflate our accomplishment; we need not serve them as eager volunteers.

Why are so many of our organizations too small, too beset with problems that consume disproportionate attention, or too dominated by a sluggish passivity and smug complacency? For an answer we must return to the nature of our original objectives. For much of the last decade we took on the task of ending conditions that had long outlived their purpose. The desegregation of most public facilities, for example, was overdue for change. It was not necessary to build a widespread organization in order to win legislative victories. Sound effort in a single city such as Birmingham or Selma produced situations that symbolized the evil everywhere and inflamed public opinion against it. Where the spotlight illuminated the evil, a legislative remedy was soon obtained that applied everywhere. As a consequence, permanent, seasoned and militant organizations did not arise out of compelling necessity.

But corrective legislation requires organization to bring it to life. Laws only declare rights; they do not deliver them. The oppressed must take hold of laws and transform them into effective mandates. Hence the absence of powerful organization has limited the degree of application and the extent of practical success.

We made easy gains and we built the kind of organizations that expect easy victories, and rest upon them. It may seem curious to speak of easy victories when some have suffered and sacrificed so much. Yet in candor and self-criticism it is necessary to acknowledge that the torturous job of organizing solidly and simultaneously in thousands of places was not a feature of our work. This is as true for the older civil rights organizations as for the newer ones. The older organizations have only acquired a mass base recently, and they still retain the flabby structures and policies that a pressureless situation made possible.

Many civil rights organizations were born as specialists in agitation and dramatic projects; they attracted massive sympathy and support; but they did not assemble and unify the support for new stages of struggle. The effect on their allies reflected their basic practices. Support waxed and waned, and people became conditioned to action in crises but inaction from day to day. We unconsciously patterned a crisis policy and program, and summoned support not for daily commitment but for explosive events alone.

Recognizing that no army can mobilize and demobilize and remain a fighting unit, we will have to build far-flung, workmanlike and experienced organizations in the future if the legislation we create and the agreements we forge are to be ably and zealously superintended. Moreover, to move to higher levels of progress we will have to emerge from crises with more than agreements and laws. We shall have to have people tied together in a long-term relationship instead of evanescent enthusiasts who lose their experience, spirit and unity because they have no mechanism that directs them to new tasks.

We have many assets to facilitate organization. Negroes are almost instinctively cohesive. We band together readily, and against white hostility we have an intense and wholesome loyalty to each other. In some of the simplest relationships we will protect a brother even at a cost to ourselves. We are loath to be witnesses against each other when the white man seeks to divide us. We are acutely conscious of the need and sharply sensitive to the importance of defending our own. Solidarity is a reality in Negro life, as it always has been among the oppressed. Sometimes, unfortunately, it is misapplied when we confuse high status with high character.

On the other hand, Negroes are capable of becoming competitive, carping and, in an expression of self-hate, suspicious and intolerant of each other. A glaring weakness in Negro life is lack of sufficient mutual confidence and trust.

Negro leaders suffer from this interplay of solidarity and divisiveness, being either exalted excessively or grossly abused. But some of those leaders who suffer from lack of sustained support are not without weaknesses that give substance to criticism. The most serious is aloofness and absence of faith in their people. The white establishment is skilled in flattering and cultivating emerging leaders. It presses its own image on them and finally, from imitation of manners, dress and style of living, a deeper strain of corruption develops. This kind of Negro leader acquires the white man's contempt for the ordinary Negro. He is often more at home with the middle-class white than he is among his own people, and frequently his physical home is moved up and away from the ghetto. His language changes, his location changes, his income changes, and ultimately he changes from the representative of the Negro to the white man into the white man's representative to the Negro. The tragedy is that too often he does not recognize what has happened to him.

I learned a lesson many years ago from a report of two men who flew to Atlanta to confer with a civil rights leader at the report. Before they could begin to talk, the porter sweeping the floor drew the local leader aside to talk about a matter that troubled him. After fifteen minutes had passed, one of the visitors said bitterly to his companion, "I am just too busy for this kind of nonsense. I haven't come a thousand miles to sit and wait while he talks to a porter."

The other replied, "When the day comes that he stops having time to talk to a porter, on that day I will not have the time to come one mile to see him."

When I heard this story, I knew I was being told something I should never forget.

We need organizations that are permeated with mutual trust, incorruptibility and militancy. Without this spirit we may have numbers but they will add up to zero. We need organizations that are responsible, efficient and alert. We lack experience because ours is a history of disorganization. But we will prevail because our need for progress is stronger than the ignorance forced upon us. If we realize how indispensable is responsible militant organization to our struggle, we will create it as we managed to create underground railroads, protest groups, self-help societies and the churches that have always been our refuge, our source of hope and our source of action.

## V

In recent years a multitude of civil rights programs have been elicited from specialists and scholars. To enhance their value and increase support for them, it is necessary that they be discussed and debated among the ordinary people affected by them. To facilitate study, I have grouped some of the more challenging proposals separately in an appendix to this volume. There is only one general proposal that I would like to examine here, because it deals with the abolition of poverty within this nation and leads logically to my final discussion of poverty on an international scale.

In the treatment of poverty nationally, one fact stands out: there are twice as many white poor as Negro poor in the United States. Therefore I will not dwell on the experiences of poverty that derive from racial discrimination, but will discuss the poverty that affects white and Negro alike.

Up to recently we have proceeded from a premise that poverty is a consequence of multiple evils: lack of education restricting job opportunities; poor housing which stultified home life and suppressed initiative; fragile family relationships which distorted personality development. The logic of this approach suggested that each of these causes be attacked one by one. Hence a housing program to transform living conditions, improved educational facilities to furnish tools for better job opportunities, and family counseling to create better personal adjustments were designed. In combination these measures were intended to remove the causes of poverty.

While none of these remedies in itself is unsound, all have a fatal disadvantage. The programs have never proceeded on a coordinated basis or at similar rates of development. Housing measures have fluctuated at the whims of legislative bodies. They have been piecemeal and pygmy. Educational reforms have been even more sluggish and entangled in bureaucratic stalling and economy-dominated decisions. Family assistance stagnated in neglect and then suddenly was discovered to be the central issue on the basis of hasty and superficial studies. At no time has a total, coordinated and fully adequate program been conceived. As a consequence, fragmentary and spasmodic reforms have failed to reach down to the profoundest needs of the poor.

In addition to the absence of coordination and sufficiency, the programs of the past all have another common failing—they are indirect. Each seeks to solve poverty by first solving something else.

I am now convinced that the simplest approach will prove to be the most effective—the solution to poverty is to abolish it directly by a now widely discussed measure: the guaranteed income.

Earlier in this century this proposal would have been greeted with ridicule and denunciation as destructive of initiative and responsibility. At that time economic status was considered the measure of the individual's abilities and talents. In the simplistic thinking of that day the absence of worldly goods indicated a want of industrious habits and moral fiber.

We have come a long way in our understanding of human motivation and of the blind operation of our economic system. Now we realize that dislocations in the market operation of our economy and the prevalence of discrimination thrust people into idleness and bind them in constant or frequent unemployment against their will. The poor are less often dismissed from our conscience today by being branded as inferior and incompetent. We also know that no matter how dynamically the economy develops and expands it does not eliminate all poverty.

We have come to the point where we must make the nonproducer a consumer or we will find ourselves drowning in a sea of consumer goods. We have so energetically mastered production that we now must give attention to distribution. Though there have been increases in purchasing power, they have lagged behind increases in production. Those at the lowest economic level, the poor white and Negro, the aged and chronically ill, are traditionally unorganized and therefore have little ability to force the necessary growth in their income. They stagnate or become even poorer in relation to the larger society.

The problem indicates that our emphasis must be twofold. We must create full employment or we must create incomes. People must be made consumers by one method or the other. Once they are placed in this position, we need to be concerned that the potential of the individual is not wasted. New forms of work that enhance the social good will have to be devised for those for whom traditional jobs are not available.

In 1879 Henry George anticipated this state of affairs when he wrote, in *Progress and Poverty*:

The fact is that the work which improves the condition of mankind, the work which extends knowledge and increases power and enriches literature, and elevates thought, is not done to secure a living. It is not the work of slaves, driven to their task either by the lash of a master or by animal necessities. It is the work of men who perform it for their own sake, and not that they may get more to eat or drink, or wear, or display. In a state of society where want is abolished, work of this sort could be enormously increased.

We are likely to find that the problems of housing and education, instead of preceding the elimination of poverty, will themselves be affected if poverty is first abolished. The poor transformed into purchasers will do a great deal on their own to alter housing decay. Negroes, who have a double disability, will have a greater effect on discrimination when they have the additional weapon of cash to use in their struggle.

Beyond these advantages, a host of positive psychological changes inevitably will result from widespread economic security. The dignity of the individual will flourish when the decisions concerning his life are in his own hands, when he has the assurance that his income is stable and certain, and when he knows that he has the means to seek self-improvement. Personal conflicts between husband, wife and children will diminish when the unjust measurement of human worth on a scale of dollars is eliminated.

Two conditions are indispensable if we are to ensure that the guaranteed income operates as a consistenly progressive measure. First, it must be pegged to the median income of society, not at the lowest levels of income. To guarantee an income at the floor would simply perpetuate welfare standards and freeze into the society poverty conditions. Second, the guaranteed income must be dynamic; it must automatically increase as the total social income grows. Were it permitted to remain static under growth conditions, the recipients would suffer a relative decline. If periodic reviews disclose that the whole national income has risen, then the guaranteed income would have to be adjusted upward by the same percentage. Without these safeguards a creeping retrogression would occur, nullifying the gains of security and stability.

This proposal is not a "civil rights" program, in the sense that that term is currently used. The program would benefit all the poor, including the two-thirds of them who are white. I hope that both Negro and white will act in coalition to effect this change, because their combined strength will be necessary to overcome the fierce opposition we must realistically anticipate.

Our nation's adjustment to a new mode of thinking will be facilitated if we realize that for nearly forty years two groups in our society have already been enjoying a guaranteed income. Indeed, it is a symptom of our confused social values that these two groups turn out to be the richest and the poorest. The wealthy who own securities have always had an assured income; and their polar opposite, the relief client, has been guaranteed an income, however minuscule, through welfare benefits.

John Kenneth Galbraith has estimated that $20 billion a year would effect a guaranteed income, which he describes as "not much more than we will spend the next fiscal year to rescue freedom and democracy and religious liberty as these are defined by 'experts' in Vietnam."[4]

The contemporary tendency in our society is to base our distribution on scarcity, which has vanished, and to compress our abundance into the overfed mouths of the middle and upper classes until they gag with superfluity. If democracy is to have breadth of meaning, it is necessary to adjust this inequity. It is not only moral, but it is also intelligent. We are wasting and degrading human life by clinging to archaic thinking.

The curse of poverty has no justification in our age. It is socially as cruel and blind as the practice of cannibalism at the dawn of civilization, when men ate each other because they had not yet learned to take food from the soil or to consume the abundant animal life around them. The time has come for us to civilize ourselves by the total, direct and immediate abolition of poverty.

## THE WORLD HOUSE (CHAPTER 6)

Some years ago a famous novelist died. Among his papers was found a list of suggested plots for future stories, the most prominently underscored being this one: "A widely separated family inherits a house in which they have to live together." This is the great new problem of mankind. We have inherited a large house, a great "world house" in which we have to live together—black and white, Easterner and Westerner, Gentile and Jew, Catholic and Protestant, Moslem and Hindu—a family unduly separated in ideas, culture and interest, who, because we can never again live apart, must learn somehow to live with each other in peace.

However deeply American Negroes are caught in the struggle to be at last at home in our homeland of the United States, we cannot ignore the larger world house in which we are also dwellers. Equality with whites will not solve the problems of either whites or Negroes if it means equality in a world society stricken by poverty and in a universe doomed to extinction by war.

All inhabitants of the globe are now neighbors. This world-wide neighborhood has been brought into being largely as a result of the modern scientific and technological revolutions. The world of today is vastly different from the world of just one hundred years ago. A century ago Thomas Edison had not yet invented the incandescent lamp to bring light to many dark places of the earth. The Wright brothers had not yet invented that fascinating mechanical bird that would spread its gigantic wings across the skies and soon dwarf distance and place time in

---

4. *The Progressive*, December 1966.

the service of man. Einstein had not yet challenged an axiom and the theory of relativity had not yet been posited.

Human beings, searching a century ago as now for better understanding, had no television, no radios, no telephones and no motion pictures through which to communicate. Medical science had not yet discovered the wonder drugs to end many dread plagues and diseases. One hundred years ago military men had not yet developed the terrifying weapons of warfare that we know today—not the bomber, an airborne fortress raining down death; nor napalm, that burner of all things and flesh in its path. A century ago there were no skyscraping buildings to kiss the stars and no gargantuan bridges to span the waters. Science had not yet peered into the unfathomable ranges of interstellar space, nor had it penetrated oceanic depths. All these new inventions, these new ideas, these sometimes fascinating and sometimes frightening developments, came later. Most of them have come within the past sixty years, sometimes with agonizing slowness, more characteristically with bewildering speed, but always with enormous significance for our future.

The years ahead will see a continuation of the same dramatic developments. Physical science will carve new highways through the stratosphere. In a few years astronauts and cosmonauts will probably walk comfortably across the uncertain pathways of the moon. In two or three years it will be possible, because of the new supersonic jets, to fly from New York to London in two and one-half hours. In the years ahead medical science will greatly prolong the lives of men by finding a cure for cancer and deadly heart ailments. Automation and cybernation will make it possible for working people to have undreamed-of amounts of leisure time. All this is a dazzling picture of the furniture, the workshop, the spacious rooms, the new decorations and the architectural pattern of the large world house in which we are living.

Along with the scientific and technological revolution, we have also witnessed a world-wide freedom revolution over the last few decades. The present upsurge of the Negro people of the United States grows out of a deep and passionate determination to make freedom and equality a reality "here" and "now." In one sense the civil rights movement in the United States is a special American phenomenon which must be understood in the light of American history and dealt with in terms of the American situation. But on another and more important level, what is happening in the United States today is a significant part of a world development.

"We live in a day," said the philosopher Alfred North Whitehead, "when civilization is shifting its basic outlook; a major turning point in history where the presuppositions on which society is structured are being analyzed, sharply challenged, and profoundly changed." What we are seeing now is a freedom explosion, the realization of "an idea whose time has come," to use Victor Hugo's phrase. The deep rumbling of discontent that we hear today is the thunder of disinherited masses, rising from dungeons of oppression to the bright hills of freedom. In one majestic chorus the rising masses are singing, in the words of our freedom song, "Ain't gonna let nobody turn us around." All over the world like a fever, freedom is spreading in the widest liberation movement in history. The great masses of people are determined to end the exploitation of their races and lands. They are awake and moving toward their goal like a tidal wave. You can hear them rumbling in every village street, on the docks, in the houses, among the students, in the churches and at political meetings. For several centuries the direction of history flowed from the nations and the societies of western Europe out into the rest of the world in "conquests" of various sorts. That period, the era of colonialism, is at an end. East is moving West. The earth is being redistributed. Yes, we are "shifting our basic outlooks."

These developments should not surprise any student of history. Oppressed people cannot remain oppressed forever. The yearning for freedom eventually manifests itself. The Bible tells the thrilling story of how Moses stood in Pharaoh's court centuries ago and cried, "Let my people go." This was an opening chapter in a continuing story. The present struggle in the United States is a later chapter in the same story. Something within has reminded the Negro of his birthright of freedom, and something without has reminded him that it can be gained. Consciously or unconsciously, he has been caught up by the spirit of the times, and with his black brothers of Africa and his brown and yellow brothers in Asia, South America and the Caribbean, the United States Negro is moving with a sense of great urgency toward the promised land of racial justice.

Nothing could be more tragic than for men to live in these revolutionary times and fail to achieve the new attitudes and the new mental outlooks that the new situation demands. In Washington Irving's familiar story of Rip Van Winkle, the one thing that we usually remember is that Rip slept twenty years. There is another important point, however, that is almost always overlooked. It was the sign on the inn in the little town on the Hudson from which Rip departed and scaled the mountain for his long sleep. When he went up, the sign had a picture of King George III of England. When he came down, twenty years later, the sign had a picture of George Washington. As he looked at the picture of the first president of the United States, Rip was confused, flustered and lost. He knew not who Washington was. The most striking thing about this story is not that Rip slept twenty years, but that he slept through a revolution that would alter the course of human history.

One of the great liabilities of history is that all too many people fail to remain awake through great periods of social change. Every society has its protectors of the status quo and its fraternities of the indifferent who are notorious for sleeping through revolutions. But today our very survival depends on our ability to stay awake, to adjust to new ideas, to remain vigilant and to face the challenge of change. The large house in which we live demands that we transform this world-wide neighborhood into a world-wide brotherhood. Together we must learn to live as brothers or together we will be forced to perish as fools.

We must work passionately and indefatigably to bridge the gulf between our scientific progress and our moral progress. One of the great problems of mankind is that we suffer from a poverty of the spirit which stands in glaring contrast to our scientific and technological abundance. The richer we have become materially, the poorer we have become morally and spiritually.

Every man lives in two realms, the internal and the external. The internal is that realm of spiritual ends expressed in art, literature, morals and religion. The external is that complex of devices, techniques, mechanisms and instrumentalities by means of which we live. Our problem today is that we have allowed the internal to become lost in the external. We have allowed the means by which we live to outdistance the ends for which we live. So much of modern life can be summarized in that suggestive phrase of Thoreau: "Improved means to an unimproved end." This is the serious predicament, the deep and haunting problem, confronting modern man. Enlarged material powers spell enlarged peril if there is not proportionate growth of the soul. When the external of man's nature subjugates the internal, dark storm clouds begin to form.

Western civilization is particularly vulnerable at this moment, for our material abundance has brought us neither peace of mind nor serenity of spirit. An Asian writer has portrayed our dilemma in candid terms:

You call your thousand material devices "labor-saving machinery," yet you are forever "busy." With the multiplying of your machinery you grow increasingly fatigued, anxious, nervous, dissatisfied. Whatever you have, you want more; and wherever you are you want to go somewhere else . . . your devices are neither time-saving nor soul-saving machinery. They are so many sharp spurs which urge you on to invent more machinery and to do more business.[1]

This tells us something about our civilization that cannot be cast aside as a prejudiced charge by an Eastern thinker who is jealous of Western prosperity. We cannot escape the indictment.

This does not mean that we must turn back the clock of scientific progress. No one can overlook the wonders that science has wrought for our lives. The automobile will not abdicate in favor of the horse and buggy, or the train in favor of the stagecoach, or the tractor in favor of

---

1. Abraham Mitrie Rihbany, *Wise Men from the East and from the West*, Houghton Mifflin, 1922, p. 137.

the hand plow, or the scientific method in favor of ignorance and superstition. But our moral and spiritual "lag" must be redeemed. When scientific power outruns moral power, we end up with guided missiles and
misguided men. When we foolishly minimize the internal of our lives
and maximize the external, we sign the warrant for our own day of
doom.

Our hope for creative living in this world house that we have inherited lies in our ability to reestablish the moral ends of our lives in personal
character and social justice. Without this spiritual and moral reawaken-
ing we shall destroy ourselves in the misuse of our own instruments.

## II

Among the moral imperatives of our time, we are challenged to work all
over the world with unshakable determination to wipe out the last vestiges of racism. As early as 1906 W. E. B. DuBois prophesied that "the
problem of the twentieth century will be the problem of the color line."
Now as we stand two-thirds into this exciting period of history we know
full well that racism is still that hound of hell which dogs the tracks of
our civilization.

Racism is no mere American phenomenon. Its vicious grasp knows no
geographical boundaries. In fact, racism and its perennial ally—economic exploitation—provide the key to understanding most of the international complications of this generation.

The classic example of organized and institutionalized racism is the
Union of South Africa. Its national policy and practice are the incarna-
tion of the doctrine of white supremacy in the midst of a population
which is overwhelmingly black. But the tragedy of South Africa is not
simply in its own policy; it is the fact that the racist government of South
Africa is virtually made possible by the economic policies of the United
States and Great Britain, two countries which profess to be the moral
bastions of our Western world.

In country after country we see white men building empires on the
sweat and suffering of colored people. Portugal continues its practices
of slave labor and subjugation in Angola; the Ian Smith government in
Rhodesia continues to enjoy the support of British-based industry and
private capital, despite the stated opposition of British government policy. Even in the case of the little country of South West Africa we find the
powerful nations of the world incapable of taking a moral position
against South Africa, though the smaller country is under the trustee-
ship of the United Nations. Its policies are controlled by South Africa
and its manpower is lured into the mines under slave-labor conditions.

During the Kennedy administration there was some awareness of the
problems that breed in the racist and exploitative conditions throughout the colored world, and a temporary concern emerged to free the
United States from its complicity, though the effort was only on a diplo-

matic level. Through our ambassador to the United Nations, Adlai Stevenson, there emerged the beginnings of an intelligent approach to the colored peoples of the world. However, there remained little or no attempt to deal with the economic aspects of racist exploitation. We have been notoriously silent about the more than $700 million of American capital which props up the system of apartheid, not to mention the billions of dollars in trade and the military alliances which are maintained under the pretext of fighting communism in Africa.

Nothing provides the communists with a better climate for expansion and infiltration than the continued alliance of our nation with racism and exploitation throughout the world. And if we are not diligent in our determination to root out the last vestiges of racism in our dealings with the rest of the world, we may soon see the sins of our fathers visited upon ours and succeeding generations. For the conditions which are so classically represented in Africa are present also in Asia and in our own back yard in Latin America.

Everywhere in Latin America one finds a tremendous resentment of the United States, and that resentment is always strongest among the poorer and darker peoples of the continent. The life and destiny of Latin America are in the hands of United States corporations. The decisions affecting the lives of South Americans are ostensibly made by their governments, but there are almost no legitimate democracies alive in the whole continent. The other governments are dominated by huge and exploitative cartels that rob Latin America of her resources while turning over a small rebate to a few members of a corrupt aristocracy, which in turn invests not in its own country for its own people's welfare but in the banks of Switzerland and the playgrounds of the world.

Here we see racism in its more sophisticated form: neocolonialism. The Bible and the annals of history are replete with tragic stories of one brother robbing another of his birthright and thereby insuring generations of strife and enmity. We can hardly escape such a judgment in Latin America, any more than we have been able to escape the harvest of hate sown in Vietnam by a century of French exploitation.

There is the convenient temptation to attribute the current turmoil and bitterness throughout the world to the presence of a Communist conspiracy to undermine Europe and America, but the potential explosiveness of our world situation is much more attributable to disillusionment with the promises of Christianity and technology.

The revolutionary leaders of Africa, Asia and Latin America have virtually all received their education in the capitals of the West. Their earliest training often occurred in Christian mission schools. Here their sense of dignity was established and they learned that all men were sons of God. In recent years their countries have been invaded by automobiles, Coca-Cola and Hollywood, so that even remote villages have become aware of the wonders and blessings available to God's white children.

Once the aspirations and appetites of the world have been whetted by the marvels of Western technology and the self-image of a people awakened by religion, one cannot hope to keep people locked out of the earthly kingdom of wealth, health and happiness. Either they share in the blessings of the world or they organize to break down and overthrow those structures or governments which stand in the way of their goals.

Former generations could not conceive of such luxury, but their children now take this vision and demand that it become a reality. And when they look around and see that the only people who do not share in the abundance of Western technology are colored people, it is an almost inescapable conclusion that their condition and their exploitation are somehow related to their color and the racism of the white Western world.

This is a treacherous foundation for a world house. Racism can well be that corrosive evil that will bring down the curtain on Western civilization. Arnold Toynbee has said that some twenty-six civilizations have risen upon the face of the earth. Almost all of them have descended into the junk heaps of destruction. The decline and fall of these civilizations, according to Toynbee, was not caused by external invasions but by internal decay. They failed to respond creatively to the challenges impinging upon them. If Western civilization does not now respond constructively to the challenge to banish racism, some future historian will have to say that a great civilization died because it lacked the soul and commitment to make justice a reality for all men.

Another grave problem that must be solved if we are to live creatively in our world house is that of poverty on an international scale. Like a monstrous octopus, it stretches its choking, prehensile tentacles into lands and villages all over the world. Two-thirds of the peoples of the world go to bed hungry at night. They are undernourished, ill-housed and shabbily clad. Many of them have no houses or beds to sleep in. Their only beds are the sidewalks of the cities and the dusty roads of the villages. Most of these poverty-stricken children of God have never seen a physician or a dentist.

There is nothing new about poverty. What is new, however, is that we now have the resources to get rid of it. Not too many years ago, Dr. Kirtley Mather, a Harvard geologist, wrote a book entitled *Enough and to Spare*.[2] He set forth the basic theme that famine is wholly unnecessary in the modern world. Today, therefore, the question on the agenda must read: Why should there be hunger and privation in any land, in any city, at any table, when man has the resources and the scientific know-how to provide all mankind with the basic necessities of life? Even

2. Harper, 1944.

deserts can be irrigated and topsoil can be replaced. We cannot complain of a lack of land, for there are 25 million square miles of tillable land on earth, of which we are using less than 7 million. We have amazing knowledge of vitamins, nutrition, the chemistry of food and the versatility of atoms. There is no deficit in human resources; the deficit is in human will.

This does not mean that we can overlook the enormous acceleration in the rate of growth of the world's population. The population explosion is very real, and it must be faced squarely if we are to avoid, in centuries ahead, a "standing room only" situation on these earthly shores. Most of the large undeveloped nations in the world today are confronted with the problem of excess population in relation to resources. But even this problem will be greatly diminished by wiping out poverty. When people see more opportunities for better education and greater economic security, they begin to consider whether a smaller family might not be better for themselves and for their children. In other words, I doubt that there can be a stabilization of the population without a prior stabilization of economic resources.

The time has come for an all-out world war against poverty. The rich nations must use their vast resources of wealth to develop the underdeveloped, school the unschooled and feed the unfed. The well-off and the secure have too often become indifferent and oblivious to the poverty and deprivation in their midst. The poor in our countries have been shut out of our minds, and driven from the mainstream of our societies, because we have allowed them to become invisible. Ultimately a great nation is a compassionate nation. No individual or nation can be great if it does not have a concern for "the least of these."

The first step in the world-wide war against poverty is passionate commitment. All the wealthy nations—America, Britain, Russia, Canada, Australia, and those of western Europe—must see it as a moral obligation to provide capital and technical assistance to the underdeveloped areas. These rich nations have only scratched the surface in their commitment. There is need now for a general strategy of support. Sketchy aid here and there will not suffice, nor will it sustain economic growth. There must be a sustained effort extending through many years. The wealthy nations of the world must promptly initiate a massive, sustained Marshall Plan for Asia, Africa and South America. If they would allocate just 2 percent of their gross national product annually for a period of ten or twenty years for the development of the underdeveloped nations, mankind would go a long way toward conquering the ancient enemy, poverty.

The aid program that I am suggesting must not be used by the wealthy nations as a surreptitious means to control the poor nations. Such an approach would lead to a new form of paternalism and a neocolonialism which no self-respecting nation could accept. Ultimately, foreign aid programs must be motivated by a compassionate and committed effort to wipe poverty, ignorance and disease from the face of the earth. Money devoid of genuine empathy is like salt devoid of savor, good for nothing except to be trodden under foot of men.

The West must enter into the program with humility and penitence and a sober realization that everything will not always "go our way." It cannot be forgotten that the Western powers were but yesterday the colonial masters. The house of the West is far from in order, and its hands are far from clean.

We must have patience. We must be willing to understand why many of the young nations will have to pass through the same extremism, revolution and aggression that formed our own history. Every new government confronts overwhelming problems. During the days when they were struggling to remove the yoke of colonialism, there was a kind of preexistent unity of purpose that kept things moving in one solid direction. But as soon as independence emerges, all the grim problems of life confront them with stark realism: the lack of capital, the strangulating poverty, the uncontrollable birth rates and, above all, the high aspirational level of their own people. The postcolonial period is more difficult and precarious than the colonial struggle itself.

The West must also understand that its economic growth took place under rather propitious circumstances. Most of the Western nations were relatively underpopulated when they surged forward economically, and they were greatly endowed with the iron ore and coal that were needed for launching industry. Most of the young governments of the world today have come into being without these advantages, and, above all, they confront staggering problems of over-population. There is no possible way for them to make it without aid and assistance.

A genuine program on the part of the wealthy nations to make prosperity a reality for the poor nations will in the final analysis enlarge the prosperity of all. One of the best proofs that reality hinges on moral foundations is the fact that when men and governments work devotedly for the good of others, they achieve their own enrichment in the process.

From time immemorial men have lived by the principle that "self-preservation is the first law of life." But this is a false assumption. I would say that other-preservation is the first law of life. It is the first law of life precisely because we cannot preserve self without being concerned about preserving other selves. The universe is so structured that things go awry if men are not diligent in their cultivation of the other-regarding dimension. "I" cannot reach fulfillment without "thou." The self cannot be self without other selves. Self-concern without other-concern is like a tributary that has no outward flow to the ocean. Stagnant, still and stale, it lacks both life and freshness. Nothing would be more disastrous and out of harmony with our self-interest than for the developed nations to travel a dead-end road of inordinate selfishness. We are in the fortunate position of having our deepest sense of morality coalesce with our self-interest.

But the real reason that we must use our resources to outlaw poverty goes beyond material concerns to the quality of our mind and spirit. Deeply woven into the fiber of our religious tradition is the conviction that men are made in the image of God, and that they are souls of infinite metaphysical value. If we accept this as a profound moral fact, we cannot be content to see men hungry, to see men victimized with ill-health, when we have the means to help them. In the final analysis, the rich must not ignore the poor because both rich and poor are tied together. They entered the same mysterious gateway of human birth, into the same adventure of mortal life.

All men are interdependent. Every nation is an heir of a vast treasury of ideas and labor to which both the living and the dead of all nations have contributed. Whether we realize it or not, each of us lives eternally "in the red." We are everlasting debtors to known and unknown men and women. When we arise in the morning, we go into the bathroom where we reach for a sponge which is provided for us by a Pacific islander. We reach for soap that is created for us by a European. Then at the table we drink coffee which is provided for us by a South American, or tea by a Chinese or cocoa by a west African. Before we leave for our jobs we are already beholden to more than half the world.

In a real sense, all life is interrelated. The agony of the poor impoverishes the rich; the betterment of the poor enriches the rich. We are inevitably our brother's keeper because we are our brother's brother. Whatever affects one directly affects all indirectly.

A final problem that mankind must solve in order to survive in the world house that we have inherited is finding an alternative to war and human destruction. Recent events have vividly reminded us that nations are not reducing but rather increasing their arsenals of weapons of mass destruction. The best brains in the highly developed nations of the world are devoted to military technology. The proliferation of nuclear weapons has not been halted, in spite of the limited-test-ban treaty.

In this day of man's highest technical achievement, in this day of dazzling discovery, of novel opportunities, loftier dignities and fuller freedoms for all, there is no excuse for the kind of blind craving for power and resources that provoked the wars of previous generations. There is no need to fight for food and land. Science has provided us with adequate means of survival and transportation, which make it possible to enjoy the fullness of this great earth. The question now is, do we have the morality and courage required to live together as brothers and not be afraid?

One of the most persistent ambiguities we face is that everybody talks about peace as a goal, but among the wielders of power peace is practically nobody's business. Many men cry "Peace! Peace!" but they refuse to do the things that make for peace.

The large power blocs talk passionately of pursuing peace while expanding defense budgets that already bulge, enlarging already awesome armies and devising ever more devastating weapons. Call the roll of those who sing the glad tidings of peace and one's ears will be surprised by the responding sounds. The heads of all the nations issue clarion calls for peace, yet they come to the peace table accompanied by bands of brigands each bearing unsheathed swords.

The stages of history are replete with the chants and choruses of the conquerors of old who came killing in pursuit of peace. Alexander, Genghis Khan, Julius Caesar, Charlemagne and Napoleon were akin in seeking a peaceful world order, a world fashioned after their selfish conceptions of an ideal existence. Each sought a world at peace which would personify his egotistic dreams. Even within the life span of most of us, another megalomaniac strode across the world stage. He sent his blitzkrieg-bent legions blazing across Europe, bringing havoc and holocaust in his wake. There is grave irony in the fact that Hitler could come forth, following nakedly aggressive expansionist theories, and do it all in the name of peace.

So when in this day I see the leaders of nations again talking peace while preparing for war, I take fearful pause. When I see our country today intervening in what is basically a civil war, mutilating hundreds of thousands of Vietnamese children with napalm, burning villages and rice fields at random, painting the valleys of tha small Asian country red with human blood, leaving broken bodies in countless ditches and sending home half-men, mutilated mentally and physically; when I see the unwillingness of our government to create the atmosphere for a negotiated settlement of this awful conflict by halting bombings in the North and agreeing unequivocally to talk with the Vietcong—and all this in the name of pursuing the goal of peace—I tremble for our world. I do so not only from dire recall of the nightmares wreaked in the wars of yesterday, but also from dreadful realization of today's possible nuclear destructiveness and tomorrow's even more calamitous prospects.

Before it is too late, we must narrow the gaping chasm between our proclamations of peace and our lowly deeds which precipitate and perpetuate war. We are called upon to look up from the quagmire of military programs and defense commitments and read the warnings on history's signposts.

One day we must come to see that peace is not merely a distant goal that we seek but a means by which we arrive at that goal. We must pursue peaceful ends through peaceful means. How much longer must we play at deadly war games before we heed the plaintive pleas of the unnumbered dead and maimed of past wars?

President John F. Kennedy said on one occasion, "Mankind must put an end to war or war will put an end to mankind." Wisdom born of experience should tell us that war is obsolete. There may have been a time when war served as a negative good by preventing the spread and growth of an evil force, but the destructive power of modern weapons eliminates even the possibility that war may serve any good at all. If we assume that life is worth living and that man has a right to survive, then we must find an alternative to war. In a day when vehicles hurtle through outer space and guided ballistic missiles carve highways of death through the stratosphere, no nation can claim victory in war. A so-called limited war will leave little more than a calamitous legacy of human suffering, political turmoil and spiritual disillusionment. A world war will leave only smoldering ashes as mute testimony of a human race whose folly led inexorably to ultimate death. If modern man continues to flirt unhesitatingly with war, he will transform his earthly habitat into an inferno such as even the mind of Dante could not imagine.

Therefore I suggest that the philosophy and strategy of nonviolence become immediately a subject for study and for serious experimentation in every field of human conflict, by no means excluding the relations between nations. It is, after all, nation-states which make war, which have produced the weapons that threaten the survival of mankind and which are both genocidal and suicidal in character.

We have ancient habits to deal with, vast structures of power, indescribably complicated problems to solve. But unless we abdicate our humanity altogether and succumb to fear and impotence in the presence of the weapons we have ourselves created, it is as possible and as urgent to put an end to war and violence between nations as it is to put an end to poverty and racial injustice.

The United Nations is a gesture in the direction of nonviolence on a world scale. There, at least, states that oppose one another have sought to do so with words instead of with weapons. But true nonviolence is more than the absence of violence. It is the persistent and determined application of peaceable power to offenses against the community—in this case the world community. As the United Nations moves ahead with the giant tasks confronting it, I would hope that it would earnestly examine the uses of nonviolent direct action.

I do not minimize the complexity of the problems that need to be faced in achieving disarmament and peace. But I am convinced that we shall not have the will, the courage and the insight to deal with such matters unless in this field we are prepared to undergo a mental and spiritual reevaluation, a change of focus which will enable us to see that the things that seem most real and powerful are indeed now unreal and have come under the sentence of death. We need to make a supreme effort to generate the readiness, indeed the eagerness, to enter into the new world which is now possible, "the city which hath foundation, whose Building and Maker is God."

It is not enough to say, "We must not wage war." It is necessary to love peace and sacrifice for it. We must concentrate not merely on the eradication of war but on the affirmation of peace. A fascinating story about Ulysses and the Sirens is preserved for us in Greek literature. The Sirens had the ability to sing so sweetly that sailors could not resist steering toward their island. Many ships were lured upon the rocks, and men forgot home, duty and honor as they flung themselves into the sea to be embraced by arms that drew them down to death. Ulysses, determined not to succumb to the Sirens, first decided to tie himself tightly to the mast of his boat and his crew stuffed their ears with wax. But finally he and his crew learned a better way to save themselves: They took on board the beautiful singer Orpheus, whose melodies were sweeter than the music of the Sirens. When Orpheus sang, who would bother to listen to the Sirens?

So we must see that peace represents a sweeter music, a cosmic melody that is far superior to the discords of war. Somehow we must transform the dynamics of the world power struggle from the nuclear arms race, which no one can win, to a creative contest to harness man's genius for the purpose of making peace and prosperity a reality for all the nations of the world. In short, we must shift the arms race into a "peace race." If we have the will and determination to mount such a peace offensive, we will unlock hitherto tightly sealed doors of hope and bring new light into the dark chambers of pessimism.

III

The stability of the large world house which is ours will involve a revolution of values to accompany the scientific and freedom revolutions engulfing the earth. We must rapidly begin the shift from a "thing"-oriented society to a "person"-oriented society. When machines and computers, profit motives and property rights are considered more important than people, the giant triplets of racism, materialism and militarism are incapable of being conquered. A civilization can flounder as readily in the face of moral and spiritual bankruptcy as it can through financial bankruptcy.

This revolution of values must go beyond traditional capitalism and communism. We must honestly admit that capitalism has often left a gulf between superfluous wealth and abject poverty, has created conditions permitting necessities to be taken from the many to give luxuries to the few, and has encouraged smallhearted men to become cold and conscienceless so that, like Dives before Lazarus, they are unmoved by suffering, poverty-stricken humanity. The profit motive, when it is the sole basis of an economic system, encourages a cutthroat competition and selfish ambition that inspire men to be more I-centered than thou-centered. Equally, communism reduces men to a cog in the wheel of the state. The communist may object, saying that in Marxian theory the state is an "interim reality" that will "wither away" when the classless society emerges. True—in theory; but it is also true that, while the state lasts, it is an end in itself. Man is a means to that end. He has no inalienable rights. His only rights are derived from, and conferred by, the state. Under such a system the fountain of freedom runs dry. Restricted are man's liberties of press and assembly, his freedom to vote and his freedom to listen and to read.

Truth is found neither in traditional capitalism nor in classical communism. Each represents a partial truth. Capitalism fails to see the truth in collectivism. Communism fails to see the truth in individualism. Capitalism fails to realize that life is social. Communism fails to realize that life is personal. The good and just society is neither the thesis of capitalism nor the antithesis of communism, but a socially conscious democracy which reconciles the truths of individualism and collectivism.

We have seen some moves in this direction. The Soviet Union has gradually moved away from its rigid communism and begun to concern itself with consumer products, art and a general increase in benefits to the individual citizen. At the same time, through constant social reforms, we have seen many modifications in laissez-faire capitalism. The problems we now face must take us beyond slogans for their solution. In the final analysis, the right-wing slogans on "government control" and "creeping socialism" are as meaningless and adolescent as the Chinese Red Guard slogans against "bourgeois revisionism." An intelligent approach to the problems of poverty and racism will cause us to see that the words of the Psalmist—"The earth is the Lord's and the fullness thereof"—are still a judgment upon our use and abuse of the wealth and resources with which we have been endowed.

A true revolution of value will soon cause us to question the fairness and justice of many of our past and present policies. We are called to play the good samaritan on life's roadside; but that will be only an initial act. One day the whole Jericho road must be transformed so that men and women will not be beaten and robbed as they make their journey through life. True compassion is more than flinging a coin to a beggar; it understands that an edifice which produces beggars needs restructuring.

A true revolution of values will soon look uneasily on the glaring contrast of poverty and wealth. With righteous indignation, it will look at thousands of working people displaced from their jobs with reduced incomes as a result of automation while the profits of the employers remain intact, and say: "This is not just." It will look across the oceans and see individual capitalists of the West investing huge sums of money in Asia, Africa and South America, only to take the profits out with no concern for the social betterment of the countries, and say: "This is not just." It will look at our alliance with the landed gentry of Latin America and say: "This is not just." The Western arrogance of feeling that it has everything to teach others and nothing to learn from them is not just. A true revolution of values will lay hands on the world order and say of war: "This way of settling differences is not just." This business of burning human beings with napalm, of filling our nation's homes with orphans and widows, of injecting poisonous drugs of hate into the veins of peoples normally humane, of sending men home from dark and bloody battlefields physically handicapped and psychologically deranged, cannot be reconciled with wisdom, justice and love. A nation that continues year after year to spend more money on military defense than on programs of social uplift is approaching spiritual death.

America, the richest and most powerful nation in the world, can well lead the way in this revolution of values. There is nothing to prevent us from paying adequate wages to schoolteachers, social workers and other servants of the public to insure that we have the best available personnel in these positions which are charged with the responsibility of guiding our future generations. There is nothing but a lack of social vision to prevent us from paying an adequate wage to every American citizen whether he be a hospital worker, laundry worker, maid or day laborer. There is nothing except shortsightedness to prevent us from guaranteeing an annual minimum—and *livable*—income for every American family. There is nothing, except a tragic death wish, to prevent us from reordering our priorities, so that the pursuit of peace will take precedence over the pursuit of war. There is nothing to keep us from remolding a recalcitrant status quo with bruised hands until we have fashioned it into a brotherhood.

This kind of positive revolution of values is our best defense against communism. War is not the answer. Communism will never be defeated by the use of atomic bombs or nuclear weapons. Let us not join those who shout war and who through their misguided passions urge the United States to relinquish its participation in the United Nations. These are days which demand wise restraint and calm reasonableness. We must not call everyone a Communist or an appeaser who advocates the seating of Red China in the United Nations, or who recognizes that hate and hysteria are not the final answers to the problems of these turbulent days. We must not engage in a negative anticommunism, but rather in a positive thrust for democracy, realizing that our greatest defense against communism is to take offensive action in behalf of justice. We must with affirmative action seek to remove those conditions of poverty, insecurity and injustice which are the fertile soil in which the seed of communism grows and develops.

These are revolutionary times. All over the globe men are revolting against old systems of exploitation and oppression, and out of the wombs of a frail world new systems of justice and equality are being born. The shirtless and barefoot people of the earth are rising up as never before. "The people who sat in darkness have seen a great light." We in the West must support these revolutions. It is a sad fact that, because of comfort, complacency, a morbid fear of communism and our proneness to adjust to injustice, the Western nations that initiated so much of the revolutionary spirit of the modern world have now become the arch antirevolutionaries. This has driven many to feel that only Marxism has the revolutionary spirit. Communism is a judgment on our failure to make democracy real and to follow through on the revolutions that we initiated. Our only hope today lies in our ability to recapture the revolutionary spirit and go out into a sometimes hostile world declaring eternal opposition to poverty, racism and militarism. With this powerful commitment we shall boldly challenge the status quo and unjust mores and thereby speed the day when "every valley shall be exalted, and every mountain and hill shall be made low: and the crooked shall be made straight and the rough places plain."

A genuine revolution of values means in the final analysis that our loyalties must become ecumenical rather than sectional. Every nation must now develop an overriding loyalty to mankind as a whole in order to preserve the best in their individual societies.

This call for a world-wide fellowship that lifts neighborly concern beyond one's tribe, race, class and nation is in reality a call for an all-embracing and unconditional love for all men. This often misunderstood and misinterpreted concept has now become an absolute necessity for the survival of man. When I speak of love, I am speaking of that force which all the great religions have seen as the supreme unifying principle of life. Love is the key that unlocks the door which leads to ultimate reality. This Hindu-Moslem-Christian-Jewish-Buddhist belief about ultimate reality is beautifully summed up in the First Epistle of Saint John:

Let us love one another: for love is of God: and every one that loveth is born of God, and knoweth God. He that loveth not knoweth not God; for God is love. . . . If we love one another, God dwelleth in us, and his love is perfected in us.

Let us hope that this spirit will become the order of the day. We can no longer afford to worship the God of hate or bow before the altar of retaliation. The oceans of history are made turbulent by the ever-rising tides of hate. History is cluttered with the wreckage of nations and individuals who pursued this self-defeating path of hate. As Arnold Toynbee once said in a speech: "Love is the ultimate force that makes for the saving choice of life and good against the damning choice of death and evil. Therefore the first hope in our inventory must be the hope that love is going to have the last word."

We are now faced with the fact that tomorrow is today. We are confronted with the fierce urgency of *now*. In this unfolding conundrum of life and history there is such a thing as being too late. Procrastination is still the thief of time. Life often leaves us standing bare, naked and dejected with a lost opportunity. The "tide in the affairs of men" does not remain at the flood; it ebbs. We may cry out desperately for time to pause in her passage, but time is deaf to every plea and rushes on. Over the bleached bones and jumbled residues of numerous civilizations are written the pathetic words: "Too late." There is an invisible book of life that faithfully records our vigilance or our neglect. "The moving finger writes, and having writ moves on. . . ." We still have a choice today: nonviolent coexistence or violent coannihilation. This may well be mankind's last chance to choose between chaos and community.

Martin Luther King, Jr., *Where Do We Go From Here: Chaos or Community?* (New York: Harper & Row, 1967).

# 57

# The Trumpet of Conscience

*The Canadian Broadcasting Corporation aired these sermons during November and December of 1967 as part of the seventh annual Massey Lectures. The lectures are named in honor of the late Rt. Hon. Vincent Massey, former governor General of Canada. After the uproar caused by his 4 April 1967 Riverside Church speech against the Vietnam War, Dr. King courageously continued to launch forthright criticisms against the Johnson administration's war policy. Many black and white leaders condemned him. They considered his stance to be anti-American and thoroughly irresponsible. Many of his closest "friends" deserted him. His stance, however, proved to be prophetic. His commitments to love, nonviolence, peace, and justice are central themes in these sermonic lectures.*

## CONSCIENCE AND THE VIETNAM WAR (CHAPTER 2)

It is many months now since I found myself obliged by conscience to end my silence and to take a public stand against my country's war in Vietnam. The considerations which led me to that painful decision have not disappeared; indeed, they have been magnified by the course of events since then. The war itself is intensified; the impact on my country is even more destructive.

I cannot speak about the great themes of violence and nonviolence, of social change and of hope for the future, without reflecting on the tremendous violence of Vietnam.

Since the spring of 1967, when I first made public my opposition to my government's policy, many persons have questioned me about the wisdom of my decision. "Why *you?*" they have said. "Peace and civil rights don't mix. Aren't you hurting the cause of your people?" And when I hear such questions, I have been greatly saddened, for they mean that the inquirers have never really known me, my commitment, or my calling. Indeed, that question suggests that they do not know the world in which they live.

In explaining my position, I have tried to make it clear that I remain perplexed—as I think everyone must be perplexed—by the complexities and ambiguities of Vietnam. I would not wish to underrate the need for a collective solution to this tragic war. I would wish neither to present North Vietnam or the National Liberation Front as paragons of virtue nor to overlook the role they can play in the successful resolution of the problem. While they both may have justifiable reasons to be suspicious of the good faith of the United States, life and history give eloquent testimony to the fact that conflicts are never resolved without trustful give-and-take on both sides.

Since I am a preacher by calling, I suppose it is not surprising that I had several reasons for bringing Vietnam into the field of my moral vision. There is at the outset a very obvious and almost facile connection between the war in Vietnam and the struggle I and others have been waging in America. A few years ago there was a shining moment in that struggle. It seemed as if there was a real promise of hope for the poor, both black and white, through the poverty program. There were experiments, hopes, new beginnings. Then came the buildup in Vietnam, and I watched the program broken and eviscerated as if it were some idle political plaything of a society gone mad on war, and I knew that America would never invest the necessary funds or energies in rehabilitation of its poor so long as adventures like Vietnam continued to draw men and skills and money like some demoniacal destructive suction tube. And so I was increasingly compelled to see the war not only as a moral outrage but also as an enemy of the poor, and to attack it as such.

Perhaps a more tragic recognition of reality took place when it became clear to me that the war was doing far more than devastating the hopes of the poor at home. It was sending their sons and their brothers and their husbands to fight and die and in extraordinarily higher proportions relative to the rest of the population. We were taking the black young men who had been crippled by our society and sending them eight thousand miles away to guarantee liberties in Southeast Asia which they had not found in southwest Georgia and east Harlem. And so we have been repeatedly faced with the cruel irony of watching Negro and white boys on TV screens as they kill and die together for a nation that has been unable to seat them together in the same schools. We watch them in brutal solidarity burning the huts of a poor village, but we realize that they would never live on the same block in Detroit. I could not be silent in the face of such cruel manipulation of the poor.

My third reason moves to an even deeper level of awareness, but it grows out of my experience in the ghettos of the North over the last three years—especially the last three summers. As I have walked among the desperate, rejected, angry young men, I have told them that Molotov cocktails and rifles would not solve their problems. I have tried to offer them my deepest compassion, while maintaining my conviction that social change comes most meaningfully through nonviolent action. But, they asked, and rightly so, what about Vietnam? They asked if our own nation wasn't using massive doses of violence to solve its problems, to bring about the changes it wanted. Their questions hit home, and I knew that I could never again raise my voice against the violence of the oppressed in the ghettos without first having spoken clearly to the greatest purveyor of violence in the world today: my own government. For the sake of those boys, for the sake of this government, for the sake of the hundreds of thousands trembling under our violence, I cannot be silent.

For those who ask the question, "Aren't you a civil rights leader?"— and thereby mean to exclude me from the movement for peace—I answer by saying that I have worked too long and hard now against segregated public accommodations to end up segregating my moral concern. Justice is indivisible. It must also be said that it would be rather absurd to work passionately and unrelentingly for integrated schools and not be concerned about the survival of a world in which to be integrated. I must say further that something in the very nature of our organizational structure in the Southern Christian Leadership Conference led me to this decision. In 1957, when a group of us formed that organization, we chose as our motto: "To save the soul of America." Now it should be incandescently clear that no one who has any concern for the integrity and life of America today can ignore the present war.

As if the weight of such a commitment were not enough, another burden of responsibility was placed upon me in 1964: I cannot forget that the Nobel Prize for Peace was also a commission—a commission to work harder than I had ever worked before for "the brotherhood of man." This is a calling which takes me beyond national allegiances, but even if it were not present, I would yet have to live with the meaning of my commitment to the ministry of Jesus Christ. To me the relationship of this ministry to the making of peace is so obvious that I sometimes marvel at those who ask me why I am speaking against the war. We are called to speak for the weak, for the voiceless, for the victims of our nation, and for those it calls enemy, for no document from human hands can make these humans any less our brothers.

And as I ponder the madness of Vietnam and search within myself for ways to understand and respond in compassion, my mind goes constantly to the people of that peninsula. I speak now not of the soldiers of each side, not of the junta in Saigon, but simply of the people who have been living under the curse of war for almost three continuous decades now. I think of them, too, because it is clear to me that there will be no meaningful solution until some attempt is made to know them and to hear their broken cries.

They must see the Americans as strange liberators. The Vietnamese people proclaimed their own independence in 1945 after a combined French and Japanese occupation and before the Communist revolution in China. They were led by Ho Chi Minh. Even though they quoted the American Declaration of Independence in their own document of freedom, we refused to recognize them. Our government felt then that the Vietnamese people weren't ready for independence, and we again fell victim to the deadly Western arrogance that has poisoned the international atmosphere for so long.

For nine years following 1945 we vigorously supported the French in their abortive attempt to recolonize Vietnam. After the French were defeated, it looked as if independence and land reform would come through the Geneva Agreements. But instead there came the United States, determined that Ho should not unify the temporarily divided nation, and the peasants watched again as we supported one of the most vicious modern dictators, Premier Diem. The peasants watched and cringed as Diem ruthlessly rooted out all opposition, supported their extortionist landlords, and refused even to discuss reunification with the North. The peasants watched as all this was presided over by U.S. influence and then by increasing numbers of U.S. troops, who came to help quell the insurgency that Diem's methods had aroused. When Diem was overthrown, they may have been happy, but the long line of military dictatorships seemed to offer no real change, especially in terms of their need for land and peace.

The only change came from America, as we increased our troop commitments in support of governments which were singularly corrupt, inept, and without popular support. All the while, the people read our leaflets and received regular promises of peace and democracy and land reform. Now they languish under our bombs and consider us—not their fellow Vietnamese—the real enemy. They move sadly and apathetically as we herd them off the land of their fathers into concentration camps where minimal social needs are rarely met. They know that they must move or be destroyed by our bombs, and they go, primarily women and children and the aged. They watch as we poison their water, as we kill a million acres of their crops, and they wander into the hospitals with at least twenty casualties from American fire power to one Vietcong-inflicted injury. They wander into the towns and see thousands of children homeless, without clothes, running in packs on the streets like animals. They see the children selling their sisters to our soldiers, soliciting for their mothers.

What do the peasants think, as we ally ourselves with the landlords, and as we refuse to put any action into our many words concerning land reform? Where are the roots of the independent Vietnam we claim to be building? Is it among these voiceless ones?

We have destroyed their two most cherished institutions: the family and the village. We have destroyed their land and their crops. We have cooperated in crushing one of the nation's only non-Communist revolutionary political forces, the United Buddhist church. We have supported the enemies of the peasants of Saigon. We have corrupted their women and children and killed their men. What liberators!

Now there is little left to build on—save bitterness. And soon the only solid physical foundations remaining will be found at our military bases and in the concrete of the concentration camps we call fortified hamlets. The peasants may well wonder if we plan to build our new Vietnam on such grounds as these; could we blame them for such thoughts? We must speak for them, and raise the questions they cannot raise. These, too, are our brothers.

Perhaps the more difficult but no less necesssary task is to speak for those who have been designated as our enemies. What of the National Liberation Front? How can they believe in our integrity when now we speak of "aggression from the North" as if there were nothing more essential to the war? How can they trust us when now we charge them with violence after the murderous reign of Diem? And charge them with violence when we pour every new weapon of death into their land? Surely we must understand their feelings, even if we do not condone their actions. How do they judge us when our officials know that their membership is less than 25 percent Communist and yet insist on giving them the blanket name? They ask how we can speak of free elections when the Saigon press is censored and controlled by the military junta. Their questions are frighteningly relevant. Is our nation planning to build on political myth again and then shore it up with the power of new violence?

Here is the true meaning and value of compassion and nonviolence, when they help us to see the enemy's point of view, to hear his questions, to know his assessment of ourselves. For from his view we may indeed see the basic weaknesses of our own condition, and if we are mature, we may learn and grow and profit from the wisdom of the brothers who are called the opposition.

So, too, with Hanoi. In the North, where our bombs now pummel the land and our mines endanger the waterways, we are met by a deep but understandable mistrust. In Hanoi are the men who led the nation to independence against the Japanese and the French. It was they who led a second struggle against French domination, and then were persuaded to give up the land they controlled between the thirteenth and seventeenth parallels as a temporary measure at Geneva. After 1954 they watched us conspire with Diem to prevent elections which would surely have brought Ho Chi Minh to power over a united Vietnam, and they realized they had been betrayed again.

When we ask why they do not leap to negotiate, these things must be remembered. Also, it must be clear that the leaders of Hanoi consider the presence of American troops in support of the Diem regime to have been the initial military breach of the Geneva Agreements concerning foreign troops. They remind us that they did not begin to send in any large number of supplies or men until American forces had moved in to the tens of thousands. Hanoi remembers how our leaders refused to tell the truth about the earlier North Vietnamese overtures for peace, how we claimed that none existed when they had clearly been made. Ho Chi Minh has watched as America has spoken of peace and built up its forces, and now he has surely heard the increasing international rumors of American plans for an invasion of the North.

At this point, I should make it clear that while I have tried in these last few minutes to give a voice to the voiceless in Vietnam and to understand the arguments of those who are called enemy, I am as deeply concerned about our own troops there as anything else. For it occurs to me that what we are submitting them to in Vietnam is not simply the brutalizing process that goes on in any war, where armies face each other and seek to destroy. We are adding cynicism to the process of death, for they must know after a short period there that none of the things we claim to be fighting for are really involved, and the more sophisticated surely realize that we are on the side of the wealthy and the secure while we create a hell for the poor.

If we continue, there will be no doubt in my mind and in the mind of the world that we have no honorable intentions in Vietnam. It will become clear that our minimal expectation is to occupy it as an American colony, and men will not refrain from thinking that our maximum hope is to goad China into a war so that we may bomb her nuclear installations.

Somehow this madness must cease. We must stop now. I speak as a child of God and brother to the suffering poor of Vietnam. I speak for those whose land is being laid waste, whose homes are being destroyed, whose culture is being subverted. I speak for the poor of America who are paying the double price of smashed hopes at home and death and corruption in Vietnam. I speak as a citizen of the world, for the world as it stands aghast at the path we have taken. I speak as an American to the leaders of my own nation. The great initiative in this war is ours. The initiative to stop it must be ours.

In the spring of 1967, I made public the steps I consider necessary for this to happen. I should add now only that while many Americans have supported the proposals, the government has so far not recognized one of them. These are the times for real choices and not false ones. We are at the moment when our lives must be placed on the line if our nation is to survive its own folly. Every man of humane convictions must decide on the protest that best suits his convictions, but we must all protest.

There is something seductively tempting about stopping there and going off on what in some circles has become a popular crusade against the war in Vietnam. I say we must enter that struggle, but I wish to go on now to say something even more disturbing. The war in Vietnam is but a symptom of a far deeper malady within the American spirit.

In 1957 a sensitive American official overseas said that it seemed to him that our nation was on the wrong side of a world revolution. I am convinced that if we are to get on the right side of the world revolution we as a nation must undergo a radical revolution of values. A true revolution of values will soon cause us to question the fairness and justice of many of our past and present policies. A true revolution of values will soon look uneasily on the glaring contrast between poverty and wealth. With righteous indignation, it will look across the seas and see individual capitalists of the West investing huge sums of money in Asia, Africa, and South America only to take the profits out with no concern for the social betterment of the countries, and say: "This is not just." It will look at our alliance with the landed gentry of Latin America and say: "This is not just." The Western arrogance of feeling that it has everything to teach others and nothing to learn from them is not just. A true revolution of values will lay hands on the world order and say of war: "This way of settling differences is not just." This business of burning human beings with napalm, of filling our nation's homes with orphans and widows, of injecting poisonous drugs of hate into the veins of peoples normally humane, of sending men home from dark and bloody battlefields physically handicapped and psychologically deranged, cannot be reconciled with wisdom, justice, and love. A nation that continues year after year to spend more money on military defense than on programs of social uplift is approaching spiritual doom.

This kind of positive revolution of values is our best defense against communism. War is not the answer. Communism will never be defeated by the use of atomic bombs or nuclear weapons.

These are revolutionary times; all over the globe men are revolting against old systems of exploitation and oppression. The shirtless and barefoot people of the land are rising up as never before. "The people that walked in darkness have seen a great light." We in the West must support these revolutions. It is a sad fact that because of comfort, complacency, a morbid fear of communism, and our proneness to adjust to injustice, the Western nations that initiated so much of the revolutionary spirit of the modern world have now become the arch-antirevolutionaries. This has driven many to feel that only Marxism has the revolutionary spirit. Therefore, communism is a judgment against our failure to make democracy real and follow through on the revolutions that we initiated. We must move past indecision to action. We must find new ways to speak for peace in Vietnam and for justice throughout the developing world, a world that borders on our doors. If we do not act, we shall surely be dragged down the long, dark, and shameful corridors of time reserved for those who possess power without compassion, might without morality, and strength without sight.


## YOUTH AND SOCIAL ACTION (CHAPTER 3)

When Paul Goodman published *Growing Up Absurd*, in 1960, he electrified the public with his description of the shattering impact on the young generation of the spiritual emptiness of contemporary society. Now, years later, it is not spiritual emptiness that is terrifying, but spiritual evil.

Today, young men of America are fighting, dying, and killing in Asian jungles in a war whose purposes are so ambiguous the whole nation seethes with dissent. They are told they are sacrificing for democracy, but the Saigon regime, their ally, is a mockery of democracy, and the black American soldier has himself never experienced democracy.

While the war devours the young abroad, at home urban outbreaks pit black youth against young soldiers and guardsmen, as racial and economic justice exhausts human endurance. Prosperity gluts the middle and upper classes, while poverty imprisons more than thirty million Americans and starvation literally stalks rural areas of the South.

Crime rises in every segment of society. As diseases are conquered and health is improved, mass drug consumption and alcoholism assume epidemic proportions.

The alienation of young people from society rises to unprecedented levels, and masses of voluntary exiles emerge as modern gypsies, aimless and empty.

This generation is engaged in a cold war, not only with the earlier generation, but with the values of its society. It is not the familiar and normal hostility of the young groping for independence. It has a new quality of bitter antagonism and confused anger which suggests basic issues are being contested.

These are unprecedented attitudes because this generation was born and matured in unprecedented conditions.

The generation of the past twenty-five years cannot be understood unless we remember that it has lived during that period through the effects of four wars: World War II, the "cold war," the Korean War, and Vietnam. No other generation of young Americans was ever exposed to a remotely similar traumatic experience. Yet as spiritually and physically abrasive as this may be, it is not the worst aspect of contemporary experience. This is the first generation to grow up in the era of the nuclear bomb, knowing that it may be the last generation of mankind.

This is the generation not only of war, but of war in its ultimate revelation. This is the generation that truly has no place to hide and no place to find security.

These are evils enough to send reason reeling. And of course they are not the only ones. All of them form part of the matrix in which this generation's character and experience were formed. The tempest of evils provides the answer for those adults who ask why this young generation is so unfathomable, so alienated, and frequently so freakish. For the young people of today, peace and social tranquillity are as unreal and remote as knight-errantry.

Under the impact of social forces unique to their times, young people have splintered into three principal groups, though of course there is some overlap among the three.

The largest group of young people is struggling to adapt itself to the prevailing values of our society. Without much enthusiasm, they accept the system of government, the economic relationships of the property system, and the social stratifications both engender. But even so, they are a profoundly troubled group, and are harsh critics of the status quo.

In this largest group, social attitudes are not congealed or determined; they are fluid and searching. Though all recent studies point to the fact that the war in Vietnam is a focus of concern, most of them are not ready to resist the draft or to take clear-cut stands on issues of violence and nonviolence. But their consciences have been touched by the feeling that is growing, all over the world, of the horror and insanity of war, of the imperative need to respect life, of the urgency of moving past war as a way to solve international problems. So while they will not glorify war, and while they feel ambiguous about America's military posture, this majority group reflects the confusion of the larger society, which is itself caught up in a kind of transitional state of conscience as it moves slowly toward the realization that war cannot be justified in the human future.

There is a second group of young people, the radicals. They range from moderate to extreme in the degree to which they want to alter the social system. All of them agree that only by *structural* change can current evils be eliminated, because the roots are in the system rather than in men or in faulty operation. These are a new breed of radicals. Very few adhere to any established ideology; some borrow from old doctrines of revolution; but practically all of them suspend judgment on what the form of a new society must be. They are in serious revolt against old values and have not yet concretely formulated the new ones. They are not repeating previous revolutionary doctrines; most of them have not even read the revolutionary classics. Ironically, their rebelliousness comes from having been frustrated in seeking change within the framework of the existing society. They tried to build racial equality and met tenacious and vicious opposition. They worked to end the Vietnam war and experienced futility. So they seek a fresh start with new rules in a new order. It is fair to say, though, that at present they know what they don't want rather than what they do want. Their radicalism is growing because the power structure of today is unrelenting in defending not only its social system but the evils it contains; so, naturally, it is intensifying the opposition.

What is the attitude of this second radical group to the problem of violence? In a word, mixed; there are young radicals today who are pacifists, and there are others who are armchair revolutionaries who insist on the political and psychological need for violence. These young theorists of violence elaborately scorn the process of dialogue in favor of the "tactics of confrontation"; they glorify the guerrilla movement and especially its new martyr, Che Guevara; and they equate revolutionary consciousness with the readiness to shed blood. But across the spectrum of attitudes toward violence that can be found among the radicals is there a unifying thread? I think there is. Whether they read Gandhi or Frantz Fanon, all the radicals understand the need for action—direct self-transforming and structure-transforming action. This may be their most creative collective insight.

The young people in the third group are currently called "hippies." They may be traced in a fairly direct line from yesterday's beatniks. The hippies are not only colorful, but complex; and in many respects their extreme conduct illuminates the negative effects of society's evils on sensitive young people. While there are variations, those who identify with this group have a common philosophy. They are struggling to disengage from society as their expression of their rejection of it. They disavow responsibility to organized society. Unlike the radicals, they are seeking not change but flight. When occasionally they merge with a peace demonstration, it is not to better the political world, but to give expression to their own world. The hardcore hippie is a remarkable contradiction. He uses drugs to turn inward, away from reality, to find peace and security. Yet he advocates love as the highest human value—love, which can exist only in communication between people, and not in the total isolation of the individual.

The importance of the hippies is not in their unconventional behavior, but in the fact that some hundreds of thousands of young people, in turning to a flight from reality, are expressing a profoundly discrediting judgment on the society they emerge from.

It seems to me that the hippies will not last long as a mass group. They cannot survive because there is no solution in escape. Some of them may persist by solidifying into a secular religious sect; their movement already has many such characteristics. We might see some of them establish utopian colonies, like the seventeenth- and eighteenth-century communities established by sects that profoundly opposed the existing order and its values. Those communities did not survive. But they were important to their contemporaries because their dream of social justice and human value continues as a dream of mankind.

In this context, one dream of the hippie group is very significant, and that is its dream of peace. Most of the hippies are pacifists, and a few have thought their way through to a persuasive and psychologically sophisticated "peace strategy." And society at large may be more ready now to learn from that dream than it was a century or two ago, to listen to the argument for peace, not as a dream, but as a practical possibility: something to choose and use.

From this quick tour of the three main groupings of our young people, it should be evident that this generation is in substantial ferment.

Even the large group that is not disaffected from society is putting forward basic questions, and its restlessness helps us understand the radicals with their angry protest and the hippies with their systematic withdrawal.

When the less sensitive supporters of the status quo try to argue against some of these condemnations and challenges, they usually cite the technological marvels our society has achieved. However, that only reveals their poverty of spirit. Mammoth productive facilities with computer minds, cities that engulf the landscape and pierce the clouds, planes that almost outrace time—these are awesome, but they cannot be spiritually inspiring. Nothing in our glittering technology can raise man to new heights, because material growth has been made an end in itself, and, in the absence of moral purpose, man himself becomes smaller as the works of man become bigger.

Another distortion in the technological revolution is that, instead of strengthening democracy at home, it has helped to eviscerate it. Gargantuan industry and government, woven into an intricate computerized mechanism, leave the person outside. The sense of participation is lost, the feeling that ordinary individuals influence important decisions vanishes, and man becomes separated and diminished.

When an individual is no longer a true participant, when he no longer feels a sense of responsibility to his society, the content of democracy is emptied. When culture is degraded and vulgarity enthroned, when the social system does not build security but induces peril, inexorably the individual is impelled to pull away from a soulless society. This process produces alienation—perhaps the most pervasive and insidious development in contemporary society.

Alienation is not confined to our young people, but it is rampant among them. Yet alienation should be foreign to the young. Growth requires connection and trust. Alienation is a form of living death. It is the acid of despair that dissolves society.

Up to now, I have been looking at the tragic factors in the quarter-century of history that today's youth has lived through. But is there another side? Are there forces in that quarter-century that could reverse the process of alienation? We must now go back over those twenty-five years to search for positive ingredients which have been there, but in relative obscurity.

Against the exaltation of technology, there has always been a force struggling to respect higher values. None of the current evils rose without resistance, nor have they persisted without opposition.

During the early 1950s the hangman operating with the cold war troops was McCarthyism. For years it decimated social organizations, throttled free expression, and intimidated into bleak silence not only liberals and radicals but men in high and protected places. A very small band of courageous people fought back, braving ostracism, slander, and loss of livelihood. Gradually and painfully, however, the democratic instinct of Americans was awakened, and the ideological brute force was routed.

However, McCarthyism left a legacy of social paralysis. Fear persisted through succeeding years, and social reform remained inhibited and defensive. A blanket of conformity and intimidation conditioned young and old to exalt mediocrity and convention. Criticism of the social order was still imbued with implications of treason. The war in Korea was unpopular, but it was never subject to the searching criticisms and mass demonstrations that currently characterize opposition to the war in Vietnam.

The blanket of fear was lifted by Negro youth. When they took their struggle to the streets, a new spirit of resistance was born. Inspired by the boldness and ingenuity of Negroes, white youth stirred into action and formed an alliance that aroused the conscience of the nation.

It is difficult to exaggerate the creative contribution of young Negroes. They took nonviolent resistance, first employed in Montgomery, Alabama, in mass dimensions, and developed original forms of application—sit-ins, freedom rides, and wade-ins. To accomplish these, they first transformed themselves. Young Negroes had traditionally imitated whites in dress, conduct, and thought in a rigid, middle-class pattern. Gunnar Myrdal described them as exaggerated Americans. Now they ceased imitating and began initiating. Leadership passed into the hands of Negroes, and their white allies began learning from them. This was a revolutionary and wholesome development for both. It is ironic that today so many educators and sociologists are seeking methods to instill middle-class values in Negro youth as the ideal in social development. It was precisely when young Negroes threw off their middle-class values that they made an historic social contribution. They abandoned those values when they put careers and wealth in a secondary role. When they cheerfully became jailbirds and troublemakers, when they took off their Brooks Brothers attire and put on overalls to work in the isolated rural South, they challenged and inspired white youth to emulate them. Many left school, not to abandon learning, but to seek it in more direct ways. They were constructive school dropouts, a variety that strengthened the society and themselves. These Negro and white youth preceded the conception of the Peace Corps, and it is safe to say that their work was the inspiration for its organization on an international scale.

The collective effort that was born out of the civil rights alliance was awesomely fruitful for this country in the first years of the 1960s. The repressive forces that had not been seriously challenged for almost a decade now faced an aroused adversary. A torrent of humanist thought and action swept across the land, scoring first small and then larger victories. The awakening grew in breadth, and the contested issues encompassed other social questions. A phalanx of reliable young activists took protest from hiding and revived a sense of responsible rebellion. A peace movement was born.

The Negro freedom movement would have been historic and worthy even if it had only served the cause of civil rights. But its laurels are greater because it stimulated a broader social movement that elevated the moral level of the nation. In the struggle against the preponderant evils of the society, decent values were preserved. Moreover, a significant body of young people learned that in opposing the tryannical forces that were crushing them they added stature and meaning to their lives. The Negro and white youth who in alliance fought bruising engagements with the status quo inspired each other with a sense of moral mission, and both gave the nation an example of self-sacrifice and dedication.

These years—the late sixties—are a most crucial time for the movement I have been describing. There is a sense in which it can be said that the civil rights and peace movements are over—at least in their first form, the protest form, which gave them their first victories. There is a sense in which the alliance of responsible young people which the movement represented has fallen apart under the impact of failures, discouragement, and consequent extremism and polarization. The movement for social change has entered a time of temptation to despair because it is clear now how deep and systemic are the evils it confronts. There is a temptation to break up into mutually suspicious extremist groups, in which blacks reject the participation of whites and whites reject the realities of their own history.

But meanwhile, as the young people face this crisis, leaders in the movement are working out programs to bring the social movements through from their early, and now inadequate, protest phase to a new stage of massive, active, nonviolent resistance to the evils of the modern system. As this work and this planning proceed, we begin to glimpse tremendous vistas of what it might mean for the world if the new programs of resistance succeed in forging an even wider alliance of today's awakened youth.

Nonviolent active resistance to social evils, including massive civil disobedience when there is need for it, can unite in a new action-synthesis the best insights of all three groups I have pointed out among our young people. From the hippies, it can accept the vision of peaceful means to a goal of peace, and also their sense of beauty, gentleness, and of the unique gifts of each man's spirit. From the radicals, it can adopt the burning sense of urgency, the recognition of the need for direct and collective action, and the need for strategy and organization. And because the emerging program is neither one of anarchy nor one of despair, it can welcome the work and insights of those young people who have not rejected our present society in its totality. They can challenge the more extreme groups to integrate the new vision into history as it actually is, into society as it actually works. They can help the movement not to break the bruised reed or to quench the smoking wick of values that are already recognized in the society that we want to change. And they can help keep open the possibility of honorable compromise.

If the early civil rights movement bore some international fruit in the formation of a peace corps, this new alliance could do far more. Already our best young workers in the United States are talking about the need to organize in international dimensions. They are beginning to form conscious connections with their opposite numbers in other countries. The conscience of an awakened activist cannot be satisfied with a focus on local problems, if only because he sees that local problems are all interconnected with world problems. The young men who are beginning to see that they must refuse to leave their country in order to fight and kill others might decide to leave their country, at least for a while, in order to share their life with others. There is as yet not even an outline in existence of what structure this growing world-consciousness might find for itself. But a dozen years ago there was not even an outline for the Negro civil rights movement in its first phase. The spirit is awake now; structures will follow, if we keep our ears open to the spirit. Perhaps the structural forms will emerge from other countries, propelled by another experience of the shaping of history.

But we do not have much time. The revolutionary spirit is already world-wide. If the anger of the peoples of the world at the injustice of things is to be channeled into a revolution of love and creativity, we must begin now to work, with all the peoples, to shape a new world.

## NONVIOLENCE AND SOCIAL CHANGE (CHAPTER 4)

There is nothing wrong with a traffic law which says you have to stop for a red light. But when a fire is raging, the fire truck goes right through that red light, and normal traffic had better get out of its way. Or, when a man is bleeding to death, the ambulance goes through those red lights at top speed.

There is a fire raging now for the Negroes and the poor of this society. They are living in tragic conditions because of the terrible economic injustices that keep them locked in as an "underclass," as the sociologists are now calling it. Disinherited people all over the world are bleeding to death from deep social and economic wounds. They need brigades of ambulance drivers who will have to ignore the red lights of the present system until the emergency is solved.

Massive civil disobedience is a strategy for social change which is at least as forceful as an ambulance with its siren on full. In the past ten years, nonviolent civil disobedience has made a great deal of history, especially in the southern United States. When we and the Southern Christian Leadership Conference went to Birmingham, Alabama, in

1963, we had decided to take action on the matter of integrated public accommodations. We went knowing that the Civil Rights Commission had written powerful documents calling for change, calling for the very rights we were demanding. But nobody did anything about the commission's report. Nothing was done until we acted on these very issues, and demonstrated before the court of world opinion the urgent need for change. It was the same story with voting rights. The Civil Rights Commission, three years before we went to Selma, had recommended the changes we started marching for, but nothing was done until, in 1965, we created a crisis the nation couldn't ignore. Without violence, we totally disrupted the system, the life style of Birmingham, and then of Selma, with their unjust and unconstitutional laws. Our Birmingham struggle came to its dramatic climax when some thirty-five hundred demonstrators virtually filled every jail in that city and surrounding communities, and some four thousand more continued to march and demonstrate nonviolently. The city knew then in terms that were crystal-clear that Birmingham could no longer continue to function until the demands of the Negro community were met. The same kind of dramatic crisis was created in Selma two years later. The result on the national scene was the Civil Rights Bill and the Voting Rights Act, as president and Congress responded to the drama and the creative tension generated by the carefully planned demonstrations.

Of course, by now it is obvious that new laws are not enough. The emergency we now face is economic, and it is a desperate and worsening situation. For the 35 million poor people in America—not even to mention, just yet, the poor in the other nations—there is a kind of strangulation in the air. In our society it is murder, psychologically, to deprive a man of a job or an income. You are in substance saying to that man that he has no right to exist. You are in a real way depriving him of life, liberty, and the pursuit of happiness, denying in his case the very creed of his society. Now, millions of people are being strangled in that way. The problem is international in scope. And it is getting worse, as the gap between the poor and the "affluent society" increases.

The question that now divides the people who want radically to change that situation is: can a program of nonviolence—even if it envisions massive civil disobedience—realistically expect to deal with such an enormous, entrenched evil?

First of all, will nonviolence work, psychologically, after the summer of 1967? Many people feel that nonviolence as a strategy for social change was cremated in the flames of the urban riots of the last two years. They tell us that Negroes have only now begun to find their true manhood in violence; that the riots prove not only that Negroes hate whites, but that, compulsively, they must destroy them.

This blood-lust interpretation ignores one of the most striking features of the city riots. Violent they certainly were. But the violence, to a startling degree, was focused against property rather than against people. There were very few cases of injury to persons, and the vast majority of the rioters were not involved at all in attacking people. The much publicized "death toll" that marked the riots, and the many injuries, were overwhelmingly inflicted on the rioters by the military. It is clear that the riots were exacerbated by police action that was designed to injure or even to kill people. As for the snipers, no account of the riots claims that more than one or two dozen people were involved in sniping. From the facts, an unmistakable pattern emerges: a handful of Negroes used gunfire substantially to intimidate, not to kill; and all of the other participants had a different target—property.

I am aware that there are many who wince at a distinction between property and persons—who hold both sacrosanct. My views are not so rigid. A life is sacred. Property is intended to serve life, and no matter how much we surround it with rights and respect, it has no personal being. It is part of the earth man walks on; it is not man.

The focus on property in the 1967 riots is not accidental. It has a message; it is saying something.

If hostility to whites were ever going to dominate a Negro's attitude and reach murderous proportions, surely it would be during a riot. But this rare opportunity for bloodletting was sublimated into arson, or turned into a kind of stormy carnival of free-merchandise distribution. Why did the rioters avoid personal attacks? The explanation cannot be fear of retribution, because the physical risks incurred in the attacks on property were no less than for personal assaults. The military forces were treating acts of petty larceny as equal to murder. Far more rioters took chances with their own lives, in their attacks on property, than threatened the life of anyone else. Why were they so violent with property then? Because property represents the white power structure, which they were attacking and trying to destroy. A curious proof of the symbolic aspect of the looting for some who took part in it is the fact that, after the riots, police received hundreds of calls from young Negroes trying to return merchandise they had taken. Those people wanted the experience of taking, of redressing the power imbalance that property represents. Possession, afterward, was secondary.

A deeper level of hostility came out in arson, which was far more dangerous than the looting. But it, too, was a demonstration and a warning. It was directed against symbols of exploitation, and it was designed to express the depth of anger in the community.

What does this restraint in the summer riots mean for our future strategy?

If one can find a core of nonviolence toward persons, even during the riots when emotions were exploding, it means that nonviolence should not be written off for the future as a force in Negro life. Many people believe that the urban Negro is too angry and too sophisticated to be nonviolent. Those same people dismiss the nonviolent marches in the South and try to describe them as processions of pious, elderly ladies. The fact is that in all the marches we have organized some men of very violent tendencies have been involved. It was routine for us to collect hundreds of knives from our own ranks before the demonstrations, in case of momentary weakness. And in Chicago last year we saw some of the most violent individuals accepting nonviolent discipline. Day after day during those Chicago marches I walked in our lines and I never saw anyone retaliate with violence. There were lots of provocations, not only the screaming white hoodlums lining the sidewalks, but also groups of Negro militants talking about guerrilla warfare. We had some gang leaders and members marching with us. I remember walking with the Blackstone Rangers while bottles were flying from the sidelines, and I saw their noses being broken and blood flowing from their wounds; and I saw them continue and not retaliate, not one of them, with violence. I am convinced that even very violent temperaments can be channeled through nonviolent discipline, if the movement is moving, if they can act constructively and express through an effective channel their very legitimate anger.

But even if nonviolence can be valid, psychologically, for the protesters who want change, is it going to be effective, strategically, against a government and a status quo that have so far resisted this summer's demands on the grounds that "we must not reward the rioters"? Far from rewarding the rioters, far from even giving a hearing to their just and urgent demands, the administration has ignored its responsibility for the causes of the riots, and instead has used the negative aspects of them to justify continued inaction on the underlying issues. The administration's only concrete response was to initiate a study and call for a day of prayer. As a minister, I take prayer too seriously to use it as an excuse for avoiding work and responsibility. When a government commands more wealth and power than has ever before been known in the history of the world, and offers no more than this, it is worse than blind, it is provocative. It is paradoxical but fair to say that Negro terrorism is incited less on ghetto street corners than in the halls of Congress.

I intended to show that nonviolence will be effective, but not until it has achieved the massive dimensions, the disciplined planning, and the intense commitment of a sustained, direct-action movement of civil disobedience on the national scale.

The dispossessed of this nation—the poor, both white and Negro— live in a cruelly unjust society. They must organize a revolution against that injustice, not against the lives of the persons who are their fellow citizens, but against the structures through which the society is refusing to take means which have been called for, and which are at hand, to lift the load of poverty.

The only real revolutionary, people say, is a man who has nothing to lose. There are millions of poor people in this country who have very little, or even nothing, to lose. If they can be helped to take action together, they will do so with a freedom and a power that will be a new and unsettling force in our complacent national life. Beginning in the new year, we will be recruiting three thousand of the poorest citizens from ten different urban and rural areas to initiate and lead a sustained, massive, direct-action movement in Washington. Those who choose to join this initial three thousand, this nonviolent army, this "freedom church" of the poor, will work with us for three months to develop nonviolent action skills. Then we will move on Washington, determined to stay there until the legislative and executive branches of the government take serious and adequate action on jobs and income. A delegation of poor people can walk into a high official's office with a carefully, collectively prepared list of demands. (If you're poor, if you're unemployed anyway, you can choose to stay in Washington as long as the struggle needs you.) And if that official says, "But Congress would have to approve this," or, "But the president would have to be consulted on that," you can say, "All right, we'll wait." And you can settle down in his office for as long a stay as necessary. If you are, let's say, from rural Mississippi, and have never had medical attention, and your children are undernourished and unhealthy, you can take those little children into the Washington hospitals and stay with them there until the medical workers cope with their needs, and in showing it your children you will have shown this country a sight that will make it stop in its busy tracks and think hard about what it has done. The many people who will come and join this three thousand, from all groups in the country's life, will play a supportive role, deciding to be poor for a time along with the dispossessed who are asking for their right to jobs or income—jobs, income, the demolition of slums, and the rebuilding by the people who live there of new communities in their place; in fact, a new economic deal for the poor.

Why camp in Washington to demand these things? Because only the federal Congress and administration can decide to use the billions of dollars we need for a real war on poverty. We need, not a new law, but a massive, new national program. This Congress has done nothing to help such measures, and plenty to hinder them. Why should Congress care about our dying cities? It is still dominated by senior representatives of the rural South, who still unite in an obstructive coalition with unprogressive northerners to prevent public funds from going where they are socially needed. We broke that coalition in 1963 and 1964, when the Civil Rights and Voting Rights laws were passed. We need to break it again by the size and force of our movement, and the best place to do that is before the eyes and inside the buildings of these same congressmen. The people of this country, if not the congressmen, are ready for a serious economic attack on slums and unemployment, as two recent polls by Lou Harris have revealed. So we have to make Congress ready to act on the plight of the poor. We will prod and sensitize the legislators, the administrators, and all the wielders of power until they have faced this utterly imperative need.

I have said that the problem, the crisis we face, is international in scope. In fact, it is inseparable from an international emergency which involves the poor, the dispossessed, and the exploited of the whole world.

Can a nonviolent, direct-action movement find application on the international level, to confront economic and political problems? I believe it can. It is clear to me that the next stage of the movement is to become international. National movements within the developed countries—forces that focus on London, or Paris, or Washington, or Ottawa—must help to make it politically feasible for their governments to undertake the kind of massive aid that the developing countries need if they are to break the chains of poverty. We in the West must bear in mind that the poor countries are poor primarily because we have exploited them through political or economic colonialism. Americans in particular must help their nation repent of her modern economic imperialism.

But movements in our countries alone will not be enough. In Latin America, for example, national reform movements have almost despaired of nonviolent methods; many young men, even many priests, have joined guerrilla movements in the hills. So many of Latin America's problems have roots in the United States of America that we need to form a solid, united movement, nonviolently conceived and carried through, so that pressure can be brought to bear on the capital and government power structures concerned, from both sides of the problem at once. I think that may be the only hope for a nonviolent solution in Latin America today; and one of the most powerful expressions of nonviolence may come out of that international coalition of socially aware forces, operating outside governmental frameworks.

Even entrenched problems like the South African government and its racial policies could be tackled on this level. If just two countries, Britain and the United States, could be persuaded to end all economic interaction with the South African regime, they could bring that government to its knees in a relatively short time. Theoretically, the British and American governments could make that kind of decision; almost every corporation in both countries has economic ties with its government which it could not afford to do without. In practice, such a decision would represent such a major reordering of priorities that we should not expect that any movement could bring it about in one year or two. Indeed, although it is obvious that nonviolent movements for social change must internationalize, because of the interlocking nature of the problems they all face, and because otherwise those problems will breed war, we have hardly begun to build the skills and the strategy, or even the commitment, to planetize our movement for social justice.

In a world facing the revolt of ragged and hungry masses of God's children; in a world torn between the tensions of East and West, white and colored, individualists and collectivists; in a world whose cultural and spiritual power lags so far behind her technological capabilities that we live each day on the verge of nuclear co-annihilation; in this world, nonviolence is no longer an option for intellectual analysis, it is an imperative for action.

Martin Luther King, Jr., *The Trumpet of Conscience* (New York: Harper & Row, 1967).

# APPENDIX:
# ADDITIONAL INTERVIEW

# 58

# Conversation with Martin Luther King

*The editor of* Conservative Judaism *introduced this transcription with the following headnote: "On the evening of March 25, 1968, ten days before he was killed, Dr. Martin Luther King appeared at the sixty-eighth annual convention of the Rabbinical Assembly. He responded to questions which had been submitted in advance to Rabbi Everett Gendler, who chaired the meeting.*

*Here is a transcript of what was said that evening, beginning with the words of Professor Abraham Joshua Heschel, who presented Dr. King to the assembled rabbis."*

*The poignant "conversation" took place in the afterglow of Rabbi Abraham Joshua Heschel's introduction of Dr. King before his fellow rabbis, and foreshadowed the broken civil rights alliance between many Jewish and African American leaders.*

DR. HESCHEL:    Where does moral religious leadership in America come from today? The politicians are astute, the establishment is proud, and the market place is busy. Placid, happy, merry, the people pursue their work, enjoy their leisure, and life is fair. People buy, sell, celebrate and rejoice. They fail to realize that in the midst of our affluent cities there are districts of despair, areas of distress.

Where does God dwell in America today? Is He at home with those who are complacent, indifferent to other people's agony, devoid of mercy? Is He not rather with the poor and the contrite in the slums?

Dark is the world for me, for all its cities and stars. If not for the few signs of God's radiance who could stand such agony, such darkness?

Where in America today do we hear a voice like the voice of the prophets of Israel? Martin Luther King is a sign that God has not forsaken the United States of America. God has sent him to us. His presence is the hope of America. His mission is sacred, his leadership of supreme importance to every one of us.

The situation of the poor in America is our plight, our sickness. To be deaf to their cry is to condemn ourselves.

Martin Luther King is a voice, a vision and a way. I call upon every Jew to harken to his voice, to share his vision, to follow in his way. The whole future of America will depend upon the impact and influence of Dr. King.

May everyone present give of his strength to this great spiritual leader, Martin Luther King.

DR. KING: I need not pause to say how very delighted I am to be here this evening and to have the opportunity of sharing with you in this significant meeting, but I do want to express my deep personal appreciation to each of you for extending the invitation. It is always a very rich and rewarding experience when I can take a brief break from the day-to-day demands of our struggle for freedom and human dignity and discuss the issues involved in that struggle with concerned friends of good will all over our nation. And so I deem this a real and a great opportunity.

Another thing that I would like to mention is that I have heard "We Shall Overcome" probably more than I have heard any other song over the last few years. It is something of the theme song of our struggle, but tonight was the first time that I ever heard "We Shall Overcome" in Hebrew, so that, too, was a beautiful experience for me, to hear that great song in Hebrew.

It is also a wonderful experience to be here on the occasion of the sixtieth birthday of a man that I consider one of the truly great men of our day and age, Rabbi Heschel. He is indeed a truly great prophet.

I've looked over the last few years, being involved in the struggle for racial justice, and all too often I have seen religious leaders stand amid the social injustices that pervade our society, mouthing pious irrelevancies and sanctimonious trivialities. All too often the religious community has been a tail light instead of a head light.

But here and there we find those who refuse to remain silent behind the safe security of stained glass windows, and they are forever seeking to make the great ethical insights of our Judeo-Christian heritage relevant in this day and in this age. I feel that Rabbi Heschel is one of the persons who is relevant at all times, always standing with prophetic insights to guide us through these difficult days.

He has been with us in many of our struggles. I remember marching from Selma to Montgomery, how he stood at my side and with us as we faced that crisis situation. I remember very well when we were in Chicago for the Conference on Religion and Race. Eloquently and profoundly he spoke on the issues of race and religion, and to a great extent this speech inspired clergymen of all the religious faiths of our country; many went out and decided to do something that they had not done before. So I am happy to be here with him, and I want to say Happy Birthday, and I hope I can be here to celebrate your one hundredth birthday.

I am not going to make a speech. We must get right to your questions. I simply want to say that we do confront a crisis in our nation, a crisis born of many problems. We see on every hand the restlessness of the comfortable and the discontent of the affluent, and somehow it seems that this mammoth ship of state is not moving toward new and more secure shores but toward old, destructive rocks.

It seems to me that all people of good will must now take a stand for that which is just, that which is righteous. Indeed, in the words of the prophet Amos, "Let justice roll down like the waters and righteousness like a mighty stream."

Our priorities are mixed up, our national purposes are confused, our policies are confused, and there must somehow be a reordering of priorities, policies and purposes. I hope, as we discuss these issues tonight, that together we will be able to find some guidelines and some sense of direction.

RABBI EVERETT GENDLER: We begin now with some of the batches of questions. And since the question of confusion came up, and the problem of politics, perhaps we can begin with two or three questions which are rather immediate and relate to some very recent developments. One question is, "At this point, who is your candidate for President?" One question is, "If as it now seems Johnson and Nixon are nominated, do you have any suggestions as an alternative for those seeking a voice in the profound moral issues of the day?" And a third question in this general area of immediacy, "Would you please comment on Congressman Powell's charge that you are a moderate, that you cater to Whitey, and also his criticism that you do not accept violence?" Some criticism!

DR. KING: Well, let me start with the first question. That is relatively easy for me because I have followed the policy of not endorsing candidates.

Somebody is saying stand, so I guess I'll have to . . .

RABBI GENDLER: Might I say that since Dr. King anticipates a good bit of footwork next month, we thought perhaps this particular evening he could remain off his feet.

DR. KING: I'll stand.

On the first question, I was about to say that I don't endorse candidates. That has been a policy in the Southern Christian Leadership Conference. We are a non-partisan organization. However, I do think the issues in this election are so crucial that it will be impossible for us to absolutely follow the past policy. I do think the voters of our nation need an alternative in the 1968 election, but I think we are in bad shape finding that alternative with simply Johnson on the one hand and Nixon on the other hand. I don't see the alternative there. Consequently, I must look elsewhere. I think in the candidacy of both Senator Kennedy and Senator McCarthy we see an alternative. It is not definite, as you know, that President Johnson will be renominated. Of course, we haven't had a situation since 1884 when an incumbent President was not renominated, if he wanted the nomination. But these are different days and it may well be that something will happen to make it possible for an alternative to develop within the Democratic party itself.

I think very highly of both Senator McCarthy and Senator Kennedy. I think they are both very competent men. I think they are both dedicated men. So I would settle with either man being nominated by the Democratic party.

On the question of Congressman Powell and his recent accusation, I must say that I would not want to engage in a public or private debate with Mr. Powell on his views concerning Martin Luther King. Frankly, I hope I am so involved in trying to do a job that has to be done that I will not come to the point of dignifying some of the statements that the Congressman has made.

I would like to say, however, on the question of being a moderate, that I always have to understand what one means. I think moderation on the one hand can be a vice; I think on the other hand it can be a virtue. If by moderation we mean moving on through this tense period of transition with wide restraint, calm reasonableness, yet militant action, then moderation is a great virtue which all leaders should seek to achieve. But if moderation means slowing up in the move for justice and capitulating to the whims and caprices of the guardians of the deadening status quo, then moderation is a tragic vice which all men of good will must condemn.

I don't see anything in the work that we are trying to do in the Southern Christian Leadership Conference which is suggestive of slowing up, which is suggestive of not taking a strong stand and a strong resistance to the evils of racial injustice. We have always stood up against injustices. We have done it militantly. Now, so often the word "militant" is misunderstood because most people think of militancy in military terms. But to be militant merely means to be demanding and to be persistent, and in this sense I think the non-violent movement has demonstrated great militancy. It is possible to be militantly non-violent.

On the question of appealing to "Whitey," I don't quite know what the Congressman means. But here again I think this is our problem which must be worked out by all people of good will, black and white. I feel that at every point we must make it clear that this isn't just a Negro problem, that white Americans have a responsibility, indeed a great responsibility, to work passionately and unrelentingly for the solution of the problem of racism, and if that means constantly reminding white society of its obligation, that must be done. If I have been accused of that, then I will have to continue to be accused.

Finally, I have not advocated violence. The Congressman is quite right. I haven't advocated violence, because I do not see it as the answer to the problem. I do not see it as the answer from a moral point of view and I do not see it as the answer from a practical point of view. I am still convinced that violence as the problematic strategy in our struggle to achieve justice and freedom in the United States would be absolutely impractical and it would lead to a dead-end street. We would end up creating many more social problems than we solve, and unborn generations would be the recipients of a long and desolate night of bitterness. Therefore, I think non-violence, militantly conceived and executed, well-organized, is the most potent weapon available to the black man in his struggle for freedom and human dignity.

RABBI GENDLER: Having raised several points that some of the questions referred to, we may proceed by a further exploration of some of these elements, Dr. King, and perhaps we could begin with several questions that relate to your evaluation of the internal mood of the black community.

Let me share some of the formulations of these questions with you. "How representative is the extremist element of the Negro community?" "How do we know who really represents the Negro community?" "If we are on a committee and there is a Negro militant and a Negro moderate, how shall a concerned white conduct himself?"

"What is your view of the thinking in some Negro circles which prefers segregation and separatism, improving the Negro's lot within this condition? How do you see Black Power in this respect?"

Black militants want complete separation. You speak of integration. How do you reconcile the two?"

"How can you work with those Negroes who are in complete opposition to your view, and I believe correct view, of integration?"

DR. KING: Let me start off with the question, "How representative are the extremist elements in the black community?" I assume when we say extremist elements we mean those who advocate violence, who advocate separatism as a goal. The fact is that these persons represent a very small segment of the Negro community at the present time. I don't know how the situation will be next year or the year after next, but at the present time the vast majority of Negroes in the United States feel that non-violence is the most effective method to deal with the problems that we face.

Polls have recently revealed this, as recently as two or three months ago. *Fortune* magazine conducted a pretty intensive poll, others have conducted such polls, and they reveal that about 92 percent of the Negroes of America feel that there must be some non-violent solution to the problem of racial injustice. The *Fortune* poll also revealed that the vast majority of the Negroes still feel that the ultimate solution to the problem will come through a meaningfully integrated society.

Now let me move into the question of integration and separation by dealing with the question of Black Power. I've said so often that I regret that the slogan Black Power came into being, because it has been so confusing. It gives the wrong connotation. It often connotes the quest for black domination rather than black equality. And it is just like telling a joke. If you tell a joke and nobody laughs at the joke and you have to spend the rest of the time trying to explain to people why they should laugh, it isn't a good joke. And that is what I have always said about the slogan Black Power. You have to spend too much time explaining what you are talking about. But it is a slogan that we have to deal with now.

I debated with Stokely Carmichael all the way down the highways of Mississippi, and I said, "Well, let's not use this slogan. Let's get the power. A lot of ethnic groups have power, and I didn't hear them marching around talking about Irish Power or Jewish Power; they just went out and got the power; let's go out and get the power." But somehow we managed to get just the slogan.

I think everybody ought to understand that there are positives in the concept of Black Power and the slogan, and there are negatives.

Let me briefly outline the positives. First, Black Power in the positive sense is a psychological call to manhood. This is desperately needed in the black community, because for all too many years black people have been ashamed of themselves. All too many black people have been ashamed of their heritage, and all too many have had a deep sense of inferiority, and something needed to take place to cause the black man not to be ashamed of himself, not to be ashamed of his color, not to be ashamed of his heritage.

It is understandable how this shame came into being. The nation made the black man's color a stigma. Even linguistics and semantics conspire to give this impression. If you look in Roget's *Thesaurus* you will find about 120 synonyms for black, and right down the line you will find words like smut, something dirty, worthless, and useless, and then you look further and find about 130 synonyms for white and they all represent something high, noble, pure, chaste—right down the line. In our language structure, a white lie is a little better than a black lie. Somebody goes wrong in the family and we don't call him a white sheep, we call him a black sheep. We don't say whitemail, but blackmail. We don't speak of white-balling somebody, but black-balling somebody.

The word black itself in our society connotes something that is degrading. It was absolutely necessary to come to a moment with a sense of dignity. It is very positive and very necessary. So if we see Black Power as a psychological call to manhood and black dignity, I think that's a positive attitude that I want my children to have. I don't want them to be ashamed of the fact that they are black and not white.

Secondly, Black Power is pooling black political resources in order to achieve our legitimate goals. I think that this is very positive, and it is absolutely necessary for the black people of America to achieve political power by pooling political resources. In Cleveland this summer we did engage in a Black Power move. There's no doubt about that. I think most people of good will feel it was a positive move. The same is true of Gary, Indiana. The fact is that Mr. Hatcher could not have been elected in Gary if black people had not voted in a bloc and then joined with a coalition of liberal whites. In Cleveland, black people voted in a bloc for Carl Stokes, joining with a few liberal whites. This was a pooling of resources in order to achieve political power.

Thirdly, Black Power in its positive sense is a pooling of black economic resources in order to achieve legitimate power. And I think there is much that can be done in this area. We can pool our resources, we can cooperate, in order to bring to bear on those who treat us unjustly. We have a program known as Operation Breadbasket in SCLC, and it is certainly one of the best programs we have. It is a very effective program and it's a simple program. It is just a program which demands a certain number of jobs from the private sector—that is, from businesses and industry. It demands a non-discriminatory policy in housing. If they don't yield, we don't argue with them, we don't curse them, we don't burn the store down. We simply go back to our people and we say that this particular company is not responding morally to the question of jobs, to the question of being just and humane toward the black people of the community, and we say that as a result of this we must withdraw our economic support.

That's Black Power in a real sense. We have achieved some very significant gains and victories as a result of this program, because the black man collectively now has enough buying power to make the difference between profit and loss in any major industry or concern of our country. Withdrawing economic support from those who will not be just and fair in their dealings is a very potent weapon.

Political power and economic power are needed, and I think these are the positives of Black Power.

I would see the negatives in two terms. First, in terms of black separatism. As I said, most Negroes do not believe in black separatism as the ultimate goal, but there are some who do and they talk in terms of totally separating themselves from white America. They talk in terms of separate states, and they really mean separatism as a goal. In this sense I must say that I see it as a negative because it is very unrealistic.

The fact is that we are tied together in an inescapable network of mutuality. Whether we like it or not and whether the racist understands it or not, our music, our cultural patterns, our poets, our material prosperity and even our food, are an amalgam of black and white, and there can be no separate black path to power and fulfillment that does not ultimately intersect white routes. There can be no separate white path to power and fulfillment, short of social disaster, that does not recognize the necessity of sharing that power with black aspirations for freedom and justice.

This leads me to say another thing, and that is that it isn't enough to talk about integration without coming to see that integration is more than something to be dealt with in esthetic or romantic terms. I think in the past all too often we did it that way. We talked of integration in romantic and esthetic terms and it ended up as merely adding color to a still predominantly white power structure.

What is necessary now is to see integration in political terms where there is sharing of power. When we see integration in political terms, then we recognize that there are times when we must see segregation as a temporary way-station to a truly integrated society. There are many Negroes who feel this; they do not see segregation as the ultimate goal. They do not see separation as the ultimate goal. They see it as a temporary way-station to put them into a bargaining position to get to that ultimate goal, which is a truly integrated society where there is shared power.

I must honestly say that there are points at which I share this view. There are points at which I see the necessity for temporary segregation in order to get to the integrated society. I can point to some cases. I've seen this in the South, in schools being integrated and I've seen it with Teachers' Associations being integrated. Often when they merge, the Negro is integrated without power. The two or three positions of power which he did have in the separate situation passed away altogether, so that he lost his bargaining position, he lost his power, and he lost his posture where he could be relatively militant and really grapple with the problems. We don't want to be integrated *out* of power; we want to be integrated *into* power.

And this is why I think it is absolutely necessary to see integration in political terms, to see that there are some situations where separation may serve as a temporary way-station to the ultimate goal which we seek, which I think is the only answer in the final analysis to the problem of a truly integrated society.

I think this is the mood which we find in the black community, generally, and this means that we must work on two levels. In every city, we have a dual society. This dualism runs in the economic market. In every city, we have two economies. In every city, we have two housing markets. In every city, we have two school systems. This duality has brought about a great deal of injustice, and I don't need to go into all that because we are all familiar with it.

In every city, to deal with this unjust dualism, we must constantly work toward the goal of a truly integrated society while at the same time we enrich the ghetto. We must seek to enrich the ghetto immediately in the sense of improving the housing conditions, improving the schools in the ghetto, improving the economic conditions. At the same time, we must be working to open the housing market so there will be one housing market only. We must work on two levels. We should gradually move to disperse the ghetto, and immediately move to improve conditions within the ghetto, which in the final analysis will make it possible to disperse it at a greater rate a few years from now.

RABBI GENDLER: Considering both the enlightenment and encouragement which I think many of us received just now from Dr. King's portrayal of the prevalent mood in the black community, we might move on to another complex of questions relating, Dr. King, to the prevailing mood in the black community which also would benefit from some clarification by you. This is what we might call the area of black and Jewish communal relations.

"What steps have been undertaken and what success has been noted in convincing anti-Semitic and anti-Israel Negroes, such as Rap Brown, Stokely Carmichael, and McKissick, to desist from their anti-Israel activity?" "What effective measures will the collective Negro community take against the vicious anti-Semitism, against the militance and the rabble-rousing of the Browns, Carmichaels, and Powells?"

"Have your contributions from Jews fallen off considerably? Do you feel the Jewish community is copping out on the civil rights struggle?"

"What would you say if you were talking to a Negro intellectual, an editor of a national magazine, and were told, as I have been, that he supported the Arabs against Israel because color is all important in this world? In the editor's opinion, the Arabs are colored Asians and the Israelis are white Europeans. Would you point out that more than half of the Israelis are Asian Jews with the same pigmentation as Arabs, or would you suggest that an American Negro should not form judgments on the basis of color? What seems to you an appropriate or an effective response?"

DR. KING: Thank you. I'm glad that question came up because I think it is one that must be answered honestly and forthrightly.

First let me say that there is absolutely no anti-Semitism in the black community in the historic sense of anti-Semitism. Anti-Semitism historically has been based on two false, sick, evil assumptions. One was unfortunately perpetuated even by many Christians, all too many as a matter of fact, and that is the notion that the religion of Judaism is anathema. That was the first basis for anti-Semitism in the historic sense.

Second, a notion was perpetuated by a sick man like Hitler and others that the Jew is innately inferior. Now in these two senses, there is virtually no anti-Semitism in the black community. There is no philosophical anti-Semitism or anti-Semitism in the sense of the historic evils of anti-Semitism that have been with us all too long.

I think we also have to say that the anti-Semitism which we find in the black community is almost completely an urban Northern ghetto phenomenon, virtually non-existent in the South. I think this comes into being because the Negro in the ghetto confronts the Jew in two dissimilar roles. On the one hand, he confronts the Jew in the role of being his most consistent and trusted ally in the struggle for justice in the civil rights movement. Probably more than any other ethnic group, the Jewish community has been sympathetic and has stood as an ally to the Negro in his struggle for justice.

On the other hand, the Negro confronts the Jew in the ghetto as his landlord in many instances. He confronts the Jew as the owner of the store around the corner where he pays more for what he gets. In Atlanta, for instance, I live in the heart of the ghetto, and it is an actual fact that my wife in doing her shopping has to pay more for food than whites have to pay out in Buckhead and Lennox. We've tested it. We have to pay five cents and sometimes ten cents a pound more for almost anything that we get than they have to pay out in Buckhead and Lennox Square where the rich people of Atlanta live.

The fact is that the Jewish storekeeper or landlord is not operating on the basis of Jewish ethics; he is operating simply as a marginal businessman. Consequently the conflicts come into being.

I remember when we were working in Chicago two years ago, we had numerous rent strikes on the West Side. And it was unfortunately true that the persons whom we had to conduct these strikes against were in most instances Jewish landlords. Now sociologically that came into being because there was a time when the West Side of Chicago was almost a Jewish community. It was a Jewish ghetto, so to speak, and when the Jewish community started moving out into other areas, they still owned the property there, and all of the problems of the landlord came into being.

We were living in a slum apartment owned by a Jew in Chicago along with a number of others, and we had to have a rent strike. We were paying $94 for four run-down, shabby rooms, and we would go out on our open housing marches on Gage Park and other places and we discovered that whites with five sanitary, nice, new rooms, apartments with five rooms out in those areas, were paying only $78 a month. We were paying twenty percent tax.

It so often happens that the Negro ends up paying a color tax, and this has happened in instances where Negroes have actually confronted Jews as the landlord or the storekeeper, or what-have-you. And I submit again that the tensions of the irrational statements that have been made are a result of these confrontations.

I think the only answer to this is for all people to condemn injustice wherever it exists. We found injustices in the black community. We find that some black people, when they get into business, if you don't set them straight, can be rascals. And we condemn them. I think when we find examples of exploitation, it must be admitted. That must be done in the Jewish community too.

I think our responsibility in the black community is to make it very clear that we must never confuse *some* with *all*, and certainly in SCLC we have consistently condemned anti-Semitism. We have made it clear that we cannot be the victims of the notion that you deal with one evil in society by substituting another evil. We cannot substitute one tyranny for another, and for the black man to be struggling for justice and then turn around and be anti-Semitic is not only a very irrational course but it is a very immoral course, and wherever we have seen anti-Semitism we have condemned it with all of our might.

We have done it through our literature. We have done it through statements that I have personally signed, and I think that's about all that we can do as an organization to vigorously condemn anti-Semitism wherever it exits.

On the Middle East crisis, we have had various responses. The response of some of the so-called young militants again does not represent the position of the vast majority of Negroes. There are some who are color-consumed and they see a kind of mystique in being colored, and anything non-colored is condemned. We do not follow that course in the Southern Christian Leadership Conference, and certainly most of the organizations in the civil rights movement do not follow that course.

I think it is necessary to say that what is basic and what is needed in the Middle East is peace. Peace for Israel is one thing. Peace for the Arab side of that world is another thing. Peace for Israel means security, and we must stand with all of our might to protect its right to exist, its territorial integrity. I see Israel, and never mind saying it, as one of the great outposts of democracy in the world, and a marvelous example of what can be done, how desert land almost can be transformed into an oasis of brotherhood and democracy. Peace for Israel means security and that security must be a reality.

On the other hand, we must see what peace for the Arabs means in a real sense of security on another level. Peace for the Arabs means the kind of economic security that they so desperately need. These nations, as you know, are part of that third world of hunger, of disease, of illiteracy. I think that as long as these conditions exist there will be tensions, there will be the endless quest to find scapegoats. So there is a need for a Marshall Plan for the Middle East, where we lift those who are at the bottom of the economic ladder and bring them into the mainstream of economic security.

This is how we have tried to answer the question and deal with the problem in the Southern Christian Leadership Conference, and I think that represents the thinking of all of those in the Negro community, by and large, who have been thinking about this issue in the Middle East.

RABBI GENDLER: Thank you very much, Dr. King. Perhaps we could share now a few questions relating to some of the domestic issues of poverty. A couple of them ask about the Kerner Report. "If the Kerner Report recommendations are implemented, will it make a difference?" "What is your opinion of the report of the Kerner Commission?"

Another raises the question of people of good intentions wanting to deal with slum problems and hardly knowing what to do, feeling that most of the simple tutoring and palliative efforts in the community may not amount to much, given the entire context of the system. It speaks of the power structure, the establishment finding funds for supersonic transports, moon projects, technological developments which are mere luxuries, for Vietnam, but not for those pressing needs which affect millions here at home. "Can you suggest why the establishment seems to work this way? Is it an accident or does it have deeper causes? What seem to you the minimal changes needed in the system in order to achieve some greater measure of social justice and equality?"

And perhaps related to this is the question of some of the realistic goals of the poor peoples' campaign to be held in Washington beginning April 22nd.

DR. KING: Thank you. I want to start this answer by reiterating something that I said earlier, and that is that we do face a great crisis in our nation. Even though the President said today that we have never had it so good, we must honestly say that for many people in our country they've never had it so bad. Poverty is a glaring, notorious reality for some forty million Americans. I guess it wouldn't be so bad for them if it were shared misery, but it is poverty amid plenty. It is poverty in the midst of an affluent society, and I think this is what makes for great frustration and great despair in the black community and the poor community of our nation generally.

In the past in the civil rights movement we have been dealing with segregation and all of its humiliation, we've been dealing with the political problem of the denial of the right to vote. I think it is absolutely necessary now to deal massively and militantly with the economic problem. If this isn't dealt with, we will continue to move as the Kerner Commission said, toward two societies, one white and one black, separate and unequal. So the grave problem facing us is the problem of economic deprivation, with the syndrome of bad housing and poor education and improper health facilities all surrounding this basic problem.

This is why in SCLC we came up with the idea of going to Washington, the seat of government, to dramatize the gulf between promise and fulfillment, to call attention to the gap between the dream and the realities, to make the invisible visible. All too often in the rush of everyday life there is a tendency to forget the poor, to overlook the poor, to allow the poor to become invisible, and this is why we are calling our campaign a poor peoples' campaign. We are going to Washington to engage in non-violent direct action in order to call attention to this great problem of poverty and to demand that the government do something, more than a token, something in a large manner to grapple with the economic problem.

We know, from my experiences in the past, that the nation does not move on questions involving genuine equality for the black man unless something is done to bring pressure to bear on Congress, and to appeal to the conscience and the self-interest of the nation.

I remember very well that we had written documents by the Civil Rights Commission at least three years before we went to Birmingham, recommending very strongly all of the things that we dramatized in our direct action in Birmingham. But the fact is that the government did not move, Congress did not move, until we developed a powerful, vibrant movement in Birmingham, Alabama.

Two years before we went into Selma, the Civil Rights Commission recommended that something be done in a very strong manner to eradicate the discrimination Negroes faced in the voting area in the South. And yet nothing was done about it until we went to Selma, mounted a movement and really engaged in action geared toward moving the nation away from the course that it was following.

I submit this evening that we have had numerous documents, numerous studies, numerous recommendations made on the economic question, and yet nothing has been done. The things that we are going to be demanding in Washington have been recommended by the President's Commission on Technology, Automation and Economic Progress. These same things were recommended at our White House Conference on Civil Rights. The Urban Coalition came into being after the Detroit riot, and recommended these things.

The Kerner Commission came out just a few days ago recommending some of the same things that we will be demanding. I think it is basically a very sound, realistic report on the conditions, with some very sound recommendations, and yet nothing has been done. Indeed, the President himself has not made any move toward implementing any of the recommendations of that Commission. I am convinced that nothing will be done until enough people of good will get together to respond to the kind of movement that we will have in Washington, and bring these issues out in the open enough so that the Congressmen, who are in no mood at the present time to do anything about this problem, will be forced to do something about it.

I have see them change in the past. I remember when we first went up and talked about a civil rights bill in 1963, right after it had been recommended by President Kennedy on the heels of the Birmingham movement. Mr. Dirksen was saying that it was unconstitutional, particularly Title I dealing with integrated public accommodations. He was showing us that it was unconstitutional. Yet we got enough people moving—we got rabbis moving, we got priests moving, we got Protestant clergymen moving, and they were going around Washington and they were staying on top of it, they were lobbying, they were saying to Mr. Dirksen and others that this must be done.

Finally, the Congress changed altogether. One day when Senator Russell saw that the civil rights bill would be passed and that the Southern wing could not defeat it, he said, "We could have blocked this thing if these preachers hadn't stayed around Washington so much."

Now the time has come for preachers and everybody else to get to Washington and get this very recalcitrant Congress to see that it must do something and that it must do it soon, because I submit that if something isn't done, similar to what it recommended by the Kerner Commission, we are going to have organized social disruption, our cities are going to continue to go up in flames, more and more black people will get frustrated, and the extreme voices calling for violence will get a greater hearing in the black community.

So far they have not influenced many, but I contend that if something isn't done very soon to deal with this basic economic problem to provide jobs and income for all America, then the extremist voices will be heard more and those who are preaching non-violence will often have their words falling on deaf ears. This is why we feel that this is such an important campaign.

We need a movement now to transmute the rage of the ghetto into a positive constructive force. And here again we feel that this movement is so necessary because the anger is there, the despair is growing every day, the bitterness is very deep, and the leader has the responsibility of trying to find an answer. I have been searching for that answer a long time, over the last eighteen months.

I can't see the answer in riots. On the other hand, I can't see the answer in tender supplications for justice. I see the answer in an alternative to both of these, and that is militant non-violence that is massive enough, that is attention-getting enough to dramatize the problems, that will be as attention-getting as a riot, that will not destroy life or property in the process. And this is what we hope to do in Washington through our movement.

We feel that there must be some structural changes now, there must be a radical re-ordering of priorities, there must be a de-escalation and a final stopping of the war in Vietnam and an escalation of the war against poverty and racism here at home. And I feel that this is only going to be done when enough people get together and express their determination through that togetherness and make it clear that we are not going to allow any military-industrial complex to control this country.

One of the great tragedies of the war in Vietnam is that it has strengthened the military-industrial complex, and it must be made clear now that there are some programs that we can cut back on—the space program and certainly the war in Vietnam—and get on with this program of a war on poverty. Right now we don't even have a skirmish against poverty, and we really need an all out, mobilized war that will make it possible for all of God's children to have the basic necessities of life.

RABBI GENDLER: Because Dr. King must still meet tonight at least briefly with certain men from particular areas in the country, and because Reverend Young must also meet with some men from the Washington area immediately after this session, regretfully we have time for only one more question.

Although Dr. King is probably a bit weary and it is even conceivable that some of you are, I must say I very much regret that we haven't more time to pick up some of the supplementary questions. Yet we have time really for only one last question, and I should imagine that, knowing the mood of the Rabbinical Assembly, the final questions have been asked in these kinds of terms, Dr. King.

One is, "What can we best do as rabbis to further the rights and equal status of our colored brethren?" Another is, "What specific role do you think we as rabbis can play in this current civil rights struggle? What role do you see for our congregants?

How can all of us who are concerned participate with you in seeking this goal of social justice?"

DR. KING: Thank you very much for raising that because I do think that is a good note to end on, and I would hope that somehow we can get some real support, not only for the over-all struggle, but for the immediate campaign ahead in the city of Washington.

Let me say that we have failed to say something to America enough. I'm very happy that the Kerner Commission had the courage to say it. However difficult it is to hear, however shocking it is to hear, we've got to face the fact that America is a racist country. We have got to face the fact that racism still occupies the throne of our nation. I don't think we will ultimately solve the problem of racial injustice until this is recognized, and until this is worked on.

Racism is the myth of an inferior race, of an inferior people, and I think religious institutions, more than any other institutions in society, must really deal with racism. Certainly we all have a responsibility—the federal government, the local governments, our educational institutions. But the religious community, being the chief moral guardian of the over-all community should really take the primary responsibility in dealing with this problem of racism, which is largely attitudinal.

So I see one specific job in the educational realm: destroying the myths and the half-truths that have constantly been disseminated about Negroes all over the country and which lead to many of these racist attitudes, getting rid once and for all of the notion of white supremacy.

I think also I might say, concerning the Washington campaign, that there is a need to interpret what we are about or will be about in Washington because the press has gone out of its way in many instances to misinterpret what we will be doing in Washington.

There is a need to interpret to all of those who worship in our congregations what poor people face in this nation, and to interpret the critical nature of the problem. We are dealing with the problem of poverty. We must be sure that the people of our country will see this as a matter of justice.

The next thing that I would like to mention is something very practical and yet we have to mention it if we are going to have movements. We are going to bring in the beginning about 3,000 people to Washington from fifteen various communities. They are going to be poor people, mainly unemployed people, some who are too old to work, some who are too young to work, some who are too physically disabled to work, some who are able to work but who can't get jobs. They are going to be coming to Washington to bring their problems, to bring their burdens to the seat of government, and to demand that the government do something about it.

Being poor, they certainly don't have any money. I was in Marks, Mississippi the other day and I found myself weeping before I knew it. I met boys and girls by the hundreds who didn't have any shoes to wear, who didn't have any food to eat in terms of three square meals a day, and I met their parents, many of whom don't even have jobs. But not only do they not have jobs, they are not even getting an income. Some of them aren't on any kind of welfare, and I literally cried when I heard men and women saying that they were unable to get any food to feed their children.

We decided that we are going to try to bring this whole community to Washington, from Marks, Mississippi. They don't have anything anyway. They don't have anything to lose. And we decided that we are going to try to bring them right up to Washington where we are going to have our Freedom School. There we are going to have all of the things that we have outlined and that we don't have time to go into now, but in order to bring them to Washington it is going to take money.

They'll have to fed after they get to Washington, and we would hope that those who are so inclined, those who have a compassion for the least of these God's children, will aid us financially. Some will be walking and we'll be using church busses to get them from point to point. Some will be coming up on mule train. We're going to have a mule train coming from Mississippi, connecting with Alabama, Georgia, going right on up, and in order to carry that out you can see that financial aid will be greatly needed.

But not only that. We need bodies to bring about the pressure that I have mentioned to get Congress and the nation moving in the right direction. The stronger the number the greater this movement will be.

We will need some people working in supportive roles, lobbying in Washington, talking with the Congressmen, talking with the various departments of government, and we will need some to march with us as we demonstrate in the city of Washington. Some have already done this, like Rabbi Gendler and others. When we first met him it was in Albany, Georgia and there along with other rabbis and Protestant clergymen and Catholic clergymen we developed a movement. And there have been others—as I said earlier, Rabbi Heschel in Selma and other movements.

The more of this kind of participation that we can get, the more helpful it will be, for after we get the 3,000 people in Washington, we want the non-poor to come in in a supportive role. Then on June fifteenth we want to have massive march on Washington. You see, the 3,000 are going to stay in Washington at least sixty days, or however long we feel it is necessary, but we want to provide an opportunity once more for thousands, hundreds of thousands of people to come to Washington, reminiscent of March 1963 when thousands of people said we are here because we endorse the demands of the poor people who have been here all of these weeks trying to get Congress to move. We would hope that as many people in your congregations as you can find will come to Washington on June fifteenth.

You can see that it is a tremendous logistics problem and it means real organization, which we are getting into. We would hope that all or our friends will go out of their way to make that a big day, indeed the largest march that has ever taken place in the city of Washington.

These are some of the things that can be done. I'm sure I've missed some, but these are the ones that are on my mind right now and I believe that this kind of support would bring new hope to those who are now in very despairing conditions. I still believe that with this kind of coalition of conscience we will be able to get something moving again in America, something that is so desperately needed.

RABBI GENDLER: I think that all of us, Dr. King, recall the words of Professor Heschel at the beginning of this evening. He spoke of the word, the vision and the way that you provide. We certainly have heard words of eloquence, words which at the same time were very much to the point, and through these I think that we have the opportunity now to share more fully in your vision.

As for the way, it is eminently clear that the paths you tread are peaceful ones leading to greater peace. You may be sure that not only have we heard your words and not only do we share your vision, but many of us will take advantage of the privilege of accompanying you in further steps on the path that all of us must tread.

Thank you, Dr. King.

*Conservative Judaism*, XXII, no. 3, Spring 1968.

# Selected Bibliography

*I. BOOKS by Martin Luther King, Jr.*

King, Jr., Martin Luther, *A Martin Luther King Treasury*, ed., Alfred E. Cain, The Negro Heritage Library. Yonkers: Educational Heritage, Inc., 1964.

——. *The Measure of a Man*. Biographical Sketch by Truman Douglas. Boston: Pilgrim Press, 1968.

——. *The Measure of a Man*. Philadelphia: Christian Education Press, 1959.

——. *Strength to Love*. New York: Harper & Row, Publishers, 1963.

——. *Stride Toward Freedom: The Montgomery Story*. New York: Harper & Row, Publishers, 1958.

——. *The Trumpet of Conscience*. Foreword by Coretta Scott King. New York: Harper & Row, Publishers, 1968.

——. *The Trumpet of Conscience*. New York: Harper & Row, Publishers, 1967.

——. *Where Do We Go from Here: Chaos or Community?* New York: Harper & Row, Publishers, 1967.

——. *Why We Can't Wait*. New York: Harper & Row, Publishers, 1963.


*II. CHAPTERS (in books) by Martin Luther King, Jr.*

King, Jr., Martin Luther, "Call to Conscience. *Representative American Speeches, 1963–1964.* " Edited by Lester Thonssen. New York: H. W. Williams, 1964.

——. "A Challenge to the Churches and Synagogues. *Race: Challenge to Religion.*" Edited by Matthew Ahmann. Chicago: Henry Regnery Co., 1963.

——. "The Day of Days, December 5." *Chronicles of Black Protest*. Edited by Bradford Chambers. New York: The New American Library, Inc., 1968.

——. "Declaration of Independence from the War in Viet Nam." *The Viet Nam War: Christian Perspectives*. Edited by Michael Hamilton. Grand Rapids: Wm. B. Eerdmans Publishing Co., 1967.

——. Foreword to *The Power of Nonviolence*, by Richard Gregg. 2d ed. New York: Schocken Books, Inc., 1959.

——. "The Future of Integration." *Crisis in Modern America*. Edited by H. John Heinz. New Haven: Yale University Press, 1959.

——. "I Have a Dream." *Chronicles of Black Protest*. Edited by Bradford Chambers. New York: The New American Library, Inc., 1968.

———. "I Have a Dream." *The Negro in Twentieth Century America*. Edited by John Hope Franklin and Isidore Starr. New York: Vintage Books—Random House, Inc., 1967.

———. Introduction to *The Negro Politician: His Success and Failure*, by Edward T. Clayton. Chicago: Johnson Publishing Co.—Book Division, 1964.

———. Introduction to *Three Lives for Mississippi*, by William Bradford Huie. New York: The New American Library Inc., 1964.

———. "Letter from the Birmingham Jail." *Nonviolence in America: A Documentary History*. Edited by Staughton Lynd. New York: The Bobbs-Merrill Co., Inc., 1966.

———. "Martin Luther King Talks with Kenneth B. Clark." *The Negro Protest*. Edited by Kenneth B. Clark. Boston: Beacon Press, 1963.

———. "Nonviolence and Racial Justice." *The Christian Century Reader*. Edited by Harold Fey and Margaret Frakes. New York: Association Press, 1957.

———. "Pilgrimage to Nonviolence." *Nonviolence in America: A Documentary History*. Edited by Staughton Lynd. New York: The Bobbs-Merrill Co., Inc., 1966.

———. "The Un-Christian Christian." *The White Problem in America*. Edited by *Ebony*. Chicago: Johnson Publishing Co.—Book Division, 1966.

———. "Where Do We Go from Here?" *Contemporary Moral Issues*." Edited by Harry K. Girvetz. Belmont, California: Wadsworth Publishing Co., Inc., 1963.

*III. ARTICLES by Martin Luther King, Jr.*

King, Jr., Martin Luther, "The Acceptance." *Dear Dr. King*. New York: Buckingham Enterprises, Inc., 1968.

———. "The American Dream." *The Negro History Bulletin* 31 (May 1968), pp. 10–15.

———. "Behind the Selma March." *Saturday Review* 48 (3 April 1965), pp. 16–17.

———. "Bold Design for a New South." *The Nation* 196 (30 March 1963), pp. 259–62.

———. "The Burning Truth in the South." *The Progressive* 24 (May 1960), pp. 8ff.

———. "The Case Against Tokenism." *The New York Times Magazine*, 5 August 1962, p. 11.

———. "The Church and the Race Crisis." *The Christian Century* 75 (8 October 1958), pp. 1140–41.

———. "Civil Right No. 1: The Right to Vote." *The New York Times Magazine*, 14 March 1965), pp. 26–27.

———. "A Comparison of the Conceptions of God in the Thinking of Paul Tillich and Henry Nelson Wieman." Ph.D. dissertation, Boston University, 1955.

———. "The Current Crisis in Race Relations." *New South*, March 1958, pp. 8ff.

———. "Dark Yesterdays, Bright Tomorrows." *The Reader's Digest* 92 (June 1968), pp. 55–58.

———. "Emancipation—1963." *Renewal* 3 (June 1963), pp. 2ff.

———. "Equality Now: The President Has the Power." *The Nation* 192 (4 February 1961), pp. 91–95.

———. "The Ethical Demands of Integration." *Religion and Labor*, May 1963, pp. 3ff.

———. "The Ethics of Love." *Religious Digest*, April 1958, pp. 1ff.

———. "An Experiment in Love." *Jubilee*, September 1958, pp. 11ff.

———. "Facing the Challenge of a New Age." *Phylon* 18 (Spring 1957), pp. 25ff.

———. "Fumbling on the New Frontier." *The Nation* 194 (3 March 1962), pp. 190–93.

———. "Gift of Love." *McCall's* 94 (December 1966), pp. 146–147.

———. "Hammer on Civil Rights." *The Nation* 198 (9 March 1964), pp. 230–34.

———. "Honoring Dr. Du Bois." *Freedomways* 8 (Spring 1968), pp. 104ff.

———. "In a Word: Now." *The New York Times Magazine* (29 September 1963), pp. 91–92.

———. "Interview: Dr. Martin Luther King, Jr." *The New York Times*, 2 April 1967.

———. "It Is Not Enough to Condemn Black Power." *The New York Times*, 26 July 1966.

———. "The Last Steep Ascent." *The Nation* 202 (14 March 1966), pp. 288ff.

———. "The Lecture." *Dear Dr. King*. Speech delivered at Oslo University, Norway, 11 December 1964. New York: Buckingham Enterprises, Inc., 1968.

———. "A Legacy of Creative Protest." *The Massachusetts Law Review* 4 (Autumn 1962), pp. 43ff.

———. "Let Justice Roll Down." *The Nation* 200 (15 March 1965), pp. 269–74.

———. "Love, Law, and Civil Disobedience." *New South*, December 1961, pp. 3ff.

———. "The Luminous Promise." *The Progressive* 26 (December 1962), pp. 34ff.

———. "Martin Luther King Defines Black Power." *The New York Times Magazine*, 11 June 1967, pp. 26–27.

———. "The Most Durable Power." *The Christian Century* 74 (5 June 1957), p. 708.

———. "My Trip to the Land of Gandhi." *Ebony* (July 1959), pp. 84ff.

———. "The Negro is Your Brother." *The Atlantic Monthly* 212 (August 1963), pp. 78–81.

———. "Negroes Are Not Moving Too Fast." *Saturday Evening Post*, 7 November 1964, pp. 8ff.

———. "New Negro Threat: Mass Disobedience." *U.S. News and World Report* 63 (28 August 1967), p. 10.

———. "A New Sense of Direction." *Worldview* 15 (April 1972), pp. 5ff.

———. "Next Stop: The North." *Saturday Review* 48 (13 November 1965), pp. 33–35.

———. "Nonviolence: The Only Road to Freedom." *Ebony* 21 (October 1966), pp. 27–30.

———. "Nonviolence and Racial Justice." *The Christian Century* 74 (6 February 1957), pp. 165–67.

———. "Our Struggle." *Liberation*, April 1956, pp. 1ff.

———. "Out of the Long Night of Segregation." *Advance* 150 (28 February 1958), pp. 14ff.

———. "Out of Segregation's Long Night: An Interpretation of a Racial Crisis." *The Churchman* 172 (February 1958), pp. 7ff.

———. "Pilgrimage to Nonviolence." *The Christian Century* 77 (13 April 1960), pp. 439–41.

———. "Playboy Interview: Martin Luther King." *Playboy*, January 1965, pp. 117ff.

———. "The Power of Nonviolence." *The Intercollegian*, May 1958, pp. 8ff.

———. "The Rising Tide of Racial Consciousness." *The YWCA Magazine*, December 1960, pp. 12ff.

———. "Say That I Was a Drum Major." *The Reader's Digest* 92 (June 1968), pp. 58–59.

———. "Showdown for Non-violence." *Look* 32 (16 April 1968), pp. 23–25.

———. "The Social Organization of Nonviolence." *Liberation*, October 1959, pp. 5ff.

———. "Suffering and Faith." *The Christian Century* 77 (27 April 1960), p. 510.

———. "A Testament of Hope." *Playboy*, January 1969, pp. 175ff.

———. "The Time for Freedom Has Come." *The New York Times Magazine*, 10 September 1961, p. 25.

———. "The Un-Christian Christian: SCLC Looks Closely at Christianity in a Troubled Land." *Ebony* 20 (August 1965), pp. 76–80.

———. "A View from the Mountaintop." *Renewal* 9 (April 1969), pp. 3ff.

———. "A View of the Dawn." *Interracial Review*, May 1957, pp. 82ff.

———. "Walk for Freedom." *Fellowship* 22 (May 1956), pp. 5ff.

———. "We Are Still Walking." *Liberation*, December 1956, pp. 6ff.

———. "Who Is Their God?" *The Nation* 195 (13 October 1962), pp. 209–10.

———. "Who Speaks for the South?" *Liberation*, March 1958, pp. 13ff.


*IV. BOOKS about Martin Luther King, Jr.*

Bennett, Lerone, Jr. *What Manner of Man.* Chicago: Johnson Publishing Co., Book Division, 1964.

Bishop, James. *The Days of Martin Luther King, Jr.* New York: G. P. Putnam's Sons, 1971.

Bleiweiss, Robert M., ed. *Marching to Freedom: The Life of Martin Luther King, Jr.* New York: The New American Library Inc, 1969.

Clayton, Edward. *The Southern Christian Leadership Conference Story.* Atlanta: SCLC, 1964.

Davis, L. G. *I Have a Dream: The Life & Times of Martin Luther King.* Chicago: Adams Press, 1969.

*I Have a Dream.* New York: Time-Life Books, 1968.

Illai, V., ed. *Indian Leaders on King.* New Delhi: Century Press, 1968.

King, Coretta Scott. *My Life with Martin Luther King, Jr.* New York: Holt, Rinehart & Winston, Inc., 1969.

Lewis, David L. *King: A Critical Biography.* Baltimore: Penguin Books, Inc., 1970.

Lincoln, C. Eric, ed. *Martin Luther King, Jr.: A Profile.* New York: Hill & Wang, Inc., 1970.

Lokos, Lionel. *House Divided: The Life and Legacy of Martin Luther King.* New Rochelle, N.Y.: Arlington House, 1968.

Lomax, Louis. *To Kill a Black Man.* Los Angeles: Holloway House Publishing Company, 1968.

*Martin Luther King, Jr.: His Life—His Death.* Fort Worth: Sepia Publishers, 1968.

*Martin Luther King, Jr., NineteenTwenty-Nine to Nineteen Sixty-Eight.* Chicago: Johnson Publishing Co., Book Division, 1968.

*Memorial—Martin Luther King.* New York: Country Wide Publications, 1968.

Miller, William Robert. *Martin Luther King, Jr.: His Life, Martyrdom and Meaning for the World.* New York: Weybright and Talley, Inc., 1968.

Muller, Gerald A. *Martin Luther King, Jr.: Civil Rights Leader.* Minneapolis: T. S. Denison, 1971.

Reddick, Lawrence D. *Crusader Without Violence: Martin Luther King, Jr.* New York: Harper & Row, Publishers, 1959.

Slack, Kenneth. *Martin Luther King.* Naperville, Ill.: Alec R. Allenson, Inc., 1970.

Uwen, Nathan. *Martin Luther King, Jr.* New York: New Dimensions Publishing Company, 1970.

Walton, Hanes, Jr. *The Political Philosophy of Martin Luther King, Jr.* Westport, Conn.: Greenwood Press, Inc., 1971.

William, John A. *The King God Didn't Save: Reflections on the Life & Death of Martin Luther King.* New York: Coward, McCann & Geoghegan, Inc., 1970.

## V. CHAPTERS (in books) about Martin Luther King, Jr.

Bartlett, Robert. "Martin Luther King, Jr." In *They Stand Invincible*, edited by Robert Bartlett. New York: Thomas Y. Crowell Company, 1959.

Curtis, C. J. "The Negro Contribution to American Theology: King." *Contemporary Protestant Thought.* New York: Bruce Books, 1970.

Griffin, John Howard. "Martin Luther King." In *Thirteen for Christ*, edited by Melville Harcourt. New York: Sheed & Ward, Inc., 1963.

Holmes, Richard. "The Ordeal of Martin Luther King." In *Listen, White Man, I'm Bleeding*, edited by Phil Hirsch. New York: Pyramid Books, 1969.

Mays, Benjamin. "Eulogy for Martin Luther King, Jr." *Disturbed About Man.* Richmond: John Knox Press, 1969.

Richardson, Herbert. "Martin Luther King, Jr.: Unsung Theologian." *New Theology No. 6*, edited by Martin Marty and Dean Peerman. New York: The Macmillan Company, 1969.

## VI. ARTICLES about Martin Luther King, Jr.

Ashmore, Harry S. "Martin Luther King, Spokesman for the Southern Negro," *New York Herald Tribune Book Review*, 21 September 1958.

Baldwin, James. "A Dangerous Road Before Martin Luther King." *Harpers* 222 (February 1961), pp. 33–42.

———. "Malcolm and Martin." *Esquire* 77 (April 1972), pp. 94–97.

Bennett, Lerone. "The King Plan for Freedom." *Ebony*, July 1956, pp. 77ff.

———. "The South and the Negro." *Ebony*, April 1957, pp. 77ff.

——. "The Martyrdom of Martin Luther King, Jr." *Ebony* 23 (May 1968), pp. 174–81.

Bowles, Chester. "What Negroes Can Learn from Gandhi." *Saturday Evening Post* 230 (1 March 1958), pp. 19–21.

Carberg, Warren. "The Story Behind the Victory." *Bostonia*, Spring 1957, pp. 7ff.

Clark, Dennis. "Toward Equality." *Commonweal* 80 (24 July 1964), pp. 518ff.

Clayton, Helen J. "Martin Luther King: The Right Man at the Right Time." *The YWCA Magazine*, June 1968.

Cleghorn, Reese. "Martin Luther King, Jr., Apostle of Crisis." *Saturday Evening Post*, 15 June 1963.

Collins, L. J. "Biography of Martin Luther King." *Contemporary Review* 208 (June 1966), pp. 326ff.

Cook, Bruce. "King in Chicago." *Commonweal* 84 (29 April 1966), pp. 175–77.

Dunbar, Ernest. "A Visit with Dr. King." *Look*, 12 February 1963.

Elder, John Dixon. "Martin Luther King and American Civil Religion." *Harvard Divinity School Bulletin* 1 (Spring 1968), pp. 17ff.

Fager, Charles E. "Dilemma for Dr. King." *The Christian Century* 83 (16 March 1966), pp. 331–32.

Galphin, Bruce M. "The Political Future of Dr. King." *The Nation* 193 (23 September 1961), pp. 177–80.

Good, Paul. "Chicago Summer: Bossism, Racism and Dr. King." *The Nation* 203 (19 September 1966), pp. 237–42.

Griffin, John Howard. "Martin Luther King's Moment." *The Sign*, April 1963, pp. 28ff.

Halberstam, David. "Second Coming of Martin Luther King." *Harpers* 235 (August 1967), pp. 39–51.

——. "Notes from the Bottom of the Mountain." *Harpers* 236 (June 1968), pp. 40–42.

Hentoff, Nat. "A Peaceful Army." *Commonweal* 72 (10 June 1960), pp. 275–78.

King, Coretta Scott. "The Legacy of Martin Luther King, Jr." *Theology Today* 28 (July 1970), pp. 129ff.

Krasnow, Erwin G. "Reflections on Martin Luther King, Jr., Versus Mister Maestro." *Georgetown Law Journal* 53 (Winter 1965), pp. 52ff.

Long, Margaret. "Martin Luther King, Jr.: 'He Kept So Plain.' " *The Progressive* 32 (May 1968), pp. 20ff.

Lynd, Staughton. "The New Negro Radicalism." *Commentary* 36 (September 1963), pp. 252ff.

Maguire, John David. "Martin Luther King and Viet Nam." *Christianity and Crisis* 27 (1 May 1967), pp. 98ff.

McClendon, James William. "Martin Luther King: Politician or American Church Father?" *Journal of Ecumenical Studies* 8 (Winter 1971), pp. 115ff.

——. "Biography as Theology." *Cross Currents* 21 (Fall 1971), pp. 415ff.

McGraw, James R. "An Interview with Andrew J. Young." *Christianity and Crisis* 27 (22 January 1968), pp. 324ff.

Meier, August. "On the Role of Martin Luther King." *New Politics* 4 (Winter 1965), pp. 52ff.

Miller, Perry. "The Mind and Faith of Martin Luther King." *The Reporter Magazine* 19 (30 October 1958), p. 40.

Miller, William Robert. "Gandhi and King: Trail Blazers in Nonviolence." *Fellowship* 35 (January 1969), pp. 5ff.

Priven, Francis P., and Cloward, Richard A. "Dissensus Politics." *New Republic* 158 (20 April 1968), pp. 20ff.

Quarles, Benjamin. "Martin Luther King in History." *The Negro History Bulletin* 31 (May 1968), p. 9.

Romero, Patricia W. "Martin Luther King and His Challenge to White America." *The Negro History Bulletin* 31 (May 1968), pp. 6–8.

Rowan, Carl T. "Heart of a Passionate Dilemma." *Saturday Review* 42 (1 August 1959), pp. 20–21.

———. "Martin Luther King's Tragic Decision." *The Reader's Digest* 91 (September 1967), pp. 37–42.

Schrag, Peter. "The Uses of Martyrdom." *Saturday Review* 51 (20 April 1968), pp. 28–29.

Schulz, William. "Martin Luther King's March on Washington." *The Reader's Digest* 92 (April 1968), pp. 65–69.

Sellers, James E. "Love, Justice and the Non-Violent Movement." *Theology Today* 18 (January 1962), pp. 422ff.

Sitton, Claude. "Doctor King, Symbol of the Segregation Struggle." *New York Times Magazine* (22 January 1961), p. 10.

Smith, Donald H. "An Exegesis of Martin Luther King, Jr.'s Social Philosophy." *Phylon* 31 (Spring 1970), pp. 89ff.

———. "Martin Luther King, Jr.: Rhetorician of Revolt." Ph.D. dissertation, University of Wisconsin, 1964.

Smith, Kenneth L. "Martin Luther King, Jr.: Reflections of a Former Teacher" *The Voice of Crozer Theological Seminary* 57 (April 1965), pp. 2ff.

Smith, Lillian. "And Suddenly Something Happened." *Saturday Review* 41 (20 September 1958), p. 21.

Smylie, James H. "On Jesus, Pharaohs, and the Chosen People: Martin Luther King as Biblical Interpreter and Humanist." *Interpretation* 24 (January 1970), pp. 74ff.

Stackhouse, Max L. "Christianity in New Formation: Reflections of a White Christian on the Death of Dr. Martin Luther King, Jr." *Andover Newton Quarterly*, November 1968.

Steinkraus, Warren E. "Martin Luther King's Personalism." *Journal of the History of Ideas* 34 (January–March 1973), pp. 97–111.

Thomas, C. W. "Nobel Peace Prize Goes to Martin Luther King." *The Negro History Bulletin* 27 (November 1964), p. 35.

Wainwright, Loudan. "Martyr of the Sit-Ins." *The Negro History Bulletin* 24 (April 1961), pp. 147–51.

*VII. NOTABLE EDITORIALS about Martin Luther King, Jr.*

"Dr. King, One Year After: He Lives, Man!" *Look* 33 (15 April 1969), pp. 29–31.

"Dr. King's Legacy." *Commonweal* 88 (19 April 1968), pp. 125–26.

"King Speaks For Peace." *The Christian Century* 84 (19 April 1967), pp. 492–93.

"The Legacy of Martin Luther King." *Life* 64 (19 April 1968), p. 4.

"The Life and Death of Martin Luther King." *Christianity Today* 12 (26 April 1968), pp. 37–40.

"Martin Luther King, Jr., and Mahatma Gandhi." *The Negro History Bulletin* 31 (May 1968), pp. 4–5.

"Martin Luther King, Jr.: 'Man of 1963.' " *The Negro History Bulletin* 27 (March 1964), pp. 136–137.

"Martin Luther King's Tropic Interlude." *Ebony* 22 (June 1967), pp. 112-14.

"Martyrdom Comes to America's Moral Leader." *The Christian Century* 85 (17 April 1968), p. 475.

## VIII. RECENT NOTABLE PUBLICATIONS

Abernathy, Ralph David. *And the Walls Came Tumbling Down: Ralph David Abernathy, An Autobiography.* New York: Harper & Row, 1989.

Ansbro, John J. *Martin Luther King, Jr.: The Making of a Mind.* Maryknoll, NY: Orbis Books, 1982.

Colaico, James A. *Martin Luther King, Jr.: Apostle of Militant Nonviolence.* New York: St. Martin's Press, 1988.

Downing, Frederick L. *To See the Promised Land: The Faith Pilgrimage of Martin Luther King, Jr.* Macon, GA: Mercer University Press, 1986.

Fairclough, Adam. *To Redeem the Soul of America: The Southern Christian Leadership Conference and Martin Luther King, Jr.* Athens, GA: University of Georgia Press, 1987.

Garrow, David J., ed. *Martin Luther King, Jr. and the Civil Rights Movement,* 18 vols. Brooklyn, NY: Carlson Publishing, Inc., 1989. [These volumes contain reprints of major articles, books, and publication of significant theses.]

Lentz, Richard. *Symbols, the News Magazines, and Martin Luther King.* Baton Rouge and London: Louisiana State University Press, 1990.

Peake, Thomas R. *Keeping the Dream Alive: A History of the Southern Christian Leadership Conference from King to the Nineteen-Eighties.* New York: Peter Lang, 1987.

One of the best studies of the history of dissent within the American religious community is Edwin Scott Gaustad, *Dissent in American Religion* (Chicago and London: University of Chicago Press, 1973), as well as the extraordinary examination of the roots of this tradition in the colonial period in William G. McLoughlin, *New England Dissent, 1630–1833: The Baptists and the Separation of Church and State,* 2 vols. (Cambridge, MA: Harvard University Press, 1971).

# Index